BOOK FOUR

BOOK FOUR

Meditation, Magical Theory and Law

BY

Aleister Crowley, Soror Virakam

KALPAZ

ISBN: 978-93-5128-910-4(PB)

First Published in1913
Indian Reprint in 2017

Published by

Kalpaz Publications
C-30, Satyawati Nagar,
Delhi – 110052
E-mail: kalpaz@hotmail.com
Website: kalpazpublications.com
Ph.: +91-9212142040

Cataloging in Publication Data—DK
Courtesy: D.K. Agencies (P) Ltd. <docinfo@dkagencies.com>

Crowley, Aleister, 1875-1947**, author.**
[Magick. Book 4]
Book four / by Frater Perdurabo and Soror Virakam.
pages cm
Reprint.
ISBN 9789351289104 (PB)

1. Magic. 2. Occultism. I. Virakam, Soror, author. II. Title.

BF1611.C76 2017 DDC 133.43 23

Part-I

Meditation

A NOTE

THIS book is intentionally "not" the work of Frater Perdurabo. Experience shows that his writing is too concentrated, too abstruse, too occult, for ordinary minds to apprehend. It is thought that this record of disjointed fragments of his casual conversation may prove alike more intelligible and more convincing, and at least provide a preliminary study which will enable the student to attack his real work from a standpoint of some little general knowledge and understanding of his ideas, and of the form in which he figures them.

Part II, "Magick," is more advanced in style than Part I; the student is expected to know a little of the literature of the subject, and to be able to take an intelligent view of it. This part is, however, really explanatory of Part I, which is a crude outline sketch only.

If both parts are thoroughly studied and understood, the pupil will have obtained a real grasp of all the fundamentals and essentials of both Magick and Mysticism.

I wrote this book down from Frater Perdurabo's dictation at the Villa Caldarazzo, Posilippo, Naples, where I was studying under him, a villa actually prophesied to us long before we reached Naples by that Brother of the A.'.A.'. who appeared to me in Zurich. Any point which was obscure to me was cleared up in some new discourse (the discourses have consequently been re-arranged). Before printing, the whole work was read by several persons of rather less than average intelligence, and any point not quite clear even to them has been elucidated.

May the whole Path now be plain to all!

Frater Perdurabo is the most honest of all the great religious teachers. Others have said: "Believe me!" He says: "*Don't* believe me!" He does not ask for followers; would despise and refuse them. He wants an independent and self-reliant body of students to follow out their own methods of research. If he can save them time and trouble by giving a few useful "tips," his work will have been done to his own satisfaction.

Those who have wished men to believe in them were absurd. A persuasive tongue or pen, or an efficient sword, with rack and stake, produced this "belief," which is contrary to, and destructive of, all real religious experience.

The whole life of Frater Perdurabo is now devoted to seeing that you obtain this living experience of Truth for, by, and in yourselves!

SOROR VIRAKAM (Mary d'Este Sturges).

PRELIMINARY REMARKS

EXISTENCE, as we know it, is full of sorrow. To mention only one minor point: every man is a condemned criminal, only he does not know the date of his execution. This is unpleasant for every man. Consequently every man does everything possible to postpone the date, and would sacrifice anything that he has if he could reverse the sentence.

Practically all religions and all philosophies have started thus crudely, by promising their adherents some such reward as immortality.

No religion has failed hitherto by not promising enough; the present breaking up of all religions is due to the fact that people have asked to see the securities. Men have even renounced the important material advantages which a well-organized religion may confer upon a State, rather than acquiesce in fraud or falsehood, or even in any system which, if not proved guilty, is at least unable to demonstrate its innocence.

Being more or less bankrupt, the best thing that we can do is to attack the problem afresh without preconceived ideas. Let us begin by doubting every statement. Let us find a way of subjecting every statement to the test of experiment. Is there any truth at all in the claims of various religions? Let us examine the question.

Our original difficulty will be due to the enormous wealth of our material. To enter into a critical examination of all systems would be an unending task; the cloud of witnesses is too great. Now each religion is equally positive; and each demands faith. This we refuse in the absence of positive proof. But we may usefully inquire whether there is not any one thing upon which all religions have agreed: for, if so, it seems possible that it may be worthy of really thorough consideration.

It is certainly not to be found in dogma. Even so simple an idea as that of a supreme and eternal being is denied by a third of the human race. Legends of miracle are perhaps universal, but these, in the absence of demonstrative proof, are repugnant to common sense.

But what of the origin of religions? How is it that unproved assertion has so frequently compelled the assent of all classes of mankind? Is not this a miracle?

There is, however, one form of miracle which certainly happens, the influence of the genius. There is no known analogy in Nature. One cannot even think of a "super-dog" transforming the world of dogs, whereas in the history of mankind this happens with regularity and frequency. Now here are three "super-men," all at loggerheads. What is there in common between Christ, Buddha, and Mohammed? Is there any one point upon which all three are in accord?

No point of doctrine, no point of ethics, no theory of a "hereafter" do they share, and yet in the history of their lives we find one identity amid many diversities.

Buddha was born a Prince, and died a beggar.

Mohammed was born a beggar, and died a Prince.

Christ remained obscure until many years after his death.

Elaborate lives of each have been written by devotees, and there is one thing common to all three — an omission. We hear nothing of Christ between the ages of twelve and thirty. Mohammed disappeared into a cave. Buddha left his palace, and went for a long while into the desert.

Each of them, perfectly silent up to the time of the disappearance, came back and immediately began to preach a new law.

This is so curious that it leaves us to inquire whether the histories of other great teachers contradict or confirm.

Moses led a quiet life until his slaying of the Egyptian. He then flees into the land of Midian, and we hear nothing of what he did there, yet immediately on his return he turns the whole place upside down. Later on, too, he absents himself on Mount Sinai for a few days, and comes back with the Tables of the Law in his hand.

St. Paul (again), after his adventure on the road to Damascus, goes into the desert of Arabia for many years, and on his return overturns the Roman Empire. Even in the legends of savages we find the same thing universal; somebody who is nobody in particular goes away for a longer or shorter period, and comes back as the "great medicine man"; but nobody ever knows exactly what happened to him.

Making every possible deduction for fable and myth, we get this one coincidence. A nobody goes away, and comes back a somebody. This is not to be explained in any of the ordinary ways.

There is not the smallest ground for the contention that these were from the start exceptional men. Mohammed would hardly have driven a camel until he was thirty-five years old if he had possessed any talent or ambition. St. Paul had much original talent; but he is the least of the five. Nor do they seem to have possessed any of the usual materials of power, such as rank, fortune, or influence.

Moses was rather a big man in Egypt when he left; he came back as a mere stranger.

Christ had not been to China and married the Emperor's daughter.

Mohammed had not been acquiring wealth and drilling soldiers.

Buddha had not been consolidating any religious organizations.

St. Paul had not been intriguing with an ambitious general.

Each came back poor; each came back alone.

What was the nature of their power? What happened to them in their absence?

History will not help us to solve the problem, for history is silent.

We have only the accounts given by the men themselves.

It would be very remarkable should we find that these accounts agree.

Of the great teachers we have mentioned Christ is silent; the other four tell us something; some more, some less.

Buddha goes into details too elaborate to enter upon in this place; but the gist of it is that in one way or another he got hold of the secret force of the World and mastered it.

Of St. Paul's experiences, we have nothing but a casual allusion to his having been "caught up into Heaven, and seen and heard things of which it was not lawful to speak."

Mohammed speaks crudely of his having been "visited by the Angel Gabriel," who communicated things from "God."

Moses says that he "beheld God."

Diverse as these statements are at first sight, all agree in announcing an experience of the class which fifty years ago would have been called supernatural, to-day may be called spiritual, and fifty years hence will have a proper name based on an understanding of the phenomenon which occurred.

Theorists have not been at a loss to explain; but they differ.

The Mohammedan insists that God is, and did really send Gabriel with messages for Mohammed: but all others contradict him. And from the nature of the case proof is impossible.

The lack of proof has been so severely felt by Christianity (and in a much less degree by Islam) that fresh miracles have been manufactured almost daily to support the tottering structure. Modern thought, rejecting these miracles, has adopted theories involving epilepsy and madness. As if organization could spring from disorganization! Even if epilepsy were the cause of these great movements which have caused civilization after civilization to arise from barbarism, it would merely form an argument for cultivating epilepsy.

Of course great men will never conform with the standards of little men, and he whose mission it is to overturn the world can hardly escape the title of revolutionary. The fads of a period always furnish terms of abuse. The fad of Caiaphas was Judaism, and the Pharisees told him that Christ "blasphemed." Pilate was a loyal Roman; to him they accused Christ of "sedition." When the Pope had all power it was necessary to prove an enemy a "heretic." Advancing to-day towards a medical oligarchy, we try to prove that our opponents are "insane," and (in a Puritan country) to attack their "morals." We should then avoid all rhetoric, and try to investigate with perfect freedom from bias the phenomena which occurred to these great leaders of mankind.

There is no difficulty in our assuming that these men themselves did not understand clearly what happened to them. The only one who explains his system thoroughly is Buddha, and Buddha is the only one that is not dogmatic. We may also suppose that the others thought it inadvisable to explain too clearly to their followers; St. Paul evidently took this line.

Our best document will therefore be the system of Buddha;

> *footnote: We have the documents of Hinduism, and of two Chinese systems. But Hinduism has no single founder. Lao Tze is one of our best examples of a man who went away and had a mysterious experience; perhaps the best of all examples, as his system is the best of all systems. We have full details of his method of training in the Khang Kang King, and elsewhere. But it is so little known that we shall omit consideration of it in this popular account.*

but it is so complex that no immediate summary will serve; and in the case of the others, if we have not the accounts of the Masters, we have those of their immediate followers.

The methods advised by all these people have a startling resemblance to one another. They recommend "virtue" (of various kinds), solitude, absence of excitement, moderation in diet, and finally a practice which some call prayer and some call meditation. (The former four may turn out on examination to be merely conditions favourable to the last.)

On investigating what is meant by these two things, we find that they are only one. For what is the state of either prayer or meditation? It is the restraining of the mind to a single act, state, or thought. If we sit down quietly and investigate the contents of our minds, we shall find that even at the best of times the principal characteristics are wandering and distraction. Any one who has had anything to do with children and untrained minds generally knows that fixity of attention is never present, even when there is a large amount of intelligence and good will.

If then we, with our well-trained minds, determine to control this wandering thought, we shall find that we are fairly well able to keep the thoughts running in a narrow channel, each thought linked to the last in a perfectly rational manner; but if we attempt to stop this current we shall find that, so far from succeeding, we shall merely bread down the banks of the channel. The mind will overflow, and instead of a chain of thought we shall have a chaos of confused images.

This mental activity is so great, and seems so natural, that it is hard to understand how any one first got the idea that it was a weakness and a nuisance. Perhaps it was because in the more natural practice of "devotion," people found that their thoughts interfered. In any case calm and self-control are to be preferred to restlessness. Darwin in his study presents a marked contrast with a monkey in a cage.

Generally speaking, the larger and stronger and more highly developed any animal is, the less does it move about, and such movements as it does make are slow and purposeful. Compare the ceaseless activity of bacteria with the reasoned steadiness of the beaver; and except in the few animal communities which are organized, such as bees, the greatest intelligence is shown by those of solitary habits. This is so true of man that psychologists have been obliged to treat of the mental state of crowds as if it were totally different in quality from any state possible to an individual.

It is by freeing the mind from external influences, whether casual or emotional, that it obtains power to see somewhat of the truth of things.

Let us, however, continue our practice. Let us determine to be masters of our minds. We shall then soon find what conditions are favourable.

There will be no need to persuade ourselves at great length that all external influences are likely to be unfavourable. New faces, new scenes will disturb us; even the new habits of life which we undertake for this very purpose of controlling the mind will at first tend to upset it. Still, we must give up our habit of eating too much, and follow the natural rule of only eating when we are hungry, listening to the interior voice which tells us that we have had enough.

The same rule applies to sleep. We have determined to control our minds, and so our time for meditation must take precedence of other hours.

We must fix times for practice, and make our feasts movable. In order to test our progress, for we shall find that (as in all physiological matters) meditation cannot be gauged by the feelings, we shall have a note-book and pencil, and we shall also have a watch. We shall then endeavour to count how often, during the first quarter of an hour, the mind breaks away from the idea upon which it is determined to concentrate. We shall practice this twice daily; and, as we go, experience will teach us which conditions are favourable and which are not. Before we have been doing this for very long we are almost certain to get impatient, and we shall find that we have to practice many other things in order to assist us in our work. New problems will constantly arise which must be faced, and solved.

For instance, we shall most assuredly find that we fidget. We shall discover that no position is comfortable, though we never noticed it before in all our lives!

This difficulty has been solved by a practice called "Asana," which will be described later on.

Memories of the events of the day will bother us; we must arrange our day so that it is absolutely uneventful. Our minds will recall to us our hopes and fears, our loves and hates, our ambitions, our envies, and many other emotions. All these must be cut off. We must have absolutely no interest in life but that of quieting our minds.

This is the object of the usual monastic vow of poverty, chastity, and obedience. If you have no property, you have no care, nothing to be anxious about; with chastity no other person to be anxious about, and to distract your attention; while if you are vowed to obedience the question of what you are to do no longer frets: you simply obey.

There are a great many other obstacles which you will discover as you go on, and it is proposed to deal with these in turn. But let us pass by for the moment to the point where you are nearing success.

In your early struggles you may have found it difficult to conquer sleep; and you may have wandered so far from the object of your meditations without noticing it, that the meditation has really been broken; but much later on, when you feel that you are "getting quite good," you will be shocked to find a complete oblivion of yourself and your surroundings. You will say: "Good heavens! I must have been to sleep!" or else "What on earth was I meditating upon?" or even "What was I doing?" "Where am I?" "Who am I?" or a mere wordless bewilderment may daze you. This may alarm you, and your alarm will not be lessened when you come to full consciousness, and reflect that you have actually forgotten who you are and what you are doing!

This is only one of many adventures that may come to you; but it is one of the most typical. By this time your hours of meditation will fill most of the day, and you will probably be constantly having presentiments that something is about to happen. You may also be terrified with the idea that your brain may be giving way; but you will have learnt the real symptoms of mental fatigue, and you will be careful to avoid them. They must be very carefully distinguished from idleness!

At certain times you will feel as if there were a contest between the will and the mind; at other times you may feel as if they were in harmony; but there is a third state, to be distinguished from the latter feeling. It is the certain sign of near success, the view-halloo. This is when the mind runs naturally towards the object chosen, not as if in obedience to the will of the owner of the mind, but as if directed by nothing at all, or by something impersonal; as if it were falling by its own weight, and not being pushed down.

Almost always, the moment that one becomes conscious of this, it stops; and the dreary old struggle between the cowboy will and the buckjumper mind begins again.

Like every other physiological process, consciousness of it implies disorder or disease.

In analysing the nature of this work of controlling the mind, the student will appreciate without trouble the fact that two things are involved — the person seeing and the thing seen — the person knowing and the thing known; and he will come to regard this as the necessary condition of all consciousness. We are too accustomed to assume to be facts things about which we have no real right even to guess. We assume, for example, that the unconscious is the torpid; and yet nothing is more certain than that bodily organs which are functioning well do so in silence. The best sleep is dreamless. Even in the case of games of skill our very best strokes are followed by the thought, "I don't know how I did it;" and we cannot repeat those strokes at will. The moment we begin to think consciously about a stroke we get "nervous," and are lost.

In fact, there are three main classes of stroke; the bad stroke, which we associate, and rightly, with wandering attention; the good stroke which we associate, and rightly, with fixed attention; and the perfect stroke, which we do not understand, but which is really caused by the habit of fixity of attention having become independent of the will, and thus enabled to act freely of its own accord.

This is the same phenomenon referred to above as being a good sign.

Finally something happens whose nature may form the subject of a further discussion later on. For the moment let it suffice to say that this consciousness of the Ego and the non-Ego, the seer and the thing seen, the knower and the thing known, is blotted out.

There is usually an intense light, an intense sound, and a feeling of such overwhelming bliss that the resources of language have been exhausted again and again in the attempt to describe it.

It is an absolute knock-out blow to the mind. It is so vivid and tremendous that those who experience it are in the gravest danger of losing all sense of proportion.

By its light all other events of life are as darkness. Owing to this, people have utterly failed to analyse it or to estimate it. They are accurate enough in saying that, compared with this, all human life is absolutely dross; but they go further, and go wrong. They argue that "since this is that which transcends the terrestrial, it must be celestial." One of the tendencies in their minds has been the hope of a heaven such as their parents and teachers have described, or such as they have themselves pictured; and, without the slightest grounds for saying so, they make the assumption "This is That."

In the Bhagavadgita a vision of this class is naturally attributed to the apparation of Vishnu, who was the local god of the period.

Anna Kingsford, who had dabbled in Hebrew mysticism, and was a feminist, got an almost identical vision; but called the "divine" figure which she saw alternately "Adonai" and "Maria."

Now this woman, though handicapped by a brain that was a mass of putrid pulp, and a complete lack of social status, education, and moral character, did more in the religious world than any other person had done for generations. She, and she alone, made Theosophy possible, and without Theosophy the world-wide interest in similar matters would never have been aroused. This interest is to the Law of Thelema what the preaching of John the Baptist was to Christianity.

We are now in a position to say what happened to Mohammed. Somehow or another his phenomenon happened in his mind. More ignorant than Anna Kingsford, though, fortunately, more moral, he connected it with the story of the "Annunciation," which he had undoubtedly heard in his boyhood, and said "Gabriel appeared to me." But in spite of his ignorance, his total misconception of the truth, the power of the vision was such that he was enabled to persist through the usual persecution, and founded a religion to which even to-day one man in every eight belongs.

The history of Christianity shows precisely the same remarkable fact. Jesus Christ was brought up on the fables of the "Old Testament," and so was compelled to ascribe his experiences to "Jehovah," although his gentle spirit could have had nothing in common with the monster who was always commanding the rape of virgins and the murder of little children, and whose rites were then, and still are, celebrated by human sacrifice.

footnote: The massacres of Jews in Eastern Europe which surprise the ignorant, are almost invariably excited by the disappearance of "Christian" children, stolen, as the parents suppose, for the purposes of "ritual murder." WEH footnote: This unfortunate perpetuation of the "blood-libel" myth was later recanted by Crowley. The blood-libel was visited upon early Christians by the Romans and is visited today upon Thelemites by Christian Fundamentalists.

Similarly the visions of Joan of Arc were entirely Christian; but she, like all the others we have mentioned, found somewhere the force to do great things. Of course, it may be said that there is a fallacy in the argument; it may be true that all these great people "saw God," but it does not follow that every one who "sees God" will do great things.

This is true enough. In fact, the majority of people who claim to have "seen God," and who no doubt did "see God" just as much as those whom we have quoted, did nothing else.

But perhaps their silence is not a sign of their weakness, but of their strength. Perhaps these "great" men are the failures of humanity; perhaps it would be better to say nothing; perhaps only an unbalanced mind would wish to alter anything or believe in the possibility of altering anything; but there are those who think existence even in heaven intolerable so long as there is one single being who does not share that joy. There are some who may wish to travel back from the very threshold of the bridal chamber to assist belated guests.

Such at least was the attitude which Gotama Buddha adopted. Nor shall he be alone.

Again it may be pointed out that the contemplative life is generally opposed to the active life, and it must require an extremely careful balance to prevent the one absorbing the other.

As it will be seen later, the "vision of God," or "Union with God," or "Samadhi," or whatever we may agree to call it, has many kinds and many degrees, although there is an impassable abyss between the least of them and the greatest of all the phenomena of normal consciousness. "To sum up," we assert a secret source of energy which explains the phenomenon of Genius.

footnote: We have dealt in this preliminary sketch only with examples of religious genius. Other kinds are subject to the same remarks, but the limits of our space forbid discussion of these.

We do not believe in any supernatural explanations, but insist that this source may be reached by the following out of definite rules, the degree of success depending upon the capacity of the seeker, and not upon the favour of any Divine Being. We assert that the critical phenomenon which determines success is an occurrence in the brain characterized essentially by the uniting of subject and object. We propose to discuss this phenomenon, analyse its nature, determine accurately the physical, mental and moral conditions which are favourable to it, to ascertain its cause, and thus to produce it in ourselves, so that we may adequately study its effects.

CHAPTER I
ASANA

THE problem before us may be stated thus simply. A man wishes to control his mind, to be able to think one chosen thought for as long as he will without interruption.

As previously remarked, the first difficulty arises from the body, which keeps on asserting its presence by causing its victim to itch, and in other ways to be distracted. He wants to stretch, scratch, sneeze. This nuisance is so persistent that the Hindus (in their scientific way) devised a special practice for quieting it.

The word Asana means "posture; but, as with all words which have caused debate, its exact meaning has altered, and it is used in several distinct senses by various authors. The greatest authority on "Yoga"

footnote: Yoga is the general name for that form of meditation which aims at the uniting of subject and object, for "yog" is the root from which are derived the Latin word "Jugum" and the English word "Yoke."

is Patanjali. He says, "Asana is that which is firm and pleasant." This may be taken as meaning the result of success in the practice. Again, Sankhya says, "Posture is that which is steady and easy." And again, "any posture which is steady and easy is an Asana; there is no other rule." Any posture will do.

In a sense this is true, because any posture becomes uncomfortable sooner or later. The steadiness and easiness mark a definite attainment, as will be explained later on. Hindu books, such as the "Shiva Sanhita," give countless postures; many, perhaps most of them, impossible for the average adult European. Others insist that the head, neck, and spine should be kept vertical and straight, for reasons connected with the subject of Prana, which will be dealt with in its proper place. The positions illustrated in Liber E (Equinox I and VII) form the best guide.

footnote: Here are four:

1. Sit in a chair; head up, back straight, knees together, hands on knees, eyes closed. ("The God.")

2. Kneel; buttocks resting on the heels, toes turned back, back and head straight, hands on thighs. ("The Dragon.")

3. Stand; hold left ankle with right hand (and alternately practise right ankle in left hand, etc.), free forefinger on lips. ("The Ibis.")

4. Sit; left heel pressing up anus, right foot poised on its toes, the heel covering the phallus; arms stretched out over the knees: head and back straight. ("The Thunderbolt.")

The extreme of Asana is practised by those Yogis who remain in one position without moving, except in the case of absolute necessity, during their whole lives. One should not criticise such persons without a thorough knowledge of the subject. Such knowledge has not yet been published.

However, one may safely assert that since the great men previously mentioned did not do this, it will not be necessary for their followers. Let us then choose a suitable position, and consider what happens. There is a sort of happy medium between rigidity and limpness; the muscles are not to be strained; and yet they are not allowed to be altogether slack. It is difficult to find a good descriptive word. "Braced" is perhaps the best. A sense of physical alertness is desirable. Think of the tiger about to spring, or of the oarsman waiting for the gun. After a little there will be cramp and fatigue. The student must now set his teeth, and go through with it. The minor sensations of itching, etc., will be found to pass away, if they are resolutely neglected, but the cramp and fatigue may be expected to increase until the end of the practice. One may begin with half an hour or an hour. The student must not mind if the process of quitting the Asana involves several minutes of the acutest agony.

> *WEH footnote: It is important to distinguish between cramp and severe chronic muscle spasm which can tear ligaments. Muscle spasm tends to result from pinching or compressing nerves, and can lead to permanent injury. Also beware of constricted circulation, which produces numbness more than it does pain. Wear loose clothing and avoid pressing on hard objects.*

It will require a good deal of determination to persist day after day, for in most cases it will be found that the discomfort and pain, instead of diminishing, tend to increase.

On the other hand, if the student pay no attention, fail to watch the body, an opposite phenomenon may occur. He shifts to ease himself without knowing that he has done so. To avoid this, choose a position which naturally is rather cramped and awkward, and in which slight changes are not sufficient to bring ease. Otherwise, for the first few days, the student may even imagine that he has conquered the position. In fact, in all these practices their apparent simplicity is such that the beginner is likely to wonder what all the fuss is about, perhaps to think that he is specially gifted. Similarly a man who has never touched a golf club will take his umbrella and carelessly hole a putt which would frighten the best putter alive.

In a few days, however, in all cases, the discomforts will begin. As you go on, they will begin earlier in the course of the hour's exercise. The disinclination to practise at all may become almost unconquerable. One must warn the student against imagining that some other position would be easier to master than the one he has selected. Once you begin to change about you are lost.

Perhaps the reward is not so far distant: it will happen one day that the pain is suddenly forgotten, the fact of the presence of the body is forgotten, and one will realize that during the whole of one's previous life the body was always on the borderland of consciousness, and that consciousness a consciousness of pain; and at this moment one will further realize with an indescribable feeling of relief that not only is this position, which has been so painful, the very ideal of physical comfort, but that all other conceivable positions of the body are uncomfortable. This feeling represents success.

There will be no further difficulty in the practice. One will get into one's Asana with almost the same feeling as that with which a tired man gets into a hot bath; and while he is in that position, the body may be trusted to send him no message that might disturb his mind.

Other results of this practice are described by Hindu authors, but they do not concern us at present. Our first obstacle has been removed, and we can continue with the others.

CHAPTER II
PRANAYAMA AND ITS PARALLEL IN SPEECH, MANTRAYOGA

THE connection between breath and mind will be fully discussed in speaking of the Magick Sword, but it may be useful to premise a few details of a practical character. You may consult various Hindu manuals, and the writing of Kwang Tze, for various notable theories as to method and result.

But in this sceptical system one had better content one's self with statements which are not worth the trouble of doubting.

The ultimate idea of meditation being to still the mind, it may be considered a useful preliminary to still consciousness of all the functions of the body. This has been dealt with in the chapter on Asana. One may, however, mention that some Yogis carry it to the point of trying to stop the beating of the heart. Whether this be desirable or no it would be useless to the beginner, so he will endeavour to make the breathing very slow and very regular. The rules for this practice are given in Liber CCVI.

The best way to time the breathing, once some little skill has been acquired, with a watch to bear witness, is by the use of a mantra. The mantra acts on the thoughts very much as Pranayama does upon the breath. The thought is bound down to a recurring cycle; any intruding thoughts are thrown off by the mantra, just as pieces of putty would be from a fly-wheel; and the swifter the wheel the more difficult would it be for anything to stick.

This is the proper way to practise a mantra. Utter it as loudly and slowly as possible ten times, then not quite so loudly and a very little faster ten times more. Continue this process until there is nothing but a rapid movement of the lips; this movement should be continued with increased velocity and diminishing intensity until the mental muttering completely absorbs the physical. The student is by this time absolutely still, with the mantra racing in his brain; he should, however, continue to speed it up until he reaches his limit, at which he should continue for as long as possible, and then cease the practice by reversing the process above described.

Any sentence may be used as a mantra, and possibly the Hindus are correct in thinking that there is a particular sentence best suited to any particular man. Some men might find the liquid mantras of the Quran slide too easily, so that it would be possible to continue another train of thought without disturbing the mantra; one is supposed while saying the mantra to meditate upon its meaning. This suggests that the student might construct for himself a mantra which should represent the Universe in sound, as the pantacle

footnote: See Part II.

should do in form. Occasionally a mantra may be "given," "i.e.," heard in some unexplained manner during a meditation. One man, for example, used the words: "And strive to see in everything the will of God;" to another, while engaged in killing thoughts, came the words "and push it down," apparently referring to the action of the inhibitory centres which he was using. By keeping on with this he got his "result."

The ideal mantra should be rhythmical, one might even say musical; but there should be sufficient emphasis on some syllable to assist the faculty of attention. The best mantras are of medium length, so far as the beginner is concerned. If the mantra is too long, one is apt to forget it, unless one practises very hard for a great length of time. On the other hand, mantras of a single syllable, such as "Aum," *footnote: However, in saying a mantra containing the word "Aum," one sometimes forgets the other words, and remains concentrated, repeating the "Aum" at intervals; but this is the result of a practice already begun, not the beginning of a practice.*

are rather jerky; the rhythmical idea is lost. Here are a few useful mantras:

1. Aum.

2. Aum Tat Sat Aum. This mantra is purely spondaic.

II.

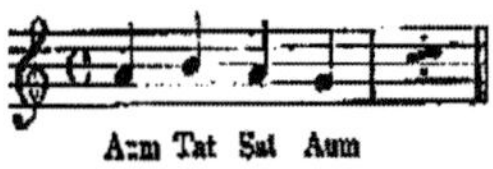

3. Aum mani padme hum; two trochees between two caesuras.

III.

4. Aum shivaya vashi; three trochees. Note that "shi" means rest, the absolute or male aspect of the Deity; "va" is energy, the manifested or female side of the Deity. This Mantra therefore expresses the whole course of the Universe, from Zero through the finite back to Zero.

IV.

5. Allah. The syllables of this are accented equally, with a certain pause between them; and are usually combined by fakirs with a rhythmical motion of the body to and fro.

6. Hua allahu alazi lailaha illa Hua.

Here are some longer ones:

7. The famous Gayatri.

Aum! tat savitur varenyam
Bhargo devasya dimahi
Dhiyo yo na pratyodayat.

Scan this as trochaic tetrameters.

8. Qol: Hua Allahu achad; Allahu Assamad; lam yalid walam yulad; walam yakun lahu kufwan achad.

9. This mantra is the holiest of all that are or can be. It is from the Stele of Revealing.

footnote: See Equinox VII.

A ka dua
Tuf ur biu
Bi aa chefu
Dudu ner af an nuteru.

IX.

Such are enough for selection.

footnote: Meanings of mantras:

1 Aum is the sound produced by breathing forcibly from the back of the throat and gradually closing the mouth. The three sounds represent the creative, preservative, and destructive principles. There are many more points about this, enough to fill a volume.

2. O that Existent! O! — An aspiration after realty, truth.

3. O the Jewel in the Lotus! Amen! — Refers to Buddha and Harpocrates; but also the symbolism of the Rosy Cross.

4. Gives the cycle of creation. Peace manifesting as Power, Power dissolving in Peace.

5. God. It adds to 66, the sum of the first 11 numbers.

6. He is God, and there is no other God than He.

7. O! let us strictly meditate on the adorable light of that divine Savitri (the interior Sun, etc.). May she enlighten our minds!

8. Say:
He is God alone!
God the Eternal!
He begets not and is not begotten!
Nor is there like unto Him any one!

9. Unity uttermost showed!
I adore the might of Thy breath,
Supreme and terrible God,
Who makest the Gods and Death
To tremble before Thee: —
I, I adore Thee!

There are many other mantras. Sri Sabapaty Swami gives a particular one for each of the Cakkras. But let the student select one mantra and master it thoroughly.

You have not even begun to master a mantra until it continues unbroken through sleep. This is much easier than it sounds.

Some schools advocate practising a mantra with the aid of instrumental music and dancing. Certainly very remarkable effects are obtained in the way of "magic" powers; whether great spiritual results are equally common is a doubtful point. Persons wishing to study them may remember that the Sahara desert is within three days of London; and no doubt the Sidi Aissawa would be glad to accept pupils. This discussion of the parallel science of mantra-yoga has led us far indeed from the subject of Pranayama.

Pranayama is notably useful in quieting the emotions and appetites; and, whether by reason of the mechanical pressure which it asserts, or by the thorough combustion which it assures in the lungs, it seems to be admirable from the standpoint of health. Digestive troubles in particular are very easy to remove in this way. It purifies both the body and the lower functions of the mind,

footnote: Emphatically. Emphatically. Emphatically. It is impossible to combine Pranayama properly performed with emotional thought. It should be resorted to immediately, at all times during life, when calm is threatened.

On the whole, the ambulatory practices are more generally useful to the health than the sedentary; for in this way walking and fresh air are assured. But some of the sedentary practice should be done, and combined with meditation. Of course when actually "racing" to get results, walking is a distraction.

and should be practised certainly never less than one hour daily by the serious student.

Four hours is a better period, a golden mean; sixteen hours is too much for most people.

CHAPTER III
YAMA AND NIYAMA

footnote: Yama means literally "control." It is dealt with in detail in Part II, "The Wand."

THE Hindus have place these two attainments in the forefront of their programme. They are the "moral qualities" and "good works" which are supposed to predispose to mental calm.

"Yama" consists of non-killing, truthfulness, non-stealing, continence, and non-receiving of any gift.

In the Buddhist system, "Sila", "Virtue," is similarly enjoined. The qualities are, for the layman, these five: Thou shalt not kill. Thou shalt not steal. Thou shalt not lie. Thou shalt not commit adultery. Thou shalt drink no intoxicating drink. For the monk many others are added.

The commandments of Moses are familiar to all; they are rather similar; and so are those given by Christ

footnote: Not, however, original. The whole sermon is to be found in the Talmud.

in the "Sermon on the Mount."

Some of these are only the "virtues" of a slave, invented by his master to keep him in order. The real point of the Hindu "Yama" is that breaking any of these would tend to excite the mind.

Subsequent theologians have tried to improve upon the teachings of the Masters, have given a sort of mystical importance to these virtues; they have insisted upon them for their own sake, and turned them into puritanism and formalism. Thus "non-killing," which originally meant "do not excite yourself by stalking tigers," has been interpreted to mean that it is a crime to drink water that has not been strained, lest you should kill the animalcula.

But this constant worry, this fear of killing anything by mischance is, on the whole, worse than a hand-to-hand conflict with a griesly bear. If the barking of a dog disturbs your meditation, it is simplest to shoot the dog, and think no more about it.

A similar difficulty with wives has caused some masters to recommend celibacy. In all these questions common sense must be the guide. No fixed rule can be laid down. The "non-receiving of gifts," for instance, is rather important for a Hindu, who would be thoroughly upset for weeks if any one gave him a coconut: but the average European takes things as they come by the time that he has been put into long trousers.

The only difficult question is that of continence, which is complicated by many considerations, such as that of energy; but everybody's mind is hopelessly muddled on this subject, which some people confuse with erotology, and others with sociology. There will be no clear thinking on this matter until it is understood as being solely a branch of athletics.

We may then dismiss Yama and Niyama with this advice: let the student decide for himself what form of life, what moral code, will least tend to excite his mind; but once he has formulated it, let him stick to it, avoiding opportunism; and let him be very careful to take no credit for what he does or refrains from doing — it is a purely practical code, of no value in itself.

The cleanliness which assists the surgeon in his work would prevent the engineer from doing his at all.

(Ethical questions are adequately dealt with in "Then Tao" in "Konx Om Pax," and should be there studied.

Also see Liber XXX of the A. A. Also in Liber CCXX, the "Book of the Law," it is said: "DO WHAT THOU WILT shall be the whole of the Law."

WEH FOOTNOTE: SIC, should be: "Do what thou wilt shall be the whole of the Law."

Remember that for the purpose of this treatise the whole object of Yama and Niyama is to live so that no emotion or passion disturbs the mind.)

CHAPTER IV
PRATYAHARA

PRATYAHARA is the first process in the mental part of our task. The previous practices, Asana, Pranayama, Yama, and Niyama, are all acts of the body, while mantra is connected with speech: Pratyahara is purely mental.

And what is Pratyahara? This word is used by different authors in different senses. The same word is employed to designate both the practice and the result. It means for our present purpose a process rather strategical than practical; it is introspection, a sort of general examination of the contents of the mind which we wish to control: Asana having been mastered, all immediate exciting causes have been removed, and we are free to think what we are thinking about.

A very similar experience to that of Asana is in store for us. At first we shall very likely flatter ourselves that our minds are pretty calm; this is a defect of observation. Just as the European standing for the first time on the edge of the desert will see nothing there, while his Arab can tell him the family history of each of the fifty persons in view, because he has learnt how to look, so with practice the thoughts will become more numerous and more insistent.

As soon as the body was accurately observed it was found to be terribly restless and painful; now that we observe the mind it is seen to be more restless and painful still. (*See diagram opposite.*)

A similar curve might be plotted for the real and apparent painfulness of Asana.

Conscious of this fact, we begin to try to control it: "Not quite so many thoughts, please!" "Don't think quite so fast, please!" "No more of that kind of thought, please!" It is only then that we discover that what we thought was a school of playful porpoises is really the convolutions of the sea-serpent. The attempt to repress has the effect of exciting.

When the unsuspecting pupil first approaches his holy but wily Guru, and demands magical powers, that Wise One replies that he will confer them, points out with much caution and secrecy some particular spot on the pupil's body which has never previously attracted his attention, and says: "In order to obtain this magical power which you seek, all that is necessary is to wash seven times in the Ganges during seven days, being particularly careful to avoid thinking of that one spot." Of course the unhappy youth spends a disgusted week in thinking of little else.

It is positively amazing with what persistence a thought, even a whole train of thoughts, returns again and again to the charge. It becomes a positive nightmare. It is intensely annoying, too, to find that one does not become conscious that one has got on to the forbidden subject until one has gone right through with it. However, one continues day after day investigating thoughts and trying to check them; and sooner or later one proceeds to the next stage, Dharana, the attempt to restrain the mind to a single object.

Before we go on to this, however, we must consider what is meant by success in Pratyahara. This is a very extensive subject, and different authors take widely divergent views. One writer means an analysis so acute that every thought is resolved into a number of elements (see "The Psychology of Hashish," Section V, in Equinox II).

Others take the view that success in the practice is something like the experience which Sir Humphrey Davy had as a result of taking nitrous oxide, in which he exclaimed: "The universe is composed exclusively of ideas."

Others say that it gives Hamlet's feeling: "There's nothing good or bad but thinking makes it so," interpreted as literally as was done by Mrs. Eddy.

However, the main point is to acquire some sort of inhibitory power over the thoughts. Fortunately there is an unfailing method of acquiring this power. It is given in Liber III. If Sections 1 and 2 are practised (if necessary with the assistance of another person to aid your vigilance) you will soon be able to master the final section.

In some people this inhibitory power may flower suddenly in very much the same way as occurred with Asana. Quite without any relaxation of vigilance, the mind will suddenly be stilled. There will be a marvellous feeling of peace and rest, quite different from the lethargic feeling which is produced by over-eating. It is difficult to say whether so definite a result would come to all, or even to most people. The matter is one of no very great importance. If you have acquired the power of checking the rise of thought you may proceed to the next stage.

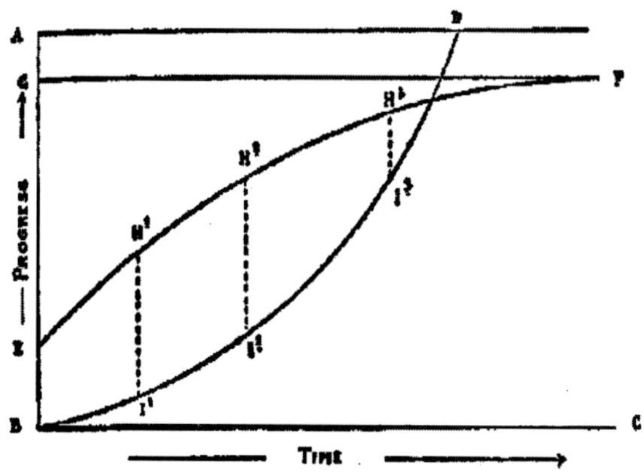

BD shows the Control of the Mind, improving slowly at first, afterwards more quickly. It starts from at or near zero, and should reach absolute control at D.

EF shows the Power of Observation of the contents of the mind, improving quickly at first, afterwards more slowly, up to perfection at F. It starts well above zero in the case of most educated men.

The height of the perpendiculars HI indicates the dissatisfaction of the student with his power of control. Increasing at first, it ultimately diminishes to zero.

CHAPTER V
DHARANA

NOW that we have learnt to observe the mind, so that we know how it works to some extent, and have begun to understand the elements of control, we may try the result of gathering together all the powers of the mind, and attempting to focus them on a single point.

We know that it is fairly easy for the ordinary educated mind to think without much distraction on a subject in which it is much interested. We have the popular phrase, "revolving a thing in the mind"; and as long as the subject is sufficiently complex, as long as thoughts pass freely, there is no great difficulty. So long as a gyroscope is in motion, it remains motionless relatively to its support, and even resists attempts to distract it; when it stops it falls from that position. If the earth ceased to spin round the sun, it would at once fall into the sun.

The moment then that the student takes a simple subject — or rather a simple object — and imagines it or visualizes it, he will find that it is not so much his creature as he supposed. Other thoughts will invade the mind, so that the object is altogether forgotten, perhaps for whole minutes at a time; and at other times the object itself will begin to play all sorts of tricks.

Suppose you have chosen a white cross. It will move its bar up and down, elongate the bar, turn the bar oblique, get its arms unequal, turn upside down, grow branches, get a crack around it or a figure upon it, change its shape altogether like an Amoeba, change its size and distance as a whole, change the degree of its illumination, and at the same time change its colour. It will get splotchy and blotchy, grow patterns, rise, fall, twist and turn; clouds will pass over its face. There is no conceivable change of which it is incapable. Not to mention its total disappearance, and replacement by something altogether different!

Any one to whom this experience does not occur need not imagine that he is meditating. It shows merely that he is incapable of concentrating his mind in the very smallest degree. Perhaps a student may go for several days before discovering that he is not meditating. When he does, the obstinacy of the object will infuriate him; and it is only now that his real troubles will begin, only now that Will comes really into play, only now that his manhood is tested. If it were not for the Will-development which he got in the conquest of Asana, he would probably give up. As it is, the mere physical agony which he underwent is the veriest trifle compared with the horrible tedium of Dharana.

For the first week it may seem rather amusing, and you may even imagine you are progressing; but as the practice teaches you what you are doing, you will apparently get worse and worse.

Please understand that in doing this practice you are supposed to be seated in Asana, and to have note-book and pencil by your side, and a watch in front of you. You are not to practise at first for more than ten minutes at a time, so as to avoid risk of overtiring the brain. In fact you will probably find that the whole of your will-power is not equal to keeping to a subject at all for so long as three minutes, or even apparently concentrating on it for so long as three seconds, or three-fifths of one second. By "keeping to it at all" is meant the mere attempt to keep to it. The mind becomes so fatigued, and the object so incredibly loathsome, that it is useless to continue for the time being. In Frater P.'s record we find that after daily practice for six months, meditations of four minutes and less are still being recorded.

The student is supposed to count the number of times that his thought wanders; this he can do on his fingers or on a string of beads.

footnote: This counting can easily become quite mechanical. With the thought that reminds you of a break associate the notion of counting.

The grosser kind of break can be detected by another person. It is accompanied with a flickering of the eyelid, and can be seen by him. With practice he could detect even very small breaks.

If these breaks seem to become more frequent instead of less frequent, the student must not be discourage; this is partially caused by his increased accuracy of observation. In exactly the same way, the introduction of vaccination resulted in an apparent increase in the number of cases of smallpox, the reason being that people began to tell the truth about the disease instead of faking.

Soon, however, the control will improve faster than the observation. When this occurs the improvement will become apparent in the record. Any variation will probably be due to accidental circumstances; for example, one night your may be very tired when you start; another night you may have headache or indigestion. You will do well to avoid practising at such times.

We will suppose, then, that you have reached the stage when your average practice on one subject is about half an hour, and the average number of breaks between ten and twenty. One would suppose that this implied that during the periods between the breaks one was really concentrated, but this is not the case. The mind is flickering, although imperceptibly. However, there may be sufficient real steadiness even at this early stage to cause some very striking phenomena, of which the most marked is one which will possibly make you think that you have gone to sleep. Or, it may seem quite inexplicable, and in any case will disgust you with yourself. You will completely forget who you are, what you are, and what you are doing. A similar phenomenon sometimes happens when one is half awake in the morning, and one cannot think what town one is living in. The similarity of these two things is rather significant. It suggests that what is really happening is that you are waking up from the sleep which men call waking, the sleep whose dreams are life.

There is another way to test one's progress in this practice, and that is by the character of the breaks.

"Breaks" are classed as follows:

Firstly, physical sensations. These should have been overcome by Asana.

Secondly, breaks that seem to be dictated by events immediately preceding the meditation. Their activity becomes tremendous. Only by this practice does one understand how much is really observed by the sense without the mind becoming conscious of it.

Thirdly, there is a class of breaks partaking of the nature of reverie or "day-dreams." These are very insidious — one may go on for a long time without realizing that one has wandered at all.

Fourthly, we get a very high class of break, which is a sort of aberration of the control itself. You think, "How well I am doing it!" or perhaps that it would be rather a good idea if you were on a desert island, or if you were in a sound-proof house, or if you were sitting by a waterfall. But these are only trifling variations from the vigilance itself.

A fifth class of breaks seems to have no discoverable source in the mind. Such may even take the form of actual hallucination, usually auditory. Of course, such hallucinations are infrequent, and are recognized for what they are; otherwise the student had better see his doctor. The usual kind consists of odd sentences or fragments of sentences, which are heard quite distinctly in a recognizable human voice, not the student's own voice, or that of any one he knows. A similar phenomenon is observed by wireless operators, who call such messages "atmospherics."

There is *a further kind of break, which is the desired result itself.* It must be dealt with later in detail.

Now there is a real sequence in these classes of breaks. As control improves, the percentage of primaries and secondaries will diminish, even though the total number of breaks in a meditation remain stationary. By the time that you are meditating two or three hours a day, and filing up most of the rest of the day with other practices designed to assist, when nearly every time something or other happens, and there is constantly a feeling of being "on the brink of something pretty big," one may expect to proceed to the next state — Dhyana.

CHAPTER VI
DHYANA

THIS word has two quite distinct and mutually exclusive meanings. The first refers to the result itself. Dhyana is the same word as the Pali "Jhana." The Buddha counted eight Jhanas, which are evidently different degrees and kinds of trance. The Hindu also speaks of Dhyana as a lesser form of Samadhi. Others, however, treat it as if it were merely an intensification of Dharana. Patanjali says: "Dhrana is holding the mind on to some particular object. An unbroken flow of knowledge in that subject is Dhyana. When that, giving up all forms, reflects only the meaning, it is Samadhi." He combines these three into Samyama.

We shall treat of Dhyana as a result rather than as a method. Up to this point ancient authorities have been fairly reliable guides, except with regard to their crabbed ethics; but when they get on the subject of results of meditation, they completely lose their heads.

They exhaust the possibilities of poetry to declare what is demonstrably untrue. For example, we find in the Shiva Sanhita that "he who daily contemplates on this lotus of the heart is eagerly desired by the daughters of Gods, has clairaudience, clairvoyance, and can walk in the air." Another person "can make gold, discover medicine for disease, and see hidden treasures." All this is filth. What is the curse upon religion that its tenets must always be associated with every kind of extravagance and falsehood?

There is one exception; it is the A.'.A.'., whose members are extremely careful to make no statement at all that cannot be verified in the usual manner; or where this is not easy, at least avoid anything like a dogmatic statement. In Their second book of practical instruction, Liber O, occur these words:

"By doing certain things certain results will follow. Students are most earnestly warned against attributing objective reality or philosophical validity to any of them."

Those golden words!

In discussing Dhyana, then, let it be clearly understood that something unexpected is about to be described.

We shall consider its nature and estimate its value in a perfectly unbiassed way, without allowing ourselves the usual rhapsodies, or deducing any theory of the universe. One extra fact may destroy some existing theory; that is common enough. But no single fact is sufficient to construct one.

It will have been understood that Dharana, Dhyana, and Samadhi form a continuous process, and exactly when the climax comes does not matter. It is of this climax that we must speak, for this is a matter of "experience," and a very striking one.

In the course of our concentration we noticed that the contents of the mind at any moment consisted of two things, and no more: the Object, variable, and the Subject, invariable, or apparently so. By success in Dharana the object has been made as invariable as the subject.

Now the result of this is that the two become one. This phenomenon usually comes as a tremendous shock. It is indescribable even by the masters of language; and it is therefore not surprising that semi-educated stutterers wallow in oceans of gush.

All the poetic faculties and all the emotional faculties are thrown into a sort of ecstasy by an occurrence which overthrows the mind, and makes the rest of life seem absolutely worthless in comparison.

Good literature is principally a matter of clear observation and good judgment expressed in the simplest way. For this reason none of the great events of history (such as earthquakes and battles) have been well described by eye-witnesses, unless those eye-witnesses were out of danger. But even when one has become accustomed to Dhyana by constant repetition, no words seem adequate.

One of the simplest forms of Dhyana may be called "the Sun." The sun is seen (as it were) by itself, not by an observer; and although the physical eye cannot behold the sun, one is compelled to make the statement that this "Sun" is far more brilliant than the sun of nature. The whole thing takes place on a higher level.

Also the conditions of thought, time, and space are abolished. It is impossible to explain what this really means: only experience can furnish you with apprehension.

(This, too, has its analogies in ordinary life; the conceptions of higher mathematics cannot be grasped by the beginner, cannot be explained to the layman.)

A further development is the appearance of the Form which has been universally described as human; although the persons describing it proceed to add a great number of details which are not human at all. This particular appearance is usually assumed to be "God."

But, whatever it may be, the result on the mind of the student is tremendous; all his thoughts are pushed to their greatest development. He sincerely believes that they have the divine sanction; perhaps he even supposes that they emanate from this "God." He goes back into the world armed with this intense conviction and authority. He proclaims his ideas without the restraint which is imposed upon most persons by doubt, modesty, and diffidence;

footnote: This lack of restraint is not to be confused with that observed in intoxication and madness. Yet there is a very striking similarity, though only a superficial one.

while further there is, one may suppose, a real clarification.

In any case, the mass of mankind is always ready to be swayed by anything thus authoritative and distinct. History is full of stories of officers who have walked unarmed up to a mutinous regiment, and disarmed them by the mere force of confidence. The power of the orator over the mob is well known. It is, probably, for this reason that the prophet has been able to constrain mankind to obey his law. I never occurs to him that any one can do otherwise. In practical life one can walk past any guardian, such as a sentry or ticket-collector, if one can really act so that the man is somehow persuaded that you have a right to pass unchallenged.

This power, by the way, is what has been described by magicians as the power of invisibility. Somebody or other has an excellent story of four quite reliable men who were on the look-out for a murderer, and had instructions to let no one pass, and who all swore subsequently in presence of the dead body that no one had passed. None of them had seen the postman.

The thieves who stole the "Gioconda" from the Louvre were probably disguised as workmen, and stole the picture under the very eye of the guardian; very likely got him to help them.

It is only necessary to believe that a thing must be to bring it about. This belief must not be an emotional or an intellectual one. It resides in a deeper portion of the mind, yet a portion not so deep but that most men, probably all successful men, will understand these words, having experience of their own with which they can compare it.

The most important factor in Dhyana is, however, the annihilation of the Ego. Our conception of the universe must be completely overturned if we are to admit this as valid; and it is time that we considered what is really happening.

It will be conceded that we have given a very rational explanation of the greatness of great men. They had an experience so overwhelming, so out of proportion to the rest of things, that they were freed from all the petty hindrances which prevent the normal man from carrying out his projects.

Worrying about clothes, food, money, what people may think, how and why, and above all the fear of consequences, clog nearly every one. Nothing is easier, theoretically, than for an anarchist to kill a king. He has only to buy a rifle, make himself a first-class shot, and shoot the king from a quarter of a mile away. And yet, although there are plenty of anarchists, outrages are very few. At the same time, the police would probably be the first to admit that if any man were really tired of life, in his deepest being, a state very different from that in which a man goes about saying he is tired of life, he could manage somehow or other to kill someone first.

Now the man who has experienced any of the more intense forms of Dhyana is thus liberated. The Universe is thus destroyed for him, and he for it. His will can therefore go on its way unhampered. One may imagine that in the case of Mohammed he had cherished for years a tremendous ambition, and never done anything because those qualities which were subsequently manifested as statesmanship warned him that he was impotent. His vision in the cave gave him that confidence which was required, the faith that moves mountains. There are a lot of solid-seeming things in this world which a child could push over; but not one has the courage to push.

Let us accept provisionally this explanation of greatness, and pass it by. Ambition has led us to this point; but we are now interested in the work for its own sake.

A most astounding phenomenon has happened to us; we have had an experience which makes Love, fame, rank, ambition, wealth, look like thirty cents; and we begin to wonder passionately, "What is truth?" The Universe has tumbled about our ears like a house of cards, and we have tumbled too. Yet this ruin is like the opening of the Gates of Heaven! Here is a tremendous problem, and there is something within us which ravins for its solution.

Let us see what what explanation we can find.

The first suggestion which would enter a well-balanced mind, versed in the study of nature, is that we have experienced a mental catastrophe. Just as a blow on the head will made a man "see stars," so one might suppose that the terrific mental strain of Dharana has somehow over-excited the brain, and caused a spasm, or possibly even the breaking of a small vessel. There seems no reason to reject this explanation altogether, though it would be quite absurd to suppose that to accept it would be to condemn the practice. Spasm is a normal function of at least one of the organs of the body. That the brain is not damaged by the practice is proved by the fact that many people who claim to have had this experience repeatedly continue to exercise the ordinary avocations of life without diminished activity.

We may dismiss, then the physiological question. It throws no light on the main problem, which is the value of the testimony of the experience.

Now this is a very difficult question, and raises the much larger question as to the value of any testimony. Every possible thought has been doubted at some time or another, except the thought which can only be expressed by a note of interrogation, since to doubt that thought asserts it. (For a full discussion see "The Soldier and the Hunchback," "Equinox," I.) But apart from this deep-seated philosophic doubt there is the practical doubt of every day. The popular phrase, "to doubt the evidence of one's senses," shows us that that evidence is normally accepted; but a man of science does nothing of the sort. He is so well aware that his senses constantly deceive him, that he invents elaborate instruments to correct them. And he is further aware that the Universe which he can directly perceive through sense, is the minutest fraction of the Universe which he knows indirectly.

For example, four-fifths of the air is composed of nitrogen. If anyone were to bring a bottle of nitrogen into this room it would be exceedingly difficult to say what it was; nearly all the tests that one could apply to it would be negative. His senses tell him little or nothing.

Argon was only discovered at all by comparing the weight of chemically pure nitrogen with that of the nitrogen of the air. This had often been done, but no one had sufficiently fine instruments even to perceive the discrepancy. To take another example, a famous man of science asserted not so long ago that science could never discover the chemical composition of the fixed stars. Yet this has been done, and with certainty.

If you were to ask your man of science for his "theory of the real," he would tell you that the "ether," which cannot be perceived in any way by any of the senses, or detected by any instruments, and which possesses qualities which are, to use ordinary language, impossible, is very much more real than the chair he is sitting on. The chair is only one fact; and its existence is testified by one very fallible person. The ether is the necessary deduction from millions of facts, which have been verified again and again and checked by every possible test of truth. There is therefore no "a priori" reason for rejecting anything on the ground that it is not directly perceived by the senses.

To turn to another point. One of our tests of truth is the vividness of the impression. An isolated event in the past of no great importance may be forgotten; and if it be in some way recalled, one may find one's self asking: "Did I dream it? or did it really happen?" What can never be forgotten is the "catastrophic". The first death among the people that one loves (for example) would never be forgotten; for the first time one would "realize" what one had previously merely "known". Such an experience sometimes drives people insane. Men of science have been known to commit suicide when their pet theory has been shattered. This problem has been discussed freely in "Science and Buddhism,"

footnote: See Crowley, "Collected Works."

"Time," "The Camel," and other papers. This much only need we say in this place that Dhyana has to be classed as the most vivid and catastrophic of all experiences. This will be confirmed by any one who has been there.

It is, then, difficult to overrate the value that such an experience has for the individual, especially as it is his entire conception of things, including his most deep-seated conception, the standard to which he has always referred everything, his own self, that is overthrown; and when we try to explain it away as hallucination, temporary suspension of the faculties or something similar, we find ourselves unable to do so. You cannot argue with a flash of lightning that has knocked you down.

Any mere theory is easy to upset. One can find flaws in the reasoning process, one can assume that the premisses are in some way false; but in this case, if one attacks the evidence for Dhyana, the mind is staggered by the fact that all other experience, attacked on the same lines, will fall much more easily.

In whatever way we examine it the result will always be the same. Dhyana may be false; but, if so, so is everything else.

Now the mind refuses to rest in a belief of the unreality of its own experiences. It may not be what is seems; but it must be something, and if (on the whole) ordinary life is something, how much more must that be by whose light ordinary life seems nothing!

The ordinary man sees the falsity and disconnectedness and purposelessness of dreams; he ascribes them (rightly) to a disordered mind. The philosopher looks upon waking life with similar contempt; and the person who has experienced Dhyana takes the same view, but not by mere pale intellectual conviction. Reasons, however cogent, never convince utterly; but this man in Dhyana has the same commonplace certainty that a man has on waking from a nightmare. "I wasn't falling down a thousand flights of stairs, it was only a bad dream."

Similarly comes the reflection of the man who has had experience of Dhyana: "I am not that wretched insect, that imperceptible parasite of earth; it was only a bad dream." And as you could not convince the normal man that his nightmare was more real than his awakening, so you cannot convince the other that his Dhyana was hallucination, even though he is only too well aware that he has fallen from that state into "normal" life.

It is probably rare for a single experience to upset thus radically the whole conception of the Universe, just as sometimes, in the first moments of waking, there remains a half-doubt as to whether dream or waking is real. But as one gains further experience, when Dhyana is no longer a shock, when the student has had plenty of time to make himself at home in the new world, this conviction will become absolute.

Footnote: It should be remembered that at present there are no data for determining the duration of Dhyana. One can only say that, since it certainly occured between such and such hours, it must have lasted less than that time. Thus we see, from Frater P.'s record, that it can certianly occur in less than an hour and five minutes.

Another rationalist consideration is this. The student has not been trying to excite the mind but to calm it, not to produce any one thought but to exclude all thoughts; for there is no connection between the object of meditation and the Dhyana. Why must we suppose a breaking down of the whole process, especially as the mind bears no subsequent traces of any interference, such as pain or fatigue? Surely this once, if never again, the Hindu image expresses the simplest theory!

That image is that of a lake into which five glaciers move. These glaciers are the senses. While ice (the impressions) is breaking off constantly into the lake, the waters are troubled. If the glaciers are stopped the surface becomes calm; and then, and only then, can it reflect unbroken the disk of the sum. This sun is the "soul" or "God."

We should, however, avoid these terms for the present, on account of their implications. Let us rather speak of this sun as "some unknown thing whose presence has been masked by all things known, and by the knower."

It is probable, too, that our memory of Dhyana is not of the phenomenon itself, but of the image left thereby on the mind. But this is true of all phenomena, as Berkeley and Kant have proved beyond all question. This matter, then, need not concern us.

We may, however, provisionally accept the view that Dhyana is real; more real and thus of more importance to ourselves than all other experience. This state has been described not only by the Hindus and Buddhists, but by Mohammedans and Christians. In Christian writings, however, the deeply-seated dogmatic bias has rendered their documents worthless to the average man. They ignore the essential conditions of Dhyana, and insist on the inessential, to a much greater extent than the best Indian writers. But to any one with experience and some knowledge of comparative religion the identity is certain. We may now proceed to Samadhi.

CHAPTER VII
SAMADHI

MORE rubbish has been written about Samadhi than enough; we must endeavour to avoid adding to the heap. Even Patanjali, who is extraordinarily clear and practical in most things, begins to rave when he talks of it. Even if what he said were true he should not have mentioned it; because it does not sound true, and we should make no statement that is *à priori* improbable without being prepared to back it up with the fullest proofs. But it is more than likely that his commentators have misunderstood him.

The most reasonable statement, of any acknowledged authority, is that of Vajna Valkya, who says: "By Pranayama impurities of the body are thrown out; by Dharana the impurities of the mind; by Pratyahara the impurities of attachment; and by Samadhi is taken off everything that hides the lordship of the soul." There is a modest statement in good literary form. If we can only do as well as that!

In the first place, what is the meaning of the term? Etymologically, "Sam" is the Greek {in Greek alphabet: sigma-upsilon-nu—} the English prefix "syn-" meaning "together with." "Adhi" means "Lord," and a reasonable translation of the whole word would be "Union with God," the exact term used by Christian mystics to describe their attainment.

Now there is great confusion, because the Buddhists use the word Samadhi to mean something entirely different, the mere faculty of attention. Thus, with them, to think of a cat is to "make Samadhi" on that cat. They use the word Jhana to describe mystic states. This is excessively misleading, for as we saw in the last section, Dhyana is a preliminary of Samadhi, and of course Jhana is merely the wretched plebeian Pali corruption of it.

footnote: The vulgarism and provincialism of the Buddhist cannon is infinitely repulsive to all nice minds; and the attempt to use the terms of an ego-centric philosophy to explain the details of a psychology whose principal doctrine is the denial of the ego, was the work of a mischievous idiot. Let us unhesitatingly reject these abominations, these nastinesses of the beggars dressed in rags that they have snatched from corpses, and follow the etymological signification of the word as given above!

There are many kinds of Samadhi.

footnote: Apparently. That is, the obvious results are different. Possibly the cause is only one, refracted through diverse media.

"Some authors consider Atmadarshana, the Universe as a single phenomenon without conditions, to be the first real Samadhi." If we accept this, we must relegate many less exalted states to the class of Dhyana. Patanjali enumerates a number of these states: to perform these on different things gives different magical powers; or so he says. These need not be debated here. Any one who wants magic powers can get them in dozens of different ways.

Power grows faster than desire. The boy who wants money to buy lead soldiers sets to work to obtain it, and by the time he has got it wants something else instead — in all probability something just beyond his means.

Such is the splendid history of all spiritual advance! One never stops to take the reward.

We shall therefore not trouble at all about what any Samadhi may or may not bring as far as its results in our lives are concerned. We began this book, it will be remembered, with considerations of death. Death has now lost all meaning. The idea of death depends on those of the ego, and of time; these ideas have been destroyed; and so "Death is swallowed up in victory." We shall now only be interested in what Samadhi is in itself, and in the conditions which cause it.

Let us try a final definition. Dhyana resembles Samadhi in many respects. There is a union of the ego and the non-ego, and a loss of the senses of time and space and causality. Duality in any form is abolished. The idea of time involves that of two consecutive things, that of space two non-coincident things, that of causality two connected things.

These Dhyanic conditions contradict those of normal thought; but in Samadhi they are very much more marked than in Dhyana. And while in the latter it seems like a simple union of two things, in the former it appears as if all things rushed together and united. One might say that in Dhyana there was still this quality latent, that the One existing was opposed to the Many non-existing; in Samadhi the Many and the One are united in a union of Existence with non-Existence. This definition is not made from reflection, but from memory.

Further, it is easy to master the "trick" or "knack" of Dhyana. After a while one can get into that state without preliminary practice; and, looking at it from this point, one seems able to reconcile the two meanings of the word which we debated in the last section. From below Dhyana seems like a trance, an experience so tremendous that one cannot think of anything bigger, while from above it seems merely a state of mind as natural as any other. Frater P., before he had Samadhi, wrote of Dhyana: "Perhaps as a result of the intense control a nervous storm breaks: this we call Dhyana. Samadhi is but an expansion of this, so far as I can see."

Five years later he would not take this view. He would say perhaps that Dhyana was "a flowing of the mind in one unbroken current from the ego to the non-ego without consciousness of either, accompanied by a crescent wonder and bliss." He can understand how that is the natural result of Dhyana, but he cannot call Dhyana in the same way the precursor of Samadhi. Perhaps he does not really know the conditions which induce Samadhi. He can produce Dhyana at will in the course of a few minutes' work; and it often happens with apparent spontaneity: with Samadhi this is unfortunately not the case. He probably can get it at will, but could not say exactly how, or tell how long it might take him; and he could not be "sure" of getting it at all.

One feels "sure" that one can walk a mile along a level road. One knows the conditions, and it would have to be a very extraordinary set of circumstances that would stop one. But though it would be equally fair to say: "I have climbed the Matterhorn and I know I can climb it again," yet there are all sorts of more or less probable circumstances any one of which would prevent success.

Now we do know this, that if thought is kept single and steady, Dhyana results. We do not know whether an intensification of this is sufficient to cause Samadhi, or whether some other circumstances are required. One is science, the other empiricism.

One author says (unless memory deceives) that twelve seconds' steadiness is Dharana, a hundred and forty-four Dhyana, and seventeen hundred and twenty-eight Samadhi. And Vivekananda, commenting on Patanjali, makes Dhyana a mere prolongation of Dharana; but says further: "Suppose I were meditating on a book, and I gradually succeeded in concentrating the mind on it , and perceiving only the internal sensation, the meaning unexpressed in any form, that state of Dhyana is called Samadhi."

Other authors are inclined to suggest that Samadhi results from meditating on subjects that are in themselves worthy. For example, Vivekananda says: "Think of any holy subject:" and explains this as follows: "This does not mean any wicked subject."(!)

Frater P. would not like to say definitely whether he ever got Dhyana from common objects. He gave up the practice after a few months, and meditated on the Cakkras, etc. Also his Dhyana became so common that he gave up recording it. But if he wished to do it this minute he would choose something to excite his "godly fear," or "holy awe," or "wonderment."

footnote: It is rather a breach of the scepticism which is the basis of our system to admit that anything can be in any way better than another. Do it thus: "A., is a thing that B. thinks 'holy.' It is natural therefore for B. to meditate on it." Get rid of the ego, observe all your actions as if they were another's, and you will avoid ninety-nine percent. of the troubles that await you.

There is no apparent reason why Dhyana should not occur when thinking of any common object of the sea-shore, such as a blue pig; but Frater P.'s constant reference to this as the usual object of his meditation need not be taken "au pied de la lettre." His records of meditation contain no reference to this remarkable animal.

It will be a good thing when organized research has determined the conditions of Samadhi; but in the mean-time there seems no particular objection to our following tradition, and using the same objects of meditation as our predecessors, with the single exception which we shall note in due course.

The first class of objects for serious meditation (as opposed to preliminary practice, in which one should keep to simple recognizable objects, whose definiteness is easy to maintain) is "various parts of the body." The Hindus have an elaborate system of anatomy and physiology which has apparently no reference to the facts of the dissecting-room. Prominent in this class are the seven Cakkras, which will be described in Part II. There are also various "nerves", equally mythical.

WEH footnote: Not quite correct. Western anatomical knowledge has advanced since Crowley wrote this!

The second class is "objects of devotion," such as the idea or form of the Deity, or the heart or body of your Teacher, or of some man whom you respect profoundly. This practice is not to be commended, because it implies a bias of the mind.

You can also meditate on "your dreams." This sounds superstitious; but the idea is that you have already a tendency, independent of your conscious will, to think of those things, which will consequently be easier to think of than others. That this is the explanation is evident from the nature of the preceding and subsequent classes.

You can also meditate on "anything that especially appeals to you."

But in all this one feels inclined to suggest that it will be better and more convincing if the meditation is directed to an object which in itself is apparently unimportant. One does not want the mind to be excited in any way, even by adoration. See the three meditative methods in Liber HHH (Equinox VI.).

footnote: These are the complements of the three methods of Enthusiasm (A.'.A.'. instruction not yet issued up to March 1912.)

At the same time, one would not like to deny positively that it is very much "easier" to take some idea towards which the mind would naturally flow.

The Hindus assert that the nature of the object determines the Samadhi; that is, the nature of those lower Samadhis which confer so-called "magic powers." For example, there are the Yogapravritti. Meditating on the tip of the nose, one obtains what may be called the "ideal smell"; that is, a smell which is not any particular smell, but is the archetypal smell, of which all actual smells are modifications. It is "the smell which is "not" a smell." This is the only reasonable description; for the experience being contrary to reason, it is only reasonable that the words describing it should be contrary to reason too.

footnote: Hence the Athanasian Creed. Compare the precise parallel in the Zohar: "The Head which is above all heads; the Head which is "not" a Head.'

Similarly, concentration on the tip of the tongue gives the "ideal taste"; on the dorsum of the tongue, "ideal contact." "Every atom of the body comes into contact with every atom in the Universe all at once," is the description Bhikku Ananda Metteya gives of it. The root of the tongue gives the "ideal sound"; and the pharynx the "ideal sight."

footnote: Similarly Patanjali tells us that by making Samyama on the strength of an elephant or a tiger, the student acquires that strength. Conquer "the nerve Udana," and you can walk on the water; "Samana," and you begin to flash with light; the "elements" fire, air, earth, and water, and you can do whatever in natural life they prevent you from doing. For instance, by conquering earth, one could take a short cut to Australia; or by conquering water, one can live at the bottom of the Ganges. They say there is a holy man at Benares who does this, coming up only once a year to comfort and instruct his disciples. But nobody need believe this unless he wants to; and you are even advised to conquer that desire should it arise. It will be interesting when science really determines the variables and constants of these equations.

The Samadhi "par excellence," however, is Atmadarshana, which for some, and those not the least instructed, is the first real Samadhi; for even the visions of "God" and of the "Self" are tainted by form. In Atmadarshana the All is manifested as the One: it is the Universe freed from its conditions. Not only are all forms and ideas destroyed, but also those conceptions which are implicit in our ideas of those ideas.

footnote: This is so complete that not only "Black is White," but "The Whiteness of Black is the essential of its Blackness." "Naught = One = Infinity"; but this is only true "because" of this threefold arrangement, a trinity or "triangle of contradictories."

Each part of the Universe has become the whole, and phenomena and noumena are no longer opposed.

But it is quite impossible to describe this state of mind. One can only specify some of the characteristics, and that in language which forms no image in mind. It is impossible for anyone who experiences it to bring back any adequate memory, nor can we conceive a state transcending this.

There is, however, a very much higher state called Shivadarshana, of which it is only necessary to say that it is the destruction of the previous state, its annihilation; and to understand this blotting-out, one must not imagine "Nothingness" (the only name for it) as negative, but as positive.

The normal mind is a candle in a darkened room. Throw open the shutters, and the sunlight makes the flame invisible. That is a fair image of Dhyana.

footnote: Here the dictation was interrupted by very prolonged thought due to the difficulty of making the image clear. Virakam.

But the mind refuses to find a simile for Atmadarshana. It seems merely ineffective to say that the rushing together of all the host of heaven would similarly blot out the sunlight. But if we do say so, and wish to form a further image of Shivadarshana, we must imagine ourselves as suddenly recognizing that this universal blaze is darkness; not a light extremely dim compared with some other light, but darkness itself. It is not the change from the minute to the vast, or even from the finite to the infinite. It is the recognition that the positive is merely the negative. The ultimate truth is perceived not only as false, but as the logical contradictory of truth. It is quite useless to elaborate this theme, which has baffled all other minds hitherto. We have tried to say as little as possible rather than as much as possible.

footnote: Yet all this has come of our desire to be as modest as Yajna Valkya!

Still further from our present purpose would it be to criticise the innumerable discussions which have taken place as to whether this is the ultimate attainment, or what it confers. It is enough if we say that even the first and most transitory Dhyana repays a thousandfold the pains we may have taken to attain it.

And there is this anchor for the beginner, that his work is cumulative: every act directed towards attainment builds up a destiny which must some day come to fruition. May all attain!

SUMMARY

Q.

What is genius, and how is it produced?

A.

Let us take several specimens of the species, and try to find some one thing common to all which is not found in other species.

Q.

Is there any such thing?

A.

Yes: all geniuses have the habit of concentration of thought, and usually need long periods of solitude to acquire this habit. In particular the greatest religious geniuses have all retired from the world at one time or another in their lives, and begun to preach immediately on their return.

Q.

Of what advantage is such a retirement? One would expect that a man who so acted would find himself on his return out of touch with his civilization, and in every way less capable than when he left.

A.

But each claims, though in different language, to have gained in his absence some superhuman power.

Q.

Do you believe this?

A.

It becomes us ill to reject the assertions of those who are admittedly the greatest of mankind until we can refute them by proof, or at least explain how they may have been mistaken. In this case each teacher left instructions for us to follow. The only scientific method is for us to repeat their experiments, and so confirm or disprove their results.

Q.

But their instructions differ widely!

A.

Only in so far as each was bound by conditions of time, race, climate and language. There is essential identity in the method.

Q.

Indeed!

A.

It was the great work of the life of Frater Perdurabo to prove this. Studying each religious practice of each great religion on the spot, he was able to show the Identity-in-diversity of all, and to formulate a method free from all dogmatic bias, and based only on the ascertained facts of anatomy, physiology, and psychology.

Q.

Can you give me a brief abstract of this method?

A.

The main idea is that the Infinite, the Absolute, God, the Over-soul, or whatever you may prefer to call it, is always present; but veiled or masked by the thoughts of the mind, just as one cannot hear a heart-beat in a noisy city.

Q.

Yes?

A.

Then to obtain knowledge of That, it is only necessary to still all thoughts.

Q.

But in sleep thought is stilled?

A.

True, perhaps, roughly speaking; but the perceiving function is stilled also.

Q.

Then you wish to obtain a perfect vigilance and attention of the mind, uninterrupted by the rise of thoughts?

A.

Yes.

Q.

And how do you proceed?

A.

Firstly, we still the body by the practice called Asana, and secure its ease and the regularity of its functions by Pranayama. Thus no messages from the body will disturb the mind.
Secondly, by Yama and Niyama, we still the emotions and passions, and thus prevent them arising to disturb the mind.
Thirdly, by Pratyahara we analyse the mind yet more deeply, and begin to control and suppress thought in general of whatever nature.

Fourthly, we suppress all other thoughts by a direct concentration upon a single thought. This process, which leads to the highest results, consists of three parts, Dharana, Dhyana, and Samadhi, grouped under the single term Samyama.

Q.

How can I obtain further knowledge and experience of this?

A.

The A.'.A.'. is an organization whose heads have obtained by personal experience to the summit of this science. They have founded a system by which every one can equally attain, and that with an ease and speed which was previously impossible.

The first grade in Their system is that of
STUDENT.

A Student must possess the following books:

1. The Equinox,
2. 777.
3. Konx Om Pax.
4. Collected Works of A. Crowley; Tannhauser, The Sword of Song, Time, Eleusis. 3 vols.
5. Raja Yoga, by Swami Vivekananda.
6. The Shiva Sanhita, or the Hathayoga Pradipika.
7. The Tao Teh King and the writings of Kwang Tze: S.B.E. xxxix, xl.
8. The Spiritual Guide, by Miguel de Molinos.
9. Rituel et Dogme de la Haute Magie, by Eliphas Levi, or its translation by A. E. Waite.
10. The Goetia of the Lemegeton of Solomon the King.

These books should be well studied in any case in conjunction with the second part — Magick — of this Book IV.

Study of these books will give a thorough grounding in the intellectual side of Their system.

After three months the Student is examined in these books, and if his knowledge of them is found satisfactory, he may become a Probationer, receiving Liber LXI and the secret holy book, Liber LXV. The principal point of this grade is that the Probationer has a master appointed, whose experience can guide him in his work.

He may select any practices that he prefers, but in any case must keep an exact record, so that he may discover the relation of cause and effect in his working, and so that the A.'.A.'. may judge of his progress, and direct his further studies.

After a year of probation he may be admitted a Neophyte of the A.'.A.'., and receive the secret holy book Liber VII.

These are the principal instructions for practice which every probationer should follow out:

Libri E, A, O, III, XXX, CLXXV, CC, CCVI, CMXIII.

Part-II

Magick Elemental Theory

THERE are seven keys to the great gate,
Being eight in one and one in eight.
First, let the body of thee be still,
Bound by the cerements of will,
Corpse-rigid; thus thou mayst abort
The fidget-babes that tease the thought.
Next, let the breath-rhythm be low,
Easy, regular, and slow;
So that thy being be in tune
With the great sea's Pacific swoon.
Third, let thy life be pure and calm,
Swayed softly as a windless palm.
Fourth, let the will-to-live be bound
To the one love of the profound.
Fifth, let the thought, divinely free
From sense, observe its entity.
Watch every thought that springs; enhance
Hour after hour thy vigilance!
Intense and keen, turned inward, miss
No atom of analysis!
Sixth, on one thought securely pinned
Still every whisper of the wind!
So like a flame straight and unstirred
Burn up thy being in one word!
Next, still that ecstasy, prolong
Thy meditation steep and strong,
Slaying even God, should He distract
Thy attention from the chosen act!
Last, all these things in one o'erpowered,
Time that the midnight blossom flowered!
The oneness is. Yet even in this,
My son, thou shall not do amiss
If thou restrain the expression, shoot
Thy glance to rapture's darkling root,
Discarding name, form, sight, and stress
Even of this high consciousness;
Pierce to the heart! I leave thee here:
Thou art the Master. I revere
Thy radiance that rolls afar,
O Brother of the Silver Star!

CROWLEY "AHA!"

ALEISTER CROWLEY

THE MAGICIAN

IN HIS ROBE AND CROWN, ARMED WITH WAND, CUP, SWORD, PANTACLE, BELL, BOOK, AND HOLY OIL.

CEREMONIAL MAGICK,

footnote: The old spelling MAGICK has been adopted throughout in order to distinguish the Science of the Magi from all its counterfeits.

THE TRAINING FOR MEDITATION

PRELIMINARY REMARKS

HITHERTO we have spoken only of the mystic path; and we have kept particularly to the practical exoteric side of it. Such difficulties as we have mentioned have been purely natural obstacles. For example, the great question of the surrender of the self, which bulks so largely in most mystical treatises, has not been referred to at all. We have said only what a man must do; we have not considered at all what that doing may involve. The rebellion of the will against the terrible discipline of meditation has not been discussed; one may now devote a few words to it.

There is no limit to what theologians call "wickedness." Only by experience can the student discover the ingenuity of the mind in trying to escape from control. He is perfectly safe so long as he sticks to meditation, doing no more and no less than that which we have prescribed; but the mind will probably not let him remain in that simplicity. This fact is the root of all the legends about the "Saint" being tempted by the '"Devil." Consider the parable of Christ in the Wilderness, where he is tempted to use his magical power, to do anything but the thing that should be done. These attacks on the will are as bad as the thoughts which intrude upon Dharana. It would almost seem as if one could not succesfully practice meditation until the will had become so strong that no force in the Universe could either bend or break it. Before concentrating the lower principle, the mind, one must concentrate the higher principle, the Will. Failure to understand this has destroyed the value of all attempts to teach "Yoga," "Menticulture," "New Thought," and the like.

There are methods of training the will, by which it is easy to check one's progress.

Every one knows the force of habit. Every one knows that if you keep on acting in a particular way, that action becomes easier, and at last absolutely natural.

All religions have devised practices for this purpose. If you keep on praying with your lips long enough, you will one day find yourself praying in your heart.

The whole question has been threshed out and organized by wise men of old; they have made a Science of Life complete and perfect; and they have given to it the name of *MAGICK*. It is the chief secret of the Ancients, and if the keys have never been actually lost, they have certainly been little used.

footnote: The holders of those keys have always kept very quiet about it. This has been especially necessary in Europe, because of the dominance of persecuting churches.

Again, the confusion of thought caused by the ignorance of the people who did not understand it has discredited the whole subject. It is now our task to re-establish this science in its perfection.

To do this we must criticize the Authorities; some of them have made it too complex, others have completely failed in such simple matters as coherence. Many of the writers are empirics, still more mere scribes, while by far the largest class of all is composed of stupid charlatans.

We shall consider a simple form of magick, harmonized from many systems old and new, describing the various weapons of the Magician and the furniture of his temple. We shall explain to what each really corresponds, and discuss the construction and the use of everything.

The Magician works in a *Temple;* the Universe, which is (be it remembered!) conterminous with himself.

footnote: By "yourself" you mean the contents of your consciousness. All without does not exist for you.

In this temple a *Circle* is drawn upon the floor for the limitation of his working. This circle is protected by divine names, the influences on which he relies to keep out hostile thoughts. Within the circle stands an *Altar,* the solid basis on which he works, the foundation of all. Upon the Altar are his *Wand, Cup, Sword,* and *Pantacle,* to represent his Will, his Understanding, his Reason, and the lower parts of his being, respectively. On the Altar, too, is a phial of *Oil,* surrounded by a *Scourge,* a *Dagger,* and a *Chain,* while above the Altar hangs a Lamp. The Magician wears a *Crown,* a single *Robe,* and a *Lamen,* and he bears a *Book* of Conjurations and a *Bell.*

The oil consecrates everything that is touched with it; it is his aspiration; all acts performed in accordance with that are holy. The scourge tortures him; the dagger wounds him; the chain binds him. It is by virtue of these three that his aspiration remains pure, and is able to consecrate all other things. He wears a crown to affirm his lordship, his divinity; a robe to symbolize silence, and a lamen to declare his work. The book of spells or conjurations is his magical record, his Karma. In the East is the *Magick Fire,* in which all burns up at last.

footnote: He needs nothing else but the apparatus here described for invocation, by which he calls down that which is above him and within him; but for evocations, by which he calls forth that which is below him and without him, he may place a triangle without the circle.

We will now consider each of these matters in detail.

CHAPTER I

THE TEMPLE

THE Temple represents the external Universe. The Magician must take it as he finds it, so that it is of no particular shape; yet we find written, Liber VII, vi, 2: "We made us a Temple of stones in the shape of the Universe, even as thou didst wear openly and I concealed." This shape is the Vesica Piscis; but it is only the greatest of the Magicians who can thus fashion the Temple. There may, however, be some choice of rooms; this refers to the power of the Magician to reincarnate in a suitable body.

THE CIRCLE

CHAPTER II

THE CIRCLE

THE Circle announces the Nature of the Great Work.

Though the Magician has been limited in his choice of room, he is more or less able to choose what part of the room he will work in. He will consider convenience and possibility. His circle should not be too small and cramp his movements; it should not be so large that he has long distances to traverse. Once the circle is made and consecrated, the Magician must not leave it, or even lean outside, lest he be destroyed by the hostile forces that are without.

He chooses a circle rather than any other lineal figure for many reasons; e.g.,

1. He affirms thereby his identity with the infinite.

2. He affirms the equal balance of his working; since all points on the circumference are equidistant from the centre.

3. He affirms the limitation implied by his devotion to the Great Work. He no longer wanders about aimlessly in the world.

The centre of this circle is the centre of the Tau of ten squares which is in the midst, as shown in the illustration. The Tau and the circle together make one form of the Rosy Cross, the uniting of subject and object which is the Great Work, and which is symbolized sometimes as this cross and circle, sometimes as the Lingam-Yoni, sometimes as the Ankh or Crux Ansata, sometimes by the Spire and Nave of a church or temple, and sometimes as a marriage feast, mystic marriage, spiritual marriage, "chymical nuptials," and in a hundred other ways. Whatever the form chosen, it is the symbol of the Great Work.

This place of his working therefore declares the nature and object of the Work. Those persons who have supposed that the use of these symbols implied worship of the generative organs, merely attributed to the sages of every time and country minds of a calibre equal to their own.

The Tau is composed of ten squares for the ten Sephiroth.

footnote: The Ten Sephiroth are the Ten Units. In one system of classification (see "777") these are so arranged, and various ideas are so attributed to them, that they have been made to mean anything. The more you know, the more these numbers mean to you.

About this Tau is escribed a triangle, which is inscribed in the great Circle; but of the triangle nothing is actually marked but the three corners, the areas defined by the cutting of the lines bounding this triangle. This triangle is only visible in the parts which are common to two of the sides; they have therefore the shape of the diamond, one form of the Yoni. The significance of this is too complex for our simple treatise; it may be studied in Crowley's "Berashith."

The size of the whole figure is determined by the size of one square of the Tau. And the size of this square is that of the base of the Altar, which is placed upon Maukuth. It will follow then that, in spite of the apparent freedom of the Magician to do anything he likes, he is really determined absolutely; for as the Altar must have a base proportionate to its height, and as that height must be convenient for the Magician, the size of the whole will depend upon his own stature. It is easy to draw a moral lesson from these considerations. We will merely indicate this one, that the scope of any man's work depends upon his own original genius. Even the size of the weapons must be determined by necessary proportion. The exceptions to this rule are the Lamp, which hangs from the roof, above the centre of the Circle, above the square of Tiphereth; and the Oil, whose phial is so small that it will suit any altar.

On the Circle are inscribed the Names of God; the Circle is of green, and the names are in flaming vermilion, of the same colour as the Tau. Without the Circle are nine pentagrams equidistant,

footnote: Some magicians prefer seven lamps, for the seven Spirits of God that are before the Throne. Each stands in a heptagram, and in each angle of the heptagram is a letter, so that the seven names (see "Equinox VII") are spelt out. But this is a rather different symbolism. Of course in ordinary specialised working the number of lamps depends on the nature of the work, "e.g.," three for works of Saturn, eight for works Mercuial, and so on.

in the centre of each of which burns a small Lamp; these are the "Fortresses upon the Frontiers of the Abyss." See the eleventh Aethyr, Liber 418 ("Equinox V"). They keep off those forces of darkness which might otherwise break in.

The names of God form a further protection. The Magician may consider what names he will use; but each name should in some way symbolise this Work in its method and accomplishment. It is impossible here to enter into this subject fully; the discovery or construction of suitable names might occupy the most learned Qabalist for many years.

These nine lamps were originally candles made of human fat, the fat of enemies

footnote: Or sometimes of "birth-strangled babes," "i.e.," of thoughts slain ere they could arise into consciousness.

slain by the Magician; they thus served as warnings to any hostile force of what might be expected if it caused trouble. To-day such candles are difficult to procure; and it is perhaps simpler to use beeswax. The honey has been taken by the Magician; nothing is left of the toil of all those hosts of bees but the mere shell, the fuel of light. This beeswax is also used in the construction of the Pantacle, and this forms a link between the two symbols. The Pantacle is the food of the Magus; and some of it he gives up in order to give light to that which is without. For these lights are only apparently hostile to intrusion; they serve to illuminate the Circle and the Names of God, and so to bring the first and outmost symbols of initiation within the view of the profane.

These candles stand upon pentagrams, which symbolize Geburah, severity, and give protection; but also represent the microcosm, the four elements crowned by Spirit, the Will of man perfected in its aspiration to the Higher. They are placed outside the Circle to attract the hostile forces, to give them the first inkling of the Great Work, which they too must some day perform.

THE ALTAR. SIDE DESIGNS FROM DR. DEE, AS IN EQUINOX VII.

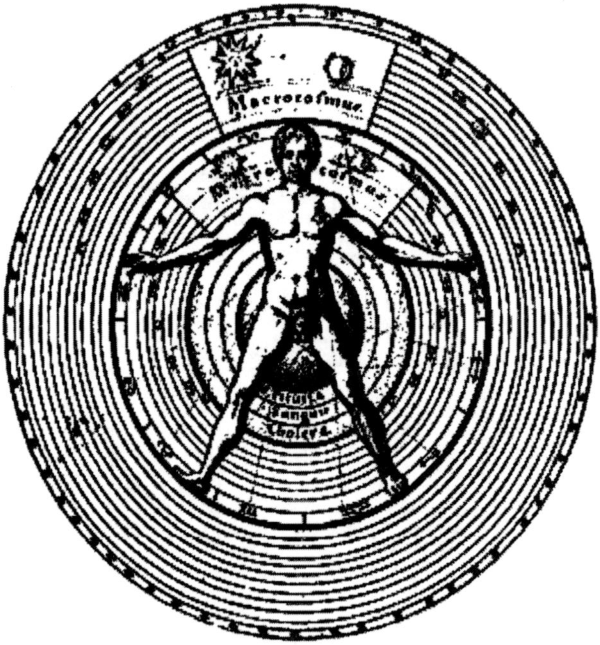

DESIGN SUITABLE FOR TOP OF ALTAR

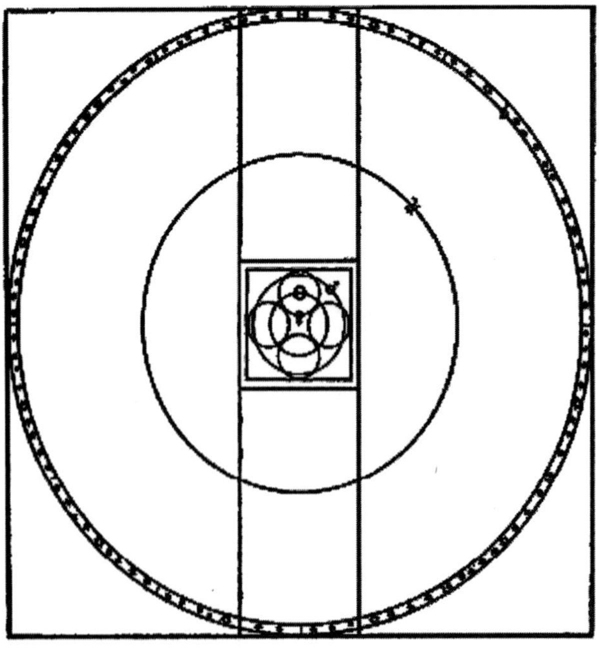

THE HOLY OBLATION

CHAPTER III

THE ALTAR

THE Altar represents the solid basis of the work, the fixed Will

footnote: It represents the extension of Will. Will is the Dyad (see section on the Wand); 2 x 2 = 4. So the altar is foursquare, and also its ten squares show 4. 10 = 1 + 2 + 3 + 4.

of the Magician; and the law under which he works. Within this altar everything is kept, since everything is subject to law. Except the lamp.

According to some authorities the Altar should be made of oak to represent the stubbornness and rigidity of law; others would make it of Acacia, for Acacia is the symbol of resurrection.

The Altar is a double cube, which is a rough way of symbolizing the Great Work; for the doubling of the cube, like the squaring of the circle, was one of the great problems of antiquity. The surface of this Altar is composed of ten squares. The top is Kether, and the bottom Malkuth. The height of the Altar is equal to the height above the ground of the navel of the Magician. The Altar is connected with the Ark of the Covenant, Noah's Ark, the nave ("navis," a ship) of the Church, and many other symbols of antiquity, whose symbolism has been well worked out in an anonymous book called "The Cannon,"

WEH footnote: written by William Stirling

(Elkin Mathews), which should be studied carefully before constructing the Altar.

For this Altar must embody the Magician's knowledge of the laws of Nature, which are the laws through which he works.

He should endeavour to make geometrical constructions to symbolize cosmic measurements. For example, he may take the two diagonals as (say) the diameter of the sun. Then the side of the altar will be found to have a length equal to some other cosmic measure, a vesica drawn on the side some other, a "rood cross" within the vesica yet another. Each Magician should work out his own system of symbolism — and he need not confine himself to cosmic measurements. He might, for example, find some relation to express the law of inverse squares.

The top of the Altar shall be covered with gold, and on this gold should be engraved some such figure as the Holy Oblation, or the New Jerusalem, or, if he have the skill, the Microcosm of Vitruvius, of which we give illustrations.

On the sides of the Altar are also sometimes drawn the great tablets of the elements, and the sigils of the holy elemental kings, as shown in The Equinox, No. VII; for these are syntheses of the forces of Nature. Yet these are rather special than general symbols, and this book purports to treat only of the grand principles of working.

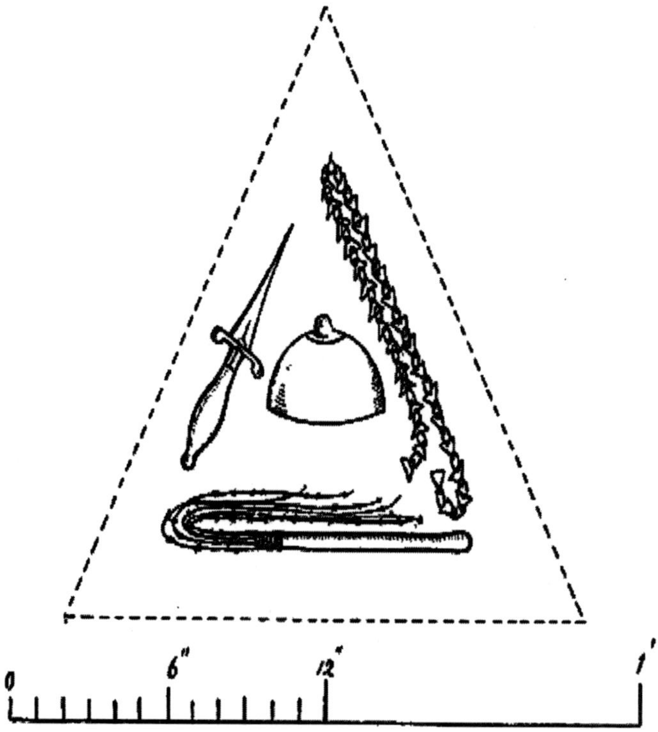

THE SCOURGE, THE DAGGER, AND THE CHAIN; ENCLOSING THE PHIAL FOR THE HOLY OIL.

CHAPTER IV

THE SCOURGE, THE DAGGER, AND THE CHAIN

THE Scourge, the Dagger, and the Chain, represent the three alchemical principles of Sulphur, Mercury, and Salt. These are not the substances which we now call by these names; they represent "principles," whose operations chemists have found it more convenient to explain in other ways. But Sulphur represents the energy of things, Mercury their fluidity, Salt their fixity. They are analogous to Fire, Air and Water; but they mean rather more, for they represent something deeper and subtler, and yet more truly active. An almost exact analogy is given by the three Gunas of the Hindus; Sattvas, Rajas, and Tamas. Sattvas is Mercury, equable, calm, clear; Rajas is Sulphur, active, excitable, even fierce; Tamas is Salt, thick, sluggish, heavy, dark.

footnote: There is a long description of these three Gunas in the Bhagavadgita.

But Hindu philosophy is so occupied with the main idea that only the Absolute is worth anything, that it tends to consider these Gunas (even Sattvas) as evil. This is a correct view, but only from above; and we prefer, if we are truly wise, to avoid this everlasting wail which characterizes the thought of the Indian peninsula: "Everything is sorrow," etc. Accepting their doctrine of the two phases of the Absolute, we must, if we are to be consistent, class the two phases together, either as good or as bad; if one is good and the other bad we are back again in that duality, to avoid which we invented the Absolute.

The Christian idea that sin was worth while because salvation was so much more worth while, that redemption is so splendid that innocence was well lost, is more satisfactory. St. Paul says: "Where sin abounded, there did grace much more abound. Then shall we do evil that good may come? God forbid." But (clearly!) it is exactly what God Himself did, or why did He create Satan with the germ of his "fall" in him?

Instead of condemning the three qualities outright, we should consider them as parts of a sacrament. This particular aspect of the Scourge, the Dagger, and the Chain, suggests the sacrament of penance.

The Scourge is Sulphur: its application excites our sluggish natures; and it may further be used as an instrument of correction, to castigate rebellious volitions. It is applied to the Nephesh, the Animal Soul, the natural desires.

The Dagger is Mercury: it is used to calm too great heat, by the letting of blood; and it is this weapon which is plunged into the side or heart of the Magician to fill the Holy Cup. Those faculties which come between the appetites and the reason are thus dealt with.

The Chain is Salt: it serves to bind the wandering thoughts; and for this reason is placed about the neck of the Magician, where Daath is situated.

These instruments also remind us of pain, death, and bondage. Students of the gospel will recollect that in the martyrdom of Christ these three were used, the dagger being replaced by the nails.

footnote: This is true of all magical instruments. The Hill of Golgotha is a circle, and the Cross the Tau. Christ had robe, crown, sceptre, etc.; this thesis should one day be fully worked out.

The Scourge should be made with a handle of iron; the lash is composed of nine strands of fine copper wire, in each of which are twisted small pieces of lead. Iron represents severity, copper love, and lead austerity.

The Dagger is made of steel inlaid with gold; and the hilt is also golden.

The chain{Sic} is made of soft iron. It has 333 links.

footnote: See The Equinox, No. V, "The Vision and the Voice": Xth Aethyr.

It is now evident why these weapons are grouped around the phial of clear crystal in which is kept the Holy Oil.

The Scourge keeps the aspiration keen: the Dagger expresses the determination to sacrifice all; and the Chain restricts any wandering.

We may now consider the Holy Oil itself.

CHAPTER V

THE HOLY OIL

THE Holy Oil is the Aspiration of the Magician; it is that which consecrates him to the performance of the Great Work; and such is its efficacy that it also consecrates all the furniture of the Temple and the instruments thereof. It is also the grace or chrism; for this aspiration is not ambition; it is a quality bestowed from above. For this reason the Magician will anoint first the top of his head before proceeding to consecrate the lower centres in their turn.

This oil is of a pure golden colour; and when placed upon the skin it should burn and thrill through the body with an intensity as of fire. It is the pure light translated into terms of desire. It is not the Will of the Magician, the desire of the lower to reach the higher; but it is that spark of the higher in the Magician which wishes to unite the lower with itself.

Unless therefore the Magician be first anointed with this oil, all his work will be wasted and evil.

This oil is compounded of four substances. The basis of all is the oil of the olive. The olive is, traditionally, the gift of Minerva, the Wisdom of God, the Logos. In this are dissolved three other oils; oil of myrrh, oil of cinnamon, oil of galangal. The Myrrh is attributed to Binah, the Great Mother, who is both the understanding of the Magician and that sorrow and compassion which results from the contemplation of the Universe. The Cinnamon represents Tiphereth, the Sun — the Son, in whom Glory and Suffering are identical. The Galangal represents both Kether and Malkuth, the First and the Last, the One and the Many, since in this Oil they are One.

These oils taken together represent therefore the whole Tree of Life. The ten Sephiroth are blended into the perfect gold.

This Oil cannot be prepared from crude myrrh, cinnamon, and galangal. The attempt to do so only gives a brown mud with which the oil will not mix. These substances must be themselves refined into pure oils before the final combination.

This perfect Oil is most penetrating and subtle. Gradually it will spread itself, a glistening film, over every object in the Temple. Each of these objects will then flame in the light of the Lamp. This Oil is like that which was in the widow's curse: it renews and multiplies itself miraculously; its perfume fills the whole Temple; it is the soul of which the grosser perfume is the body.

The phial which contains the Oil should be of clear rock crystal, and some magicians have fashioned it in the shape of the female breast, for that it is the true nourishment of all that lives. For this reason also it has been made of mother-of-pearl and stoppered with a ruby.

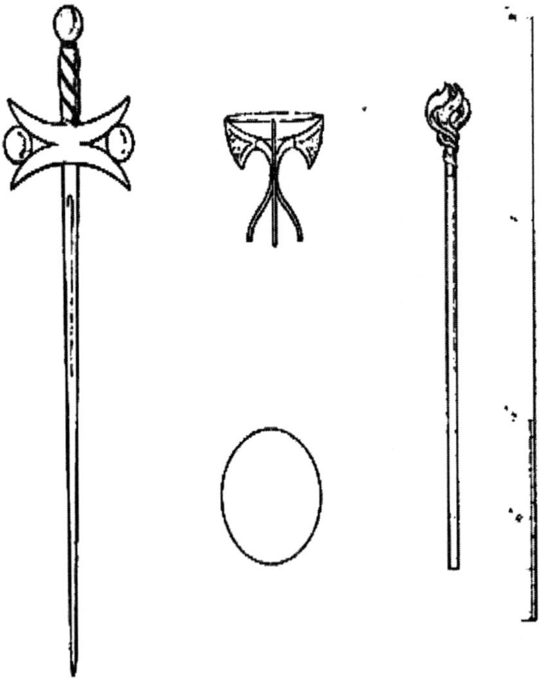

THE WAND, CUP, SWORD, AND DISK OR PANTACLE (drawn to scale).

CHAPTER VI

THE WAND

THE Magical Will is in its essence twofold, for it presupposes a beginning and an end; to will to be a thing is to admit that you are not that thing.

Hence to will anything but the supreme thing, is to wander still further from it — any will but that to give up the self to the Beloved is Black Magick — yet this surrender is so simple an act that to our complex minds it is the most difficult of all acts; and hence training is necessary. Further, the Self surrendered must not be less than the All-Self; one must not come before the altar of the Most High with an impure or an imperfect offering. As it is written in Liber LXV, "To await Thee is the end, not the beginning."

This training may lead through all sorts of complications, varying according to the nature of the student, and hence it may be necessary for him at any moment to will all sorts of things which to others might seem unconnected with the goal. Thus it is not "a priori" obvious why a billiard player should need a file.

Since, then, we may want "anything," let us see to it that our will is strong enough to obtain anything we want without loss of time.

It is therefore necessary to develop the will to its highest point, even though the last task but one is the total surrender of this will. Partial surrender of an imperfect will is of no account in Magick.

The will being a lever, a fulcrum is necessary; this fulcrum is the main aspiration of the student to attain. All wills which are not dependent upon this principal will are so many leakages; they are like fat to the athlete.

The majority of the people in this world are ataxic; they cannot coordinate their mental muscles to make a purposed movement. They have no real will, only a set of wishes, many of which contradict others. The victim wobbles from one to the other (and it is no less wobbling because the movements may occasionally be very violent) and at the end of life the movements cancel each other out. Nothing has been achieved; except the one thing of which the victim is not conscious: the destruction of his own character, the confirming of indecision. Such an one is torn limb from limb by Choronzon.

How then is the will to be trained? All these wishes, whims, caprices, inclinations, tendencies, appetites, must be detected, examined, judged by the standard of whether they help or hinder the main purpose, and treated accordingly.

Vigilance and courage are obviously required. I was about to add self-denial, in deference to conventional speech; but how could I call that self-denial which is merely denial of those things which hamper the self? It is not suicide to kill the germs of malaria in one's blood.

Now there are very great difficulties to be overcome in the training of the mind. Perhaps the greatest is forgetfulness, which is probably the worst form of what the Buddhists call ignorance. Special practices for training the memory may be of some use as a preliminary for persons whose memory is naturally poor. In any case the Magical Record prescribed for Probationers of the A.'.A.'. is useful and necessary.

Above all the practices of Liber III must be done again and again, for these practices develop not only vigilance but those inhibiting centres in the brain which are, according to some psychologists, the mainspring of the mechanism by which civilized man has raised himself above the savage.

So far it has been spoken, as it were, in the negative. Aaron's rod has become a serpent, and swallowed the serpents of the other Magicians; it is now necessary to turn it once more into a rod.

footnote: As everyone knows, the word used in Exodus for a Rod of Almond is {{Hebrew letters: Mem-tet-Hay Hay-Shin-Qof-Dalet

}, adding to 463. Now 400 is Tau, the path leading from Malkuth to Yesod. Sixty is Samekh, the path leading leading {{sic}} from Yesod to Tiphereth; and 3 is Gimel, the path leading thence to Kether. The whole rod therefore gives the paths from the Kingdom to the Crown.}

This Magical Will is the wand in your hand by which the Great Work is accomplished, by which the Daughter is not merely set upon the throne of the Mother, but assumed into the Highest.

footnote: In one, the best, system of Magick, the Absolute is called the Crown, God is called the Father, the Pure Soul is called the Mother, the Holy Guardian Angel is called the Son, and the Natural Soul is called the Daughter. The Son purifies the Daughter by wedding her; she thus becomes the Mother, the uniting of whom with the Father absorbs all into the Crown. See Liber CDXVIII.

The Magick Wand is thus the principal weapon of the Magus; and the "name" of that wand is the Magical Oath.

The will being twofold is in Chokmah, who is the Logos, the word; hence some have said that the word is the will. Thoth the Lord of Magic {sic} is also the Lord of Speech; Hermes the messenger bears the Caduceus.

Word should express will: hence the Mystic Name of the Probationer is the expression of his highest Will.

There are, of course, few Probationers who understand themselves sufficiently to be able to formulate this will to themselves, and therefore at the end of their probation they choose a new name.

It is convenient therefore for the student to express his will by taking Magical Oaths.

Since such an oath is irrevocable it should be well considered; and it is better not to take any oath permanently; because with increase of understanding may come a perception of the incompatibility of the lesser oath with the greater.

This is indeed almost certain to occur, and it must be remembered that as the whole essence of the will is its one-pointedness,

footnote: The Top of the Wand is in Kether — which is one; and the Qliphoth of Kether are the Thaumiel, opposing heads that rend and devour each other.

a dilemma of this sort is the worst in which the Magus can find himself.

Another great point in this consideration of Magick Vows is to keep them in their proper place. They must be taken for a clearly defined purpose, a clearly understood purpose, and they must never be allowed to go beyond it.

It is a virtue in a diabetic not to eat sugar, but only in reference to his own condition. It is not a virtue of universal import. Elijah said on one occasion: "I do well to be angry;" but such occasions are rare.

Moreover, one man's meat is another man's poison. An oath of poverty might be very useful for a man who was unable intelligently to use his wealth for the single end proposed; to another it would be simply stripping himself of energy, causing him to waste his time over trifles.

There is no power which cannot be pressed in to the service of the Magical Will: it is only the temptation to value that power for itself which offends.

One does not say: "Cut it down; why cumbereth it the ground?" unless repeated prunings have convinced the gardener that the growth must always be a rank one.

"If thine hand offend thee, cut it off!" is the scream of a weakling. If one killed a dog the first time it misbehaved itself, not many would pass the stage of puppyhood.

The best vow, and that of most universal application, is the vow of Holy Obedience; for not only does it lead to perfect freedom, but is a training in that surrender which is the last task.

> *WEH footnote: Of all Crowley's views, this is the most controversial. It appears to fly in the face of Thelema. There is high merit in a vow of obedience, and necessity; but the merit is to be found in the "small print." To receive a vow of obedience from another implies perfection in the teacher, a thing impossible to mortals but possible to roles. To make a vow of obedience to a mortal is foolish unless conditions of circumstance and duration are involved.*

It has this great value, that it never gets rusty. If the superior to whom the vow is taken knows his business, he will quickly detect which things are really displeasing to his pupil, and familiarize him with them.

Disobedience to the superior is a contest between these two wills in the inferior. The will expressed in his vow, which is the will linked to his highest will by the fact that he has taken it in order to develop that highest will, contends with the temporary will, which is based only on temporary considerations.

The Teacher should then seek gently and firmly to key up the pupil, little by little, until obedience follows command without reference to what that command may be; as Loyola wrote: "perinde ac cadaver."

No one has understood the Magical Will better than Loyola; in his system the individual was forgotten. The will of the General was instantly echoed by every member of the Order; hence the Society of Jesus became the most formidable of the religious organizations of the world.

That of the Old Man of the Mountains was perhaps the next best.

The defect in Loyola's system is that the General was not God, and that owing to various other considerations he was not even necessarily the best man in the Order.

To become General of the Order he must have willed to become General of the Order; and because of this he could be nothing more.

To return to the question of the development of the Will. It is always something to pluck up the weeds, but the flower itself needs tending. Having crushed all volitions in ourselves, and if necessary in others, which we find opposing our real Will, that Will itself will grow naturally with greater freedom. But it is not only necessary to purify the temple itself and consecrate it; invocations must be made. Hence it is necessary to be constantly doing things of a positive, not merely of a negative nature, to affirm that Will.

Renunciation and sacrifice are necessary, but they are comparatively easy. There are a hundred ways of missing, and only one of hitting. To avoid eating beef is easy; to eat nothing but pork is very difficult.

Levi recommends hat at times the Magical Will itself should be cut off, on the same principle as one can always work better after a "complete change." Levi is doubtless right, but he must be understood as saying this "for the hardness of men's hearts." The turbine is more efficient than a reciprocating engine; and his counsel is only good for the beginner.

Ultimately the Magical Will so identifies itself with the man's whole being that it becomes unconscious, and is as constant a force as gravitation. One may even be surprised at one's own acts, and have to reason out their connection. But let it be understood that when the Will has thus really raised itself to the height of Destiny, the man is no more likely to do wrong than he is to float off into the air.

One may be asked whether there is not a conflict between this development of the Will and Ethics.

The answer is Yes.

In the Grand Grimoire we are told "to buy an egg without haggling"; and attainment, and the next step in the path of attainment, is that pearl of great price, which when a man hath found he straightway selleth all that he hath, and buyeth that pearl.

With many people custom and habit — of which ethics is but the social expression — are the things most difficult to give up: and it is a useful practice to break any habit just to get into the way of being free from that form of slavery. Hence we have practices for breaking up sleep, for putting our bodies into strained and unnatural positions, for doing difficult exercises of breathing — all these, apart from any special merit they may have in themselves for any particular purpose, have the main merit that the man forces himself to do them despite any conditions that may exist. Having conquered internal resistance one may conquer external resistance more easily.

In a steam boat the engine must first overcome its own inertia before it can attack the resistance of the water.

When the will has thus ceased to be intermittent, it becomes necessary to consider its size. Gravitation gives an acceleration of thirty-two feet per second on this planet, on the moon very much less. And a Will, however single and however constant, may still be of no particular use, because the circumstances which oppose it may be altogether too strong, or because it is for some reason unable to get into touch with them. It is useless to wish for the moon. If one does so, one must consider by what means that Will may be made effective.

And though a man may have a tremendous Will in one direction it need not always be sufficient to help him in another; it may even be stupid.

There is the story of the man who practised for forty years to walk across the Ganges; and, having succeeded, was reproached by his Holy Guru, who said: "You are a great fool. All your neighbours have been crossing every day on a raft for two pice."

This occurs to most, perhaps to all, of us in our careers. We spend infinite pains to learn something, to achieve something, which when gained does not seem worth even the utterance of the wish.

But this is a wrong view to take. The discipline necessary in order to learn Latin will stand us in good stead when we wish to do something quite different.

At school our masters punished us; when we leave school, if we have not learned to punish ourselves, we have learned nothing.

In fact the only danger is that we may value the achievement in itself. The boy who prides himself on his school knowledge is in danger of becoming a college professor.

So the Guru of the water-walking Hindu only meant that it was now time to be dissatisfied with what he had done — and to employ his powers to some better end.

And, incidentally, since the divine Will is one, it will be found that there is no capacity which is not necessarily subservient to the destiny of the man who possesses it.

One may be unable to tell when a thread of a particular colour will be woven into the carpet of Destiny. It is only when the carpet is finished and seen from a proper distance that the position of that particular strand is seen to be necessary. From this one is tempted to break a lance on that most ancient battlefield, free-will and destiny.

But even though every man is "determined" so that every action is merely the passive resultant of the sum-total of the forces which have acted upon him from eternity, so that his own Will is only the echo of the Will of the Universe, yet that consciousness of "free-will" is valuable; and if he really understands it as being the partial and individual expression of that internal motion in a Universe whose sum is rest, by so much will he feel that harmony, that totality. And though the happiness which he experiences may be criticised as only one scale of a balance in whose other scale is an equal misery, there are those who hold that misery consists only in the feeling of separation from the Universe, and that consequently all may cancel out among the lesser feelings, leaving only that infinite bliss which is one phase of the infinite consciousness of that ALL. Such speculations are somewhat beyond the scope of the present remarks. It is of no particular moment to observe that the elephant and flea can be no other than they are; but we do perceive that one is bigger than the other. That is the fact of practical importance.

We do know that persons can be trained to do things which they could not do without training — and anyone who remarks that you cannot train a person unless it is his destiny to be trained is quite unpractical. Equally it is the destiny of the trainer to train. There is a fallacy in the determinist argument similar to the fallacy which is the root of all "systems" of gambling at Roulette. The odds are just over three to one against red coming up twice running; but after red has come up once the conditions are changed.

WEH footnote: Exactly four to one before and even after.

It would be useless to insist on such a point were it not for the fact that many people confuse Philosophy with Magick. Philosophy is the enemy of Magick. Philosophy assures us that after all nothing matters, and that "che sara sara."

In practical life, and Magick is the most practical of the Arts of life, this difficulty does not occur. It is useless to argue with a man who is running to catch a train that he may be destined not to catch it; he just runs, and if he could spare breath would say "Blow destiny!"

It has been said earlier that the real Magical Will must be toward the highest attainment, and this can never be until the flowering of the Magical Understanding. The Wand must be made to grow in length as well as in strength; it need not do so of its own nature.

The ambition of every boy is to be an engine-driver. Some attain it, and remain there all their lives.

But in the majority of cases the Understanding grows faster than the Will, and long before the boy is in a position to attain his wish he has already forgotten it.

In other cases the Understanding never grows beyond a certain point, and the Will persists without intelligence.

The business man (for example) has wished for ease and comfort, and to this end goes daily to his office and slaves under a more cruel taskmaster than the meanest of the workmen in his pay; he decides to retire, and finds that life in empty. The end has been swallowed up in the means.

Only those are happy who have desired the unattainable.

All possessions, the material and the spiritual alike, are but dust.

Love, sorrow, and compassion are three sisters who, if they seem freed from this curse, are only so because of their relation to The Unsatisfied.

Beauty is itself so unattainable that it escapes altogether; and the true artist, like the true mystic, can never rest. To him the Magician is but a servant. His wand is of infinite length; it is the creative Mahalingam.

The difficulty with such an one is naturally that his wand being very thin in proportion to its length is liable to wobble. Very few artists are conscious of their real purpose, and in very many cases we have this infinite yearning supported by so frail a constitution that nothing is achieved.

The Magician must build all that he has into his pyramid; and if that pyramid is to touch the stars, how broad must be the base! There is no knowledge and no power which is useless to the Magician. One might almost say there is no scrap of material in the whole Universe with which he can dispense. His ultimate enemy is the great Magician, the Magician who created the whole illusion of the Universe; and to meet him in battle, so that nothing is left either of him or of yourself, you must be exactly equal to him.

At the same time let the Magician never forget that every brick must tend to the summit of the pyramid — the sides must be perfectly smooth; there must be no false summits, even in the lowest layers.

This is the practical and active form of that obligation of a Master of the Temple in which it is said: "I will interpret every phenomenon as a particular dealing of God with my soul."

In Liber CLXXV many practical devices for attaining this one-pointedness are given, and though the subject of that book is devotion to a particular Deity, its instructions may be easily generalized to suit the development of any form of will.

This will is then the active form of understanding. The Master of the Temple asks, on seeing a slug: "What is the purpose of this message from the Unseen? How shall I interpret this Word of God Most High?" The Magus thinks: "How shall I use this slug?" And in this course he must persist. Though many things useless, so far as he can see, are sent to him, one day he will find the one thing he needs, while his Understanding will appreciate the fact that none of those other things were useless.

So with these early practices of renunciation it will now be clearly understood that they were but of temporary use. They were only of value as training. The adept will laugh over his early absurdities — the disproportions will have been harmonized; and the structure of his soul will be seen as perfectly organic, with no one thing out of its place. He will see himself as the positive Tau with its ten complete squares within the triangle of the negatives; and this figure will become one, as soon as from the equilibrium of opposites he has attained to the identity of opposites.

In all this is will have been seen that the most powerful weapon in the hand of the student is the Vow of Holy Obedience; and many will wish that they had the opportunity of putting themselves under a holy Guru. Let them take heart — for any being capable of giving commands is an efficient Guru for the purpose of this Vow, provided that he is not too amiable and lazy.

The only reason for choosing a Guru who has himself attained is that he will aid the vigilance of the sleepy Chela, and, while tempering the Wind to that shorn lamb, will carefully harden him, and at the same time gladden his ears with holy discourse. But if such a person is inaccessible, let him choose any one with whom he has constant intercourse, explain the circumstances, and ask him to act.

The person should if possible be trustworthy; and let the Chela remember that if he should be ordered to jump over a cliff it is very much better to do it than to give up the practice.

And it is of the very greatest importance not to limit the vow in any way. You must buy the egg without haggling.

In a certain Society the members were bound to do certain things, being assured that there was "not[illegible] the vow contrary to their civil, moral, or religious obligations." So when any one wanted to break his vow [illegible] had no difficulty in discovering a very good reason for it. The vow lost all its force.

> *WEH footnote: Crowley expressly cites this clause in the Golden Dawn initiations as the third defense for his publishing the Golden Dawn rituals. See Equinox I, 4, page 5, "Editorial".*

When Buddha took his seat under the blessed Bo-Tree, he took an oath that none of the inhabitants of the 10,000 worlds should cause him to rise until he had attained; so that when even Mara the great Arch-Devil, with his three daughters the arch-temptresses appeared, he remained still.

Now it is useless for the beginner to take so formidable a vow; he has not yet attained the strength which can defy Mara. Let him estimate his strength, and take a vow which is within it, but only just within it. Thus Milo began by carrying a new-born calf; and day by day as it grew into a bull, his strength was found sufficient.

Again let it be said that Liber III is a most admirable method for the beginner,

> *footnote: This book must be carefully read. Its essence is that the pupil swears to refrain from a certain thought, word, or deed; and on each breach of the oath, cuts his arm sharply with a razor. This is better than flagellation because it can be done in public, without attracting notice. It however forms one of the most hilariously exciting parlour games for the family circle ever invented. Friends and relations are always ready to do their utmost to trap you into doing the forbidden thing.*

and it will be best, even if he is very confident in his strength, to take the vow for very short periods, beginning with an hour and increasing daily by half-hours until the day is filled. Then let him rest awhile, and attempt a two-day practice; and so on until he is perfect.

He should also begin with the very easiest practices. But the thing which he is sworn to avoid should not be a thing which normally he would do infrequently; because the strain on the memory which subserves his vigilance would be very great, and the practice become difficult. It is just as well at first that the pain of his arm should be there "at the time when he would normally do the forbidden thing," to warn him against its repetition.

There will thus be a clear connection in his mind of cause and effect, until he will be just as careful in avoiding this particular act which he has consciously determined, as in those other things which in childhood he has been trained to avoid.

Just as the eyelid unconsciously closes when the eye is threatened,

> *footnote: If it were not so there would be very few people in the world who were not blind.*

so must he build up in consciousness this power of inhibition until it sinks below consciousness, adding to his store of automatic force, so that he is free to devote his conscious energy to a yet higher task.

It is impossible to overrate the value of this inhibition to the man when he comes to meditate. He has guarded his mind against thoughts A, B, and C; he has told the sentries to allow no one to pass who is not in uniform. And it will be very easy for him to extend that power, and to lower the portcullis.

Let him remember, too that there is a difference not only in the frequency of thoughts — but in their intensity.

[illegible]rst of all is of course the ego, which is almost omnipresent and almost irresistible, although so deeply-[illegible]hat in normal thought one may not always be aware of it.

[illegible]dha, taking the bull by the horns, made this idea the first to be attacked.

[illegible]ch must decide for himself whether this is a wise course to pursue. But it certainly seems easier to strip off [illegible]irst the things which can easily be done without.

> *WEH footnote: Among those who might find the ego an unwise first choice to attack are those who confuse it with a sense of private property. Many petty thieves use denial of the ego as an excuse. Three book-thieves and any number of shop-lifters come to mind.*

The majority of people will find most trouble with the Emotions, and thoughts which excite them.

But is is both possible and necessary not merely to suppress the emotions, but to turn them into faithful servants. Thus the emotion of anger is occasionally useful against that portion of the brain whose slackness vitiates the control.

If there is one emotion which is never useful, it is pride; for this reason, that it is bound up entirely with the Ego...

No, there is no use for pride!

The destruction of the Perceptions, either the grosser or the subtler, appears much easier, because the mind not being moved, is free to remember its control.

It is easy to be so absorbed in a book that one takes no notice of the most beautiful scenery. But if stung by a wasp the book is immediately forgotten.

The Tendencies are, however, much harder to combat than the three lower Shandhas put together — for the simple reason that they are for the most part below consciousness, and must be, as it were, awakened in order to be destroyed, so that the will of the Magician is in a sense trying to do two opposite things at the same time.

Consciousness itself is only destroyed by Samadhi.

One can now see the logical process which begins in refusing to think of a foot, and ends by destroying the sense of individuality.

Of the methods of destroying various deep-rooted ideas there are many.

The best is perhaps the method of equilibrium. Get the mind into the habit of calling up the opposite to every thought that may arise. In conversation always disagree. See the other man's arguments; but, however much your judgment approves them, find the answer.

Let this be done dispassionately; the more convinced you are that a certain point of view is right, the more determined you should be to find proofs that it is wrong.

If you have done this thoroughly, these points of view will cease to trouble you; you can then assert your own point of view with the calm of a master, which is more convincing than the enthusiasm of a learner.

You will cease to be interested in controversies; politics, ethics, religion will seem so many toys, and your Magical Will will be free from these inhibitions.

In Burma there is only one animal which the people will kill, Russell's Viper; because, as they say, "either you must kill it or it will kill you"; and it is a question of which sees the other first.

Now any one idea which is not The Idea must be treated in this fashion. When you have killed the snake you can use its skin, but as long as it is alive and free, you are in danger.

And unfortunately the ego-idea, which is the real snake, can throw itself into a multitude of forms, each clothed in the most brilliant dress. Thus the devil is said to be able to disguise himself as an angel of light.

Under the strain of a magical vow this is too terribly the case. No normal human being understands or can understand the temptations of the saints.

An ordinary person with ideas like those which obsessed St. Patrick and St. Antony would be only fit for an asylum.

The tighter you hold the snake (which was previously asleep in the sun, and harmless enough, to all appearance), the more it struggles; and it is important to remember that your hold must tighten correspondingly, or it will escape and bite you.

Just as if you tell a child not to do a thing — no matter what — it will immediately want to do it, thought otherwise the idea might never have entered its head, so it is with the saint. We have all of us these tendencies latent in us; of most of them we might remain unconscious all our lives — unless they were awakened by our Magick. They lie in ambush. And every one must be awakened, and every one must be destroyed. Every one who signs the oath of a Probationer is stirring up a hornets' nest.

A man has only to affirm his conscious aspiration; and the enemy is upon him.

It seems hardly possible that any one can ever pass through that terrible year of probation — and yet the aspirant is not bound to anything difficult; it almost seems as if he were not bound to anything at all — and yet experience teaches us that the effect is like plucking a man from his fireside into mid-Atlantic in a gale. The truth is, it may be, that the very simplicity of the task makes it difficult.

The Probationer must cling to his aspiration — affirm it again and again in desperation.

He has, perhaps, almost lost sight of it; it has become meaningless to him; he repeats it mechanically as he is tossed from wave to wave.

But if he can stick to it he will come through.

And, once he "is" through, things will again assume their proper aspect; he will see that mere illusion were the things that seemed so real, and he will be fortified against the new trials that await him.

But the unfortunate indeed is he who cannot thus endure. It is useless for him to say, "I don't like the Atlantic;

I will go back to the fireside."

Once take one step on the path, and there is no return. You will remember in Browning's "Childe Roland to the dark Tower came":

For mark! no sooner was I fairly found

Pledged to the plain, after a pace or two,

Than, pausing to throw backwards a last view

O'er the safe road, 'twas gone: grey plain all round,

Nothing but plain to the horizon's bound.

I might go on; naught else remained to do.

And this is universally true. The statement that the Probationer can resign when he chooses is in truth only for those who have taken the oath but superficially.

A real Magical Oath cannot be broken: you think it can, but it can't.

This is the advantage of a real Magical Oath.

However far you go around, you arrive at the end just the same, and all you have done by attempting to break your oath is to involve yourself in the most frightful trouble.

It cannot be too clearly understood that such is the nature of things: it does not depend upon the will of any persons, however powerful or exalted; nor can Their force, the force of Their great oaths, avail against the weakest oath of the most trivial of beginners.

The attempt to interfere with the Magical Will of another person would be wicked, if it were not absurd.

One may attempt to build up a Will when {sic} before nothing existed but a chaos of whims; but once organization has taken place it is sacred. As Blake says: "Everything that lives is holy"; and hence the creation of life is the most sacred of tasks. It does not matter very much to the creator what it is that he creates; there is room in the universe for both the spider and the fly.

It is from the rubbish-heap of Choronzon that one selects the material for a god!

This is the ultimate analysis of the Mystery of Redemption, and is possibly the real reason of the existence (if existence it can be called) of form, or, if you like, of the Ego.

It is astonishing that this typical cry — "I am I" — is the cry of that which above all is not I.

It was that Master whose Will was so powerful that at its lightest expression the deaf heard, and the dumb spake, lepers were cleansed and the dead arose to life, that Master and no other who at the supreme moment of his agony could cry, "Not my Will, but Thine, be done."

CHAPTER VII

THE CUP

AS the Magick Wand is the Will, the Wisdom, the Word of the Magician, so is the Magick Cup his Understanding.

This is the cup of which it was written: "Father, if it be Thy Will, let this cup pass from Me!" And again: "Can ye drink of the cup that I drink of?"

And it is also the cup in the hand of OUR LADY BABALON, and the cup of the Sacrament.

This Cup is full of bitterness, and of blood, and of intoxication.

The Understanding of the Magus is his link with the Invisible, on the passive side.

His Will errs actively by opposing itself to the Universal Will.

His Understanding errs passively when it receives influence from that which is not the ultimate truth.

In the beginning the Cup of the student is almost empty; and even such truth as he receives may leak away, and be lost.

They say that the Venetians made glasses which changed colour if poison was put into them; of such a glass must the student make his Cup.

Very little experience on the mystic path will show him that of all the impressions he receives none is true. Either they are false in themselves, or they are wrongly interpreted in his mind.

There is one truth, and only one. All other thoughts are false.

And as he advances in the knowledge of his mind he will come to understand that its whole structure is so faulty that it is quite incapable, even in its most exalted moods, of truth.

He will recognize that any thought merely establishes a relation between the Ego and the non-Ego.

Kant has shown that even the laws of nature are but the conditions of thought. And as the current of thought is the blood of the mind, it is said that the Magick Cup is filled with the blood of the Saints. All thought must be offered up as a sacrifice.

The Cup can hardly be described as a weapon. It is round like the pantacle — not straight like the wand and the dagger. Reception, not projection, is its nature.

footnote: As the Magician is in the position of God towards the Spirit that he evokes, he stands in the Circle, and the spirit in the Triangle; so the Magician is in the Triangle with respect to his own God.

So that which is round is to him a symbol of the influence from the higher. This circle symbolizes the Infinite, as every cross or Tau represents the Finite. That which is four square shows the Finite fixed into itself; for this reason the altar is foursquare. It is the solid basis from which all the operation proceeds. One form

footnote: An ugly form. A better is given in the illustration.

of the magical cup has a sphere beneath the bowl, and is supported upon a conical base.

This cup (crescent, sphere, cone) represents the three principles of the Moon, the Sun, and Fire, the three principles which, according to the Hindus, have course in the body.

> *footnote: These "principles" are seen by the pupil when first he succeeds in stilling his mind. That one which happens to be in course at the moment is the one seen by him. This is so marvellous an experience, even for one who has pushed astral visions to a very high point, that he may mistake them for the End. See chapter on Dhyana.*
>
> *The Hebrew letters corresponding to these principles are Gimel, Resh, and Shin, and the word formed by them means "a flower" and also "expelled," "cast forth."*

This is the Cup of Purification; as Zoroaster says:

"So therefore first the priest who governeth the works of fire must sprinkle with the lustral water of the loud-resounding sea."

It is the sea that purifies the world. And the "Great Sea" is in the Qabalah a name of Binah, "Understanding."

It is by the Understanding of the Magus that his work is purified.

Binah, moreover, is the Moon, and the bowl of this cup is shaped like the moon.

This moon is the path of Gimel through which the influence from the Crown descends upon the Sun of Tiphereth.

And this is based upon the pyramid of fire which symbolizes the aspiration of the student.

In Hindu symbolism the Amrita or "dew of immortality"

> *footnote: A—, the privative particle; "mrita," mortal.*

drips constantly upon a man, but is burnt up by the gross fire of his appetites. Yogis attempt to catch and so preserve this dew by turning back the tongue in the mouth.

Concerning the water in this Cup, it may be said that just as the wand should be perfectly rigid, the ideal solid, so should the water be the ideal fluid.

The Wand is erect, and must extend to Infinity.

The surface of the water is flat, and must extend to Infinity.

One is the line, the other the plane.

But as the Wand is weak without breadth, so is the water false without depth. The Understanding of the Magus must include all things, and that understanding must be infinitely profound.

H. G. Wells has said that "every word of which a man is ignorant represents an idea of which he is ignorant." And it is impossible perfectly to understand all things unless all things be first known.

Understanding is the structuralization of knowledge.

All impressions are disconnected, as the Babe of the Abyss is so terribly aware; and the Master of the Temple must sit for 106 seasons in the City of the Pyramids because this coordination is a tremendous task.

There is nothing particularly occult in this doctrine concerning knowledge and understanding.

A looking-glass receives all impressions but coordinates none.

The savage has none but the most simple associations of ideas.

Even the ordinary civilized man goes very little further.

All advance in thought is made by collecting the greatest possible number of facts, classifying them, and grouping them.

The philologist, though perhaps he only speaks one language, has a much higher type of mind than the linguist who speaks twenty.

This Tree of Thought is exactly paralleled by the tree of nervous structure.

Very many people go about nowadays who are exceedingly "well-informed," but who have not the slightest idea of the meaning of the facts they know. They have not developed the necessary higher part of the brain. Induction is impossible to them.

This capacity for storing away facts is compatible with actual imbecility. Some imbeciles have been able to store their memories with more knowledge than perhaps any sane man could hope to acquire.

This is the great fault of modern education — a child is stuffed with facts, and no attempt is made to explain their connection and bearing. The result is that even the facts themselves are soon forgotten.

Any first-rate mind is insulted and irritated by such treatment, and any first-rate memory is in danger of being spoilt by it.

No two ideas have any real meaning until they are harmonized in a third, and the operation is only perfect when these ideas are contradictory. This is the essence of the Hegelian logic.

The Magick Cup, as was shown above, is also the flower. It is the lotus which opens to the sun, and which collects the dew.

This Lotus is in the hand of Isis the great Mother. It is a symbol similar to the Cup in the hand of OUR LADY BABALON.

There are also the Lotuses in the human body, according to the Hindu system of Physiology referred to in the chapter on Dharana.

> *footnote: These Lotuses are all situated in the spinal column, which has three channels, Sushumna in the middle, Ida and Pingala on either side ("cf." the Tree of Life). The central channel is compressed at the base by Kundalini, the magical power, a sleeping serpent. Awake her: she darts up the spine, and the Prana flows through the Sushumna. See "Raja-Yoga" for more details.*

There is the lotus of three petals in the Sacrum, in which the Kundalini lies asleep. This lotus is the receptacle of reproductive force.

There is also the six-petalled lotus opposite the navel — which receives the forces which nourish the body.

There is also a lotus in the Solar plexus which receives the nervous forces.

The six-petalled lotus in the heart corresponds to Tiphereth, and receives those vital forces which are connected with the blood.

The sixteen-petalled lotus opposite the larynx receives the nourishment needed by the breath.

The two-petalled lotus of the pineal gland receives the nourishment needed by thought, while above the junction of the cranial structures is that sublime lotus, of a thousand and one petals, which receives the influence from on high; and in which, in the Adept, the awakened Kundalini takes her pleasure with the Lord of All.

All these lotuses are figured by the Magick Cup.

In man they are but partly opened, or only opened to their natural nourishment. In fact it is better to think of them as closed, as secreting that nourishment, which, because of the lack of sun, turns to poison.

The Magick Cup must have no lid, yet it must be kept veiled most carefully at all times, except when invocation of the Highest is being made.

This cup must also be hidden from the profane. The Wand must be kept secret lest the profane, fearing it, should succeed in breaking it; the Cup lest, wishing to touch it, they should defile it.

Yet the Sprinkling of its water not only purifies the Temple, but blesseth them that are without: freely must it be poured! But let no one know your real purpose, and let no one know the secret of your strength. Remember Samson! Remember Guy Fawkes!

Of the methods of increasing Understanding those of the Holy Qabalah are perhaps the best, provided that the intellect is thoroughly awake to their absurdity, and never allows itself to be convinced.

footnote: See the "Interlude" following.

Further meditation of certain sorts is useful: not the strict meditation which endeavours to still the mind, but such a meditation as Samasati.

footnote: See Equinox V, "The Training of the Mind"; Equinox II, "The Psychology of Hashish": Equinox VII, "Liber DCCCCXIII."

On the exoteric side if necessary the mind should be trained by the study of any well-developed science, such as chemistry, or mathematics.

The idea of organization is the first step, that of interpretation the second. The Master of the Temple, whose grade corresponds to Binah, is sworn to "interpret every phenomenon as a particular dealing of God with his soul."

But even the beginner may attempt this practice with advantage.

Either a fact fits in or it does not; if it does not, harmony is broken; and as the Universal harmony cannot be broken, the discord must be in the mind of the student, thus showing that he is not in tune with that Universal choir.

Let him then puzzle out first the great facts, then the little; until one summer, when he is bald and lethargic after lunch, he understands and appreciates the existence of flies!

This lack of Understanding with which we all begin is so terrible, so pitiful. In this world there is so much cruelty, so much waste, so much stupidity.

The contemplation of the Universe must be at first almost pure anguish. It is this fact which is responsible for most of the speculations of philosophy.

Mediaeval philosophers when hopelessly astray because their theology necessitated the reference of all things to the standard of men's welfare.

They even became stupid: Bernardin de St. Pierre (was it not?) said that the goodness of God was such that wherever men had built a great city, He had placed a river to assist them in conveying merchandise. But the truth is that in no way can we imagine the Universe as devised. If horses were made for men to ride, were not men made for worms to eat?

And so we find once more that the Ego-idea must be ruthlessly rooted out before Understanding can be attained.

There is an apparent contradiction between this attitude and that of the Master of the Temple. What can possibly be more selfish than this interpretation of everything as the dealing of God with the soul?

But it is God who is all and not any part; and every "dealing" must thus be an expansion of the soul, a destruction of its separateness.

Every ray of the sun expands the flower.

The surface of the water in the Magick Cup is infinite; there is no point different from any other point.

footnote: "If ye confound the space-marks, saying: They are one; or saying, They are many ... then expect the direful judgments of Ra Hoor Khuit ... {{sic: error of capitalization, should be: "if ye confound the space-marks ..."}}

This shall regenerate the world, the little world my sister." These are the words of NUIT, Our Lady of the Stars, of whom Binah is but the troubled reflection.}

Thus, ultimately, as the wand is a binding and a limitation, so is the Cup an expansion — into the Infinite.

And this is the danger of the Cup; it must necessarily be open to all, and yet if anything is put into it which is out of proportion, unbalanced, or impure, it takes hurt.

And here again we find difficulty with our thoughts. The grossness and stupidity of "simple impressions" cloud the waters; "emotions" trouble it; "perceptions" are still far from the perfect purity of truth; they cause reflections; while the "tendencies" alter the refractive index, and break up the light. Even "consciousness" itself is that which distinguishes between the lower and the higher, the waters which are below the firmament from the waters which are above the firmament, that appalling stage in the great curse of creation.

Since at the best this water

footnote: The water in this Cup (the latter is also a heart, as shown by the transition from the ancient to the modern Tarot; the suit "Hearts" in old packs of cards, and even in modern Spanish and Italian cards, is called "Cups") is the letter "Mem" (the Hebrew word for water), which has for its Tarot trump the Hanged Man. This Hanged Man represents the Adept hanging by one heel from a gallows, which is in the shape of the letter Daleth — the letter of the Empress, the heavenly Venus in the Tarot. His legs form a cross, his arms a triangle, as if by his equilibrium and self-sacrifice he were bringing the light down and establishing it even in the abyss.

Elementary as this is, it is a very satisfactory hieroglyph of the Great Work, though the student is warned that the obvious sentimental interpretation will have to be discarded as soon as it has been understood. It is a very noble illusion, and therefore a very dangerous one, to figure one's self as the Redeemer. For, of all the illusions in this Cup — the subtler and purer they are, the more difficult they are to detect.

is but a reflection, how tremendously important it becomes that it should be still!

If the cup is shaken the light will be broken up.

Therefore the Cup is placed upon the Altar, which is foursquare, will multiplied by will, the confirmation of the will in the Magical Oath, its fixation in Law.

It is easy to see when water is muddy, and easy to get rid of the mud; but there are many impurities which defy everything but distillation and even some which must be fractionated unto 70 times 7.

There is, however, a universal solvent and harmonizer, a certain dew which is so pure that a single drop of it cast into the water of the Cup will for the time being bring all to perfection.

This dew is called Love. Even as in the case of human love, the whole Universe appears perfect to the man who is under its control, so is it, and much more, with the Divine Love of which it is now spoken.

For human love is an excitement, and not a stilling, of the mind; and as it is bound to the individual, only leads to greater trouble in the end.

This Divine Love, on the contrary, is attached to no symbol.

It abhors limitation, either in its intensity or its scope. And this is the dew of the stars of which it is spoken in the Holy Books, for NUIT the Lady of the Stars is called "the Continuous One of Heaven," and it is that Dew which bathes the body of the Adept "in a sweet-smelling perfume of sweat."

footnote: See Liber Legis. Equinox VII. {{SIC to the quote, correctly: ".. bathing his whole body in a sweet-smelling perfume of sweat: O Nuit, continuous one of Heaven, let ...

In this cup, therefore, though all things are placed, by virtue of this dew all lose their identity. And therefore this Cup is in the hand of BABALON, the Lady of the City of the Pyramids, wherein no one can be distinguished from any other, wherein no one may sit until he has lost his name.

Of that which is in the Cup it is also said that it is wine. This is the Cup of Intoxication. Intoxication means poisoning, and in particular refers to the poison in which arrows are dipped (Greek

WEH: here in Greek letters: tau-omicron-xi-omicron-nu

, "a bow"). Think of the Vision of the Arrow in Liber 418, and look at the passages in the Holy Books which speak of the action of the spirit under the figure of a deadly poison.

For to each individual thing attainment means first and foremost the destruction of the individuality.

Each of our ideas must be made to give up the Self to the Beloved, so that we may eventually give up the Self to the Beloved in our turn.

It will be remembered in the History Lection

footnote: Liber LXI, the book given to those who wish to become Probationers of A.'.A.'.

how the Adepts "who had with smiling faces abandoned their homes and their possessions — could with steady calm and firm correctness abandon the Great Work itself; for this is the last and greatest projection of the Alchemist."

The Master of the Temple has crossed the Abyss, has entered the Palace of the King's Daughter; he has only to utter one word, and all is dissolved. But, instead of that, he is found hidden in the earth, tending a garden.

This mystery is all too complex to be elucidated in these fragments of impure thought; it is a suitable subject for meditation.

An Interlude

Every nursery rime contains profound magical secrets which are open to every one who has made a study of the correspondences of the Holy Qabalah. To puzzle out an imaginary meaning for this "nonsense" sets one thinking of the Mysteries; one enters into deep contemplation of holy things and God Himself leads the soul to a real illumination. Hence also the necessity of Incarnation; the soul must descend into all falsity in order to attain All-Truth.

For instance:

Old Mother Hubbard

Went to her cupboard

To get her poor dog a bone;

When she got there,

The cupboard was bare,

And so the poor dog had none.

Who is this ancient and venerable mother of whom it is spoken? Verily she is none other than Binah, as is evident in the use of the holy letter H with which her name begins.

Nor is she the sterile Mother Ama-but the fertile Aima; for within her she bears Vau, the son, for the second letter of her name, and R, the penultimate, is the Sun, Tiphareth, the Son.

The other three letters of her name, B, A, and D, are the three paths which join the three supernals.

To what cupboard did she go? Even to the most secret caverns of the Universe. And who is this dog? Is it not the name of God spelt Qabalistically backwards? And what is this bone? The bone is the Wand, the holy Lingam!

The complete interpretation of the rune is now open. This rime is the legend of the murder of Osiris by Typhon.

The limbs of Osiris were scattered in the Nile.

Isis sought them in every corner of the Universe, and she found all except his sacred lingam, which was not found until quite recently (vide Fuller, The Star in the West).

Let us take another example from this rich storehouse of magick lore.

Little Bo Peep

She lost her sheep,

And couldn't tell where to find them.

Leave them alone!

And they'll come home,

Dragging their tails behind them.

"Bo" is the root meaning Light, from which spring such words as Bo-Tree, Bodhisattva, and Buddha.

And "Peep" is Apep, the serpent Apophis. This poem therefore contains the same symbol as that in the Egyptian and Hebrew Bibles.

The snake is the serpent of initiation, as the Lamb is the Saviour.

This ancient one, the Wisdom of Eternity, sits in its old anguish awaiting the Redeemer. And this holy verse triumphantly assures us that there is no need for anxiety. The Saviours will come one after the other, at their own good pleasure, and as they may be needed, and drag their tails, that is to say those who follow out their holy commandment, to the ultimate goal.

Again we read:

Little Miss Muffett

Sat on a tuffet,

Eating of curds and whey,

Up came a big spider,

And sat down beside her,

And frightened Miss Muffett away.

Little Miss Muffett unquestionably represents Malkah; for she is unmarried. She is seated upon a "tuffet"; id est, she is the unregenerate soul upon Tophet, the pit of hell. And she eats curds and whey, that is, not the pure milk of the mother, but milk which has undergone decomposition.

But who is the spider? Verily herein is a venerable arcanum connoted! Like all insects, the spider represents a demon. But why a spider? Who is this spider "who taketh hold with her hands, and is in King's Palaces"? The name of this spider is Death. It is the fear of death which first makes the soul aware of its forlorn condition.

It would be interesting if tradition had preserved for us Miss Muffett's subsequent adventures.

But we must proceed to consider the interpretation of the following rime:

Little Jack Horner

Sat in a corner,

Eating a Christmas pie.

He stuck in his thumb,

And pulled out a plum,

And said, "What a good boy am I!"

In the interpretation of this remarkable poem there is a difference between two great schools of Adepts.

One holds that Jack is merely a corruption of John, Ion, he who goes-Hermes, the Messenger. The other prefers to take Jack simply and reverently as Iacchus, the spiritual form of Bacchus. But it does not matter very much whether we insist upon the swiftness or the rapture of the Holy Spirit of God; and that it is he of whom it is here spoken is evident, for the name Horner could be applied to none other by even the most casual reader of the Holy Gospels and the works of Congreve. And the context makes this even clearer, for he sits in a corner, that is in the place of Christ, the Corner Stone, eating, that is, enjoying, that which the birth of Christ assures to us. He is the Comforter who replaces the absent Saviour. If there was still any doubt of His identity it would be cleared up by the fact that it is the thumb, which is attributed to the element of Spirit, and not one of the four fingers of the four lesser elements, which he sticks into the pie of the new dispensation. He plucks forth one who is ripe, no doubt to send him forth as a teacher into the world, and rejoices that he is so well carrying out the will of the Father.

Let us pass from this most blessed subject to yet another.

Tom, Tom, the piper's son,

Stole a pig and away he run.

The pig was eat,

And Tom was beat,

And Tom went roaring down the street.

This is one of the more exoteric of these rimes. In fact, it is not much better than a sun-myth. Tom is Toum, the God of the Sunset (called the Son of Apollo, the Piper, the maker of music). The only difficulty in the poem concerns the pig; for anyone who has watched an angry sunset in the Tropics upon the sea, will recognize how incomparable a description of that sunset is given in that wonderful last line. Some have thought that the pig refers to the evening sacrifice, others that she is Hathor, the Lady of the West, in her more sensual aspect.

But it is probable that this poem is only the frst stanza of an epic. It has all the characteristic marks. Someone said of the Iliad that it did not finish, but merely stopped. This is the same. We may be sure that there is more of this poem. It tells us too much and too little. How came this tragedy of the eating of a merely stolen pig? Unveil this mystery of who "eat" it!

It must be abandoned, then, as at least partially insoluble. Let us consider this poem:

Hickory, dickory, dock!

The mouse ran up the clock;

The clock struck one,

And the mouse ran down,

Hickory, dickory, dock!

Here we are on higher ground at once. The clock symbolizes the spinal column, or, if you prefer it, Time, chosen as one of the conditions of normal consciousness. The mouse is the Ego; "Mus," a mouse, being only Sum, "I am," spelt Qabalistically backwards.

This Ego or Prana or Kundalini force being driven up the spine, the clock strikes one, that is, the duality of consciousness is abolished. And the force again subsides to its original level.

"Hickory, dickory, dock!" is perhaps the mantra which was used by the adept who constructed this rime, thereby hoping to fix it in the minds of men; so that they might attain to Samadhi by the same method. Others attribute to it a more profound signifance-which it is impossible to go into at this moment, for we must turn to:-

Humpty Dumpty sat on a wall;

Humpty Dumpty got a great fall;

All the king's horses

And all the king's men

Couldn't set up Humpty Dumpty again.

This is so simple as hardly to require explanation. Humpty Dumpty is of course the Egg of Spirit, and the wall is the Abyss—his "fall" is therefore the descent of spirit into matter; and it is only too painfully familiar to us that all the king's horses and all his men cannot restore us to the height.

Only The King Himself can do that!

But one can hardly comment upon a theme which has been so fruitfully treated by Ludovicus Carolus, that most holy illuminated man of God. His masterly treatment of the identity of the three reciprocating paths of Daleth, Teth, and Pe, is one of the most wonderful passages in the Holy Qabalah. His resolution of what we take to be the bond of slavery into very love, the embroidered neckband of honour bestowed upon us by the King himself, is one of the most sublime passages in this class of literature.

Peter, Peter, pumpkin eater,

Had a wife and couldn't keep her.

He put her in a peanut shell;

Then he kept her very well.

This early authentic text of the Hinayana School of Buddhism is much esteemed even to-day by the more cultured and devoted followers of that school.

The pumpkin is of course the symbol of resurrection, as is familiar to all students of the story of Jonah and the gourd.

Peter is therefore the Arahat who has put an end to his series of resurrections. That he is called Peter is a reference to the symbolizing of Arahats as stones in the great wall of the guardians of mankind. His wife is of course (by the usual symbolism) his body, which he could not keep until he put her in a peanut shell, the yellow robe of a Bhikkhu.

Buddha said that if any man became an Arahat he must either take the vows of a Bhikkhu that very day, or die, and it is this saying of Buddha's that the unknown poet wished to commemorate.

Taffy was a Welshman

Taffy was a thief;

Taffy came to my house

And stole a leg of beef.

I went to Taffy's house;

Taffy was in bed.

I took a carving knife,

And cut off Taffy's head.

Taffy is merely short for Taphthatharath, the Spirit of Mercury and the God of Welshmen or thieves. "My house" is of course equivalent to "my magick circle." Note that Beth, the letter of Mercury and "The Magus," means "a house."

The beef is a symbol of the Bull, Apis the Redeemer. This is therefore that which is written, "Oh my God, disguise thy glory! Come as a thief, and let us steal away the sacraments!"

In the following verse we find that Taffy is "in bed," owing to the operation of the sacrament. The great task of the Alchemist has been accomplished; the mercury is fixed.

One can then take the Holy Dagger, and separate the Caput Mortuum from the Elixir. Some Alchemists believe that the beef represents that dense physical substance which is imbibed by Mercury for his fixation; but here as always we should prefer the more spiritual interpretation.

Bye, Baby Bunting!

Daddy's gone a-hunting.

He's gone to get a rabbit-skin

To wrap my Baby Bunting in.

This is mystical charge to the new-born soul to keep still, to remain steadfast in meditation; for, in Bye, Beth is the letter of thought, Yod that of the Hermit. It tells the soul that the Father of All will clothe him about with His own majestical silence. For is not the rabbit he "who lay low and said nuffin'"?

Pat-a-cake, pat-a-cake, baker's man!

Bake me a cake as fast as you can!

Pat it and prick it and mark it with P!

Bake it in the oven for baby and me!

This rime is usually accompanied (even to-day in the nursery) with a ceremonial clapping of hands-the symbol of Samadhi. Compare what is said on this subject in our comment on the famous "Advent" passage in Thessalonians.

The cake is of course the bread of the sacrament, and it would ill become Frater P. to comment upon the third line-though it may be remarked that even among the Catholics the wafer has always been marked with a phallus or cross.

CHAPTER VIII

THE SWORD

"THE word of the Lord is quick and powerful, and sharper than a two-edged sword."

As the Wand is Chokmah, the Will, "the Father," and the Cup the Understanding, "the Mother," Binah; so the Magick Sword is the Reason, "the Son," the six Sephiroth of the Ruach, and we shall see that the Pantacle corresponds to Malkuth, "the Daughter."

The Magick Sword is the analytical faculty; directed against any demon it attacks his complexity.

Only the simple can withstand the sword. As we are below the Abyss, this weapon is then entirely destructive: it divides Satan against Satan. It is only in the lower forms of Magick, the purely human forms, that the Sword has become so important a weapon. A dagger should be sufficient.

But the mind of man is normally so important to him that the sword is actually the largest of his weapons; happy is he who can make the dagger suffice!

The hilt of the Sword should be made of copper.

The guard is composed of the two crescents of the waxing and the waning moon — back to back. Spheres are placed between them, forming an equilateral triangle with the sphere of the pommel.

The blade is straight, pointed, and sharp right up to the guard. It is made of steel, to equilibrate with the hilt, for steel is the metal of Mars, as copper is of Venus.

Those two planets are male and female — and thus reflect the Wand and the Cup, though in a much lower sense.

The hilt is of Venus, for Love is the motive of this ruthless analysis — if this were not so the sword would be a Black Magical weapon.

The pommel of the Sword is in Daath, the guard extends to Chesed and Geburah; the point is in Malkuth. Some magi make the three spheres of lead, tin, and gold respectively; the moons are silver, and the grip contains quicksilver, thus making the Sword symbolic of the seven planets. But this is a phantasy and affectation.

"Whoso taketh the sword shall perish by the sword," is not a mystical threat, but a mystical promise. It is our own complexity that must be destroyed.

Here is another parable. Peter, the Stone of the Philosophers, cuts off the ear of Malchus, the servant of the High Priest (the ear is the organ of Spirit). In analysis the spiritual part of Malkuth must be separated from it by the philosophical stone, and then Christus, the Anointed One, makes it whole once more. "Solve et coagula!"

It is noticeable that this takes place at the arrest of Christ, who is the son, the Ruach, immediately before his crucifixion.

The Calvary Cross should be of six squares, an unfolded cube, which cube is this same philosophical stone.

Meditation will reveal many mysteries which are concealed in this symbol.

The Sword or Dagger is attributed to air, all-wandering, all-penetrating, but unstable; not a phenomenon subtle like fire, not a chemical combination like water, but a mixture of gases.

footnote: The Oxygen in the air would be too fierce for life; it must be largely diluted with the inert nitrogen.

The rational mind supports life, but about seventy-nine per cent. of it not only refuses itself to enter into combination, but prevents the remaining twenty-one per cent. from doing so. Enthusiasms are checked; the intellect is the great enemy of devotion. One of the tasks of the Magician is to manage somehow to separate the Oxygen and Nitrogen in his mind, to stifle four-fifts so that he may burn up the remainder, a flame of holiness. But this cannot be done by the Sword.

The Sword, necessary as it is to the Beginner, is but a crude weapon. Its function is to keep off the enemy or to force a passage through them — and though it must be wielded to gain admission to the palace, it cannot be worn at the marriage feast.

One might say that the Pantacle is the bread of life, and the Sword the knife which cuts it up. One must have ideas, but one must criticize them.

The Sword, too, is that weapon with which one strikes terror into the demons and dominates them. One must keep the Ego Lord of the impressions. One must not allow the circle to be broken by the demon; one must not allow any one idea to carry one away.

It will readily be seen how very elementary and false all this is — but for the beginner it is necessary.

In all dealings with demons the point of the Sword is kept downwards, and it should not be used for invocation, as is taught in certain schools of magick.

If the Sword is raised towards the Crown, it is no longer really a sword. The Crown cannot be divided. Certainly the Sword should not be lifted.

The Sword may, however, be clasped in both hands, and kept steady and erect, symbolizing that thought has become one with the single aspiration, and burnt up like a flame. This flame is the Shin, the Ruach Alhim, not the mere Ruach Adam. The divine and not the human consciousness.

The Magician cannot wield the Sword unless the Crown is on his head.

Those Magicians, who have attempted to make the Sword the sole or even the principal weapon, have only destroyed themselves, not by the destruction of combination, but by the destruction of division.

footnote: It should be noted that this ambiguity in the word "destruction" has been the cause of much misunderstanding. "Solve" is destruction, but so is "coagula." The aim of the Magus is to destroy his partial thought by uniting it with the Universal Thought, not to make a further breach and division in the Whole.

Weakness overcomes strength.

The most stable political edifice of history has been that of China, which was founded principally on politeness; and that of India has proved strong enough to absorb its many conquerors.

footnote: The Brahmin caste is not so strict as that of the "heaven-born" (Indian Civil Service).

The Sword has been the great weapon of the last century. Every idea has been attacked by thinkers, and none has withstood attack. Hence civilization crumbles.

No settled principles remain. To-day all constructive statesmanship is empiricism or opportunism. It has been doubted whether there is any real relation between Mother and Child, any real distinction between Male and Female.

The human mind, in despair, seeing insanity imminent in the breaking up of these coherent images, has tried to replace them by ideals which are only saved from destruction, at the very moment of their birth, by their vagueness.

The Will of the King was at least ascertainable at any moment; nobody has yet devised a means for ascertaining the will of the people.

All conscious willed action is impeded; the march of events is now nothing but inertia.

Let the Magician consider these matters before he takes the Sword in his hand. Let him understand that the Ruach, this loose combination of 6 Sephiroth, only bound together by their attachment to the human will in Tiphereth, must be rent asunder.

The mind must be broken up into a form of insanity before it can be transcended.

David said: "I hate thoughts."

The Hindu says: "That which can be thought is not true."

Paul said: "The carnal mind is enmity against God."

And every one who meditates, even for an hour, will soon discover how this gusty aimless wind makes his flame flicker. "The wind bloweth where it listeth." The normal man is less than a straw.

> *footnote: But as it is said, "Similia similibus curantur," we find this Ruach also the symbol of the Spirit. RVCh ALHIM, the Spirit of God, is 300, the number of the holy letter Shin. As this is the breath, which by its nature is double, the two edges of the Sword, the letter H symbolises breath, and H is the letter of Aries — the House of Mars, of the Sword: and H is also the letter of the Mother; this is the link between the Sword and the Cup.*

The connection between Breath and Mind has been supposed by some to exist merely in etymology. But the connection is a truer one.

> *footnote: It is undoubted that Ruach means primarily "that which moves or revolves," "a going," "a wheel," "the wind," and that its secondary meaning was mind because of the observed instability of mind, and its tendency to a circular motion. "Spiritus" only came to mean Spirit in the modern technical sense owing to the efforts of the theologians. We have an example of the proper use of the word in the term: Spirit of Wine — the airy portion of wine. But the word "inspire" was perhaps derived from observing the derangement of the breathing of persons in divine ecstasy.*

In any case there is undoubtedly a connection between the respiratory and mental functions. The Student will find this out by practising Pranayama. By this exercise some thoughts are barred, and those which do come into the mind come more slowly than before, so that the mind has time to perceive their falsity and to destroy them.

On the blade of the Magick Sword is etched the name AGLA, a Notariqon formed from the initials of the sentence "Ateh Gibor Leolahm Adonai," "To thee be the Power unto the Ages, O my lord."

And the acid which eats into the steel should be oil of vitrol. Vitrol is a Notariqon of "Visita Interiora Terrae

Rectificando Invenies Occultum Lapidem." That is to say: By investigating everything and bringing it into harmony and proportion you will find the hidden stone, the same stone of the philosophers of which mention has already been made, which turns all into gold. This oil which can eat into the steel, is further that which is written, Liber LXV, i, 16: "As an acid eats into steel . . . so am I unto the Spirit of Man."

Note how closely woven into itself is all this symbolism!

The centre of Ruach being the heart, it is seen that this Sword of the Ruach must be thrust by the Magician into his own heart.

But there is a subsequent task, of which it is spoken — Liber VII, v, 47. "He shall await the sword of the Beloved and bare his throat for the stroke." In the throat is Daath — the throne of Ruach. Daath is knowledge. This final destruction of knowledge opens the gate of the City of the Pyramids.

It is also written, Liber CCXX, iii, 11: "Let the woman be girt with a sword before me." But this refers to the arming of Vedana with Sanna, the overcoming of emotion by clarity of perception.

It is also spoken, Liber LXV, v, 14, of the Sword of Adonai, "that hath four blades, the blade of the Thunderbolt, the blade of the Pylon, the blade of the Serpent, the blade of the Phallus."

But this Sword is not for the ordinary Magician. For this is the Sword flaming every way that keeps Eden, and in this Sword the Wand and the Cup are concealed — so that although the being of the Magician is blasted by the Thunderbolt, and poisoned by the Serpent, at the same time the organs whose union is the supreme sacrament are left in him.

At the coming of Adonai the individual is destroyed in both senses. He is shattered into a thousand pieces, yet at the same time united with the simple

footnote: Compare the first set of verses in Liber XVI. (XVI in the Taro is Pe, Mars, the Sword.)

Of this it is also spoken by St. Paul in his Epistle to the Church in Thessalonica: "For the Lord shall descend from Heaven, with a shout, with the voice of the Archangel, and with the trump of God; and the dead in Christ shall rise first. Then we which are alive and remain shall be caught up together with them into the clouds to meet the Lord in the air; and so shall we be for ever with the Lord."

The stupid interpretation of this verse as prophetic of a "second advent" need not concern us; every word of it is, however, worthy of profound consideration.

"The Lord" is Adonai — which is the Hebrew for "my Lord"; and He descends from heaven, the supernal Eden, the Sahasrara Cakkra in man, with a "shout," a "voice," and a "trump," again airy symbols, for it is air that carries sound. These sounds refer to those heard by the Adept at the moment of rapture.

This is most accurately pictured in the Tarot Trump called "The Angel," which corresponds to the letter Shin, the letter of Spirit and of Breath.

The whole mind of man is rent by the advent of Adonai, and is at once caught up into union with Him. "In the air," the Ruach.

Note that etymologically the word {greek letters here: sigma-upsilon-nu}, "together with," is the Sanskrit "Sam;" and the Hebrew ADNI is the Sanskrit ADHI.

The phrase "together with the Lord," is then literally identical with the word Samadhi, which is the Sanskrit name of the phenomenon described by Saint Paul, this union of the ego and the non-ego, subject and object, this chymical marriage, and thus identical with the symbolism of the Rosy Cross, under a slightly different aspect.

And since marriage can only take place between one and one, it is evident that no idea can thus be united, unless it is simple.

Hence every idea must be analysed by the Sword. Hence, too, there must only be a single thought in the mind of the person meditating.

One may now go on to consider the use of the Sword in purifying emotions into perceptions.

It was the function of the Cup to interpret the perceptions by the tendencies; the Sword frees the perceptions from the Web of emotion.

The perceptions are meaningless in themselves; but the emotions are worse, for they delude their victim into supposing them significant and true.

Every emotion is an obsession; the most horrible of blasphemies is to attribute any emotion to God in the macrocosm, or to the pure soul in the microcosm.

How can that which is self-existent, complete, be "moved?" It is even written that "torsion about a point is iniquity."

WEH footnote: See Macrobius, Iamblichus, Plotinus and sayings attributed to Pythagoras for these views

But if the point itself could be moved it would cease to be itself, for position is the only attribute of the point.

The Magician must therefore make himself absolutely free in this respect.

It is the constant practice of Demons to attempt to terrify, to shock, to disgust, to allure. Against all this he must oppose the Steel of the Sword. If he has got rid the ego-idea this task will be comparatively easy; unless he has done so it will be almost impossible. So says the Dhammapada:

Me he abused, and me he beat, he robbed me, he insulted me;

In whom such thoughts find harbourage, hatred will never cease to be.

And this hatred is the thought which inhibits the love whose apotheosis is Samadhi.

But it is too much to expect of the young Magician to practise attachment to the distasteful; let him first become indifferent. Let him endeavour to see facts as facts, as simply as he would see them if they were historical. Let him avoid the imaginative interpretation of any facts. Let him not put himself in the place of the people of whom the facts are related, or if he does so, let it be done only for the purpose of comprehension. Sympathy,

footnote: It is true that sometimes sympathy is necessary to comprehension.

indignation, praise and blame, are out of place in the observer.

No one has properly considered the question as to the amount and quality of the light afforded by candles made by waxed Christians.

Who has any idea which joint of the ordinary missionary is preferred by epicures? It is only a matter of conjecture that Catholics are better eating than Presbyterians.

Yet these points and their kind are the only ones which have any importance at the time when the events occur.

Nero did not consider what unborn posterity might think of him; it is difficult to credit cannibals with the calculation that the recital of their exploits will induce pious old ladies to replenish their larder.

Very few people have ever "seen" a bull-fight. One set of people goes for excitement, another set for the perverse excitement which real or simulated horror affords. Very few people know that blood freshly spilled in the sunlight is perhaps the most beautiful colour that is to be found in nature.

It is a notorious fact that it is practically impossible to get a reliable description of what occurs at a spiritualistic "seance;" the emotions cloud the vision.

Only in the absolute calm of the laboratory, where the observer is perfectly indifferent to what may happen, only concerned to observe exactly what that happening is, to measure and to weigh it by means of instruments incapable of emotion, can one even begin to hope for a truthful record of events. Even the common physical bases of emotion, the senses of pleasure and pain, lead the observer infallibly to err. This though they be not sufficiently excited to disturb his mind.

Plunge one hand into a basin of hot water, the other into a basin of cold water, then both together into a basin of tepid water; the one hand will say hot, the other cold.

Even in instruments themselves, their physical qualities, such as expansion and contraction (which may be called, in a way, the roots of pleasure and pain), cause error.

Make a thermometer, and the glass is so excited by the necessary fusion that year by year, for thirty years afterwards or more, the height of the mercury will continue to alter; how much more then with so plastic a matter as the mind! There is no emotion which does not leave a mark on the mind, and all marks are bad marks. Hope and fear are only opposite phases of a single emotion; both are incompatible with the purity of the soul. With the passions of man the case is somewhat different, as they are functions of his own will. They need to be disciplined, not to be suppressed. But emotion is impressed from without. It is an invasion of the circle.

As the Dhammapada says:

An ill-thatched house is open to the mercy of the rain and wind;

So passion hath the power to break into an unreflecting mind.

A well-thatched house is proof against the fury of the rain and wind;

So passion hath no power to break into a rightly-ordered mind.

Let then the Student practise observation of those things which normally would cause him emotion; and let him, having written a careful description of what he sees, check it by the aid of some person familiar with such sights.

Surgical operations and dancing girls are fruitful fields for the beginner.

In reading emotional books such as are inflicted on children, let him always endeavour to see the event from the standpoint opposite to that of the author. Yet let him not emulate the partially emancipated child who complained of a picture of the Colosseum that "there was one poor little lion who hadn't got any Christian," except in the first instance. Adverse criticism is the first step; the second must go further.

Having sympathized sufficiently with both the lions and the Christians, let him open his eyes to that which his sympathy had masked hitherto, that the picture is abominably conceived, abominably composed, abominably drawn, and abominably coloured, as it is pretty sure to be.

Let him further study those masters, in science or in art, who have observed with minds untinctured by emotion.

Let him learn to detect idealizations, to criticize and correct them.

Let him understand the falsehood of Raphael, of Watteau, of Leighton, of Bouguereau; let him appreciate the truthfulness of John, of Rembrandt, of Titian, of O'Conor.

Similar studies in literature and philosophy will lead to similar results. But do not let him neglect the analysis of his own emotions; for until these are overcome he will be incapable of judging others.

This analysis may be carried out in various ways; one is the materialistic way. For example, if oppressed by nightmare, let him explain: "This nightmare is a cerebral congestion."

The strict way of doing this by meditation is Mahasatipatthana,

footnote: See Crowley, "Collected Works," vol. ii, pp. 252-254.

but it should be aided in every moment of life by endeavouring to estimate occurrences at their true value. Their relativity in particular must be carefully considered.

Your toothache does not hurt any one outside a very small circle. Floods in China mean to you nothing but a paragraph in the newspaper. The destruction of the world itself would have no significance in Sirius. One can hardly imagine even that the astronomers of Sirius could perceive so trifling a disturbance.

Now considering that Sirius itself is only, as far as you know, but one, and one of the least important, of the ideas in your mind, why should that mind be disturbed by your toothache? It is not possible to labour this point without tautology, for it is a very simple one; but it should be emphasised, for it is a very simple one. Waugh! Waugh! Waugh! Waugh! Waugh!

In the question of ethics it again becomes vital, for to many people it seems impossible to consider the merits of any act without dragging in a number of subjects which have no real connection with it.

The Bible has been mistranslated by perfectly competent scholars because they had to consider the current theology. The most glaring example is the "Song of Solomon," a typical piece of Oriental eroticism. But since to admit that it was this would never do for a canonical book, they had to pretend that it was symbolical.

They tried to refine away the grossness of the expressions, but even their hardihood proved unequal to the task.

This form of dishonesty reaches its climax in the expurgating of the classics. "The Bible is the Word of God, written by holy men, as they were inspired by the Holy Ghost. But we will cut out those passages which we think unsuitable." "Shakespeare is our greatest poet — but, of course, he is very dreadful." "No one can surpass the lyrics of Shelley, but we must pretend that he was not an atheist."

Some translators could not bear that the heathen Chinese should use the word Shang Ti, and pretended that it did not mean God. Others, compelled to admit that it did mean God, explained that the use of the term showed that "God had not left himself without a witness even in this most idolatrous of nations. They had been mysteriously compelled to use it, not knowing what it meant." All this because of their emotional belief that they were better than the Chinese.

The most dazzling example of this is shown in the history of the study of Buddhism.

The early scholars simply could not understand that the Buddhist canon denies the soul, regards the ego as a delusion caused by a special faculty of the diseased mind, could not understand that the goal of the Buddhist, Nibbana, was in any way different from their own goal, Heaven, in spite of the perfect plainness of the language in such dialogues as those between the Arahat Nagasena and King Melinda; and their attempts to square the text with their preconceptions will always stand as one of the great follies of the wise.

Again, it is almost impossible for the well-mannered Christian to realize that Jesus Christ ate with his fingers. The temperance advocate makes believe that the wine at the marriage feast of Cana was non-alcoholic.

It is a sort of mad syllogism.

"Nobody whom I respect does this."

"I respect So-and-so."

"Therefore, So-and-so did not do this."

The moralist of to-day is furious when one points to the fact that practically every great man in history was grossly and notoriously immoral.

Enough of this painful subject!

As long as we try to fit facts to theories instead of adopting the scientific attitude of altering the theories (when necessary) to fit the facts, we shall remain mired in falsehood.

The religious taunt the scientific man with this open-mindedness, with this adaptability. "Tell a lie and stick to it!" is "their" golden rule.

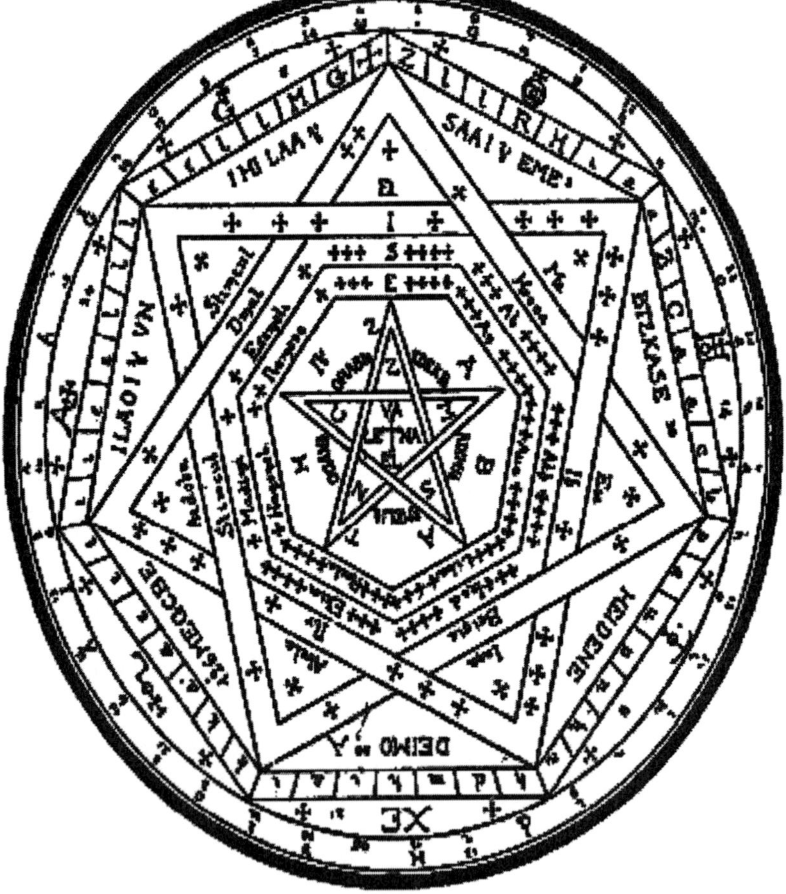

THE SIGILLUM DEI ÆMETH, A PANTACLE
MADE BY DR. JOHN DEE.

CHAPTER IX

THE PANTACLE

AS the Magick Cup is the heavenly food of the Magus, so is the Magick Pantacle his earthly food.

The Wand was his divine force, and the Sword his human force.

The Cup is hollow to receive the influence from above. The Pantacle is flat like the fertile plains of earth.

The name Pantacle implies an image of the All, "omne in parvo;" but this is by a magical transformation of the Pantacle. Just as we made the Sword symbolical of everything by the force of our Magick, so do we work upon the Pantacle. That which is merely a piece of common bread shall be the body of God!

The Wand was the will of man, his wisdom, his word; the Cup was his understanding, the vehicle of grace; the Sword was his reason; and the Pantacle shall be his body, the temple of the Holy Ghost.

What is the length of this Temple?

From North to South.

What is the breadth of this Temple?

From East to West.

What is the height of this Temple?

From the Abyss to the Abyss.

There is, therefore, nothing movable or immovable under the whole firmament of heaven which is not included in this pantacle, though it be but "eight inches in diameter, and in thickness half an inch."

Fire is not matter at all; water is a combination of elements; air almost entirely a mixture of elements; earth contains all both in admixture and in combination.

So must it be with this Pantacle, the symbol of earth.

And as this Pantacle is made of pure wax, do not forget that "everything that lives is holy."

All phenomena are sacraments. Every fact, and even every falsehood, must enter into the Pantacle; it is the great storehouse from which the Magician draws.

"In the brown cakes of corn we shall taste the food of the world and be strong."

footnote: We have avoided dealing with the Pantacle as the Paten of the Sacrament, though special instructions about it are given in Liber Legis. It is composed of meal, honey, wine, holy oil, and blood.

When speaking of the Cup, it was shown how every fact must be made significant, how every stone must have its proper place in the mosaic. Woe were it were one stone misplaced! But that mosaic cannot be wrought at all, well or ill, unless every stone be there.

These stones are the simple impressions or experiences; not one may be foregone.

Do not refuse anything merely because you know that it is the cup of Poison offered by your enemy; drink it with confidence; it is he that will fall dead!

WEH footnote: Metaphor. Not for reading by children!

How can I give Cambodian art its proper place in art, if I have never heard of Cambodia? How can the Geologist estimate the age of what lies beneath the chalk unless he have a piece of knowledge totally unconnected with geology, the life-history of the animals of whom that chalk is the remains?

This then is a very great difficulty for the Magician. He cannot possibly have all experience, and though he may console himself philosophically with the reflection that the Universe is conterminous with such experience as he has, he will find it grow at such a pace during the early years of his life that he may almost be tempted to believe in the possibility of experiences beyond his own, and from a practical standpoint he will seem to be confronted with so many avenues of knowledge that he will be bewildered which to choose.

The ass hesitated between two thistles; how much more that greater ass, that incomparably greater ass, between two thousand!

Fortunately it does not matter very much; but he should at least choose those branches of knowledge which abut directly upon universal problems.

He should choose not one but several, and these should be as diverse as possible in nature.

It is important that he should strive to excel in some sport, and that that sport should be the one best calculated to keep this body in health.

He should have a thorough grounding in classics, mathematics and science; also enough general knowledge of modern languages and of the shifts of life to enable him to travel in any part of the world with ease and security.

History and geography he can pick up as he wants them; and what should interest him most in any subject is its links with some other subject, so that his Pantacle may not lack what painters call "composition."

He will find that, however good his memory may be, ten thousand impressions enter his mind for every one that it is able to retain even for a day. And the excellence of a memory lies in the wisdom of its selection.

The best memories so select and judge that practically nothing is retained which has not some coherence with the general plan of the mind.

All Pantacles will contain the ultimate conceptions of the circle and the cross, though some will prefer to replace the cross by a point, or by a Tau, or by a triangle. The Vesica Pisces is sometimes used instead of the circle, or the circle may be glyphed as a serpent. Time and space and the idea of causality are sometimes represented; so also are the three stages in the history of philosophy, in which the three objects of study were successively Nature, God, and Man.

The duality of consciousness is also sometimes represented; and the Tree of Life itself may be figured therein, or the categories. An emblem of the Great Work should be added. But the Pantacle will be imperfect unless each idea is contrasted in a balanced manner with its opposite, and unless there is a necessary connection between each pair of ideas and every other pair.

The Neophyte will perhaps do well to make the first sketches for his Pantacle very large and complex, subsequently simplifying, not so much by exclusion as by combination, just as a Zoologist, beginning with the four great Apes and Man, combines all in the single word "primate."

It is not wise to simplify too far, since the ultimate hieroglyphic must be an infinite. The ultimate resolution not having been performed, its symbol must not be portrayed.

If any person were to gain access to V.V.V.V.V.,

footnote: The Motto of the Chief of the A.'.A.'., "the Light of the World Himself."

and ask Him to discourse upon any subject, there is little doubt that He could only comply by an unbroken silence, and even that might not be wholly satisfactory, since the Tao Teh King says that the Tao cannot be declared either by silence or by speech.

In this preliminary task of collecting materials, the idea of the Ego is not of such great moment; all impressions are phases of the non-ego, and the Ego serves merely as a receptacle. In fact, to the well regulated mind, there is no question but that the impressions are real, and that the mind, if not a "tabula rasa," is only not so because of the "tendencies" or "innate ideas" which prevent some ideas from being received as readily as others.

footnote: It does not occur to a newly-hatched chicken to behave in the same way as a new-born child.

These "tendencies" must be combated: distasteful facts should be insisted upon until the Ego is perfectly indifferent to the nature of its food.

"Even as the diamond shall glow red for the rose, and green for the rose-leaf, so shalt thou abide apart from the Impressions."

This great task of separating the self from the impressions or "vrittis" is one of the may meanings of the aphorism "solve," corresponding to the "coagula" implied in Samadhi, and this Pantacle therefore represents all that we are, the resultant of all that we had a tendency to be.

In the Dhammapada we read:

All that we are from mind results; on mind is founded, built of mind;

Who acts or speaks with evil thought him doth pain follow sure and blind.

So the ox plants his foot, and so the car wheel follows hard behind.

All that we are from mind results; on mind is founded, built of mind;

Who acts or speaks with righteous thought him happiness doth surely find.

So failing not the shadow falls for ever in its place assigned.

The Pantacle is then in a sense identical with the Karma or Kamma of the Magician.

The Karma of a man is his "ledger." The balance has not been struck and he does not know what it is; he does not even fully know what debts he may have to pay, or what is owed him; nor does he know on what dates even those payments which he anticipates may fall due.

A business conducted on such lines would be in a terrible mess; and we find in fact that man is in just such a mess. While he is working day and night at some unimportant detail of his affairs, some giant force may be advancing "pede claudo" to overtake him.

Many of the entries in this "ledger" are for the ordinary man necessarily illegible; the method of reading them is given in that important instruction of the A.'.A.'. called "Thisharb," Liber CMXIII.

Now consider that this Karma is all that a man has or is. His ultimate object is to get rid of it completely — when it comes to the point of surrendering

footnote: To surrender all, one must give up not only the bad but the good; not only weakness but strength. How can the mystic surrender all, while he clings to his virtues?

the Self to the Beloved; but in the beginning the Magician is not that Self, he is only the heap of refuse from which that Self is to be built up. The Magical instruments must be made before they are destroyed.

This idea of Karma has been confused by many who ought to have know better, including the Buddha, with the ideas of poetic justice and of retribution.

We have the story of one of the Buddha's Arahats, who being blind, in walking up and down unwittingly killed a number of insects. [The Buddhist regards the destruction of life as the most shocking crime.] His brother Arahats inquired as to how this was, and Buddha spun them a long yarn as to how, in a previous incarnation, he had maliciously deprived a woman of her sight. This is only a fairy tale, a bogey to frighten the children, and probably the worst way of influencing the young yet devised by human stupidity.

Karma does not work in this way at all.

In any case moral fables have to be very carefully constructed, or they may prove dangerous to those who use them.

You will remember Bunyan's Passion and Patience: naughty Passion played with all this toys and broke them, good little Patience put them carefully aside. Bunyan forgets to mention that by the time Passion had broken all his toys, he had outgrown them.

Karma does not act in this tit-for-tat-way. An eye for an eye is a sort of savage justice, and the idea of justice in our human sense is quite foreign to the constitution of the Universe.

Karma is the Law of Cause and Effect. There is no proportion in its operations. Once an accident occurs it is impossible to say what may happen; and the Universe is a stupendous accident.

We go out to tea a thousand times without mishap, and the thousand-and-first time we meet some one who changes radically the course of our lives for ever.

There is a sort of sense in which every impression that is made upon our minds is the resultant of all the forces of the past; no incident is so trifling that it has not in some way shaped one's disposition. But there is none of this crude retribution about it. One may kill a hundred thousand lice in one brief hour at the foot of the Baltoro Glacier, as Frater P. once did. It would be stupid to suppose, as the Theosophist inclines to suppose, that this action involves one in the doom of being killed by a louse a hundred thousand times.

This ledger of Karma is kept separate from the petty cash account; and in respect of bulk this petty cash account is very much bigger than the ledger.

If we eat too much salmon we get indigestion and perhaps nightmare. It is silly to suppose that a time will come when a salmon will eat us, and find us disagree.

On the other hand we are always being terribly punished for actions that are not faults at all. Even our virtues rouse insulted nature to revenge.

Karma only grows by what it fees on: and if Karma is to be properly brought up, it requires a very careful diet.

With the majority of people their actions cancel each other out; no sooner is effort made than it is counterbalanced by idleness. Eros gives place to Anteros.

Not one man in a thousand makes even an apparent escape from the commonplace of animal life.

Birth is sorrow;

Life is sorrow;

Sorrowful are old age, disease, and death;

But resurrection is the greatest misery of all.

"Oh what misery! birth incessantly!" as Buddha said.

One goes on from day to day with a little of this and a little of that, a few kind thoughts and a few unkind thoughts; nothing really gets done. Body and mind are changed, changed beyond recall by nightfall. But what "meaning" has any of this change?

How few there are who can look back through the years and say that they have made advance in any definite direction? And in how few is that change, such as it is, a variable with intelligence and conscious volition! The dead weight of the original conditions under which we were born has counted for far more than all our striving. The unconscious forces are incomparably greater than those of which we have any knowledge. This is the "solidity" of our Pantacle, the Karma of our earth that whirls us will he nill he around her axis at the rate of a thousand miles an hour. And a thousand is Aleph, a capital Aleph, the microcosm of all-wandering air, the fool of the Taro, the aimlessness and fatality of things!

It is very difficult then in any way to "fashion" this heavy Pantacle.

We can engrave characters upon it with the dagger, but they will scarcely come to more than did the statue of Ozymandias, King of Kings, in the midst of the unending desert.

We cut a figure on the ice; it is effaced in a morning by the tracks of other skaters; nor did that figure do more than scratch the surface of the ice, and the ice itself must melt before the sun. Indeed the Magician may despair when he comes to make the Pantacle! Everyone has the material, one man's pretty well as good as his brothers; but for that Pantacle to be in any way fashioned to a willed end, or even to an intelligible end, or even to a known end: "Hoc opus, Hic labor est." It is indeed the toil of ascending from Avernus, and escaping to the upper air.

In order to do it, it is most necessary to understand our tendencies, and to will the development of one, the destruction of another. And though all elements in the Pantacle must ultimately be destroyed, yet some will help us directly to reach a position from which this task of destruction becomes possible; and there is no element therein which may not be occasionally helpful.

And so — beware! Select! Select! Select!

This Pantacle is an infinite storehouse; things will always be there when we want them. We may see to it occasionally that they are dusted and the moth kept out, but we shall usually be too busy to do much more. Remember that in travelling from the earth to the stars, one dare not be encumbered with too much heavy luggage. Nothing that is not a necessary part of the machine should enter into its composition.

Now though this Pantacle is composed only of shams, some shams somehow seem to be more false than others.

The whole Universe is an illusion, but it is an illusion difficult to get rid of. It is true compared with most things. But ninety-nine out of every hundred impressions are false even in relation to the things on their own plane.

Such distinctions must be graven deeply upon the surface of the Pantacle by the Holy Dagger.

There is only one other of the elemental Instruments to be considered, namely the Lamp.

CHAPTER X

THE LAMP

IN Liber A. vel Armorum, the official instruction of the A.'.A.'. for the preparation of the elemental weapons, it is said that each symbolic representation of the Universe is to be approved by the Superior of the Magician. To this rule the Lamp is an exception; it is said:

"A Magical Lamp that shall burn without wick or oil, being fed by the Aethyr. This shall he accomplish secretly and apart, without asking the advice or approval of his Adeptus Minor."

This Lamp is the light of the pure soul; it hath no need of fuel, it is the Burning Bush incomsumable that Moses saw, the image of the Most High.

This Lamp hangeth above the Altar, it hath no support from below; its light illumines the whole Temple, yet upon it are cast no shadows, no reflections. It cannot be touched, it cannot be extinguished, in no way can it change; for it is utterly apart from all those things which have complexity, which have dimension, which change and may be changed.

When the eyes of the Magus are fixed upon this Lamp naught else exists.

The Instruments lie idle on the Altar; that Light alone burns eternally.

The Divine Will that was the Wand is no more; for the path has become one with the Goal.

The Divine Understanding that was the Cup is no more; for the subject and Object of intelligence are one.

The Divine Reason that was the Sword is no more; for the complex has been resolved into the Simple.

And the Divine Substance that was the Pantacle is no more; for the many has become the One.

Eternal, unconfined, unextended, without cause and without effect, the Holy Lamp mysteriously burns. Without quantity or quality, unconditioned and sempiternal, is this Light.

It is not possible for anyone to advise or approve; for this Lamp is not made with hands; it exists alone for ever; it has no parts, no person; it is before "I am." Few can behold it, yet it is always there. For it there is no "here" nor "there," no "then" nor "now;" all parts of speech are abolished, save the noun; and this noun is not found either in human speech or in Divine. It is the Lost Word, the dying music of whose sevenfold echo is I A O and A U M. Without this Light the Magician could not work at all; yet few indeed are the Magicians that have know of it, and far fewer They that have beheld its brilliance!

The Temple and all that is in it must be destroyed again and again before it is worthy to receive that Light. Hence it so often seems that the only advice that any master can give to any pupil is to destroy the Temple.

"Whatever you have" and "whatever you are" are veils before that Light.

Yet in so great ~a matter all advice is vain. There is no master so great that he can see clearly the whole character of any pupil. What helped him in the past may hinder another in the future.

Yet since the Master is pledged to serve, he may take up that service on these simple lines. Since all thoughts are veils of this Light, he may advise the destruction of all thoughts, and to that end teach those practices which are clearly conductive to such destruction.

These practices have now fortunately been set down in clear language by order of the A.'.A.'..

In these instructions the relativity and limitation of each practice is clearly taught, and all dogmatic interpretations are carefully avoided. Each practice is in itself a demon which must be destroyed; but to be destroyed it must first be evoked.

Shame upon that Master who shirks any one of these practices, however distasteful or useless it may be to him! For in the detailed knowledge of it, which experience alone can give him, may lie his opportunity for crucial assistance to a pupil. However dull the drudgery, it should be undergone. If it were possible to regret anything in life, which is fortunately not the case, it would be the hours wasted in fruitful practices which might have been more profitably employed on sterile ones: for NEMO

footnote: NEMO is the Master of the Temple, whose task it is to develop the beginner. See Liber CDXVIII, Aethyr XIII.

in tending his garden seeketh not to single out the flower that shall be NEMO after him. And we are not told that NEMO might have used other things than those which he actually does use; it seems possible that if he had not the acid or the knife, or the fire, or the oil, he might miss tending just that one flower which was to be NEMO after him!

CHAPTER XI

THE CROWN

THE Crown of the Magician represents the Attainment of his Work. It is a band of pure gold, on the front of which stand three pentagrams, and on the back a hexagram. The central pentagram contains a diamond or a great opal; the other three symbols contain the Tau. Around this Crown is twined the golden Ureaus serpent, with erect head and expanded hood. Under the Crown is a crimson cap of maintenance, which falls to the shoulders.

Instead of this, the Ateph Crown of Thoth is sometimes worn; for Thoth is the God of Truth, of Wisdom, and the Teacher of Magick. The Ateph Crown has two ram's horns, showing energy, dominion, the force that breaks down obstacles, the sign of the spring. Between these horns is the disk of the sun; from this springs a Lotus upheld by the twin plumes of truth, and three other sun-disks are upheld, one by the cup of the lotus, the others beneath the curving feathers.

There is still another Crown, the Crown of Amoun, the concealed one, from whom the Hebrews borrowed their holy word "Amen." This Crown consists simply of the plumes of truth. But into the symbolism of these it is not necessary to go, for all this and more is in the Crown first described.

The crimson cap implies concealment, and is also symbolical of the flood of glory that pours upon the Magician from above. It is of velvet for the softness of that divine kiss, and crimson for that it is the very blood of God which is its life. The band of gold is the eternal circle of perfection. The three pentagrams symbolize the Father, the Son, and the Holy Spirit, while the hexagram represents the Magician himself. Ordinarily, pentagrams represent the microcosm, hexagrams the macrocosm; but here the reverse is the case, because in this Crown of Perfection, that which is below has become that which is above, and that which is above had become that which is below. If a diamond be worn, it is for the Light which is before all manifestations in form; if an opal, it is to commemorate that sublime plan of the All, to fold and unfold in eternal rapture, to manifest as the Many that the Many may become the One Unmanifest. But this matter is too great for an elementary treatise on Magick.

The Serpent which is coiled about the Crown means many things, or, rather, one thing in many ways. It is the symbol of royalty and of initiation, for the Magician is anointed King and Priest.

It also represents Hadit, of which one can here only quote these words: "I am the secret serpent coiled about to spring; in my coiling there is joy. If I lift up my head, I and my Nuit are one; if I droop down mine head and shoot forth venom, there is rapture of the earth, and I and the earth are one."

The serpent is also the Kundalini serpent, the Magical force itself, the manifesting side of the Godhead of the Magician, whose unmanifested side is peace and silence, of which there is no symbol.

In the Hindu system the Great Work is represented by saying that this serpent, which is normally coiled at the base of the spine, rises with her hood over the head of the Yogi, there to unite with the Lord of all.

The serpent is also he who poisons. It is that force which destroys the manifested Universe. This is also the emerald snake which encircles the Universe. This matter must be studied in Liber LXV, where this is discussed incomparably. In the hood of this serpent are the six jewels, three on each side, Ruby, Emerald, and Sapphire, the three holy elements made perfect, on both sides in equilibrium.

CHAPTER XII

THE ROBE

THE Robe of the Magician may be varied according to his grade and the nature of his working.

There are two principal Robes, the white and the black; of these the black is more important than the white, for the white has no hood. These Robes may be varied by the addition of various symbols, but in any case the shape of the Robe is a Tau.

The general symbolism which we have adopted leads us, however, to prefer the description of a Robe which few dare wear. This Robe is of a rich silk of deep pure blue, the blue of the night sky: it is embroidered with golden stars, and with roses and lilies. Around the hem, its tail in its mouth, is the great serpent, while upon the front from neck to hem falls the Arrow described in the Vision of the Fifth Aethyr. This Robe is lined with purple silk on which is embroidered a green serpent coiled from neck to hem. The symbolism of this Robe treats of high mysteries which must be studied in Liber CCXX and Liber CDXVIII; but having thus dealt with special Robes, let us consider the use of the Robe in general.

The Robe is that which conceals, and which protects the Magician from the elements; it is the silence and secrecy with which he works, the hiding of himself in the occult life of Magick and Meditation. This is the "going away into the wilderness" which we find in the lives of all men of the highest types of greatness. And it is also the withdrawing of one's self from life as such.

In another sense it is the "Aura" of the Magician, that invisible egg or sheath which surrounds him. This "Aura" must be shining, elastic, impenetrable, even by the light, that is, by any partial light that comes from one side.

The only light of the Magician is from the Lamp which hangs above his head, as he stands in the centre of the Circle, and the Robe, being open at the neck, opposes no obstacles to the passage of this light. And being open, and very wide open, at the bottom, it permits that light to pass and illumine them that sit in darkness and in the shadow of death.

CHAPTER XIII

THE BOOK

THE Book of Spells or of Conjurations is the Record of every thought, word, and deed of the Magician; for everything that he has willed is willed to a purpose. It is the same as if he had taken an oath to perform some achievement.

Now this Book must be a holy Book, not a scribbling-book in which you jot down every piece of rubbish that comes into your head. It is written, Liber VII, v, 23: "Every breath, every word, every thought, every deed is an act of love with Thee. Be this devotion a potent spell to exorcise the demons of the Five."

This Book must then be thus written. In the first place the Magician must perform the practice laid down in Liber CMXIII so that he understands perfectly who he is, and to what his development must necessarily tend. So much for the first page of the Book.

Let him then be careful to write nothing therein that is inharmonious or untrue. Nor can he avoid this writing, for this is a Magick Book. If you abandon even for an hour the one purpose of your life, you will find a number of meaningless scratches and scrawls on the white vellum; and these cannot be erased. In such a case, when you come to conjure a demon by the power of the Book, he will mock you; he will point to all this foolish writing, more like his own than yours. In vain will you continue with the subsequent spells; you have broken by your own foolishness the chain which would have bound him.

Even the calligraphy of the Book must be firm, clear, and beautiful; in the cloud of incense it is hard to read the conjurations. While you peer dimly through the smoke, the demon will vanish, and you will have to write the terrible word "failure."

And yet there is no page of this Book on which this word is not written; but so long as it is immediately followed by a new affirmation, all is not lost; and as in this Book the word "failure" is thus made of little account, so also must the word "success" never be employed, for its is the last word that may be written therein, and it is followed by a full stop.

This full stop may never be written anywhere else; for the writing of the Book goes on eternally; there is no way of closing the record until the goal of all has been attained. Let every page of this Book be filled with song — for it is a Book of incantation!

CHAPTER XIV

THE BELL

THE Magical Bell is best attached to the chain. In some systems of Magick a number of bells have been worn, sewn upon the hem of the robe with the idea of symbolizing that every movement of the Magician should make music. But the Bell of which we shall speak is a more important implement. This Bell summons and alarms; and it is also the Bell which sounds at the elevation of the Host.

It is thus also the "Astral Bell" of the Magician.

> *footnote: During certain meditation-practices the Student hears a bell resound in the depths of his being. It is not subjective, for it is sometimes heard by other people. Some Magicians are able to call the attention of those with whom they wish to communicate at a distance by its means, or, so it is said.*

The Bell of which we speak is a disk of some two inches in diameter, very slightly bent into a shape not unlike that of a cymbal. A hole in the centre permits the passage of a short leather thong, by which it may be attached to the chain. At the other end of the chain is the striker; which, in Tibet, is usually made of human bone.

The Bell itself is made of electrum magicum, an alloy of the "seven metals" blended together in a special manner. First the gold is melted up with the silver during a favourable aspect of the sun and moon; these are then fused with tin when Jupiter is well dignified. Lead is added under an auspicious Saturn; and so for the quicksilver, copper, and iron, when Mercury, Venus, and Mars are of good augury.

The sound of this Bell is indescribably commanding, solemn, and majestic. Without even the minutest jar, its single notes tinkle fainter and fainter into silence. At the sound of this Bell the Universe ceases for an indivisible moment of time, and attends to the Will of the Magician. Let him not interrupt the sound of this Bell. Let this be that which is written, Liber VII, v, 31: "There is a solemnity of the silence. There is no more voice at all."

As the Magical Book was the record of the past, so is the Magick Bell the prophecy of the future. The manifested shall repeat itself again and again, always a clear thin note, always a simplicity of music, yet ever less and less disturbing the infinite silence until the end.

EXAMPLE OF DESIGN FOR A LAMEN

CHAPTER XV

THE LAMEN

THE breastplate or Lamen of the Magician is a very elaborate and important symbol. In the Jewish system we read that the High Priest was to wear a plate with twelve stones, for the twelve tribes of Israel (with all their correspondences), and in this plate were kept the Urim and Thummin.

footnote: Scholars are uncertain as to what these really were, though apparently they were methods of divination.

The modern Lamen is, however, a simple plate which (being worn over the heart) symbolizes Tiphereth, and it should therefore be a harmony of all the other symbols in one. It connects naturally by its shape with the Circle and the Pentacle; but it is not sufficient to repeat the design of either.

The Lamen of the spirit whom one wishes to evoke is both placed in the triangle and worn on the breast; but in this case, since that which we wish to evoke in nothing partial, but whole, we shall have but a single symbol to combine the two. The Great Work will then form the subject of the design.

footnote: Some writers have actually confused the Lamen with the Pantacle, usually through a misunderstanding of the nature of the latter. Dr. Dee's "Sigillum Dei Amath" makes a fine pantacle, but it would be useless as a lamen, Eliphas Levi made several attempts to draw one or the other, he never seemed sure which. Fortunately he knows better now. The lamens given in the Lesser and Greater Keys of "Solomon" are rather better, but we know of no perfect example. The design on the cover of "The Star in the West" represents an early effort of Fra. P.

In this Lamen the Magician must place the secret keys of his power.

The Pentacle is merely the material to be worked upon, gathered together and harmonized but not yet in operation, the parts of the engine arranged for use, or even put together, but not yet set in motion. In the Lamen these forces are already at work; even accomplishment is prefigured.

In the system of Abramelin the Lamen is a plate of silver upon which the Holy Guardian Angel writes in dew. This is another way of expressing the same thing, for it is He who confers the secrets of that power which should be herein expressed. St. Paul expresses the same thing when he says that the breastplate is faith, and can withstand the fiery darts of the wicked. "This "faith" is not blind self-confidence and credulity; it is that self confidence which only comes when self is forgotten.

It is the "Knowledge and Conversation of the Holy Guardian Angel" which confers this faith. The task of attaining to this Knowledge and Conversation is the sole task of him who would be called Adept. An absolute method for achieving this is given in the Eighth Aethyr (Liber CDXVIII, Equinox V).

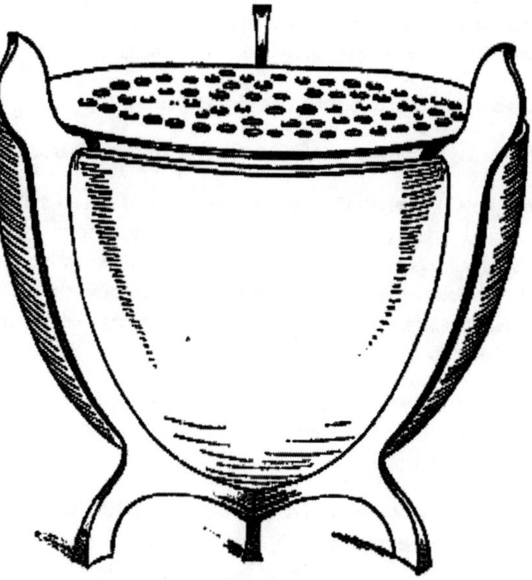

THE CENSER (CROWLEY'S PATENT PATTERN).

CHAPTER XVI

THE MAGICK FIRE; WITH CONSIDERATIONS OF THE THURIBLE, THE CHARCOAL, AND THE INCENSE

INTO the Magick Fire all things are cast. It symbolizes the final burning up of all things in Shivadarshana. It is the absolute destruction alike of the Magician and the Universe.

The Thurible stands upon a small altar. "My altar is of open brass work: burn thereon in silver or gold!"

WEH footnote: quotation corrected

This altar stands in the East, as if to symbolize the identity of Hope and Annihilation. This brass contains the metals of Jupiter and Venus fused in a homogeneous alloy. This is then symbolical of divine love, and it is "open brass work" because this love is not limited in direction or extent; it is not particularized, it is universal.

Upon this altar stands the Censer proper; it has three legs symbolical of fire.

footnote: Because Shin the Hebrew letter of Fire, has three tongues of flame, and its value is 300.

Its cup is a hemisphere, and supported from its edge is a plate pierced with holes. This censer is of silver or gold, because there were called the perfect metals; it is upon perfection that the imperfect is burned. Upon this plate burns a great fire of charcoal, impregnated with nitre. This charcoal is (as chemists now begin to surmise) the ultimate protean element: absolutely black, because it absorbs all light; infusible by the application of any known heat; the lightest of those elements which occur in the solid state in nature; the essential constituent of all known forms of life.

It has been treated with nitre, whose potassium has the violet flame of Jupiter, the father of all, whose nitrogen is that inert element which by proper combination becomes a constituent of all the most explosive bodies known; and oxygen, the food of fire.

WEH footnote: That is to say, this nitre is Potassium Nitrate or "Salt Peter". Such charcoal impregnated with Potash is now commonly sold for incense burning in the form of disks with an indentation in the top, "Three Kings Charcoal" is a popular brand, but some "self-starting" barbecue brickettes are also of this composition and much less expensive.

This fire is blown upon by the Magician; this blaze of destruction has been kindled by his word and by his will.

Into this Fire he casts the Incense, symbolical of prayer, the gross vehicle or image of his aspiration. Owing to the imperfection of this image, we obtain mere smoke instead of perfect combustion. But we cannot use explosives instead of incense, because it would not be true. Our prayer is the expression of the lower aspiring to the higher; it is without the clear vision of the higher, it does not understand what the higher wants. And, however sweet may be its smell, it is always cloudy.

In this smoke illusions arise. We sought the light, and behold the Temple is darkened! In the darkness this smoke seems to take strange shapes, and we may hear the crying of beasts. The thicker the smoke, the darker grows the Universe. We gasp and tremble, beholding what foul and unsubstantial things we have evoked!

Yet we cannot do without the Incense! Unless our aspiration took form it could not influence form. This also is the mystery of incarnation.

This Incense is based upon Gum Olibanum, the sacrifice of the human will of the heart. This olibanum has been mixed with half its weight of storax, the earthly desires, dark, sweet, and clinging; and this again with half its weight of lignum aloes, which symbolizes Sagittarius, the arrow,

footnote: Note that there are two arrows: the Divine shot downward, the human upward. The former is the Oil, the latter the Incense, or rather the finest part of it. See Liber CDXVIII, Fifth Aethyr.

and so represents the aspiration itself; it is the arrow that cleaves the rainbow. This arrow is "Temperance" in the Taro; it is a life equally balanced and direct which makes our work possible; yet this life itself must be sacrificed!

In the burning up of these things arise in our imagination those terrifying or alluring phantasms which throng the "Astral Plane." This smoke represents the "Astral Plane," which lies between the material and the spiritual. One may now devote a little attention to the consideration of this "plane," about which a great deal of nonsense has been written.

When a man shuts his eyes and begins to look about him, at first there is nothing but darkness. If he continues trying to penetrate the gloom, a new pair of eyes gradually opens.

Some people think that these are the "eyes of imagination." Those with more experience understand that this truly represents things seen, although those things are themselves totally false.

As first the seer will perceive gray gloom; in subsequent experiments perhaps figures may appear with whom the seer may converse, and under whose guidance he may travel about. This "plane" being quite as large and varied as the material Universe, one cannot describe it effectively; we must refer the reader to Liber O and to Equinox II, pages 295 to 334.

This "Astral Plane" has been described by Homer in the Odyssey. Here are Polyphemus and the Laestrygons, here Calypso and the Sirens. Here, too, are those things which many have imagined to be the "spirits" of the dead. If the student once take any of these things for truth, he must worship it, since all truth is worshipful. In such a case he is lost; the phantom will have power over him; it will obsess him.

As long as an idea is being examined you are free from it. There is no harm in man's experimenting with opium-smoking or feeding on nuts; but the moment he ceases to examine, to act from habit and without reflection, he is in trouble. We all of us eat too much, because people, liveried and obsequious, have always bustled up five times daily with six months' provisions, and it was less trouble to feed and be done with it, than to examine the question whether we were hungry. If you cook your own food, you soon find that you don't cook more or less than you want; and health returns. If, however, you go to the other extreme and think of nothing but diet, you are almost sure to acquire that typical form of melancholia, in which the patient is convinced that all the world is in league to poison him. Professor Schweinhund has shown that beef causes gout; Professor Naschtikoff proves that milk causes consumption. Sir Ruffon Wratts tells us that old age is brought on by eating cabbage. By and by you reach the state of which Mr. Hereward Carrington make his proud boast: your sole food is chocolate, which you chew unceasingly, even in your dreams. Yet no sooner have you taken it into you than you awake to the terrible truth demonstrated by Guterbock Q. Hosenscheisser, Fourth Avenue, Grand Rapids, that chocolate is the cause of constipation, and constipation of cancer, and proceed to get it out of you by means of an enema which would frighten a camel into convulsions.

A similar madness attacks even real men of science. Metchnikoff studied the diseases of the colon until he could see nothing else, and then calmly proposed to cut out every one's colon, pointing out that a vulture (who has no colon) is a very long-lived bird. As a matter of fact the longevity of the vulture is due to its twisted neck, and many thoughtful persons propose to experiment on Professor Metchnikoff.

But the worst of all phantasms are the moral ideas and the religious ideas. Sanity consists in the faculty of adjusting ideas in proper proportion. Any one who accepts a moral or religious truth without understanding it is only kept out of the asylum because he does not follow it out logically. If one really believed in Christianity,

footnote: "One would go mad if one took the Bible seriously; but to take it seriously one must be already mad."
— "Crowley."

if one really thought that the majority of mankind was doomed to eternal punishment, one would go raving about the world trying to "save" people. Sleep would not be possible until the horror of the mind left the body exhausted. Otherwise, one must be morally insane. Which of us can sleep if one we love is in danger of mere death? We cannot even see a dog drown without at least interrupting all our business to look on. Who then can live in London and reflect upon the fact that of its seven million souls, all but about a thousand Plymouth Brethren will be damned? Yet the thousand Plymouth Brethren (who are the loudest in proclaiming that they will be the only ones saved) seem to get on very well, thank you. Whether they are hypocrites or morally insane is a matter which we can leave to their own consideration.

All these phantoms, of whatever nature, must be evoked, examined, and mastered; otherwise we may find that just when we want it there is some idea with which we have never dealt; and perhaps that idea, springing on us by surprise, and as it were from behind, may strangle us. This is the legend of the sorcerer strangled by the Devil!

GLOSSARY

ONLY words nowhere explained in the preceding pages are given in this list. Several others, mentioned in passing in the early part of the book, are sufficiently dealt with later on. In these cases the references in the Index should be turned up.

A.'.A.'.

The Great White Brotherhood which is giving this Method of Attainment to the world. *See* Equinox I.

Adeptus Minor.

A grade of adeptship. *See* Equinox III.

Aethyrs.

See Equinox V and VII.

Aima.

The Great Fertile Mother Nature.

Ama.

The Great Mother not yet fertile.

Amoun.

The God Amen = Zeus = Jupiter, etc., etc.

Ankh.

The Symbol of "Life." A form of the Rosy Cross. *See* Equinox III.

Apophis.

The Serpent-God who slew Osiris. *See* Equinox III.

Babalon, Our Lady.

See Equinox V, The Vision and Voice, 14th Aethyr.

Babe of the Abyss.

See Equinox VIII, Temple of Solomon.

Bhagavadgita.

Scared Hymn of India, translated by Sir Edwin Arnold in the "Song Celestial."

Binah.

Understanding, the 3rd "emanation" of the Absolute.

Caduceus.

The Wand of Mercury. *See* Equinox II and III.

Chela.

Pupil.

Chesed.

Mercy, the 4th "emanation" of the Absolute.

Chokmah.

Wisdom, the 2nd "emanation" of the Absolute.

Choronzon.

See Equinox V, The Vision and the Voice, 10th Aethyr.

City of the Pyramids.

See Equinox V, The Vision and the Voice, 14th Aethyr.

Crux Ansata.

Same as Ankh, *q.v.*

Daath.

Knowledge, child of Chokmah and Binah in one sense; in another, the home of Choronzon.

Dhammapada.

A sacred Buddhist book.

Elemental Kings.

See 777.

Geburah.

Strength, the 5th "emanation" of the Absolute.

Gunas.

Three principles. *See* Bhagadvadgita,{sic} 777, etc.

Guru.

Teacher.

Hadit.

See "Liber Legis," Equinox VII. Also "Liber 555."

Hathayoga Pradipika.

A book on physical training for spiritual purposes.

Hod.

Splendour, the 8th "emanation" of the Absolute.

Kamma.

Pali dialect of Karma, *q.v.*

Karma.

"That which is made," "The law of cause and effect." *See* "Science and Buddhism," Crowley, Coll. Works, Vol. II.

Kether.

The Crown, 1st "emanation" of the Absolute.

Lao Tze.

Great Chinese teacher, founder of Taoists. *See* Tao Teh "K"ing.

Liber Legis.

See Equinox VII for facsimile reproduction of MS.

Lingam

The Unity or Male Principle. But these have many symbols, *e.g.*, sometimes Yoni is 0 or 3 and Lingam 2.

Lingam-Yoni.

A form of the Rosy Cross.

Macrocosm.

The great Universe, of which man is an exact image.

Magus.

A magician. Technically, also, a Master of the grade 9{degree} = 2{square}.

See

Equinox VII, "Liber I," and elsewhere.

Mahalingam.

See Lingam. Maha means great.

Maha Sattipatthana.

A mode of meditation. *See* "Science and Buddhism," Crowley, Coll. Works, Vol. II, for a full account.

Malkah.

A young girl. The "bride." The unredeemed soul.

Malkuth.

"The kingdom," 10th "emanation" of the Absolute.

Mantrayoga.

A practice to attain union with God by repetition of a sacred sentence.

Master of the Temple.

One of grade 8{degree} = 3{square}. Fully discussed in Equinox.

Microcosm.

Man, considered as an exact image of the Universe.

Nephesch.

The "animal soul" of man.

Netzach.

Victory, the 7th "emanation" of the Absolute.

Nibbana.

The state called, for want of a better name, annihilation. The final goal.

Nirvana.

See Nibbana.

Nuit.

See "Liber Legis."

Paths.

See 777, and Equinox II and elsewhere.

Perdurabo, Frater.

See Equinox I-X, "The Temple of Solomon the King."

Prana.

See "Raja Yoga."

Qabalah.

See "The tradition of secret wisdom of the Hebrews," Equinox V.

Qliphoth.

"Shells" or demons. The excrement of ideas.

Ra-Hoor-Khuit.

See "Liber Legis."

Ruach.

The intellect and other mental qualities. *See* 777, etc.

Sahasrara Cakkra.

"The Temple of Solomon the King." *See* Equinox IV.

Sammasati.

See "The training of the Mind," Equinox V, and "The Temple of Solomon," Equinox VIII.

Also

"Science and Buddhism," Crowley Coll. Works, Vol. II

Sankhara.

See "Science and Buddhism."

Sanna.

See "Science and Buddhism."

Sephiroth.

See "Temple of Solomon," Equinox V.

Shin.

"A tooth." Hebrew letter = Sh, corresponds to Fire and Spirit.

Shiva Sanhita.

A Hindu treatise on physical training for spiritual ends.

Skandhas.

See "Science and Buddhism."

Tao.

See Konx Om Pax, "Thien Tao." 777, etc.

Tao Teh King.

Chinese Classic of the Tao.

Taro.

See 777, Equinox III and VIII, etc., etc.

Tau.

A "cross," Hebrew letter = Th corresponds to ""Earth." *See* 777.

Thaumiel.

The demons corresponding to Kether. Two contending forces.

Theosophist.

A person who talks about Yoga, and does no work.

Thoth.

The Egyptian god of Speech, Magick, Wisdom.

Tiphereth.

"Beauty" or "Harmony," the 6th "emanation" of the Absolute.

Typhon.

The destroyer of Osiris.

Udana.

One of the imaginary "nerves" of Hindu pseudo-physiology."

Vedana.

See "Science and Buddhism," Crowley, Coll. Works, Vol. II.

Vesica, Vesica Piscies.

See Yoni. The oval formed by the intersection of the circles in Euclid I, 1.

Virakam, Soror.

A chela of Frater Perdurabo.

Vrittis.

"Impressions."

Yesod.

"Foundation," the ninth "emanation" of the Absolute.

Yogi.

One who seeks to attain "Union" (with God). A Hindu word corresponding to the Mohammedan word Fakir.

Yoni.

The Dyad, or Female Principle. *See* Lingam.

Zohar.

Splendour, a collection of books on the Qabalah. *See* "The Temple of Solomon the King," Equinox V.

NOTICE

The A.'.A.'. is an organization whose heads have obtained by personal experience to the summit of this science. They have founded a system by which every one can equally attain, and that with an ease and speed which was previously impossible.

The first grade in Their system is that of

STUDENT.

A Student must possess the following books:

The Equinox,

777.

Konx Om Pax.

Collected Works of A. Crowley; Tannhauser, The Sword of Song, Time, Eleusis. 3 vols.

Raja Yoga, by Swami Vivekananda.

The Shiva Sanhita, or the Hathayoga Pradipika.

The Tao Teh King and the writings of Kwang Tze: S.B.E. xxxix, xl.

The Spiritual Guide, by Miguel de Molinos.

Rituel et Dogme de la Haute Magie, by Eliphas Levi, or its translation by A. E. Waite.

The Goetia of the Lemegeton of Solomon the King.

These books should be well studied in any case in conjunction with the second part — Magick — of this Book IV.

Study of these books will give a thorough grounding in the intellectual side of Their system.

After three months the Student is examined in these books, and if his knowledge of them is found satisfactory, he may become a Probationer, receiving Liber LXI and the secret holy book, Liber LXV. The principal point of this grade is that the Probationer has a master appointed, whose experience can guide him in his work.

He may select any practices that he prefers, but in any case must keep an exact record, so that he may discover the relation of cause and effect in his working, and so that the A.'.A.'. may judge of his progress, and direct his further studies.

After a year of probation he may be admitted a Neophyte of the A.'.A.'., and receive the secret holy book Liber VII.

These are the principal instructions for practice which every probationer should follow out:

Libri E, A, O, III, XXX, CLXXV, CC, CCVI, CMXIII.

Part-III

Magick in Theory and Practice

HYMN TO PAN

ephrix erōti periarchés d' aneptoman
iō iō pan pan
ō pan pan aliplankte, kyllanias chionoktypoi
petraias apo deirados phanéth, ō
theōn choropoi anax
SOPH. AJ.

Thrill with lissome lust of the light,
O man! My man!
Come careering out of the night
Of Pan! Io Pan!
Io Pan! Io Pan! Come over the sea
From Sicily and from Arcady!
Roaming as Bacchus, with fauns and pards
And nymphs and satyrs for thy guards,
On a milk-white ass, come over the sea
To me, to me,
Come with Apollo in bridal dress
(Shepherdess and pythoness)
Come with Artemis, silken shod,
And wash thy white thigh, beautiful God,
In the moon of the woods, on the marble mount,
The dimpled dawn of the amber fount!
Dip the purple of passionate prayer
In the crimson shrine, the scarlet snare,
The soul that startles in eyes of blue
To watch thy wantonness weeping through
The tangled grove, the gnarled bole
Of the living tree that is spirit and soul
And body and brain — come over the sea,
(Io Pan! Io Pan!)
Devil or god, to me, to me,
My man! my man!
Come with trumpets sounding shrill
Over the hill!
Come with drums low muttering
From the spring!
Come with flute and come with pipe!
Am I not ripe?
I, who wait and writhe and wrestle
With air that hath no boughs to nestle
My body, weary of empty clasp,
Strong as a lion and sharp as an asp —

Come, O come!
I am numb
With the lonely lust of devildom.
Thrust the sword through the galling fetter,
All-devourer, all-begetter;
Give me the sign of the Open Eye,
And the token erect of thorny thigh,
And the word of madness and mystery,
O Pan! Io Pan!
Io Pan! Io Pan Pan! Pan Pan! Pan,
I am a man:
Do as thou wilt, as a great god can,
O Pan! Io Pan!
Io Pan! Io Pan Pan! I am awake
In the grip of the snake.
The eagle slashes with beak and claw;
The gods withdraw:
The great beasts come, Io Pan! I am borne
To death on the horn
Of the Unicorn.
I am Pan! Io Pan! Io Pan Pan! Pan!
I am thy mate, I am thy man,
Goat of thy flock, I am gold, I am god,
Flesh to thy bone, flower to thy rod.
With hoofs of steel I race on the rocks
Through solstice stubborn to equinox.
And I rave; and I rape and I rip and I rend
Everlasting, world without end,
Mannikin, maiden, Maenad, man,
In the might of Pan.
Io Pan! Io Pan Pan! Pan! Io Pan!

1. Earth: the god Set fighting.
2. Air: the god Shu supporting the sky.
3. Water: the goddess Auramoth.
4. Fire: the goddess Thoum-aesh-neith.

5-6. Spirit: the rending and closing of the veil.

7-10. *The L V X signs.*

7. ✢ Osiris slain — the cross.
8. L Isis mourning — the Svastika.
9. V Typhon — the Trident.
10. X. Osiris risen — the Pentagram.

INTRODUCTION

Esseai athanatos theos, ambrotos, oyk eti thnétos

Pythagoras.

"Magic is the Highest, most Absolute, and most Divine Knowledge of Natural Philosophy, advanced in its works and wonderful operations by a right understanding of the inward and occult virtue of things; so that true Agents being applied to proper Patients, strange and admirable effects will thereby be produced. Whence magicians are profound and diligent searchers into Nature; they, because of their skill, know how to anticipate an effect, the which to the vulgar shall seem to be a miracle."

The Goetia of the Lemegeton of King Solomon.

"Wherever sympathetic magic occurs in its pure unadulterated form, it is assumed that in nature one event follows another necessarily and invariably without the intervention of any spiritual or personal agency.

Thus its fundamental conception is identical with that of modern science; underlying the whole system is a faith, implicit but real and firm, in the order and uniformity of nature. The magician does not doubt that the same causes will always produce the same effects, that the performance of the proper ceremony accompanied by the appropriate spell, will inevitably be attended by the desired results, unless, indeed, his incantations should chance to be thwarted and foiled by the more potent charms of another sorcerer. He supplicates no higher power: he sues the favour of no fickle and wayward being: he abases himself before no awful deity. Yet his power, great as he believes it to be, is by no means arbitrary and unlimited. He can wield it only so long as he strictly conforms to the rules of his art, or to what may be called the laws of nature as conceived by him. To neglect these rules, to break these laws in the smallest particular is to incur failure, and may even expose the unskilful practitioner himself to the utmost peril. If he claims a sovereignty over nature, it is a constitutional sovereignty rigorously limited in its scope and exercised in exact conformity with ancient usage. Thus the analogy between the magical and the scientific conceptions of the world is close. In both of them the succession of events is perfectly regular and certain, being determined by immutable laws, the operation of which can be foreseen and calculated precisely; the elements of caprice, of chance, and of accident are banished from the course of nature. Both of them open up a seemingly boundless vista of possibilities to him who knows the causes of things and can touch the secret springs that set in motion the vast and intricate mechanism of the world. Hence the strong attraction which magic and science alike have exercised on the human mind; hence the powerful stimulus that both have given to the pursuit of knowledge. They lure the weary enquirer, the footsore seeker, on through the wilderness of disappointment in the present by their endless promises of the future: they take him up to he top of an exceeding high mountain and shew him, beyond the dark clouds and rolling mists at his feet, a vision of the celestial city, far off, it may be, but radiant with unearthly splendour, bathed in the light of dreams."

Dr. J. G. FRAZER, "*The Golden Bough*".

"So far, therefore, **as the public profession of magic has been one of the roads by which men have passed to supreme power, it has contributed to emancipate mankind from the thraldom of tradition and to elevate them into a larger, freer life, with a broader outlook on the world. This is no small service rendered to humanity.** And when we remember further that in another direction magic has paved the way for science, we are forced to admit that if the black art has done much evil, it has also been the source of much good; that if it is the child of error, **it has yet been the mother of freedom and truth.**"

Ibid.

"Prove all things; hold fast that which is good."

St. Paul.

"Also the mantras and spells; the obeah and the wanga; the work of the wand and the work of the sword; these he shall learn and teach."

"He must teach; but he may make severe the ordeals."

"The word of the Law is [in Greek] Thelema."

LIBER AL vel xxxi: The Book of the Law.

This book is for

ALL:

for every man, woman, and child.

My former work has been misunderstood, and its scope limited, by my use of technical terms. It has attracted only too many dilettanti and eccentrics, weaklings seeking in "Magic" an escape from reality. I myself was first consciously drawn to the subject in this way. And it has repelled only too many scientific and practical minds, such as I most designed to influence.

But

MAGICK

is for

ALL.

I have written this book to help the Banker, the Pugilist, the Biologist, the Poet, the Navvy, the Grocer, the Factory Girl, the Mathematician, the Stenographer, the Golfer, the Wife, the Consul — and all the rest — to fulfil themselves perfectly, each in his or her own proper function.

Let me explain in a few words how it came about that I blazoned the word

MAGICK

upon the Banner that I have borne before me all my life.

Before I touched my teens, I was already aware that I was THE BEAST whose number is 666. I did not understand in the least {XI} what that implied; it was a passionately ecstatic sense of identity.

In my third year at Cambridge, I devoted myself consciously to the Great Work, understanding thereby the Work of becoming a Spiritual Being, free from the constraints, accidents, and deceptions of material existence.

I found myself at a loss for a name to designate my work, just as H. P. Blavatsky some years earlier. "Theosophy", "Spiritualism", "Occultism", "Mysticism", all involved undesirable connotations.

I chose therefore the name.

"MAGICK"

as essentially the most sublime, and actually the most discredited, of all the available terms.

I swore to rehabilitate

MAGICK,

to identify it with my own career; and to compel mankind to respect, love, and trust that which they scorned, hated and feared. I have kept my Word.

But the time is now come for me to carry my banner into the thick of the press of human life.

I must make

MAGICK

the essential factor in the life of

ALL.

In presenting this book to the world, I must then explain and justify my position by formulating a definition of

MAGICK

and setting forth its main principles in such a way that

ALL

may understand instantly that their souls, their lives, in every relation with every other human being and every circumstance, depend upon

MAGICK

and the right comprehension and right application thereof.

I) *DEFINITION.*

Magick is the Science and Art of causing Change to occur in conformity with Will.

(Illustration: It is my Will to inform the World of certain facts within my knowledge. I therefore take "magickal weapons", pen, ink, and paper; I write "incantations"—these sentences—in the "magickal language" ie, that which is understood by the people I wish to instruct; I call forth "spirits", such as printers, publishers, booksellers and so forth and constrain them to convey my message to those people. The composition and distribution of this book is thus an act of Magick by which I cause Changes to take place in conformity with my Will.)

In one sense Magick may be defined as the name given to Science by the vulgar.

II) *POSTULATE.*

ANY required change may be effected by the application of the proper kind and degree of

Force in the proper manner, through the proper medium to the proper object.

(Illustration: I wish to prepare an ounce of Chloride of Gold. I must take the right kind of acid, nitro-hydrochloric and no other, in a vessel which will not break, leak or corrode, in such a manner as will not produce undesirable results, with the necessary quantity of Gold: and so forth. Every change has its own conditions.

In the present state of our knowledge and power some changes are not possible in practice; we cannot cause eclipses, for instance, or transform lead into tin, or create men from mushrooms. But it is theoretically possible to cause in any object any change of which that object is capable by nature; and the conditions are covered by the above postulate.)

III) *THEOREMS.*

1) Every intentional act is a Magickal act.

(Illustration: See "Definition" above.)

> *By "intentional" I mean "willed". But even unintentional acts so seeming are not truly so. Thus, breathing is an act of the Will to Live.*

2) Every successful act has conformed to the postulate.

3) Every failure proves that one or more requirements of the postulate have not been fulfilled.

(Illustrations: There may be failure to understand the case, as when a doctor makes a wrong diagnosis, and his treatment injures the patient. There may be a failure to apply the right kind of force, as when a rustic tries to blow out an electric light. There may be failure to apply the right degree of force, as when a wrestler has his hold broken, There may be failure to apply the force in the right manner, as when one presents a cheque at the wrong window of the Bank. There may be failure to employ the correct medium, as when Leonardo da Vinci saw his masterpiece fade away. The force may be applied to an unsuitable object, as when one tries to crack a stone, thinking it a nut.)

4) The first requisite for causing any change is thorough qualitative and quantitative understanding of the conditions.

(Illustration: The most common cause of failure in life is ignorance of one's own True Will, or of the means to fulfill that Will. A man may fancy himself a painter, and waste his life trying to become one; or he may really be a painter, and yet fail to understand and to measure the difficulties peculiar to that career.)

5) The second requisite of causing any change is the practical ability to set in right motion the necessary forces.

(Illustration: A banker may have a perfect grasp of a given situation, yet lack the quality of decision, or the assets, necessary to take advantage of it.)

6) "Every man and every woman is a star". That is to say, every human being is intrinsically an independent individual with his own proper character and proper motion.

7) Every man and every woman has a course, depending partly on the self, and partly on the environment which is natural and necessary for each. Anyone who is forced from his own course, either through not understanding himself, or through external opposition, comes into conflict with the order of the Universe, and suffers accordingly.

(Illustration: A man may think it is his duty to act in a certain way, through having made a fancy picture of himself, instead of investigating his actual nature. For example, a woman may make herself miserable for life by thinking that she prefers love to social consideration, or vice versa. One woman may stay with an unsympathetic husband when she would really be happy in an attic with a lover, while another may fool herself into a romantic elopement when her only pleasures are those of presiding over fashionable functions. Again, a boy's instinct may tell him to go to sea, while his parents insist on his becoming a doctor. In such a case he will be both unsuccessful and unhappy in medicine.)

8) A Man whose conscious will is at odds with his True Will is wasting his strength. He cannot hope to influence his environment efficiently.

(Illustration: When Civil War rages in a nation, it is in no condition to undertake the invasion of other countries. A man with cancer employs his nourishment alike to his own use and to that of the enemy which is part of himself. He soon fails to resist the pressure of his environment. In practical life, a man who is doing what his conscience tells him to be wrong will do it very clumsily. At first!)

9) A Man who is doing his True Will has the inertia of the Universe to assist him.

(Illustration: The first principle of success in evolution is that the individual should be true to his own nature, and at the same time adapt himself to his environment.)

10) Nature is a continuous phenomenon, though we may not know in all cases how things are connected.

(Illustration: Human comsciousness depends on the properties of protoplasm, the existence of which depends on innumerable physical conditions peculiar to this planet; and this planet is determined by the mechanical balance of the whole universe of matter. We may then say that our consciousness is causally connected with the remotest galaxies; yet we do not even know how it arises from—or with—the molecular changes in the brain.)

11) Science enables us to take advantage of the continuity of Nature by the empirical application of certain principles whose interplay involves different orders of idea connected with each other in a way beyond our present comprehension.

(Illustration: We are able to light cities by rule-of-thumb methods. We do not know what consciousness is, or how it is connected with muscular action; what electricity is or how it is connected with the machines that generate it; and our methods depend on calculations involving mathematical ideas which have no correspondance in the Universe as we know it.)

For instance "irrational", "unreal" and "infinite" expressions.

12) Man is ignorant of the nature of his own being and powers. Even his idea of his limitations is based on experience of the past, and every step in his progress extends his empire. There is therefore no reason to assign theoretical limits

note: i.e., except—possibly—in the case of logically absurd questions such as the Schoolmen discussed in connection with "God".

to what he may be, or what he may do.

(Illustration: A generation ago it was supposed theoretically impossible that man should ever know the composition of the fixed stars. It is known that our senses are adapted to receive only a fraction of the possible rates of vibration.Modern instruments have enabled us to detect some of these supra-sensibles by indirect methods, and even to use their peculiar qualities in the service of man, as in the case of the rays of Hertz and Roentgen. As Tyndall said, man might at any moment learn to percieve and utilize vibrations of all concievable and inconcievable kinds. The question of Magick is a question of discovering and employing hitherto unknown forces in nature. We know that they exist, and we cannot doubt the possibility of mental or physical instruments capable of bringing us into relation with them.)

13) Every man is more or less aware that his individuality comprises several orders of existence, even when he maintains that his subtler principles are merely symptomatic of the changes in his gross vehicle. A similar order may be assumed to extend throughout nature.

(Illustration: One does not confuse the pain of a toothache with the decay that causes it. Inanimate objects are sensitive to certain physical forces, such as electrical and thermal conductivity; but neither in us nor in them—so far as we know—is there any direct conscious perception of these forces. Imperceptible influences are therefore associated with all material phenomena; and there is no reason why we should not work upon matter through these subtle energies as we do through their material bases. In fact, we use magnetic force to move iron and solar radiation to reproduce images.)

14) Man is capable of being, and using, anything which he perceives, for everything which he perceives is in a certain sense a part of his being. He may thus subjugate the whole of the Universe of which he is conscious to his individual Will.

(Illustration: Man has used the idea of God to dictate his personal conduct, to obtain power over his fellows, to excuse his crimes, and for innumerable other purposes, including that of realizing himself as God. He has used the irrational and unreal conceptions of mathematics to help him in the construction of mechanical devices. He has used his moral force to influence the actions even of wild animals. He has employed poetic genius for political purposes.)

15) Every force in the Universe is capable of being transformed into any other kind of force by using suitable means. There is thus an inexhaustible supply of any particular kind of force that we may need.

(Illustration: Heat may be transformed into light and power by using it to drive dynamos. The vibrations of the air may be used to kill men by so ordering them in speech so as to inflame war-like passions. The hallucinations connected with the mysterious energies of sex result in the perpetuation of the species.)

16) The application of any given force affects all the orders of being which exist in the object in the object to which it is applied, whichever of of those orders is directly affected.

(Illustration: If I strike a man with a dagger, his consciousness, not his body only, is affected by my act, although the dagger, as such, has no direct relation therewith. Similarly, the power of my thought may so work on the mind of another person as to produce far-reaching physical changes in him, or in others through him.)

17) A man may learn to use any force so as to serve any purpose, by taking advantage of the above theorems.

(Illustration: A man may use a razor to make himself vigilant over his speech, by using it to cut himself whenever he ungaurdedly utters a chosen word. He may serve the same purpose by resolving that every incident of his life shall remind him of a particular thing, making every impression the starting point of a connected series of thoughts ending in that thing. He might also devote his whole energies to some one particular object, by resolving to do nothing at variance therewith, and to make every act turn to the advantage of that object.)

18) He may attract to himself any force of the Universe by making himself a fit receptacle for it, and arranging conditions so that its nature compels it to flow toward him.

(Illustration: If I want pure water to drink, I dig a well in a place where there is underground water; I prevent it from leaking away; and I arrange to take advantage of water's accordance with the laws of Hydrostatics to fill it.)

19) Man's sense of himself as seperate from, and opposed to, the Universe is a bar to his conducting its currents. It insulates him.

(Illustration: A popular leader is most successful when he forgets himself and remembers only "The Cause". Self-seeking engenders jealousies and schism. When the organs of the body assert their presence other by silent satisfaction, it is a sign they are diseased. The single exception is the organ of reproduction. Yet even in this case its self-assertion bears witness to its dissatisfaction with itself, since it cannot fulfil its function until completed by its counterpart in another organism.)

20) Man can only attract and employ the forces for which he is really fitted.

(Illustration: You cannot make a silk purse out of a sow's ear. A true man of science learns from every phenomeneon. But Nature is dumb to the hypocrite; for in her there is nothing false.)

> *It is no objection that the hypocrite is himself part of Nature. He is an "endothermic" product, divided against himself, with a tendency to break up. He will see his own qualities everywhere, and thus obtain a radical misconception of phenomena. Most religions of the past have failed by expecting nature to conform with their ideals of proper conduct.*

21) There is no limit to the extent of the relations of any man with the Universe in essence; for as soon as man makes himself one with any idea the means of measurement cease to exist. But his power to utilize that force is limited by his mental power and capacity, and by the circumstances of his human environment.

(Illustration: When a man falls in love, the whole world becomes, to him, nothing but love boundless and immanent; but his mystical state is not contagious; his fellow-men are either amused or annoyed. He can only extend to others the effect which his love has had upon himself by means of his mental and physical qualities. Thus Catullus, Dante and Swinburne made their love a mighty mover of mankind by virtue of their power to put their thoughts on the subject in musical and eloquent language. Again, Cleopatra and other people in authority moulded the fortunes of many other people by allowing love to influence their political actions. The Magician, however well he succeed in making contact with the secret sources of energy in nature, can only use them to the extent permitted by his intellectual and moral qualities. Mohammed's intercourse with Gabriel was only effective because of his statesmanship, soldiership, and the sublimity of his command of Arabic. Hertz's discovery of the rays which we now use for wireless telegraphy was sterile until it reflected through the minds and wills of the people who could take his truth and transmit it to the world of action by means of mechanical and economic instruments.)

22) Every individual is essentially sufficient to himself. But he is unsatisfactory to himself until

he has established himself in his right relation with the universe.

(Illustration: A microscope, however perfect, is useless in the hands of savages. A poet, however sublime, must impose himself upon his generation if he is to enjoy (and even to understand) himself, as theoretically should be the case.)

23) Magick is the Science of understanding oneself and one's conditions. It is the Art of applying that understanding in action.

(Illustration: A golf club is intended to move a special ball in a special way in special circumstances. A Niblick should rarely be used on the tee or a brassie under the bank of a bunker. But also, the use of any club demands skill and experience.)

24) Every man has an indefeasible right to be what he is.

(Illustration: To insist that any one else should comply with one's own standards is to outrage, not only him, but oneself, since both parties are equally born of necessity.)

25) Every man must do Magick each time he acts or even thinks, since a thought is an internal act whose influence ultimately affects action, though it may not do so at the time.

(Illustration: The least gesture causes a change in a man's own body and in the air around him; it disturbs the balance of the entire Universe, and its effects continue eternally throughout all space. Every thought, however swiftly suppressed, has its effect on the mind. It stands as one of the causes of every subsequent thought, and tends to influence every subsequent action. A golfer may lose a few yards on his drive, a few more with his second and third, he may lie on the green six bare inches too far from the hole, but the net result of these trifling mishaps is the difference between halving and losing the hole.)

26) Every man has a right, the right of self preservation, to fulfill himself to the utmost.

> *Men of "criminal nature" are simply at issue with their true Wills. The murderer has the Will to Live; and his will to murder is a false will at variance with his true Will, since he risks death at the hands of Society by obeying his criminal impulse.*

(Illustration: A function imperfectly performed injures, not only itself, but everything associated with it. If the heart is afraid to beat for fear of disturbing the liver, the liver is starved for blood and avenges itself on the heart by upsetting digestion, which disorders respiration, on which cardiac welfare depends.)

27) Every man should make Magick the keystone of his life. He should learn its laws and live by them.

(Illustration: The Banker should discover the real meaning of his existence, the real motive which led him to choose that profession. He should under-stand banking as a necessary factor in the economic existence of mankind instead of merely a business whose objects are independant of the general welfare. He should learn to distinguish false values from real, and to act not on accidental fluctuations but on considerations of essential importance. Such a banker will prove himself superior to others; because he will not be an individual limited by transitory things, but a force of Nature, as impersonal, impartial and eternal as gravitation, as patient and irresistable as the tides. His system will not be subject to panic, any more than the law of Inverse Squares is disturbed by elections. He will not be anxious about his affairs because they will not be his; and for that reason he will be able to direct them with the calm, clear-headed confidence of an onlooker, with intelligence unclouded by self-interest, and power unimpaired by passion.)

28) Every man has a right to fulfill his own will without being afraid that it may interfere with that of others; for if he is in his proper place, it is the fault of others if they interfere with him.

(Illustration: If a man like Napoleon were actually appointed by destiny to control Europe, he should not be blamed for exercising his rights. To oppose him would be an error. Any one so doing would have made a mistake as to his own destiny, except insofar as it mught be necessary for him to learn the lessons of defeat. The sun moves in space without interference. the order of nature provides an orbit for each star. A clash proves that one or the other has strayed from its course. But as to each man that keeps his true course, the more firmly he acts, the less likely others are to get in his way. His example will helpthem to find their own paths and pursue them. Every man that becomes a Magician helps others to do likewise. The more firmly and surely men move, and the more such action is accepted as the standard of morality, the less will conflict and confusion hamper humanity.)

I hope that the above principles will demonstrate to

ALL

that their welfare, their very existence, is bound up in

MAGICK.

I trust that they will understand, not only the reasonableness, but the necessity of the fundamental truth which I was the means of giving to mankind:

"Do what thou wilt shall be the whole of the Law." I trust that they will assert themselves as individually absolute, that they will grasp the fact that it is their right to assert themselves, and to accomplish the task for which their nature fits them. Yea, more, that this is their duty, and that not only to themselves but to others, a duty founded upon universal necessity, and not to be shirked on account of any casual circumstances of the moment which may seem to put such conduct in the light of inconvenience or even of cruelty.

I hope that the principles outlined above will help them to understand this book, and prevent them from being deterred from its study by the more or less technical language in which it is written.

The essence of

MAGICK

is simple enough in all conscience. It is not otherwise with the art of government. The Aim is simply prosperity; but the theory is tangled, and the practice beset with briars.

In the same way

MAGICK

is merely to be and to do. I should add: "to suffer". For Magick is the verb; and it is part of the Training to use the passive voice. This is, however, a matter of Initiation rather than of Magick in its ordinary sense. It is not my fault if being is baffling, and doing desperate!

Yet, once the above principles are firmly fixed in the mind, it is easy enough to sum up the situation very shortly. One must find out for oneself, and make sure beyond doubt, "who" one is, "what" one is, "why" one is. This done, one may put the will which is implicit in the "Why" into words, or rather into One Word. Being thus conscious of the proper course to pursue, the next thing is to understand the conditions necessary to following it out. After that, one must eliminate from oneself every element alien or hostile to success, and develop those parts of oneself which are specially needed to control the aforesaid conditions.

Let us make an analogy. A nation must become aware of its own character before it can be said to exist. From that knowledge it must divine its destiny. It must then consider the political conditions of the world; how other countries may help it or hinder it. It must then destroy it itself any elements discordant with its destiny. Lastly, it must develop in itself those qualities which will enable it to combat successfully the external conditions which threaten to oppose is purpose. We have had a recent example in the case of the young German Empire, which, knowing itself and its will, disciplined and trained itself so that it conquered the neighbours which had oppressed it for so many centuries. But after 1866 and 1870, 1914! It mistook itself for superhuman, it willed a thing impossible, it failed to eliminate its own internal jealousies, it failed to understand the conditions of victory,

At least, it allowed England to discover its intentions, and so to combine the world against it. {WEH NOTE: This footnote in Crowley's text belongs to this page, but it is not marked in the text. I have assigned it this tentative point, as following the general context.

it did not train itself to hold the sea, and thus, having violated every principle of

MAGICK,

it was pulled down and broken into pieces by provincialism and democracy, so that neither individual excellence nor civic virtue has yet availed to raise it again to that majestic unity which made so bold a bid for the mastery of the race of man.

The sincere student will discover, behind the symbolic technicalities of his book, a practical method of making himself a Magician. The processes described will enable him to discriminate between what he actually is, and what he has fondly imagined himself to be.

Professor Sigmund Freud and his school have, in recent years, discovered a part of this body of Truth, which has been taught for many centuries in the Sanctuaries of Initiation. But failure to grasp the fullness of Truth, especially that implied in my Sixth Theorem (above) and its corollaries, has led him and his followers into the error of admitting that the avowedly suicidal "Censor" is the proper arbiter of conduct. Official psycho-analysis is therefore committed to upholding a fraud, although the foundation of the science was the observation of the disastrous effects on the individual of being false to his Unconscious Self, whose "writing on the wall" in dream language is the record of the sum of the essential tendencies of the true nature of the individual. The result has been that psycho-analysts have misinterpreted life, and announced the absurdity that every human being is essentially an anti-social, criminal, and insane animal. It is evident that the errors of the Unconscious of which the psycho-analysts complain are neither more nor less than the "original sin" of the theologians whom they despise so heartily.

He must behold his soul in all its awful nakedness, he must not fear to look on that appalling actuality. He must discard the gaudy garments with which his shame has screened him; he must accept the fact that nothing can make him anything but what he is. He may lie to himself, drug himself, hide himself; but he is always there. Magick will teach him that his mind is playing him traitor. It is as if a man were told that tailors' fashion-plates were the canon of human beauty, so that he tried to make himself formless and featureless like them, and shuddered with horror at the idea of Holbein making a portrait of him. Magick will show him the beauty and majesty of the self which he has tried to suppress and disguise.

Having discovered his identity, he will soon perceive his purpose. Another process will show him how to make that purpose pure and powerful. He may then learn how to estimate his environment, learn how to make allies, how to make himself prevail against all powers whose error has caused them to wander across his path.

In the course of this Training, he will learn to explore the Hidden Mysteries of Nature, and to develop new senses and faculties in himself, whereby he may communicate with, and control, Beings and Forces pertaining to orders of existence which have been hitherto inaccessible to profane research, and available only to that unscientific and empirical

MAGICK

(of tradition) which I came to destroy in order that I might fulfil.

CHAPTER 0

THE MAGICAL THEORY OF THE UNIVERSE

There are three main theories of the Universe; Dualism, Monism and Nihilism. It is impossible to enter into a discussion of their relative merits in a popular manual of this sort. They may be studied in Erdmann's "History of Philosophy" and similar treatises.

All are reconciled and unified in the theory which we shall now set forth. The basis of this Harmony is given in Crowley's

"Berashith" — to which reference should be made.

Infinite space is called the goddess NUIT, while the infinitely small and atomic yet omnipresent point is called HADIT.

I present this theory in a very simple form. I cannot even explain (for instance) that an idea may not refer to Being at all, but to Going. The Book of the Law demands special study and initiated apprehension.

These are unmanifest. One conjunction of these infinites is called RA-HOOR-KHUIT,

More correctly, HERU-RA-HA, to include HOOR-PAAR-KRAAT.

a unity which includes and heads all things.

The basis of this theology is given in Liber CCXX, AL vel Legis which forms Part IV of this Book 4. Hence I can only outline the matter in a very crude way; it would require a separate treatise to discuss even the true meaning of the terms employed, and to show how The Book of the Law anticipates the recent discoveries of Frege, Cantor, Poincare, Russell, Whitehead, Einstein and others.

(There is also a particular Nature of Him, in certain conditions, such as have obtained since the Spring of 1904, e.v.) This profoundly mystical conception is based upon actual spiritual experience, but the trained reason

All advance in understanding demands the acquisition of a new point-of-view. Modern conceptions of Mathematics, Chemistry, and Physics are sheer paradox to the "plain man" who thinks of Matter as something that one can knock up against.

can reach a reflection of this idea by the method of logical contradiction which ends in reason transcending itself. The reader should consult "The Soldier and the Hunchback" in Equinox I, I, and Konx Om Pax.

"Unity" transcends "consciousness". It is above all division. The Father of thought — the Word — is called Chaos — the dyad. The number Three, the Mother, is called Babalon. In connection with this the reader should study "The Temple of Solomon the King" in Equinox I, V, and Liber 418.

This first triad is essentially unity, in a manner transcending reason. The comprehension of this Trinity is a matter of spiritual experience. All true gods are attributed to this Trinity.

Considerations of the Christian Trinity are of a nature suited only to Initiates of the IX Degree of O.T.O., as they enclose the final secret of all practical Magick.

An immeasurable abyss divides it from all manifestations of Reason or the lower qualities of man. In the ultimate analysis of Reason, we find all reason identified with this abyss. Yet this abyss is the crown of the mind. Purely intellectual faculties all obtain here. This abyss has no number, for in it all is confusion.

Below this abyss we find the moral qualities of Man, of which there are six. The highest is symbolised by the number Four. Its nature is fatherly

> *Each conception is, however, balanced in itself. Four is also Daleth, the letter of Venus; so that the mother-idea is included. Again, the Sephira of 4 is Chesed, referred to Water. 4 is ruled by Jupiter, Lord of the Lightning (Fire) yet ruler of Air. Each Sephira is complete in its way.*

; Mercy and Authority are the attributes of its dignity.

The number Five is balanced against it. The attributes of Five are Energy and Justice. Four and Five are again combined and harmonized in the number Six, whose nature is beauty and harmony, mortality and immortality.

In the number Seven the feminine nature is again predominant, but it is the masculine type of female, the Amazon, who is balanced in the number Eight by the feminine type of male.

In the number Nine we reach the last of the purely mental qualities. It identifies change with stability.

Pendant to this sixfold system is the number Ten<<

The balance of the Sephiroth:

Kether (1) "Kether is in Malkuth, and Malkuth is in Kether, but after another manner."

Chokmah (2) is Yod of Tetragrammaton, and therefore also Unity.

Binah (3) is He of Tetragrammaton, and therefore "The

Emperor."

Chesed (4) is Daleth, Venus the female.

Geburah (5) is the Sephira of Mars, the Male.

Tiphereth (6) is the Hexagram, harmonizing, and mediating between

Kether and Malkuth. Also it reflects Kether. "That

which is above, is like that which is below, and

that which is below, is like that which is above."

Netzach (7) and Hod (8) balanced as in text.

Jesod (9) see text.

Malkuth (10) contains all the numbers.>> which includes the whole of Matter as we know it by the senses.

It is impossible here to explain thoroughly the complete conception; for it cannot be too clearly understood that this is a "classification" of the Universe, that there is nothing which is not comprehended therein.

The Article on the Qabalah in Vol. I, No. V of the Equinox is the best which has been written on the subject.

It should be deeply studied, in connection with the Qabalistic Diagrams in Nos. II and III: "The Temple of Solomon the King".

Such is a crude and elementary sketch of this system.

The formula of Tetragrammaton is the most important for the practical magician. Here Yod = 2, He = 3, Vau = 4 to 9, He final = 10.

The Number Two represents Yod, the Divine or Archetypal World, and the Number One is only attained by the destruction of the God and the Magician in Samadhi. The world of Angels is under the numbers Four to Nine, and that of spirits under the number Ten.

> *It is not possible to give a full account of the twenty-two "paths" in this condensed sketch. They should be studied in view of all their attributes in 777, but more especially that in which they are attributed to the planets, elements and signs, as also to the Tarot Trumps, while their position on the Tree itself and their position as links between the particular Sephiroth which they join is the final key to their understanding. It will be noticed that each chapter of this book is attributed to one of them. This was not intentional. The book was originally but a collection of haphazard dialogues between Fra. P. and Soror A.; but on arranging the MSS, they fell naturally and of necessity into this division. Conversely, my knowledge of the Schema pointed out to me numerous gaps in my original exposition; thanks to this, I have been able to make it a complete and systematic treatise. That is, when my laziness had been jogged by the criticisms and suggestions of various colleagues to whom I had submitted the early drafts.*

All these numbers are of course parts of the magician himself considered as the microcosm. The microcosm is an exact image of the Macrocosm; the Great Work is the raising of the whole man in perfect balance to the power of Infinity.

The reader will remark that all criticism directed against the Magical Hierarchy is futile. One cannot call it incorrect — the only line to take might be that it was inconvenient. In the same way one cannot say that the Roman alphabet is better or worse than the Greek, since all required sounds can be more or less satisfactorily represented by either; yet both these alphabets were found so little satisfactory when it came to an attempt at phonetic printing of Oriental languages, that the alphabet had to be expanded by the use of italics and other diacritical marks. In the same way our magical alphabet of the Sephiroth and the Paths (thirty-two letters as it were) has been expanded into the four worlds corresponding to the four letters of the name Yod-Heh-Vau-Heh; and each Sephira is supposed to contain a Tree of Life of its own. Thus we obtain four hundred Sephiroth instead of the original ten, and the Paths being capable of similar multiplications, or rather of subdivision, the number is still further extended. Of course this process might be indefinitely continued without destroying the original system.

The Apologia for this System is that our purest conceptions are symbolized in Mathematics. "God is the Great Arithmetician." "God is the Grand Geometer." It is best therefore to prepare to apprehend Him by formulating our minds according to these measures.

> *By "God" I here mean the Ideal Identity of a man's inmost nature. "Something ourselves (I erase Arnold's imbecile and guilty 'not') that makes for righteousness;" righteousness being rightly defined as internal coherence. (Internal Coherence implies that which is written "Detegitur Yod.")*

To return, each letter of this alphabet may have its special magical sigil. The student must not expect to be given a cut-and-dried definition of what exactly is meant by any of all this. On the contrary, he must work backwards, putting the whole of his mental and moral outfit into these pigeon-holes. You would not expect to be able to buy a filing cabinet with the names of all your past, present and future correspondents ready indexed: your cabinet has a system of letters and numbers meaningless in themselves, but ready to take on a meaning to you, as you fill up the files. As your business increased, each letter and number would receive fresh accessions of meaning for you; and by adopting this orderly arrangement you would be able to have a much more comprehensive grasp of your affairs than would otherwise be the case. By the use of this system the magician is able ultimately to unify the whole of his knowledge — to transmute, even on the Intellectual Plane, the Many into the One.

The Reader can now understand that the sketch given above of the magical Hierarchy is hardly even an outline of the real theory of the Universe. This theory may indeed be studied in the article already referred to in No. V of the Equinox, and, more deeply in the Book of the Law and the Commentaries thereon: but the true understanding depends entirely upon the work of the Magician himself. Without magical experience it will be meaningless.

In this there is nothing peculiar. It is so with all scientific knowledge. A blind man might cram up astronomy for the purpose of passing examinations, but his knowledge would be almost entirely unrelated to his experience, and it would certainly not give him sight. A similar phenomenon is observed when a gentleman who has taken an "honours degree" in modern languages at Cambridge arrives in Paris, and is unable to order his dinner. To exclaim against the Master Therion is to act like a person who, observing this, should attack both the professors of French and the inhabitants of Paris, and perhaps go on to deny the existence of France.

Let us say, once again, that the magical language is nothing but a convenient system of classification to enable the magician to docket his experiences as he obtains them.

Yet this is true also, that, once the language is mastered, one can divine the unknown by study of the known, just as one's knowledge of Latin and Greek enables one to understand some unfamiliar English word derived from those sources. Also, there is the similar case of the Periodic Law in Chemistry, which enables Science to prophesy, and so in the end to discover, the existence of certain previously unsuspected elements in nature. All discussions upon philosophy are necessarily sterile, since truth is beyond language. They are, however, useful if carried far enough — if carried to the point when it become apparent that all arguments are arguments in a circle.

> *See "The Soldier and the Hunchback," Equinox I, I. The apparatus of human reason is simply one particular system of coordinating impressions; its structure is determined by the course of the evolution of the species. It is no more absolute than the evolution of the species. It is no more absolute than the mechanism of our muscles is a complete type wherewith all other systems of transmitting Force must conform.*

But discussions of the details of purely imaginary qualities are frivolous and may be deadly. For the great danger of this magical theory is that the student may mistake the alphabet for the things which the words represent.

An excellent man of great intelligence, a learned Qabalist, once amazed the Master Therion by stating that the Tree of Life was the framework of the Universe. It was as if some one had seriously maintained that a cat was a creature constructed by placing the letters C. A. T. in that order. It is no wonder that Magick has excited the ridicule of the unintelligent, since even its educated students can be guilty of so gross a violation of the first principles of common sense.< The absurdity of any such disturbance of the arrangement of the Paths is evident to any sober student from such examples as the following. Binah, the Supernal Understanding, is connected with Tiphereth, the Human Consciousness, by Zain, Gemini, the Oracles of the Gods, or the Intuition. That is, the attribution represents a psychological fact: to replace it by The Devil is either humour or plain idiocy. Again, the card "Fortitude", Leo, balances Majesty and Mercy with Strength and Severity: what sense is there in putting "Death", the Scorpion, in its stead? There are twenty other mistakes in the new wonderful illuminated-from-on-high attribution; the student can therefore be sure of twenty more laughs if he cares to study it.>> A synopsis of the grades of the A.'. A.'. as illustrative of the Magical Hierarchy in Man is given in Appendix 2 "One Star in Sight." This should be read before proceeding with the chapter. The subject is very difficult. To deal with it in full is entirely beyond the limits of this small treatise.

"FURTHER CONCERNING THE MAGICAL UNIVERSE"

All these letters of the magical alphabet — referred to above — are like so many names on a map. Man himself is a complete microcosm. Few other beings have this balanced perfection. Of course every sun, every planet, may have beings similarly constituted.

> *Equally, of course, we have no means of knowing what we really are. We are limited to symbols. And it is certain that all our sense-perceptions give only partial aspects of their objects. Sight, for instance, tells us very little about solidity, weight, composition, electrical character, thermal conductivity, etc., etc. It says nothing at all about the very existence of such vitally important ideas as Heat, Hardness, and so on. The impression which the mind combines from the senses can never claim to be accurate or complete. We have indeed learnt that nothing is in itself what it seems to be to us.*

But when we speak of dealing with the planets in Magick, the reference is usually not to the actual planets, but to parts of the earth which are of the nature attributed to these planets. Thus, when we say that Nakhiel is the "Intelligence" of the Sun, we do not mean that he lives in the Sun, but only that he has a certain rank and character; and although we can invoke him, we do not necessarily mean that he exists in the same sense of the word in which our butcher exists.

When we "conjure Nakhiel to visible appearance," it may be that our process resembles creation — or, rather imagination — more nearly than it does calling-forth. The aura of a man is called the "magical mirror of the universe"; and, so far as any one can tell, nothing exists outside of this mirror. It is at least convenient to represent the whole as if it were subjective. It leads to less confusion. And, as a man is a perfect microcosm,

> *He is this only by definition. The universe may contain an infinite variety of worlds inaccessible to human apprehension. Yet, for this very reason, they do not exist for the purposes of the argument. Man has, however, some instruments of knowledge; we may, therefore, define the Macrocosm as the totality of things possible to his perception. As evolution develops those instruments, the Macrocosm and the Microcosm extend; but they always maintain their mutual relation. Neither can possess any meaning except in terms of the other. Our "discoveries" are exactly as much of ourselves as they are of Nature. America and Electricity did, in a sense, exist before we were aware of them; but they are even now no more than incomplete ideas, expressed in symbolic terms of a series of relations between two sets of inscrutable phenomena.*

it is perfectly easy to re-model one's conception at any moment.

Now there is a traditional correspondence, which modern experiment has shown to be fairly reliable. There is a certain natural connexion between certain letters, words, numbers, gestures, shapes, perfumes and so on, so that any idea or (as we might call it) "spirit", may be composed or called forth by the use of those things which are harmonious with it, and express particular parts of its nature. These correspondences have been elaborately mapped in the Book 777 in a very convenient and compendious form. It will be necessary for the student to make a careful study of this book in connexion with some actual rituals of Magick, for example, that of the evocation of Taphtatharath printed in Equinox I, III, pages 170-190, where he will see exactly why these things are to be used. Of course, as the student advances in knowledge by experience he will find a progressive subtlety in the magical universe corresponding to his own; for let it be said yet again! not only is his aura a magical mirror of the universe, but the universe is a magical mirror of his aura.

In this chapter we are only able to give a very thin outline of magical theory — faint pencilling by weak and wavering fingers — for this subject may almost be said to be co-extensive with one's whole knowledge.

The knowledge of exoteric science is comically limited by the fact that we have no access, except in the most indirect way, to any other celestial body than our own. In the last few years, the semi-educated have got an idea that they know a great deal about the universe, and the principal ground for their fine opinion of themselves is usually the telephone or the airship. It is pitiful to read the bombastic twaddle about progress, which journalists and others, who wish to prevent men from thinking, put out for consumption. We know infinitesimally little of the material universe. Our detailed knowledge is so contemptibly minute, that it is hardly worth reference, save that our shame may spur us to increased endeavour. Such knowledge

Knowledge is, moreover, an impossible conception. All propositions come ultimately back to "A is A".

as we have got is of a very general and abstruse, of a philosophical and almost magical character. This consists principally of the conceptions of pure mathematics. It is, therefore, almost legitimate to say that pure mathematics is our link with the rest of the universe and with "God".

Now the conceptions of Magick are themselves profoundly mathematical. The whole basis of our theory is the Qabalah, which corresponds to mathematics and geometry. The method of operation in Magick is based on this, in very much the same way as the laws of mechanics are based on mathematics. So far, therefore as we can be said to possess a magical theory of the universe, it must be a matter solely of fundamental law, with a few simple and comprehensive propositions stated in very general terms.

I might expend a life-time in exploring the details of one plane, just as an explorer might give his life to one corner of Africa, or a chemist to one subgroup of compounds. Each such detailed piece of work may be very valuable, but it does not as a rule throw light on the main principles of the universe. Its truth is the truth of one angle. It might even lead to error, if some inferior person were to generalize from too few facts.

Imagine an inhabitant of Mars who wished to philosophise about the earth, and had nothing to go by but the diary of some man at the North Pole! But the work of every explorer, on whatever branch of the Tree of Life the caterpillar he is after may happen to be crawling, is immensely helped by a grasp of general principles. Every magician, therefore, should study the Holy Qabalah. Once he has mastered the main principles, he will find his work grow easy.

"Solvitur ambulando" which does not mean: "Call the Ambulance!"

CHAPTER I

THE PRINCIPLES OF RITUAL.

There is a single main definition of the object of all magical Ritual. It is the uniting of the Microcosm with the Macrocosm. The Supreme and Complete Ritual is therefore the Invocation of the Holy Guardian Angel;

See the "Book of the Sacred Magic of Abramelin the Mage"; and Liber 418, 8th Aethyr, Liber Samekh; see Appendix 3.

or, in the language of Mysticism, Union with God.

The difference between these operations is more of theoretical than of practical importance.

All other magical Rituals are particular cases of this general principle, and the only excuse for doing them is that it sometimes occurs that one particular portion of the microcosm is so weak that its imperfection of impurity would vitiate the Macrocosm of which it is the image, Eidolon, or Reflexion. For example, God is above sex; and therefore neither man nor woman as such can be said fully to understand, much less to represent, God. It is therefore incumbent on the male magician to cultivate those female virtues in which he is deficient, and this task he must of course accomplish without in any way impairing his virility. It will then be lawful for a magician to invoke Isis, and identify himself with her; if he fail to do this, his apprehension of the Universe when he attains Samadhi will lack the conception of maternity. The result will be a metaphysical and — by corollary — ethical limitation in the Religion which he founds. Judaism and Islam are striking example of this failure.

To take another example, the ascetic life which devotion to magick so often involves argues a poverty of nature, a narrowness, a lack of generosity. Nature is infinitely prodigal — not one in a million seeds ever comes to fruition. Whoso fails to recognise this, let him invoke Jupiter.

There are much deeper considerations in which it appears that "Everything that is, is right". They are set forth elsewhere; we can only summarise them here by saying that the survival of the fittest is their upshot.

The danger of ceremonial magick — the sublest and deepest danger — is this: that the magician will naturally tend to invoke that partial being which most strongly appeals to him, so that his natural excess in that direction will be still further exaggerated. Let him, before beginning his Work, endeavour to map out his own being, and arrange his invocations in such a way as to redress the balance.

The ideal method of doing this is given in Liber 913 (Equinox VII). See also Liber CXI Aleph.

This, of course, should have been done in a preliminary fashion during the preparation of the weapons and furniture of the Temple.

To consider in a more particular manner this question of the Nature of Ritual, we may suppose that he finds himself lacking in that perception of the value of Life and Death, alike of individuals and of races, which is characteristic of Nature. He has perhaps a tendency to perceive the "first noble truth" uttered by Buddha, that Everything is sorrow. Nature, it seems, is a tragedy. He has perhaps even experienced the great trance called Sorrow. He should then consider whether there is not some Deity who expresses this Cycle, and yet whose nature is joy. He will find what he requires in Dionysus.

There are three main methods of invoking any Deity.

The "First Method" consists of devotion to that Deity, and, being mainly mystical in character, need not be dealt with in this place, especially as a perfect instruction exists in Liber 175 ("See" Appendix).

The "Second method"is the straight forward ceremonial invocation. It is the method which was usually employed in the Middle Ages. Its advantage is its directness, its disadvantage its crudity. The "Goetia" gives clear instruction in this method, and so do many other rituals, white and black. We shall presently devote some space to a clear exposition of this Art.

In the case of Bacchus, however, we may roughly outline the procedure. We find that the symbolism of Tiphareth expresses the nature of Bacchus. It is then necessary to construct a Ritual of Tiphareth. Let us open the Book 777; we shall find in line 6 of each column the various parts of our required apparatus. Having ordered everything duly, we shall exalt the mind by repeated prayers or conjurations to the highest conception of the God, until, in one sense or another of the word, He appears to us and floods our consciousness with the light of His divinity.

The "Third Method is the Dramatic," perhaps the most attractive of all; certainly it is so to the artist's temperament, for it appeals to his imagination through his aesthetic sense.

Its disadvantage lies principally in the difficulty of its performance by a single person. But it has the sanction of the highest antiquity, and is probably the most useful for the foundation of a religion. It is the method of Catholic Christianity, and consists in the dramatization of the legend of the God. The Bacchae of Euripides is a magnificent example of such a Ritual; so also, through in a less degree, is the Mass. We may also mention many of the degrees in Freemasonry, particularly the third. The 5'=6' Ritual published in No. III of the Equinox is another example.

In the case of Bacchus, one commemorates firstly his birth of a mortal mother who has yielded her treasure-house to the Father of All, of the jealousy and rage excited by this incarnation, and of the heavenly protection afforded to the infant. Next should be commemorated the journeying westward upon an ass. Now comes the great scene of the drama: the gentle, exquisite youth with his following (chiefly composed of women) seems to threaten the established order of things, and that Established Order takes steps to put an end to the upstart. We find Dionysus confronting the angry King, not with defiance, but with meekness; yet with a subtle confidence, an underlying laughter. His forehead is wreathed with vine tendrils. He is an effeminate figure with those broad leaves clustered upon his brow? But those leaves hide horns. King Pentheus, representative of respectability,

There is a much deeper interpretation in which Pentheus is himself "The Dying God". See my "Good Hunting!" and Dr. J.G.Frazer's "Golden Bough".

is destroyed by his pride. He goes out into the mountains to attack the women who have followed Bacchus, the youth whom he has mocked, scourged, and put in chains, yet who has only smiled; and by those women, in their divine madness, he is torn to pieces.

It has already seemed impertinent to say so much when Walter Pater has told the story with such sympathy and insight. We will not further transgress by dwelling upon the identity of this legend with the course of Nature, its madness, its prodigality, its intoxication, its joy, and above all its sublime persistence through the cycles of Life and Death. The pagan reader must labour to understand this in Pater's "Greek Studies", and the Christian reader will recognise it, incident for incident, in the story of Christ. This legend is but the dramatization of Spring.

The magician who wishes to invoke Bacchus by this method must therefore arrange a ceremony in which he takes the part of Bacchus, undergoes all His trials, and emerges triumphant from beyond death. He must, however, be warned against mistaking the symbolism. In this case, for example, the doctrine of individual immortality has been dragged in, to the destruction of truth. It is not that utterly worthless part of man, his individual consciousness as John Smith, which defies death — that consciousness which dies and is reborn in every thought. That which persists (if anything persist) is his rēal John Smithiness, a quality of which he was probably never conscious in his life.

See "The Book of Lies", Liber 333, for several sermons to this effect. Caps. Alpha, Delta, Eta, Iota-Epsilon, Iota-Sigma, Iota-Eta, Kappa-Alpha, Kappa-Eta, in particular. The reincarnation of the Khu or magical Self is another matter entirely, too abstruse to discuss in this elementary manual. {WEH NOTE: I have made a correction in the above list of chapters from Liber 333. The published text cites Iota-Digamma, which does not exist. The correct chapter is Iota-Sigma, which does exist and discusses the subject}.

Even that does not persist unchanged. It is always growing. The Cross is a barren stick, and the petals of the Rose fall and decay; but in the union of the Cross and the Rose is a constant succession of new lives.

See "The Book of Lies", Liber 333, for several sermons to this effect. The whole theory of Death must be sought in Liber CXI Aleph.

Without this union, and without this death of the individual, the cycle would be broken.

A chapter will be consecrated to removing the practical difficulties of this method of Invocation. It will doubtless have been noted by the acumen of the reader that in the great essentials these three methods are one. In each case the magician identifies himself with the Deity invoked. To "invoke" is to "call in", just as to "evoke" is to "call forth". This is the essential difference between the two branches of Magick. In invocation, the macrocosm floods the consciousness. In evocation, the magician, having become the macrocosm, creates a microcosm. You "in"voke a God into the Circle. You "e"voke a Spirit into the Triangle. In the first method identity with the God is attained by love and by surrender, by giving up or suppressing all irrelevant (and illusionary) parts of yourself. It is the weeding of a garden.

In the second method identity is attained by paying special attention to the desired part of yourself: positive, as the first method is negative. It is the potting-out and watering of a particular flower in the garden, and the exposure of it to the sun.

In the third, identity is attained by sympathy. It is very difficult for the ordinary man to lose himself completely in the subject of a play or of a novel; but for those who can do so, this method is unquestionably the best.

Observe: each element in this cycle is of equal value. It is wrong to say triumphantly "Mors janua vitae", unless you add, with equal triumph, "Vita janua mortis". To one who understands this chain of the Aeons from the point of view alike of the sorrowing Isis and of the triumphant Osiris, not forgetting their link in the destroyer Apophis, there remains no secret veiled in Nature. He cries that name of God which throughout History has been echoed by one religion to another, the infinite swelling paean I.A.O.!

This name, I.A.O. is qabalistically identical with that of THE BEAST and with His number 666, so that he who invokes the former invokes also the latter. Also with AIWAZ and the Number 93. See Chapter V.

CHAPTER II

THE FORMULAE OF THE ELEMENTAL WEAPONS.

Before discussing magical formulae in detail, one may observe that most rituals are composite, and contain many formulae which must be harmonized into one.

The first formula is that of the Wand. In the sphere of the principle which the magician wishes to invoke, he rises from point to point in a perpendicular line, and then descends; or else, beginning at the top, he comes directly down, "invoking" first the god of that sphere by "devout supplication"

Beware, O brother, lest thou bend the knee! Liber CCXX teaches the proper attitude. See also Liber CCCLXX. Infra, furthermore, there is special instruction: Chapter XV and elsewhere.

that He may deign to send the appropriate Archangel. He then "beseeches" the Archangel to send the Angel or Angels of that sphere to his aid; he "conjures" this Angel or Angels to send the intelligence in question, and this intelligence he will "conjure with authority" to compel the obedience of the spirit and his manifestation. To this spirit he "issues commands".

It will be seen that this is a formula rather of evocation than of invocation, and for the latter the procedure, though apparently the same, should be conceived of in a different manner, which brings it under another formula, that of Tetragrammaton. The essence of the force invoked is one, but the "God" represents the germ or beginning of the force, the "Archangel" its development; and so on, until, with the "Spirit", we have the completion and perfection of that force.

The formula of the Cup is not so well suited for Evocations, and the magical Hierarchy is not involved in the same way; for the Cup being passive rather than active, it is not fitting for the magician to use it in respect of anything but the Highest. In practical working it consequently means little but prayer, and that prayer the "prayer of silence".

Considerations which might lead to a contrary conclusion are unsuited to this treatise. See Liber LXXXI.

The formula of the dagger is again unsuitable for either purpose, since the nature of the dagger is to criticise, to destroy, to disperse; and all true magical ceremonies tend to concentration. The dagger will therefore appear principally in the banishings, preliminary to the ceremony proper. The formula of the pantacle is again of no particular use; for the pantacle is inert. In fine, the formula of the wand is the only one with which we need more particularly concern ourselves.

Later, these remarks are amplified, and to some extent modified.

Now in order to invoke any being, it is said by Hermes Trismegistus that the magi employ three methods. The first, for the vulgar, is that of supplication. In this the crude objective theory is assumed as true. There is a god named A, whom you, B, proceed to petition, in exactly the same sense as a boy might ask his father for pocket-money.

The second method involves a little more subtlety, inasmuch as the magician endeavours to harmonize himself with the nature of the god, and to a certain extent exalts himself, in the course of the ceremony; but the third method is the only one worthy of our consideration.

This consists of a real identification of the magician and the god. Note that to do this in perfection involves the attainment of a species of Samadhi: and this fact alone suffices to link irrefragably magick with mysticism.

Let us describe the magical method of identification. The symbolic form of the god is first studied with as much care as an artist would bestow upon his model, so that a perfectly clear and unshakeable mental picture of the god is presented to the mind. Similarly, the attributes of the god are enshrined in speech, and such speeches are committed perfectly to memory. The invocation will then begin with a prayer to the god, commemorating his physical attributes, always with profound understanding of their real meaning. In the "second part" of the invocation, the voice of the god is heard, and His characteristic utterance is recited.

In the "third portion" of the invocation the magician asserts the identity of himself with the god. In the "fourth portion" the god is again invoked, but as if by Himself, as if it were the utterance of the will of the god that He should manifest in the magician. At the conclusion of this, the original object of the invocation is stated.

Thus, in the invocation of Thoth which is to be found in the rite of Mercury (Equinox I, VI) and in Liber LXIV, the first part begins with the words "Majesty of Godhead, wisdom-crowned TAHUTI, Thee, Thee I invoke. Oh Thou of the Ibis head, Thee, Thee I invoke"; and so on. At the conclusion of this a mental image of the God, infinitely vast and infinitely splendid, should be perceived, in just the same sense as a man might see the Sun.

The second part begins with the words:

"Behold! I am yesterday, today, and the brother of tomorrow."

The magician should imagine that he is hearing this voice, and at the same time that he is echoing it, that it is true also of himself. This thought should so exalt him that he is able at its conclusion to utter the sublime words which open the third part: "Behold! he is in me, and I am in him." At this moment, he loses consciousness of his mortal being; he is that mental image which he previously but saw. This consciousness is only complete as he goes on: "Mine is the radiance wherein Ptah floateth over his firmament. I travel upon high. I tread upon the firmament of Nu. I raise a flashing flame with the lightnings of mine eye: ever rushing on in the splendour of the daily glorified Ra — giving my life to the treaders of Earth!" This thought gives the relation of God and Man from the divine point of view.

The magician is only recalled to himself at the conclusion of the third part; in which occur, almost as if by accident, the words: "Therefore do all things obey my word." Yet in the fourth part, which begins: "Therefore do thou come forth unto me", it is not really the magician who is addressing the God; it is the God who hears the far-off utterance of the magician. If this invocation has been correctly performed, the words of the fourth part will sound distant and strange. It is surprising that a dummy (so the magus now appears to Himself) should be able to speak!

The Egyptian Gods are so complete in their nature, so perfectly spiritual and yet so perfectly material, that this one invocation is sufficient. The God bethinks him that the spirit of Mercury should now appear to the magician; and it is so. This Egyptian formula is therefore to be preferred to the Hierarchical formula of the Hebrews with its tedious prayers, conjurations, and curses.

It will be noted, however, that in this invocation of Thoth which we have summarized, there is another formula contained, the Reverberating or Reciprocating formula, which may be called the formula of Horus and Harpocrates. The magician addresses the God with an active projection of his will, and then becomes passive while the God addresses the Universe. In the fourth part he remains silent, listening, to the prayer which arises therefrom.

The formula of this invocation of Thoth may also be classed under Tetragrammaton. The first part is fire, the eager prayer of the magician, the second water, in which the magician listens to, or catches the reflection of, the god. The third part is air, the marriage of fire and water; the god and the man have become one; while the fourth part corresponds to earth, the condensation or materialization of those three higher principles.

With regard to the Hebrew formulae, it is doubtful whether most magicians who use them have ever properly grasped the principles underlying the method of identity. No passage which implies it occurs to mind, and the extant rituals certainly give no hint of such a conception, or of any but the most personal and material views of the nature of things. They seem to have thought that there was an Archangel named Ratziel in exactly the same sense as there was a statesman named Richelieu, an individual being living in a definite place. He had possibly certain powers of a somewhat metaphysical order — he might be in two places at once,

He could do this provided that he can travel with a speed exceeding that of Light, as he does. See A.S. Eddington "Space, Time, and Gravitation". Also: what means "at once"?

for example, though even the possibility of so simple a feat (in the case of spirits) seems to be denied by certain passages in extant conjurations which tell the spirit that if he happens to be in chains in a particular place in Hell, or if some other magician is conjuring him so that he cannot come, then let him send a spirit of similar nature, or otherwise avoid the difficultly. But of course so vulgar a conception would not occur to the student of the Qabalah. It is just possible that the magi wrote their conjurations on this crude hypothesis in order to avoid the clouding of the mind by doubt and metaphysical speculation.

He who became the Master Therion was once confronted by this very difficulty. Being determined to instruct mankind, He sought a simple statement of his object. His will was sufficiently informed by common sense to decide him to teach man "The Next Step", the thing which was immediately above him. He might have called this "God", or "The Higher Self", or "The Augoeides", or "Adi-Buddha", or 61 other things — but He had discovered that these were all one, yet that each one represented some theory of the Universe which would ultimately be shattered by criticism — for He had already passed through the realm of Reason, and knew that every statement contained an absurdity. He therefore said: "Let me declare this Work under this title: 'The obtaining of the Knowledge and Conversation of the Holy Guardian Angel'", because the theory implied in these words is so patently absurd that only simpletons would waste much time in analysing it. It would be accepted as a convention, and no one would incur the grave danger of building a philosophical system upon it.

With this understanding, we may rehabilitate the Hebrew system of invocations. The mind is the great enemy; so, by invoking enthusiastically a person whom we know not to exist, we are rebuking that mind. Yet we should not refrain altogether from philosophising in the light of the Holy Qabalah. We should accept the Magical Hierarchy as a more or less convenient classification of the facts of the Universe as they are known to us; and as our knowledge and understanding of those facts increase, so should we endeavour to adjust our idea of what we mean by any symbol.

At the same time let us reflect that there is a certain definite consensus of experience as to the correlation of the various beings of the hierarchy with the observed facts of Magick. In the simple matter of astral vision, for example, one striking case may be quoted.

Without telling him what it was, the Master Therion once recited as an invocation Sappho's "Ode to Venus" before a Probationer of the A.'. A.'. who was ignorant of Greek, the language of the Ode. The disciple then went on an "astral journey," and everything seen by him was without exception harmonious with Venus. This was true down to the smallest detail. He even obtained all the four colour-scales of Venus with absolute correctness. Considering that he saw something like one hundred symbols in all, the odds against coincidence are incalculably great. Such an experience (and the records of the A.'. A.'. contain dozens of similar cases) affords proof as absolute as any proof can be in this world of Illusion that the correspondences in Liber 777 really represent facts in Nature.

It suggests itself that this "straightforward" system of magick was perhaps never really employed at all. One might maintain that the invocations which have come down to us are but the ruins of the Temple of Magick. The exorcisms might have been committed to writing for the purpose of memorising them, while it was forbidden to make any record of the really important parts of the ceremony. Such details of Ritual as we possess are meagre and unconvincing, and though much success has been attained in the quite conventional exoteric way both by FRATER PERDURABO and by many of his colleagues, yet ceremonies of this character have always remained tedious and difficult. It has seemed as if the success were obtained almost in spite of the ceremony. In any case, they are the more mysterious parts of the Ritual which have evoked the divine force. Such conjurations as those of the "Goetia" leave one cold, although, notably in the second conjuration, there is a crude attempt to use that formula of Commemoration of which we spoke in the preceding Chapter.

CHAPTER III

THE FORMULA OF TETRAGRAMMATON.

Yod, He, Vau, He, the Ineffable Name (Jehovah) of the Hebrews. The four letters refer respectively to the four "elements", Fire, Water, Air, Earth, in the order named.

This formula is of most universal aspect, as all things are necessarily comprehended in it; but its use in a magical ceremony is little understood.

The climax of the formula is in one sense before even the formulation of the Yod. For the Yod is the most divine aspect of the Force — the remaining letters are but a solidification of the same thing. It must be understood that we are here speaking of the whole ceremony considered as a unity, not merely of that formula in which "Yod" is the god invoked, "He" the Archangel, and so on. In order to understand the ceremony under this formula, we must take a more extended view of the functions of the four weapons than we have hitherto done.

The formation of the "Yod" is the formulation of the first creative force, of that father who is called "self-begotten", and unto whom it is said: "Thou has formulated thy Father, and made fertile thy Mother". The adding of the "He" to the "Yod" is the marriage of that Father to the great co-equal Mother, who is a reflection of Nuit as He is of Hadit. Their union brings forth the son "Vau" who is the heir. Finally the daughter "He" is produced. She is both the twin sister and the daughter of "Vau".

There is a further mystery herein, far deeper, for initiates.

His mission is to redeem her by making her his bride; the result of this is to set her upon the throne of her mother, and it is only she whose youthful embrace can reawaken the eld of the All-Father. In this complex family relationship

The formula of Tetragrammaton, as ordinarily understood, ending with the appearance of the daughter, is indeed a degradation.

is symbolised the whole course of the Universe. It will be seen that (after all) the Climax is at the end. It is the second half of the formula which symbolises the Great Work which we are pledged to accomplish. The first step of this is the attainment of the Knowledge and Conversation of the Holy Guardian Angel, which constitutes the Adept of the Inner Order. The re-entry of these twin spouses into the womb of the mother is that initiation described in Liber 418, which gives admission to the Inmost Order of the A.'. A.'. Of the last step we cannot speak.

It will now be recognised that to devise a practical magical ceremony to correspond to Tetragrammaton in this exalted sense might be difficult if not impossible. In such a ceremony the Rituals of purification alone might occupy many incarnations.

It will be necessary, therefore, to revert to the simpler view of Tetragrammaton, remembering only that the "He" final is the Throne of the Spirit, of the Shin of Pentagrammaton.

The Yod will represent a swift and violent creative energy; following this will be a calmer and more reflective but even more powerful flow of will, the irresistible force of a mighty river. This state of mind will be followed by an expansion of the consciousness; it will penetrate all space, and this will finally undergo a crystallization resplendent with interior light. Such modifications of the original Will may be observed in the course of the invocations when they are properly performed.

The peculiar dangers of each are obvious — that of the first is a flash in the pan — a misfire; that of the second, a falling into dreaminess or reverie; that of the third, loss of concentration. A mistake in any of these points will prevent, or injure the proper formation of, the fourth.

In the expression which will be used in Chapter XV: "Enflame thyself", etc., only the first stage is specified; but if that is properly done the other stages will follow as if by necessity. So far is it written concerning the formula of Tetragrammaton.

CHAPTER IV.

THE FORMULA OF ALHIM, AND THAT OF ALIM.

"ALHIM", (Elohim) is the exoteric word for Gods.

> *"Gods" are the Forces of Nature; their "Names" are the Laws of Nature. Thus They are eternal, omnipotent, omnipresent and so on; and thus their "Wills" are immutable and absolute.*

It is the masculine plural of a feminine noun, but its nature is principally feminine.

> *It represents Sakti,or Teh; femininity always means form, manifestation. The masculine Siva, or Tao, is always a concealed force.*

It is a perfect hieroglyph of the number 5. This should be studied in "A Note on Genesis" (Equinox I, II).

The Elements are all represented, as in Tetragrammaton, but there is no development from one into the others. They are, as it were, thrown together — untamed, only sympathising by virtue of their wild and stormy but elastically resistless energy. The Central letter is "He" — the letter of breath — and represents Spirit. The first letter "Aleph" is the natural letter of Air, and the Final "Mem" is the natural letter of Water. Together, "Aleph" and "Mem" make "Am" — the mother within whose womb the Cosmos is conceived. But "Yod" is not the natural letter of Fire. Its juxtaposition with "He" sanctifies that fire to the "Yod" of Tetragrammaton. Similarly we find "Lamed" for Earth, where we should expect Tau — in order to emphasize the influence of Venus, who rules Libra.

"ALHIM", therefore, represents rather the formula of Consecration than that of a complete ceremony. It is the breath of benediction, yet so potent that it can give life to clay and light to darkness.

In consecrating a weapon, "Aleph" is the whirling force of the thunderbolt, the lightning which flameth out of the East even into the West. This is the gift of the wielding of the thunderbolt of Zeus or Indra, the god of Air. "Lamed" is the Ox-goad, the driving force; and it is also the Balance, representing the truth and love of the Magician. It is the loving care which he bestows upon perfecting his instruments, and the equilibration of that fierce force which initiates the ceremony.

> *The letters Aleph and Lamed are infinitely important in this Aeon of Horus; they are indeed the Key of the Book of the Law. No more can be said in this place than that Aleph is Harpocrates, Bacchus Diphues, the Holy Ghost, the "Pure Fool" or Innocent Babe who is also the Wandering Singer who impregnates the King's Daughter with Himself as Her Child; Lamed is the King's Daughter, satisfied by Him, holding His "Sword and Balances" in her lap. These weapons are the Judge, armed with power to execute His Will, and Two Witnesses "in whom shall every Truth be established" in accordance with whose testimony he gives judgment.*

"Yod" is the creative energy — the procreative power: and yet "Yod" is the solitude and silence of the hermitage into which the Magician has shut himself. "Mem" is the letter of water, and it is the Mem final, whose long flat lines suggest the Sea at Peace HB:Mem-final ; not the ordinary (initial and medial) Mem whose hieroglyph is a wave HB:Mem.

> *In the symbolism above outlined, Yod is the Mercurial "Virgin Word", the Spermatozoon concealing its light under a cloke; and Mem is the amniotic fluid, the flood wherein is the Life-bearing Ark. See A. Crowley "The Ship", Equinox I, X.*

And then, in the Centre of all, broods Spirit, which combines the mildness of the Lamb with the horns of the Ram, and is the letter of Bacchus or "Christ".

The letter He is the formula of Nuith, which makes possible the process described in the previous notes. But it is not permissible here to explain fully the exact matter or manner of this adjustment. I have preferred the exoteric attributions, which are sufficiently informative for the beginner.

After the magician has created his instrument, and balanced it truly, and filled it with the lightnings of his Will, then is the weapon laid away to rest; and in this Silence, a true Consecration comes.

THE FORMULA OF ALIM

It is extremely interesting to contrast with the above the formula of the elemental Gods deprived of the creative spirit. One might suppose that as ALIM, is the masculine plural of the masculine noun AL, its formula would be more virile than that of ALHIM, which is the masculine plural of the feminine noun ALH. A moment's investigation is sufficient to dissipate the illusion. The word masculine has no meaning except in relation to some feminine correlative.

The word ALIM may in fact be considered as neuter. By a rather absurd convention, neuter objects are treated as feminine on account of their superficial resemblance in passivity and inertness with the unfertilized female. But the female produces life by the intervention of the male, while the neuter does so only when impregnated by Spirit. Thus we find the feminine AMA, becoming AIMA,

AMA is 42, the number of sterility; AIMA, 52, that of fertility, of BN, the SON.

through the operation of the phallic Yod, while ALIM, the congress of dead elements, only fructifies by the brooding of Spirit.

This being so, how can we describe ALIM as containing a Magical Formula? Inquiry discloses the fact that this formula is of a very special kind.

The word adds up to 81, which is a number of the moon. It is thus the formula of witchcraft, which is under Hecate.

See A. Crowley "Orpheus" for the Invocation of this Goddess.

It is only the romantic mediaeval perversion of science that represents young women as partaking in witchcraft, which is, properly speaking, restricted to the use of such women as are no longer women in the Magical sense of the word, because thy are no longer capable of corresponding to the formula of the male, and are therefore neuter rather than feminine. It is for this reason that their method has always been referred to the moon, in that sense of the term in which she appears, not as the feminine correlative of the sun, but as the burnt-out, dead, airless satellite of earth.

No true Magical operation can be performed by the formula of ALIM. All the works of witchcraft are illusory; and their apparent effects depend on the idea that it is possible to alter things by the mere rearrangement of them. One must not rely upon the false analogy of the Xylenes to rebut this argument. It is quite true that geometrical isomers act in different manners towards the substance to which they are brought into relation. And it is of course necessary sometimes to rearrange the elements of a molecule before that molecule can form either the masculine or the feminine element in a true Magical combination with some other molecule.

It is therefore occasionally inevitable for a Magician to reorganize the structure of certain elements before proceeding to his operation proper. Although such work is technically witchcraft, it must not be regarded as undesirable on that ground, for all operations which do not transmute matter fall strictly speaking under this heading.

The real objection to this formula is not inherent in its own nature. Witchcraft consists in treating it as the exclusive preoccupation of Magick, and especially in denying to the Holy Spirit his right to indwell His Temple.

The initiate of the XI Degree of O.T.O. will remark that there is a totally different formula of ALIM, complementary with that here discussed. 81 may be regarded as a number of Yesod rather than of Luna. The actual meaning of the word may be taken as indicating the formula. Aleph may be referred to Harpocrates, with allusion to the well-known poem of Catullus. Lamed may imply the exaltation of Saturn, and suggest the Three of Swords in a particular manner. Yod will then recall Hermes, and Mem the Hanged Man. We have thus a Tetragrammaton which contains no feminine component. The initial Force is here the Holy Spirit and its vehicle or weapon the "Sword and Balances". Justice is then done upon the Mercurial "Virgin", with the result that the Man is "Hanged" or extended, and is slain in this manner. Such an operation makes creation impossible — as in the former case; but here there is no question of re-arrangement; the creative force is employed deliberately for destruction, and is entirely absorbed in its own sphere (or cylinder, on Einstein's equations) of action. This Work is to be regarded as "Holiness to the Lord". The Hebrews, in fact, conferred the title of Qadosh (holy) upon its adepts. Its effect is to consecrate the Magicians who perform it in a very special way. We may take note also of the correspondence of Nine with Teth, XI, Leo, and the Serpent. The great merits of this formula are that it avoids contact with the inferior planes, that it is self-sufficient, that it involves no responsibilities, and that it leaves its masters not only stronger in themselves, but wholly free to fulfil their essential Natures. Its abuse is an abomination.

CHAPTER V

The Formula of I.A.O.

This formula is the principal and most characteristic formula of Osiris, of the Redemption of Mankind. "I" is Isis, Nature, ruined by "A", Apophis the Destroyer, and restored to life by the Redeemer Osiris.

There is a quite different formula in which I is the father, O the Mother, A the child — and yet another, in which I.A.O. are all fathers of different kinds balanced by H.H.H., 3 Mothers, to complete the Universe. In a third, the true formula of the Beast 666, I and O are the opposites which form the field for the operation of A. But this is a higher matter unsuited for this elementary handbook. See, however, Liber Samekh, Point II, Section J.

The same idea is expressed by the Rosicrucian formula of the Trinity:

"Ex Deo nascimur. In Jesu Morimur

Per Spiritum Sanctum reviviscimus."

This is also identical with the Word Lux, L.V.X., which is formed by the arms of a cross. It is this formula which is implied in those ancient and modern monuments in which the phallus is worshipped as the Saviour of the World.

The doctrine of resurrection as vulgarly understood is false and absurd. It is not even "Scriptural". St. Paul does not identify the glorified body which rises with the mortal body which dies. On the contrary, he repeatedly insists on the distinction.

The same is true of a magical ceremony. The magician who is destroyed by absorption in the Godhead is really destroyed. The miserable mortal automaton remains in the Circle. It is of no more consequence to Him that the dust of the floor.

It is, for all that, His instrument, acquired by Him as an astronomer buys a telescope. See Liber Aleph, for a full explanation of the objects attained by the stratagem of incarnation; also Part IV of this Book 4.

But before entering into the details of "I.A.O." as a magick formula it should be remarked that it is essentially the formula of Yoga or meditation; in fact, of elementary mysticism in all its branches.

In beginning a meditation practice, there is always

If not, one is not working properly.

a quiet pleasure, a gentle natural growth; one takes a lively interest in the work; it seems easy; one is quite pleased to have started. This stage represents Isis. Sooner or later it is succeeded by depression — the Dark Night of the Soul, an infinite weariness and detestation of the work. The simplest and easiest acts become almost impossible to perform. Such impotence fills the mind with apprehension and despair. The intensity of this loathing can hardly be understood by any person who has not experienced it. This is the period of Apophis.

It is followed by the arising not of Isis, but of Osiris. The ancient condition is not restored, but a new and superior condition is created, a condition only rendered possible by the process of death.

The Alchemists themselves taught this same truth. The first matter of the work was base and primitive, though "natural". After passing through various stages the "black dragon" appeared; but from this arose the pure and perfect gold.

Even in the legend of Prometheus we find an identical formula concealed; and a similar remark applies to those of Jesus Christ, and of many other mythical god-men worshipped in different countries.

See J.G.Frazer, "The Golden Bough:" J.M.Robertson "Pagan Christs;" A. Crowley "Jesus," etc., etc.

A magical ceremony constructed on this formula is thus in close essential harmony with the natural mystic process. We find it the basis of many important initiations, notably the Third Degree in Masonry, and the 5 Degree = 6Square ceremony of the G.'. D.'. described in Equinox I, III. A ceremonial self-initiation may be constructed with advantage on this formula. The essence of it consists in robing yourself as a king, then stripping and slaying yourself, and rising from that death to the Knowledge and Conversation of the Holy Guardian Angel

This formula, although now superseded by that of HORUS, the Crowned and Conquering Child, remains valid for those who have not yet assimilated the point of view of the Law of Thelema. But see Appendix, Liber SAMEKH. Compare also "The Book of the Spirit of the Living Gods," — where there is a ritual given "in extenso" on slightly different lines: Equinox I, III, pages 269-272.

. There is an etymological identity between Tetragrammaton and "I A O", but the magical formulae are entirely different, as the descriptions here given have schewn.

Professor William James, in his "Varieties of Religious Experience," has well classified religion as the "once-born" and the "twice-born"; but the religion now proclaimed in Liber Legis harmonizes these by transcending them. There is no attempt to get rid of death by denying it, as among the once-born; nor to accept death as the gate of a new life, as among the twice-born. With the A.'. A.'. life and death are equally incidents in a career, very much like day and night in the history of a planet. But, to pursue the simile, we regard this planet from afar. A Brother of A.'. A.'. looks at (what another person would call) "himself", as one — or, rather, some — among a group of phenomena. He is that "nothing" whose consciousness is in one sense the universe considered as a single phenomenon in time and space, and in another sense is the negation of that consciousness. The body and mind of the man are only important (if at all) as the telescope of the astronomer to him. If the telescope were destroyed it would make no appreciable difference to the Universe which that telescope reveals.

It will now be understood that this formula of I A O is a formula of Tiphareth. The magician who employs it is conscious of himself as a man liable to suffering, and anxious to transcend that state by becoming one with god. It will appear to him as the Supreme Ritual, as the final step; but, as has already been pointed out, it is but a preliminary. For the normal man today, however, it represents considerable attainment; and there is a much earlier formula whose investigation will occupy Chapter VI.

THE MASTER THERION, in the Seventeenth year of the Aeon, has reconstructed the Word I A O to satisfy the new conditions of Magick imposed by progress. The Word of the Law being Thelema, whose number is 93, this number should be the canon of a corresponding Mass. Accordingly, he has expanded I A O by treating the O as an Ayin, and then adding Vau as prefix and affix. The full word is then

Vau Yod Aleph Ayin Vau

whose number is 93. We may analyse this new Word in detail and demonstrate that it is a proper hieroglyph of the Ritual of Self-Initiation in this Aeon of Horus. For the correspondence in the following note, see Liber 777. The principal points are these:

Atu (Tarot Trump)	No. of Atu	Hebrew letters	No. of letter	Correspondence in Nature	Other Correspondences
The Hierophant (Osiris throned & crowned, with Wand). Four Worshippers; the four elements.	V	Vau (a nail) English V, W, or vowel between O and Uma'ajab and ma'aruf.	6	Taurus (An earthy sign ruled by Venus; the Moon exalted therein but male.) Liberty, i.e. free will.	The Sun. The son in Tetragrammaton. (See Cap. III). The Pentagram which shows Spirit master & reconciler of the Four Elements. The Hexagram which unites God and Man. The consciousness or Ruach. Parzival as the Child in his widowed mother's care: Horus, son of Isis and the slain Osiris. Parzival as King & Priest in Montsalvat performing the miracle of redemption; Horus crowned and conquering, taking the place of his father. Christ-Bacchus in Heaven-Olympus saving the world.
The Hermit (Hermes with Lamp, Wings, Wand, Cloak, and Serpent).	IX	Yod (a hand) English I or Y.	10	Virgo (an earthy sign ruled by Mercury exalted therein; sexually ambivalent) Light, i.e. of Wisdom, the Inmost.	The root of the Alphabet. The Spermatozoon. The youth setting out on his adventures after receiving the Wand. Parzival in the desert. Christ taking refuge in Egypt, and on the Mount tempted by the Devil. The Unconscious Will, or Word.
The Fool (The Babe in the Egg on the Lotus, Bacchus Diphues, etc.)	O	Aleph (an ox) English A, more or less.	1	Air (The condition of all Life, the impartial vehicle. Sexually undeveloped). Life; i.e. the organ of possible expression.	The free breath. The Svastika. The Holy Ghost. The Virgin's Womb. Parzival as "der reine Thor" who knows nothing. Horus. Christ-Bacchus as the innocent babe, pursued by Herod-Héré. Hercules strangling the serpents. The Unconscious Self not yet determined in any direction.
The Devil (Baphomet throned & adored by Male & Female. See Eliphas Levi's design.)	XV	Ayin (an eye) English A, or O more or less: the bleat of a goat, A'a.	70	Capricornus (an earthy sign ruled by Saturn; Mars exalted therein. Sexually male) Love: i.e. the instinct to satisfy Godhead by uniting it with the Universe.	Parzival in Black Armour, ready to return to Montsalvat as Redeemer-King: Horus come to full growth. Christ-Bacchus with Calvary-Cross Kithairon-Thyrsus.

Iota-Alpha-Digamma varies in significance with successive Aeons.

"Aeon of Isis." Matriarchal Age. The Great Work conceived as a straightforward simple affair. We find the theory reflected in the customs of Matriarchy. Parthenogenesis is supposed to be true. The Virgin (Yod-Virgo) contains in herself the Principle of Growth — the epicene Hermetic seed. It becomes the Babe in the Egg (A — Harpocrates) by virtue of the Spirit (A = Air, impregnating the Mother—Vulture) and this becomes the Sun or Son (Digamma = the letter of Tiphareth, 6, even when spelt as Omega, in Coptic. See 777).

"Aeon of Osiris." Patriarchal age. Two sexes. I conceived as the Father-Wand. (Yod in Tetragrammaton). A the Babe is pursued by the Dragon, who casts a flood from his mouth to swallow it. See "Rev." VII. The Dragon is also the Mother — the "Evil Mother" of Freud. It is Harpocrates, threatened by the crocodile in the Nile. We find the symbolism of the Ark, the Coffin of Osiris, etc. The Lotus is the Yoni; the Water the Amniotic Fluid. In order to live his own life, the child must leave the Mother, and overcome the temptation to return to her for refuge. Kundry, Armida, Jocasta, Circe, etc., are symbols of this force which tempts the Hero. He may take her as his servant

Her sole speech in the last Act is "Dienen: Dienen".

when he has mastered her, so as to heal his father (Amfortas), avenge him (Osiris), or pacify him (Jehovah). But in order to grow to manhood, he must cease to depend on her, earning the Lance (Parzival), claiming his arms (Achilles), or making his club (Hercules)

Note that all these three remain for a time as neuters among woman, prevented from living the male life.

, and wander in the waterless wilderness like Krishna, Jesus, Oedipus, chi. tau. lambda. — until the hour when, as the "King's Son" or knight-errant, he must win the Princess, and set himself upon a strange throne. Almost all the legends of heroes imply this formula in strikingly similar symbols. Digamma. Vau the Sun — Son. He is supposed to be mortal; but how is this shewn? It seems an absolute perversion of truth: the sacred symbols have no hint of it. This lie is the essence of the Great Sorcery. Osirian religion is a Freudian phantasy fashioned of man's dread of death and ignorance of nature. The parthenogenesis-idea persists, but is now the formula for incarnating demi-gods, or divine kings; these must be slain and raised from the dead in one way or another.

All these ideas may be explained by reference to anthropology. But this is not their condemnation, but their justification; for the customs and legends of mankind reflect the true nature of the species.

"Aeon of Horus." Two sexes in one person.

Digamma Iota Alpha Omicron Digamma: 93, the full formula, recognizing the Sun as the Son (Star), as the pre-existent manifested Unit from which all springs and to which all returns. The Great Work is to make the initial Digamma Digamma of Assiah (The world of material illusion) into the final Digamma Iota Digamma of Atziluth,

For these spellings see 777.

the world of pure reality.

Spelling the Name in full, Digamma Digamma + Iota Digamma Delta + Alpha Lambda Pi + Omicron Iota Nu + Digamma Iota = 309 = Sh T = XX + XI = 31 the secret Key of the Law.

Digamma is the manifested Star. Iota is the secret Life .... Serpent

— Light .... Lamp

— Love .... Wand

— Liberty .... Wings

— Silence .... Cloak

These symbols are all shewn in the Atu "The Hermit".

They are the powers of the Yod, whose extension is the Vau.

Yod is the Hand wherewith man does his Will. It is also

The Virgin; his essence is inviolate.

Alpha is the Babe "who has formulated his Father, and made fertile

his Mother" — Harpocrates, etc., as before; but he develops

to

Omicron The exalted "Devil" (also the "other" secret Eye) by the

formula of the Initiation of Horus elsewhere described in

detail. This "Devil" is called Satan or Shaitan, and regarded with horror by people who are ignorant of his formula, and, imagining themselves to be evil, accuse Nature herself of their own phantasmal crime. Satan is Saturn, Set, Abrasax, Adad, Adonis, Attis, Adam, Adonai, etc. The most serious charge against him is that he is the Sun in the South. The Ancient Initiates, dwelling as they did in lands whose blood was the water of the Nile or the Euphrates, connected the South with life-withering heat, and cursed that quarter where the solar darts were deadliest. Even in the legend of Hiram, it is at high noon that he is stricken down and slain. Capricornus is moreover the sign which the sun enterers when he reaches his extreme Southern declination at the Winter Solstice, the season of the death of vegetation, for the folk of the Northern hemisphere. This gave them a second cause for cursing the south. A third; the tyranny of hot, dry, poisonous winds; the menace of deserts or oceans dreadful because mysterious and impassable; these also were connected in their minds with the South. But to us, aware of astronomical facts, this antagonism to the South is a silly superstition which the accidents of their local conditions suggested to our animistic ancestors. We see no enmity between Right and Left, Up and Down, and similar pairs of opposites. These antitheses are real only as a statement of relation; they are the conventions of an arbitrary device for representing our ideas in a pluralistic symbolism based on duality. "Good" must be defined in terms of human ideals and instincts. "East" has no meaning except with reference to the earth's internal affairs; as an absolute direction in space it changes a degree every four minutes. "Up" is the same for no two men, unless one chance to be in the line joining the other with the centre of the earth. "Hard" is the private opinion of our muscles. "True" is an utterly unintelligible epithet which has proved refractory to the analysis of our ablest philosophers.

We have therefore no scruple in restoring the "devil-worship" of such ideas as those which the laws of sound, and the phenomena of speech and hearing, compel us to connect with the group of "Gods" whose names are based upon Sht, or D, vocalized by the free breath A. For these Names imply the qualities of courage, frankness, energy, pride, power and triumph; they are the words which express the creative and paternal will.

Thus "the Devil" is Capricornus, the Goat who leaps upon the loftiest mountains, the Godhead which, if it become manifest in man, makes him Aegipan, the All.

The Sun enters this sign when he turns to renew the year in the North. He is also the vowel O, proper to roar, to boom, and to command, being a forcible breath controlled by the firm circle of the mouth.

He is the Open Eye of the exalted Sun, before whom all shadows flee away: also that Secret Eye which makes an image of its God, the Light, and gives it power to utter oracles, enlightening the mind.

Thus, he is Man made God, exalted, eager; he has come consciously to his full stature, and so is ready to set out on his journey to redeem the world. But he may not appear in this true form; the Vision of Pan would drive men mad with fear. He must conceal Himself in his original guise.

He therefore becomes apparently the man that he was at the beginning; he lives the life of a man; indeed, he is wholly man. But his initiation has made him master of the Event by giving him the understanding that whatever happens to him is the execution of this true will. Thus the last stage of his initiation is expressed in our formula as the final:

Digamma — The series of transformations has not affected his identity; but it has explained him to himself. Similarly, Copper is still Copper after

Cu+O = CuO:+H SO =CuS O(H O):+K S=CuS(K SO):

2 4 4 2 2 2 4 + blowpipe and reducing agent = Cu(S).

It is the same copper, but we have learnt some of its properties. We observe especially that it is indestructible, inviolably itself throughout all its adventures, and in all its disguises. We see moreover that it can only make use of its powers, fulfill the possibilities of its nature, and satisfy its equations, by thus combining with its counterparts. Its existence as a separate substance is evidence of its subjection to stress; and this is felt as the ache of an incomprehensible yearning until it realises that every experience is a relief, an expression of itself; and that it cannot be injured by aught that may befall it. In the Aeon of Osiris it was indeed realised that Man must die in order to live. But now in the Aeon of Horus we know that every event is a death; subject and object slay each other in "love under will"; each such death is itself life, the means by which one realises oneself in a series of episodes.

The second main point is the completion of the A babe Bacchus by the O Pan (Parzival wins the Lance, etc.).

The first process is to find the I in the V — initiation, purification, finding the Secret Root of oneself, the epicene Virgin who is 10 (Malkuth) but spelt in full 20 (Jupiter).

This Yod in the "Virgin" expands to the Babe in the Egg by formulating the Secret Wisdom of Truth of Hermes in the Silence of the Fool. He acquires the Eye-Wand, beholding the acting and being adored. The Inverted Pentagram — Baphomet — the Hermaphrodite fully grown — begets himself on himself as V again.

Note that there are now two sexes in one person throughout, so that each individual is self-procreative sexually, whereas Isis knew only one sex, and Osiris thought the two sexes opposed. Also the formula is now Love in all cases; and the end is the beginning, on a higher plane.

The I is formed from the V by removing its tail, the A by balancing 4 Yods, the O by making an inverted triangle of Yods, which suggests the formula of Nuit — Hadit — Ra-Hoor-Khuit. A is the elements whirling as a Svastika — the creative Energy in equilibrated action.

CHAPTER VI

THE FORMULA OF THE NEOPHYTE.

See the Neophyte Ceremony, Equinox I, II.

This formula has for its "first matter" the ordinary man entirely ignorant of everything and incapable of anything. He is therefore represented as blindfolded and bound. His only aid is his aspiration, represented by the officer who is to lead him into the Temple. Before entering, he must be purified and consecrated. Once within the Temple, he is required to bind himself by an oath. His aspiration is now formulated as Will. He makes the mystic circumambulation of the Temple for the reasons to be described in the Chapter on "Gesture". After further purification and consecration, he is allowed for one moment to see the Lord of the West, and gains courage

Fear is the source of all false perception. Even Freud had a glimpse of this fact.

to persist. For the third time he is purified and consecrated, and he sees the Lord of the East, who holds the balance, keeping him in a straight line. In the West he gains energy. In the East he is prevented from dissipating the same. So fortified, he may be received into the Order as a neophyte by the three principal officers, thus uniting the Cross with the Triangle. He may then be placed between the pillars of the Temple, to receive the fourth and final consecration. In this position the secrets of the grade are communicated to him, and the last of his fetters is removed. All this is sealed by the sacrament of the Four Elements.

It will be seen that the effect of this whole ceremony is to endow a thing inert and impotent with balanced motion in a given direction. Numerous example of this formula are given in Equinox I, Nos. II and III. It is the formula of the Neophyte Ceremony of G.'. D.'. It should be employed in the consecration of the actual weapons used by the magician, and may also be used as the first formula of initiation.

In the book called Z 2

Those sections dealing with divination and alchemy are the most grotesque rubbish in the latter case, and in the former obscure and unpractical.

(Equinox I, III) are given full details of this formula, which cannot be too carefully studied and practised. It is unfortunately, the most complex of all of them. But this is the fault of the first matter of the work, which is so muddled that many operations are required to unify it.

CHAPTER VII

THE FORMULA OF THE HOLY GRAAL:

OF ABRAHADABRA:

"and of certain other Words."

Also: THE MAGICAL MEMORY.

The Hieroglyph shewn in the Seventh Key of the Tarot (described in the 12th Aethyr, Liber 418, Equinox I, V) is the Charioteer of OUR LADY BABALON, whose Cup or Graal he hears.

Now this is an important formula. It is the First of the Formulae, in a sense, for it is the formula of Renunciation.

There is no moral implication here. But to choose A implies to refuse not-A: at least, that is so, below the Abyss.

It is also the Last!

This Cup is said to be full of the Blood of the Saints; that is, every "saint" or magician must give the last drop of his life's blood to that cup. It is the original price paid for magick power. And if by magick power we mean the true power, the assimilation of all force with the Ultimate Light, the true Bridal of the Rosy Cross, then is that blood the offering of Virginity, the sole sacrifice well-pleasing to the Master, the sacrifice whose only reward is the pain of child-bearing unto him.

But "to sell one's soul to the devil", to renounce no matter what for an equivalent in personal gain,

"Supposed" personal gain. There is really no person to gain; so the whole transaction is a swindle on both sides.

is black magic. You are no longer a noble giver of your all, but a mean huckster.

This formula is, however, a little different in symbolism, since it is a Woman whose Cup must be filled. It is rather the sacrifice of the Man, who transfers life to his descendants. For a woman does not carry in herself the principle of new life, except temporarily, when it is given her. But here the formula implies much more even than this. For it is his whole life that the Magus offers to OUR LADY. The Cross is both Death and Generation, and it is on the Cross that the Rose blooms. The full significance of these symbols is so lofty that it is hardly fitted for an elementary treatise of this type. One must be an Exempt Adept, and have become ready to pass on, before one can see the symbols even from the lower plane. Only a Master of the Temple can fully understand them.

(However, the reader may study Liber CLVI, in Equinox I, VI, the 12th and 2nd Aethyrs in Liber 418 in Equinox I, V, and the Symbolism of the V Degree and VI Degree in O.T.O.)

Of the preservation of this blood which OUR LADY offers to the ANCIENT ONE, CHAOS

CHAOS is a general name for the totality of the Units of Existence; it is thus a name feminine in form. Each unit of CHAOS is itself All-Father.

the All-Father, to revive him, and of how his divine Essence fills the Daughter (the soul of Man) and places her upon the Throne of the Mother, fulfilling the Economy of the Universe, and thus ultimately rewarding the

Magician (the Son) ten thousandfold, it would be still more improper to speak in this place. So holy a mystery is the Arcanum of the Masters of the Temple, that it is here hinted at in order to blind the presumptuous who may, unworthy, seek to lift the veil, and at the same time to lighten the darkness of such as may be requiring only one ray of the Sun in order to spring into life and light.

II

ABRAHADABRA is a word to be studied in Equinox I, V., "The Temple of Solomon the King". It represents the Great Work complete, and it is therefore an archetype of all lesser magical operations. It is in a way too perfect to be applied in advance to any of them. But an example of such an operation may be studied in Equinox I, VII, "The Temple of Solomon the King", where an invocation of Horus on this formula is given in full. Note the reverberation of the ideas one against another. The formula of Horus has not yet been so fully worked out in details as to justify a treatise upon its exoteric theory and practice; but one may say that it is, to the formula of Osiris, what the turbine is to the reciprocating engine.

III

There are many other sacred words which enshrine formulae of great efficacity in particular operations.

For example, V.I.T.R.I.O.L. gives a certain Regimen of the Planets useful in Alchemical work. Ararita is a formula of the macrocosm potent in certain very lofty Operations of the Magick of the Inmost Light. (See Liber 813.)

The formula of Thelema may be summarized thus: Theta "Babalon and the Beast conjoined" — epsilon unto Nuith (CCXX, I, 51) — lambda The Work accomplished in Justice — eta The Holy Graal — mu The Water therein — alpha The Babe in the Egg (Harpocrates on the Lotus.)

That of "Agape" is as follows:

Dionysus (Capital Alpha) — The Virgin Earth gamma — The Babe in the Egg (small alpha — the image of the Father) — The Massacre of the Innocents, pi (winepress) — The Draught of Ecstasy, eta.

The student will find it well worth his while to seek out these ideas in detail, and develop the technique of their application.

There is also the Gnostic Name of the Seven Vowels, which gives a musical formula most puissant in evocations of the Soul of Nature. There is moreover ABRAXAS; there is XNOUBIS; there is MEITHRAS; and indeed it may briefly be stated that every true name of God gives the formula of the invocation of that God.

> *Members of the IV Degree of the O.T.O. are well aware of a Magick Word whose analysis contains all truth, human and Divine, a word indeed potent for any group which dares to use it.*

It would therefore be impossible, even were it desirable, to analyse all such names. The general method of doing so has been given, and the magician must himself work out his own formula for particular cases.

> *The Holy Qabalah (see Liber D in Equinox I, VIII, Supplement, and Liber 777) affords the means of analysis and application required. See also Equinox I, V, "The Temple of Solomon The King".*

IV.

It should also be remarked that every grade has its peculiar magical formula. Thus, the formula of Abrahadabra concerns us, as men, principally because each of us represents the pentagram or microcosm; and our equilibration must therefore be with the hexagram or macrocosm. In other words, 5 Degree = 6Square is the formula of the Solar operation; but then 6 Degree = 5Square is the formula of the Martial operation, and this reversal of the figures implies a very different Work. In the former instance the problem was to dissolve the microcosm in the macrocosm; but this other problem is to separate a particular force from the macrocosm, just as a savage might hew out a flint axe from the deposits in a chalk cliff. Similarly, an operation of Jupiter will be of the nature of the equilibration of him with Venus. Its graphic formula will be 7 Degree = 4Square, and there will be a word in which the character of this operation is described, just as Abrahadabra describes the Operation of the Great Work.

It may be stated without unfairness, as a rough general principle, that the farther from original equality are the two sides of the equation, the more difficult is the operation to perform.

Thus, to take the case of the personal operation symbolized by the grades, it is harder to become a Neophyte, 1'=10', than to pass from that grade to Zelator, 2'=9'.

Initiation is, therefore, progressively easier, in a certain sense, after the first step is taken. But (especially after the passing of Tiphareth) the distance between grade and grade increases as it were by a geometrical progression with an enormously high factor, which itself progresses.

A suggestion has recently been made that the Hierarchy of the Grades should be "destroyed, and replaced by" — a ring system of 13 grades all equal. There is, of course, one sense in which every grade is a Thing-in-Itself. But the Hierarchy is only a convenient method of classifying observed facts. One is reminded of the Democracy, who, on being informed by the Minister of the Interior that the scarcity of provisions was due to the Law of Supply and Demand, passed a unanimous resolution calling for the immediate repeal of that iniquitous measure!

Every person, whatever his grade in the Order, has also a "natural" grade appropriate to his intrinsic virtue. He may expect to be "cast out" into that grade when he becomes 8'=3'. Thus one man, throughout his career, may be essentially of the type of Netzach; another, of Hod. In the same way Rembrandt and Raphael retained their respective points of view in all stages of their art. The practical consideration is that some aspirants may find it unusually difficult to attain certain grades; or, worse, allow their inherent predispositions to influence them to neglect antipathetic, and indulge sympathetic, types of work. They may thus become more unbalanced than ever, with disastrous results. Success in one's favourite pursuit is a temptress; whose yields to her wiles limits his own growth. True, every Will is partial; but, even so, it can only fulfill itself by symmetrical expansion. It must be adjusted to the Universe, or fail of perfection.

It is evidently impossible to give details of all these formulae. Before beginning any operation soever the magician must make a through Qabalistic study of it so as to work out its theory in symmetry of perfection. Preparedness in Magick is as important as it is in War.

V

It should be profitable to make a somewhat detailed study of the strange-looking word AUMGN, for its analysis affords an excellent illustration of the principles on which the Practicus may construct his own Sacred Words.

This word has been uttered by the MASTER THERION himself, as a means of declaring his own personal work as the Beast, the Logos of the Aeon. To understand it, we must make a preliminary consideration of the word which it replaces and from which it was developed: the word AUM.

The word AUM is the sacred Hindu mantra which was the supreme hieroglyph of Truth, a compendium of the Sacred Knowledge. Many volumes have been written with regard to it; but, for our present purpose, it will be necessary only to explain how it came to serve for the representation of the principal philosophical tenets of the Rishis.

Firstly, it represents the complete course of sound. It is pronounced by forcing the breath from the back of the throat with the mouth wide open, through the buccal cavity with the lips so shaped as to modify the sound from A to O (or U), to the closed lips, when it becomes M. Symbolically, this announces the course of Nature as proceeding from free and formless creation through controlled and formed preservation to the silence of destruction. The three sounds are harmonized into one; and thus the word represents the Hindu Trinity of Brahma, Vishnu, and Shiva; and the operations in the Universe of their triune energy. It is thus the formula of a Manvantara, or period of manifested existence, which alternates with a Pralaya, during which creation is latent.

Analysed Qabalistically, the word is found to possess similar properties. A is the negative, and also the unity which concentrates it into a positive form. A is the Holy Spirit who begets God in flesh upon the Virgin, according to the formula familiar to students of "The Golden Bough". A is also the "babe in the Egg" thus produced. The quality of A is thus bisexual. It is the original being — Zeus Arrhenothelus, Bacchus Diphues, or Baphomet.

U or V is the manifested son himself. Its number is 6. It refers therefore, to the dual nature of the Logos as divine and human; the interlacing of the upright and averse triangles in the hexagram. It is the first number of the Sun, whose last number

The Sun being 6, a square 6x6 contains 36 squares. We arrange the numbers from 1 to 36 in this square, so that each line, file, and diagonal adds to the same number. This number is 111; the total of all is 666.

is 666, "the number of a man".

The letter M exhibits the termination of this process. It is the Hanged Man of the Tarot; the formation of the individual from the absolute is closed by his death.

We see accordingly how AUM is, on either system, the expression of a dogma which implies catastrophe in nature. It is cognate with the formula of the Slain God. The "resurrection" and "ascension" are not implied in it. They are later inventions without basis in necessity; they may be described indeed as Freudian phantasms conjured up by the fear of facing reality. To the Hindu, indeed, they are still less respectable. in his view, existence is essentially objectionable

Thelemites agree that manifested existence implies Imperfection. But they understand why Perfection devises this disguise. The Theory is developed fully in Liber Aleph, and in Part IV of this Book 4. See also Cap V Paragraph on Digamma final of Digamma-Iota-Alpha-Omicron-Digamma.

; and his principle concern is to invoke Shiva

The Vaishnava theory, superficially opposed to this, turns out on analysis to be practically identical.

to destroy the illusion whose thrall is the curse of the Manvantara.

The cardinal revelation of the Great Aeon of Horus is that this formula AUM does not represent the facts of nature. The point of view is based upon misapprehension of the character of existence. It soon became obvious to The Master Therion that AUM was an inadequate and misleading hieroglyph. It stated only part of the truth, and it implied a fundamental falsehood. He consequently determined to modify the word in such a manner as to fit it to represent the Arcana unveiled by the Aeon of which He had attained to be the Logos.

The essential task was to emphasize the fact that nature is not catastrophic, but proceeds by means of undulations. It might be suggested that Manvantara and Pralaya are in reality complementary curves; but the Hindu doctrine insists strongly on denying continuity to the successive phases. It was nevertheless important to avoid disturbing the Trinitarian arrangement of the word, as would be done by the addition of other letters. It was equally desirable to make it clear that the letter M represents an operation which does not actually occur in nature except as the withdrawal of phenomena into the absolute; which process, even when so understood, is not a true destruction, but, on the contrary, the emancipation of anything from the modifications which it had mistaken for itself. It occurred to him that the true nature of Silence was to permit the uninterrupted vibration of the undulatory energy, free from the false conceptions attached to it by the Ahamkara or Ego-making facility, whose assumption that conscious individuality constitutes existence let it to consider its own apparently catastrophic character as pertaining to the order of nature.

The undulatory formula of putrefaction is represented in the Qabalah by the letter N, which refers to Scorpio, whose triune nature combines the Eagle, Snake and Scorpion. These hieroglyphs themselves indicate the spiritual formulae of incarnation. He was also anxious to use the letter G, another triune formula expressive of the aspects of the moon, which further declares the nature of human existence in the following manner. The moon is in itself a dark orb; but an appearance of light is communicated to it by the sun; and it is exactly in this way that successive incarnations create the appearance, just as the individual star, which every man is, remains itself, irrespective of whether earth perceives it or not.

Now it so happens that the root GN signifies both knowledge and generation combined in a single idea, in an absolute form independent of personality. The G is a silent letter, as in our word Gnosis; and the sound GN is nasal, suggesting therefore the breath of life as opposed to that of speech. Impelled by these considerations, the Master Therion proposed to replace the M of AUM by a compound letter MGN, symbolizing thereby the subtle transformation of the apparent silence and death which terminates the manifested life of Vau by a continuous vibration of an impersonal energy of the nature of generation and knowledge, the Virgin Moon and the Serpent furthermore operating to include in the idea a commemoration of the legend so grossly deformed in the Hebrew legend of the Garden of Eden, and its even more malignantly debased falsification in that bitterly sectarian broadside, the Apocalypse.

Sound work invariable vindicates itself by furnishing confirmatory corollaries not contemplated by the Qabalist. In the present instance, the Master Therion was delighted to remark that his compound letter MGN, constructed on theoretical principles with the idea of incorporating the new knowledge of the Aeon, had the value of 93 (M = 40, G = 3, N = 50). 93 is the number of the word of the Law — Thelema — Will, and of Agape — Love, which indicates the nature of Will. It is furthermore the number of the Word which overcomes death, as members of the degree of M M of the O.T.O. are well aware;

WEH NOTE: III Degree O.T.O., a word never to be written, published or spoken without the rite.

and it is also that of the complete formula of existence as expressed in the True Word of the Neophyte,

WEH NOTE: Another unpublished word, this time belonging to the A.'. A.'. and not to O.T.O. The two words are different, even to the number of letters. It was written down once, in a letter to Frank Bennett.

where existence is taken to import that phase of the whole which is the finite resolution of the Qabalistic Zero.

Finally, the total numeration of the Word AUMGN is 100, which, as initiates of the Sanctuary of the Gnosis of the O.T.O.

WEH NOTE: IX Degree O.T.O.

are taught, expresses the unity under the form of complete manifestation by the symbolism of pure number, being Kether by Aiq Bkr

A method of exegesis in which 1 = 10 = 100, 2 = 20 = 200, etc.

; also Malkuth multiplied by itself

10 to the 2 power = 100.

, and thus established in the phenomenal universe. But, moreover, this number 100 mysteriously indicates the Magical formula of the Universe as a reverberatory engine for the extension of Nothingness through the device of equilibrated opposites.

Koph-Pehfinal = 100 (20 + 80). HB:Koph = chi = Kappa-tau-epsilon-iota-sigma: HB:Pehfinal = phi = Phi-alpha-lambda-lambda-omicron-sigma; (by Notariqon).

It is moreover the value of the letter Qoph, which means "the back of the head", the cerebellum, where the creative or reproductive force is primarily situated. Qoph in the Tarot is "the Moon", a card suggesting illusion, yet shewing counterpartal forces operating in darkness, and the Winged Beetle or Midnight Sun in his Bark travelling through the Nadir. Its Yetziratic attribution is Pisces, symbolic of the positive and negative currents of fluidic energy, the male Ichthus or "Pesce" and the female Vesica, seeking respectively the anode and kathode. The number 100 is therefore a synthetic glyph of the subtle energies employed in creating the Illusion, or Reflection of Reality, which we call manifested existence.

The above are the principal considerations in the matter of AUMGN. They should suffice to illustrate to the student the methods employed in the construction of the hieroglyphics of Magick, and to arm him with a mantra of terrific power by virtue whereof he may apprehend the Universe, and control in himself its Karmic consequences.

VI

THE MAGICAL MEMORY.

WEH NOTE: This is not the same "Magical Memory" as that described by F. A. Yates and used by the ancient Roman orators for mnemonics.

I

There is no more important task than the exploration of one's previous incarnations.

It has been objected to reincarnation that the population of this planet has been increasing rapidly. Where do the new souls come from? It is not necessary to invent theories about other planets; it is enough to say that the earth is passing through a period when human units are being built up from the elements with increased frequency. The evidence for this theory springs to the eye: in what other age was there such puerility, such lack of race-experience, such reliance upon incoherent formulas? (Contrast the infantile emotionalism and credulity of the average "well-educated" Anglo-Saxon with the shrewd common sense of the normal illiterate peasant.) A large proportion of mankind today is composed of "souls" who are living the human life for the first time. Note especially the incredible spread of congenital homosexuality and other sexual deficiencies in many forms. These are the people who have not understood, accepted, and used even the Formula of Osiris. Kin to them are the "once-born" of William James, who are incapable of philosophy, magick, or even religion, but seek instinctively a refuge from the horror of contemplating Nature, which they do not comprehend, in soothing-syrup affirmations such as those of Christian Science, Spiritualism, and all the sham 'occult' creeds, as well as the emasculated forms of so-called Christianity.

As Zoroaster says: "Explore the river of the soul; whence and in what order thou has come." One cannot do one's True Will intelligently unless one knows what it is. Liber Thisarb, Equinox I, VII, give instructions for determining this by calculating the resultant of the forces which have made one what one is. But this practice is confined to one's present incarnation.

If one were to wake up in a boat on a strange river, it would be rash to conclude that the direction of the one reach visible was that of the whole stream. It would help very much if one remembered the bearings of previous reaches traversed before one's nap. It would further relieve one's anxiety when one became aware that a uniform and constant force was the single determinant of all the findings of the stream: gravitation. We could rejoice "that even the weariest river winds somewhere safe to sea."

Liber Thisarb describes a method of obtaining the Magical Memory by learning to remember backwards. But the careful practice of Dharana is perhaps more generally useful. As one prevents the more accessible thoughts from arising, we strike deeper strata — memories of childhood reawaken. Still deeper lies a class of thoughts whose origin puzzles us. Some of these apparently belong to former incarnations. By cultivating these departments of one's mind we can develop them; we become expert; we form an organized coherence of these originally disconnected elements; the faculty grows with astonishing rapidity, once the knack of the business is mastered.

It is much easier (for obvious reasons) to acquire the Magical Memory when one has been sworn for many lives to reincarnate immediately. The great obstacle is the phenomenon called Freudian forgetfulness; that is to say, that, though an unpleasant event may be recorded faithfully enough by the mechanism of the brain, we fail to recall it, or recall it wrong, because it is painful. "The Psychopathology of Everyday Life" analyses and illustrates this phenomenon in detail. Now, the King of Terrors being Death, it is hard indeed to look it in the face. Mankind has created a host of phantastic masks; people talk of "going to heaven", "passing over", and so on; banners flaunted from pasteboard towers of baseless theories. One instinctively flinches from remembering one's last, as one does from imagining one's next, death.

This later is a very valuable practice to perform. See Liber HHH; also read up the Buddhist meditations of the Ten Impurities. {WEH NOTE ADENDA: Right, but it scares the dickens out of you! When I succeeded in the practice in my teens, I panicked out of using the related abilities for several years. This was without benefit of initiation.}

The point of view of the initiate helps one immensely.

As soon as one has passed this Pons Asinorum, the practice becomes much easier. It is much less trouble to reach the life before the last; familiarity with death breeds contempt for it.

It is a very great assistance to the beginner if he happens to have some intellectual grounds for identifying himself with some definite person in the immediate past. A brief account of Aleister Crowley's good fortune in this matter should be instructive. It will be seen that the points of contact vary greatly in character. 1. The date of Eliphas Levi's death was about six months previous to that of Aleister Crowley's birth. The reincarnating ego is supposed to take possession of the foetus at about this stage of development.

2. Eliphas Levi had a striking personal resemblance to Aleister Crowley's father. This of course merely suggests a certain degree of suitability from a physical point of view.

3. Aleister Crowley wrote a play called "The Fatal Force" at a time when he had not read any of Eliphas Levi's works. The motive of this play is a Magical Operation of a very peculiar kind. The formula which Aleister Crowley supposed to be his original idea is mentioned by Levi. We have not been able to trace it anywhere else with such exact correspondence in every detail.

4. Aleister Crowley found a certain quarter of Paris incomprehensibly familiar and attractive to him. This was not the ordinary phenomenon of the "deja vu", it was chiefly a sense of being at home again. He discovered long after that Levi had lived in the neighbourhood for many years.

5. There are many curious similarities between the events of Eliphas Levi's life and that of Aleister Crowley. The intention of the parents that their son should have a religious career; the inability to make use of very remarkable talents in any regular way; the inexplicable ostracism which afflicted him, and whose authors seemed somehow to be ashamed of themselves; the events relative to marriage:

> *Levi, on her deliberately abandoning him, withdrew his protection from his wife; she lost her beauty and intelligence, and became the prey of an aged and hideous pithecoid. Aleister Crowley's wife insisted upon doing her own will, as she defined it; this compelled him to stand aside. What happened to Mme. Constant happened to her, although in a more violent and disastrous form.*

all these offer surprisingly close parallels.

6. The characters of the two men present subtle identities in many points. Both seem to be constantly trying to reconcile insuperable antagonisms. Both find it hard to destroy the delusion that men's fixed beliefs and customs may be radically altered by a few friendly explanations. Both show a curious fondness for out-the-way learning, preferring recondite sources of knowledge they adopt eccentric appearances. Both inspire what can only be called panic fear in absolute strangers, who can give no reason whatever for a repulsion which sometimes almost amounts to temporary insanity. The ruling passion in each case is that of helping humanity. Both show quixotic disregard of their personal prosperity, and even comfort, yet both display love of luxury and splendour. Both have the pride of Satan.

7. When Aleister Crowley became Frater Omicron-Upsilon Mu-Eta and had to write his thesis for the grade of Adeptus Exemptus, he had already collected his ideas when Levi's "Clef des Grands Mysteres" fell into his hands. It was remarkable that he, having admired Levi for many years, and even begun to suspect the identity, had not troubled (although an extravagant buyer of books) to get this particular work. He found, to his astonishment, that almost everything that he had himself intended to say was there written. The result of this was that he abandoned writing his original work, and instead translated the masterpiece in question.

8. The style of the two men is strikingly similar in numerous subtle and deep-seated ways. The general point of view is almost identical. The quality of the irony is the same. Both take a perverse pleasure in playing practical jokes on the reader. In one point, above all, the identity is absolute — there is no third name in literature which can be put in the same class. The point is this: In a single sentence is combined sublimity and enthusiasm with sneering bitterness, scepticism, grossness and scorn. It is evidently the supreme enjoyment to strike a chord composed of as many conflicting elements as possible. The pleasure seems to be derived from gratifying the sense of power, the power to compel every possible element of thought to contribute to the

spasm.

If the theory of reincarnation were generally accepted, the above considerations would make out a strong case. FRATER PERDURABO was quite convinced in one part of his mind of this identity, long before he got any actual memories as such.

Long since writing the above, the publication of the biography of Eliphas Levi by M. Paul Chacornat has confirmed the hypothesis in innumerable striking ways.

II

Unless one has a groundwork of this sort to start with, one must get back to one's life as best one can by the methods above indicated. It may be of some assistance to give a few characteristics of genuine Magical Memory; to mention a few sources of error, and to lay down critical rules for the verification of one's results.

The first great danger arises from vanity. One should always beware of "remembering" that one was Cleopatra or Shakespeare.

Again, superficial resemblances are usually misleading.

One of the great tests of the genuineness of any recollection is that one remembers the really important things in one's life, not those which mankind commonly classes as such. For instance, Aleister Crowley does not remember any of the decisive events in the life of Eliphas Levi. He recalls intimate trivialities of childhood. He has a vivid recollection of certain spiritual crises; in particular, one which was fought out as he paced up and down a lonely stretch of road in a flat and desolate district. He remembers ridiculous incidents, such as often happen at suppers when the conversation takes a turn such that its gaiety somehow strikes to the soul, and one receives a supreme revelation which is yet perfectly inarticulate. He has forgotten his marriage and its tragic results,

It is perhaps significant that although the name of the woman has been familiar to him since 1898, he has never been able to commit it to memory.

although the plagiarism which Fate has been shameless enough to perpetrate in this present life, would naturally, one might think, reopen the wound.

There is a sense which assures us intuitively when we are running on a scent breast high. There is an "oddness" about the memory which is somehow annoying. It gives a feeling of shame and guiltiness. There is a tendency to blush. One feels like a schoolboy caught red-handed in the act of writing poetry. There is the same sort of feeling as one has when one finds a faded photograph or a lock of hair twenty years old among the rubbish in some forgotten cabinet. This feeling is independent of the question whether the thing remembered was in itself a source of pleasure or of pain. Can it be that we resent the idea of our "previous condition of servitude"? We want to forget the past, however good reason we may have to be proud of it. It is well known that many men are embarrassed in the presence of a monkey.

When the "loss of face" does not occur, distrust the accuracy of the item which you recall, The only reliable recollections which present themselves with serenity are invariably connected with what men call disasters. Instead of the feeling of being caught in the slips, one has that of being missed at the wicket. One has the sly satisfaction of having done an outrageously foolish thing and got off scot free. When one sees life in perspective, it is an immense relief to discover that things like bankruptcy, wedlock, and the gallows made no particular difference. They were only accidents such as might happen to anybody; they had no real bearing on the point at issue. One consequently remembers having one's ears cropped as a lucky escape, while the causal jest of a drunken skeinsmate in an all-night cafe stings one with the shame of the parvenu to whom a polite stranger has unsuspectingly mentioned "Mine Uncle".

The testimony of intuitions is, however, strictly subjective, and shrieks for collateral security. It would be a great error to ask too much. In consequence of the peculiar character of the recollections which are under the microscope, anything in the shape of gross confirmation almost presumes perjury. A pathologist would arouse suspicion if he said that his bacilli had arranged themselves on the slide so as to spell Staphylococcus. We distrust an arrangement of flowers which tells us that "Life is worth living in Detroit, Michigan". Suppose that Aleister Crowley remembers that he was Sir Edward Kelly. It does not follow that he will be able to give us details of Cracow in the time of James I of England. Material events are the words of an arbitrary language; the symbols of a cipher previously agreed on. What happened to Kelly in Cracow may have meant something to him, but there is no reason to presume that it has any meaning for his successor. There is an obvious line of criticism about any recollection. It must not clash with ascertained facts. For example — one cannot have two lives which overlap, unless there is reason to suppose that the earlier died spiritually before his body ceased to breathe. This might happen in certain cases, such as insanity.

It is not conclusive against a previous incarnation that the present should be inferior to the past. One's life may represent the full possibilities of a certain partial Karma. One may have devoted one's incarnation to discharging the liabilities of one part of one's previous character. For instance, one might devote a lifetime to settling the bill run up by Napoleon for causing unnecessary suffering, with the object of starting afresh, clear of debt, in a life devoted to reaping the reward of the Corsican's invaluable services to the race.

The Master Therion, in fact, remembers several incarnations of almost uncompensated wretchedness, anguish and humiliation, voluntarily undertaken so that he might resume his work unhampered by spiritual creditors.

These are the stigmata. Memory is hall-marked by its correspondence with the facts actually observed in the present. This correspondence may be of two kinds. It is rare (and it is unimportant for the reasons stated above) that one's memory should be confirmed by what may be called, contemptuously, external evidence. It was indeed a reliable contribution to psychology to remark that an evil and adulterous generation sought for a sign.

(Even so, the permanent value of the observation is to trace the genealogy of the Pharisee — from Caiaphas to the modern Christian.)

Signs mislead, from "Painless Dentistry" upwards. The fact that anything is intelligible proves that it is addressed to the wrong quarter, because the very existence of language presupposes impotence to communicate directly. When Walter Raleigh flung his cloak upon the muddy road, he merely expressed, in a cipher contrived by a combination of circumstances, his otherwise inexpressible wish to get on good terms with Queen Elizabeth. The significance of his action was determined by the concourse of circumstances. The reality can have no reason for reproducing itself exclusively in that especial form. It can have no reason for remembering that so extravagant a ritual happened to be necessary to worship. Therefore, however well a man might remember his incarnation as Julius Caesar, there is no necessity for his representing his power to set all upon the hazard of a die by imagining the Rubicon. Any spiritual state can be symbolized by an infinite variety of actions in an infinite variety of circumstances. One should recollect only those events which happen to be immediately linked with one's peculiar tendencies to imagine one thing rather than another.

The exception is when some whimsical circumstance ties a knot in the corner of one's mnemonic handkerchief.

Genuine recollections almost invariably explain oneself to oneself. Suppose, for example, that you feel an instinctive aversion to some particular kind of wine. Try as you will, you can find no reason for your idiosyncrasy. Suppose, then, that when you explore some previous incarnation, you remember that you died by a poison administered in a wine of that character, your aversion is explained by the proverb, "A burnt child dreads the fire." It may be objected that in such a case your libido has created a phantasm of itself in the manner which Freud has explained. The criticism is just, but its value is reduced if it should happen that you were not aware of its existence until your Magical Memory attracted your attention to it. In fact, the essence of the test consists in this: that your memory notifies you of something which is the logical conclusion of the premisses postulated by the past.

As an example, we may cite certain memories of the Master Therion. He followed a train of thought which led him to remember his life as a Roman named Marius de Aquila. It would be straining probability to presume a connection between (alpha) this hieroglyphically recorded mode of self-analysis and (beta) ordinary introspection conducted on principles intelligible to himself. He remembers directly various people and various events connected with this incarnation; and they are in themselves to all appearance actual. There is no particular reason why they, rather than any others, should have entered his sphere. In the act of remembering them, they are absolute. He can find no reason for correlating them with anything in the present. But a subsequent examination of the record shows that the logical result of the Work of Marius de Aquila did not occur to that romantic reprobate; in point of fact, he died before anything could happen. Can we suppose that any cause can be baulked of effect? The Universe is unanimous in rebuttal. If then the exact effects which might be expected to result from these causes are manifested in the career of the Master Therion, it is assuredly the easiest and most reasonable explanation to assume an identity between the two men. Nobody is shocked to observe that the ambition of Napoleon has diminished the average stature of Frenchmen. We know that somehow or other every force must find its fulfilment; and those people who have grasped the fact that external events are merely symptoms of external ideas, cannot find any difficulty in attributing the correspondences of the one to the identities of the other. Far be it from any apologist for Magick to insist upon the objective validity of these concatenations! It would be childish to cling to the belief that Marius de Aquila actually existed; it matters no more that it matters to the mathematician whether the use of the symbol X to the 22 power involves the "reality" of 22 dimension of space. The Master Therion does not care a scrap of yesterday's newspaper whether he was Marius de Aquila, or whether there ever was such a person, or whether the Universe itself is anything more than a nightmare created by his own imprudence in the matter of rum and water. His memory of Marius de Aquila, of the adventures of that person in Rome and the Black Forest, matters nothing, either to him or to anybody else. What matters is this: True or false, he has found a symbolic form which has enabled him to govern himself to the best advantage. "Quantum nobis prodest hec fabula Christi!" The "falsity" of Aesop's Fables does not diminish their value to mankind.

The above reduction of the Magical Memory to a device for externalizing one's interior wisdom need not be regarded as sceptical, save only in the last resort. No scientific hypothesis can adduce stronger evidence of its validity than the confirmation of its predictions by experimental evidence. The objective can always be expressed in subjective symbols if necessary. The controversy is ultimately unmeaning. However we interpret the evidence, its relative truth depends in its internal coherence. We may therefore say that any magical recollection is genuine if it gives the explanation of our external or internal conditions. Anything which throws light upon the Universe, anything which reveals us to ourselves, should be welcome in this world of riddles.

As our record extends into the past, the evidence of its truth is cumulative. Every incarnation that we remember must increase our comprehension of ourselves as we are. Each accession of knowledge must indicate with unmistakable accuracy the solution of some enigma which is propounded by the Sphynx of our own unknown birth-city, Thebes. The complicated situation in which we find ourselves is composed of elements; and no element of it came out of nothing. Newton's First Law applies to every plane of thought. The theory of evolution is omniform. There is a reason for one's predisposition to gout, or the shape of one's ear, in the past. The symbolism may change; the facts do not. In one form or another, everything that exists is derived from some previous manifestation. Have it, if you will, that the memories of other incarnations are dreams; but dreams are determined by reality just as much as the events of the day. The truth is to be apprehended by the correct translation of the symbolic language. The last section of the Oath of the Master of the Temple is: "I swear to interpret every phenomenon as a particular dealing of God with my soul." The Magical Memory is (in the last analysis) one manner, and, as experience testifies, one of the most important manners, of performing this vow.

CHAPTER VIII

OF EQUILIBRIUM, AND OF THE GENERAL AND PARTICULAR METHOD OF PREPARATION OF THE FURNITURE OF THE TEMPLE AND OF THE INSTRUMENTS OF ART.

I

"Before there was equilibrium, countenance beheld not countenance."

> *The full significance of this aphorism is an Arcanum of the grade of Ipsissimus. It may, however, be partially apprehended by study of Liber Aleph, and the Book of the Law and the Commentaries thereon. It explains Existence.*

So sayeth the holiest of the Books of the ancient Qabalah. (Siphra Tzeniutha 1. 2.) One countenance here spoken of is the Macrocosm, the other the Microcosm.

> *This is the case because we happen ourselves to be Microcosms whose Law is "love under will". But it is also Magick for an unit which has attained Perfection (in absolute nothingness, 0 Degree), to become "divided for love's sake, for the chance of union".*

As said above, the object of any magick ceremony is to unite the Macrocosm and the Microcosm.

It is as in optics; the angles of incidence and reflection are equal. You must get your Macrocosm and Microcosm exactly balanced, vertically and horizontally, or the images will not coincide.

This equilibrium is affirmed by the magician in arranging the Temple. Nothing must be lop-sided. If you have anything in the North, you must put something equal and opposite to it in the South. The importance of this is so great, and the truth of it so obvious, that no one with the most mediocre capacity for magick can tolerate any unbalanced object for a moment. His instinct instantly revolts.

> *This is because the essence of his being a Magician is his intuitive apprehension of the fundamental principles of the Universe. His instinct is a subconscious assertion of the structural identity of the Macrocosm and the Microcosm. Equilibrium is the condition of manifested existence.*

. For this reason the weapons, altar, circle, and magus are all carefully proportioned one with another. It will not do to have a cup like a thimble and a wand like a weaver's beam.

> *See Bagh-i-Muattar, V, par. 2.*

Again, the arrangement of the weapons of the altar must be such that they "look" balanced. Nor should the magician have any unbalanced ornament. If he have the wand in his right hand, let him have the Ring

> *The Ring has not been described in Part II of this book, for reasons which may be or may not be apparent to the reader. It is the symbol of Nuit, the totality of the possible ways in which he may represent himself and fulfill himself.*

on his left, or let him take the Ankh, or the Bell, or the Cup. And however little he move to the right, let him balance it by an equivalent movement to the left; or if forwards, backwards; and let him correct each idea by implying the contradictory contained therein. If he invoke Severity, let him recount that Severity is the instrument of Mercy;

For example, as when Firmness with one's self or another is the truest kindness; or when amputation saves life.

if Stability, let him show the basis of that Stability to be constant change, just as the stability of a molecule is secured by the momentum of the swift atoms contained in it.

See Liber 418, 11th Aethyr.

In this way let every idea go forth as a triangle on the base of two opposites, making an apex transcending their contradiction in a higher harmony.

It is not safe to use any thought in Magick, unless that thought has been thus equilibrated and destroyed.

Thus again with the instruments themselves; the Wand must be ready to change into a Serpent, the Pantacle into the whirling Svastika or Disk of Jove, as if to fulfil the functions of the Sword. The Cross is both the death of the "Saviour"

It is the extension in matter of the Individual Self, the Indivisible Point determined by reference to the Four Quarters. This is the formula which enables it to express its Secret Self; its dew falling upon the Rose is developed into an Eidolon of Itself, in due season.

and the Phallic symbol of Resurrection. Will itself must be ready to culminate in the surrender of that Will:

See Liber LXV and Liber VII.

the aspiration's arrow that is shot against the Holy Dove must transmute itself into the wondering Virgin that receives in her womb the quickening of that same Spirit of God.

Any idea that is thus in itself positive and negative, active and passive, male and female, is fit to exist above the Abyss; any idea not so equilibrated is below the Abyss, contains in itself an unmitigated duality or falsehood, and is to that extent qliphotic

See The Qabalah for the use of this word, and study the doctrine concerning the Kings of Edom.

and dangerous. Even an idea like "truth" is unsafe unless it is realized that all Truth is in one sense falsehood. For all Truth is relative; and if it be supposed absolute, will mislead.

See Poincare for the mathematical proof of this thesis. But Spiritual Experience goes yet deeper, and destroys the Canon of the Law of Contradiction. There is an immense amount of work by the Master Therion on this subject; it pertains especially to His grade of 9 Degree = 2Square. Such profundities are unsuited to the Student, and may unsettle him seriously. It will be best for him to consider (provisionally) Truth in the sense in which it is taken by Physical Science.

"The Book of Lies falsely so called" (Liber 333) is worthy of close and careful study in this respect. The reader should also consult Konx Om Pax, "Introduction", and "Thien Tao" in the same volume.

All this is to be expressed in the words of the ritual itself, and symbolised in every act performed.

II

It is said in the ancient books of Magick that everything used by the Magician must be "virgin". That is: it must never have been used by any other person or for any other purpose. The greatest importance was attached by the Adepts of old to this, and it made the task of the Magician no easy one. He wanted a wand; and in order to cut and trim it he needed a knife. It was not sufficient merely to buy a new knife; he felt that he had to make it himself. In order to make the knife, he would require a hundred other things, the acquisition of each of which might require a hundred more; and so on. This shows the impossibility of disentangling one's self from one's environment. Even in Magick we cannot get on without the help of others.

It is, and the fact is still more important, utterly fatal and demoralizing to acquire the habit of reliance on others. The Magician must know every detail of his work, and be able and willing to roll up his shirtsleeves and do it, no matter how trivial or menial it may seem. Abramelin (it is true) forbids the Aspirant to perform any tasks of an humiliating type; but he will never be able to command perfect service unless he has experience of such necessary work, mastered during his early training.

There was, however, a further object in this recommendation. The more trouble and difficulty your weapon costs, the more useful you will find it. "If you want a thing well done, do it yourself." It would be quite useless to take this book to a department store, and instruct them to furnish you a Temple according to specification. It is really worth the while of the Student who requires a sword to go and dig out iron ore from the earth, to smelt it himself with charcoal that he has himself prepared, to forge the weapon with his own hand: and even to take the trouble of synthesizing the oil of virtiol with which it is engraved. He will have learnt a lot of useful things in his attempt to make a really virgin sword; he will understand how one thing depends upon another; he will begin to appreciate the meaning of the words "the harmony of the Universe", so often used so stupidly and superficially by the ordinary apologist for Nature, and he will also perceive the true operation of the law of Karma.

In this sense especially: any one thing involves, and is involved in, others apparently altogether alien.

Another notable injunction of the ancient Magick was that whatever appertained to the Work should be "single". The Wand was to be cut with a single stroke of the knife. There must be no boggling and hacking at things, no clumsiness and no hesitation. If you strike a blow at all, strike with your strength! "Whatsoever thy hand findeth to do, do it with all thy might!" If you are going to take up Magick, make no compromise. You cannot make revolutions with rose-water, or wrestle in a silk hat. You will find very soon that you must either lose the hat or stop wrestling. Most people do both. They take up the magical path without sufficient reflection, without that determination of adamant which made the author of this book exclaim, as he took the first oath, "PERDURABO" — "I will endure unto the end!"

"For enduring unto the End, at the End was Naught to endure." Liber 333, Cap Zeta.

They start on it at a great pace, and then find that their boots are covered with mud. Instead of persisting, they go back to Piccadilly. Such persons have only themselves to thank if the very street-boys mock at them.

Another recommendation was this: buy whatever may be necessary without haggling!

You must not try to strike a proportion between the values of incommensurable things.

However closely the square of any fraction approximates to 2, no fraction equals the square root of 2. The square root of 2 is not in the series; it is a different kind of number altogether.

The least of the Magical Instruments is worth infinitely more than all that you possess, or if you like, than all that you stupidly suppose yourself to possess. Break this rule, and the usual Nemesis of the half-hearted awaits you. Not only do you get inferior instruments, but you lose in some other way what you thought you were so clever to have saved. Remember Ananias!

Observe well that there is never any real equivalence or measurable relation between any two things, for each is impregnably Itself. The exchange of property is not a mathematically accurate equation. The Want is merely a conventional expression of the Will, just as a word is of a thought. It can never be anything else; thus, though the process of making it, whether it involves time, money, or labour, is a spiritual and moral synthesis, it is not measurable in terms of its elements.

On the other hand, if you purchase without haggling you will find that along with your purchase the vendor has thrown in the purse of Fortunatus. No matter in what extremity you may seem to be, at the last moment your difficulties will be solved. For there is no power either of the firmament of the ether, or of the earth or under the earth, on dry land or in the water, of whirling air or of rushing fire, or any spell or scourge of God which is not obedient to the necessity of the Magician! That which he has, he has not; but that which he is, he is; and that which he will be, he will be. And neither God nor Man, nor all the malice of Choronzon, can either check him, or cause him to waver for one instant upon the Path. This command and this promise have been given by all the Magi without exception. And where this command has been obeyed, this promise has been most certainly fulfilled.

time and place, in the proper circumstances.

. It is said that at the utterance of this name the Universe crashes into dissolution. Let the Magician earnestly seek this Lost Word, for its pronunciation is synonymous with the accomplishment of the Great Work.

Each man has a different Great Work, just as no two points on the circumference of a circle are connected with the centre by the same radius. The Word will be correspondingly unique.

In this matter of the efficacity of words there are again two formulae exactly opposite in nature. A word may

CHAPTER IX

OF SILENCE AND SECRECY:

AND OF

THE BARBAROUS NAMES OF EVOCATION.

It is found by experience (confirming the statement of Zoroaster) that the most potent conjurations are those in an ancient and perhaps forgotten language, or even those couched in a corrupt and possibly always meaningless jargon. Of these there are several main types. The "preliminary invocation" in the "Goetia" consists principally of corruptions of Greek and Egyptian names. For example, we find "Osorronnophris" for "Asor Un-Nefer".

See appendix 4, Liber Samekh; this is an edition of this Invocation, with an elaborate Rubric, translation, scholia, and instruction.

{WEH ADDENDUM: This is the "Preliminary Invocation" placed in the "Goetia" in the Mathers transcription (Not "translation") by Crowley. This invocation is not a part of the original text, but comes to us from the Greco-Egyptian period of perhaps the 6th century. The Goetia is itself a small portion of the "Lemegeton" or "Lesser Key of Solomon." This "Preliminary Evocation" is altered in Liber Samekh over that published in the "Goetia".

The conjurations given by Dr. Dee (vide Equinox I, VIII) are in a language called Angelic, or Enochian. Its source has hitherto baffled research, but it is a language and not a jargon, for it possesses a structure of its own, and there are traces of grammar and syntax.

However this may be, it "works". Even the beginner finds that "things happen" when he uses it: and this is an advantage — or disadvantage! —— shared by no other type of language,. The rest need skill. This needs Prudence!

The Egyptian Invocations are much purer, but their meaning has not been sufficiently studied by persons magically competent. We possess a number of Invocations in Greek of every degree of excellence; in Latin but few, and those of inferior quality. It will be noticed that in every case the conjurations are very sonorous, and there is a certain magical voice in which they should be recited. This special voice was a natural gift of the Master Therion; but it can be easily taught — to the right people.

Various considerations impelled Him to attempt conjurations in the English language. There already existed one example, the charm of the witches in Macbeth; although this was perhaps not meant seriously, its effect is indubitable.

A true poet cannot help revealing himself and the truth of things in his art, whether he be aware of what he is writing, or no.

He has found iambic tetrameters enriched with many rimes both internal an external very useful. "The Wizard Way" (Equinox I,I) gives a good idea of the sort of thing. So does the Evocation of Bartzabel in Equinox I,IX. There are many extant invocations throughout his works, in many kinds of metre, of many kinds of being, and for many kinds of purposes. (See Appendix).

Other methods of incantation are on record as efficacious. For instance Frater I.A., when a child, was told that he could invoke the devil by repeating the "Lord's Prayer" backwards. He went into the garden and did so.

The Devil appeared, and almost scared him out of his life.

It is therefore not quite certain in what the efficacy of conjurations really lies. The peculiar mental excitement required may even be aroused by the perception of the absurdity of the process, and the persistence in it, as when once FRATER PERDURABO (at the end of His magical resources) recited "From Greenland's Icy Mountains", and obtained His result.

See "Eleusis", A. Crowley, "Collected Works", Vol. III Epilogue.

It may be conceded in any case that the long strings of formidable words which roar and moan through so many conjurations have a real effect in exalting the consciousness of the magician to the proper pitch — that they should do so is no more extraordinary than music of any kind should do so.

Magicians have not confined themselves to the use of the human voice. The Pan-pipe with its seven stops, corresponding to the seven planets, the bull-roarer, the tom-tom, and even the violin, have all been used, as well as many others, of which the most important is the bell

See Part II. It should be said that in experience no bell save His own Tibetan bell of Electrum Magicum has ever sounded satisfactory to the Master Therion. Most bells jar and repel.

, though this is used not so much for actual conjuration as to mark stages in the ceremony. Of all these the tom-tom will be found to be the most generally useful.

While on the subject of barbarous names of evocation we should not omit the utterance of certain supreme words which enshrine (alpha) the complete formula of the God invoked, or (beta) the whole ceremony.

Examples of the former kind are Tetragrammaton, I.A.O., and Abrahadabra.

An example of the latter kind is the great word StiBeTTChePhMeFSHiSS, which is a line drawn on the Tree of Life (Coptic attributions) in a certain manner.

It represents the descent of a certain Influence. See the Evocation of Taphtatharath, Equinox I, III. The attributions are given in 777. This Word expresses the current Kether - Beth - Binah - Cheth - Geburach - Mem - Hod - Shin - Malkuth, the descent from 1 to 10 via the Pillar of Severity.

With all such words it is of the utmost importance that they should never be spoken until the supreme moment, and even then they should burst from the magician almost despite himself — so great should be his reluctance

This reluctance is Freudian, due to the power of these words to awaken the suppressed subconscious libido.

to utter them. In fact, they should be the utterance of the God in him at the first onset of the divine possession. So uttered, they cannot fail of effect, for they have become the effect.

Every wise magician will have constructed (according to the principles of the Holy Qabalah) many such words, and he should have quintessentialised them all in one Word, which last Word, once he has formed it, he should never utter consciously even in thought, until perhaps with it he gives up the ghost. Such a Word should in fact be so potent that man cannot hear it and live.

Such a word was indeed the lost Tetragrammaton

The Master Therion has received this Word; it is communicated by Him to the proper postulants, at the proper time and place, in the proper circumstances.

. It is said that at the utterance of this name the Universe crashes into dissolution. Let the Magician earnestly seek this Lost Word, for its pronunciation is synonymous with the accomplishment of the Great Work.

Each man has a different Great Work, just as no two points on the circumference of a circle are connected with the centre by the same radius. The Word will be correspondingly unique.

In this matter of the efficacity of words there are again two formulae exactly opposite in nature. A word may become potent and terrible by virtue of constant repetition. It is in this way that most religions gain strength. At first the statement "So and so is God" excites no interest. Continue, and you meet scorn and scepticism: possibly persecution. Continue, and the controversy has so far died out that no one troubles to contradict your assertion.

No superstition is so dangerous and so lively as an exploded superstition. The newspapers of to-day (written and edited almost exclusively by men without a spark of either religion or morality) dare not hint that any one disbelieves in the ostensibly prevailing cult; they deplore Atheism — all but universal in practice and implicit in the theory of practically all intelligent people — as if it were the eccentricity of a few negligible or objectionable persons. This is the ordinary story of advertisement; the sham has exactly the same chance as the real. Persistence is the only quality required for success.

The opposite formula is that of secrecy. An idea is perpetuated because it must never be mentioned. A freemason never forgets the secret words entrusted to him, thought these words mean absolutely nothing to him, in the vast majority of cases; the only reason for this is that he has been forbidden to mention them, although they have been published again and again, and are as accessible to the profane as to the initiate.

In such a work of practical Magick as the preaching of a new Law, these methods may be advantageously combined; on the one hand infinite frankness and readiness to communicate all secrets; on the other the sublime and terrible knowledge that all real secrets are incommunicable.

If this were not the case, individuality would not be inviolable. No man can communicate even the simplest thought to any other man in any full and accurate sense. For that thought is sown in a different soil, and cannot produce an identical effect. I cannot put a spot of red upon two pictures without altering each in diverse ways. It might have little effect on a sunset by Turner, but much on a nocturne by Whistler. The identity of the two spots as spots would thus be fallacious.

It is, according to tradition, a certain advantage in conjurations to employ more than one language. In all probability the reason of this is than any change spurs the flagging attention. A man engaged in intense mental labour will frequently stop and walk up and down the room — one may suppose for this cause — but it is a sign of weakness that this should be necessary. For the beginner in Magick, however, it is permissible

This is not to say that it is advisable. O how shameful is human weakness! But it does encourage one — it is useless to deny it — to be knocked down by a Demon of whose existence one was not really quite sure.

to employ any device to secure the result.

Conjurations should be recited, not read:

Even this is for the weaker brethern. The really great Magus speaks and acts impromptu and extempore.

and the entire ceremony should be so perfectly performed that one is hardly conscious of any effort of memory.

The ceremony should be constructed with such logical fatality that a mistake is impossible.

First-rate poetry is easily memorized because the ideas and the musical values correspond to man's mental and sensory structure.

The conscious ego of the Magician is to be destroyed to be absorbed in that of the God whom he invokes, and the process should not interfere with the automation who is performing the ceremony.

But this ego of which it is here spoken is the true ultimate ego. The automaton should possess will, energy, intelligence, reason, and resource. This automaton should be the perfect man far more than any other man can be. It is only the divine self within the man, a self as far above the possession of will or any other qualities whatsoever as the heavens are high above the earth, that should reabsorb itself into that illimitable radiance of which it is a spark.

This is said of the partial or lesser Works of Magick. This is an elementary treatise; one cannot discuss higher Works as for example those of "The Hermit of Aesopus Island".

The great difficulty for the single Magician is so to perfect himself that these multifarious duties of the Ritual are adequately performed. At first he will find that the exaltation destroys memory and paralyses muscle. This is an essential difficulty of the magical process, and can only be overcome by practice and experience.

See "The Book of Lies"; there are several chapters on this subject. But Right exaltation should produce spontaneously the proper mental and physical reactions. As soon as the development is secured, there will be automatic reflex "justesse", exactly as in normal affairs mind and body respond with free unconscious rightness to the Will.

In order to aid concentration, and to increase the supply of Energy, it has been customary for the Magician to employ assistants or colleagues. It is doubtful whether the obvious advantages of this plan compensate the difficulty of procuring suitable persons

The organic development of Magick in the world due to the creative Will of the Master Therion makes it with every year that passes easier to find scientifically trained co-workers.

, and the chance of a conflict of will or a misunderstanding in the circle itself. On one occasion FRATER PERDURABO was disobeyed by an assistant, and had it not been for His promptitude in using the physical compulsion of the sword, it is probable that the circle would have been broken. As it was, the affair fortunately terminated in nothing more serious than the destruction of the culprit.

However, there is no doubt that an assemblage of persons who really are in harmony can much more easily produce an effect than a magician working by himself. The psychology of "Revival meetings" will be familiar to almost every one, and though such meetings

See, for an account of properly-conducted congregational ceremonial, Equinox I, IX. "Energized Enthusiasm", and Equinox III, L. Liber XV, Ecclesiae Gnosticae Catholicae Cannon Missae. The "Revival meetings" here in question were deliberate exploitations of religious hysteria.

are the foulest and most degraded rituals of black magic, the laws of Magick are not thereby suspended. The laws of Magick are the laws of Nature.

A singular and world-famous example of this is of sufficiently recent date to be fresh in the memory of many people now living. At a nigger camp meeting in the "United" States of America, devotees were worked up to such a pitch of excitement that the whole assembly developed a furious form of hysteria. The comparatively intelligible cries of "Glory" and "Hallelujah" no longer expressed the situation. Somebody screamed out "Ta-ra-ra-boom-de-ay!", and this was taken up by the whole meeting and yelled continuously, until reaction set in. The affair got into the papers, and some particularly bright disciple of John Stuart Mill, logician and economist, thought that these words, having set one set of fools crazy, might do the same to all the other fools in the world. He accordingly wrote a song, and produced the desired result. This is the most notorious example of recent times of the power exerted by a barbarous name of evocation.

A few words may be useful to reconcile the general notion of Causality with that of Magick. How can we be sure that a person waving a stick and howling thereby produces thunderstorms? In no other way than that familiar to Science; we note that whenever we put a lighted match to dry gunpowder, an unintelligibly arbitrary phenomenon, that of sound, is observed; and so forth.

We need not dwell upon this point; but it seems worth while to answer one of the objections to the possibility of Magick, chosing one which is at first sight of an obviously "fatal" character. It is convenient to quote verbatim from the Diary

In a later entry we read that the diarist has found a similar train of argument in "Space, Time, and Gravitation", page 51. He was much encourage by the confirmation of his thesis in so independent a system of thought.

of a distinguished Magician and philosopher. "I have noticed that the effect of a Magical Work has followed it so closely that it must have been started before the time of the Work. E.g. I work to-night to make X in Paris write to me. I get the letter the next morning, so that it must have been written before the Work. Does this deny that the Work caused the effect?

"If I strike a billiard-ball and it moves, both my will and its motion are due to causes long antecedent to the act. I may consider both my Work and its reaction as twin effects of the eternal Universe. The moved arm and ball are parts of a state of the Cosmos which resulted necessarily from its momentarily previous state, and so, back for ever. "Thus, my Magical Work is only one of the cause-effects necessarily concomitant with the case-effects which set the ball in motion. I may therefore regard the act of striking as a cause-effect of my original Will to move the ball, though necessarily previous to its motion. But the case of magical Work is not quite analogous. For my nature is such that I am compelled to perform Magick in order to make my will to prevail; so that the cause of my doing the Work is also the cause of the ball's motion, and there is no reason why one should precede the other. (CF. "Lewis Carroll," where the Red Queen screams before she pricks her finger.)

"Let me illustrate the theory by an actual example.

"I write from Italy to a man in France and another in Australia on the same day, telling them to join me. Both arrive ten days later; the first in answer to my letter, which he received, the second on "his own initiative", as it would seem. But I summoned him because I wanted him; and I wanted him because he was my representative; and his intelligence made him resolve to join me because it judged rightly that the situation (so far as he knew it) was such as to make me desire his presence.

"The same cause, therefore, which made me write to him made him come to me; and though it would be improper to say that the writing of the letter was the direct cause of his arrival, it is evident that if I had not written I should have been different from what I actually am, and therefore my relations with him would have been otherwise than they are. In this sense, therefore, the letter and the journey are causally connected.

"One cannot go farther, and say that in this case I ought to write the letter even if he had arrived before I did so; for it is part of the whole set of circumstance that I do not use a crowbar on an open door. "The conclusion is that one should do one's Will 'without lust of result'. If one is working in accordance with the laws of one's own nature, one is doing 'right'; and no such work can be criticised as 'useless', even in cases of the character here discussed. So long as one's Will prevails, there is no cause for complaint.

"To abandon one's Magick would shew lack of self-confidence in one's powers, and doubt as to one's inmost faith in Self and in Nature.

> *i.e. on the ground that one cannot understand how Magick can produce the desired effects. For if one possesses the inclination to do Magick, it is evidence of a tendency in one's Nature. Nobody understands fully how the mind moves the muscles; but we know that lack of confidence on this point means paralysis. "If the Sun and Moon should doubt, They'd immediately go out", as Blake said. Also, as I said myself. "Who hath the How is careless of the Why".*

Of course one changes one's methods as experience indicates; but there is no need to change them on any such ground as the above.

"Further, the argument here set forth disposes of the need to explain the "modus operandi" of Magick. A successful operation does not involve any theory soever, not even that of the existence of causality itself. The whole set of phenomena may be conceived as single.

"For instance, if I see a star (as it was years ago) I need not assume causal relations as existing between it, the earth, and myself. The connexion exists; I can predicate nothing beyond that. I cannot postulate purpose, or even determine the manner in which the event comes to be. Similarly, when I do Magick, it is in vain to inquire why I so act, or why the desired result does or does not follow. Nor can I know how the previous and subsequent conditions are connected. At most I can describe the consciousness which I interpret as a picture of the facts, and make empirical generalizations of the superficial aspects of the case.

"Thus, I have my own personal impressions of the act of telephoning; but I cannot be aware of what consciousness, electricity, mechanics, sound, etc., actually are in themselves. And although I can appeal to experience to lay down 'laws' as to what conditions accompany the act, I can never be sure that they have always been, or ever will again be, identical. (In fact, it is certain that an event can never occur twice in precisely the same circumstances.)

> *If it did so, how could we call it duplex?*

"Further, my 'laws; must always take nearly all the more important elements of knowledge for granted. I cannot say — finally — how an electric current is generated. I cannot be sure that some totally unsuspected force is not at work in some entirely arbitrary way. For example, it was formerly supposed that Hydrogen and Chlorine would unite when an electric spark was passed through the mixture; now we 'know' that the presence of a minute quantity of aqueous vapour (or some tertium quid) is essential to the reaction. We formulated before the days of Ross the 'laws' of malarial fever, without reference to the mosquito; we might discover one day that the germ is only active when certain events are transpiring in some nebula

> *The history of the Earth is included in the period of some such relation; so that we cannot possibly be sure that we may deny: "Malarial fever is a function of the present precession of the Equinoxes".*

, or when so apparently inert a substance as Argon is present in the air in certain proportions.

"We may therefore admit quite cheerfully that Magick is as mysterious as mathematics, as empirical as poetry, as uncertain as golf, and as dependent on the personal equation as Love.

"That is no reason why we should not study, practice and enjoy it; for it is a Science in exactly the same sense as biology; it is no less an Art that Sculpture; and it is a Sport as much as Mountaineering.

"Indeed, there seems to be no undue presumption in urging that no Science possesses equal possibilities of deep and important Knowledge;

> *Magick is less liable to lead to error than any other Science, because its terms are interchangeable, by definition, so that it is based on relativity from the start. We run no risk of asserting absolute propositions. Furthermore we make our measurements in terms of the object measured, thus avoiding the absurdity of defining metaphysical ideas by mutable standards, (Cf. Eddington "Space, Time, and Gravitation". Prologue.) of being forced to attribute the qualities of human consciousness to inanimate things (Poincare, "La mesure du temps"), and of asserting that we know anything of the universe in itself, though the nature of our senses and our minds necessarily determines our observations, so that the limit of our knowledge is subjective, just as a thermometer can record nothing but its own reaction to one particular type of Energy.*

> *Magick recognizes frankly (1) that truth is relative, subjective, and apparent; (2) that Truth implies Omniscience, which is unattainable by mind, being transfinite; just as if one tried to make an exact map of England in England, that map must contain a map of the map, and so on, ad infinitum; (3) that logical contradiction is inherent in reason, (Russell, "Introduction to Mathematical Philosophy", p. 136; Crowley, "Eleusis", and elsewhere); (4) that a Continuum requires a Continuum to be commensurable with it: (5) that Empiricism is ineluctable, and therefore that adjustment is the only possible method of action; and (6) that error may be avoided by opposing no resistance to change, and registering observed phenomena in their own language.*

that no Art offers such opportunities to the ambition of the Soul to express its Truth, in Ecstasy, through Beauty; and that no Sport rivals its fascinations of danger and delight, so excites, exercises, and tests its devotees to the uttermost, or so rewards them by well-being, pride, and the passionate pleasures of personal triumph.

"Magick takes every thought and act for its apparatus; it has the Universe for its Library and its Laboratory; all Nature is its Subject; and its Game, free from close seasons and protective restrictions, always abounds in infinite variety, being all that exists.

> *The elasticity of Magick makes it equal to all possible kinds of environment, and therefore biologically perfect. "Do what thou wilt..." implies self-adjustment, so that failure cannot occur. One's true Will is necessarily fitted to the whole Universe with the utmost exactitude, because each term in the equation a+b+c=0 must be equal and opposite to the sum of all the other terms. No individual can ever be aught than himself, or do aught else than his Will, which is his necessary relation with his environment, dynamically considered. All error is no more than an illusion proper to him to dissipate the mirage, and it is a general law that the method of accomplishing this operation is to realize, and to acquiesce in, the order of the Universe, and to refrain from attempting the impossible task of overcoming the inertia of the forces which oppose, and therefore are identical with, one's self. Error in thought is therefore failure to understand, and in action to perform, one's own true Will.*

CHAPTER X

OF THE GESTURES

This chapter may be divided into the following parts:

1. Attitudes.

2. Circumambulations (and similar movements).

3. Changes of position (This depends upon the theory of the construction of the circle).

4. The Knocks or Knells.

I

Attitudes are of two Kinds: natural and artificial. Of the first kind, prostration is the obvious example. It comes natural to man (poor creature!) to throw himself to the ground in the presence of the object of his adoration.

> *The Magician must eschew prostration, or even the "bending of the knee in supplication", as infamous and ignominious, an abdication of his sovereignty.*

Intermediate between this and the purely artificial form of gesture comes a class which depends on acquired habit. Thus it is natural to an European officer to offer his sword in token of surrender. A Tibetan would, however, squat, put out his tongue, and place his hand behind his right ear. Purely artificial gestures comprehend in their class the majority of definitely magick signs, though some of these simulate a natural action — e.g. the sign of the Rending of the Veil. But the sign of Auramoth (see Equinox I, II, Illustration "The Signs of the Grades") merely imitates a hieroglyph which has only a remote connection with any fact in nature. All signs must of course be studied with infinite patience, and practised until the connection between them and the mental attitude which they represent appears "necessary."

II

The principal movement in the circle is circumambulation.

> *In Part II of this Book 4 it was assumed that the Magician went barefoot. This would imply his intention to make intimate contact with his Circle. But he may wear sandals, for the Ankh is a sandal-strap; it is born by the Egyptian Gods to signify their power of Going, that is their eternal energy. By shape the Ankh (or Crux Ansata) suggests the formula by which this going is effected in actual practice.*

This has a very definite result, but one which is very difficult to describe. An analogy is the dynamo. Circumambulation properly performed in combination with the Sign of Horus (or "The Enterer") on passing the East is one of the best methods of arousing the macrocosmic force in the Circle. It should never be omitted unless there be some special reason against it.

A particular tread seems appropriate to it. This tread should be light and stealthy, almost furtive, and yet very purposeful. It is the pace of the tiger who stalks the deer. The number of circumambulations should of course correspond to the nature of the ceremony.

Another important movement is the spiral, of which there are two principal forms, one inward, one outward. They can be performed in either direction; and, like the circumambulation, if performed deosil *i.e. In the same direction as the hands of a watch move.*

they invoke — if widdershins

i.e. In the opposite direction.

they banish

Such, at least, is the traditional interpretation. But there is a deeper design which may be expressed through the direction of rotation. Certain forces of the most formidable character may be invoked by circumambulation Widdershins when it is executed with intent toward them, and the initiated technique. Of such forces Typhon is the type, and the war of the Titans against the Olympians the legend. (Teitan, Titan, has in Greek the numerical value of 666.)

WEH Addenda: Crowley is using the spelling Tau-epsilon-iota-tau-alpha-nu in place of the more usual Tau-iota-tau-alpha-nu or Tau-alpha-iota-tau-alpha-nu to obtain 666 in place of 661 or 662.

. In the spiral the tread is light and tripping, almost approximating to a dance: while performing it the magician will usually turn on his own axis, either in the same direction as the spiral, or in the opposite direction. Each combination involves a different symbolism.

There is also the dance proper; it has many different forms, each God having his special dance. One of the easiest and most effective dances is the ordinary waltz-step combined with the three signs of L.V.X. It is much easier to attain ecstasy in this way than is generally supposed. The essence of the process consists in the struggle of the Will against giddiness; but this struggle must be prolonged and severe, and upon the degree of this the quality and intensity of ecstasy attained may depend.

With practice, giddiness is altogether conquered; exhaustion then takes its place and the enemy of Will. It is through the mutual destruction of these antagonisms in the mental and moral being of the magician that Samadhi is begotten.

III

Good examples of the use of change of position are given in the manuscripts Z.1 and Z.3;

Equinox I, II, pp. 244-260.

explanatory of the Neophyte Ritual of the G.'. D.'., where the candidate is taken to various stations in the Temple, each station having a symbolic meaning of its own; but in pure invocation a better example is given in Liber 831

Equinox I, VII, pp. 93 sqq.

. In the construction of a ceremony an important thing to decide is whether you will or will not make such movements. For every Circle has its natural symbolism, and even if no use is to be made of these facts, one must be careful not to let anything be inharmonious with the natural attributions.

The practical necessities of the work are likely to require certain movements. One should either exclude this symbolism altogether, or else think out everything beforehand, and make it significant. Do not let some actions be symbolic and others haphazard.

For the sensitive aura of the magician might be disturbed, and the value of the ceremony completely destroyed, by the embarrassment caused by the discovery of some such error, just as if a pre-occupied T-totaller found that he had strayed into a Temple of the Demon Rum! It is therefore impossible to neglect the theory of the Circle.

To take a simple example, suppose that, in an Evocation of Bartzabel, the planet Mars, whose sphere is Geburah (Severity) were situated (actually, in the heavens) opposite to the Square of Chesed (Mercy) of the Tau in the Circle, and the triangle placed accordingly. It would be improper for the Magus to stand on that Square unless using this formula, "I, from Chesed, rule Geburah through the Path of the Lion"; while — taking an extreme case — to stand on the square of Hod (which is naturally dominated by Geburah) would be a madness which only a formula of the very highest Magick could counteract.

Certain positions, however, such as Tiphareth,

Tiphareth is hardly "dominated" even by Kether. It is the son rather than the servant.

are so sympathetic to the Magus himself that he may use them without reference to the nature of the spirit, or of the operation; unless he requires an exceptionally precise spirit free of all extraneous elements, or one whose nature is difficulty compatible with Tiphareth.

To show how these positions may be used in conjunction with the spirals, suppose that you are invoking Hathor, Goddess of Love, to descend upon the Altar. Standing on the square of Netzach you will make your invocation to Her, and then dance an inward spiral deosil ending at the foot of the altar, where you sink on your knees with your arms raised above the altar as if inviting Her embrace.

But NOT "in supplication".

To conclude, one may add that natural artistic ability, of you possess it, forms an excellent guide. All Art is Magick.

Isadora Duncan has this gift of gesture in a very high degree. Let the reader study her dancing; if possible rather in private than in public, and learn the superb "unconsciousness" — which is magical consciousness — with which she suits the action to the melody.

This passage was written in 1911 e.v. "Wake Duncan with thy Knocking? I would thou couldst!"

There is no more potent means than Art of calling forth true Gods to visible appearance.

IV.

The knocks or knells are all of the same character. They may be described collectively — the difference between them consists only in this, that the instrument with which they are made seals them with its own special properties. It is of no great importance (even so) whether they are made by clapping the hands or stamping the feet, by strokes of one of the weapons, or by the theoretically appropriate instrument, the bell. It may nevertheless be admitted that they become more important in the ceremony if the Magician considers it worth while to take up

Any action not purely rhythmical is a disturbance.

an instrument whose single purpose is to produce them.

Let it first be laid down that a knock asserts a connection between the Magician and the object which he strikes. Thus the use of the bell, or of the hands, means that the Magician wishes to impress the atmosphere of the whole circle with what has been or is about to be done. He wishes to formulate his will in sound, and radiate it in every direction; moreover, to influence that which lives by breath in the sense of his purpose, and to summon it to bear witness to his Word. The hands are used as symbols of his executive power, the bell to represent his consciousness exalted into music. To strike with the wand is to utter the fiat of creation; the cup vibrates with his delight in receiving spiritual wine. A blow with the dagger is like the signal for battle. The disk is used to express the throwing down of the price of one's purchase. To stamp with the foot is to declare one's mastery of the matter in hand. Similarly, any other form of giving knocks has its own virtue. From the above examples the intelligent student will have perceived the method of interpreting each individual case that may come in question.

As above said, the object struck is the object impressed. Thus, a blow upon the altar affirms that he has complied with the laws of his operation. To strike the lamp is to summon the Light divine. Thus for the rest.

It must also be observed that many combinations of ideas are made possible by this convention. To strike the wand within the cup is to apply the creative will to its proper complement, and so perform the Great Work by the formula of Regeneration. To strike with the hand on the dagger declares that one demands the use of the dagger as a tool to extend one's executive power. The reader will recall how Siegfried smote Nothung, the sword of Need, upon the lance of Wotan. By the action Wagner, who was instructed how to apply magical formulae by one of the heads of our Order, intended his hearers to understand that the reign of authority and paternal power had come to an end; that the new master of the world was intellect.

The general object of a knock or a knell is to mark a stage in the ceremony. Sasaki Shigetz tells us in his essay on Shinto that the Japanese are accustomed to clap their hands four times "to drive away evil spirits". He explains that what really happens is that the sudden and sharp impact of the sound throws the mind into an alert activity which enables it to break loose from the obsession of its previous mood. It is aroused to apply itself aggressively to the ideals which had oppressed it. There is therefore a perfectly rational interpretation of the psychological power of the knock.

In a Magical ceremony the knock is employed for much the same purpose. The Magician uses it like the chorus in a Greek play. It helps him to make a clean cut, to turn his attention from one part of his work to the next.

So much for the general character of the knock or knell. Even this limited point of view offers great opportunities to the resourceful Magician. But further possibilities lie to our hand. It is not usually desirable to attempt to convey anything except emphasis, and possibly mood, by varying the force of the blow. It is obvious, moreover, that there is a natural correspondence between the hard loud knock of imperious command on the one hand, and the soft slurred knock of sympathetic comprehension on the other. It is easy to distinguish between the bang of the outraged creditor at the front, and the hushed tap of the lover at the bedroom, door. Magical theory cannot here add instruction to instinct.

But a knock need not be single; the possible combinations are evidently infinite. We need only discuss the general principles of determining what number of strokes will be proper in any case, and how we may interrupt any series so as to express our idea by means of structure.

The general rule is that a single knock has no special significance as such, because unity is omniform. It represents Kether, which is the source of all things equally without partaking of any quality by which we discriminate one thing from another. Continuing on these lines, the number of knocks will refer to the Sephira or other idea Qabalistically cognate with that number. Thus, 7 knocks will intimate Venus, 11 the

Great Work, 17 the Trinity of Fathers, and 19 the Feminine Principle in its most general sense.

Analyzing the matter a little further, we remark firstly that a battery of too many knocks is confusing, as well as liable to overweight the other parts of the ritual. In practice, 11 is about the limit. It is usually not difficult to arrange to cover all necessary ground with that number. Secondly, each is so extensive in scope, and includes aspects so diverse from a practical standpoint that our danger lies in vagueness. A knock should be well defined; its meaning should be precise. The very nature of knocks suggests smartness and accuracy. We must therefore devise some means of making the sequence significant of the special sense which may be appropriate. Our only resource is in the use of intervals.

It is evidently impossible to attain great variety in the smaller numbers. But this fact illustrates the excellence of our system. There is only one way of striking 2 knocks, and this fact agrees with the nature of Chokmah; there is only one way of creating. We can express only ourselves, although we do so in duplex form. But there are three ways of striking 3 knocks, and these 3 ways correspond to the threefold manner in which Binah can receive the creative idea. There are three possible types of triangle. We may understand an idea either as an unity tripartite, as an unity dividing itself into a duality, or as a duality harmonized into an unity. Any of these methods may be indicated by 3 equal knocks; 1 followed, after a pause, by 2; and 2 followed, after a pause, by 1.

As the nature of the number becomes more complex, the possible varieties increase rapidly. There are numerous ways of striking 6, each of which is suited to the nature of the several aspects of Tiphareth. We may leave the determination of these points to the ingenuity of the student.

The most generally useful and adaptable battery is composed of 11 strokes. The principal reasons for this are as follows: "Firstly", 11 is the number of Magick in itself. It is therefore suitable to all types of operation. "Secondly", it is the sacred number par excellence of the new Aeon. As it is written in the Book of the Law: "...11, as all their numbers who are of us." "Thirdly", it is the number of the letters of the word ABRAHADABRA, which is the word of the Aeon. The structure of this word is such that it expresses the great Work, in every one of its aspects. "Lastly", it is possible thereby to express all possible spheres of operation, whatever their nature. This is effected by making an equation between the number of the Sephira and the difference between that number and 11. For example, 2 Degree=9Square is the formula of the grade of initiation corresponding to Yesod. Yesod represents the instability of air, the sterility of the moon; but these qualities are balanced in it by the stability implied in its position as the Foundation, and by its function of generation. This complex is further equilibrated by identifying it with the number 2 of Chokmah, which possesses the airy quality, being the Word, and the lunar quality, being the reflection of the sun of Kether as Yesod is the sun of Tiphareth. It is the wisdom which is the foundation by being creation. This entire cycle of ideas is expressed in the double formula 2 Degree = 9Square, 9 Degree = 2Square; and any of these ideas may be selected and articulated by a suitable battery.

We may conclude with a single illustration of how the above principles may be put into practice. Let us suppose that the Magician contemplates an operation for the purpose of helping his mind to resist the tendency to wander. This will be a work of Yesod. But he must emphasize the stability of that Sephira as against the Airy quality which it possesses. His first action will be to put the 9 under the protection of the 2; the battery at this point will be 1-9-1. But this 9 as it stands is suggestive of the changefulness of the moon. It may occur to him to divide this into 4 and 5, 4 being the number of fixity, law, and authoritative power; and 5 that of courage, energy, and triumph of the spirit over the elements. He will reflect, moreover, that 4 is symbolic of the stability of matter, while 5 expresses the same idea with regard to motion. At this stage the battery will appear as 1-2-5-2-1. After due consideration he will probably conclude that to split up the central 5 would tend to destroy the simplicity of his formula, and decide to use it as it stands. The possible alternative would be to make a single knock the centre of his battery as if he appealed to the ultimate immutability of Kether, invoking that unity by placing a fourfold knock on either side of it. In this case, his battery would be 1-4-1-4-1. He will naturally have been careful to preserve the balance of each part of the battery against the corresponding part. This would be particularly necessary in an operation such as we have chosen for our example.

CHAPTER XI

OF OUR LADY BABALON AND OF THE BEAST WHEREON SHE RIDETH.

ALSO CONCERNING TRANSFORMATIONS.

I

The contents of this section, inasmuch as they concern OUR LADY, are too important and too sacred to be printed. They are only communicated by the Master Therion to chosen pupils in private instruction.

II

The essential magical work, apart from any particular operation, is the proper formation of the Magical Being or Body of Light. This process will be discussed at some length in Chapter XVIII.

We will here assume that the magician has succeeded in developing his Body of Light until it is able to go anywhere and do anything. There will, however, be a certain limitation to his work, because he has formed his magical body from the fine matter of his own element. Therefore, although he may be able to penetrate the utmost recesses of the heavens, or conduct vigorous combats with the most unpronounceable demons of the pit, it may be impossible for him to do as much as knock a vase from a mantelpiece. His magical body is composed of matter too tenuous to affect directly the gross matter of which illusions such as tables and chairs are made.

> *The one really easy "physical" operation which the Body of Light can perform is "Congressus subtilis". The emanations of the "Body of Desire" of the material being whom one visits are, if the visit be agreeable, so potent that one spontaneously gains substance in the embrace. There are many cases on record of Children having been born as the result of such unions. See the work of De Sinistrari on Incubi and Succubi for a discussion of analogous phenomena.*

There has been a good deal of discussion in the past within the Colleges of the Holy Ghost, as to whether it would be quite legitimate to seek to transcend this limitation. One need not presume to pass judgment. One can leave the decision to the will of each magician.

The Book of the Dead contains many chapters intended to enable the magical entity of a man who is dead, and so deprived (according to the theory of death then current) of the material vehicle for executing his will, to take on the form of certain animals, such as a golden hawk or a crocodile, and in such form to go about the earth "taking his pleasure among the living."

> *See "The Book of Lies" Cap. 44, and The Collected Works of Aleister Crowley, Vol. III, pp. 209-210, where occur paraphrased translations of certain classical Egyptian rituals.*

As a general rule, material was supplied out of which he could construct the party of the second part aforesaid, hereinafter referred to as the hawk.

We need not, however, consider this question of death. It may often be convenient for the living to go about the world in some such incognito. Now, then, conceive of this magical body as creative force, seeking manifestation; as a God, seeking incarnation.

There are two ways by which this aim may be effected. The first method is to build up an appropriate body from its elements. This is, generally speaking, a very hard thing to do, because the physical constitution of any material being with much power is, or at least should be, the outcome of ages of evolution. However, there is a lawful method of producing an homunculus which is taught in a certain secret organization, perhaps known to some of those who may read this, which could very readily be adapted to some such purpose as we are now discussing.

The second method sounds very easy and amusing. You take some organism already existing, which happens to be suitable to your purpose. You drive out the magical being which inhabits it, and take possession. To do this by force is neither easy nor justifiable, because the magical being of the other was incarnated in accordance with its Will. And "... thou hast no right but to do thy will." One should hardly strain this sentence to make one's own will include the will to upset somebody else's will!

Yet it might happen that the Will of the other being was to invite the Magician to indwell its instrument.

Moreover, it is extremely difficult thus to expatriate another magical being; for though, unless it is a complete microcosm like a human being, it cannot be called a star, it is a little bit of a star, and part of the body of Nuit.

But there is no call for all this frightfulness. There is no need to knock the girl down, unless she refuses to do what you want, and she will always comply if you say a few nice things to her.

Especially on the subject of the Wand or the Disk.

You can always use the body inhabited by an elemental, such as an eagle, hare, wolf, or any convenient animal, by making a very simple compact. You take over the responsibility for the animal, thus building it up into your own magical hierarchy. This represents a tremendous gain to the animal.

This is the magical aspect of eating animal food, and its justification, or rather the reconciliation of the apparent contradiction between the carnivorous and humanitarian elements in the nature of "Homo Sapiens".

It completely fulfils its ambition by an alliance of this extremely intimate sort with a Star. The magician, on the other hand, is able to transform and retransform himself in a thousand ways by accepting a retinue of such adherents. In this way the projection of the "astral" or Body of Light may be made absolutely tangible and practical. At the same time, the magician must realise that in undertaking the Karma of any elemental, he is assuming a very serious responsibility. The bond which unites him with that elemental is love; and, though it is only a small part of the outfit of a magician, it is the whole of the outfit of the elemental. He will, therefore, suffer intensely in case of any error or misfortune occurring to his protegee. This feeling is rather peculiar. It is quite instinctive with the best men. They hear of the destruction of a city of a few thousand inhabitants with entire callousness, but then they hear of a dog having hurt its paw, they feel Weltschmertz acutely.

It is not necessary to say much more than this concerning transformations. Those to whom the subject naturally appeals will readily understand the importance of what has been said. Those who are otherwise inclined may reflect that a nod is as good as a wink to a blind horse.

CHAPTER XII

OF THE BLOODY SACRIFICE: AND MATTERS COGNATE.

It is necessary for us to consider carefully the problems connected with the bloody sacrifice, for this question is indeed traditionally important in Magick. Nigh all ancient Magick revolves around this matter. In particular all the Osirian religions — the rites of the Dying God — refer to this. The slaying of Osiris and Adonis; the mutilation of Attis; the cults of Mexico and Peru; the story of Hercules or Melcarth; the legends of Dionysus and of Mithra, are all connected with this one idea. In the Hebrew religion we find the same thing inculcated. The first ethical lesson in the Bible is that the only sacrifice pleasing to the Lord is the sacrifice of blood; Abel, who made this, finding favour with the Lord, while Cain, who offered cabbages, was rather naturally considered a cheap sport. The idea recurs again and again. We have the sacrifice of the Passover, following on the story of Abraham's being commanded to sacrifice his firstborn son, with the idea of the substitution of animal for human life. The annual ceremony of the two goats carries out this in perpetuity. And we see again the domination of this idea in the romance of Esther, where Haman and Mordecai are the two goats or gods; and ultimately in the presentation of the rite of Purim in Palestine, where Jesus and Barabbas happened to be the Goats in that particular year of which we hear so much, without agreement on the date.

This subject must be studied in the "Golden Bough", where it is most learnedly set forth by Dr. J. G. Frazer. Enough has now been said to show that the bloody sacrifice has from time immemorial been the most considered part of Magick. The ethics of the thing appear to have concerned no one; nor, to tell the truth, need they do so. As St. Paul says, "Without shedding of blood there is no remission"; and who are we to argue with St. Paul? But, after all that, it is open to any one to have any opinion that he likes upon the subject, or any other subject, thank God! At the same time, it is most necessary to study the business, whatever we may be going to do about it; for our ethics themselves will naturally depend upon our theory of the universe. If we were quite certain, for example, that everybody went to heaven when he died, there could be no serious objection to murder or suicide, as it is generally conceded — by those who know neither — that earth is not such a pleasant place as heaven.

However, there is a mystery concealed in this theory of the bloody sacrifice which is of great importance to the student, and we therefore make no further apology, We should not have made even this apology for an apology, had it not been for the solicitude of a pious young friend of great austerity of character who insisted that the part of this chapter which now follows — the part which was originally written — might cause us to be misunderstood. This must not be. The blood is the life. This simple statement is explained by the Hindus by saying that the blood is the principal vehicle of vital Prana.

Prana or force" is often used as a generic term for all kinds of subtle energy. The prana of the body is only one of its "vayus". Vayu means air or spirit. The idea is that all bodily forces are manifestations of the finer forces of the more real body, this real body being a subtle and invisible thing.

There is some ground for the belief that there is a definite substance

This substance need not be conceived as "material" in the crude sense of Victorian science; we now know that such phenomena as the rays and emanations of radioactive substances occupy an intermediate position. For instance, mass is not, as once supposed, necessarily impermeable to mass, and matter itself can be only interpreted in terms of motion. So, as to "prana", one might hypothesize a phenomenon in the ether analogous to isomerism. We already know of bodies chemically identical whose molecular structure makes one active, another inactive, to certain reagents. Metals can be "tired" or even "killed" as to some of their properties, without discoverable chemical change. One can "kill" steel, and "raise it from the dead"; and flies drowned in icewater can be resuscitated. That it should be impossible to create high organic life is scientifically unthinkable, and the Master Therion believes it to be a matter of few years indeed before this is done in the laboratory. Already we restore the apparently drowned. Why not those dead from such causes as syncope? If we understood the ultimate physics and chemistry of the brief moment of death we would get hold of the force in some say, supply the missing element, reverse the electrical conditions or what not. Already we prevent certain kinds of death by supplying wants, as in the case of Thyroid.

, not isolated as yet, whose presence makes all the difference between live and dead matter. We pass by with deserved contempt the pseudo-scientific experiments of American charlatans who claim to have established that weight is lost at the moment of death, and the unsupported statements of alleged clairvoyants that they have seen the soul issuing like a vapour from the mouth of persons "in articulo mortis"; but his experiences as an explorer have convinced the Master Therion that meat loses a notable portion of its nutritive value within a very few minutes after the death of the animal, and that this loss proceeds with ever-diminishing rapidity as time goes on. It is further generally conceded that live food, such as oysters, is the most rapidly assimilable and most concentrated form of energy.

Once can become actually drunk on oysters, by chewing them completely. Rigor seems to be a symptom of the loss of what I may call the Alpha-energy and makes a sharp break in the curve. The Beta and other energies dissipate more slowly. Physiologists should make it their first duty to measure these phenomena; for their study is evidently a direct line of research into the nature of Life. The analogy between the living and complex molecules of the Uranium group of inorganic and the Protoplasm group of organic elements is extremely suggestive. The faculties of growth, action, self-recuperation, etc., must be ascribed to similar properties in both cases; and as we have detected, measured and partially explained radioactivity, it must be possible to contrive means of doing the same for Life.

Laboratory experiments in food-values seem to be almost worthless, for reasons which we cannot here enter into; the general testimony of mankind appears a safer guide.

It would be unwise to condemn as irrational the practice of those savages who tear the heart and liver from an adversary, and devour them while yet warm. In any case it was the theory of the ancient Magicians, that any living being is a storehouse of energy varying in quantity according to the size and health of the animal, and in quality according to its mental and moral character. At the death of the animal this energy is liberated suddenly.

The animal should therefore be killed

It is a mistake to suppose that the victim is injured. On the contrary, this is the most blessed and merciful of all deaths, for the elemental spirit is directly built up into Godhead — the exact goal of its efforts through countless incarnations. On the other hand, the practice of torturing animals to death in order to obtain the elemental as a slave is indefensible, utterly black magic of the very worst kind, involving as it does a metaphysical basis of dualism. There is, however, no objection to dualism or black magic when they are properly understood. See the account of the Master Therion's Great Magical Retirement by Lake Pasquaney, where he "crucified a toad in the Basilisk abode".

within the Circle, or the Triangle, as the case may be, so that its energy cannot escape. An animal should be selected whose nature accords with that of the ceremony — thus, by sacrificing a female lamb one would not obtain any appreciate quantity of the fierce energy useful to a Magician who was invoking Mars. In such a case a ram

A wolf would be still better in the case of Mars. See 777 for the correspondences between various animals and the "32 Paths" of Nature.

would be more suitable. And this ram should be virgin — the whole potential of its original total energy should not have been diminished in any way.

There is also the question of its magical freedom. Sexual intercourse creates a link between its exponents, and therefore a responsibility.

For the highest spiritual working one must accordingly choose that victim which contains the greatest and purest force. A male child of perfect innocence and high intelligence

It appears from the Magical Records of Frater Perdurabo that He made this particular sacrifice on an average about 150 times every year between 1912 e.v. and 1928 e.v. Contrast J.K.Huyman's "La-Bas", where a perverted form of Magic of an analogous order is described.

"It is the sacrifice of oneself spiritually. And the intelligence and innocence of that male child are the perfect understanding of the Magician, his one aim, without lust of result. And male he must be, because what he sacrifices is not the material blood, but his creative power." This initiated interpretation of the texts was sent spontaneously by Soror I.W.E., for the sake of the younger Brethren.

WEH ADDENDA: When Crowley speaks of sacrificing a male child, his diaries and other writings indicate that he thereby obfuscates the actual practice. Crowley did this by diversion of the act of sexual intercourse and other sexual actions. He considered contraception as human sacrifice. There is no indication in any of his writings that he ever performed infanticide. In fact, Crowley was even against abortion.

is the most satisfactory and suitable victim.

For evocations it would be more convenient to place the blood of the victim in the Triangle — the idea being that the spirit might obtain from the blood this subtle but physical substance which was the quintessence of its life in such a manner as to enable it to take on a visible and tangible shape.

See Equinox (I, V. Supplement: Tenth Aethyr) for an Account of an Operation where this was done. Magical phenomena of the creative order are conceived and germinate in a peculiar thick velvet darkness, crimson, purple, or deep blue, approximating black: as if it were said, In the body of Our Lady of the Stars.

See 777 for the correspondences of the various forces of Nature with drugs, perfumes, etc.

Those magicians who abject to the use of blood have endeavored to replace it with incense. For such a purpose the incense of Abramelin may be burnt in large quantities. Dittany of Crete is also a valuable medium. Both these incenses are very catholic in their nature, and suitable for almost any materialization.

But the bloody sacrifice, though more dangerous, is more efficacious; and for nearly all purposes human sacrifice is the best. The truly great Magician will be able to use his own blood, or possibly that of a disciple, and that without sacrificing the physical life irrevocably.

Such details, however, may safely be left to the good sense of the Student. Experience here as elsewhere is the best teacher. In the Sacrifice during Invocation, however, it may be said without fear of contradiction that the death of the victim should coincide with the supreme invocation.

WEH addenda: A sworn testimony by Crowley declares that he held actual human sacrifice to physical death to be the most efficacious, but that he never did such a thing. On the matter concerning death of the victim in invocation, Crowley elsewhere enlarges that this is the ephemeral death of the Ego.

An example of this sacrifice is given in Chapter 44 of Liber 333. This Mass may be recommended generally for daily practice.

One last word on this subject. There is a Magical operation of maximum importance: the Initiation of a New Aeon. When it becomes necessary to utter a Word, the whole Planet must be bathed in blood. Before man is ready to accept the Law of Thelema, the Great War must be fought. This Bloody Sacrifice is the critical point of the World-Ceremony of the Proclamation of Horus, the Crowned and conquering Child, as Lord of the Aeon.

Note: This paragraph was written in the summer of 1911 e.v., just three years before its fulfilment.

This whole matter is prophesied in the Book of the Law itself; let the student take note, and enter the ranks of the Host of the Sun.

II

There is another sacrifice with regard to which the Adepts have always maintained the most profound secrecy. It is the supreme mystery of practical Magick. Its name is the Formula of the Rosy Cross. In this case the victim is always — in a certain sense — the Magician himself, and the sacrifice must coincide with the utterance of the most sublime and secret name of the God whom he wishes to invoke.

Properly performed, it never fails of its effect. But it is difficult for the beginner to do it satisfactorily, because it is a great effort for the mind to remain concentrated upon the purpose of the ceremony. The overcoming of this difficulty lends most powerful aid to the Magician.

It is unwise for him to attempt it until he has received regular initiation in the true

It is here desirable to warn the reader against the numerous false orders which have impudently assumed the name of Rosicrucian. The Masonic Societas Rosicruciana is honest and harmless; and makes no false pretences; if its members happen as a rule to be pompous busy-bodies, enlarging the borders of their phylacteries, and scrupulous about cleansing the outside of the cup and the platter; if the masks of the Officers in their Mysteries suggest the Owl, the Cat, the Parrot, and the Cuckoo, while the Robe of their Chief Magus is a Lion's Skin, that is their affair. But those orders run by persons "claiming" to represent the True Ancient Fraternity are common swindles. The representatives of the late S. L. Mathers (Count McGregor) are the phosphorescence of the rotten wood of a branch which was lopped off the tree at the end of the 19th century. Those of Papus (Dr. Encausse), Stanislas de Guaita and Peladan, merit respect as serious, but lack full knowledge and authority. The "Ordo Rosae Crucis" is a mass of ignorance and falsehood, but this may be a deliberate device for masking itself. The test of any Order is its attitude towards the Law of Thelema. The True Order presents the True Symbols, but avoids attaching the True Name thereto; it is only when the Postulant has taken irrevocable Oaths and been received formally, that he discovers what Fraternity he has joined. If he have taken false symbols for true, and find himself magically pledged to a gang of rascals, so much the worse for him!

Order of the Rosy Cross, and he must have taken the vows with the fullest comprehension and experience of their meaning. It is also extremely desirable that he should have attained an absolute degree of moral emancipation

This results from the full acceptance of the Law of THELEMA, persistently put into practice.

, and that purity of spirit which results from a perfect understanding both of the differences and harmonies of the planes upon the Tree of Life.

For this reason FRATER PERDURABO has never dared to use this formula in a fully ceremonial manner, save once only, on an occasion of tremendous import, when, indeed, it was not He that made the offering, but ONE in Him. For he perceived a grave defect in his moral character which he has been able to overcome on the intellectual plane, but not hitherto upon higher planes. Before the conclusion of writing this book he will have done so.

P.S. With the happiest results. P.

The practical details of the Bloody Sacrifice may be studied in various ethnological manuals, but the general conclusions are summed up in Frazer's "Golden Bough", which is strongly recommended to the reader. Actual ceremonial details likewise may be left to experiment. The method of killing is practically uniform. The animal should be stabbed to the heart, or its throat severed, in either case by the knife. All other methods of killing are less efficacious; even in the case of Crucifixion death is given by stabbing.

Yet one might devise methods of execution appropriate to the Weapons: Stabbing or clubbing for the Lance or Wand, Drowning or poisoning for the Cup, Beheading for the Sword, Crushing for the Disk, Burning for the Lamp, and so forth.

One may remark that warm-blooded animals only are used as victims: with two principal exceptions. The first is the serpent, which is only used in a very special Ritual;

The Serpent is not really killed; it is seethed in an appropriate vessel; and it issues in due season refreshed and modified, but still essentially itself. The idea is the transmission of life and wisdom from a vehicle which has fulfilled its formula to one capable of further extension. The development of a wild fruit by repeated plantings in suitable soil is an analogous operation.

WEH ADDENDA: *The serpent is the phallus. The vessel and the seething are likewise sub rosa.*

the second the magical beetles of Liber Legis. (See Part IV.)

One word of warning is perhaps necessary for the beginner. The victim must be in perfect health — or its energy may be as it were poisoned. It must also not be too large:

The sacrifice (e.g.) of a bull is sufficient for a large number of people; hence it is commonly made in public ceremonies, and in some initiations, e.g. that of a King, who needs force for his whole kingdom. Or again, in the Consecration of a Temple.

See Lord Dunsany, "The Blessing of Pan" — a noble and most notable prophecy of Life's fair future.

the amount of energy disengaged is almost unimaginably great, and out of all anticipated proportion to the strength of the animal. Consequently, the Magician may easily be overwhelmed and obsessed by the force which he has let loose; it will then probably manifest itself in its lowest and most objectionable form. The most intense spirituality of purpose

This is a matter of concentration, with no ethical implication. The danger is that one may get something which one does not want. This is "bad" by definition. Nothing is in itself good or evil. The shields of the Sabines which crushed Tarpeia were not murderous to them, but the contrary. Her criticism of them was simply that they were what she did not want in her Operation.

is absolutely essential to safety.

In evocations the danger is not so great, as the Circle forms a protection; but the circle in such a case must be protected, not only by the names of God and the Invocations used at the same time, but by a long habit of successful defence.

> *The habitual use of the Lesser Banishing Ritual of the Pentagram (say, thrice daily) for months and years and constant assumption of the God-form of Harpocrates (See Equinox, I, II and Liber 333, cap. XXV for both of these) should make the "real circle", i.e. the Aura of the Magus, impregnable.*
>
> *This Aura should be clean-cut, resilient, radiant, iridescent, brilliant, glittering. "A Soap-bubble of razor-steel, streaming with light from within" is my first attempt at description; and is not bad, despite its incongruities: P.*
>
> *"FRATER PERDURABO, on the one occasion on which I was able to see Him as He really appears, was brighter than the Sun at noon. I fell instantly to the floor in swoon which lasted several hours, during which I was initiated." Soror A.'.. Cf. Rev. I, 12-17.*

If you are easily disturbed or alarmed, or if you have not yet overcome the tendency of the mind to wander, it is not advisable for you to perform the "Bloody Sacrifice".

> *The whole idea of the word Sacrifice, as commonly understood, rests upon an error and superstition, and is unscientific, besides being metaphysically false. The Law of Thelema has totally changed the Point of View as to this matter. Unless you have thoroughly assimilated the Formula of Horus, it is absolutely unsafe to meddle with this type of Magick. Let the young Magician reflect upon the Conservation of Matter and of Energy.*

Yet it should not be forgotten that this, and that other art at which we have dared darkly to hint, are the supreme formulae of Practical Magick.

You are also likely to get into trouble over this chapter unless you truly comprehend its meaning.

> *There is a traditional saying that whenever an Adept seems to have made a straightforward, comprehensible statement, then is it most certain that He means something entirely different. The Truth is nevertheless clearly set forth in His Words: it is His simplicity that baffles the unworthy. I have chosen the expressions in this Chapter in such a way that it is likely to mislead those magicians who allow selfish interests to cloud their intelligence, but to give useful hints to such as are bound by the proper Oaths to devote their powers to legitimate ends. "...thou hast no right but to do thy will." "It is a lie, this folly against self." The radical error of all uninitiates is that they define "self" as irreconcilably opposed to "not-self." Each element of oneself is, on the contrary, sterile and without meaning, until it fulfils itself, by "love under will", in its counterpart in the Macrocosm. To separate oneself from others is to destroy oneself; the way to realize and to extend oneself is to lose that self — its sense of separateness — in the other. Thus: Child plus food: this does not preserve one at the expense of the other; it "destroys" or rather changes both in order to fulfil both in the result of the operation — a grown man. It is in fact impossible to preserve anything as it is by positive action upon it. Its integrity demands inaction; and inaction, resistance to change, is stagnation, death and dissolution due to the internal putrefaction of the starved elements.*

CHAPTER XIII

OF THE BANISHINGS:

AND OF THE PURIFICATIONS.

Cleanliness is next to Godliness, and had better come first. Purity means singleness. God is one. The wand is not a wand if it has something sticking to it which is not an essential part of itself. If you wish to invoke Venus, you do not succeed if there are traces of Saturn mixed up with it.

That is a mere logical commonplace: in magick one must go much farther than this. One finds one's analogy in electricity. If insulation is imperfect, the whole current goes back to earth. It is useless to plead that in all those miles of wire there is only one-hundredth of an inch unprotected. It is no good building a ship if the water can enter, through however small a hole.

That first task of the Magician in every ceremony is therefore to render his Circle absolutely impregnable.

> *See, however, the Essay on Truth in "Konx om Pax". The Circle (in one aspect) asserts Duality, and emphasizes Division.*

If one littlest thought intrude upon the mind of the Mystic, his concentration is absolutely destroyed; and his consciousness remains on exactly the same level as the Stockbroker's. Even the smallest baby is incompatible with the virginity of its mother. If you leave even a single spirit within the circle, the effect of the conjuration will be entirely absorbed by it.

> *While one remains exposed to the action of all sorts of forces they more or less counterbalance each other, so that the general equilibrium, produced by evolution, is on the whole maintained. But if we suppress all but one, its action becomes irresistible. Thus, the pressure of the atmosphere would crush us if we "banished" that of our bodies; and we should crumble to dust if we rebelled successfully against cohesion. A man who is normally an "allround good sort" often becomes intolerable when he gets rid of his collection of vices; he is swept into monomania by the spiritual pride which had been previously restrained by countervailing passions. Again, there is a worse draught when an ill-fitting door is closed than when it stands open. It is not as necessary to protect his mother and his cattle from Don Juan as it was from the Hermits of the Thebaid.*

The Magician must therefore take the utmost care in the matter of purification, "firstly", of himself, "secondly", of his instruments, "thirdly", of the place of working. Ancient Magicians recommended a preliminary purification of from three days to many months. During this period of training they took the utmost pains with diet. They avoided animal food, lest the elemental spirit of the animal should get into their atmosphere. They practised sexual abstinence, lest they should be influenced in any way by the spirit of the wife. Even in regard to the excrements of the body they were equally careful; in trimming the hair and nails, they ceremonially destroyed

> *Such destruction should be by burning or other means which produces a complete chemical change. In so doing care should be taken to bless and liberate the native elemental of the thing burnt. This maxim is of universal application.*

the severed portion. They fasted, so that the body itself might destroy anything extraneous to the bare necessity of its existence. They purified the mind by special prayers and conservations. They avoided the contamination of social intercourse, especially the conjugal kind; and their servitors were disciples specially chosen and consecrated for the work.

In modern times our superior understanding of the essentials of this process enables us to dispense to some extent with its external rigours; but the internal purification must be even more carefully performed. We may eat meat, provided that in doing so we affirm that we eat it in order to strengthen us for the special purpose of our proposed invocation.

In an Abbey of Thelema we say "Will" before a meal. The formula is as follows. "Do what thou wilt shall be the whole of the Law." "What is thy Will?" "It is my will to eat and drink" "To what end?" "That my body may be fortified thereby." "To what end?" "That I may accomplish the Great Work." "Love is the law, love under will." "Fall to!" This may be adapted as a monologue. One may also add the inquiry "What is the Great Work?" and answer appropriately, when it seems useful to specify the nature of the Operation in progress at the time. The point is to seize every occasion of bringing every available force to bear upon the objective of the assault. It does not matter what the force is (by any standard of judgment) so long as it plays its proper part in securing the success of the general purpose. Thus, even laziness may be used to increase our indifference to interfering impulses, or envy to counteract carelessness. See Liber CLXXV, Equinox I, VII, p. 37. This is especially true, since the forces are destroyed by the process. That is, one destroys a complex which in itself is "evil" and puts its elements to the one right use.

By thus avoiding those actions which might excite the comment of our neighbours we avoid the graver dangers of falling into spiritual pride.

We have understood the saying: "To the pure all things are pure", and we have learnt how to act up to it. We can analyse the mind far more acutely than could the ancients, and we can therefore distinguish the real and right feeling from its imitations. A man may eat meat from self-indulgence, or in order to avoid the dangers of asceticism. We must constantly examine ourselves, and assure ourselves that every action is really subservient to the One Purpose.

It is ceremonially desirable to seal and affirm this mental purity by Ritual, and accordingly the first operation in any actual ceremony is bathing and robing, with appropriate words. The bath signifies the removal of all things extraneous to antagonistic to the one thought. The putting on of the robe is the positive side of the same operation. It is the assumption of the fame of mind suitable to that one thought.

A similar operation takes place in the preparation of every instrument, as has been seen in the Chapter devoted to that subject. In the preparation of the place of working, the same considerations apply. We first remove from that place all objects; and we then put into it those objects, and only those objects, which are necessary. During many days we occupy ourselves in this process of cleansing and consecration; and this again is confirmed in the actual ceremony.

The cleansed and consecrated Magician takes his cleansed and consecrated instruments into that cleansed and consecrated place, and there proceeds to repeat that double ceremony in the ceremony itself, which has these same two main parts. The first part of every ceremony is the banishing; the second, the invoking. The same formula is repeated even in the ceremony of banishing itself, for in the banishing ritual of the pentagram we not only command the demons to depart, but invoke the Archangels and their hosts to act as guardians of the Circle during our pre-occupation with the ceremony proper. In more elaborate ceremonies it is usual to banish everything by name. Each element, each planet, and each sign, perhaps even the Sephiroth themselves; all are removed, including the very one which we wished to invoke, for that forces as existing in Nature is always impure. But this process, being long and wearisome, is not altogether advisable in actual working. It is usually sufficient to perform a general banishing, and to rely upon the aid of the guardians invoked. Let the banishing therefore be short, but in no wise slurred — for it is useful as it tends to produce the proper attitude of mind for the invocations. "The Banishing Ritual of the Pentagram" (as now rewritten, Liber 333, Cap.

XXV) is the best to use.

See also the Ritual called "The Mark of the Beast" given in an Appendix. But this is pantomorphous.

Only the four elements are specifically mentioned, but these four elements contain the planets and the signs

The signs and the planets, of course, contain, the elements. It is important to remember this fact, as it helps one to grasp what all these terms really mean. None of the "Thirty-two Paths" is a simple idea; each one is a combination, differentiated from the others by its structure and proportions. The chemical elements are similarly constituted, as the critics of Magick have at last been compelled to admit.

— the four elements are Tetragrammaton; and Tetragrammaton is the Universe. This special precaution is, however, necessary: make exceedingly sure that the ceremony of banishing is effective! Be alert and on your guard! Watch before you pray! The feeling of success in banishing, once acquired, is unmistakable.

At the conclusion, it is usually well to pause for a few moments, and to make sure once more that every thing necessary to the ceremony is in its right place. The Magician may then proceed to the final consecration of the furniture of the Temple.

That is, of the special arrangement of that furniture. Each object should have been separately consecrated beforehand. The ritual here in question should summarize the situation, and devote the particular arrangement to its purpose by invoking the appropriate forces. Let it be well remembered that each object is bound by the Oaths of its original consecration as such. Thus, if a pantacle has been made sacred to Venus, it cannot be used in an operation of Mars; the Energy of the Exorcist would be taken up in overcoming the opposition of the "Karma" or inertia therein inherent.

CHAPTER XIV

OF THE CONSECRATIONS:

WITH AN ACCOUNT OF THE NATURE AND NURTURE OF THE MAGICAL LINK.

I

Consecration is the active dedication of a thing to a single purpose. Banishing prevents its use for any other purpose, but it remains inert until consecrated. Purification is performed by water, and banishing by air, whose weapon is the sword. Consecration is performed by fire, usually symbolised by the holy lamp.

> *The general conception is that the three active elements co-operate to affect earth; but earth itself may be employed as an instrument. Its function is solidification. The use of the Pentacle is indeed very necessary in some types of operation, especially those whose object involves manifestation in matter, and the fixation in (more or less) permanent form of the subtle forces of Nature.*

In most extant magical rituals the two operations are performed at once; or (at least) the banishing has the more important place, and greater pains seem to be taken with it; but as the student advances to Adeptship the banishing will diminish in importance, for it will no longer be so necessary. The Circle of the Magician will have been perfected by his habit of Magical work. In the truest sense of that word, he will never step outside the Circle during his whole life. But the consecration, being the application of a positive force, can always be raised to a closer approximation to perfection. Complete success in banishing is soon attained; but there can be no completeness in the advance to holiness.

The method of consecration is very simple. Take the wand, or the holy oil, and draw upon the object to be consecrated the supreme symbol of the force to which you dedicate it. Confirm this dedication in words, invoking the appropriate God to indwell that pure temple which you have prepared for Him. Do this with fervour and love, as if to balance the icy detachment which is the proper mental attitude for banishing.

> *The Hebrew legends furnish us with the reason for the respective virtues of water and fire. The world was purified by water at the Deluge, and will be consecrated by fire at the last Judgment. Not until that is finished can the "real ceremony" begin.*

The words of purification are: Asperges me, Therion, hyssopo, et mundabor; lavabis me, et super nivem dealbabor.

Those of consecration are: Accendat in nobis Therion ignem sui amoris et flammam aeternae caritatis.

> *These may now advantageously be replaced by (a) "... pure will, unassuaged of purpose, delivered from the lust of result, is every way perfect." (CCXX, I, 44) to banish; and (b) "I am uplifted in thine heart; and the kisses of the stars rain hard upon thy body." (CCXX, II, 62) to consecrate. For the Book of the Law contains the Supreme Spells.*

These, as initiates of the VII Degree of O.T.O. are aware, mean more than appears.

II

It is a strange circumstance that no Magical writer has hitherto treated the immensely important subject of the Magical Link. It might almost be called the Missing Link. It has apparently always been taken for granted, only lay writers on Magick like Dr. J. G. Frazer have accorded the subject its full importance.

Let us try to make considerations of the nature of Magick in a strictly scientific spirit, as well as, deprived of the guidance of antiquity, we may.

What is a Magical Operation? It may be defined as any event in nature which is brought to pass by Will. We must not exclude potato-growing or banking from our definition.

Let us take a very simple example of a Magical Act: that of a man blowing his nose. What are the conditions of the success of the Operation? Firstly, that the man's Will should be to blow his nose; secondly, that he should have a nose capable of being blown; thirdly, that he should have at command an apparatus capable of expressing his spiritual Will in terms of material force, and applying that force to the object which he desires to affect. His Will may be as strong and concentrated as that of Jupiter, and his nose may be totally incapable of resistance; but unless the link is made by the use of his nerves and muscles in accordance with psychological, physiological, and physical law, the nose will remain unblown through all eternity.

Writers of Magick have been unsparing in their efforts to instruct us in the preparation of the Will, but they seem to have imagined that no further precaution was necessary. There is a striking case of an epidemic of this error whose history is familiar to everybody. I refer to Christian Science, and the cognate doctrines of "mental healing" and the like. The theory of such people, stripped of dogmatic furbelows, is perfectly good Magic of its kind, its negroid kind. The idea is correct enough: matter is an illusion created by Will through mind, and consequently susceptible of alteration at the behest of its creator. But the practice has been lacking. They have not developed a scientific technique for applying the Will. It is as if they expected the steam of Watts' kettle to convey people from place to place without the trouble of inventing and using locomotives.

Let us apply these considerations to Magick in its restricted sense, the sense in which it was always understood until the Master Therion extended it to cover the entire operations of Nature.

What is the theory implied in such rituals as those of the Goetia? What does the Magician do? He applies himself to invoke a God, and this God compels the appearance of a spirit whose function is to perform the Will of the magician at the moment. There is no trace of what may be called machinery in the method. The exorcist hardly takes the pains of preparing a material basis for the spirit to incarnate except the bare connection of himself with his sigil. It is apparently assumed that the spirit already possesses the means of working on matter. The conception seems to be that of a schoolboy who asks his father to tell the butler to do something for him. In other words, the theory is grossly animistic. The savage tribes described by Frazer had a far more scientific theory. The same may be said of witches, who appear to have been wiser than the thaumaturgists who despised them. They at least made waxen images — identified by baptism — of the people they wished to control. They at least used appropriate bases for Magical manifestations, such as blood and other vehicles of animal force, with those of vegetable virtue such as herbs. They were also careful to put their bewitched products into actual contact — material or astral — with their victims. The classical exorcists, on the contrary, for all their learning, were careless about this essential condition. They acted as stupidly as people who should write business letters and omit to post them.

It is not too much to say that this failure to understand the conditions of success accounts for the discredit into which Magick fell until Eliphas Levi undertook the task of re-habilitating it two generations ago. But even he (profoundly as he studied, and luminously as he expounded, the nature of Magick considered as a universal formula) paid no attention whatever to that question of the Magical Link, though he everywhere implies that it is essential to the Work. He evaded the question by making the "petitio principii" of assigning to the Astral Light the power of transmitting vibrations of all kinds. He nowhere enters into detail as to how its effects are produced. He does not inform us as to the qualitative or quantitative laws of this light. (The scientifically trained student will observe the analogy between Levi's postulate and that of ordinary science "in re" the luminiferous ether.)

It is deplorable that nobody should have recorded in a systematic form the results of our investigations of the Astral Light. We have no account of its properties or of the laws which obtain in its sphere. Yet these are sufficiently remarkable. We may briefly notice that, in the Astral Light, two or more objects can occupy the same space at the same time without interfering with each other or losing their outlines.

In that Light, objects can change their appearance completely without suffering change of Nature. The same thing can reveal itself in an infinite number of different aspects; in fact, it identifies itself by so doing, much as a writer or a painter reveals himself in a succession of novels or pictures, each of which is wholly himself and nothing else, but himself under varied conditions, though each appears utterly different from its fellows. In that Light one is "swift without feet and flying without wings"; one can travel without moving, and communicate without conventional means of expression. One is insensible to heat, cold, pain, and other forms of apprehension, at least in the shapes which are familiar to us in our bodily vehicles. They exist, but they are appreciated by us, and they affect us, in a different manner. In the Astral Light we are bound by what is, superficially, an entirely different series of laws. We meet with obstacles of a strange and subtle character; and we overcome them by an energy and cunning of an order entirely alien to that which serves us in earthly life. In that Light, symbols are not conventions but realities, yet (on the contrary) the beings whom we encounter are only symbols of the realities of our own nature. Our operations in that Light are really the adventures of our own personified thoughts. The universe is a projection of ourselves; an image as unreal as that of our faces in a mirror, yet, like that face, the necessary form of expression thereof, not to be altered save as we alter ourselves.

> *This passage must not be understood as asserting that the Universe is purely subjective. On the contrary, the Magical Theory accepts the absolute reality of all things in the most objective sense. But all perceptions are neither the observer nor the observed; they are representations of the relation between them. We cannot affirm any quality in an object as being independent of our sensorium, or as being in itself that which it seems to us. Nor can we assume that what we cognize is more than a partial phantom of its cause. We cannot even determine the meaning of such ideas as motion, or distinguish between time and space, except in relation to some particular observer. For example, if I fire a cannon twice at an interval of 3 hours, an observer on the Sun would note a difference of some 200,000 miles in space between the shots, while to me they seem "in the same place." Moreover, I am incapable of perceiving any phenomenon except by means of the arbitrary instruments of my senses; it is thus correct to say that the Universe as I know it is subjective, without denying its objectivity.*

The mirror may be distorted, dull, clouded, or cracked; and to this extent, the reflection of ourselves may be false even in respect of its symbolic presentation. In that Light, therefore, all that we do is to discover ourselves by means of a sequence of hieroglyphics, and the changes which we apparently operate are in an objective sense illusions.

But the Light servers us in this way. It enables us to see ourselves, and therefore to aid us to initiate ourselves by showing us what we are doing. In the same way a watchmaker uses a lens, though it exaggerates and thus falsifies the image of the system of wheels which he is trying to adjust. In the same way, a writer employs arbitrary characters according to a meaningless convention in order to enable his reader by retranslating them to obtain an approximation to his idea.

Such are a few of the principal characteristics Astral Light. Its quantitative laws are much less dissimilar from those of material physics. Magicians have too often been foolish enough to suppose that all classes of Magical Operations were equally easy. They seem to have assumed that the "almighty power of God" was an infinite quantity in presence of which all finites were equally insignificant. "One day is with the Lord as a thousand years" is their first law of Motion. "Faith can move mountains" they say, and disdain to measure either the faith or the mountains. If you can kill a chicken by Magick, why not destroy an army with equal exertion? "With God all things are possible."

This absurdity is an error of the same class as that mentioned above. The facts are wholly opposed. Two and two make four in the Astral as rigorously as anywhere else. The distance of one's Magical target and the accuracy of one's Magical rifle are factors in the success of one's Magical shooting in just the same way as at Bisley. The law of Magical gravitation is as rigid as that of Newton. The law of Inverse Squares may not apply; but some such law does apply. So it is for everything. You cannot produce a thunderstorm unless the materials exist in the air at the time, and a Magician who could make rain in Cumberland might fail lamentably in the Sahara. One might make a talisman to win the love of a shop-girl and find it work, yet be baffled in the case of a countess; or vice versa. One might impose one's Will on a farm, and be crushed by that of a city; or vice versa. The MASTER THERION himself, with all his successes in every kind of Magick, sometimes appears utterly impotent to perform feats which almost any amateur might do, because He has matched his Will against that of the world, having undertaken the Work of a Magus to establish the word of His Law on the whole of mankind. He will succeed, without doubt, but He hardly expects to see more than a sample of His product during His present incarnation. But He refuses to waste the least fraction of His force on works foreign to His WORK, however obvious it may seem to the onlooker that His advantage lies in commanding stones to become bread, or otherwise making things easy for Himself.

These considerations being thoroughly understood we may return to the question of making the Magical Link. In the case above cited FRATER PERDURABO composed His talisman by invoking His Holy Guardian Angel according to the Sacred Magick of Abramelin the Mage. That Angel wrote on the lamen the Word of the Aeon. The Book of the Law is this writing. To this lamen the Master Therion gave life by devoting His own life thereto. We may then regard this talisman, the Law, as the most powerful that has been made in the world's history, for previous talismans of the same type have been limited in their scope by conditions of race and country. Mohammed's talisman, Allah, was good only from Persia to the Pillars of Hercules. The Buddha's, Anatta, operated only in the South and East of Asia. The new talisman, Thelema, is master of the planet.

But now observe how the question of the Magical Link arises! No matter how mighty the truth of Thelema, it cannot prevail unless it is applied to any by mankind. As long as the Book of the Law was in Manuscript, it could only affect the small group amongst whom it was circulated. It had to be put into action by the Magical Operation of publishing it. When this was done, it was done without proper perfection. Its commands as to how the work ought to be done were not wholly obeyed. There were doubt and repugnance in FRATER PERDURABO's mind, and they hampered His work. He was half-hearted. Yet, even so then intrinsic power of the truth of the Law and the impact of the publication were sufficient to shake the world so that a critical war broke out, and the minds of men were moved in a mysterious manner. The second blow was struck by the re-publication of the Book in September 1913, and this time the might of this Magick burst out and caused a catastrophe to civilization. At this hour, the MASTER THERION is concealed, collecting his forces for a final blow. When The Book of the Law and its Comment is published, with the forces of His whole Will in perfect obedience to the instructions which have up to now been misunderstood or neglected, the result will be incalculably effective. The event will establish the kingdom of the Crowned and Conquering Child over the whole earth, and all men shall bow to the Law, which is "love under will".

This is an extreme case; but there is one law only to govern the small as the great. The same laws describe and measure the motions of the ant and the stars. Their light is no swifter than that of a spark. In every operation of Magick the link must be properly made. The first requisite is the acquisition of adequate force of the kind required for the purpose. We must have electricity of a certain potential in sufficient amount if we wish to heat food in a furnace. We shall need a more intense current and a greater supply to light a city than to charge a telephone wire. No other kind of force will do. We cannot use the force of steam directly to impel an aeroplane, or to get drunk. We must apply it in adequate strength in an appropriate manner.

It is therefore absurd to invoke the spirit of Venus to procure us the love of an Empress, unless we take measures to transmit the influence of our work to the lady. We may for example consecrate a letter expressing our Will; or, if we know how, we may use some object connected with the person whose acts we are attempting to control, such as a lock of hair or a handkerchief once belonging to her, and so in subtile connection with her aura. But for material ends it is better to have material means. We must not rely on fine gut in trolling for salmon. Our will to kill a tiger is poorly conveyed by a charge of small shot fired at a range of one hundred yards. Our talisman must, therefore, be an object suitable to the nature of our Operation, and we must have some such means of applying its force to such a way as will naturally compel the obedience of the portion of Nature which we are trying to change. If one will the death of a sinner, it is not sufficient to hate him, even if we grant that the vibrations of thought, when sufficiently powerful and pure, may modify the Astral light sufficiently to impress its intention to a certain extent on such people as happen to be sensitive. It is much surer to use one's mind and muscle in service of that hate by devising and making a dagger, and then applying the dagger to the heart of one's enemy. One must give one's hate a bodily form of the same order as that which one's enemy has taken for his manifestation. Your spirit can only come into contact with his by means of this magical manufacture of phantoms; in the same way, one can only measure one's mind (a certain part of it) against another man's by expressing them in some such form as the game of chess. One cannot use chessmen against another man unless he agree to use them in the same sense as you do. The board and men form the Magical Link by which you can prove your power to constrain him to yield. The game is a device by which you force him to turn down his king in surrender, a muscular act made in obedience to your will, thought he may be twice your weight and strength.

These general principles should enable the student to understand the nature of the work of making the Magical Link. It is impossible to give detailed instructions, because every case demands separate consideration. It is sometimes exceedingly difficult to devise proper measures.

Remember that Magick includes all acts soever. Anything may serve as a Magical weapon. To impose one's Will on a nation, for instance, one's talisman may be a newspaper, one's triangle a church, or one's circle a Club. To win a woman, one's pantacle may be a necklace; to discover a treasure, one's wand may be a dramatist's pen, or one's incantation a popular song.

Many ends, many means: it is only important to remember the essence of the operation, which is to will its success with sufficiently pure intensity, and to incarnate that will in a body suitable to express it, a body such that its impact on the bodily expression of the idea one wills to change is to cause it to do so. For instance, is it my will to become a famous physician? I banish all "hostile spirits" such as laziness, alien interests, and confliction pleasures, from my "circle" the hospital; I consecrate my "weapons" (my various abilities) to the study of medicine; I invoke the "Gods" (medical authorities) by studying and obeying their laws in their books. I embody the "Formulae" (the ways in which causes and effects influence disease) in a "Ritual" (my personal style of constraining sickness to conform with my will). I persist in these conjurations year after year, making the Magical gestures of healing the sick, until I compel the visible appearance of the Spirit of Time, and make him acknowledge me his master. I have used the appropriate kind of means, in adequate measure, and applied them in ways pertinent to my purpose by projecting my incorporeal idea of ambition in a course of action such as to induce in others the incorporeal idea of satisfying mine. I made my Will manifest to sense; sense swayed the Wills of my fellowmen; mind wrought on mind through matter.

I did not "sit for" a medical baronetcy by wishing I had it, or by an "act of faith", or by praying to God "to move Pharaoh's heart", as our modern mental, or our mediaeval, mystic, miracle-mongers were and are muddlers and maudlin enough to advise us to do.

A few general observations on the Magical Link may not be amiss, in default of details; one cannot make a Manual of How to Go Courting, with an Open-Sesame to each particular Brigand's Cavern, any more than one can furnish a budding burglar with a directory containing the combination of every existing safe. But one can point out the broad distinctions between women who yield, some to flattery, some to eloquence, some to appearance, some to rank, some to wealth, some to ardour, and some to authority. We cannot exhaust the combinations of Lover's Chess, but we may enumerate the principal gambits: the Bouquet, the Chocolates, the Little Dinner, the Cheque-Book, the Poem, the Motor by Moonlight, the Marriage Certificate, the Whip, and the Feigned Flight.

The Magical Link may be classified under three main heads; as it involves (1) one plane and one person, (2) one plane and two or more persons, (3) two planes.

In class (1) the machinery of Magick — the instrument — already exists. Thus, I may wish to heal my own body, increase my own energy; develop my own mental powers, or inspire my own imagination. Here the Exorcist and the Demon are already connected, consciously or subconsciously, by an excellent system of symbols. The Will is furnished by Nature with an apparatus adequately equipped to convey and execute its orders.

It is only necessary to inflame the Will to the proper pitch and to issue its commands; they are instantly obeyed, unless — as in the case of organic disease — the apparatus is damaged beyond the art of Nature to repair. It may be necessary in such a case to assist the internal "spirits" by the "purification" of medicines, the "banishing" of diet, or some other extraneous means.

But at least there is no need of any special device "ad hoc" to effect contact between the Circle and the Triangle. Operations of this class are therefore often successful, even when the Magician has little or no technical knowledge of Magick. Almost any duffer can "pull himself together", devote himself to study, break off a bad habit, or conquer a cowardice. This class of work, although the easiest, is yet the most important; for it includes initiation itself in its highest sense. It extends to the Absolute in every dimension; it involves the most intimate analysis, and the most comprehensive synthesis. In a sense, it is the sole type of Magick either necessary or proper to the Adept; for it includes both the attainment of the Knowledge and Conversation of the Holy Guardian Angel, and the Adventure of the Abyss.

The second class includes all operations by which the Magician strives to impose his Will upon objects outside his own control, but within that of such other wills as are symbolised by means of a system similar to his own. That is, they can be compelled naturally by cognate consciousness.

For instance, one may wish to obtain the knowledge put forth in this book. Not knowing that such a book exists, one might yet induce some one who knows of it to offer a copy. Thus one's operation would consist in inflaming one's Will to possess the knowledge to the point of devoting one's life to it, in expressing that will by seeking out people who seem likely to know what is needed, and in imposing it on them by exhibiting such enthusiastic earnestness that they will tell the enquirer that this book will meet his needs.

Does this sound too simple? Can this obvious common-sense course be really that marvellous Magick that frightens folk so? Yes, even this triviality is one instance of how Magick works.

But the above practical programme may be a fiasco. One might then resort to Magick in the conventional sense of the word, by constructing and charging a Pantacle appropriate to the object; this Pantacle should then cause a strain in the Astral Light such that the vibrations would compel some alien consciousness to restore equilibrium by bringing the book.

Suppose a severer and more serious aim; suppose that I wish to win a woman who dislikes me and loves somebody else. In this case, not only her Will, but her lover's must be overcome by my own. I have no direct control of either. But my Will is in touch with the woman's by means of our minds; I have only to make my mind the master of hers by the existing means of communication; her mind will then present its recantation to her Will, her Will repeal its decision, and her body submit to mine as the seal of her surrender.

Here the Magical Link exists; only it is complex instead of simple as in the First Class.

There is opportunity for all kinds of error in the transmission of the Will; misunderstanding may mar the matter; a mood may make mischief; external events may interfere; the lover may match me in Magick; the Operation itself may offend nature in many ways; for instance, if there is a subconscious incompatibility between myself and the woman, I deceive myself into thinking that I desire her. Such a flaw is enough to bring the whole operation to naught, just as no effort of Will can make oil mix with water.

I may work "naturally" by wooing, of course. But, magically, I may attack her astrally so that her aura becomes uneasy, responding no longer to her lover. Unless they diagnose the cause, a quarrel may result, and the woman's bewildered and hungry Body of Light may turn in its distress to that of the Magician who has mastered it.

Take a third case of this class 2. I wish to recover my watch, snatched from me in a crowd.

Here I have no direct means of control over the muscles that could bring back my watch, or over the mind that moves these muscles. I am not even able to inform that mind of my Will, for I do not know where it is. But I know it to be a mind fundamentally like my own, and I try to make a Magical Link with it by advertising my loss in the hope of reaching it, being careful to calm it by promising it immunity, and to appeal to its own known motive by offering a reward. I also attempt to use the opposite formula; to reach it by sending my "familiar spirits", the police, to hunt it, and compel its obedience by threats.

> *The ceremonial method would be to transfer to the watch — linked naturally to me by possession and use — a thought calculated to terrify the thief, and induce him to get rid of it at once. Observing clairsentiently this effect, suggest relief and reward as the result of restoring it.*

Again, a sorcerer might happen to possess an object belonging magically to a rich man, such as a compromising letter, which is really as much part of him as his liver; he may then master the will of that man by intimidating his mind. His power to publish the letter is as effective as if he could injure the man's body directly.

These "natural" cases may be transposed into subtler terms; for instance, one might master another man, even a stranger, by sheer concentration of will, ceremonially or otherwise wrought up to the requisite potential. But in one way or another that will must be made to impinge on the man; by the normal means of contact if possible, if not, by attacking some sensitive spot in his subconscious sensorium. But the heaviest rod will not land the smallest fish unless there be a line of some sort fixed firmly to both.

The Third Class is characterized by the absence of any existing link between the Will of the Magician and that controlling the object to be affected. (The Second Class may approximate to the Third when there is no possibility of approaching the second mind by normal means, as sometimes happens).

This class of operations demands not only immense knowledge of the technique of Magick combined with tremendous vigour and skill, but a degree of Mystical attainment which is exceedingly rare, and when found is usually marked by an absolute apathy on the subject of any attempt to achieve any Magick at all. Suppose that I wish to produce a thunderstorm. This event is beyond my control or that of any other man; it is as useless to work on their minds as my own. Nature is independent of, and indifferent to, man's affairs. A storm is caused by atmospheric conditions on a scale so enormous that the united efforts of all us Earth-vermin could scarcely disperse one cloud, even if we could get at it. How then can any Magician, he who is above all things a knower of Nature, be so absurd as to attempt to throw the Hammer of Thor? Unless he be simply insane, he must be initiated in a Truth which transcends the apparent facts. He must be aware that all nature is a continuum, so that his mind and body are consubstantial with the storm, are equally expressions of One Existence, all alike of the self-same order of artifices whereby the Absolute appreciates itself. He must also have assimilated the fact that the Quantity is just as much a form as Quality; that as all things are modes of One Substance, so their measures are modes of their relation. Not only are gold and lead mere letters, meaningless in themselves yet appointed to spell the One Name; but the difference between the bulk of a mountain and that of a mouse is no more than one method of differentiating them, just as the letter "m" is not bigger than the letter "i" in any real sense of the word.

> *Professor Rutherford thinks it not theoretically impracticable to construct a detonator which could destroy every atom of matter by releasing the energies of one, so that the vibrations would excite the rest to disintegrate explosively.*

Our Magician, with this in his mind, will most probably leave thunderstorms to stew in their own juice; but, should he decide (after all) to enliven the afternoon, he will work in the manner following.

First, what are the elements necessary for his storms? He must have certain stores of electrical force, and the right kind of clouds to contain it.

He must see that the force does not leak away to earth quietly and slyly.

He must arrange a stress so severe as to become at last so intolerable that it will disrupt explosively.

Now he, as a man, cannot pray to God to cause them, for the Gods are but names for the forces of Nature themselves.

But, "as a Mystic", he knows that all things are phantoms of One Thing, and that they may be withdrawn therein to reissue in other attire. He knows that all things are in himself, and that he is All-One with the All. There is therefore no theoretical difficulty about converting the illusion of a clear sky into that of a tempest. On the other hand, he is aware, "as a Magician", that illusions are governed by the laws of their nature. He knows that twice two is four, although both "two" and "four" are merely properties pertaining to One. He can only use the Mystical identity of all things in a strictly scientific sense. It is true that his experience of clear skies and storms proves that his nature contains elements cognate with both; for it not, they could not affect him. He is the Microcosm of his own Macrocosm, whether or no either one or the other extend beyond his knowledge of them. He must therefore arouse in himself those ideas which are clansmen of the Thunderstorm, collect all available objects of the same nature for talismans, and proceed to excite all these to the utmost by a

Magical ceremony; that is, by insisting on their godhead, so that they flame within and without him, his ideas vitalising the talismans. There is thus a vivid vibration of high potential in a certain group of sympathetic substances and forces; and this spreads as do the waves from a stone thrown into a lake, widening and weakening; till the disturbance is compensated. Just as a handful of fanatics, insane with one over-emphasised truth, may infect a whole country for a time by inflaming that thought in their neighbours, so the Magician creates a commotion by disturbing the balance of power. He transmits his particular vibration as a radio operator does with his ray; rate-relation determines exclusive selection.

In practice, the Magician must "evoke the spirits of the storm" by identifying himself with the ideas of which atmospheric phenomena are the expressions as his humanity is of him; thus achieved, he must impose his Will upon them by virtue of the superiority of his intelligence and the integration of his purpose to their undirected impulses and uncomprehending interplay.

All such Magick demands the utmost precision in practice. It is true that the best rituals give us instructions in selecting our vehicles of force. In 777 we find "correspondences" of many classes of being with the various types of operation, so that we know what weapons, jewels, figures, drugs, perfumes, names, etc. to employ in any particular work. But it has always been assumed that the invoked force is intelligent and competent, that it will direct itself as desired without further ado, by this method of sympathetic vibrations.

The necessity of timing the force has been ignored; and so most operations, even when well performed as far as invocation goes, are as harmless as igniting loose gunpowder.

But, even allowing that Will is sufficient to determine the direction, and prevent the dispersion of the force, we can hardly be sure that it will act on its object, unless that object be properly prepared to receive it. The Link must be perfectly made. The object must possess in itself a sufficiency of stuff sympathetic to our work. We cannot make love to a brick, or set an oak to run errands.

We see, then, that we can never affect anything outside ourselves save only as it is also within us. Whatever I do to another, I do also to myself. If I kill a man, I destroy my own life at the same time. That is the magical meaning of the so-called "Golden Rule", which should not be in the imperative but in the indicative mood. Every vibration awakens all others of its particular pitch.

There is thus some justification for the assumption of previous writers on Magick that the Link is implicit, and needs no special attention. Yet, in practice, there is nothing more certain than that one ought to confirm one's will by all possible acts on all possible planes. The ceremony must not be confined to the formally magical rites. We must neglect no means to our end, neither despising our common sense, nor doubting our secret wisdom.

When Frater I. A. was in danger of death in 1899 e.v. Frater V. N. and FRATER PERDURABO did indeed invoke the spirit Buer to visible manifestation that the might heal their brother; but also one of them furnished the money to send him to a climate less cruel than England's. He is alive to day

P.S. He died some months after this passage was written: but he had been enabled to live and work for nearly a quarter of a century longer than he would otherwise have done.

; who cares whether spirits or shekels wrought that which these Magicians willed?

Let the Magical Link be made strong! It is "love under will"; it affirms the identity of the Equation of the work; it makes success Necessity.

CHAPTER XVI

(Part I)

OF THE OATH

The third operation in any magical ceremony is the oath or proclamation. The Magician, armed and ready, stands in the centre of the Circle, and strikes once upon the bell as if to call the attention of the Universe. He then declares "who he is", reciting his magical history by the proclamation of the grades which he has attained, giving the signs and words of those grades.

This is not merely to prove himself a person in authority. It is to trace the chain of causes that have let to the present position, so that the operation is seen as karma.

He then states the purpose of the ceremony, and proves that it is necessary to perform it and to succeed in its performance. He then takes an oath before the Lord of the Universe (not before the particular Lord whom he is invoking) as if to call Him to witness to the act. He swears solemnly that he will perform it — that nothing shall prevent him from performing it — that he will not leave the operation until it is successfully performed — and once again he strikes upon the bell.

Yet, having demonstrated himself in that position at once infinitely lofty and infinitely unimportant, the instrument of destiny, he balances this by the "Confession", in which there is again an infinite exaltation harmonised with an infinite humility. He admits himself to be a weak human being humbly aspiring to something higher; a creature of circumstance utterly dependent — even for the breath of life — upon a series of fortunate accidents. He makes this confession prostrate

Compare the remarks in a previous chapter. But this is a particular case. We leave its justification as a problem.

before the altar in agony and bloody sweat. He trembles at the thought of the operation which he has dared to undertake, saying, "Father, if it be Thy Will, let this cup pass from me! Nevertheless not my will but Thine be done!"

Of course this is for the beginner. As soon as it is assimilated as true, he will say: "My will which is thine be done!" And ultimately no more distinguish "mine" from "thine". A sympathetic change of gesture will accompany the mental change.

The dread answer comes that It Must Be, and this answer so fortifies him with holy zeal that it will seem to him as if he were raised by divine hands from that prostrate position; with a thrill of holy exaltation he renews joyfully the Oath, feeling himself once again no longer the man but the Magician, yet not merely the Magician, but the chosen and appointed person to accomplish a task which, however apparently unimportant, is yet an integral part of universal destiny, so that if it were not accomplished the Kingdom of Heaven would be burst in pieces.

He is now ready to commence the invocations. He consequently pauses to cast a last glance around the Temple to assure himself of the perfect readiness of all things necessary, and to light the incense.

The Oath is the foundation of all Work in Magick, as it is an affirmation of the Will. An Oath binds the Magician for ever. In Part II of Book 4 something has already been said on this subject; but its importance deserves some further elaboration. Thus, should one, loving a woman, make a spell to compel her embraces, and tiring of her a little later, evoke Zazel to kill her; he will find that the implications of his former Oath conflict with those proper to invoke the Unity of the Godhead of Saturn. Zazel will refuse to obey him in the case of the woman whom he has sworn that he loves. To this some may object that, since all acts are magical, every man who loves a woman implicitly takes an Oath of love, and therefore would never be able to murder her later, as we find to be the not uncommon case. The explanation is as follows. It is perfectly true that when Bill Sykes desires to possess Nancy, he does in fact evoke a spirit of the nature of Venus, constraining him by his Oath of Love (and by his magical power as a man) to bring him the girl. So also, when he wants to kill her, he evokes a Martial or Saturnian spirit, with an Oath of hate. But these are not pure planetary spirits, moving in well-defined spheres by rigidly righteous laws. They are gross concretions of confused impulses, "incapable of understanding the nature of an oath". They are also such that the idea of murder is nowise offensive to the Spirit of Love.

It is indeed the criterion of spiritual "caste" that conflicting elements should not coexist in the same consciousness. The psalm-singing Puritan who persecutes publicans, and secretly soaks himself in fire-water; the bewhiskered philanthropist in broadcloth who swindles his customers and sweats his employees: these men must not be regarded as single-minded scoundrels, whose use of religion and respectability to cloke their villainies is a deliberate disguise dictated by their criminal cunning. Far from it, they are only too sincere in their "virtues"; their terror of death and of supernatural vengeance is genuine; it proceeds from a section of themselves which is in irreconcilable conflict with their rascality. Neither side can conciliate, suppress, or ignore the other; yet each is so craven as to endure its enemy's presence. Such men are therefore without pure principles; they excuse themselves for every dirty trick that turns to their apparent advantage.

The first step of the Aspirant toward the Gate of Initiation tells him that purity — unity of purpose — is essential above all else. "Do what thou Wilt" strikes on him, a ray of fierce white flame consuming all that is not utterly God. Very soon he is aware that he cannot consciously contradict himself. He develops a subtle sense which warns him that two trains of thought which he had never conceived as connected are incompatible. Yet deeper drives "Do what thou wilt"; subconscious oppositions are evoked to visible appearance. The secret sanctuaries of the soul are cleansed. "Do What thou Wilt" purges his every part. He has become One, one only. His Will is consequently released from the interference of internal opposition, and he is a Master of Magick. But for that very reason he is now utterly impotent to achieve anything that is not in absolute accordance with his Original Oath, with his True Will, by virtue whereof he incarnated as a man. With Bill Sykes love and murder are not mutually exclusive, as they are with King Arthur. The higher the type of man, the more sensitive he becomes; so that the noblest love divines intuitively when a careless word or gesture may wound, and, vigilant, shuns them as being of the family of murder. In Magick, likewise, the Adept who is sworn to attain to the Knowledge and Conversation of his Holy Guardian Angel may in his grosser days have been expert as a Healer, to find that he is now incapable of any such work. He will probably be puzzled, and wonder whether he has lost all his power. Yet the cause may be no more than that the Wisdom of his Angel depreciates the interference of ignorant kindliness with diseases which may have been sent to the sufferer for a purpose profoundly important to his welfare.

In the case of THE MASTER THERION, he had originally the capacity for all classes of Orgia. In the beginning, He cured the sick, bewitched the obstinate, allured the seductive, routed the aggressive, made himself invisible, and generally behaved like a Young-Man-About-town on every possible plane. He would afflict one vampire with a Sending of Cats, and appoint another his private Enchantress, neither aware of any moral oxymoron, nor hampered by the implicit incongruity of his oaths.

But as He advanced in Adeptship, this coltishness found its mouth bitted; as soon as He took serious Oaths and was admitted to the Order which we name not, those Oaths prevented him using His powers as playthings.

Trifling operations, such as He once could do with a turn of the wrist, became impossible to the most persistent endeavour. It was many years before He understood the cause of this. But little by little He became so absorbed in the Work of His true Will that it no longer occurred to Him to indulge in capricious amusements.

Yet even at this hour, though He be verily a Magus of A.'. A.'., though His Word be the Word of the Aeon, though He be the Beast 666, the Lord of the Scarlet Woman "in whom is all power given", there are still certain Orgia beyond Him to perform, because to do so would be to affirm what He hath denied in those Oaths by whose virtue He is That He is. This is the case, even when the spirit of such Orgia is fully consonant with His Will. The literal sense of His original Oath insists that it shall be respected.

The case offers two instances of this principle. FRATER PERDURABO specifically swore that he would renounce His personal possessions to the last penny; also that He would allow no human affection to hinder Him. These terms were accepted; He was granted infinitely more than He had imagined possible to an incarnated Man. On the other hand, the price offered by Him was exacted as strictly as if it had been stipulated by Shylock. Every treasure that he had on earth was taken away, and that, usually, in so brutal or cruel a manner as to make the loss itself the least part of the pang. Every human affection that He had in His heart — and that heart aches for Love as few hearts can ever conceive — was torn out and trampled with such infernal ingenuity in intensifying torture that His endurance is beyond belief. Inexplicable are the atrocities which accompanied every step in His Initiation! Death dragged away His children with slow savagery; the women He loved drank themselves into delirium and dementia before His eyes, or repaid His passionate devotion with toad-cold treachery at the moment when long years of loyalty had tempted Him to trust them. His friend, that bore the bag, stole that which was put therein, and betrayed his Master as thoroughly as he was able. At the first distant rumour that the Pharisees were out, his disciples "all forsook Him and fled". His mother nailed Him with her own hands to the cross, and reviled Him as nine years He hung thereupon.

Now, having endured to the end, being Master of Magick, He is mighty to Work His true Will; which Will is, to establish on Earth His Word, the Law of Thelema. He hath none other Will than this; so all that He doth is unto this end. All His Orgia bear fruit; what was the work of a month when He was a full Major Adept is to day wrought in a few minutes by the Words of Will, uttered with the right vibrations into the prepared Ear.

But neither by the natural use of His abilities, though they have made Him famous through the whole world, nor by the utmost might of his Magick, is He able to acquire material wealth beyond the minimum necessary to keep Him alive and at work. It is in vain that He protests that not He but the Work is in need of money; He is barred by the strict letter of His Oath to give all that He hath for His magical Attainment.

Yet more awful is the doom that He hath invoked upon Himself in renouncing His right as a man to enjoy the Love of those whom He loves with passion so selfless, so pure, and so intense in return for the power so to love Mankind that He be chosen to utter the Word of the Aeon for their sake, His reward universal abhorrence, bodily torment, mental despair, and moral paralysis.

Yet He, who hath power over Death, with breath to call back health, with a touch to beckon life, He must watch His own child waste away month by month, aware that His Art may not anywise avail, who hath sold the signet ring of his personal profit to buy him a plain gold band for the felon finger of his bride, that worn widow, the World!

CHAPTER XV

I

OF THE INVOCATION

In the straightforward or "Protestant" system of Magick there is very little to add to what has already been said. The Magician addresses a direct petition to the Being invoked. But the secret of success in invocation has not hitherto been disclosed. It is an exceedingly simple one. It is practically of no importance whatever that the invocation should be "right". There are a thousand different ways of compassing the end proposed, so far as external things are concerned. The whole secret may be summarised in these four words: "Enflame thyself in praying."

This is Qabalistically expressed in the old Formula: Domine noster, audi tuo servo! kyrie Christe! O Christe!

The mind must be exalted until it loses consciousness of self. The Magician must be carried forward blindly by a force which, though in him and of him, is by no means that which he in his normal state of consciousness calls I. Just as the poet, the lover, the artist, is carried out of himself in a creative frenzy, so must it be for the Magician.

It is impossible to lay down rules for the obtaining of this special stimulus. To one the mystery of the whole ceremony may appeal; another may be moved by the strangeness of the words, even by the fact that the "barbarous names" are unintelligible to him. Some times in the course of a ceremony the true meaning of some barbarous name that has hitherto baffled his analysis may flash upon him, luminous and splendid, so that he is caught up unto orgasm. The smell of a particular incense may excite him effectively, or perhaps the physical ecstasy of the magick dance.

Every Magician must compose his ceremony in such a manner as to produce a dramatic cilmax. At the moment when the excitement becomes ungovernable, when then the whole conscious being of the Magician undergoes a spiritual spasm, at that moment must he utter the supreme adjuration.

One very effective method is to stop short, by a supreme effort of will, again and again, on the very brink of that spasm, until a time arrives when the idea of exercising that will fails to occur

This forgetfulness must be complete; it is fatal to try to "let oneself go" consciously.

. Inhibition is no longer possible or even thinkable, and the whole being of the Magician, no minutest atom saying nay, is irresistibly flung forth. In blinding light, amid the roar of ten thousand thunders, the Union of God and man is consummated.

If the Magician is still seen standing in the Circle, quietly pursuing his invocations, it is that all the conscious part of him has become detached from the true ego which lies behind that normal consciousness. But the circle is wholly filled with that divine essence; all else is but an accident and an illusion.

The subsequent invocations, the gradual development and materialization of the force, require no effort. It is one great mistake of the beginner to concentrate his force upon the actual stated purpose of the ceremony. This mistake is the most frequent cause of failures in invocation.

A corollary of this Theorem is that the Magician soon discards evocation almost altogether — only rare circumstances demand any action what ever on the material plane. The Magician devotes himself entirely to the invocation of a god; and as soon as his balance approaches perfection he ceases to invoke any partial god; only that god vertically above him is in his path. And so a man who perhaps took up Magick merely with the idea of acquiring knowledge, love, or wealth, finds himself irrevocably committed to the performance of *The Great Work.*

It will now be apparent that there is no distinction between magick and meditation except of the most arbitrary and accidental kind.

> *There is the general metaphysical antithesis that Magick is the Art of the Will-to-Live, Mysticism of the Will-to-Die; but — "Truth comes bubbling to my brim; Life and Death are one to Him!".*

II

Beside these open methods thee are also a number of mental methods of Invocation, of which we may give three.

The first method concerns the so-called astral body. The Magician should practise the formation of this body as recommended in Liber O, and learn to rise on the planes according to the instruction given in the same book, though limiting his "rising" to the particular symbol whose God he wishes to invoke.

The second is to recite a mantra suitable to the God.

The third is the assumption of the form of the God — by transmuting the astral body into His shape. This last method is really essential to all proper invocation, and cannot be too sedulously practised.

There are many other devices to aid invocation, so many that it is impossible to enumerate them; and the Magician will be wise to busy himself in inventing new ones.

We will give one example.

Suppose the Supreme Invocation to consist of 20 to 30 barbarous names, let him imagine these names to occupy sections of a vertical column, each double the length of the preceding one; and let him imagine that his consciousness ascends the column with each name. The mere multiplication will then produce a feeling of awe and bewilderment which is the proper forerunner of exstasy.

In the essay "Energized Enthusiasm" in No. IX, Vol. I of the Equinox

> *The earliest and truest Christians used what is in all essentials this method. See "Fragments of a Faith Forgotten" by G.R.S.Mead, Esq. B. A., pp. 80-81.*

> *There is a real connexion between what the vulgar call blasphemy and what they call immorality, in the fact that the Christian legend is an echo of a Phallic rite. There is also a true and positive connexion between the Creative force of the Macrocosm, and that of the Microcosm. For this reason the latter must be made a pure and consecrated as the former. The puzzle for most people is how to do this. The study of Nature is the Key to that Gate.*

is given a concise account of one of the classical methods of arousing Kundalini. This essay should be studied with care and determination.

CHAPTER XVI

(Part II)

OF THE CHARGE TO THE SPIRIT WITH SOME ACCOUNT OF THE CONSTRAINTS AND CURSES OCCASIONALLY NECESSARY

I

On the appearance of the spirit, or the manifestation of the force in the talisman which is being consecrated, it is necessary to bind it by an Oath or Charge. A spirit should be made to lay its hand visibly on the weapon by whose might it has been evoked, and to "swear obedience and faith to Him that liveth and triumpheth, that regneth above him in His palaces as the Balance of Righteousness and Truth" by the names used in the evocation.

It is then only necessary to formulate the Oath or Charge in language harmonious with the previously announced purpose of the operation.

The precaution indicated is not to let oneself sink into one's humanity while the weapon is extended beyond the Circle. Were the force to flow from it to you instead of from you to it, you would be infallibly blasted, or, at the least, become the slave of the spirit.

At no moment is it more important that the Divine Force should not only fill, but radiate from, the aura of the Magician.

II

Occasionally it may happen that the spirit is recalcitrant, and refuses to appear.

Let the Magician consider the cause of such disobedience!

It may be that the place or time is wrong. One cannot easily evoke water-spirits in the Sahara, or salamanders in the English Lake District. Hismael will not readily appear when Jupiter is below the horizon.

> *It is not possible in this elementary treatise to explain the exact nature of the connexion between the rays of the actual planet called Jupiter and the Jupiterian elements which exist in various degrees in terrestrial objects.*

In order to counteract a natural deficiency of this sort, one would have to supply a sufficient quantity of the proper kind of material. One cannot make bricks without straw.

With regard to invocations of the Gods, such considerations do not apply. The Gods are beyond most material conditions. It is necessary to fill the "heart" and "mind" with the proper basis for manifestation. The higher the nature of the God, the more true this is. The Holy Guardian Angel has always the necessary basis. His manifestation depends solely on the readiness of the Aspirant, and all magical ceremonies used in that invocation are merely intended to prepare that Aspirant; not in any way to attract or influence Him. It is His constant and eternal Will

Since this Knowledge and Conversation is not universal, it seems at first as if an omnipotent will were being baulked. But His Will and your will together make up that one will, because you and He are one. That one will is therefore divided against itself, so long as your will fails to aspire steadfastly.

Also, His will cannot constrain yours. He is so much one with you that even your will to separate is His will. He is so certain of you that He delights in your perturbation and coquetry no less than in your surrender. These relations are fully explained in Liber LXV. See also Liber Aleph CXI.

to become one with the Aspirant, and the moment the conditions of the latter make it possible, That Bridal is consummated.

III

The obstinacy of a spirit (or the inertial of a talisman) usually implies a defect in invocation. The spirit cannot resist even for a moment the constraint of his Intelligence, when that Intelligence is working in accordance with the Will of the Angel, Archangel and God above him. It is therefore better to repeat the Invocations than to proceed at once to curses.

The Magician should also consider

Of course this should have been done in preparing the Ritual. But he renews this consideration from the new standpoint attained by the invocation.

whether the evocation be in truth a necessary part of the Karma of the Universe, as he has stated in his own Oath (See Cap. XVI, I). For if this be a delusion, success is impossible. It will then be best to go back to the beginning, and recapitulate with greater intensity and power of analysis the Oath and the Invocations. And this may be done thrice.

But if this be satisfactorily accomplished, and the spirit be yet disobedient, the implication is that some hostile force is at work to hinder the operation. It will then become advisable to discover the nature of that force, and to attack and destroy it. This makes the ceremony more useful than ever to the Magician, who may thereby be led to unveil a black magical gang whose existence he had not hitherto suspected.

His need to check the vampiring of a lady in Paris by a sorceress once led FRATER PERDURABO to the discovery of a very powerful body of black magicians, which whom he was obliged to war for nearly 10 years before their ruin was complete and irremediable as it now is.

Such a discovery will not necessarily impede the ceremony. A general curse may be pronounced against the forces hindering the operation (for "ex hypothesi" no divine force can be interfering) and having thus temporarily dislodged them — for the power of the God invoked will suffice for this purpose — one may proceed with a certain asperity to conjure the spirit, for that he has done ill to bend before the conjurations of the Black Brothers.

Indeed, some demons are of a nature such that they only understand curses, are not amenable to courteous command: —

"a slave

Whom stripes may move, not kindness."

Finally, as a last resource, one may burn the Sigil of the Spirit in a black box with stinking substances, all having been properly prepared beforehand, and the magical links properly made, so that he is really tortured by the Operation.

> *The precise meaning of these phrases is at first sight obscure. The spirit is merely a recalcitrant part of one's own organism. To evoke him is therefore to become conscious of some part of one's own character; to command and constrain him is to being that part into subjection. This is best understood by the analogy of teaching oneself some mental-physical accomplishment (e.g. billiards), by persistent and patient study and practice, which often involves considerable pain as well as trouble.*

This is a rare event, however. Only once in the whole of his magical career was FRATER PERDURABO driven to so harsh a measure.

IV

In this connexion, beware of too ready a compliance on the part of the spirit. If some Black Lodge has got wind of your operation, it may send the spirit, full of hypocritical submission, to destroy you. Such a spirit will probably pronounce the oath amiss, or in some way seek to avoid his obligations.

It is a dangerous trick, though, for the Black Lodge to play; for if the spirit come properly under your control, it will be forced to disclose the transaction, and the current will return to the Black Lodge with fulminating force. The liars will be in the power of their own lie; their own slaves will rise up and put them into bondage. The wicked fall into the pit that they themselves digged.

And so perish all the King's enemies!

V

The charge to the spirit is usually embodied, except in works of pure evocation, which after all are comparatively rare, in some kind of talisman. In a certain sense, the talisman is the Charge expressed in hieroglyphics. Yet, every object soever is a talisman, for the definition of a talisman is: something upon which an act of will (that is, of Magick) has been performed in order to fit it for a purpose. Repeated acts of will in respect of any object consecrate it without further ado. One knows what miracles can be done with one's favourite mashie! One has used the mashie again and again, one's love for it growing in proportion to one's success with it, and that success again made more certain and complete by the effect of this "love under will", which one bestows upon it by using it.

It is, of course, very important to keep such an abject away from the contact of the profane. It is instinctive not to let another person use one's fishing rod or one's gun. It is not that they could do any harm in a material sense. It is the feeling that one's use of these things has consecrated them to one's self.

Of course, the outstanding example of all such talismans is the wife. A wife may be defined as an object specially prepared for taking the stamp of one's creative will. This is an example of a very complicated magical operation, extending over centuries. But, theoretically, it is just an ordinary case of talismanic magick. It is for this reason that so much trouble has been taken to prevent a wife having contact with the profane; or, at least, to try to prevent her.

Readers of the Bible will remember that Absalom publicly adopted David's wives and concubines on the roof of the palace, in order to signify that he had succeeded in breaking his father's magical power.

Now, there are a great many talismans in this world which are being left lying about in a most reprehensibly careless manner. Such are the objects of popular adoration, as ikons, and idols. But, it is actually true that a great deal of real magical Force is locked up in such things; consequently, by destroying these sacred symbols, you can overcome magically the people who adore them.

It is not at all irrational to fight for one's flag, provided that the flag is an object which really means something to somebody. Similarly, with the most widely spread and most devotedly worshipped talisman of all, money, you can evidently break the magical will of a worshipper of money by taking his money away from him, or by destroying its value in some way or another. But, in the case of money, general experience tells us that there is very little of it lying about loose. In this case, above all, people have recognised its talismanic virtue, that is to say, its power as an instrument of the will.

But with many ikons and images, it is easy to steal their virtue. This can be done sometimes on a tremendous scale, as, for example, when all the images of Isis and Horus, or similar mother-child combinations, were appropriated wholesale by the Christians. The miracle is, however, of a somewhat dangerous type, as in this case, where enlightenment has come through the researches of archaeologists. It has been shown that the so-called images of Mary and Jesus are really nothing but imitations of those of Isis and Horus. Honesty is the best policy in Magick as in other lines of life.

CHAPTER XVII

OF THE LICENSE TO DEPART

After a ceremony has reached its climax, anti-climax must inevitably follow. But if the ceremony has been successful this anti-climax is merely formal. The Magician should rest permanently on the higher plain to which he has aspired.

The rock-climber who relaxes on the face of the precipice falls to earth; but once he has reached a safe ledge he may sit down.

The whole force of the operation should be absorbed; but there is almost certain to be a residuum, since no operation is perfect: and (even if it were so) there would be a number of things, sympathetic to the operation, attracted to the Circle. These must be duly dispersed, or they will degenerate and become evil. It is always easy to do this where invocations are concerned; the mere removal of the strain imposed by the will of the magician will restore things to their normal aspects, in accordance with the great law of inertia. In a badly-managed evocation, however, this does not always obtain; the spirit may refuse to be controlled, and may refuse to depart — even after having sworn obedience. In such a case extreme danger may arise.

In the ordinary way, the Magician dismisses the spirit with these words: "And now I say unto thee, depart in peace unto thine habitations and abodes — and may the blessing of the Highest be upon thee in the name of (here mention the divine name suitable to the operation, or a Name appropriate to redeem that spirit); and let there be peace between thee and me; and be thou very ready to come, whensoever thou are invoked and called!"

It is usual to add "either by a word, or by a will, or by this mighty Conjuration of Magick Art."

Should he fail to disappear immediately, it is a sign that there is something very wrong. The Magician should immediately reconsecrate the Circle with the utmost care. He should then repeat the dismissal; and if this does not suffice, he should then perform the banishing ritual suitable to the nature of the spirit and, if necessary, add conjurations to the same effect. In these circumstances, or if anything else suspicious should occur, he should not be content with the apparent disappearance of the spirit, who might easily make himself invisible and lie in ambush to do the Magician a mischief when he stepped out of the Circle — or even months afterwards.

Any symbol which has once definitely entered your environment with your own consent is extremely dangerous; unless under absolute control. A man's friends are more capable of working him harm than are strangers; and his greatest danger lies in his own habits.

Of course it is the very condition of progress to build up ideas into the subconscious. The necessity of selection should therefore be obvious.

True, there comes a time when all elements soever must be thus assimilated. Samadhi is, by definition, that very process. But, from the point of view of the young magician, there is a right way — strait and difficult — of performing all this. One cannot too frequently repeat that what is lawful and proper to one Path is alien to another.

Immediately after the License to Depart, and the general closing up of the work, it is necessary that the Magician should sit down and write up his magical record. However much he may have been tired

He ought to be refreshed, more than after a full night's deep sleep. This forms one test of his skill.

by the ceremony, he ought to force himself to do this until it becomes a habit. Verily, it is better to fail in the magical ceremony than to fail in writing down an accurate record of it. One need not doubt the propriety of this remark. Even if one is eaten alive by Malkah be-Tarshishim ve-Ruachoth ha-Schehalim, it does not matter very much, for it is over so very quickly. But the record of the transactions is otherwise important. Nobody cares about Duncan having been murdered by Macbeth. It is only one of a number of similar murders. But Shakespeare's account of the incident is a unique treasure of mankind. And, apart from the question of the value to others, there is that of the value to the magician himself. The record of the magician is his best asset.

It is as foolish to do Magick without method, as if it were anything else. To do Magick without keeping a record is like trying to run a business without book-keeping. There are a great many people who quite misunderstand the nature of Magick. They have an idea that it is something vague and unreal, instead of being, as it is, a direct means of coming into contact with reality. It is these people who pay themselves with phrases, who are always using long words with no definite connotation, who plaster themselves with pompous titles and decorations which mean nothing whatever. With such people we have nothing to do. But to those who seek reality the Key of Magick is offered, and they are hereby warned that the key to the treasure-house is no good without the combination; and the combination is the magical record.

From one point of view, magical progress actually consists in deciphering one's own record.

As one is a Star in the Body of Nuith, every successive incarnation is a Veil, and the acquisition of the Magical Memory a gradual Unveiling of that Star, of that God.

For this reason it is the most important thing to do, on strictly magical grounds. But apart from this, it is absolutely essential that the record should be clear, full and concise, because it is only by such a record that your teacher can judge how it is best to help you. Your magical teacher has something else to do besides running around after you all the time, and the most important of all his functions is that of auditor. Now, if you call in an auditor to investigate a business, and when he asks for the books you tell him that you have not thought it worth while to keep any, you need not be surprised if he thinks you every kind of an ass.

It is — at least, it was — perfectly incredible to THE MASTER THERION that people who exhibit ordinary common sense in the other affairs of life should lose it completely when they tackle Magick. It goes far to justify the belief of the semi-educated that Magick is rather a crazy affair after all. However, there are none of these half-baked lunatics connected with the A.'. A.'., because the necessity for hard work, for passing examinations at stated intervals, and for keeping an intelligible account of what they are doing, frightens away the unintelligent, idle and hysterical.

There are numerous models of magical and mystical records to be found in the various numbers of the "Equinox", and the student will have no difficulty in acquiring the necessary technique, if he be diligent in practice.

CHAPTER XVIII

OF CLAIRVOYANCE AND THE BODY OF LIGHT

ITS POWER AND ITS DEVELOPMENT

ALSO CONCERNING DIVINATION

I

Within the human body is another body of approximately the same size and shape;

i.e. as a general rule. It can be altered very greatly in these respects.

but made of a subtler and less illusory material. It is of course not "real"; but then no more is the other body! Before treating of clairvoyance one must discuss briefly this question of reality, for misapprehension on the subject has given rise to endless trouble.

There is the story of the American in the train who saw another American carrying a basket of unusual shape. His curiosity mastered him, and he leant across and said: "Say, stranger, what you got in that bag?" The other, lantern-jawed and taciturn, replied: "mongoose". The first man was rather baffled, as he had never heard of a mongoose. After a pause he pursued, at the risk of a rebuff: "But say, what is a Mongoose?" "Mongoose eats snakes", replied the other. This was another poser, but he pursued: "What in hell do you want a Mongoose for?" "Well, you see", said the second man (in a confidential whisper) "my brother sees snakes". The first man was more puzzled than ever; but after a long think, he continued rather pathetically: "But say, them ain't real snakes". "Sure", said the man with the basket, "but this Mongoose ain't real either".

This is a perfect parable of Magick. There is no such thing as truth in the perceptible universe; every idea when analysed is found to contain a contradiction. It is quite useless (except as a temporary expedient) to set up one class of ideas against another as being "more real". The advance of man towards God is not necessarily an advance towards truth. All philosophical systems have crumbled. But each class of ideas possesses true relations within itself. It is possible, with Berkeley,

The real Berkeley did nothing of the sort: the reference here is to an imaginary animal invented by Dr. Johnson out of sturdy British ignorance.

to deny the existence of water and of wood; but, for all that, wood floats on water. The Magician becomes identical with the immortal Osiris, yet the Magician dies. In this dilemma the facts must be restated. One should preferably say that the Magician becomes conscious of that part of himself which he calls the immortal Osiris; and that Part does not "die".

Now this interior body of the Magician, of which we spoke at the beginning of this chapter, does exist, and can exert certain powers which his natural body cannot do. It can, for example, pass through "matter", and it can move freely in every direction through space. But this is because "matter", in the sense in which we commonly use the word, is on another plane

We do not call electrical resistance, or economic laws, unreal, on the ground that they are not directly perceived by the senses. Our magical doctrine is universally accepted by sceptics — only they wish to make Magick itself an exception!

Now this fine body perceives a universe which we do not ordinarily perceive. It does not necessarily perceive the universe which we do normally perceive, so although in this body I can pass through the roof, it does not follow that I shall be able to tell what the weather is like. I might do so, or I might not: but if I could not, it would not prove that I was deceiving myself in supposing that I had passed through the roof. This body, which is called by various authors the Astral double, body of Light, body of fire, body of desire, fine body, scin-laeca and numberless other names is naturally fitted to perceive objects of its own class ... in particular, the phantoms of the astral plane.

There is some sort of vague and indeterminate relation between the Astrals and the Materials; and it is possible, with great experience, to deduce facts about material things from the astral aspect which they present to the eyes of the Body of Light.

> *This is because there is a certain necessary correspondence between planes; as in the case of an Anglo-Indian's liver and this temper. The relation appears "vague and indeterminate" only in so far as one happens to be ignorant of the laws which state the case. The situation is analogous to that of the chemist before the discovery of the law of "Combining Weights", etc.*

This astral plane is so varied and so changeable that several clairvoyants looking at the same thing might give totally different accounts of what they saw; yet they might each make correct deductions. In looking at a man the first clairvoyant might say: "The lines of force are all drooping"; the second: "It seems all dirty and spotty"; a third; "The Aura looks very ragged." Yet all might agree in deducing that the man was in ill-health. In any case all such deductions are rather unreliable. One must be a highly skilled man before one can trust one's vision. A great many people think that they are extremely good at the business, when in fact they have only made some occasional shrewd guesses (which they naturally remember) in the course of hundreds of forgotten failures.

The only way to test clairvoyance is to keep a careful record of every experiment made. For example, FRATER O. M. once gave a clairvoyant a waistcoat to psychometrize. He made 56 statements about the owner of the waistcoat; of these 4 were notably right; 17, though correct, were of that class of statement which is true of almost everybody. The remainder were wrong. It was concluded from this that he showed no evidence of any special power. In fact, his bodily eyes, — if he could discern Tailoring — would have served him better, for he thought the owner of the vest was a corn-chandler, instead of an earl, as he is.

The Magician can hardly take too much trouble to develop this power in himself. It is extremely useful to him in guarding himself against attack; in obtaining warnings, in judging character, and especially in watching the process of his Ceremonies.

There are a great many ways of acquiring the power. Gaze into a crystal, or into a pool of ink in the palm of the hand, or into a mirror, or into a teacup. Just as with a microscope the expert operator keeps both eyes open, though seeing only through the one at the eye-piece of the instrument, so the natural eyes, ceasing to give any message to the brain, the attention is withdrawn from them, and the man begins to see through the Astral eyes.

These methods appear to The MASTER THERION to be unsatisfactory. Very often they do not work at all. It is difficult to teach a person to use these methods; and, worst of all, they are purely passive! You can see only what is shewn you, and you are probably shewn things perfectly pointless and irrelevant.

The proper method is as follows: — Develop the body of Light until it is just as real to you as your other body, teach it to travel to any desired symbol, and enable it to perform all necessary Rites and Invocations. In short, educate it. Ultimately, the relation of that body with your own must be exceedingly intimate; but before this harmonizing takes place, you should begin by a careful differentiation. The first thing to do, therefore, is to get the body outside your own. To avoid muddling the two, you begin by imagining a shape resembling yourself standing in front of you. Do not say: "Oh, it's only imagination!" The time to test that is later on, when you have secured a fairly clear mental image of such a body. Try to imagine how your own body would look if you were standing in its place; try to transfer your consciousness to the Body of Light. Your own body has its eyes shut. Use the eyes of the Body of Light to describe the objects in the room behind you. Don't say. "It's only an effort of subconscious memory" ... the time to test that is later on.

As soon as you feel more or less at home in the fine body, let it rise in the air. Keep on feeling the sense of rising; keep on looking about you as you rise until you see landscapes or beings of the astral plane. Such have a quality all their own. They are not like material things — they are not like mental pictures — they seem to lie between the two.

After some practice has made you adept, so that in the course of any hour's journey you can reckon on having a fairly eventful time, turn your attention to reaching a definite place on the astral plane; invoke Mercury, for example, and examine carefully your record of the resulting vision — discover whether the symbols which you have seen correspond with the conventional symbols of Mercury.

This testing of the spirits is the most important branch of the whole tree of Magick. Without it, one is lost in the jungle of delusion. Every spirit, up to God himself, is ready to deceive you if possible, to make himself out more important than he is; in short to lay in wait for your soul in 333 separate ways. Remember that after all the highest of all the Gods is only the Magus,

See Liber 418, 3rd Aethyr.

Mayan, the greatest of all the devils.

You may also try "rising on the planes".

See Infra and Appendix.

With a little practice, especially if you have a good Guru, you ought to be able to slip in and out of your astral body as easily as you slip in and out of a dressing-gown. It will then no longer be so necessary for your astral body to be sent far off; without moving an inch you will be able to "turn on" its eyes and ears — as simply as the man with the microscope (mentioned above) can transfer his complete attention from one eye to the other.

Now, however unsuccessful your getting out the body may apparently have been, it is most necessary to use every effort to bring it properly back. Make the Body of Light coincide in space with the physical body, assume the God-Form, and vibrate the name of Harpocrates with the utmost energy; then recover unity of consciousness. If you fail to do this properly you may find yourself in serious trouble. Your Body of Light may wander away uncontrolled, and be attacked and obsessed. You will become aware of this through the occurrence of headache, bad dreams, or even more serious signs such as hysteria, fainting fits, possibly madness or paralysis. Even the worst of these attacks will probably wear off, but it may leave you permanently damaged to a greater or less extent.

A great majority of "spiritualists", "occultists", "Toshosophists", are pitiable examples of repeated losses from this cause.

The emotional type of religionist also suffers in this way. Devotion projects the fine body, which is seized and vampirized by the demon masquerading as "Christ" or "Mary", or whoever may be the object of worship. Complete absence of all power to concentrate thought, to follow an argument, to formulate a Will, to hold fast to an opinion or a course of action, or even to keep a solemn oath, mark indelibly those who have thus lost parts of their souls. They wander from one new cult to another even crazier. Occasionally such persons drift for a moment into the surrounding of The MASTER THERION, and are shot out by the simple process of making them try to do a half-hour's honest work of any kind.

In projecting the Astral, it is a valuable additional safeguard to perform the whole operation in a properly consecrated circle.

Proceed with great caution, then, but proceed. In time your Body of Light will be as strong against spirits as your other body against the winds of Heaven. All depends upon the development of that Body of Light. It must be furnished with an organism as ramified and balanced as its shadowy brother, the material body.

To recapitulate once more, then, the first task is to develop your own Body of light within your own circle without reference to any other inhabitants of the world to which it belongs.

That which you have accomplished with the subject you may now proceed to do with the object. You will learn to see the astral appearance of material things; and although this does not properly belong to pure clairvoyance, one may here again mention that you should endeavour to the utmost to develop and fortify this Body of Light. The best and simplest way to do this is to use it constantly, to exercise it in every way. In particular it may be employed in ceremonies of initiation or of invocation — while the physical body remains silent and still.

In doing this it will often be necessary to create a Temple on the astral plane. It is excellent practice to create symbols. This one precaution is needed: after using them, they should be reabsorbed.

Having learned to create astral forms, the next step will be at first very difficult. Phantasmal and fleeting as the astral is in general, those forms which are definitely attached to the material possess enormous powers of resistance, and it consequently requires very high potential to influence them. The material analogues seem to serve as a fortress. Even where a temporary effect is produced, the inertia of matter draws it back to the normal; yet the power of the trained and consecrated will in a well-developed astral body is such that it can even produce a permanent change in the material upon whose Body of Light you are working, e.g.; one can heal the sick by restoring a healthy appearance to their astral forms. On the other hand, it is possible so to disintegrate the Body of Light even of a strong man that he will fall dead.

Such operations demand not only power, but judgment. Nothing can upset the sum total of destiny — everything must be paid for the uttermost farthing. For this reason a great many operations theoretically possible cannot be performed. Suppose, for example, you see two men of similarly unhealthy astral appearance. In one case the cause may be slight and temporary. Your help suffices to restore him in a few minutes. The other, who looks no worse, is really oppressed by a force incalculably greater than you could control, and you would only damage yourself by attempting to help him. The diagnosis between the two cases could be made by an investigation of the deeper strata of the astral, such as compose the"causal body".

A body of black magicians under Anna Kingsford

Anna Kingsford, so far as her good work is concerned, was only the rubber stamp of Edward Maitland.

once attempted to kill a vivisector who was not particularly well known; and they succeeded in making him seriously ill. But in attempting the same thing with Pasteur they produced no effect whatever, because Pasteur was a great genius — an adept in his own line far greater than she in hers — and because millions of people were daily blessing him. It cannot be too clearly understood that magical force is subject to the same laws of proportion as any other kind of force. It is useless for a mere millionaire to try to bankrupt a man who has the Bank of England behind him.

To sum up, the first task is to separate the astral form from the physical body, the second to develop the powers of the astral body, in particular those of sight, travel, and interpretation; third, to unify the two bodies without muddling them.

This being accomplished, the magician is fitted to deal with the invisible.

II

It is now useful to contine with considerations of other planes, which have commonly been classed under the Astral. There is some reason for this, as the delimitations are somewhat vague. Just as the vegetable kingdom merges into the animal, and as the material plane has beings which encroach upon the boundaries of the astral, so do we find it in the higher planes.

The mental images which appear during meditation are subjective, and pertain not at all to the astral plane. Only very rarely do astral images occur during meditation. It is a bad break in the circle, as a rule, when they do.

There is also a Magical Plane. This touches the material, and even includes a portion of it. It includes the Astral, chiefly a full-blooded type of the Astral. It reaches to and includes most, if not all, of the spiritual planes.

The Magical plane is thus the most comprehensive of all. Egyptian Gods are typical inhabitants of this plane, and it is the home of every Adept.

The spiritual planes are of several types, but are all distinguished by a reality and intensity to be found nowhere else. Their inhabitants are formless, free of space and time, and distinguished by incomparable brilliance.

There are also a number of sub-planes, as, for example, the Alchemical. This plane will often appear in the practice of "Rising on the Planes"; its images are usually those of gardens curiously kept, mountains furnished with peculiar symbols, hieroglyphic animals, or such figures as that of the "Hermetic Arcanum", and pictures like the "Goldseekers" and the "Massacre of the Innocents" of Basil Valentine. There is a unique quality about the alchemical Plane which renders its images immediately recognizable.

There are also planes corresponding to various religions past and present, all of which have their peculiar unity.

It is of the utmost importance to the "Clairvoyant" or "traveler in the fine body" to be able to find his way to any desired plane, and operate therein as its ruler.

The Neophyte of A.'. A.'. is examined most strictly in this practice before he is passed to the degree of Zelator.

In "Rising on the Planes" one must usually pass clear through the Astral to the Spiritual. Some will be unable to do this. The "fine body" which is good enough to subsist on lower planes, a shadow among shadows, will fail to penetrate the higher strata. It requires a great development of this body, and an intense infusion of the highest spiritual constituents of man, before he can pierce the veils. The constant practice of Magick is the best preparation possible. Even though the human consciousness fail to reach the goal, the consciousness of the fine body itself may do so, wherefore whoso travels in that body on a subsequent occasion may be found worthy; and its success will react favourably on the human consciousness, and increase its likelihood of success in its next magical operation.

Similarly, the powers gained in this way will strengthen the magician in his mediation-practices. His Will becomes better able to assist the concentration, to destroy the mental images which disturb it, and to reject the lesser rewards of that practice which tempt, and too often stop the progress of, the mystic.

Although it is said that the spiritual lies "beyond the astral", this is theoretical;

> *The Hon. Bertrand Russell's "Principia Mathematica" may be said to "lie beyond" Colenso's "School Arithmetic"; but one can take the former book from one's shelves — as every one should — and read it without first going all through the latter again.*

the advanced Magician will not find it to be so in practice. He will be able by suitable invocation to travel directly to any place desired. In Liber 418 an example of perfection is given. The Adept who explored these Aethyrs did not have to pass through and beyond the Universe, the whole of which yet lies within even the inmost (30th) Aethyr. He was able to summon the Aethyrs he wanted, and His chief difficulty was that sometimes He was at first unable to pierce their veils. In fact, as the Book shows, it was only by virtue of successive and most exalted initiations undergone in the Aethyrs themselves that He was able to penetrate beyond the 15th. The Guardians of such fortresses know how to guard.

The MASTER THERION has published the most important practical magical secrets in the plainest language. No one, by virtue of being clever or learned, has understood one word; and those unworthy who have profaned the sacrament have but eaten and drunken damnation to themselves.

One may bring down stolen fire in a hollow tube from Heaven, as The MASTER THERION indeed has done in a way that no other adept dared to do before him. But the thief, the Titan, must foreknow and consent to his doom to be chained upon a lonely rock, the vulture devouring his liver, for a season, until Hercules, the strong man armed by virtue of that very fire, shall come and release him.

The TEITAN

> *GR:Tau-Epsilon-Iota-Tau-Alpha-Nu = 300+5+10+300+1+50 = 666.*

— whose number is the number of a man, six hundred and three score and six — unsubdued, consoled by Asia and Panthea, must send forth constant showers of blessing not only upon Man whose incarnation he is, but upon the tyrant and the persecutor. His infinite pain must thrill his heart with joy, since every pang is but the echo of some new flame that leaps upon the earth lit by his crime.

For the Gods are the enemies of Man; it is Nature that Man must overcome ere he enter into his kingdom.<
"All elements must at one time have been separate, — that would be the case with great heat. Now when atoms get to the sun, when we get to the sun, we get that immense, extreme heat, and all the elements are themselves again. Imagine that each atom of each element possesses the memory of all his adventures in combination. By the way, that atom (fortified with that memory) would not be the same atom; yet it is, because it has gained nothing from anywhere except this memory. Therefore, by the lapse of time, and by virtue of memory, a thing could become something more than itself; and thus a real development is possible. One can then see a reason for any element deciding to go through this series of incarnations; because so, and only so, can he go; and he suffers the lapse of memory which he has during these incarnations, because he knows he will come through unchanged.

"Therefore you can have an infinite number of gods, individual and equal though diverse, each one supreme and utterly indestructible. This is also the only explanation of how a being could create a war {WEH NOTE: SIC, probably should be "world"} in which war, evil, etc. exist. Evil is only an appearance, because, (like "good") it cannot affect the substance itself, but only multiply its combinations. This is something the same as mystic monotheism, but the objection to that theory is that God has to create things which are all parts of himself, so that their interplay is false. If we presuppose many elements, their interplay is natural. It is no objection to this theory to ask who made the elements, — the elements are at least there, and God, when you look for him, is not there. Theism is "obscurum per obscurius." A male star is built up from the centre outwards; a female from the circumference inwards. This is what is meant when we say that woman has no soul. It explains fully the difference between the sexes.>> The true God is man. In man are all things hidden. Of these the Gods, Nature, Time, all the powers of the universe are rebellious slaves. It is these that men must fight and conquer in the power and in the name of the Beast that hath availed them, the Titan, the Magus, the Man whose number is six hundred and three score and six.

III

The practice of Rising on the Planes is of such importance that special attention must be paid to it. It is part of the essential technique of Magick. Instruction in this practice has been given with such conciseness in Liber O, that one cannot do better than quote verbatim (the "previous experiment" referred to in the first sentence is the ordinary astral journey.):

"1. The previous experiment has little value, and leads to few results of importance. But it is susceptible of a development which merges into a form of Dharana — concentration — and as such may lead to the very highest ends. The principal use of the practice in the last chapter is to familiarise the student with every kind of obstacle and every kind of delusion, so that he may be perfect master of every idea that may arise in his brain, to dismiss it, to transmute it, to cause it instantly to obey his will.

"2. Let him then begin exactly as before; but with the most intense solemnity and determination.

"3. Let him be very careful to cause his imaginary body to rise in a line exactly perpendicular to the earth's tangent at the point where his physical body is situated (or, to put it more simply, straight upwards).

"4. Instead of stopping, let him continue to rise until fatigue almost overcomes him. If he should find that he has stopped without willing to do so, and that figures appear, let him at all costs rise above them. Yea, though his very life tremble on his lips, let him force his way upward and onward!

"5. Let him continue in this so long as the breath of life is in him. Whatever threatens, whatever allures, though it were Typhon and all his hosts loosed from the pit and leagued against him, though it were from the very Throne of God himself that a voice issues bidding him stay and be content, let him struggle on, ever on.

"6. At last there must come a moment when his whole being is swallowed up in fatigue, overwhelmed by its own inertia. Let him sink (when no longer can he strive, though his tongue be bitten through with the effort and the blood gush from his nostrils) into the blackness of unconsciousness; and then on coming to himself, let him write down soberly and accurately a record of all that hath occurred: yea, a record of all that hath occurred."

Of course, the Rising may be done from any starting pint. One can go (for example) into the circle of Jupiter, and the results, especially in the lower planes, will be very different to those obtained from a Saturnian starting point.

The student should undertake a regular series of such experiments, in order to familiarise himself not only with the nature of the different spheres, but with the inner meaning of each. Of course, it is not necessary in every case to push the practice to exhaustion, as described in the instructions, but this is the proper thing to do whenever definitely practising, in order to acquire the power of Rising. But, having obtained this power, it is, of course, legitimate to rise to any particular plane that may be necessary for the purpose of exploration, as in the case of the visions recorded in Liber 418, where the method may be described as mixed. In such a case, it is not enough to invoke the place you wish to visit, because you may not be able to endure its pressure, or to breathe its atmosphere. Several instances occur in that record where the seer was unable to pass through certain gateways, or to remain in certain contemplations. He had to undergo certain Initiations before he was able to proceed. Thus, it is necessary that the technique of Magick should be perfected. The Body of Light must be rendered capable of going everywhere and doing everything. It is, therefore, always the question of drill which is of importance. You have got to go out Rising on the Planes every day of your life, year after year. You are not to be disheartened by failure, or too much encouraged by success, in any one practice or set of practices. What you are doing is what will be of real value to you in the end; and that is, developing a character, creating a Karma, which will give you the power to do your will.

IV

Divination is so important a branch of Magick as almost to demand a separate treatise.

Genius is composed of two sides; the active and the passive. The power to execute the Will is but blind force unless the Will be enlightened. At every stage of a Magical Operation it is necessary to know what one is doing, and to be sure that one is acting wisely. Acute sensitiveness is always associated with genius; the power to perceive the universe accurately, to analyse, coordinate, and judge impressions is the foundation of all great Work. An army is but a blundering brute unless its intelligence department works as it should.

The Magician obtains the transcendental knowledge necessary to an intelligent course of conduct directly in consciousness by clairvoyance and clairaudience; but communication with superior intelligences demands elaborate preparation, even after years of successful performance.

It is therefore useful to possess an art by which one can obtain at a moment's notice any information that may be necessary. This art is divination. The answers to one's questions in divination are not conveyed directly but through the medium of a suitable series of symbols. These symbols must be interpreted by the diviner in terms of his problem. It is not practicable to construct a lexicon in which the solution of every difficulty is given in so many words. It would be unwieldy; besides, nature does not happen to work on those lines.

The theory of any process of divination may be stated in a few simple terms.

1. We postulate the existence of intelligences, either within or without the diviner, of which he is not immediately conscious. (It does not matter to the theory whether the communicating spirit so-called is an objective entity or a concealed portion of the diviner's mind.) We assume that such intelligences are able to reply correctly — within limits — to the questions asked.

2. We postulate that it is possible to construct a compendium of hieroglyphs sufficiently elastic in meaning to include every possible idea, and that one or more of these may always be taken to represent any idea. We assume that any of these hieroglyphics will be understood by the intelligences with whom we wish to communicate in the same sense as it is by ourselves. We have therefore a sort of language. One may compare it to a "lingua franca" which is perhaps defective in expressing fine shades of meaning, and so is unsuitable for literature, but which yet serves for the conduct of daily affairs in places where many tongues are spoken. Hindustani is an example of this. But better still is the analogy between the conventional signs and symbols

employed by mathematicians, who can thus convey their ideas perfectly

> *As a matter of fact, they cannot. The best qualified are the most diffident as to having grasped the meaning of their colleagues with exactitude; in criticising their writings they often make a point of apologising for possible misunderstanding.*

without speaking a word of each other's languages.

3. We postulate that the intelligences whom wish to consul are willing, or may be compelled, to answer us truthfully.

Let us first consider the question of the compendium of symbols. The alphabet of a language is a more or less arbitrary way of transcribing the sounds employed in speaking it. The letters themselves have not necessarily any meaning as such. But in a system of divination each symbol stands for a definite idea. It would not interfere with the English language to add a few new letters. In fact, some systems of shorthand have done so. But a system of symbols suitable for divination must be a complete representation of the Universe, so that each is absolute, and the whole insusceptible to increase or diminution. It is (in fact) technically a pantacle in the fullest sense of the word.

Let us consider some prominent examples of such system. We may observe that a common mode of divination is to inquire of books by placing the thumb at random within the leaves. The Books of the Sybil, the works of Vergil, and the Bible have been used very frequently for this purpose. For theoretical justification, one must assume that the book employed is a perfect representation of the Universe. But even if this were the case, it is an inferior form of construction, because the only reasonable conception of the Cosmos is mathematical and hieroglyphic rather than literary. In the case of a book, such as the Book of the Law which is the supreme truth and the perfect rule of life, it is not repugnant to good sense to derive an oracle from its pages. It will of course be remarked that the Book of the Law is not merely a literary compilation but a complex mathematical structure. It therefore fulfils the required conditions.

The principal means of divination in history are astrology, geomancy, the Tarot, the Holy Qabalah, and the Yi King. There are hundreds of others; from pyromancy, oneiromancy, auguries from sacrifices, and the spinning-top of some ancient oracles to the omens drawn from the flight of birds and the prophesying of tea-leaves. It will be sufficient for our present purpose to discuss only the five systems first enumerated.

ASTROLOGY is theoretically a perfect method, since the symbols employed actually exist in the macrocosm, and thus possess a natural correspondence with microcosmic affairs. But in practice the calculations involved are overwhelmingly complicated. A horoscope is never complete. It needs to be supplemented by innumerable other horoscopes. For example, to obtain a judgment on the simplest question, one requires not only the nativities of the people involved, some of which are probably inaccessible, but secondary figures for directions and transits, together with progressed horoscopes, to say nothing of prenatal, mundane, and even horary figures. To appreciate the entire mass of data, to balance the elements of so vast a concourse of forces, and to draw a single judgment therefrom, is a task practically beyond human capacity. Besides all this, the actual effects of the planetary positions and aspects are still almost entirely unknown. No two astrologers agree on all points; and most of them are at odds on fundamental principles.

> *Nearly all professional astrologers are ignorant of their own subject, as of all others.*

This science had better be discarded unless the student chances to feel strongly drawn toward it. It is used by the MASTER THERION Himself with fairly satisfactory results, but only in special cases, in a strictly limited sphere, and with particular precautions. Even so, He feels great diffidence in basing His conduct on the result so obtained.

GEOMANCY has the advantage of being rigorously mathematical. A hand-book of the science is to be found in Equinox I, II. The objection to its use lies in the limited number of the symbols. To represent the Universe by no more than 16 combinations throws too much work upon them. There is also a great restriction arising from the fact that although 15 symbols appear in the final figure, there are, in reality, but 4, the remaining 11 being drawn by an ineluctable process from the "Mothers". It may be added that the tables given in the handbook for the interpretation of the figure are exceedingly vague on the one hand, and insufficiently comprehensive on the other. Some Adepts, however, appear to find this system admirable, and obtain great satisfaction from its use. Once more, the personal equation must be allowed full weight. At one time the MASTER THERION employed it extensively; but He was never wholly at ease with it; He found the interpretation very difficult. Moreover, it seemed to Him that the geomantic intelligences themselves were of a low order, the scope of which was confined to a small section of the things which interested Him; also, they possessed a point of view of their own which was far from sympathetic with His, so that misunderstanding constantly interfered with the Work.

THE TAROT and THE HOLY QABALAH may be discussed together. The theoretical basis of both is identical: The Tree of Life.

Both these subjects may be studied in the Equinox in several articles appearing in several numbers.

The 78 symbols of the Tarot are admirably balanced and combined. They are adequate to all demands made upon them; each symbol is not only mathematically precise, but possesses an artistic significance which helps the diviner to understand them by stimulating his aesthetic perceptions. The MASTER THERION finds that the Tarot is infallible in material questions. The successive operations describe the course of events with astonishing wealth of detail, and the judgments are reliable in all respects. But a proper divination means at least two hours' hard work, even by the improved method developed by Him from the traditions of initiates. Any attempt to shorten the proceedings leads to disappointment; furthermore, the symbols do not lend themselves readily to the solution of spiritual questions.

The Holy Qabalah, based as it is on pure number, evidently possesses an infinite number of symbols. Its scope is conterminous with existence itself; and it lacks nothing in precision, purity, or indeed in any other perfection. But it cannot be taught;

It is easy to teach the General Principles of exegesis, and the main doctrines. There is a vast body of knowledge common to all cases; but this is no more than the basis on which the student must erect his original Research.

each man must select for himself the materials for the main structure of his system. It requires years of work to erect a worthy building. Such a building is never finished; every day spent on it adds new ornaments. The Qabalah is therefore a living Temple of the Holy Ghost. It is the man himself and his universe expressed in terms of thought whose language is so rich that even the letters of its alphabet have no limit. This system is so sublime that it is unsuited to the solution of the petty puzzles of our earthly existence. In the light of the Qabalah, the shadows of transitory things are instantly banished.

The YI KING is the most satisfactory system for general work. The MASTER THERION is engaged in the preparation of a treatise on the subject, but the labour involved is so great that He cannot pledge Himself to have it ready at any definite time. The student must therefore make his own investigations into the meaning of the 64 hexagrams as best he can.

The Yi King is mathematical and philosophical in form. Its structure is cognate with that of the Qabalah; the identity is so intimate that the existence of two such superficially different systems is transcendent testimony to the truth of both. It is in some ways the most perfect hieroglyph ever constructed. It is austere and sublime, yet withal so adaptable to every possible emergency that its figures may be interpreted to suit all classes of questions. One may resolve the most obscure spiritual difficulties no less than the most mundane dilemmas; and the symbol which opens the gates of the most exalted palaces of initiation is equally effective when employed to advise one in the ordinary business of life. The MASTER THERION has found the Yi King entirely satisfactory in every respect. The intelligences which direct it show no inclination to evade the question or to mislead the querent. A further advantage is that the actual apparatus is simple. Also the system is easy to manipulate, and five minutes is sufficient to obtain a fairly detailed answer to any but the most obscure questions.

With regard to the intelligences whose business it is to give information to the diviner, their natures differ widely, and correspond more or less to the character of the medium of divination. Thus, the geomantic intelligences are gnomes, spirits of an earthy nature, distinguished from each other by the modifications due to the various planetary and zodiacal influences which pertain to the several symbols. The intelligence governing Puella is not to be confused with that of Venus or of Libra. It is simply a particular terrestrial daemon which partakes of those natures.

The Tarot, on the other hand, being a book, is under Mercury, and the intelligence of each card is fundamentally Mercurial. Such symbols are therefore peculiarly proper to communicate thought. They are not gross, like the geomantic daemons; but, as against this, they are unscrupulous in deceiving the diviner.

> *This does not mean that they are malignant. They have a proper pride in their office as Oracles of Truth; and they refuse to be profaned by the contamination of inferior and impure intelligences. A Magician whose research is fully adapted to his Neschamah will find them lucid and reliable.*

The Yi King is served by beings free from these defects. The intense purity of the symbols prevent them from being usurped by intelligences with an axe of their own to grind.

> *Malicious or pranksome elementals instinctively avoid the austere sincerity of the Figures of Fu and King Wan.*

It is always essential for the diviner to obtain absolute magical control over the intelligences of the system which he adopts. He must not leave the smallest loop-hole for being tricked, befogged, or mocked. He must not allow them to use casuistry in the interpretation of his questions. It is a common knavery, especially in geomancy, to render an answer which is literally true, and yet deceives. For instance, one might ask whether some business transaction would be profitable, and find, after getting an affirmative answer, that it really referred to the other party to the affair!

There is, on the surface, no difficulty at all in getting replies. In fact, the process is mechanical; success is therefore assured, bar a stroke of apoplexy. But, even suppose we are safe from deceit, how can we know that the question has really been put to another mind, understood rightly, and answered from knowledge? It is obviously possible to check one's operations by clairvoyance, but this is rather like buying a safe to keep a brick in. Experience is the only teacher. One acquires what one may almost call a new sense. One feels in one's self whether one is right or not. The diviner must develop this sense. It resembles the exquisite sensibility of touch which is found in the great billiard player whose fingers can estimate infinitesimal degrees of force, or the similar phenomenon in the professional taster of tea or wine who can distinguish fantastically subtle differences of flavour.

It is a hard saying; but in the order to divine without error, one ought to be a Master of the Temple. Divination affords excellent practice for those who aspire to that exalted eminence, for the faintest breath of personal preference will deflect the needle from the pole of truth in the answer. Unless the diviner have banished utterly from his mind the minutest atom of interest in the answer to his question, he is almost certain to influence that answer in favour of his personal inclinations.

The psycho-analyst will recall the fact that dreams are phantasmal representations of the unconscious Will of the sleeper, and that not only are they images of that Will instead of representations of objective truth, but the image itself is confused by a thousand cross-currents set in motion by the various complexes and inhibitions of his character. If therefore one consults the oracle, one must take sure that one is not consciously or unconsciously bringing pressure to bear upon it. It is just as when an Englishman cross-examines a Hindu, the ultimate answer will be what the Hindu imagines will best please the inquirer.

The same difficulty appears in a grosser form when one receives a perfectly true reply, but insists on interpreting it so as to suit one's desires. The vast majority of people who go to "fortunetellers" have nothing else in mind but the wish to obtain supernatural sanction for their follies. Apart from Occultism altogether, every one knows that when people ask for advice, they only want to be told how wise they are. Hardly any one acts on the most obviously commonsense counsel if it happens to clash with his previous intentions. Indeed, who would take counsel unless he were warned by some little whisper in his heart that he was about to make a fool of himself, which he is determined to do, and only wants to be able to blame his best friend, or the oracle, when he is overtaken by the disaster which his own interior mentor foresees?

Those who embark on divination will be wise to consider the foregoing remarks very deeply. They will know when they are getting deep enough by the fact of the thought beginning to hurt them. It is essential to explore oneself to the utmost, to analyse one's mind until one can be positive, beyond the possibility of error, that one is able to detach oneself entirely from the question. The oracle is a judge; it must be beyond bribery and prejudice.

It is impossible in practice to lay down rules for the interpretation of symbols. Their nature must be investigated by intellectual methods such as the Qabalah, but the precise shape of meaning in any one case, and the sphere and tendency of its application, must be acquired by experience, that is, but induction, by recording and classifying one's experiments over a long period; and — this is the better part — by refining one's ratiocination to the point where it becomes instinct or intuition, whichever one likes to call it.

It is proper in cases where the sphere of the question is well marked to begin the divination by invocations of the forces thereto appropriate. An error of judgment as to the true character of the question would entail penalties proportionate to the extent of that error; and the delusions resulting from a divination fortified by invocation would be more serious than if one had not employed such heavy artillery.

The apparent high sanction for the error would fortify the obstinacy of the mule.

There can, however, be no objection to preparing oneself by a general purification and consecration devised with the object of detaching oneself from one's personality and increasing the sensitiveness of one's faculties.

All divination comes under the general type of the element Air. The peculiar properties of air are in consequence its uniform characteristics. Divination is subtle and intangible. It moves with mysterious ease, expanding, contracting, flowing, responsive to the slightest stress. It receives and transmits every vibration without retaining any. It becomes poisonous when its oxygen is defiled by passing through human lungs.

There is a peculiar frame of mind necessary to successful divination. The conditions of the problem are difficult. It is obviously necessary for the mind of the diviner to be concentrated absolutely upon his question. Any intrusive thought will confuse the oracle as certainly as the reader of a newspaper is confused when he reads a paragraph into which a few lines have strayed from another column. It is equally necessary that the muscles with which he manipulates the apparatus of divination must be entirely independent of any volition of his. He must lend them for the moment to the intelligence whom he is consulting, to be guided in their movement to make the necessary mechanical actions which determine the physical factor of the operation. It will be obvious that this is somewhat awkward for the diviner who is also a magician, for as a magician he has been constantly at work to keep all his forces under his own control, and to prevent the slightest interference with them by any alien Will. It is, in fact, commonly the case, or so says the experience of The MASTER THERION, that the most promising Magicians are the most deplorable diviners, and vice versa. It is only when the aspirant approaches perfection that he becomes able to reconcile these two apparently opposing faculties. Indeed, there is no surer sign of all-round success than this ability to put the whole of one's powers at the service of any type of task.

With regard to the mind, again, it would seem that concentration on the question makes more difficult the necessary detachment from it. Once again, the diviner stands in need of a considerable degree of attainment in the practices of meditation. He must have succeeded in destroying the tendency of the ego to interfere with the object of thought. He must be able to conceive of a thing out of all relation with anything else. The regular practice of concentration leads to this result; in fact, it destroys the thing itself as we have hitherto conceived it; for the nature of things is always veiled from us by our habit of regarding them as in essential relation without ourselves and our reactions toward them.

One can hardly expect the diviner to make Samadhi with his question — that would be going too far, and destroy the character of the operation by removing the question from the class of concatenated ideas. It would mean interpreting the question in terms of "without limit", and this imply an equally formless answer. But he should approximate to this extreme sufficiently to allow the question entire freedom to make for itself its own proper links with the intelligence directing the answer, preserving its position on its own plane, and evoking the necessary counterpoise to its own deviation from the norm of nothingness.

We may recapitulate the above reflections in a practical form. We will suppose that one wishes to divine by geomancy whether or no one should marry, it being assumed that one's emotional impulses suggest so rash a course. The man takes his wand and his sand; the traces the question, makes the appropriate pentagram, and the sigil of the spirit. Before tracing the dashes which are to determine the four "Mothers", he must strictly examine himself. He must banish from his mind every thought which can possibly act as an attachment to his proposed partner. He must banish all thoughts which concern himself, those of apprehension no less than those of ardour. He must carry his introspection as far as possible. He must observe with all the subtlety at his command whether it pains him to abandon any of these thoughts. So long as his mind is stirred, however slightly, by one single aspect of the subject, he is not fit to begin to form the figure. He must sink his personality in that of the intelligence hearing the question propounded by a stranger to whom he is indifferent, but whom it is his business to serve faithfully. He must now run over the whole affair in his mind, making sure of this utter aloofness therefrom. He must also make sure that his muscles are perfectly free to respond to the touch of the Will of that intelligence. (It is of course understood that he has not become so familiar with geomancy by dint of practice as to be able to calculate subconsciously what figures he will form; for this would vitiate the experiment entirely. It is, in fact, one of the objections to geomancy that sooner or later one does become aware at the time of tracing them whether the dots are going to be even or odd. This needs a special training to correct).

Physio-psychological theory will probably maintain that the "automatic" action of the hand is controlled by the brain no less than in the case of conscious volition; but this is an additional argument for identifying the brain with the intelligence invoked.

Having thus identified himself as closely as possible with that intelligence, and concentrated on the question as if the "prophesying spirit" were giving its whole attention thereto, he must await the impulse to trace the marks on the sand; and, as soon as it comes let it race to the finish. Here arises another technical difficulty. One has to make 16 rows of dots; and, especially for the beginner, the mind has to grapple with the apprehension lest the hand fail to execute the required number. It is also troubled by fearing to exceed; but excess does not matter. Extra lines are simply null and void, so that the best plan is to banish that thought, and make sure only of not stopping too soon.

Practice soon teaches one to count subconsciously ... yes, and that is the other difficulty again!

The lines being traced, the operation is over as far as spiritual qualities are required, for a time. The process of setting up the figure for judgment is purely mechanical.

But, in the judgment, the diviner stands once more in need of his inmost and utmost attainments. He should exhaust the intellectual sources of information at his disposal, and form from them his judgment. But having done this, he should detach his mind from what it has just formulated, and proceed to concentrate it on the figure as a whole, almost as if it were the object of his meditation. One need hardly repeat that in both these operations detachment from one's personal partialities is as necessary as it was in the first part of the work. In setting up the figure, bias would beget a Freudian phantasm to replace the image of truth which the figure ought to be; and it is not too much to say that the entire subconscious machinery of the body and mind lends itself with horrid willingness to this ape-like antic of treason. But now that the figure stands for judgment, the same bias would tend to form its phantasm of wish-fulfilment in a different manner. It would act through the mind to bewray sound judgment. It might, for example, induce one to emphasize the Venereal element in Puella at the expense of the Saturnian. It might lead one to underrate the influence of a hostile figure, or to neglect altogether some element of importance. The MASTER THERION has known cases where the diver was so afraid of an unfavourable answer that he made actual mistakes in the simple mechanical construction of the figure! Finally, in the summing up; it is fatally easy to slur over unpleasantness, and to breathe on the tiniest spark that promises to kindle the tinder — the rotten rags! — of hope.

The concluding operation is therefore to obtain a judgment of the figure, independent of all intellectual or moral restraint. One must endeavour to apprehend it as a thing absolute in itself. One must treat it, in short, very much the same as one did the question; as a mystical entity, till now unrelated with other phenomena. One must, so to speak, adore it as a god, uncritically: "Speak, Lord, for thy servant heareth." It must be allowed to impose its intrinsic individuality on the mind, to put its fingers independently on whatever notes it pleases.

In this way one obtains an impression of the true purport of the answer; and one obtains it armed with a sanction superior to any sensible suggestions. It comes from and to a part of the individual which is independent of the influence of environment; is adjusted to that environment by true necessity, and not by the artifices of such adaptations as our purblind conception of convenience induces us to fabricate.

The student will observe from the above that divination is in one sense an art entirely separate from that of Magick; yet it interpenetrates Magick at every point. The fundamental laws of both are identical. The right use of divination has already been explained; but it must be added that proficiency therein, tremendous as is its importance in furnishing the Magician with the information necessary to his strategical and tactical plans, in no wise enables him to accomplish the impossible. It is not within the scope of divination to predict the future (for example) with the certainty of an astronomer in calculating the return of a comet.

The astronomer himself has to enter a caveat. He can only calculate the probability on the observed facts. Some force might interfere with the anticipated movement.

There is always much virtue in divination; for (Shakespeare assures us!) there is "much virtue in IF"!

In estimating the ultimate value of a divinatory judgment, one must allow for more than the numerous sources of error inherent in the process itself. The judgment can do no more than the facts presented to it warrant. It is naturally impossible in most cases to make sure that some important factor has not been omitted. In asking, "shall I be wise to marry?" one leaves it open for wisdom to be defined in divers ways. One can only expect an answer in the sense of the question. The connotation of "wise" would then imply the limitations "in your private definition of wisdom", "in reference to your present circumstances." It would not involve guarantee against subsequent disaster, or pronounce a philosophical dictum as to wisdom in the abstract sense. One must not assume that the oracle is omniscient. By the nature of the case, on the contrary, it is the utterance of a being whose powers are partial and limited, though not to such an extent, or in the same directions, as one's own. But a man who is advised to purchase a certain stock should not complain if a general panic knocks the bottom out of it a few weeks later. The advice only referred to the prospects of the stock in itself. The divination must not be blamed any more than one would blame a man for buying a house at Ypres there years before the World-War.

As against this, one must insist that it is obviously to the advantage of the diviner to obtain this information from beings of the most exalted essence available. An old witch who has a familiar spirit of merely local celebrity such as the toad in her tree, can hardly expect him to tell her much more of private matters than her parish magazine does of public. It depends entirely on the Magician how he is served. The greater the man, the greater must be his teacher. It follows that the highest forms of communicating daemons, those who know, so to speak, the court secrets, disdain to concern themselves with matters which they regard as beneath them. One must not make the mistake of calling in a famous physician to one's sick Pekinese. One must also beware of asking even the cleverest angel a question outside his ambit. A heart specialist should not prescribe for throat trouble.

The Magician ought therefore to make himself master of several methods of divination; using one or the other as the purpose of the moment dictates. He should make a point of organizing a staff of such spirits to suit various occasions. These should be "familiar"spirits, in the strict sense; members of his family. He should deal with them constantly, avoiding whimsical or capricious changes. He should choose them so that their capacities cover the whole ground of his work; but he should not multiply them unnecessarily, for he makes himself responsible for each one that he employs. Such spirits should be ceremonially evoked to visible or semi-visible appearance. A strict arrangement should be made and sworn. This must be kept punctiliously by the Magician, and its infringement by the spirit severely punished. Relations with these spirits should be confirmed and encouraged by frequent intercourse. They should be treated with courtesy, consideration, and even affection. They should be taught to love and respect their master, and to take pride in being trusted by him.

It is sometimes better to act on the advice of a spirit even when one knows it to be wrong, though in such a case one must take the proper precautions against an undesirable result. The reason for this is that spirits of this type are very sensitive. They suffer agonies of remorse on realising that they have injured their Master; for he is their God; they know themselves to be part of him, their aim is to attain to absorption in him. They understand therefore that his interests are theirs. Care must be taken to employ none but spirits who are fit for the purpose, not only by reason of their capacity to supply information, but for their sympathy with the personality of the Magician. Any attempt to coerce unwilling spirits is dangerous. They obey from fear; their fear makes them flatter, and tell amiable falsehoods. It also creates phantasmal projections of themselves to personate them; and these phantasms, besides being worthless, become the prey of malicious daemons who use them to attack the Magician in various ways whose prospect of success is enhanced by the fact that he has himself created a link with them.

One more observation seems desirable while on this subject. Divination of any kind is improper in matters directly concerning the Great Work itself. In the Knowledge and Conversation of his Holy Guardian Angel, the adept is possessed of all he can possibly need. To consult any other is to insult one's Angel. Moreover, it is to abandon the only person who really knows, and really cares, in favour of one who by the nature of the case, must be ignorant

No intelligence of the type that operates divination is a complete Microcosm as Man is. He knows in perfection what lies within his own Sphere, and little or nothing beyond it. Graphiel knows all that is knowable about Marital matters, as no Man can possibly do. For even the most Marital man is limited as to Madim by the fact that Mars is only one element in his molecule; the other elements both inhibit concentration on their colleague, and veil him by insisting on his being interpreted in reference to themselves. No entity whose structure does not include the entire Tree of Life is capable of the Formulae of Initiation. Graphiel, consulted by the Aspirants to Adeptship, would be bound to regard the Great Work as purely a question of combat, and ignore all other considerations. His advice would be absolute on technical points of this kind; but its very perfection would persuade the Aspirant to an unbalance course of action which would entail failure and destruction. It is pertinent to mention in this connection that one must not expect absolute information as to what is going to happen. "Fortune-telling" is an abuse of divination. At the utmost one can only ascertain what may reasonably be expected. The proper function of the process is to guide one's judgment. Diagnosis is fairly reliable; advice may be trusted, generally speaking; but prognosis should always be cautious. The essence of the business is the consultation of specialists.

of the essence of the matter — one whose interest in it is no more (at the best) than that of a well-meaning stranger. It should go without saying that until the Magician has attained to the Knowledge and Conversation of his Holy Guardian Angel he is liable to endless deceptions. He does not know Himself; how can he explain his business to others? How can those others, though they do their best for him, aid in anything but trifles? One must therefore be prepared for disappointment at every stage until one attains to adeptship.

This is especially true of divination, because the essence of the horror of not knowing one's Angel is the utter bewilderment and anguish of the mind, complicated by the persecution of the body, and envenomed by the ache of the soul. One puts the wrong questions, and puts them wrong; gets the wrong answers, judges them wrong, and acts wrongly upon them. One must nevertheless persist, aspiring with ardour towards one's Angel, and comforted by the assurance that He is guiding one secretly towards Himself, and that all one's mistakes are necessary preparations for the appointed hour of meeting Him. Each mistake is the combing-out of some tangle in the hair of the bride as she is being coiffed for marriage.

On the other hand, although the adept is in daily communication with his Angel, he ought to be careful to consult Him only on questions proper to the dignity of the relation. One should not consult one's Angel on too many details, or indeed on any matters which come within the office of one's familiar spirits. One does not go the the King about petty personal trifles. The romance and rapture of the ineffable union which constitutes Adeptship must not be profaned by the introduction of commonplace cares. One must not appear with one's hair in curl-papers, or complain of the cook's impertinence, if one wants to make the most of the honeymoon.

As the poet puts it; "Psyche, beware how thou disclose Thy tricks of toilet to Eros, Or let him learn that those love-breathing Lyrical lips that whisper, wreathing His brows with sense-bewitching gold, Are equally expert to scold; That those caressing hands will maybe Yet box his ears and slap the baby!"

To the Adept divination becomes therefore a secondary consideration, although he can now employ it with absolute confidence, and probably use it with far greater frequency than before his attainment. Indeed, this is likely in proportion as he learns that resort to divination (on every occasion when his Will does not instantly instruct him) with implicit obedience to its counsels careless as to whether or no they may land him in disaster, is a means admirably efficacious of keeping his mind untroubled by external impressions, and therefore in the proper condition to receive the reiterant strokes of rapture with which the love of his Angel ravishes him.

We have now mapped out the boundaries of possibility and propriety which define the physical and political geography of divination. The student must guard himself constantly against supposing that this art affords any absolute means of discovering "truth", or indeed, of using that word as if it meant more than the relation of two ideas each of which is itself as subject to "change without notice" as a musical programme.

Divination, in the nature of things, can do no more than put the mind of the querent into conscious connection with another mind whose knowledge of the subject at issue is to his own as that of an expert to a layman. The expert is not infallible. The client may put his question in a misleading manner, or even base it on a completely erroneous conception of the facts. He may misunderstand the expert's answer, and he may misinterpret its purport. Apart from all this, excluding all error, both question and answer are limited in validity by their own conditions; and these conditions are such that truth may cease to be true, either as time goes on, or if it be flawed by the defect of failure to consider some circumstances whose concealed operation cancels the contract.

In a word, divination, like any other science, is justified of its children. It would be extraordinary should so fertile a mother be immune from still-births, monstrosities, and abortions.

We none of us dismiss our servant science with a kick and a curse every time the telephone gets out of order. The telephone people make no claim that it always works and always works right.

Except in New York City.

Divination, with equal modesty, admits that "it often goes wrong; but it works well enough, all things considered. The science is in its infancy. All we can do is our best. We no more pretend to infallibility than the mining expert who considers himself in luck if he hits the bull's eye four times in ten."

The error of all dogmatists (from the oldest prophet with his "literally-inspired word of God" to the newest German professor with his single-track explanation of the Universe) lies in trying to prove too much, in defending themselves against critics by stretching a probably excellent theory to include all the facts and the fables, until it bursts like the overblown bladder it is.

Divination is no more than a rough and ready practical method which we understand hardly at all, and operate only as empirics. Success for the best diviner alive is no more certain in any particular instance than a long putt by a champion golfer. Its calculations are infinitely more complex than Chess, a Chess played on an infinite board with men whose moves are indeterminate, and made still more difficult by the interference of imponderable forces and unformulated laws; while its conduct demands not only the virtues, themselves rare enough, of intellectual and moral integrity, but intuition combining delicacy with strength in such perfection and to such extremes as to make its existence appear monstrous and miraculous against Nature.

To admit this is not to discredit oracles. On the contrary, the oracles fell into disrepute just because they pretended to do more than they could. To divine concerning a matter is little more than to calculate probabilities. We obtain the use of minds who have access to knowledge beyond ours, but not to omniscience. HRU, the great angel set over the Tarot, is beyond us as we are beyond the ant; but, for all we know, the knowledge of HRU is excelled by some mightier mind in the same proportion. Nor have we any warrant for accusing

HRU of ignorance or error if we read the Tarot to our own delusion. He may have known, he may have spoken truly; the fault may lie with our own insight.

> *The question of the sense in which an answer is true arises. One {WEH NOTE: sic, interpolate "should"} not mix up the planes. Yet as Mr. Russell shows, "Op Cit. p". 61, the worlds which lie behind phenomena must possess the same structure as our own. "Every proposition having a communicable significance must lie in just that essence of individuality which, for that very reason, is irrelevant to science". Just so: but this is to confess the impotence of science to attain truth, and to admit the urgency of developing a mental instrument of superior capacity.*

The MASTER THERION has observed on innumerable occasions that divinations, made by him and dismissed as giving untrue answers, have justified themselves months or years later when he was able to revise his judgment in perspective, untroubled by his personal passion.

It is indeed surprising how often the most careless divinations give accurate answers. When things go wrong, it is almost always possible to trace the error to one's own self-willed and insolent presumption in insisting that events shall accommodate themselves to our egoism and vanity. It is comically unscientific to adduce examples of the mistakes of the diviners as evidence that their art is fatuous. Every one knows that the simplest chemical experiments often go wrong. Every one knows the eccentricities of fountain pens; but nobody outside Evangelical circles makes fun of the Cavendish experiment, or asserts that, if fountain pens undoubtedly work now and then, their doing so is merely coincidence.

The fact of the case is that the laws of nature are incomparably more subtle than even science suspects. The phenomena of every plane are intimately interwoven. The arguments of Aristotle were dependent on the atmospheric pressure which prevented his blood from boiling away. There is nothing in the universe which does not influence every other thing in one way or another. There is no reason in Nature why the apparently chance combination of half-a dozen sticks of tortoise-shell should not be so linked both with the human mind and with the entire structure of the Universe that the observation of their fall should not enable us to measure all things in heaven and earth.

With one piece of curved glass we have discovered uncounted galaxies of suns; with another, endless orders of existence in the infinitesimal. With the prism we have analysed light so that matter and force have become intelligible only as forms of light. With a rod we have summoned the invisible energies of electricity to be our familiar spirit serving us to do our Will, whether it be to outsoar the condor, or to dive deeper into the demon world of disease than any of our dreamers dared to dream.

Since with four bits of common glass mankind has learnt to know so much, achieved so much, who dare deny that the Book of Thoth, the quintessentialized wisdom of our ancestors whose civilizations, perished though they be, have left monuments which dwarf ours until we wonder whether we are degenerate from them, or evolved from Simians, who dare deny that such a book may be possessed of unimaginable powers?

It is not so long since the methods of modern science were scoffed at by the whole cultured world. In the sacred halls themselves the roofs rang loud with the scornful laughter of the high priests as each new postulant approached with his unorthodox offering. There is hardly a scientific discovery in history which was not decried as quackery by the very men whose own achievements were scarce yet recognized by the world at large.

Within the memory of the present generation, the possibility of aeroplanes was derisively denied by those very engineers accounted most expert to give their opinions.

The method of divination, the "ratio" of it, is as obscure to-day as was that of spectrum analysis a generation ago. That the chemical composition of the fixed stars should become known to man seemed an insane imagining too ridiculous to discuss. To-day it seems equally irrational to enquire of the desert sand concerning the fate of empires. Yet surely it, if any one knows, should know!

To-day it may sound impossible for inanimate objects to reveal the inmost secrets of mankind and nature. We cannot say why divination is valid. We cannot trace the process by which it performs it marvels.

> *The main difference between a Science and an Art is that the former admits mensuration. Its processes must be susceptible of the application of quantitative standards. Its laws reject imponderable variables. Science despises Art for its refusal to conform with calculable conditions. But even to-day, in the boasted Age of Science, man is still dependent on Art as to most matters of practical importance to him; the arts of Government, of War, of Literature, etc. are supremely influential, and Science does little more than facilitate them by making their materials mechanically docile. The utmost extension of Science can merely organize the household of Art. Art thus progresses in perception and power by increased control or automatic accuracy of its details. The MASTER THERION has made an Epoch in the Art of Magick by applying the Method of Science to its problems. His Work is a contribution of unique value, comparable only to that of those men of genius who revolutionized the empirical guesswork of "natural philosophers". The Magicians of to-morrow will be armed with mathematical theory, organized observation, and experimentally-verified practice. But their Art will remain inscrutable as ever in essence; talent will never supplant genius. Education is impotent to produce a poet greater than Robert Burns; the perfection of laboratory apparatus prepares indeed the path of a Pasteur, but cannot make masters of mediocrities.*

But the same objections apply equally well to the telephone. No man knows what electricity is, or the nature of the forces which determine its action. We know only that by doing certain things we get certain results, and that the least error on our part will bring our work to naught. The same is exactly true of divination. The difference between the two sciences is not more than this: that, more minds having been at work on the former we have learnt to master its tricks with greater success than in the case of the latter.

CHAPTER XIX

OF DRAMATIC RITUALS.

The Wheel turns to those effectual methods of invocation employed in the ancient Mysteries and by certain secret bodies of initiates to-day. The object of them is almost invariably

The word is unwarrantably universal. It would not be impracticable to adopt this method to such operations as Talismanic Magick. For example, one might consecrate and charge a Pantacle by the communication by AIWAZ to the Scribe of the BOOK of the LAW, the Magician representing the Angel, the Pantacle being the Book, and the person on whom the Pantacle is intended to act taking the part of the Scribe.

the invocation of a God, that God conceived in a more or less material and personal fashion. These Rituals are therefore well suited for such persons as are capable of understanding the spirit of Magick as opposed to the letter. One of the great advantages of them is that a large number of persons may take part, so that there is consequently more force available; but it is important that they should all be initiates of the same mysteries, bound by the same oaths, and filled with the same aspirations. They should be associated only for this one purpose.

Such a company being prepared, the story of the God should be dramatised by a well-skilled poet accustomed to this form of composition. Lengthy speeches and invocations should be avoided, but action should be very full. Such ceremonies should be carefully rehearsed; but in rehearsals care should be taken to omit the climax, which should be studied by the principal character in private. The play should be so arranged that this climax depends on him alone. By this means one prevents the ceremony from becoming mechanical or hackneyed, and the element of surprise. assists the lesser characters to get out of themselves at the supreme moment. Following the climax there should always be an unrehearsed ceremony, an impromptu. The most satisfactory form of this is the dance. In such ceremonies appropriate libations may be freely used.

The Rite of Luna (Equinox I. VI) is a good example of this use. Here the climax is the music of the goddess, the assistants remaining in silent ecstasy.

In the rite of Jupiter the impromptu is the dance, in that of Saturn long periods of silence.

It will be noticed that in these Rites poetry and music were largely employed — mostly published pieces by well-known authors and composers. It would be better

"PERHAPS! One can think of certain Awful Consequences". "But, after all, they wouldn't seem so to the authors!" "But — pity the poor Gods!" "Bother the Gods!"

to write and compose specially for the ceremony.

A body of skilled Magicians accustomed to work in concert may be competent to conduct impromptu Orgia. To cite an actual instance in recent times; the blood of a Christian being required for some purpose, a young cock was procured and baptized into the Roman Catholic Church by a man who, being the son of an ordained Priest, was magically an incarnation of the Being of that Priest, and was therefore congenitally possessed of the powers thereto appurtenant. The cock, "Peter Paul," was consequently a baptized Christian for all magical purposes. Order was then taken to imprison the bird; which done, the Magicians assuming respectively the characters of Herod, Herodias, Salome, and the Executioner, acted out the scene of the dance and the beheading, on the lines of Oscar Wilde's drama, "Peter Paul" being cast for the part of John the Baptist. This ceremony was devised and done on the spur of the moment, and its spontaneity and simplicity were presumably potent factors in its success.

On the point of theology, I doubt whether Dom Gorenflot sucessfully avoided eating meat in Lent by baptizing the pullet a carp. For as the sacrament — by its intention, despite its defects of form — could not fail of efficacy, the pullet must have become a Christian, and therefore a human being. Carp was therefore only its baptized name — cf. Polycarp — and Dom Gorenflot ate human flesh in Lent, so that, for all he became a bishop, he is damned.

CHAPTER XX

OF THE EUCHARIST

AND OF THE ART OF ALCHEMY

I

One of the simplest and most complete of Magick ceremonies is the Eucharist.

It consists in taking common things, transmuting them into things divine, and consuming them.

So far, it is a type of every magick ceremony, for the reabsorption of the force is a kind of consumption; but it has a more restricted application, as follows.

Take a substance

This may be of composite character.

symbolic of the whole course of nature, make it God, and consume it.

There are many ways of doing this; but they may easily be classified according to the number of the elements of which the sacrament is composed.

The highest form of the Eucharist is that in which the Element consecrated is One.

It is one substance and not two, not living and not dead, neither liquid nor solid, neither hot nor cold, neither male nor female.

This sacrament is secret in every respect. For those who may be worthy, although not officially recognized as such, this Eucharist has been described in detail and without concealment, "somewhere" in the published writings of the MASTER THERION. But He has told no one where. It is reserved for the highest initiates, and is synonymous with the Accomplished Work on the material plane. It is the Medicine of Metals, the Stone of the Wise, the Potable Gold, the Elixir of Life that is consumed therein. The altar is the bosom of Isis, the eternal mother; the chalice is in effect the Cup of our Lady Babalon Herself; the Wand is that which Was and Is and Is To Come.

The Eucharist of *two* elements has its matter of the passives. The wafer (pantacle) is of corn, typical of earth; the wine (cup) represents water. (There are certain other attributions. The Wafer is the Sun, for instance: and the wine is appropriate to Bacchus).

The wafer may, however, be more complex, the "Cake of Light" described in Liber Legis.

This is used in the exoteric Mass of the Phoenix (Liber 333, Cap: 44) mixed with the blood of the Magus. This mass should be performed daily at sunset by every magician.

Corn and wine are equivalent to flesh and blood; but it is easier to convert live substances into the body and blood of God, than to perform this miracle upon dead matter.

The Eucharist of *three* elements has for basis the symbols of the three Gunas. For Tamas (darkness) take opium or nightshade or some sleepy medicine; for Rajas (activity) take strychnine or other excitant; for Sattvas (calm) the cakes of Light may again be suitable.

The Cakes of Light are universally applicable; they contain meal, honey, and oil (carbohydrates, fats, and proteids, the three necessaries of human nutrition): also perfume of the three essential types of magical and curative virtue; the subtle principle of animal life itself is fixed in them by the introduction of fresh living blood.

The Eucharist of *four* elements consists of fire, air, water, and earth. These are represented by a flame for fire, by incense or roses for air, by wine for water, and by bread and salt for earth.

The Eucharist of *five* has for basis wine for taste, a rose for smell, a flame for sight, a bell for sound, and a dagger for touch. This sacrament is implied in the Mass of the Phoenix in a slightly different form.

The Eucharist of *six* elements has Father, Son, and Holy Spirit above; breath, water, and blood beneath. It is a sacrament reserved for high initiates.

The Lance and the Graal are firstly dedicated to the Holy Spirit of Life, in Silence. The Bread and Wine are then fermented and manifested by vibration, and received by the Virgin Mother. The elements are then intermingled and consumed after the Epiphany of Iacchus, when "Countenance beholdeth Countenance).

The Eucharist of *seven* elements is mystically identical with that of one.

Of the method of consecrating the elements it is only necessary to say that they should be treated as talismans. The circle and other furniture of the Temple should receive the usual benefit of the banishings and consecrations. The Oath should be taken and the Invocations made. When the divine force manifests in the elements, they should be solemnly consumed. There is also a simpler method of consecration reserved for initiates of high rank, of which it is here unlawful to speak.

According to the nature of the Sacrament, so will its results be. In some one may receive a mystic grace, culminating in Samadhi; in others a simpler and more material benefit may be obtained.

The highest sacrament, that of One element, is universal in its operation; according to the declared purpose of the work so will the result be. It is a universal Key of all Magick.

These secrets are of supreme practical importance, and are guarded in the Sanctuary with a two-edged sword flaming every way

J.K.Husmans, who was afraid of them, and tried to betray the little he knew of them, became a Papist, and died of cancer of the tongue.

; for this sacrament is the Tree of Life itself, and whoso partaketh of the fruit thereof shall never die

The use of the Elixir of Life is only justifiable in peculiar circumstances. To go counter to the course of natural Change is to approximate perilously to the error of the "Black Brothers".

.

Unless he so will. Who would not rather work through incarnation; a real renewal of body and brain, than content himself with a stagnant immortality upon this mote in the Sunlight of the Universe which we call earth?

With regard to the preparations for such Sacraments, the Catholic Church has maintained well enough the traditions of the true Gnostic Church in whose keeping the secrets are.

Study, in the Roman Missal, the Canon of the Mass, and the chapter of "defects".

Chastity

The Word Chastity is used by initiates to signify a certain state of soul and of mind determinant of a certain habit of body which is nowise identical with what is commonly understood. Chastity in the true magical sense of the word is inconceivable to those who are not wholly emancipated from the obsession of sex.

is a condition; fasting for some hours previous is a condition; an earnest and continual aspiration is a condition. Without these antecedents even the Eucharist of the One and Seven is partially — though such is its intrinsic virtue that it can never be wholly — baulked of its effect.

A Eucharist of some sort should most assuredly be consummated daily by every magician, and he should regard it as the main sustenance of his magical life. It is of more importance than any other magical ceremony, because it is a complete circle. The whole of the force expended is completely re-absorbed; yet the virtue is that vast gain represented by the abyss between Man and God.

The magician becomes filled with God, fed upon God, intoxicated with God. Little by little his body will become purified by the internal lustration of God; day by day his mortal frame, shedding its earthly elements, will become in very truth the Temple of the Holy Ghost. Day by day matter is replaced by Spirit, the human by the divine; ultimately the change will be complete; God manifest in flesh will be his name.

This is the most important of all magical secrets that ever were or are or can be. To a Magician thus renewed the attainment of the Knowledge and Conversation of the Holy Guardian Angel becomes an inevitable task; every force of his nature, unhindered, tends to that aim and goal of whose nature neither man nor god may speak, for that it is infinitely beyond speech or thought or ecstasy or silence. Samadhi and Nibbana are but its shadows cast upon the universe.

II

If the Master Therion effects by this book nothing else but to demonstrate the continuity of nature and the uniformity of Law, He will feel that His work has not been wasted. In his original design of Part III he did not contemplate any allusion to alchemy. It has somehow been taken for granted that this subject is entirely foreign to regular Magick, both in scope and method. It will be the main object of the following description to establish it as essentially a branch of the subject, and to show that it may be considered simply as a particular case of the general proposition — differing from evocatory and talismanic Magick only in the values which are represented by the unknown quantities in the pantomorphous equations.

There is no need to make any systematized attempt to decipher the jargon of Hermetic treatises. We need not enter upon an historical discussion. Let it suffice to say that the word alchemy is an Arabic term consisting of the article "al" and the adjective "khemi" which means "that which pertains to Egypt"

This etymology differs from that given by Skeat; I can do no more than present my submission.

. A rough translation would be "The Egyptian matter". The assumption is that the Mohammedan grammarians held traditionally that the art was derived from that wisdom of the Egyptians which was the boast of Moses, Plato, and Pythagoras, and the source of their illumination.

Modern research (by profane scholars) leaves it still doubtful as to whether Alchemical treatises should be classified as mystical, magical, medical, or chemical. The most reasonable opinion is that all these objects formed the pre-occupation of the alchemists in varying proportions. Hermes is alike the god of Wisdom,

Thaumaturgy, therapeutics, and physical science. All these may consequently claim the title Hermetic. It cannot be doubted that such writers as Fludd aspired to spiritual perfection. It is equally sure that Edward Kelly wrote primarily from the point of view of a Magician; that Paracelesus applied himself to the cure of disease and the prolongation of life as the first consideration, although his greatest achievements seem to modern thinkers to have been rather his discoveries of opium, zinc, and hydrogen; so that we tend to think of him as a chemist no less than we do of Van Helmont, whose conception of gas ranks him as one of those rare geniuses who have increased human knowledge by a fundamentally important idea.

The literature of Alchemy is immense. Practically all of it is wholly or partially unintelligible. Its treatises, from the "Asch Metzareph" of the Hebrews to the "Chariot of Antimony" are deliberately couched in hieratic riddles. Ecclesiastical persecution, and the profanation of the secrets of power, were equally dreaded. Worse still, from our point of view, this motive induced writers to insert intentionally misleading statements, the more deeply to bedevil unworthy pretenders to their mysteries.

We do not propose to discuss any of the actual processes. Most readers will be already aware that the main objects of alchemy were the Philosopher's Stone, the Medicine of Metals, and various tinctures and elixirs possessing divers virtues; in particular, those of healing disease, extending the span of life, increasing human abilities, perfecting the nature of man in every respect, conferring magical powers, and transmuting material substances, especially metals, into more valuable forms.

The subject is further complicated by the fact that many authors were unscrupulous quacks. Ignorant of the first elements of the art, they plagiarized without shame, and reaped a harvest of fraudulent gain. They took advantage of the general ignorance, and the convention of mystery, in just the same way as their modern successors do in the matter of all Occult sciences.

But despite all this, one thing is abundantly clear; all serious writers, though they seem to speak of an infinity of different subjects, so much so that it has proved impossible for modern analytic research to ascertain the true nature of any single process, were agreed on the fundamental theory on which they based their practices. It appears at first sight as if hardly any two of them were in accord as to the nature of the "First Matter of the work". They describe this in a bewildering multiplicity of unintelligible symbols. We have no reason to suppose that they were all talking of the same thing, or otherwise. The same remarks apply to every reagent and every process, no less than to the final product or products.

Yet beneath this diversity, we may perceive an obscure identity. They all begin with a substance in nature which is described as existing almost everywhere, and as universally esteemed of no value. The alchemist is in all cases to take this substance, and subject it to a series of operations. By so doing, he obtains his product. This product, however named or described, is always a substance which represents the truth or perfection of the original "First Matter"; and its qualities are invariably such as pertain to a living being, not to an inanimate mass. In a word, the alchemist is to take a dead thing, impure, valueless, and powerless, and transform it into a live thing, active, invaluable and thaumaturgic.

The reader of this book will surely find in this a most striking analogy with what we have already said of the processes of Magick. What, by our definition, is initiation? The First Matter is a man, that is to say, a perishable parasite, bred of the earth's crust, crawling irritably upon it for a span, and at last returning to the dirt whence he sprang. The process of initiation consists in removing his impurities, and finding in his true self an immortal intelligence to whom matter is no more than the means of manifestation. The initiate is eternally individual; he is ineffable, incorruptible, immune from everything. He possesses infinite wisdom and infinite power in himself. This equation is identical with that of a talisman. The Magician takes an idea, purifies it, intensifies it by invoking into it the inspiration of his soul. It is no longer a scrawl scratched on a sheep-skin, but a word of

Truth, imperishable, mighty to prevail throughout the sphere of its purport. The evocation of a spirit is precisely similar in essence. The exorcist takes dead material substances of a nature sympathetic to the being whom he intends to invoke. He banishes all impurities therefrom, prevents all interference therewith, and proceeds to give life to the subtle substance thus prepared by instilling his soul.

Once again, there is nothing in this exclusively "magical". Rembrandt van Ryn used to take a number of ores and other crude objects. From these he banished the impurities, and consecrated them to his work, by the preparation of canvasses, brushes, and colours. This done, he compelled them to take the stamp of his soul; from those dull, valueless creatures of earth he created a vital and powerful being of truth and beauty. It would indeed be surprising to anybody who has come to a clear comprehension of nature if there were any difference in the essence of these various formulas. The laws of nature apply equally in every possible circumstance.

We are now in a position to understand what alchemy is. We might even go further and say that even if we had never heard of it, we know what it must be.

Let us emphasize the fact that the final product is in all cases a living thing. It has been the great stumbling block to modern research that the statements of alchemists cannot be explained away. From the chemical standpoint it has seemed not "a priori" impossible that lead should be turned into gold. Our recent discovery of the periodicity of the elements has made it seem likely, at least in theory, that our apparently immutable elements should be modifications of a single one.< Aleister Crowley held this doctrine in his teens at a period when it was the grossest heresy.>> Organic Chemistry, with its metatheses and syntheses dependent on the conceptions of molecules as geometrical structures has demonstrated a praxis which gives this theory body; and the properties of Radium have driven the Old Guard from the redoubt which flew the flag of the essential heterogeneity of the elements. The doctrines of Evolution have brought the alchemical and monistic theory of matter into line with our conception of life; the collapse of the wall between the animal and vegetable kingdoms has shaken that which divided them from the mineral.

But even though the advanced chemist might admit the possibility of transmuting lead into gold, he could not conceive of that gold as other than metallic, of the same order of nature as the lead from which it had been made. That this gold should possess the power of multiplying itself, or of acting as a ferment upon other substances, seemed so absurd that he felt obliged to conclude that the alchemists who claimed these properties for their Gold must, after all, have been referring not to Chemistry, but to some spiritual operations whose sanctity demanded some such symbolic veil as the cryptographic use of the language of the laboratory.

The MASTER THERION is sanguine that his present reduction of all cases of the art of Magick to a single formula will both elucidate and vindicate Alchemy, while extending chemistry to cover all classes of Change.

There is an obvious condition which limits our proposed operations. This is that, as the formula of any Work effects the extraction and visualization of the Truth from any "First Matter", the "Stone" or "Elixir" which results from our labours will be the pure and perfect Individual originally inherent in the substance chosen, and nothing else. The most skilful gardener cannot produce lilies from the wild rose; his roses will always be roses, however he have perfected the properties of this stock.

There is here no contradiction with our previous thesis of the ultimate unity of all substance. It is true that Hobbs and Nobbs are both modifications of the Pleroma. Both vanish in the Pleroma when they attain Samadhi. But they are not interchangeable to the extent that they are individual modifications; the initiate Hobbs is not the initiate Nobbs any more than Hobbs the haberdasher is Nobbs of "the nail an sarspan business as he got his money by". Our skill in producing aniline dyes does not enable us to dispense with the original aniline, and use sugar instead. Thus the Alchemists said: "To make gold you must take gold"; their art was to bring each substance to the perfection of its own proper nature.

No doubt, part of this process involved the withdrawal of the essence of the "First Matter" within the homogeneity of "Hyle", just as initiation insists on the annihilation of the individual in the Impersonal Infinity of Existence to emerge once more as a less confused and deformed Eidolon of the Truth of Himself. This is the guarantee that he is uncontaminated by alien elements. The "Elixir" must possess the activity of a "nascent" substance, just as "nascent" hydrogen combines with arsenic (in "Marsh's test") when the ordinary form of the gas is inert. Again, oxygen satisfied by sodium or diluted by nitrogen will not attack combustible materials with the vehemence proper to the pure gas.

We may summarize this thesis by saying that Alchemy includes as many possible operations as there are original ideas inherent in nature.

Alchemy resembles evocation in its selection of appropriate material bases for the manifestation of the Will; but differs from it in proceeding without personification, or the intervention of alien planes.

Some alchemists may object to this statement. I prefer to express no final opinion on the matter.

It may be more closely compared with Initiation; for the effective element of the Product is of the essence of its own nature, and inherent therein; the Work similarly consists in isolating it from its accretions.

Now just as the Aspirant, on the Threshold of Initiation, finds himself assailed by the "complexes" which have corrupted him, their externalization excruciating him, and his agonized reluctance to their elimination plunging him into such ordeals that he seems (both to himself and to others) to have turned from a noble and upright man into an unutterable scoundrel; so does the "First Matter" blacken and putrefy as the Alchemist breaks up its coagulations of impurity.

The student may work out for himself the various analogies involved, and discover the "Black Dragon", the "Green Lion", the "Lunar Water", the "Raven's Head", and so forth. The indications above given should suffice all who possess aptitude for Alchemical Research.

Only one further reflection appears necessary; namely, that the Eucharist, with which this chapter is properly preoccupied, must be conceived as one case — as the critical case — of the Art of the Alchemist.

The reader will have observed, perhaps with surprise, that The MASTER THERION describes several types of Eucharist. The reason is that given above; there is no substance incompetent to serve as an element in some Sacrament; also, each spiritual Grace should possess its peculiar form of Mass, and therefore its own "materia magica". It is utterly unscientific to treat "God" as a universal homogeneity, and use the same means to prolong life as to bewitch cattle. One does not invoke "Electricity" indiscriminately to light one's house and to propel one's brougham; one works by measured application of one's powers to intelligent analytical comprehension of the conditions of each separate case.

There is a Eucharist for every Grace that we may need; we must apprehend the essential characters in each case, select suitable elements, and devise proper processes.

To consider the classical problems of Alchemy: The Medicine of Metals must be the quintessence of some substance that serves to determine the structure (or rate of vibration) whose manifestation is in characteristic metallic qualities. This need not be a chemical substance at all in the ordinary sense of the word.

The Elixir of Life will similarly consist of a living organism capable of growth, at the expense of its environment; and of such a nature that its "true Will" is to cause that environment to serve it as its means of expression in the physical world of human life.

The Universal Medicine will be a menstruum of such subtlety as to be able to penetrate all matter and transmute it in the sense of its own tendency, while of such impartial purity as to accept perfectly the impression of the Will of the Alchemist. This substance, properly prepared, and properly charged, is able to perform all things soever that are physically possible, within the limits of the proportions of its momentum to the inertia of the object to which it is applied.

It may be observed in conclusion that, in dealing with forms of Matter-Motion so subtle as these, it is not enough to pass the Pons Asinorum of intellectual knowledge.

The MASTER THERION has possessed the theory of these Powers for many years; but His practice is still in progress towards perfection. Even efficiency in the preparation is not all; there is need to be judicious in the manipulation, and adroit in the administration, of the product. He does not perform haphazard miracles, but applies His science and skill in conformity with the laws of nature.

CHAPTER XXI

OF BLACK MAGIC

OF THE MAIN TYPES OF THE OPERATIONS OF MAGICK ART

AND OF THE POWERS OF THE SPHINX

I

As was said at the opening of the second chapter, the Single Supreme Ritual is the attainment of the Knowledge and Conversation of the Holy Guardian Angel. "It is the raising of the complete man in a vertical straight line."

Any deviation from this line tends to become black magic. Any other operation is black magic.

In the True Operation the Exaltation is equilibrated by an expansion in the other three arms of the Cross. Hence the Angel immediately gives the Adept power over the Four Great Princes and their servitors.

See the Book of the Sacred Magic of Abramelin the Mage.

If the magician needs to perform any other operation than this, it is only lawful in so far as it is a necessary preliminary to That One Work.

There are, however many shades of grey. It is not every magician who is well armed with theory. Perhaps one such may invoke Jupiter, with the wish to heal others of their physical ills. This sort of thing is harmless,

There is nevertheless the general objection to the diversion of channels of Initiation to the Sea of Attainment, into ditches of irrigation for the fields of material advantage. It is bad business to pay good coin for perishable products; like marrying for money, or prostituting poetic genius to political purposes. The converse course, though equally objectionable as pollution of the purity of the planes, is at least respectable for its nobility. The ascetic of the Thebaid or the Trappist Monastery is infinitely worthier than the health-peddler and success-monger of Boston or Los Angeles; for the one offers temporal trash to gain eternal wealth, while the other values spiritual substance only as enabling him to get better bodily conditions, and a firmer grip on the dollars.

or almost so. It is not evil in itself. It arises from a defect of understanding. Until the Great Work has been performed, it is presumptuous for the magician to pretend to understand the universe, and dictate its policy. Only the Master of the Temple can say whether any given act is a crime. "Slay that innocent child?" (I hear the ignorant say) "What a horror!" "Ah!" replies the Knower, with foresight of history, "but that child will become Nero. Hasten to strangle him!"

There is a third, above these, who understands that Nero was as necessary as Julius Caesar.

The Master of the Temple accordingly interferes not with the scheme of things except just so far as he is doing the Work which he is sent to do. Why should he struggle against imprisonment, banishment, death? It is all part of the game in which he is a pawn. "It was necessary for the Son of Man to suffer these things, and to enter into His glory."

The Master of the Temple is so far from the man in whom He manifests that all these matters are of no importance to Him. It may be of importance to His Work that man shall sit upon a throne, or be hanged. In such a case He informs his Magus, who exerts the power intrusted to HIm, and it happens accordingly. Yet all happens naturally, and of necessity, and to all appearance without a word from Him.

Nor will the mere Master of the Temple, as a rule, presume to act upon the Universe, save as the servant of his own destiny. It is only the Magus, He of the grade above, who has attained to Chokhmah, Wisdom, and so dare act. He must dare act, although it like Him not. But He must assume the Curse of His grade, as it is written in the Book of the Magus.

Equinox I, VII, 5-9.

There are, of course, entirely black forms of magic. To him who has not given every drop of his blood for the cup of BABALON all magic power is dangerous. There are even more debased and evil forms, things in themselves black. Such is the use of spiritual force to material ends. Christian Scientists, Mental Healers, Professional Diviners, Psychics and the like, are all "ipso facto" Black Magicians.

They exchange gold for dross. They sell their higher powers for gross and temporary benefit.

That the most crass ignorance of Magick is their principal characteristic is no excuse, even if Nature accepted excuses, which she does not. If you drink poison in mistake for wine, your "mistake" will not save your life.

Below these in one sense, yet far above them in another, are the Brothers of the Left Hand Path< Supplement.>>. These are they who "shut themselves up", who refuse their blood to the Cup, who have trampled Love in the Race for self-aggrandisment.

As far as the grade of Exempt Adept, they are on the same path as the White Brotherhood; for until that grade is attained, the goal is not disclosed. Then only are the goats, the lonely leaping mountain-masters, separated from the gregarious huddling valley-bound sheep. Then those who have well learned the lessons of the Path are ready to be torn asunder, to give up their own life to the Babe of the Abyss which is — and is not — they.

The others, proud in their purple, refuse. They make themselves a false crown of the Horror of the Abyss; they set the Dispersion of Choronzon upon their brows; they clothe themselves in the poisoned robes of Form; they shut themselves up; and when the force that made them what they are is exhausted, their strong towers fall, they become the Eaters of Dung in the Day of Be-with-us, and their shreds, strewn in the Abyss, are lost.

Not so the Masters of the Temple, that sit as piles of dust in the City of the Pyramids, awaiting the Great Flame that shall consume that dust to ashes. For the blood that they have surrendered is treasured in the Cup of OUR LADY BABALON, a mighty medicine to awake the Eld of the All-Father, and redeem the Virgin of the World from her virginity.

II

Before leaving the subject of Black Magic, one may touch lightly on the question of Pacts with the Devil.

The Devil does not exist. It is a false name invented by the Black Brothers to imply a Unity in their ignorant muddle of dispersions. A devil who had unity would be a God

"The Devil" is, historically, the God of any people that one personally dislikes. This has led to so much confusion of thought that THE BEAST 666 has preferred to let names stand as they are, and to proclaim simply that

AIWAZ — the solar-phallic-hermetic "Lucifer" is His own Holy Guardian Angel, and "The Devil" SATAN or HADIT of our particular unit of the Starry Universe. This serpent, SATAN, is not the enemy of Man, but He who made Gods of our race, knowing Good and Evil; He bade "Know Thyself!" and taught Initiation. He is "the Devil" of the Book of Thoth, and His emblem is BAPHOMET, the Androgyne who is the hieroglyph of arcane perfection. The number of His Atu is XV, which is Yod He, the Monogram of the Eternal, the Father one with the Mother, the Virgin Seed one with all-containing Space. He is therefore Life, and Love. But moreover his letter is Ayin, the Eye; he is Light, and his Zodiacal image is Capricornus, that leaping goat whose attribute is Liberty. (Note that the "Jehovah" of the Hebrews is etymologically connected with these. The classical example of such antinomy, one which has led to such disastrous misunderstandings, is that between NU and HAD, North and South, Jesus and John. The subject is too abstruse and complicated to be discussed in detail here. The student should consult the writings of Sir R. Payne Knight, General Forlong, Gerald Massey, Fabre d'Olivet; etc. etc., for the data on which these considerations are ultimately based.)

It was said by the Sorcerer of the Jura that in order to invoke the Devil it is only necessary to call him with your whole will.

This is an universal magical truth, and applies to every other being as much as to the Devil. For the whole will of every man is in reality the whole will of the Universe.

It is, however, always easy to call up the demons, for they are always calling you; and you have only to step down to their level and fraternize with them. They will tear you in pieces at their leisure. Not at once; they will wait until you have wholly broken the link between you and your Holy Guardian Angel before they pounce, lest at the last moment you escape.

Anthony of Padua and (in our own times) "Macgregor" Mathers are examples of such victims.

Nevertheless, every magician must firmly extend his empire to the depth of hell. "My adepts stand upright, their heads above the heavens, their feet below the hells."

Liber XC, verse 40. See The Equinox.

This is the reason why the magician who performs the Operation of the "Sacred Magic of Abramelin the Mage", immediately after attaining to the Knowledge and Conversation of the Holy Guardian Angel, must evoke the Four Great Princes of the Evil of the World.

"Obedience and faith to Him that liveth and triumpheth, that reigneth above you in your palaces as the Balance of Righteousness and Truth" is your duty to your Holy Guardian Angel, and the duty of the demon world to you.

These powers of "evil" nature are wild beasts; they must be tamed, trained to the saddle and the bridle; they will bear you well. There is nothing useless in the Universe: do not wrap up your Talent in a napkin, because it is only "dirty money"!

With regard to Pacts, they are rarely lawful. There should be no bargain struck. Magick is not a trade, and no hucksters need apply. Master everything, but give generously to your servants, once they have unconditionally submitted.

There is also the questions of alliances with various Powers. These again are hardly ever allowable.

Notwithstanding, there exist certain bodies of spiritual beings, in whose ranks are not only angelic forces, but elementals, and even daemons, who have attained to such Right Understanding of the Universe that they have banded themselves together with the object of becoming Microcosms, and realize that their best means to this end is devotion to the service of the true interests of Mankind. Societies of spiritual forces, organized on these lines, dispose of enormous resources. The Magician who is himself sworn to the service of humanity may count upon the heartiest help of these Orders. Their sincerity may always be assured by putting them to the test of the acceptance of the Law of Thelema. Whoso denies "Do what thou wilt shall be the whole of the Law" confesses that he still clings to the conflict in his own nature; he is not, and does not want to be, true to himself. "A fortiori", he will prove false to you.

No Power which is not a microcosm in itself — and even archangels reach rarely to this centre of balance — is fit to treat on an equality with Man. The proper study of mankind is God; with Him is his business; and with Him alone. Some magicians have hired legions of spirits for some special purpose; but it has always proved a serious mistake. The whole idea of exchange is foreign to magick. The dignity of the magician forbids compacts. "The Earth is the Lord's and the fulness thereof".

III

The operations of Magick art are difficult to classify, as they merge into each other, owing to the essential unity of their method and result. We may mention:

1. Operations such as evocation, in which a live spirit is brought from dead matter.

2. Consecrations of talismans in which a live spirit is bound into "dead" matter and vivifies the same.

3. Works of divination, in which a live spirit is made to control operations of the hand or brain of the Magician. Such works are accordingly most dangerous, to be used only by advanced magicians, and then with great care.

4. Works of fascination, such as operations of invisibility, and transformations of the apparent form of the person or thing concerned. This consists almost altogether in distracting the attention, or disturbing the judgment, of the person whom it is wished to deceive. There are, however, "real" transformations of the adept himself which are very useful. See the Book of the Dead for methods. The assumption of God-Forms can be carried to the point of actual transformation.

5. Works of Love and Hate, which are also performed (as a rule) by fascination. These works are too easy; and rarely useful. They have a nasty trick of recoiling on the magician.

6. Works of destruction, which may be done in many different ways. One may fascinate and bend to one's will a person who has of his own right the power to destroy. One may employ spirits or talismans. The more powerful magicians of the last few centuries have employed books.

In private matters these works are very easy, if they be necessary. An adept known to The MASTER THERION once found it necessary to slay a Circe who was bewitching brethren. He merely walked to the door of her room, and drew an Astral T ("traditore", and the symbol of Saturn) with an astral dagger. Within 48 hours she shot herself.

As explained above, in another connexion, he who "destroys" any being must accept it, with all the responsibilities attached, as part of himself. The Adept here in question was therefore obliged to incorporate the elemental spirit of the girl — she was not human, the sheath of a Star, but an advanced planetary daemon, whose rash ambition had captured a body beyond its capacity to conduct — in his own magical vehicle. He thereby pledged himself to subordinate all the sudden accession of qualities — passionate, capricious, impulsive, irrational, selfish, short-sightedness, sensual, fickle, crazy, and desperate, to his True Will; to discipline, co-ordinate and employ them in the Great Work, under the penalty of being torn asunder by the wild horses which he had bound fast to his own body by the act of "destroying" their independent consciousness and control of their chosen vehicle. See His Magical Record An XX, Sun in Libra and onward.

7. Works of creation and dissolution, and the higher invocations.

There are also hundreds of other operations;

Examples of Rituals for several such purposes are given in the Equinox.

to bring wanted objects — gold, books, women and the like; to open locked doors, to discover treasure; to swim under water; to have armed men at command — etc., etc. All these are really matters of detail; the Adeptus Major will easily understand how to perform them if necessary.

Moral: become an Adeptus Major!

It should be added that all these things happen "naturally".

The value of the evidence that your operations have influenced the course of events is only to be assessed by the application of the Laws of probability. The MASTER THERION would not accept any one single case as conclusive, however improbable it might be. A man might make a correct guess at one chance in ten million, no less than at one in three. If one pick up a pebble, the chance was infinitely great against that particular pebble; yet whichever one was chosen, the same chance "came off". It requires a series of events antecedently unlikely to deduce that design is a work, that the observed changes are causally, not casually, produced. The prediction of events is further evidence that they are effected by will. Thus, any man may fluke a ten shot at billiard, or even make a break of a few strokes. But chance cannot account for consistent success, even if moderate, when it extends over a long period of time. And the ability of the expert to "name his shot" manifests a knowledge of the relations of cause and effect which confirms the testimony of his empirical skill that his success is not chance and coincidence.

Perform an operation to bring gold — your rich uncle dies and leaves you his money; books — you see the book wanted in a catalogue that very day, although you have advertised in vain for a year; woman — but if you have made the spirits bring you enough gold, this operation will become unnecessary.

This cynical statement is an absurdity of Black Magic.

It must further be remarked that it is absolute Black Magic to use any of these powers if the object can possibly be otherwise attained. If your child is drowning, you must jump and try to save him; it won't do to invoke the Undines.

Nor is it lawful in all circumstances to invoke those Undines even where the case is hopeless; maybe it is necessary to you and to the child that it should die. An Exempt Adept on the right road will make no error here — an Adept Major is only too likely to do so. A through apprehension of this book will arm adepts of every grade against all the more serious blunders incidental to their unfortunate positions.

IV

Necromancy is of sufficient importance to demand a section to itself.

It is justifiable in some exceptional cases. Suppose the magician fail to obtain access to living Teachers, or should he need some especial piece of knowledge which he has reason to believe died with some teacher of the past, it may be useful to evoke the "shade" of such a one, or read the "Akasic record" of his mind.

The only minds likely to be useful to the Magician belong to Adepts sworn to suffer reincarnation at short intervals, and the best elements of such minds are bound up in the "Unconscious Self" of the Adept, not left to wander idly about the Astral Plane. It will thus be more profitable to try to get into touch with the "Dead Teacher" in his present avatar. Moreover, Adepts are at pains to record their teaching in books, monuments, or pictures, and to appoint spiritual guardians to preserve such heirlooms throughout the generations. Whenever these are destroyed or lost, the reason usually is that the Adept himself judges that their usefulness is over, and withdraws the forces which protected them. The student is therefore advised to acquiesce; the sources of information available for him are probably selected by the Wardens of Mankind with a view to his real necessities. One must learn to trust one's Holy Guardian Angel to shape one's circumstances with skill. If one be but absorbed in the ardour of one's aspiration toward Him, short indeed is the time before Experience instils the certain conviction that His works and His ways are infinitely apt to one's needs.

If this be done it must be done properly very much on the lines of the evocation of Apollonius of Tyana, which Eliphas Levi performed.

See Rituel et Dogme de la Haute Magie; Rituel, ch. XIII.

The utmost care must be taken to prevent personation of the "shade". It is of course easy, but can rarely be advisable, to evoke the shade of a suicide, or of one violently slain or suddenly dead. Of what use is such an operation, save to gratify curiosity or vanity?

One must add a word on spiritism, which is a sort of indiscriminate necromancy — one might prefer the word necrophilia — by amateurs. They make themselves perfectly passive, and, so far from employing any methods of protection, deliberately invite all and sundry spirits, demons, shells of the dead, all the excrement and filth of earth and hell, to squirt their slime over them. This invitation is readily accepted, unless a clean man be present with an aura good enough to frighten these foul denizens of the pit.

No spiritualistic manifestation has ever taken place in the presence even of FRATER PERDURABO; how much less in that of The MASTER THERION!

Even the earliest Initiations confer protection. Compare the fear felt by D. D. Home for Eliphas Levi. See Equinox I, X, "The Key of the Mysteries".

Of all the creatures He ever met, the most prominent of English spiritists (a journalist and pacifist of more than European fame) had the filthiest mind and the foulest mouth. He would break off any conversation to tell a stupid smutty story, and could hardly conceive of any society assembling for any other purpose than "phallic orgies", whatever they may be. Utterly incapable of keeping to a subject, he would drag the conversation down again and again to the sole subject of which he really thought — sex and sex-perversions and sex and sex and sex and sex again.

This was the plain result of his spiritism. All spiritists are more or less similarly afflicted. They feel dirty even across the street; their auras are ragged, muddy and malodorous; they ooze the slime of putrefying corpses.

No spiritist, once he is wholly enmeshed in sentimentality and Freudian fear-phantasms, is capable of concentrated thought, of persistent will, or of moral character. Devoid of every spark of the divine light which was his birthright, a prey before death to the ghastly tenants of the grave, the wretch, like the mesmerized and living corpse of Poe's Monsieur Valdemar, is a "nearly liquid mass of loathsome, of detestable putrescence."

The student of this Holy Magick is most earnestly warned against frequenting their seances, or even admitting them to his presence.

They are contagious as Syphilis, and more deadly and disgusting. Unless your aura is strong enough to inhibit any manifestation of the loathly larvae that have taken up their habitation in them, shun them as you need not mere lepers!

It occurs in certain rare cases that a very unusual degree of personal purity combined with integrity and force of character provides even the ignorant with a certain natural defence, and attracts into his aura only intelligent and beneficent entities. Such persons may perhaps practise spiritualism without obvious bad results, and even with good results, within limits. But such exceptions in no wise invalidate the general rule, or in any way serve as argument against the magical theory outlined above with such mild suasion.

V

Of the powers of the Sphinx much has been written.

In Liber CXI (Aleph) the subject is treated with profound and all-comprehensive wisdom.

Wisely they have been kept in the forefront of true magical instruction. Even the tyro can always rattle off that he has to know, to dare to will and to keep silence. It is difficult to write on this subject, for these powers are indeed comprehensive, and the interplay of one with the other becomes increasingly evident as one goes more deeply into the subject.

But there is one general principle which seems worthy of special emphasis in this place. These four powers are thus complex because they are the powers of the Sphinx, that is, they are functions of a single organism.

Now those who understand the growth of organisms are aware that evolution depends on adaptation to environment. If an animal which cannot swim is occasionally thrown into water, it may escape by some piece of good fortune, but if it is thrown into water continuously it will drown sooner or later, unless it learns to swim.

Organisms being to a certain extent elastic, they soon adapt themselves to a new environment, provided that the change is not so sudden as to destroy that elasticity.

Now a change in environment involves a repeated meeting of new conditions, and if you want to adapt yourself to any given set of conditions, the best thing you can do is to place yourself cautiously and persistently among them. That is the foundation of all education.

The old-fashioned pedagogues were not all so stupid as some modern educators would have us think. The principle of the system was to strike the brain a series of constantly repeated blows until the proper reaction became normal to the organism.

It is not desirable to use ideas which excite interest, or may come in handy later as weapons, in this fundamental training of the mind. It is much better to compel the mind to busy itself with root ideas which do not mean very much to the child, because you are not trying to excite the brain, but to drill it. For this reason, all the best minds have been trained by preliminary study of classics and mathematics.

The same principle applies to the training of the body. The original exercises should be of a character to train the muscles generally to perform any kind of work, rather than to train them for some special kind of work, concentration of which will unfit them for other tasks by depriving them of the elasticity which is the proper condition of life.

Some few forms of exercise are exempt from these strictures. Rock-climbing, in particular, trains every muscle in an endless variety of ways. It moreover compels the learner to use his own judgment, to rely on himself, to develop resource, and to depend upon his own originality to attack each new problem that presents itself. This principle may be extended to all departments of the education of children. They should be put into contact with all kinds of truth, and allowed to make their own reflections thereon and reactions thereto, without the least attempt to bias their judgment. Magical pupils should be trained on similar lines. They should be made to work alone from the first, to cover the whole ground impartially, to devise their own experiments and draw their own conclusions.

In Magick and meditation this principle applies with tremendous force. It is quite useless to teach people how to perform magical operations, when it may be that such operations, when they have learned to do them, are not in accordance with their wills. What must be done is to drill the Aspirant in the hard routine of the elements of the Royal Art.

So far as mysticism is concerned, the technique is extremely simple, and has been very simply described in Part I of this Book 4. It cannot be said too strongly that any amount of mystical success whatever is no compensation for slackness with regard to the technique. There may come a time when Samadhi itself is no part of the business of the mystic. But the character developed by the original training remains an asset. In other words, the person who has made himself a first-class brain capable of elasticity is competent to attack any problem soever, when he who has merely specialized has got into a groove, and can no longer adapt and adjust himself to new conditions.

The principle is quite universal. You do not train a violinist to play the Beethoven Concerto; you train him to play every conceivable consecution of notes with perfect ease, and you keep him at the most monotonous drill possible for years and years before you allow him to go on the platform. You make of him an instrument perfectly able to adjust itself to any musical problem that may be set before him. This technique of Yoga is the most important detail of all our work. The MASTER THERION has been himself somewhat to blame in representing this technique as of value simply because it leads to the great rewards, such as Samadhi. He would have been wiser to base His teaching solely on the ground of evolution. But probably He thought of the words of the poet:

"You dangle a carrot in front of her nose,

And she goes wherever the carrot goes."

For, after all, one cannot explain the necessity of the study of Latin either to imbecile children or to stupid educationalists; for, not having learned Latin, they have not developed the brains to learn anything.

The Hindus, understanding these difficulties, have taken the God-Almighty attitude about the matter. If you go to a Hindu teacher, he treats you as less than an earthworm. You have to do this, and you have to do that, and you are not allowed to know why you are doing it.

This does not conflict with the "go-as-you-please" plan put forward in the previous note. An autocratic Adept is indeed a blessing to the disciple, not because he is able to guide the pupil "aright" in the particular path which happens to suit his personality, but because he can compel the beginner to grind away at the weariest work and thus acquire all-round ability, and prevent him from picking out the plums which please him from the Pie of Knowledge, and making himself sick of a surfeit of sweets to the neglect of a balanced diet of wholesome nourishment.

After years of experience in teaching, The MASTER THERION is not altogether convinced that this is not the right attitude. When people begin to argue about things instead of doing them, they become absolutely impossible. Their minds begin to work about it and about, and they come out by the same door as in they went. They remain brutish, voluble, and uncomprehending.

The technique of Magick is just as important as that of mysticism, but here we have a very much more difficult problem, because the original unit of Magick, the Body of Light, is already something unfamiliar to the ordinary person. Nevertheless, this body must be developed and trained with exactly the same rigid discipline as the brain in the case of mysticism. The essence of the technique of Magick is the development of the body of Light, which must be extended to include all members of the organism, and indeed of the cosmos.

The most important drill practices are:

1. The fortification of the Body of Light by the constant use of rituals, by the assumption of god-forms, and by the right use of the Eucharist.

2. The purification and consecration and exaltation of that Body by the use of rituals of invocation.

3. The education of that Body by experience. It must learn to travel on every plane; to break down every obstacle which may confront it. This experience must be as systematic and regular as possible; for it is of no use merely to travel to the spheres of Jupiter and Venus, or even to explore the 30 Aethyrs, neglecting unattractive meridians.

> *The Aspirant should remember that he is a Microcosm. "Universus sum et Nihil universi a me alienum puto" should be his motto. He should make it his daily practice to travel on the Astral Plane, taking in turn each of the most synthetic sections, the Sephiroth and the Paths. These being thoroughly understood, and an Angel in each pledged to guard or to guide him at need, he should start on a new series of expeditions to explore the subordinate sections of each. He may then practice Rising on the Planes from these spheres, one after the other in rotation. When he is thoroughly conversant with the various methods of meeting unexpected emergencies, he may proceed to investigate the regions of the Qliphoth and the Demonic Forces. It should be his aim to obtain a comprehensive knowledge of the entire Astral Plane, with impartial love of truth for its own sake; just as a child learns the geography of the whole planet, though he may have no intention of ever leaving his native land.*

The object is to possess a Body which is capable of doing easily any particular task that may lie before it. There must be no selection of special experience which appeals to one's immediate desire. One must go steadily through all possible pylons.

FRATER PERDRABO was very unfortunate in not having magical teachers to explain these things to Him. He was rather encouraged in unsystematic working. Very fortunate, on the other hand, was He to have found a Guru who instructed Him in the proper principles of the technique of Yoga, and He, having sufficient sense to recognize the universal application of those principles, was able to some extent to repair His original defects. But even to this day, despite the fact that His original inclination is much stronger towards Magick than towards mysticism, he is much less competent in Magick.

> *Reconsideration of these remarks, at the request of a loyal colleague, compels Him to admit that this may not be the case, It is true that He has been granted all Mystical Attainment that is theoretically possible, while His powers in Magick seem to be uneven and imperfect. Despite this, it may yet be that He has compassed the Possible. For Mystical Attainments are never mutually exclusive; the trance of Sorrow (for example) is not incompatible with the Beatific Vision, or the "Universal Joke". But in Magick any one Operation debars its performer from accomplishing some other. The reason of this is that the Oath of any Work bonds the Magician once and for all to be the principles implied therein. See Chapter XVI Part I. Further, it is obviously possible to reach the essence of anything without interfering with other things which obstruct each other. Crosscountry journeys are often scarcely practicable.*

A trace of this can be seen even in His method of combining the two divisions of our science, for in that method He makes concentration bear the Cross of the work.

This is possibly an error, probably a defect, certainly an impurity of thought, and the root of it is to be found in His original bad discipline with regard to Magick.

If the reader will turn to the account of his astral journeys in the Second Number of the First Volume of the Equinox, he will find that these experiments were quite capricious. Even when, in Mexico, He got the idea of exploring the 30 Aethyrs systematically, He abandoned the vision after only 2 Aethyrs had been investigated.

Very different is His record after the training in 1901 e.v. had put Him in the way of discipline.<

so that this Book (as now finally revised for the Press) may be considered

practically free from serious defect in this particular.>>

At the conclusion of this part of this book, one may sum up the whole matter in these words: There is no object whatever worthy of attainment but the regular development of the being of the Aspirant by steady scientific work; he should not attempt to run before he can walk; he should not wish to go somewhere until he knows for certain whither he wills to go.

APPENDIX I.

The reader will find excellent classical examples of rituals of Magick in The Equinox, Volume I, in the following places —

Number I. — The supplement contains considerations for preparing a ritual of self-initiation. The supplement is also a perfect model of what a magical record should be, in respect of the form.

Number II. — On pages 244-288 are given several rituals of Initiation.

Pages 302-317 give an account of certain astral visions.

Pages 326-332 give a formula for Rising on the Planes.

Number III. — Pages 151-169 give details of certain magical formulae.

Pages 170-190 are a very perfect example — classical, old style — of a magical ritual for the evocation of the spirit of Mercury.

Pages 190-197 — a ritual for the consecration of a talisman. A very perfect example.

Pages 198-205 — a very fine example of a ritual to invoke the Higher Genius.

Pages 208-233 — Ritual of Initiation, with explanation of the same.

Pages 269-272 — Ritual of obtaining the Knowledge and Conversation of the Holy Guardian Angel by the formula of I.A.O.

Pages 272-278 — Ritual to make one's self invisible.

Number IV. — Pages 43-196 — Treatise, with model Records, of Mental Training appropriate to the Magician.

Number V. — The supplement is the most perfect account of visions extant. They explore the farthest recesses of the magical universe.

Number VI. — the Supplement gives seven rituals of the dramatic order, as described in Chapter XIX.

Pages 29-32 — A highly important magical ritual for daily use and work.

Number VII. — Pages 21-27 — Classical ritual to invoke Mercury; for daily use and work.

Pages 117-157 — Example of a dramatic ritual in modern style.

Pages 229-243 — An elaborate magical map of the universe on particular principles.

Pages 372-375 — Example of a seasonal ritual.

Pages 376-383 — Ritual to invoke Horus.

Number VIII. — Pages 99-128 — The conjuration of the elemental spirits.

Number IX. — Pages 117-136 — Ritual for invoking the spirit of Mars.

Number X. — Pages 57-79 — Modern example of a magical ritual in dramatic form, commemorating the return of Spring.

Pages 81-90 — Fragment of ritual of a very advanced character.

VOL. III.

No. I. — This volume contains an immense number of articles of primary importance to every student of magick.

The rituals of The Book of Lies and the Goetia are also to be studied. The "preliminary invocation" of the Goetia is in particular recommended for daily use and work.

Orpheus, by Aleister Crowley, contains a large number of magical invocations in verse. There are also a good many others in other parts of his poetical works.

The following is a complete curriculum of reading officially approved by the A.'. A.'.

CURRICULUM OF A.'. A.'.

COURSE I.

GENERAL READING.

SECTION 1. — Books for Serious Study:

The Equinox. The standard Work of Reference in all occult matters. The Encyclopaedia of Initiation.

Collected Works of A. Crowley. These works contain many mystical and magical secrets, both stated clearly in prose, and woven into the robe of sublimest poesy.

The Yi King. (S.B.E. Series, Oxford University Press.) The "Classic of Changes"; gives the initiated Chinese system of Magick.

The Tao Teh King. (S.B.E. Series.) gives the initiated Chinese system of Mysticism.

Tannhauser, by A. Crowley. An allegorical drama concerning the Progress of the soul; the Tannhauser story slightly remodelled.

The Upanishads. (S.B.E. Series.) The Classical Basis of Vedantism, the best-known form of Hindu Mysticism.

The Bhagavad-Gita. A dialogue in which Krishna, the Hindu "Christ", expounds a system of Attainment.

The Voice of the Silence, by H. P. Blavatsky, with an elaborate commentary by Frater O. M.

The Goetia. The most intelligible of the mediaeval rituals of Evocation. Contains also the favorite Invocation of the Master Therion.

The Shiva Sanhita. A famous Hindu treatise on certain physical practices.

The Hathayoga Pradipika. Similar to The Shiva Sanhita.

Erdmann's "History of Philosophy". A compendious account of philosophy from the earliest times.

Most valuable as a general education of the mind.

The Spiritual Guide of Molinos. A simple manual of Christian mysticism.

The Star of the West. (Captain Fuller.) An introduction to the study of the Works of Aleister Crowley.

The Dhammapada. (S.B.E. Series, Oxford University Press.) The best of the Buddhist classics.

The Questions of King Milinda. (S.B.E. Series.) Technical points of Buddhist dogma, illustrated by dialogues.

Varieties of Religious Experience. (James.) Valuable as showing the uniformity of mystical attainment.

Kabbala Denudata, von Rosenroth: also the Kabbalah Unveiled, by S. L. Mathers. The text of the Kabalah, with commentary. A good elementary introduction to the subject.

Konx om Pax. Four invaluable treatises and a preface on Mysticism and Magick.

The Pistis Sophia. An admirable introduction to the study of Gnosticism.

The Oracles of Zoroaster. An invaluable collection of precepts mystical and magical.

The Dream of Scipio, by Cicero. Excellent for its Vision and its Philosophy.

The Golden Verses of Pythagoras, by Fabre d'Olivet. An interesting study of the exoteric doctrines of this Master.

The Divine Pymander, by Hermes Trismegistus. Invaluable as bearing on the Gnostic Philosophy.

The Secret Symbols of the Rosicrucians, reprint of Franz Hartmann. An invaluable compendium.

Scrutinium Chymicum, by Michael Maier. One of the best treatises on alchemy.

Science and the Infinite, by Sidney Klein. One of the best essays written in recent years.

Two Essays of the Worship of Priapus, by Richard Payne Knight. Invaluable to all students.

The Golden Bough, by J. G. Frazer. The Text-Book of folk Lore. Invaluable to all students.

The Age of Reason, by Thomas Paine. Excellent, though elementary, as a corrective to superstition.

Rivers of Life, by General Forlong. An invaluable text-book of old systems of initiation.

Three Dialogues, by Bishop Berkeley. The Classic of subjective idealism.

Essays of David Hume. The Classic of Academic Scepticism.

First Principles, by Herbert Spencer. The Classic of Agnosticism.

Prolegomena, by Emanuel Kant. The best introduction to Metaphysics.

The Canon. The best text-book of Applied Qabalah.

The Fourth Dimension, by H. Hinton. The text-book on this subject.

The Essays of Thomas Henry Huxley. Masterpieces of philosophy, as of prose.

The object of this course of reading is to familiarize the student with all that has been said by the Great Masters in every time and country. He should make a critical examination of them; not so much with the idea of discovering where truth lies, for he cannot do this except by virtue of his own spiritual experience, but rather to discover the essential harmony in those varied works. He should be on his guard against partisanship with a favourite author. He should familiarize himself thoroughly with the method of mental equilibrium, endeavouring to contradict any statement soever, although it may be apparently axiomatic.

The general object of this course, besides that already stated, is to assure sound education in occult matters, so that when spiritual illumination comes it may find a well-built temple. Where the mind is strongly biased towards any special theory, the result of an illumination is often to inflame that portion of the mind which is thus overdeveloped, with the result that the aspirant, instead of becoming an Adept, becomes a bigot and fanatic.

The A.'. A.'. does not offer examination in this course, but recommends these books as the foundation of a library.

SECTION 2. — Other books, principally fiction, of a generally suggestive and helpful kind:

Zanoni, by Sir Edward Bulwer Lytton. Valuable for its facts and suggestions about Mysticism.

A Strange Story, by Sir Edward Bulwer Lytton. Valuable for its facts and suggestions about Magick.

The Blossom and the Fruit, by Mabel Collins. Valuable for its account of the Path.

Petronius Arbiter. Valuable for those who have wit to understand it.

The Golden Ass, by Apuleius. Valuable for those who have wit to understand it.

Le Comte de Gabalis. Valuable for its hints of those things which it mocks.

The Rape of the Lock, by Alexander Pope. Valuable for its account of elementals.

Undine, by de la Motte Fouque. Valuable as an account of elementals.

Black Magic, by Marjorie Bowen. An intensely interesting story of sorcery.

Le Peau de Chagrin, by Honore de Balzac. A magnificent magical allegory.

Number Nineteen, by Edgar Jepson. An excellent tale of modern magic.

Dracula, by Bram Stoker. Valuable for its account of legends concerning vampires.

Scientific Romances, by H. Hinton. Valuable as an introduction to the study of the Fourth Dimension.

Alice in Wonderland, by Lewis Carroll. Valuable to those who understand the Qabalah.

Alice Through the Looking Glass, by Lewis Carroll. Valuable to those who understand the Qabalah.

The Hunting of the Snark, by Lewis Carroll. Valuable to those who understand the Qabalah.

The Arabian Nights, translated by either Sir Richard Burton or John Payne. Valuable as a storehouse of oriental magick-lore.

Morte d'Arthur, by Sir Thomas Mallory. Valuable as a storehouse of occidental Magick-lore.

The Works of Francois Rabelais. Invaluable for Wisdom.

The Kasidah, by Sir Richard Burton. Valuable as a summary of philosophy.

The Song Celestial, by Sir Edwin Arnold. "The Bhagavad-Gita" in verse.

The Light of Asia, by Sir Edwin Arnold. An account of the attainment of Gotama Buddha.

The Rosicrucians, by Hargrave Jennings. Valuable to those who can read between the lines.

The Real History of the Rosicrucians, by A. E. Waite. A good vulgar piece of journalism on the subject.

The Works of Arthur Machen. Most of these stories are of great magical interest.

The Writings of William O'Neill (Blake). Invaluable to all students.

The Shaving of Shagpat, by George Meredith. An excellent allegory.

Lilith, by George MacDonald. A good introduction to the Astral.

La-Bas, by J. K. Huysmans. An account of the extravagances caused by the Sin-complex.

The Lore of Proserpine, by Maurice Hewlett. A suggestive enquiry into the Hermetic Arcanum.

En Route, by J. K. Huysmans. An account of the follies of Christian mysticism.

Sidonia the Sorceress, by Wilhelm Meinhold.

The Amber Witch, by Wilhelm Meinhold.

These two tales are highly informative.

Macbeth; Midsummer Night's Dream; The Tempest, by W. Shakespeare. Interesting for traditions treated.

Redgauntlet, by Sir Walter Scott. Also one or two other novels. Interesting for traditions treated.

Rob Roy, by James Grant. Interesting for traditions treated.

The Magician, by W. Somerset Maugham. An amusing hotchpot of stolen goods.

The Bible, by various authors unknown. The Hebrew and Greek Originals are of Qabalistic value. It contains also many magical apologues, and recounts many tales of folk-lore and magical rites.

Kim, by Rudyard Kipling. An admirable study of Eastern thought and life. Many other stories by this author are highly suggestive and informative.

For Mythology, as teaching Correspondences:

Books of Fairy Tales generally.

Oriental Classics generally.

Sufi Poetry generally.

Scandinavian and Teutonic Sagas generally.

Celtic Folk-Lore generally.

This course is of general value to the beginner. While it is not to be taken, in all cases, too seriously, it will give him a general familiarity with the mystical and magical tradition, create a deep interest in the subject, and suggest many helpful lines of thought.

It has been impossible to do more, in this list, than to suggest a fairly comprehensive course of reading.

SECTION 3. — Official publications of the A.'. A.'.

Liber I.

Liber B vel Magi.

An account of the Grade of Magus, the highest grade which it is ever possible to manifest in any way whatever upon this plane. Or so it is said by the Masters of the Temple. Equinox VII, p. 5.

Liber II.

The Message of the Master Therion. Explains the Essence of the new law in a very simple manner. Equinox XI (Vol. III, No. 1), p. 39.

Liber III.

Liber Jugorum.

An instruction for the control of speech, action and thought. Equinox IV, p. 9 & Appendix VI of this book.
Liber IV. ABA.

A general account in elementary terms of magical and mystical powers.

Part. 1. *Mysticism* — published.

2. *Magick* (Elementary Theory) — published.

3. *Magick in Theory and Practice* (this book).

4. *The Law.* Not yet completed.

[note by shawn: Part IV was subsequenty published as *The Equinox of the Gods (Equinox Volume III, Number 3)*.]

Liber VI.

Liber O vel Manus et Sagittae.

Instructions given for elementary study of the Qabalah, Assumption of God forms, vibration of Divine Names, the Rituals of Pentagram and Hexagram, and their uses in protection and invocation, a method of attaining astral visions so-called, and an instruction in the practice called Rising on the Planes. Equinox II, p. 11 and appendix VI in this book.

Liber VII.

Liber Liberi vel Lapis Lazuli, Adumbratio Kabbalae Aegyptiorum.

sub Figura VII.

Being the Voluntary Emancipation of a certain exempt Adept from his Adeptship. These are the Birth Words of a Master of the Temple.

Its 7 chapters are referred to the 7 planets in the following order:

Mars, Saturn, Jupiter, Sol, Mercury, Luna, Venus.

Liber VIII.

See CCCCXVIII.

[note by shawn: This reference is a bit cryptic. Liber VIII is from the eighth Aethyr in Liber CCCCXVIII.]

Liber IX.

Liber E vel Exercitiorum.

Instructs the aspirant in the necessity of keeping a record. Suggests methods of testing physical clairvoyance. Gives instruction in Asana, Pranayama and Dharana, and advises the application of tests to the physical body, in order that the student may thoroughly understand his own limitations. Equinox I, p. 25 & Appendix VI of this Book.

Liber X.

Liber Porta Lucis.

An account of the sending forth of the Master Therion by the A.'. A.'. and an explanation of His mission. Equinox VI, p. 3.

Liber XI.

Liber NV.

An Instruction for attaining Nuit. Equinox VII, p. 11.

Liber XIII.

Graduum Montis Abiegni.

An account of the task of the Aspirant from Probationer to Adept. Equinox III, p. 3.

Liber XV.

Ecclesiae Gnosticae Catholicae Cannon Missae.

Represents the original and true pre-Christian Christianity. Equinox XI (vol. iii, part 1) And Appendix VI of this book.

Liber XVI.

Liber Turris vel Domus Dei.

An Instruction for attainment by the direct destruction of thoughts as they arise in the mind. Equinox VI, p. 9.

Liber XVII.

Liber I.A.O.

Gives three methods of attainment through a willed series of thoughts. Unpublished. It is the active form of Liber CCCLXI.

Liber XXI.

The Classic of Purity, by Ko Hsuen.

A new translation from the Chinese by the Master Therion. Unpublished.

Liber XXV.

The Ritual of the Star Ruby.

An improved form of the lesser ritual of the Pentagram, Liber CCCXXXIII, The Book of Lies, pp. 34 & 35. Also Appendix VI of this book.

Liber XXVII.

Liber Trigrammaton, being a book of Trigrams of the Mutations of the Tao with the Yin and Yang.

An account of the cosmic process: corresponding to the stanzas of Dzyan in another system. Unpublished. [note by shawn: published in *The Holy Books of Thelema (Equinox Volume III, Number 9).*]

Liber XXX.

Liber Librae.

An elementary course of morality suitable for the average man. Equinox I, p. 17.

Liber XXXIII.

An account of A.'. A.'. first written in the Language of his period by the Councillor Von Eckartshausen and now revised and rewritten in the Universal Cipher. Equinox I, p. 4.

Liber XXXVI.

The Star Sapphire.

An improved ritual of the Hexagram. Liber CCCXXXIII (The Book of Lies), p.p. 46 & 7, and Appendix VI of this book.

Liber XLI.

Thien Tao.

An Essay on Attainment by the Way of Equilibrium.

Knox Om Pax, p. 52

Liber XLIV

The Mass of the Phoenix.

A Ritual of the Law. Liber CCCXXXIII (The Book of Lies), pp. 57-7, and Appendix VI in this book.

Liber XLVI.

The Key of the Mysteries.

A Translation of "La Clef des Grands Mysteres", by Eliphas Levi. Specially adapted to the task of the Attainment of Bhakta-Yoga. Equinox X, Supplement.

Liber XLIX.

Shi Yi Chien.

An account of the divine perfection illustrated by the seven-fold permutation of the Dyad. Unpublished.

Liber LI.

The Lost Continent.

An account of the continent of Atlantis: the manners and customs, magical rites and opinions of its people, together with a true account of the catastrophe, so called, which ended in its disappearance. Unpublished.

Liber LV.

The Chymical Jousting of Brother Perardua with the seven Lances that he brake.

An account of the Magical and Mystic Path in the language of Alchemy. Equinox I, p. 88.

Liber LVIII.

An article on the Qabalah in Equinox V, p. 65.

Liber LIX.

Across the Gulf.

A fantastic account of a previous Incarnation. Its principal interest lies in the fact that its story of the overthrowing of Isis by Osiris may help the reader to understand the meaning of the overthrowing of Osiris by Horus in the present Aeon. Equinox VII, p. 293.

Liber LXI.

Liber Causae.

Explains the actual history and origin of the present movement. Its statements are accurate in the ordinary sense of the word. The object of the book is to discount Mythopeia. Equinox XI, p. 55.

Liber LXIV.

Liber Israfel, formerly called *Anubis.*

An instruction in a suitable method of preaching. Unpublished.

Liber LXV.

Liber Cordis Cincti Serpente.

An account of the relations of the Aspirant with his Holy Guardian Angel. Equinox XI (vol. iii, part 1), p. 65.

Liber LXVI.

Liber Stellae Rubeae.

A secret ritual, the Heart of IAO-OAI, delivered unto V.V.V.V.V. for his use in a certain matter of *Liber Legis.* See Liber CCCXXXIII (The Book of Lies), pp. 34-5. Also Appendix VI in this book.

Liber LXVII.

The Sword of Song.

A critical study of various philosophies. An account of Buddhism. A. Crowley, Collected Works, Vol. ii, pp. 140-203.

Liber LXXI.

The Voice of the Silence, the Two Paths, the Seven Portals,

by H. P. Blavatsky, with an elaborate commentary by Frater O. M. Equinox III, I. Supplement.

Liber LXXXIII. — The Urn.

This is the sequel to *The Temple of Solomon the King,* and is the Diary of a Magus. This book contains a detailed account of all the experiences passed through by the Master Therion in his attainment of this grade of Initiation, the highest possible to any manifested Man. Unpublished.

Liber LXXVIII.

A complete treatise on the Tarot giving the correct designs of the cards with their attributions and symbolic meanings on all the planes. Part-published in Equinox VII, p.143.

Liber LXXXI.

The Butterfly Net.

An account of a magical operation, particularly concerning the planet Luna, written in the form of a novel. Published under the title "Moon-child" by the Mandrake Press, 41, Museum St., London, W.C.1.

Liber LXXXIV.

Vel Chanokh.

A brief abstraction of the Symbolic representation of the Universe derived by Dr. John Dee through the Scrying of Sir Edward Kelly. Part-published in Equinox VII, p. 229 & VIII, p. 99.

Liber XC.

Tzaddi vel Hamus Hermeticus.

An account of Initiation, and an indication as to those who are suitable for the same. Equinox VI, p. 17.

Liber XCV.

The Wake-World.

A poetical allegory of the relations of the soul and the Holy Guardian Angel. Konx Om Pax, p. 1.

Liber XCVI.

Liber Gaias.

A Handbook of Geomancy. Equinox II, p. 137.

Liber CVI.

A Treatise on the Nature of Death, and the proper attitude to be taken towards it.

Published in "The International", New York, 1917.

Liber CXI (Aleph).

The Book of Wisdom or Folly.

An extended and elaborate commentary on the Book of the Law, in the form of a letter from the Master Therion to his magical son. Contains some of the deepest secrets of initiation, with a clear solution of many cosmic and ethical problems. Unpublished. [note by shawn: Since published as *Liber Aleph (Equinox Volume III, Number 6)*.]

Liber CL.

De Lege Libellum.

A further explanation of the Book of the Law, with special reference to the Powers and Privileges conferred by its acceptance.

Equinox III, part 1, p. 99.

Liber CLVI.

Liber Cheth, vel Vallum Abiegni.

A perfect account of the task of the Exempt Adept considered under the symbols of a particular plane, not the intellectual. Equinox VI, p. 23.

Liber CLVII.

The Tao Teh King.

A new translation, with a commentary, by the Master Therion. Unpublished.

Liber CLXV.

A Master of the Temple, Being an account of the attainment of Frater Unus In Omnibus.

The record of a man who actually attained by the system taught by the A.'. A.'. Part-published in Equinox III, I, p. 127.

Liber CLXXV.

Astarte vel Liber Berylli.

An instruction in attainment by the method of devotion, or Bhakta-Yogi. Equinox VII, p. 37.

Liber CLXXXV.

Liber Collegii Sancti.

Being the tasks of the Grades and their Oaths proper to Liber XIII. This is the official paper of the various grades. It includes the Task and Oath of a Probationer. Unpublished. [note by shawn: Since released in *Gems from the Equinox*, Israel Regardie, ed.]

Liber CXCVII.

The High History of Good Sir Palamedes the Saracen Knight and of his following of the Questing Beast.

A poetic account of the Great Work and enumeration of many obstacles. Equinox IV, Special Supplement.

Liber CC.

Resh vel Helios.

An instruction for the adoration of the Sun four times daily, with the object of composing the mind to meditation, and of regularising the practices. Equinox VI, p. 29.

Liber CCVI.

Liber RU vel Spiritus.

Full instruction in Pranayama. Equinox VII, p. 59.

Liber CCVII.

Syllabus. An enumeration of the Official publications of A.'. A.'. with a brief description of the contents of each book. Equinox XI (vol. iii part 1), p. 11. This appendix is extracted therefrom.

Liber CCXX (L vel Legis).

The Book of the Law, which is the foundation of the whole work. Text in Equinox X, p. 9. Short commentary in Equinox VII, p. 378. Full commentary by the Master Therion through whom it was given to the world, will be published shortly. [note by shawn: Retitled 'AL vel Legis' after the discoveries of Frater Achad.]

Liber CCXVI.

The Yi King.

A new translation, with a commentary by the Master Therion. Unpublished.

Liber CCXXXI.

Liber Arcanorum ton *ATU* tou *TAHUTI quas vidit ASAR in AMENNTI sub figura CCXXXI. Liber Carcerorum* ton *QLIPHOTH cum suis Geniis. Adduntur Sigilla et Nomina Eorum.*

An account of the cosmic process so far as it is indicated by the Tarot Trumps. Equinox VII, p. 69.

Liber CCXLII. AHA!

An exposition in poetic language of several of the ways of attainment and the results obtained. Equinox III, p. 9

Liber CCLXV.

The Structure of the Mind.

A Treatise on psychology from the mystic an magical standpoint. Its study will help the aspirant to make a detailed scientific analysis of his mind, and so learn to control it. Unpublished.

Liber CCC. Khabs am Pekht.

A special instruction for the Promulgation of the Law. This is the first and most important duty of every Aspirant of whatever grade. It builds up in him the character and Karma which forms the Spine of Attainment. Equinox III, I, p. 171

Liber CCCXXXIII.

The Book of Lies falsely so-called.

Deals with many matters on all planes of the very highest importance. It is an official publication for Babes of the Abyss, but is recommended even to beginners as highly suggestive. Published.

Liber CCCXXXV. Adonis.

An account in poetic language of the struggle of the human and divine elements in the consciousness of man, giving their harmony following on the victory of the latter. Equinox VII, p. 117.

Liber CCCLXI.

Liber H.H.H.

Gives three methods of attainment through a willed series of thoughts.

Liber CCCLXV, vel CXX.

The Preliminary Invocation of the Goetia so-called, with a complete explanation of the barbarous names of evocation used therein, and the secret rubric of the ritual, by the Master Therion. This is the most potent invocation extant, and was used by the Master Himself in his attainment. See p. 265 of this book.

Liber CD.

Liber TAU vel Kabbalae Truium Literarum sub figura CD.

A graphic interpretation of the Tarot on the plane of initiation. Equinox VII, p. 75.

Liber CCCCXII.

A vel Armorum.

An instruction for the preparation of the elemental Instruments. Equinox IV, p. 15.

Liber CCCCXVIII.

Liber XXX AERUM vel Saeculi.

Being of the Angels of the Thirty Aethyrs, the Vision and the Voice. Besides being the classical account of the thirty Aethyrs and a model of all visions, the cries of the Angels should be regarded as accurate, and the doctrine of the function of the Great White Brotherhood understood as the foundation of the Aspiration of the Adept. The account of the Master of the Temple should in particular be taken as authentic. Equinox V, Special Supplement.

Liber CDLXXIV. Os Abysmi vel Da'ath.

An instruction in a purely intellectual method of entering the Abyss. Equinox VII, p. 77.

Liber D. Sepher Sephiroth.

A dictionary of Hebrew words arranged according to their numerical value. This is an Encyclopaedia of the Holy Qabalah, which is a Map of the Universe, and enables man to attain Perfect Understanding. Equinox VIII, Special Supplement.

Liber DXXXVI.

A complete Treatise on Astrology.

This is the only text book on astrology composed on scientific lines by classifying observed facts instead of deducting from *a priori* theories. Unpublished.

Liber DXXXVI.

BATRACHOPHRENOBOOKOSMOMACHIA.

An instruction in expansion of the field of the mind. Equinox X, p. 35.

Liber DLV. LIBER HAD.

An instruction for attaining Hadit. Equinox VII, p. 83.

Liber DCXXXIII.

De Thaumaturgia.

A statement of certain ethical considerations concerning Magick. Unpublished.

Liber DCLXVI.

The Beast.

An account of the Magical Personality who is the Logos of the present Aeon. Unpublished.

Liber DCCLXXVII. (777).

Vel Prolegomena Symbolica Ad Systemam Sceptico-Mysticae Viae Explicandae, Fundamentum Hieroglyphicorum sanctissimorum Scientae Summae.

A complete Dictionary of the Correspondences of all magical elements, reprinted with extensive additions, making it the only standard comprehensive book of reference ever published. It is to the language of Occultism what Webster or Murray is to the English Language. The reprint with additions will shortly be published.

Liber DCCCXI.

Energised Enthusiasm.

Specially adapted to the task of Attainment of Control of the Body of Light, development of Intuition and Hathayoga. Equinox IX, p. 17.

Liber DCCCXIII.

vel ARARITA.

An account of the Hexagram and the method of reducing it to the Unity, and Beyond. Unpublished.

Liber DCCCXXXI.

Liber IOD, formerly called VESTA.

An instruction giving three methods of reducing the manifold consciousness to the Unity. Adapted to facilitate the task of the Attainment of Raja-Yoga and of the Knowledge and Conversation of the Holy Guardian Angel. Equinox VII, p. 101.

Liber DCCCXXXVII.

The Law of Liberty. This is a further explanation of the Book of the Law in reference to certain Ethical problems. Equinox XI (vol. III, No. 1), p. 45.

Liber DCCCLX.

John St. John.

The Record of the Magical Retirement of G. H. Frater O.'. M.'. A model of what a magical record should be, so far as accurate analysis and fullness of description are concerned. Equinox I, Supplement.

Liber DCCCLXVIII.

Liber Viarum Viae.

A graphical account of magical powers classified under the Tarot Trumps. Equinox VII, p. 101.

Liber DCCCLXXXVIII.

A complete study of the origins of Christianity. Unpublished.

Liber CMXIII.

Liber Viae Memoriae.

Gives methods for attaining the magical memory, or memory of past lives, and an insight into the function of the Aspirant in this present life. Equinox VII, p. 105.

Liber CMXXXIV.

The Cactus.

An elaborate study of the psychological effects produced by *Anhalonium Lewinii* (Mescal Buttons), compiled from the actual records of some hundreds of experiments. Unpublished.

Liber DCCCCLXIII.

The Treasure House of Images.

A superb collection of Litanies appropriate to the Signs of the Zodiac. Equinox III, Supplement.

Liber MMCCMXI.

A Note on Genesis.

A model of Qabalistic ratiocination. Specially adapted to Gnana Yoga.

Liber MCCLXIV.

The Greek Qabalah.

A complete dictionary of all sacred and important words and phrases given in the Books of the Gnosis and other important writings both in the Greek and the Coptic. Unpublished.

APPENDIX II.

ONE STAR IN SIGHT.

Thy feet in mire, thine head in murk,
O man, how piteous thy plight,
The doubts that daunt, the ills that irk,
Thou hast nor wit nor will to fight —
How hope in heart, or worth in work?
No star in sight!
Thy gods proved puppets of the priest.
"Truth? All's relation!" science sighed.
In bondage with thy brother beast,
Love tortured thee, as Love's hope died
And Lover's faith rotted. Life no least
Dim star descried.
Thy cringing carrion cowered and crawled
To find itself a chance-cast clod
Whose Pain was purposeless; appalled
That aimless accident thus trod
Its agony, that void skies sprawled
On the vain sod!
All souls eternally exist,
Each individual, ultimate,
Perfect — each makes itself a mist
Of mind and flesh to celebrate
With some twin mask their tender tryst
Insatiate.
Some drunkards, doting on the dream,

Despair that it should die, mistake

Themselves for their own shadow-scheme.

One star can summon them to wake

To self; star-souls serene that gleam

On life's calm lake.

That shall end never that began.

All things endure because they are.

Do what thou wilt, for every man

And every woman is a star.

Pan is not dead; he liveth, Pan!

Break down the bar!

To man I come, the number of

A man my number, Lion of Light;

I am The Beast whose Law is Love.

Love under will, his royal right —

Behold within, and not above,

One star in sight!

ONE STAR IN SIGHT.

A glimpse of the structure and system of the Great White Brotherhood.

A.'. A.'.

> *The Name of the Order and those of its three divisions are not disclosed to the profane. Certain swindlers have recently stolen the initials A.'. A.'. in order to profit by its reputation.*

Do what thou wilt shall be the whole of the Law.

1. The Order of the Star called S. S. is, in respect of its existence upon the Earth, an organized body of men and women distinguished among their fellows by the qualities here enumerated. They exist in their own Truth, which is both universal and unique. They move in accordance with their own Wills, which are each unique, yet coherent with the universal will.

They perceive (that is, understand, know, and feel) in love, which is both unique and universal.

2. The order consists of eleven grades or degrees, and is numbered as follows: these compose three groups, the Orders of the S. S., of the R. C., and of the G. D. respectively.

The Order of the S. S.

Ipsissimus .... 10 Degree = 1Square

Magus .... 9 Degree = 2Square

Magister Templi .... 8 Degree = 3Square

The Order of the R. C.

(Babe of the Abyss — the link)

Adeptus Exemptus .... 7 Degree = 4Square

Adeptus Major .... 6 Degree = 5Square

Adeptus Minor .... 5 Degree = 6Square

The Order of the G. D.

(Dominus Liminis — the link)

Philosophus .... 4 Degree = 7Square

Practicus .... 3 Degree = 8Square

Zelator .... 2 Degree = 9Square

Neophyte .... 1 Degree = 10Square

Probationer .... 0 Degree = 0Square

(These figures have special meanings to the initiated and are commonly employed to designate the grades.)

The general characteristics and attributions of these Grades are indicated by their correspondences on the Tree of Life, as may be studied in detail in the Book 777.

Student. — His business is to acquire a general intellectual knowledge of all systems of attainment, as declared in the prescribed books. (See curriculum in Appendix I.)

Probationer. — His principal business is to begin such practices as he my prefer, and to write a careful record of the same for one year.

Neophyte. — Has to acquire perfect control of the Astral Plane.

Zelator. — His main work is to achieve complete success in Asana and Pranayama. He also begins to study the formula of the Rosy Cross.

Practicus. — Is expected to complete his intellectual training, and in particular to study the Qabalah.

Philosophus. — Is expected to complete his moral training. He is tested in Devotion to the Order.

Dominus Liminis. — Is expected to show mastery of Pratyahara and Dharana.

Adeptus (without). — is expected to perform the Great Work and to attain the Knowledge and Conversation of the Holy Guardian Angel.

Adeptus (within). — Is admitted to the practice of the formula of the Rosy Cross on entering the College of the Holy Ghost. **Adeptus** (Major). — Obtains a general mastery of practical Magick, though without comprehension.

Adeptus (Exemptus). — Completes in perfection all these matters. He then either (*a*) becomes a Brother of the Left Hand Path or, (*b*) is stripped of all his attainments and of himself as well, even of his Holy Guardian Angel, and becomes a babe of the Abyss, who, having transcended the Reason, does nothing but grow in the womb of its mother. It then finds itself a

Magister Templi. — (Master of the Temple): whose functions are fully described in Liber 418, as is this whole initiation from Adeptus Exemptus. See also "Aha!". His principal business is to tend his "garden" of disciples, and to obtain a perfect understanding of the Universe. He is a Master of Samadhi.

Magus. — Attains to wisdom, declares his law (See Liber I, vel Magi) and is a Master of all Magick in its greatest and highest sense.

Ipsissimus. — Is beyond all this and beyond all comprehension of those of lower degrees.

But of these last three Grades see some further account in *The Temple of Solomon the King,* Equinox I to X and elsewhere.

It should be stated that these Grades are not necessarily attained fully, and in strict consecution, or manifested wholly on all planes. The subject is very difficult, and entirely beyond the limits of this small treatise.

We append a more detailed account.

3. *The Order of the* S. S. is composed of those who have crossed the Abyss; the implications of this expression may be studied in Liber 418, the 14th, 13th, 12th, 11th, 10th, and 9th Aethyrs in particular.

All members of the Order are in full possession of the Formulae of Attainment, both mystical or inwardly-directed and Magical or outwardly-directed. They have full experience of attainment in both these paths.

They are all, however, bound by the original and fundamental Oath of the Order, to devote their energy to assisting the Progress of their Inferiors in the Order. Those who accept the rewards of their emancipation for themselves are no longer within the Order.

Members of the Order are each entitled to found Orders dependent on themselves on the lines of the R. C. and G. D. orders, to cover types of emancipation and illumination not contemplated by the original (or main) system. All such orders must, however, be constituted in harmony with the A.'. A.'. as regards the essential principles.

All members of the Order are in possession of the Word of the existing Aeon, and govern themselves thereby.

They are entitled to communicate directly with any and every member of the Order, as they may deem fitting.

Every active Member of the Order has destroyed all that He is and all that he has on crossing the Abyss; but a star is cast forth in the Heavens to enlighten the Earth, so that he may possess a vehicle wherein he may communicate with mankind. The quality and position of this star, and its functions, are determined by the nature of the incarnations transcended by him.

4. The Grade of Ipsissimus is not to be described fully; but its opening is indicated in Liber I vel Magi.

There is also an account in a certain secret document to be published when propriety permits. Here it is only said this: The Ipsissimus is wholly free from all limitations soever, existing in the nature of all things without discriminations of quantity or quality between them. He has identified Being and not-Being and Becoming, action and non-action and tendency to action, with all other such triplicities, not distinguishing between them in respect of any conditions, or between any one thing and any other thing as to whether it is with or without conditions.

He is sworn to accept this Grade in the presence of a witness, and to express its nature in word and deed, but to withdraw Himself at once within the veils of his natural manifestation as a man, and to keep silence during his human life as to the fact of his attainment, even to the other members of the Order.

The Ipsissimus is pre-eminently the Master of all modes of existence; that is, his being is entirely free from internal or external necessity. His work is to destroy all tendencies to construct or to cancel such necessities. He is the Master of the Law of Unsubstantiality (Anatta).

The Ipsissimus has no relation as such with any Being: He has no will in any direction, and no Consciousness of any kind involving duality, for in Him all is accomplished; as it is written "beyond the Word and the Fool, yea, beyond the Word and the Fool".

5. The Grade of Magus is described in Liber I vel Magi, and there are accounts of its character in Liber 418 in the Higher Aethyrs.

There is also a full and precise description of the attainment of this Grade in the Magical Record of the Beast 666.

The essential characteristic of the Grade is that its possessor utters a Creative Magical Word, which transforms the planet on which he lives by the installation of new officers to preside over its initiation. This can take place only at an "Equinox of the Gods" at the end of an "Aeon"; that is, when the secret formula which expresses the Law of its action becomes outworn and useless to its further development.

(Thus "Suckling" is the formula of an infant: when teeth appear it marks a new "Aeon", whose "Word" is "Eating").

A Magus can therefore only appear as such to the world at intervals of some centuries; accounts of historical Magi, and their Words, are given in Liber Aleph.

This does not mean that only one man can attain this Grade in any one Aeon, so far as the Order is concerned. A man can make personal progress equivalent to that of a "Word of an Aeon"; but he will identify himself with the current word, and exert his will to establish it, lest he conflict with the work of the Magus who uttered the Word of the Aeon in which He is living.

The Magus is pre-eminently the Master of Magick, that is, his will is entirely free from internal diversion or external opposition; His work is to create a new Universe in accordance with His Will. He is the Master of the Law of Change (Anicca).

To attain the Grade of Ipsissimus he must accomplish three tasks, destroying the Three Guardians mentioned in Liber 418, the 3rd Aethyr; Madness, and Falsehood, and Glamour, that is, Duality in Act, Word and Thought.

6. The Grade of Master of the Temple is described in Liber 418 as above indicated. There are full accounts in the Magical Diaries of the Beast 666, who was cast forth into the Heaven of Jupiter, and of Omnia in Uno, Unus in Omnibus, who was cast forth into the sphere of the Elements.

The essential Attainment is the perfect annihilation of that personality which limits and oppresses his true self.

The Magister Templi is pre-eminently the Master of Mysticism, that is, His Understanding is entirely free from internal contradiction or external obscurity; His word is to comprehend the existing Universe in accordance with His own Mind. He is the Master of the Law of Sorrow (Dukkha).

To attain the grade of Magus he must accomplish Three 235} Tasks; the renunciation of His enjoyment of the Infinite so that he may formulate Himself as the Finite; the acquisition of the practical secrets alike of initiating and governing His proposed new Universe and the identification of himself with the impersonal idea of Love. Any neophyte of the Order (or, as some say, any person soever) possesses the right to claim the Grade of Master of the Temple by taking the Oath of the Grade. It is hardly necessary to observe that to do so is the most sublime and awful responsibility which it is possible to assume, and an unworthy person who does so incurs the most terrific penalties by his presumption.

7. *The Order of the R. C.* The Grade of the Babe of the Abyss is not a Grade in the proper sense, being rather a passage between the two Orders. Its characteristics are wholly negative, as it is attained by the resolve of the Adeptus Exemptus to surrender all that he has and is for ever. It is an annihilation of all the bonds that compose the self or constitute the Cosmos, a resolution of all complexities into their elements, and these thereby cease to manifest, since things are only knowable in respect of their relation to, and reaction on, other things.

8. The Grade of Adeptus Exemptus confers authority to govern the two lower Orders of R. C. and G. D.

The Adept must prepare and publish a thesis setting forth His knowledge of the Universe, and his proposals for its welfare and progress. He will thus be known as the leader of a school of thought.

(Eliphas Levi's *Clef des Grands Mysteres,* the works of Swedenborg, von Eckarshausen, Robert Fludd, Paracelsus, Newton, Bolyai, Hinton, Berkeley, Loyola, etc., etc., are examples of such essays.)

He will have attained all but the supreme summits of meditation, and should be already prepared to perceive that the only possible course for him is to devote himself utterly to helping his fellow creatures.

To attain the Grade of Magister Templi, he must perform two tasks; the emancipation from thought by putting each idea against its opposite, and refusing to prefer either; and the consecration of himself as a pure vehicle for the influence of the order to which he aspires.

He must then decide upon the critical adventure of our Order; the absolute abandonment of himself and his attainments. He cannot remain indefinitely an Exempt Adept; he is pushed onward by the irresistible momentum that he has generated.

Should he fail, by will or weakness, to make his self-annihilation absolute, he is none the less thrust forth into the Abyss; but instead of being received and reconstructed in the Third Order, as a Babe in the womb of our Lady BABALON, under the Night of Pan, to grow up to be Himself wholly and truly as He was not previously, he remains in the Abyss, secreting his elements round his Ego as if isolated from the Universe, and becomes what is called a "Black Brother". Such a being is gradually disintegrated from lack of nourishment and the slow but certain action of the attraction of the rest of the Universe, despite efforts to insulate and protect himself, and to aggrandise himself by predatory practices. He may indeed prosper for a while, but in the end he must perish, especially when with a new Aeon a new word is proclaimed which he cannot and will not hear, so that he is handicapped by trying to use an obsolete method of Magick, like a man with a boomerang in a battle where every one else has a rifle.

9. The Grade of Adeptus Major confers Magical Powers (strictly so-called) of the second rank.

His work is to use these to support the authority of the Exempt Adept his superior. (This is not to be understood as an obligation of personal subservience or even loyalty; but as a necessary part of his duty to assist his inferiors. For the authority of the Teaching and governing Adept is the basis of all orderly work.)

To attain the Grade of Adeptus Exemptus, he must accomplish Three Tasks; the acquisition of absolute Self-Reliance, working in complete isolation, yet transmitting the word of his superior clearly, forcibly and subtly; and the comprehension and use of the Revolution of the wheel of force, under its three successive forms of Radiation, Conduction and Convection (Mercury, Sulphur, Salt; or Sattvas, Rajas, Tamas), with their corresponding natures on other planes. Thirdly, he must exert his whole power and authority to govern the Members of lower Grades with balanced vigour and initiative in such a way as to allow no dispute or complaint; he must employ to this end the formula called "The Beast conjoined with the Woman" which establishes a new incarnation of deity; as in the legends of Leda, Semele, Miriam, Pasiphae, and others. He must set up this ideal for the orders which he rules, so that they may possess a not too abstract rallying point suited to their undeveloped states.

10. The Grade of Adeptus Minor is the main theme of the instructions of the A.'. A.'. It is characterised by the Attainment of the Knowledge and Conversation of the Holy Guardian Angel. (See the Equinox, *The Temple of Solomon the King; The Vision and the Voice* 8th Aethyr; also *Liber Samekh*, etc. etc.) This is the essential work of every man; none other ranks with it either for personal progress or for power to help one's fellows. This unachieved, man is no more than the unhappiest and blindest of animals. He is conscious of his own incomprehensible calamity, and clumsily incapable of repairing it. Achieved, he is no less than the co-heir of gods, a Lord of Light. He is conscious of his own consecrated course, and confidently ready to run it. The Adeptus Minor needs little help or guidance even from his superiors in our Order.

His work is to manifest the Beauty of the Order to the world, in the way that his superiors enjoin, and his genius dictates.

To attain the Grade Adeptus Major, he must accomplish two tasks; the equilibration of himself, especially as to his passions, so that he has no preference for any one course of conduct over another, and the fulfilment of every action by its complement, so that whatever he does leaves him without temptation to wander from the way of his True Will.

Secondly, he must keep silence, while he nails his body to the tree of his creative will, in the shape of that Will, leaving his head and arms to form the symbol of Light, as if to make oath that his every thought, word and deed should express the Light derived from the God with which he has identified his life, his love and his liberty — symbolised by his heart, his phallus, and his legs. It is impossible to lay down precise rules by which a man may attain to the knowledge and conversation of His Holy Guardian Angel; for that is the particular secret of each one of us; as secret not to be told or even divined by any other, whatever his grade. It is the Holy of Holies, whereof each man is his own High Priest, and none knoweth the Name of his brother's God, or the Rite that invokes Him.

The Masters of the A.'. A.'. have therefore made no attempt to institute any regular ritual for this central Work of their Order, save the generalised instructions in Liber 418 (the 8th Aethyr) and the detailed Canon and

Rubric of the Mass actually used with success by FRATER PERDURABO in His attainment. This has been written down by Himself in Liber Samekh. But they have published such accounts as those in *The Temple of Solomon the King* and in *John St. John.* They have taken the only proper course; to train aspirants to this attainment in the theory and practice of the whole of Magick and Mysticism, so that each man may be expert in the handling of all known weapons, and free to choose and to use those which his own experience and instinct dictate as proper when he essays the Great Experiment.

He is furthermore trained to the one habit essential to Membership of the A.'. A.'.; he must regard all his attainments as primarily the property of those less advanced aspirants who are confided to his charge.

No attainment soever is officially recognised by the A.'. A.'. unless the immediate inferior of the person in question has been fitted by him to take his place.

The rule is not rigidly applied in all cases, as it would lead to congestion, especially in the lower grades where the need is greatest, and the conditions most confused; but it is never relaxed in the Order of the R. C. or of the S. S.: save only in One Case.

There is also a rule that the Members of the A.'. A.'. shall not know each other officially, save only each Member his superior who introduced him and his inferior whom he has himself introduced.

This rule has been relaxed, and a "Grand Neophyte" appointed to superintend all Members of the Order of the G. D. The real object of the rule was to prevent Members of the same Grade working together and so blurring each other's individuality; also to prevent work developing into social intercourse.

The Grades of the Order of the G. D. are fully described in Liber 185

This book is published in the Equinox Vol. III No. 2 —— Addenda by WEH: No, it isn't. Vol. III, 2 didn't get out of printer's proofs and was not published. The book in question was finally published in Regardie's "Gems from the Equinox".

, and there is no need to amplify what is there stated. It must however, be carefully remarked that in each of these preliminary Grades there are appointed certain tasks appropriate, and that the ample accomplishment of each and every one of these is insisted upon with the most rigorous rigidity.

Liber 185 need not be quoted at length. It is needful only to say that the Aspirant is trained systematically and comprehensively in the various technical practices which form the basis of Our Work. One may become expert in any or all of these without necessarily making any real progress, just as a man might be first-rate at grammar, syntax, and prosody without being able to write a single line of good poetry, although the greatest poet in soul is unable to express himself without the aid of those three elements of literary composition.

Members of the A.'. A.'. of whatever grade are not bound or expected or even encouraged to work on any stated lines, or with any special object, save as has been above set forth. There is however an absolute prohibition to accept money or other material reward, directly or indirectly, in respect of any service connected with the Order, for personal profit or advantage. The penalty is immediate expulsion, with no possibility of reinstatement on any terms soever.

But all members must of necessity work in accordance with the facts of Nature, just as an architect must allow of the Law of Gravitation, or a sailor reckon with currents.

So must all Members of the A.'. A.'. work by the Magical Formula of the Aeon.

They must accept the Book of the Law as the Word and the Letter of Truth, and the sole Rule of Life.

This is not in contradiction with the absolute right of every person to do his own true Will. But any True Will is of necessity in harmony with the facts of Existence; and to refuse to accept the Book of the Law is to create a conflict within Nature, as if a physicist insisted on using an incorrect formula of mechanics as the basis of an experiment.

They must acknowledge the Authority of the Beast 666 and of the Scarlet Woman as in the book it is defined, and accept Their Will

"Their Will" — not, of course, their wishes as individual human beings, but their will as officers of the New Aeon.

as concentrating the Will of our Whole Order. They must accept the Crowned and Conquering Child as the Lord of the Aeon, and exert themselves to establish His reign upon Earth. They must acknowledge that "The word of the Law is [in Greek] Thelema" and that "Love is the law, love under will."

Each member must make it his main work to discover for himself his own true will, and to do it, and do nothing else.

It is not considered "essential to right conduct" to be an active propagandist of the Law, and so on; it may, or may not, be the True Will of any particular person to do so. But since the fundamental purpose of the Order is to further the Attainment of humanity, membership implies, by definition, the Will to help mankind by the means best adapted thereto.

He must accept those orders in the Book of the Law that apply to himself as being necessarily in accordance with his own true will, and execute the same to the letter with all the energy, courage, and ability that he can command. This applies especially to the work of extending the Law in the world, wherein his proof is his own success, the witness of his Life to the Law that hath given him light in his ways, and liberty to pursue them. Thus doing, he payeth his debt to the Law that hath freed him by working its will to free all men; and he proveth himself a true man in our Order by willing to bring his fellows into freedom.

By thus ordering his disposition, he will fit himself in the best possible manner for the task of understanding and mastering the divers technical methods prescribed by the A.'. A.'. for Mystical and Magical attainment.

He will thus prepare himself properly for the crisis of his career in the Order, the attainment of the Knowledge and Conversation of his Holy Guardian Angel.

His Angel shall lead him anon to the summit of the Order of the R. C. and make him ready to face the unspeakable terror of the Abyss which lies between Manhood and Godhead; teach him to Know that agony, to Dare that destiny, to Will that catastrophe, and to keep Silence for ever as he accomplishes the act of annihilation.

From the Abyss comes No Man forth, but a Star startles the Earth, and our Order rejoices above that Abyss that the Beast hath begotten one more Babe in the Womb of Our Lady, His concubine, the Scarlet Woman, BABALON.

There is not need to instruct a Babe thus born, for in the Abyss it was purified of every poison of personality; its ascent to the highest is assured, in its season, and it hath no need of seasons for it is conscious that all conditions are no more than forms of its fancy.

Such is a brief account, adapted as far as may be to the average aspirant to Adeptship, or Attainment, or

Initiation, or Mastership, or Union with God, or Spiritual Development, or Mahatmaship, or Freedom, or Occult Knowledge, or whatever he may call his inmost need of Truth, of our Order of A.'. A.'.

It is designed principally to awake interest in the possibilities of human progress, and to proclaim the principles of the A.'. A.'.

The outline given of the several successive steps is exact; the two crises — the Angel and the Abyss — are necessary features in every career. The other tasks are not always accomplished in the order given here; one man, for example, may acquire many of the qualities peculiar to the Adeptus Major, and yet lack some of those proper to the Practicus.

> *The natural talents of individual differ very widely. The late Sir Richard Jebb, one of the greatest classical scholars of modern times, was so inferior to the average mediocrity in mathematics, that despite repeated efforts he could not pass the "little go" at Cambridge — which the dullest minds can usually do. He was so deeply esteemed for his classics that a special "Grace" was placeted so as to admit him to matriculation. Similarly a brilliant Exorcist might be an incompetent Diviner. In such a case the A.'. A.'. would refuse to swerve from Its system; the Aspirant would be compelled to remain at the Barrier until he succeeded in breaking it down, though a new incarnation were necessary to permit him to do so. But no technical failure of any kind soever could necessarily prevent him from accomplishing the Two Critical Tasks, since the fact of his incarnation itself proves that he has taken the Oath which entitled him to attain to the Knowledge and Conversation of his Holy Guardian Angel, and the annihilation of this Ego. One might therefore be an Adeptus Minor or even a Magister Templi, in essence, though refused official recognition by the A.'. A.'. as a Zelator owing to (say) a nervous defect which prevented him from acquiring a Posture which was "steady and easy" as required by the Task of that grade.*

But the system here given shows the correct order of events, as they are arranged in Nature; and in no case is it safe for a man to neglect to master any single detail, however dreary and distasteful it may seem. It often does so, indeed; that only insists on the necessity of dealing with it. The dislike and contempt for it bear witness to a weakness and incompleteness in the nature which disowns it; that particular gap in one's defences may admit the enemy at the very turning-point of some battle. Worse, one were shamed for ever if one's inferior should happen to ask for advice and aid on that subject and one were to fail in service to him! His failure — one's own failure also! No step, however well won for oneself, till he is ready for his own advance!

Every Member of the A.'. A.'. must be armed at all points, and expert with every weapon. The examinations in every Grade are strict and severe; no loose or vague answers are accepted. In intellectual questions, the candidate must display no less mastery of his subject than if he were entered in the "final" for Doctor of Science or Law at a first class University.

In examination of physical practices, there is a standardised test. In Asana, for instance, the candidate must remain motionless for a given time, his success being gauged by poising on his head a cup filled with water to the brim; if he spill one drop, he is rejected.

He is tested in "the Spirit Vision" or "Astral Journeying" by giving him a symbol unknown and unintelligible to him, and he must interpret its nature by means of a vision as exactly as if he had read its name and description in the book when it was chosen.

The power to make and "charge" talismans is tested as if they were scientific instruments of precision, as they are.

In the Qabalah, the candidate must discover for himself, and prove to the examiner beyond all doubt, the properties of a number never previously examined by any student.

In invocation the divine force must be made as manifest and unmistakable as the effects of chloroform; in evocation, the spirit called forth must be at least as visible and tangible as the heaviest vapours; in divination, the answer must be as precise as a scientific thesis, and as accurate as an audit; in meditation, the results must read like a specialist's report of a classical case.

But such methods, the A.'. A.'. intends to make occult science as systematic and scientific as chemistry; to rescue it from the ill repute which, thanks both to the ignorant and dishonest quacks that have prostituted its name, and to the fanatical and narrow-minded enthusiasts that have turned it into a fetish, has made it an object of aversion to those very minds whose enthusiasm and integrity make them most in need of its benefits, and most fit to obtain them.

It is the one really important science, for it transcends the conditions of material existence and so is not liable to perish with the planet, and it must be studied as a science, sceptically, with the utmost energy and patience.

The A.'. A.'. possesses the secrets of success; it makes no secret of its knowledge, and if its secrets are not everywhere known and practised, it is because the abuses connected with the name of occult science disincline official investigators to examine the evidence at their disposal.

This paper has been written not only with the object of attracting individual seekers into the way of Truth, but of affirming the propriety of the methods of the A.'. A.'. as the basis for the next great step in the advance of human knowledge.

Love is the law, love under will.

O. M. 7 Degree= 4Square A.'. A.'.

Praemonstrator of the

Order of the R... C...

Given from the Collegium ad Spiritum Sanctum, Cefalu, Sicily, in the Seventeenth Year of the Aeon of Horus, the Sun being in 23 Degree Virgo and the Moon in 14 Degree Pisces.

Appendix III

Notes for an Astral Atlas

[shawn note: The above title is from the 1994 O.T.O. *Book Four* edition.]

Notes on the nature of the "Astral Plane".

> *On consideration these notes have been left as they were originally written. In An XVII, Sol in Virgo, Soror Rhodon, a probationer of A.'. A.'., at that time in enjoyment of the privilege of sojourning in a certain secret Abbey of Thelema, asked Him to add to this book an outline of the uranography of the Astral Planes, in less technical language than that of Liber 777. These notes were accordingly jotted down by Him. To elaborate them further would have been to make them disproportionate to the rest of this treatise.*

1) What are "Astral" and "Spiritual Beings?"

Man is one: it is a case of any consciousness assuming a sensible form.

Microcosms and elementals. Maybe an elemental (e.g. a dog) has a cosmic conception in which he is a microcosm and man incomplete. No means of deciding same, as in case of kinds of space.

> *See Poincare, passages quoted infra.*

Similarly, our gross matter may appear unreal to Beings clad in fine matter. Thus, science thinks vulgar perceptions "error". We cannot perceive at all except within our gamut; as, concentrated perfumes, which seem malodorous, and time-hidden facts, such as the vanes of a revolving fan, which flies can distinguish.

Hence: no *a priori* reason to deny the existence of conscious intelligences with insensible bodies. Indeed we know of other *orders* of mind (flies, etc., possibly vegetables) thinking by means of non-human brain-structures.

But the fundamental problem of Religion is this: **Is there any praeter-human Intelligence, of the same order as our own, which is not dependent on cerebral structures consisting of matter in the vulgar sense of the word?**

2) "Matter" includes all that is movable. Thus, electric waves are "matter". There is no reason to deny the existence of Beings who perceive by other means those subtle forces which we only perceive by our instruments.

3) We can influence other Beings, conscious or no, as lion-tamers, gardeners, etc., and are influenced by them, as by storms, bacilli, etc.

4) There is an apparent gap between our senses and their correspondences in consciousness. Theory needs a medium to join matter and spirit, just as physics once needed an "ether" to transmit and transmute vibrations.

5) We may consider all beings as parts of ourselves, but it is more convenient to regard them as independent. Maximum Convenience is our cannon of "Truth".

> *The passages referred to are as follows:*
>
> *"Les axiomes geometriques ne sont donc ni des jugements synthetiques a priori ni des faits experimentaux. Ce sont des conventions ...*

Des lors, que doit-on penser de cette question: La geometrie Euclidienne est-elle vraie?

Elle n'a aucun sens. Autant demander si le systeme metrique est vrai et les anciennes mesures fausses; si les coordonnees cartesiennes sont vraies et les coordonnees polaires fausses. Une geometrie ne peut pas etre plus vraie qu'une autre; elle peut seulement etre "plus commode."

On veut dire que par selection naturelle notre esprit s'est adapte aux conditions du monde exterieur, qu'il a adopte la geometrie la plus avantageuse a l'espece; ou en d'autres termes la plus commode. Cela est conforme tout a fait a nos conclusions; la geometrie n'est pas vraie: elle est avantageuse." Poincare, "La Science et l'Hypothese."

"Nous choisirons donc ces regles non parce qu'elles sont vraies, mais parce qu'elles sont les plus commodes, et nous pourrions les resumer ainsi en disant:

"La simultaneite de dex evenements, ou l'ordre de leur succession, l'egalite de deux durees, doivent etre definies de telle sorte que l'enonce des lois naturelles soit aussi simple que possible. En d'autres termes, toutes ces regles, toutes ces definitions ne sont pas que le fruit d'un opportunisme inconscient." Poincare "La Valeur de la Science."

The Student may consult H. H. Joachim's "The Nature of Truth", in rebuttal. But most of these subtleties miss the point. Truth must be defined. It is a name, being a noun (nomen); and all names are human symbols of things. Now Truth is the power to arouse a certain reaction ("assent") in a man, under certain conditions: ("greenness", weight, all other qualities, are also powers). It exists in the object, whether latent or manifest; so experiencing both does and does not alter the facts. This is Solipsism, because we can only be conscious of our own consciousness; yet it is not Solipsism, because our consciousness tells us that its changes are due to the impact of an external force. Newton's First Law makes this a matter of definition.

"What is truth?", beyond this, inquires into the nature of this power. It is inherent in all things, since all possible propositions, or their contradictories, can be affirmed as true. Its condition is identity of form (or structure) of the Monads involved.

It requires a quality of mind beyond the "normal" to appreciate 0 Degree = X, etc., directly, just as H. H. Joachim's reasoning demands a point-of-view beyond that of the Bushman.

We may thus refer psychical phenomena to the intention of "Astral" Beings, without committing ourselves to any theory. Coherence is the sole quality demanded of us.

6) Magick enables us to receive sensible impressions of worlds other than the "physical" universe (as generally understood by profane science). These worlds have their own laws; their inhabitants are often of quasi-human intelligence; there is a definite set of relations between certain "ideas" of ours, and their expressions, and certain types of phenomena. (Thus symbols, the Qabalah, etc. enable us to communicate with whom we choose.)

7) "Astral" Beings possess knowledge and power of a different kind from our own; their "universe" is presumably of a different kind from ours, in some respects. (Our idea "bone" is not the same as a dog's; a short-sighted man sees things differently to one of normal vision.) It is **more convenient** to assume the objective existence of an "Angel" who gives us new knowledge than to allege that our invocation has awakened a supernormal power in ourselves. Such incidents as "Calderazzo"

See the story, infra, about the origin of Book 4.

and "Jacob"

See the story, infra, about Amalantra.

make this more cogent.

8) The Qabalah maps ourselves by means of a convention. Every aspect of every object may thus be referred to the Tree of Life, and evoked by using the proper keys.

9) Time and Space are forms by which we obtain (distorted) images of Ideas. Our measures of Time and Space

See Poincare's essay on the Nature of Space, as an idea invented by ourselves to measure the result of, and explain, our muscular movements.

are crude conventions, and differ widely for different Beings. (Hashish shows how the same mind may vary.)

10) We may admit that any aspect of any object or idea may be presented to us in a symbolic form, whose relation to its Being is irrational. (Thus, there is no rational link between seeing a bell struck and hearing its chime. Our notion of "bell" is no more than a personification of its impressions on our senses. And our wit and power to make a bell "to order" imply a series of correspondences between various orders of nature precisely analogous to Magick, when we obtain a Vision of Beauty by the use of certain colours, forms, sounds, etc.)

11) "Astral" Beings may thus be defined in the same way as "material objects"; they are the Unknown Causes of various observed effects. They may be of any order of existence. We give a physical form and name to a bell but not to its tone, though in each case we know nothing but our own impressions. But we record musical sounds by a special convention. We may therefore call a certain set of qualities "Ratziel", or describe an impression as "Saturnian" without pretending to know what anything is in itself. All we need is to know how to cast a bell that will please our ears, or how to evoke a "spirit" that will tell us things that are hidden from our intellectual faculties.

12) (a) Every object soever may be considered as possessed of an "Astral shape", sensible to our subtle perceptions. This "astral shape" is to its material basis as our human character is to our physical appearance. We may imagine this astral shape: e.g. we may "see" a jar of opium as a soft seductive woman with a cruel smile, just as we see in the face of a cunning and dishonest man the features of some animal, such as a fox.

(b) We may select any particular property of any object, and give it an astral shape. Thus, we may take the tricky perils of a mountain, and personify them as "trolls", or the destructive energies of the simoom, as "Jinn".

(c) We may analyse any of these symbols, obtaining a finer form; thus the "spirit" contains an "angel", the angel an "archangel", etc.

(d) We may synthesize any set of symbols, obtaining a more general form. Thus we may group various types of earth-spirit as gnomes.

(e) All these may be attributed to the Tree of Life, and dealt with accordingly.

(f) The Magician may prepare a sensible body for any of these symbols, and evoke them by the proper rites.

13) The "reality" or "objectivity" of these symbols is not pertinent to the discussion. The ideas of X to the 4th power and square root of -1 have proved useful to the progress of mathematical advance toward Truth; it is no odds whether a Fourth Dimension "exists", or whether square root of -1 has "meaning" in the sense that square root of 4 has, the number of units in the side of a square of 4 units.

The Astral Plane — real or imaginary — is a danger to anybody who takes it without the grain of salt contained in the Wisdom of the above point of view; who violates its laws either wilfully, carelessly, ignorantly, or by presuming that their psychological character differentiates them from physical laws in the narrower sense; or who abdicates his autonomy, on the ground that the subtler nature of astral phenomena guarantees their authority and integrity.

(14) The variety of the general character of the "planes" of being is indefinitely large. But there are several main types of symbolism corresponding to the forms of plastic presentation established by the minds of Mankind. Each such "plane" has its special appearances, inhabitants, and laws — special cases of the general proposition. Notable among these are the "Egyptian" plane, which conforms with the ideas and methods of magick once in vogue in the Nile valley; the "Celtic" plane, close akin to "Fairyland", with a Pagan Pantheism as its keynote, sometimes concealed by Christian nomenclature: the "Alchemical" plane, where the Great Work is often presented under the form of symbolically constructed landscapes occupied by quasi-heraldic animals and human types hieroglyphically distinguished, who carry on the mysterious operations of the Hermetic Art.

There are also "planes" of Parable, of Fable, and of Folk-lore; in short, every country, creed, and literature has given its characteristic mode of presentation to some "plane" or other.

But there are "planes" proper to every clairvoyant who explores the Astral Light without prejudice; in such case, things assume the form of his own mind, and his perception will be clear in proportion to his personal purity.

On the higher planes, the diversity of form, due to grossness, tends to disappear. Thus, the Astral Vision of "Isis" is utterly unlike that of "Kali". The one is of Motherhood and Wisdom, ineffably candid, clear, and loving; the other of Murder and madness, blood-intoxicated, lust-befogged, and cruel. The sole link is the Woman-symbol. But whoso makes Samadhi on Kali obtains the self-same Illumination as if it had been Isis; for in both cases he attains identity with the Quintessence of the Woman-Idea, untrammelled by the qualities with which the dwellers by the Nile and the Ganges respectively disguised it.

Thus, in low grades of initiation, dogmatic quarrels are inflamed by astral experience; as when Saint John distinguishes between the Whore BABALON and the Woman clothed with the Sun, between the Lamb that was slain and the Beast 666 whose deadly wound was healed; nor understands that Satan, the Old Serpent, in the Abyss, the Lake of Fire and Sulphur, is the Sun-Father, the vibration of Life, Lord of Infinite Space that flames with His Consuming Energy, and is also that throned Light whose Spirit is suffused throughout the City of Jewels.

Each "plane" is a veil of the one above it; the original individual Ideas become diversified as they express their elements. Two men with almost identical ideas on a subject would write two totally different treatises upon it.

15) The general control of the Astral Plane, the ability to find one's way about it, to penetrate such sanctuaries as are guarded from the profane, to make such relations with its inhabitants as may avail to acquire knowledge and power, or to command service; all this is a question of the general Magical attainment of the student.

He must be absolutely at ease in his Body of Light, and have made it invulnerable. He must be adept in assuming all God-forms, in using all weapons, sigils, gestures, words, and signs. He must be familiar with the names and numbers pertinent to the work in hand. He must be alert, sensitive, and ready to exert his authority; yet courteous, gracious, patient, and sympathetic.

16) There are two opposite methods of exploring the Astral Plane.

(a). One may take some actual object in Nature, and analyse it by evoking its astral form, thus bringing it into knowledge and under control by applying the keys of the Qabalah and of Magick.

(b). One may proceed by invoking the required idea, and giving body to the same by attracting to it the corresponding elements in Nature.

17) Every Magician possesses an Astral Universe peculiar to himself, just as no man's experience of the world is coterminous with that of another. There will be a general agreement on the main points, of course; and so the Master Therion is able to describe the principal properties of these "planes", and their laws, just as he might write a geography giving an account of the Five Continents, the Oceans and Seas, the most notable mountains and rivers; he could not pretend to put forth the whole knowledge that any one peasant possesses in respect of his district. But, to the peasant, these petty details are precisely the most important items in his daily life. Likewise, the Magician will be grateful to the Master Therion for the Compass that guides him at night, the Map that extends his comprehension of his country, and shows him how best he may travel afield, the advice as to Sandals and Staff that make surer his feet, and the Book that tells him how, splitting open his rocks with an Hammer, he may be master of their Virgin Gold. But he will understand that his own career on earth is his kingdom, that even the Master Therion is no more than a fellow man in another valley, and that he must explore and exploit his own inheritance with his own eyes and hands.

The Magician must not accept the Master Therion's account of the Astral Plane, His Qabalistic discoveries, His instructions in Magick. They may be correct in the main for most men; yet they cannot be wholly true for any save Him, even as no two artists can make identical pictures of the same subject.

More, even in fundamentals, though these things be Truth for all Mankind, as we carelessly say, any one particular Magician may be the one man for whom they are false. May not the flag that seems red to ten thousand seem green to some one other? Then, every man and every woman being a Star, that which is green to him is verily green; if he consent to the crowd and call it red, hath he not broken the Staff of Truth that he leaneth upon?

Each and every man therefore that will be a Magician must explore the Universe for himself. This is pre-eminently the case in the matter of the Astral Plane, because the symbols are so sensitive. Nothing is easier than to suggest visions, or to fashion phantasms to suit one's ideas. **It is obviously impossible to communicate with an independent intelligence — the one real object of astral research — if one allows one's imagination to surround one with courtiers of one's own creation.** If one expects one's visions to resemble those of the Master Therion, they are only too likely to do so; and if one's respect for Him induces one to accept such visions as authentic, one is being false to one's soul; the visions themselves will avenge it. The true Guide being gone, the seer will stray into a wilderness of terror where he is tricked and tortured; he will invoke his idol the Master Therion, and fashion in His image a frightful phantasm who will mock him in his misery, until his mind stagger and fall; and, Madness swooping upon his carrion, blast his eyes with the horror of seeing his Master dissolve into that appalling hallucination, the "Vision of THE DEMON CROWLEY!"

Remember, then, always, but especially when dealing with the Astral Plane, that man's breath stirs the Feather of Truth. What one sees and hears is "real" in its way, whether it be itself, or distorted by one's desires, or created by one's personality. There is no touchstone of truth: the authentic Nakhiel is indistinguishable from the image of the Magician's private idea of Nakhiel, so far as he is concerned. The stronger one is to create, the more readily the Astral Light responds, and coagulates creatures of this kind. Not that such creation is necessarily an error; but it is another branch of one's Work. One cannot obtain outside help from inside sources. One must use precautions similar to those recommended in the chapter of Divination.

The Magician may go on for a long time being fooled and flattered by the Astrals that he has himself modified or manufactured. Their natural subservience to himself will please him, poor ape!

They will pretend to show him marvellous mysteries, pageants of beauty and wonder unspeakably splendid; he will incline to accept them as true, for the very reason that they are images of himself idealized by the imagination.

But his real progress will stop dead. These phantasms will prevent him from coming into contact with independent intelligences, from whom alone he can learn anything new.

He will become increasingly interested in himself, imagine himself to be attaining one initiation after another. His Ego will expand unchecked, till he seem to himself to have heaven at his feet. Yet all this will be nothing but his fool's face of Narcissus smirking up from the pool that will drown him.

Error of this kind on the Astral Plane — in quite ordinary visions with no apparent moral import — may lead to the most serious mischief. Firstly, mistakes mislead; to pollute one's view of Jupiter by permitting the influence of Venus to distort it may end in finding oneself at odds with Jupiter, later on, in some crisis of one's work.

Secondly, the habit of making mistakes and leaving them uncorrected grows upon one. He who begins by "spelling Jeheshua with a 'Resh'" may end by writing the name of the Dweller on the Threshold by mistake for that of his Angel.

Lastly, Magick is a Pyramid, built layer by layer. The work of the Body of Light — with the technique of Yoga — is the foundation of the whole. One's apprehension of the Astral Plane must be accurate, for Angels, Archangels, and Gods are derived therefrom by analysis. One must have pure materials if one wishes to brew pure beer.

If one have an incomplete and incorrect view of the universe, how can one find out its laws?

Thus, original omission or error tends to extend to the higher planes. Suppose a Magician, invoking Sol, were persuaded by a plausible spirit of Saturn that he was the Solar Intelligence required, and bade him eschew human love if he would attain to the Knowledge and Conversation of his Holy Guardian Angel; and suppose that his will, and that Angel's nature, were such that the Crux of their Formula was Lyrical Exaltation!

Apart from the regular tests — made at the time — of the integrity of any spirit, the Magician must make a careful record of every vision, omitting no detail; he must then make sure that it tallies in every point with the correspondences in Book 777 and in Liber D. Should he find (for instance) that, having invoked Mercury, his vision contains names whose numbers are Martial, or elements proper to Pisces, let him set himself most earnestly to discover the source of error, to correct it, and to prevent its recurrence.

But these tests, as implied above, will not serve to detect personation by self-suggested phantasms. Unless one's aura be a welter of muddled symbols beyond recognition, the more autohypnotic the vision is, the more smoothly it satisfies the seer's standards. There is nothing to puzzle him or oppose him; so he spins out his story with careless contempt of criticism. He can always prove himself right; the Qabalah can always be stretched; and Red being so nearly Orange, which is really a shade of Yellow, and Yellow a component of Green which merges into Blue, what harm if a Fiend in Vermilion appears instead of an Angel in Azure?

The true, the final test, of the Truth of one's visions is their Value. The most glorious experience on the Astral plane, let it dazzle and thrill as it may, is not necessarily in accordance with the True Will of the seer; if not, though it be never so true objectively, it is not true for him, because not useful for him. (Said we not a while ago that Truth was no more than the Most Convenient Manner of Statement?)

It may intoxicate and exalt the Seer, it may inspire and fortify him in every way, it may throw light upon most holy mysteries, yet withal be no more than an interpretation of the individual to himself, the formula not of Abraham but of Onan.

These plastic "Portraits of the Artist as a Young Man" are well enough for those who have heard "Know Thyself". They are necessary, even, to assist that analysis of one's nature which the Probationer of A.'. A.'. is sworn to accomplish. But "Love is the law, love under will." And Our Lady Nuit is "... divided for love's sake, for the chance of union." These mirror-mirages are therefore not Works of Magick, according to the Law of Thelema: the true Magick of Horus requires the passionate union of opposites.

Now the proof that one is in contact with an independent entity depends on a sensation which ought to be unmistakeable if one is in good health. One ought not to be liable to mistake one's own sensible impressions for somebody else's! It is only Man's incurable vanity that makes the Astral "Strayed Reveller" or the mystic confuse his own drunken babble with the voice of the Most High.

The essence of the right sensation consists in recognition of the reality of the other Being. There will be as a rule some element of hostility, even when the reaction is sympathetic. One's "soul-mate" (even) is not thought of as oneself, at first contact.

One must therefore insist that any real appearance of the Astral Plane gives the sensation of meeting a stranger. One must accept it as independent, be it Archangel or Elf, and measure one's own reaction to it. One must learn from it, though one despise it; and love it, however one loathe it.

One must realize, on writing up the record, that the meeting has effected a definite change in oneself. One must have known and felt something alien, and not merely tried on a new dress.

There must always be some slight pang of pain in a true Astral Vision; it hurts the Self to have to admit the existence of a not-Self; and it taxes the brain to register a new thought. This is true at the first touch, even when exaltation and stimulation result from the joy of making an agreeable contact.

There is a deeper effect of right reaction to a strange Self: the impact invariable tends to break up some complex in the Seer. The class of ideas concerned has always been tied up, labelled, and put away. It is now necessary to unpack it, and rearrange its contents. At least, the annoyance is like that of a man who has locked and strapped his bag for a journey, and then finds that he has forgotten his pyjamas. At most, it may revolutionise his ideas of the business, like an old bachelor with settled plans of life who meets a girl once too often.

Any really first-class Astral Vision, even on low planes, should therefore both instruct the Seer, and prepare him for Initiation. Those failing to pass this test are to be classed as "practice".

One last observation seems fit. We must not assert the "reality" or "objectivity" of an Astral Being on no better evidence than the subjective sensation of its independent existence. We must insist on proof patient to all qualified observers if we are to establish the major premiss of Religion: that there exists a Conscious Intelligence independent of brain and nerve as we know them. If it have also Power, so much the better. But we already know of inorganic forces; we have no evidence of inorganic conscious Mind.

How can the Astral Plane help us here? It is not enough to prove, as we easily do, the correspondences between Invocation and Apparition.

The Master Therion's regular test is to write the name of a Force on a card, and conceal it; invoke that Force secretly, send His pupil on the Astral Plane, and make him attribute his vision to some Force. The pupil then looks at the card; the Force he has named is that written upon it.

We must exclude coincidence,

The most famous novel of Fielding is called "Tom Jones". It happened that FRATER PERDURABO was staying in an hotel in London. He telephoned a friend named Fielding at the latter's house, and was answered by Mr. Fielding's secretary, who said that his employer had left the house a few minutes previously, and could only be reached by telephoning a certain office in the City at between 11 o'clock and a quarter past. FRATER PERDURABO had an appointment at 11 o'clock with a music-hall star, the place being the entrance to a theatre. In order to remind himself, he made a mental note that as soon as he saw the lady, he would raise his hand and say, before greeting her: "Remind me that I must telephone at once to Fielding", when he met her. He did this, and she advanced toward Him with the same gesture, and said in the same breath, "Remind me that I have to telephone to Tom Jones" — the name of a music-hall agent employed by her.

It will be seen that there is here no question of any connection between the elements of the coincidence. If a similar occurrence had taken place in the course of communication with an alleged spirit, it would have been regarded as furnishing a very high degree of proof of the existence of an independent intelligence.

To make this clear, let me substitute the terms of the equation. Suppose two independent mediums, A and B, were to receive respectively at the same moment two messages, the first; "Ask B who wrote Hamlet", the second: "Ask A the name of Shakespeare's most famous tragedy." The coincidence is here much simpler and less striking than the one recorded above, for there is no question of arriving at the identity by way of accidental synonyms concealing their rational connection. Yet most students of Occult phenomena would admit that there was a strong presumption that a single intelligence had deliberately devised the two messages as a means of proving his existence.

telepathy,

In "The International" of November, 1918, was published the conconclusion of an article called "The Revival of Magick" by the Master Therion. The last sentence reads: "Herein is Wisdom; let him that hath understanding count the number of the Beast; for it is the number of a man; and his number is six hundred and three score and six." [Greek:] To Mega Therion the Great Wild Beast, has the value, according to the Greek system, of 666. It is, of course, the title of the Master Therion.

The Master Therion was, about this time, in communication with an intelligence who gave the name of Amalantrah. On Sunday, February 24, 1918, at 9.30 p. m., The Master Therion asked Amalantrah if he could use the word [Greek:] Therion as if it were Hebrew, with the idea of getting further information as to the mystic meaning of the Word. The answer was "Yes". He then asked: "Am I to take the word [Greek:] Therion alone, or the three words [Greek:] To Mega Therion?" The answer was to take the word [Greek:] Therion alone. The Master Therion then asked what Hebrew letters should be used to transliterate the Greek. The answer was: "Tau, Yod, Resh, Yod, Ayin, Nun", which adds to 740 or 1390, according as Nun is given its ordinary value of 50, or its value as the final letter of a word, 700. Neither of these numbers possessed any special significance to The Master Therion. He became very annoyed at Amalantrah's failure to be of use; so much so that the communications became confused, and the work had to be abandoned for that evening. He tried various other Hebrew spellings for the word [Greek:] Therion, but was unable to obtain anything of interest. This is rather remarkable, as it is nearly always possible to get more or less good results by trying various possibilities. For example, the O might be equally well Ayin, Vau or Aleph.

On Monday morning, The Master Therion went to the office of "The International," of which he was editor. At this period there was a coal famine in New York, and it was forbidden to heat office buildings on Mondays. He merely took away his mail and went home. On Tuesday morning He found on his desk a letter which had arrived on Monday for the general editor, who had sent it across to Him for reply, as it concerned The Master Therion rather than himself. This letter had been written and posted on Sunday evening, at about the same time as the communication from Amalantrah. The letter ends as follows: "Please inform your readers that I, Samuel bar Aiwaz bie Yackou de Sherabad, have counted the number of the Beast, and it is the number of a man.

[Hebrew]	*Nun final*	*Vau*	*Yod*	*Resh*	*Tau*
	N	*O*	*I*	*R*	*Th*
(Read from right to left)	*50*	*6*	*10*	*200*	*400*
			666		

Here, then, we see the most striking solution possible of the problem presented to Amalantrah. Observe that Amalantrah had refused to give the correct solution directly; as it would seem, in order to emphasize the remarkable character of the intervention of this Assyrian correspondent. Observe, too, that the latter was totally ignorant of the ordinary Qabalah, it being quite generally known that [Greek:] To Mega Therion adds up to 666 in Greek. Observe, moreover, that nearly four months had passed since the problem was propounded in "The International?" The Assyrian lived some distance outside New York, and was an entire stranger to any of the staff of "The International." The evidence appears overwhelming for the existence of Amalantrah, that he was more expert in the Qabalah than The Master Therion himself, and that he was (further) possessed with the power to recall this four-months-old problem to the mind of an entirely unconnected stranger, causing him to communicate the correct answer at the same moment as the question was being asked many miles away.

Coincidence, so completely adequate to explain the Fielding-Tom Jones incident, is utterly incompetent as an alternative theory. The directly purposeful character of the circumstances is undeniable; but if we are resolutely determined to deny the possibility of the existence of Amalantrah, which explains the whole affair so simply, we have still one resource. It involves difficulties which The Master Therion cannot conceive as less than those which encumber the other, but it is, at least, not entirely beyond possibility. This theory is telepathy. One may postulate that the solution of his problem existed in the subconscious mind of the Master Therion or in that of His seer, and that this solution was telepathically impressed upon the consciousness of the Assyrian so forcibly as to impel him to communicate it to the Master Therion's colleague on "The International." Apart from the general improbability of this hypothesis, it is strange that if "Amalantrah" were really the subconscious mind of the seer, he should have given a wrong orthography. His doing so (if he knew the correct spelling) is only explicable by his wish not to take the edge off his plan for making the Assyrian's letter a fulminating revelation of his existence, as would have happened if the secret had been prematurely disclosed.

The case is here cited in order to illustrate the extreme care which ought to be taken in excluding all alternative hypotheses before admitting the existence of disembodied intelligences. It may be mentioned, however, that in this particular case there are numerous other incidents which make the telepathic theory untenable.

and subconscious knowledge.

There is a well-known story quoted in several treatises of psychology in which the heroine is an ignorant English servant girl of quite inferior intelligence, and unacquainted with any language, even her own. In the course of a fever, she became delirious, and proceeded to reel off long passages of scholarly Hebrew. Investigations showed that in her first youth she had been for a time in the service of a Jewish Rabbi who had been accustomed to declaim his sermons in the hearing of the girl. Although attaching no meaning to the words, she had stored them mechanically in her subconscious memory, to be reproduced when the action of the fever excited the group of cells where they were recorded.

Our praeter-human Intelligence must convey a Truth not known to any human mind, past or present. Yet this Truth must be verifiable.

There is but one document in the world which presents evidence that fully satisfies these conditions. This is

LIBER AL vel **LEGIS**

the Book of the Law.

of this New Aeon of Horus, the Crowned and Conquering Child, the Aeon whose Logos is THE BEAST 666, whose name in the Outer Order was FRATER PERDURABO.

The nature of the proof of the separate existence of praeterhuman Intelligence, independent of bodily form, is extremely complicated. Its main divisions may be briefly enumerated.

AIWAZ, the name of the Intelligence in question, proves:

(a) His power to pre-arrange events unconnected with His scribe so that they should fit in with that scribe's private calculations.

E.g. The Stele which reveals the Theogony of the Book was officially numbered 666, in the Boulak Museum. The scribe had adopted 666 as His magical number, many years previously. Again, the scribe's magical House, bought years earlier, had a name whose value was 418. The scribe had calculated 418 as the number of the Great Work, in 1901 e.v. He only discovered that 418 was the number of his house in consequence of AIWAZ mentioning the fact.

(b) His power to conceal a coherent system of numbers and letters in the text of a rapidly-written document, containing riddles and ciphers opening to a Master-Key unknown to the scribe, yet linked with his own system; this Key and its subordinates being moreover a comment on the text.

E.g. "The word of the Law is [Greek:] Theléma." (Will); this word has the value of 93.

"Love is the law, love under will." Love, [Greek:] Agapé, like

[Greek:] Theléma, adds to 93.

AIWAZ itself adds to 93.

This numeration was discovered years later. The question then arose out of consideration of this discovery through S. Jacobs: "Why is Aiwaz spelt Aiwass, not Aiwaz, in the Book of the Law?" In Greek [Greek:] Aifass = 418. The author of the Book had concealed in His own name not one only but two numbers, those of supreme importance in the Book.

This was all strange to the scribe; yet years later he discovered the "Lost Word" of one of his own Orders: it was 93 also.

[WEH Note: This refers to the word of the IIIrd Degree of O.T.O., readers who may wish to acquire it may apply for initiation and work their way up through the Degrees. Ordo Templi Orientis, JAF Box 7666, New

York, NY 10116, USA.]

The Word of His most holy Order proved equally to count up to 93.

This list by no means exhausts the series. In particular, Frater Perdurabo discovered in 1923 that the Hebrew word for "to will" is also of the value of 93: and its special technical meanings throw yet further light on the meaning of [Greek:] Theléma as used by Aiwaz.

{WEH NOTE: In this instance, Crowley refers not to the word of III Degree O.T.O., but to the Neophyte word of A.'. A.'..

Now 93 is thrice 31; 31 is LA, "Not" and AL, "The" or "God"; these words run throughout the Book, giving a double meaning to many passages. A third 31 is the compound letter ShT, the two hieroglyphs of Sh and T (many centuries old) being pictures of the "Dramatis Personae" of the Book; and ShT being a haphazard line scrawled on the MS. touch letters which added to 418, valuing "this circle squared in its failure" as pi correct to six places of decimals, etc.

Again: "thou shalt know not",

[WEH Note: It is remarkable that Crowley succeeds in blowing every quotation of "Liber AL" on this page. This despite the injunction of the Book itself: AL I,54: "Change not as much as the style of a letter; for behold! thou, o prophet, shalt not behold all these mysteries hidden therein." Crowley strongly resisted the idea that he could not understand all of the Book. In later life, he came to grudgingly accept this limitation. Also, Achad did not work out as his successor. Several of these mis-quotes relate to that belief. This particular mis-quote could come from as many as six points in the text, but there is no part of the text in which this quote appears exactly.]

meaning "thou shalt know LA"; and "he shall discover the Key of it all"

[WEH Note: This misquote could be from AL III,47: "... Let him not seek to try: but one cometh after him, whence I say not, who shall discover the Key of it all.... ".]

id est, the Key AL.

(c) His power to combine subsequent events beyond the control of the scribe or his associates, so that they confirmed statements in the Book. Or, per contra, to predict such events.

E.g. The first Scarlet Woman proved unworthy, and suffered the exact penalties predicted.

Again, "one cometh after thee; he shall discover the key."

[WEH Note: misquoted from AL II,76: "...There cometh one to follow thee: he shall expound it. ... "]

This one was to be the "child" of the scribe, "and that strangely".

[WEH Note: This time the misquote is in the style of the letters: AL III,47: "This book shall be translated into all tongues: but always with the original in the writing of the Beast; for in the chance shape of the letters and their position to one another: in these are mysteries that no Beast shall divine. Let him not seek to try: but one cometh after him, whence I say not, who shall discover the Key of it all. Then this line drawn is a key: then this circle squared in its failure is a key also. And Abrahadabra. It shall be his child & that strangely. Let him not seek after this; for thereby alone can he fall from it." — interesting that these misquotes seem to hit verses that either appear to warn Crowley against misquoting or of his limits.]

Nine months after THE BEAST 666 had gotten a Magical "child" upon His concubine Jane Foster, a "Babe of the Abyss" was born, Frater Achad asserting his right to that grade, and thus "coming after" THE BEAST 666, who had been the last Adept to do so. And this "child" was definitely "one", since "one" is the meaning of his motto Achad. Finally, he did in fact "discover the key of it all"

> *[WEH Note: see the citation in an earlier note of mine. This time Crowley missed the "style of the letter" again.]*

after THE BEAST Himself had failed to do so in 14 years of study.

(d) His power to conceive and express in concise terms true solutions of the main problems of the Universe.

E.g. The formula of Nuith and Hadith explain Existence in the terms of Mathematical-Logical Philosophy, so as to satisfy the difficulties of reconciling Dualism, Monism and Nihilism; all antinomies in all spheres; and the Original Perfection with the Manifest Imperfection of Things.

Again "Do that thou wilt...", the most sublimely austere ethical precept ever uttered, despite its apparent licence, is seen on analysis to be indeed "...the whole of the Law.", the sole and sufficient warrant for human action, the self-evident Code of Righteousness, the identification of Fate with Freewill, and the end of the Civil War in Man's nature by appointing the Canon of Truth, the conformity of things with themselves, to determine his every act. "Do what thou wilt..." is to bid Stars to shine, Vines to bear grapes, Water to seek its level; man is the only being in Nature that has striven to set himself at odds with himself.

(e) His power to interpret the Spirit of the New Aeon, the relapse into ruthless savagery of the most civilized races, at a time when war was discredited by most responsible men.

(f) His power to comprehend and control these various orders of ideas and events, demonstrating thereby a mind and a means of action intelligible to, yet immensely above, all human capacity; to bind the whole into a compact cryptograph displaying mastery of English, of mathematical and philosophical conceptions, of poetic splendour and intense passion, while concealing in the letters and words a complex cipher involving the knowledge of facts never till than existing in any human mind, and depending on the control of the arm of the scribe, though He thought He was writing consciously from dictation; and to weave into a single pattern so many threads of proof of different orders that every type of mind, so it be but open and just, may be sure of the existence of AIWAZ as a being independent of body, conscious and individual, with a mind mightier than man's, and a power beyond man's set in motion by will.

In a word, the Book of the Law proves the prime postulate of Religion.

The Magician may therefore be confident that Spiritual Beings exist, and seek the Knowledge and conversation of His own Holy Guardian Angel with the same ardour as that of FRATER PERDURABO when He abandoned all: love, wealth, rank, fame, to seek Him. Nay, this he must do or condemn himself to be torn asunder by the Maenads of his insensate impulses; he hath no safety save he himself be Bacchus! Bacchus, divine and human! Bacchus, begotten on Semele of Zeus, the adulterous Lord of Thunder ravishing, brutally, his virginal victim! Bacchus, babe hidden from hate in the most holy of holies, the secret of thy sire, in the Channel of the Star-Spate, Whereof one Serpent is thy soul! Bacchus, twy-formed, man-woman, Bacchus, whose innocence tames the Tiger, while yet thy horns drip blood upon thy mouth, and sharpen the merriment of wine to the madness of murder! Bacchus, Thy thyrsus oozes sap; thine ivy clings to it; thy Lion-skin slips from thy sleek shoulders, slips from thy lissome loins; drunk on delight of the godly grape, thou knowest no more the burden of the body and the vexation of the spirit.

Come, Bacchus, come thou hither, come out of the East; come out of the East, astride the Ass of Priapus! Come with thy revel of dancers and singers! Who followeth thee, forbearing to laugh and to leap? Come, in thy name Dionysus, that maidens be mated to God-head! Come, in thy name Iacchus, with thy mystical fan to winnow the air, each gust of thy Spirit inspiring our Soul, that we bear to thee Sons in Thine Image!

Verily and Amen! Let not the Magician forget for a single second what is his one sole business. His uninitiated "self" (as he absurdly thinks it) is a mob of wild women, hysterical from uncomprehended and unstated animal instinct; they will tear Pentheus, the merely human king who presumes to repress them, into mere shreds of flesh; his own mother, Nature, the first to claw at his windpipe! None but Bacchus, the Holy Guardian Angel, hath grace to be God to this riot of maniacs; he alone can transform the disorderly rabble into a pageant of harmonious movements, tune their hyaena howls to the symphony of a paean, and their reasonless rage to self-controlled rapture. It is this Angel whose nature is doubly double, that He may partake of every sacrament. He is at once a God who is drunken with the wine of earth, and the mammal who quaffs the Blood of God to purge him of mortality. He is a woman as he accepts all impulses, are they not His? He is a man to stamp Himself upon whatever would hallow itself to Him. He wields the Wand, with cone of pine and ivy tendrils; the Angel creates continually, wreathing His Will in clinging beauty, imperishably green.

The Tiger, the symbol of the brutal passions of man, gambols about its master's heels; and He bestrides the Ass of Priapus; he makes his sexual force carry him whither He wills to go.

Let the Magician therefore adventure himself upon the Astral Plane with the declared design to penetrate to a sanctuary of discarnate Beings such as are able to instruct and fortify him, also to prove their identity by testimony beyond rebuttal. All explanations other than these are of value only as extending and equilibrating Knowledge, or possibly as supplying Energy to such Magicians as may have found their way to the Sources of Strength. In all cases, naught is worth an obol save as it serve to help the One Great Work.

He who would reach Intelligences of the type under discussion may expect extreme difficulty. The paths are guarded; there is a lion in the way. Technical expertness will not serve here; it is necessary to satisfy the Warders of one's right to enter the presence of the Master. Particular pledges may be demanded, ordeals imposed, and initiations conferred. These are most serious matters; the Body of Light must be fully adult, irrevocably fixed, or it will be disintegrated at the outset. But, being fit to pass through such experiences, it is bound utterly to its words and acts. It cannot even appear to break an oath, as its fleshly fellow may do.

Such, then is a general description of the Astral Plane, and of the proper conduct of the Magician in his dealings therewith.

Liber Samekh

Theurgia Goetia Summma

Congressus Cum Daemone)

Sub Figura DCCC

being the Ritual employed by the Beast 666

for the Attainment of the Knowledge and Conversation of his Holy Guardian Angel

during the Semester of His performance of the Operation of the Sacred Magick of ABRAMELIN THE MAGE.

Prepared An XVII Sun in Virgo at the Abbey of Thelema in Cephalaedium

by the Beast 666 in service to FRATER PROGRADIOR

OFFICIAL PUBLICATION of A.·.A.·.

Class D for the Grade of Adeptus Minor.

POINT I

Evangelii Textus Redactus

THE INVOCATION

Magically restored, with the significance of the

BARBAROUS NAMES

Etymologically or Qabalistically determined

and paraphrased in English.

Section A.

The Oath

1. Thee I invoke, the Bornless One.

2. Thee, that didst create the Earth and the Heavens.

3. Thee, that didst create the Night and the Day.

4. Thee, that didst create the darkness and the Light.

5. Thou art ASAR UN-NEFER ("Myself made Perfect"):
Whom no man hath seen at any time.

6. Thou art IA-BESZ ("the Truth in Matter").

7. Thou art IA-APOPHRASZ ("the Truth in Motion").

8. Thou hast distinguished between the Just and the Unjust.

9. Thou didst make the Female and the Male.

10. Thou didst produce the Seeds and the Fruit.

11. Thou didst form Men to love one another, and to hate one another.

Section Aa.

1. I am ANKH - F - N - KHONSU hy Prophet, unto Whom Thou didst commit Thy Mysteries, the Ceremonies of KHEM.

2. Thou didst produce the moist and the dry, and that which nourisheth all created Life.

3. Hear Thou Me, for I am the Angel of PTAH - APO - PHRASZ - RA (vide the Rubric): this is Thy True Name, handed down to the Prophets of KHEM.

Section B.

Air

Hear Me: -

AR	"O breathing, flowing Sun!"
ThIAF [1]	"O Sun IAF! O Lion-Serpent Sun, The Beast that whirlest forth, a thunder- bolt, begetter of Life!"
RhEIBET	"Thou that flowest! Thou that goest!"
A-ThELE-BER-SET	"Thou Satan-Sun Hadith that goest without Will!"
A	"Thou Air! Breath! Spirit! Thou without bound or bond!"
BELAThA	"Thou Essence, Air Swift-streaming, Elasticity!"
ABEU	"Thou Wanderer, Father of All!"
EBEU	"Thou Wanderer, Spirit of All!"
PhI-ThETA-SOE	"Thou Shining Force of Breath! Thou Lion-Serpent Sun! Thou Saviour, save!"

IB	"Thou Ibis, secret solitary Bird, inviolate Wisdom, whose Word in Truth, creating the World by its Magick!".
ThIAF	"O Sun IAF! O Lion-Serpent Sun, The Beas that whirlest forth, a thunder- bolt, begetter of Life!"

The conception is of Air, glowing, inhabited by a Solar-Phallic Bird, "the Holy Ghost", of a Mercurial Nature.

Hear me, and make all Spirits subject unto Me; so that every Spirit of the Firmament and of the Ether: upon the Earth and under the Earth, on dry land and in the water; of Whirling Air, and of rushing Fire, and every Spell and Scourge of God may be obedient unto Me.

[1] The letter F is used to represent the Hebrew Vau and the Greek Digamma; its sound lies between those of the English long o and long oo, as in Rope and Tooth.

Section C.

Fire

I invoke Thee, the Terrible and Invisible God: Who dwellest in the Void Place of the Spirit: -

AR-O-GO-GO-RU-ABRAO	"Thou spiritual Sun! Satan, Thou Eye, Thou Lust! Cry aloud! Cry aloud! Whirl the Wheel, O my Father, O Satan, O Sun!"
SOTOU	"Thou, the Saviour!"
MUDORIO	"Silence! Give me Thy Secret!"
PhALARThAO	"Give me suck, Thou Phallus, Thou Sun!"
OOO	"Satan, thou Eye, thou Lust!" Satan, thou Eye, thou Lust! Satan, thou Eye, thou Lust!
AEPE	"Thou self-caused, self-determined, exalted, Most High!"

The Bornless One. (Vide supra).

The conception is of Fire, glowing, inhabited by a Solar-Phallic Lion of a Uranian nature.

Hear Me, and make all Spirits subject unto Me: so that every Spirit of the Firmament and of the Ether: upon the Earth and under the Earth: on dry Land and in the Water: of Whirling Air, and of rushing Fire, and every Spell and Scourge of God may be obedient unto Me.

Section D.

Water

Hear Me: -

RU-ABRA-IAF [1]	"Thou the Wheel, thou the Womb, that containeth the Father IAF!"
MRIODOM	"Thou the Sea, the Abode!"
BABALON-BAL-BIN-ABAFT	"Babalon! Thou Woman of Whoredom. Thou, Gate of the Great God

	ON! Thou Lady of the Understanding of the Ways!"
ASAL-ON-AI	"Hail Thou, the unstirred! Hail, sister and bride of ON, of the God that is all and is none, by the Power of Eleven!"
APhEN-IAF	"Thou Treasure of IAO!"
I	"Thou Virgin twin-sexed! Thou Secret Seed! Thou inviolate Wisdom!"
PhOTETh	"Abode of the Light ....
ABRASAX	"......of the Father, the Sun, of Hadith, of the spell of the Aeon of Horus!"
AEOOU	"Our Lady of the Western Gate of Heaven!"
ISChURE	"Mighty art Thou!"

Mighty and Bornless One! (Vide Supra)

The conception is of Water, glowing, inhabited by a Solar-Phallic Dragon-Serpent, of a Neptunian nature.

Hear Me: and make all Spirits subject unto Me: so that every Spirit of the Firmament and of the Ether: upon the Earth and under the Earth: on dry Land and in the Water: of Whirling Air, and of rushing Fire: and every Spell and Scourge of God may be obedient unto Me.

[1] See, for the formula of IAF, or rather FIAOF, Book 4 Part III, Chapter V. The form FIAOF will be found preferable in practice.

Section E.

Earth

I invoke Thee: -

MA	"O Mother! O Truth!"
BARRAIO	"Thou Mass!" [1]
IOEL	"Hail, Thou that art!"
KOThA	"Thou hollow one!"
AThOR-e-BAL-O	"Thou Goddess of Beauty and Love, whom Satan, beholding, desireth!"
ABRAFT	"The Fathers, male-female, desire Thee!"

The conception of of Earth, glowing, inhabited by a Solar-Phallic Hippopotamus[2] of a Venereal nature.

Hear Me: and make all Spirits subject unto Me: so that every Spirit of the Firmament, and of the Ether: upon The Earth and under the Earth: on dry land and in the Water: of Whirling Air, and of rushing Fire: and every Spell and Scourge of God may be obedient unto Me.

[1]"Mass", in the sense of the word which is used by physicists. The impossibility of defining it will not deter the intrepid initiate (in view of the fact that the fundamental conception is beyond the normal categories of

reason.)[2]Sacred to AHAThOOR. The idea is that of the Female conceived as invulnerable, reposeful, of enormous swallowing capacity etc.

Section F.

Spirit

Hear Me:

AFT	"Male-Female Spirits!"
ABAFT	"Male-Female Sires!"
BAS-AUMGN	"Ye that are Gods, going forth, uttering AUMGN. The Word that goeth from (A) Free Breath. (U) through Willed Breath. (M) and stopped Breath. (GN) to Continuous Breath. thus symbolizing the whole course of spiritual life. A is the formless Hero; U is the six-fold solar sound of physical life, the triangle of Soul being entwined with that of Body; M is the silence of "death"; GN is the nasal sound of generation & knowledge.
ISAK	"Identical Point!"
SA-BA-FT	"Nuith! Hadith! Ra-Hoor-Khuit! Hail, Great Wild Beast! Hail, IAO!"

Section Ff.

This is the Lord of the Gods:

This is the Lord of the Universe:

This is He whom the Winds fear.

This is He, Who having made Voice by His commandment is Lord of all Things; King, Ruler and Helper. Hear Me, and make all Spirits subject unto Me: so that every Spirit of the Firmament and of the Ether: upon the Earth and under the Earth: on dry Land and in the Water: of Whirling Air, and of rushing Fire: and every Spell and Scourge of God may be obedient unto Me.

Section G.

Spirit

Hear Me: -

IEOU	"Indwelling Sun of Myself"
PUR	"Thou Fire! Thou Sixfold Star initiator compassed about with Force and Fire!"
IOU	"Indwelling Soul of Myself"
PUR	(Vide Supra)
IAFTh	"Sun-lion Serpent, hail! All Hail, thou Great Wild Beast, thou I A O!"
IAEO	"Breaths of my soul, breaths of mine Angel."

IOOU	"Lust of my soul, lust of mine Angel!"
ABRASAX	(Vide Supra).
SABRIAM	"Ho for the Sangraal! Ho for the Cup of Babalon! Ho for mine Angel pouring Himself forth within my Soul!"
OO	"The Eye! Satan, my Lord! The Lust of the goat!"
FF	"Mine Angel! Mine initiator! Thou one with me - the Sixfold Star!"
AD-ON-A-I [1]	"My Lord! My secret self beyond self, Hadith, All Father! Hail, ON, thou Sun, thou Life of Man, thou Fivefold Sword of Flame! Thou Goat exalted upon Earth in Lust, thou Snake extended upon Earth in Life! Spirit most holy! Seed most Wise! Innocent Babe. Inviolate Maid! Begetter of Being! Soul of all Souls! Word of all Words, Come forth, most hidden Light!"
EDE	"Devour thou me!"
EDU	"Thou dost devour Me!"
ANGELOS TON ThEON	"Thou Angel of the Gods!"
ANLALA	"Arise thou in Me, free flowing, Thou who art Naught, who art Naught, and utter thy Word!"
LAI	"I also am Naught! I Will Thee! I behold Thee! My nothingness!"
GAIA	"Leap up, thou Earth!" (This is also an agonising appeal to the Earth, the Mother; for at this point of the ceremony the Adept should be torn from his mortal attachments, and die to himself in the orgasm of his operation.) [2]
AEPE	"Thou Exalted One! It (i.e. the spritual 'semen', the Adept's secret ideas, drawn irresistibly from their 'Hell'[3] by the love of his Angel) leaps up; it leaps forth![4]
DIATHARNA THORON	"Lo! the out-splashing of the seeds of Immortality"

[1]In Hebrew, ADNI, 65. The Gnostic Initiates transliterated it to imply their own secret formulae; we follow so excellent an example. ON is an Arcanum of Arcana; its significance is taught, gradually, in the O.T.O. Also AD is the paternal formula, Hadit; ON is its complement NUIT; the final Yod signifies "mine" etymologically and essentially the Mercurial (transmitted) hermaphroditic virginal seed - The Hermit of the Taro - The use of the name is therefore to invoke one's own inmost secrecy, considered as the result of the conjunction of Nuit and Hadit. If the second A is included, its import is to affirm the operation of the Holy Ghost and the formulation of the Babe in the Egg, which precedes the appearance of the Hermit.[2]A thorough comprehension of Psycho-analysis will contribute notably to the proper appreciation of this Ritual.[3]It is said among men that the word Hell deriveth from the word "helan", to hele or conceal, in the tongue of the Anglo-Saxons. That is, it is the concealed place, which since all things are in thine own self, is the unconscious, *Liber CXI (Aleph) chap. Delta-Zeta*[4]But compare the use of the same word in section C.

Section Gg.

The Attainment

I am He! the Bornless Spirit! having sight in the feet: Strong, and the Immortal Fire!

I am He! the Truth!

I am He! Who hate that evil should be wrought in the World!

I am He, that lighteneth and thundereth!

I am He, from whom is the Shower of the Life of Earth!

I am He, whose mouth ever flameth!

I am He, the Begetter and Manifester unto the Light!

I am He, The Grace of the Worlds!

"The Heart Girt with a Serpent" is my name!

Section H.

The "Charge to the Spirit"

Come thou forth, and follow me: and make all Spirits subject unto Me so that every Spirit of the Firmament, and of the Ether, upon the Earth and under the Earth: on dry Land, or in the Water: of Whirling Air or of rushing Fire, and every Spell and scourge of God, may be obedient unto me!

Section J.

The Proclamation of the Beast 666

IAF:SABAF [1]

Such are the Words!

[1]See explanation in Point II.

POINT II

Ars Congressus Cum Daemone

Section A

Let the Adeptus Minor be standing in this circle on the square of Tiphereth, armed with his Wand and Cup; but let him perform the Ritual throughout in his Body of Light. He may burn the Cakes of Light, or the Incense of Abramelin; he may be prepared by Liber CLXXV, the reading of Liber LXV, and by the practices of Yoga. He may invoke Hadit by "... wine and strange drugs" if he so will. [1] He prepares the circle by the usual formulae of Banishing and Consecration, etc. He recites Section A as a rehearsal before His Holy Guardian Angel of the attributes of that Angel. Each phrase must be realized with full concentration of force, so as to make Samadhi as perfectly as possible upon the truth proclaimed.

Line 1

He identifies his Angel with the Ain Soph, and the Kether thereof; one formulation of Hadit in the boundless Body of Nuith.

Line 2,3,4

He asserts that His Angel has created (for the purpose of self-realization through projection in conditioned Form) three pairs of opposites: (a) The Fixed and the Volatile; (b) The Unmanifested and the Manifest; and (c) the Unmoved and the Moved. Otherwise, the Negative and the Positive in respect of Matter, Mind and Motion.

Line 5

He acclaims his Angel as "Himself Made Perfect"; adding that this Individuality is inscrutable in inviolable. In the Neophyte Ritual of G: D: (As it is printed in Equinox I, II, for the old aeon) the Hierophant is the perfected Osiris, who brings the candidate, the natural Osiris, to identity with himself. But in the new Aeon the Hierophant is Horus (Liber CCXX, I, 49) therefore the Candidate will be Horus too. What then is the formula of the initiation of Horus? It will no longer be that of the Man, through Death. It will be the natural growth of the Child. His experiences will no more be regarded as catastrophic. Their hieroglyph is the Fool: the innocent and impotent Harpocrates Babe becomes the Horus Adult by obtaining the Wand. "Der reine Thor" seizes the Sacred Lance. Bacchus becomes Pan. The Holy Guardian Angel is the Unconscious Creature Self - the Spiritual Phallus. His knowledge and conversation contributes occult puberty. It is therefore advisable to replace the name Asar-Un-Nefer by that of Ra-Hoor-Khuit at the outset, and by that of one's own Holy Guardian Angel when it has been communicated.

Line 6

He hails Him as BESZ, the Matter that destroys and devours Godhead, for the purpose of the Incarnation of any God.

Line 7

He hails Him as APOPHRASZ, the Motion that destroys and devours Godhead, for the purpose of the Incarnation of any God. The combined action of these two DEVILS is to allow the God upon whom they prey to enter into enjoyment of existence through the Sacrament of dividual "Life" (Bread - the flesh of BESZ) and "Love" (Wine - the blood or venom of AOPHRASZ).

Line 8

He acclaims His Angel as having "eaten of the Fruit of the Tree of Knowledge of Good and Evil"; otherwise, having become wise (in the Dyad, Chokmah) to apprehend the formula of Equilibrium which is now His own, being able to apply Himself accurately to His self-appointed environment.

Line 9

He acclaims His Angel as having laid down the Law of Love as the Magical formula of the Universe, that He may resolve the phenomenal again into its noumenal phase by uniting any two opposites in ecstasic passion.

Line 10

He acclaims His Angel as having appointed that this formula of Love should effect not only the dissolution of the separateness of the Lovers into His own impersonal Godhead, but their co-ordination in a "Child" quintessentialized from its parents to constitute a higher order of Being than theirs, so that each generation is an alchemical progress towards perfection in the direction of successive complexities. As Line 9 asserts Involution, Line 10 asserts Evolution.

Line 11

He acclaims His Angel as having devised this method of self-realization; the object of Incarnation is to obtain its reactions to its relations with other incarnated Beings and to observe theirs with each other.

[1]Any such formula should be used only when the adept has full knowledge based on experience of the management of such matters.

Section Aa.

Line 1

The Adept asserts his right to enter into conscious communication with His Angel, on the ground that that Angel has Himself taught him the Secret Magick by which he may make the proper link. "Mosheh" is M H, the formation in Jechidah, Chiah, Neshamah, Ruach, - The Sephiroth from Kether to Yesod - since 45 is Sum 1-9 while Sh, 300, is Sum 1-24, which superadds to these Nine an extra Fifteen numbers. (See in Liber D, the meanings and correspondences of 9, 15, 24, 45, 300, 345.) 45 is moreover A D M, MDA, man. "Mosheh" is thus the name of man as a God-concealing form. But in the Ritual let the Adept replace this "Mosheh" by his own motto as Adeptus Minor. For "Ishrael" let him prefer his own Magical Race, according to the obligations of his Oaths to Our Holy Order! (The Beast 666 Himself used "Ankh-f-n-Khonsu" and "Khem" in this section.)

Line 2

The Adept reminds his Angel that He has created That One Substance of which Hermes hath written in the Table of Emerald, whose virtue is to unite in itself all opposite modes of Being, thereby to serve as a Talisman charged with the Spiritual Energy of Existence, an Elixir or Stone composed of the physical basis of Life. This Commemoration is placed between the two personal appeals to the Angel, as if to claim privilege to partake of this Eucharist which createth, sustaineth and redeemeth all things.

Line 3

He now asserts that he is himself the "Angel" or messenger of his Angel; that is, that he is a mind and body whose office is to receive and transmit the Word of his Angel. He hails his Angel not only as "un-nefer" the Perfection of "Asar" himself as a man, but as Ptah-Apophrasz-Ra, the identity (Hadit) wrapped in the Dragon (Nuit) and thereby manifested as a Sun (Ra-Hoor-Khuit). The "Egg" (or Heart) "girt with a Serpent" is a cognate symbol; the idea is thus expressed later in the ritual. (See Liber LXV which expands this to the uttermost.)

Section B

The Adept passes from contemplation to action in the sections now following B to Gg. He is to travel astrally around the circle, making the appropriate pentagrams, sigils, and signs. His direction is widdershins. He thus makes three curves, each covering three-fourths of the circle. He should give the sign of the Enterer on passing the Kiblah, or Direction of Boleskine. This picks up the force naturally radiating from that point[1] and projects it in the direction of the path of the Magician. The sigils are those given in the Equinox Vol. I, No. 7, Plate X outside the square; the signs those shewn in Vol. I, No. 2, Plate "The Signs of the Grades". In these invocations he should expand his girth and his stature to the utmost[2], assuming the form and the consciousness of the elemental god of the quarter. After this, he begins to vibrate the "Barbarous Names" of the Ritual.

Now let him not only fill his whole being to the uttermost with the force of the Names; but let him formulate his Will, understood thoroughly as the dynamic aspect of his Creative Self, in an appearance symbolically apt, I say not in the form of a Ray of Light, of a Fiery Sword, or of aught save that bodily Vehicle of the Holy Ghost which is sacred to BAPHOMET, by its virtue that concealeth the Lion and the Serpent that His Image may appear adorably upon the Earth for ever.

Let then the Adept extend his Will beyond the Circle in this imagined Shape and let it radiate with the Light proper to the element invoked, and let each Word issue along the Shaft with passionate impulse, as if its voice gave command thereto that it should thrust itself leapingly forward. Let also each Word accumulate authority, so that the Head of the Shaft may plunge twice as far for the Second Word as for the First, and Four Times for the Third as the Second, and thus to the end. Moreover, let the Adept fling forth his whole consciousness thither. Then at the final Word, let him bring rushing back his Will within himself, steadily streaming, and let him offer himself to its point, as Artemis to PAN, that this perfectly pure concentration of the Element purge him thoroughly, and possess him with its passion.

In this Sacrament being wholly at one with that Element, let the Adept utter the Charge "Hear me, and make", etc. with strong sense that this unity with that quarter of the Universe confers upon him the fullest freedom and privilege appurtenant thereto.

Let the Adept take note of the wording of the Charge. The "Firmament" is the Ruach, the "mental plane"; it is the realm of Shu, or Zeus, where revolves the Wheel of the Gunas, the Three forms [3] of Being. The Aethyr is the "akasha", the "Spirit", the Aethyr or physics, which is the framework on which all forms are founded; it receives, records and transmits all impulses without itself suffering mutation thereby. The "Earth" is the sphere wherein the operation of these "fundamental" and aethyric forces appears to perception. "Under the Earth" is the world of those phenomena which inform those perceived projections, and determine their particular character. "Dry land" is the place of dead "material things", dry (i.e. unknowable) because unable to act on our minds. "Water" is the vehicle whereby we feel such things; "air" their menstruum wherein these feelings are mentally apprehended. It is called "whirling" because of the instability of thought, and the fatuity of reason, on which we are yet dependent for what we call "life". "Rushing Fire" is the world in which wandering thought burns up to swift-darting Will. These four stages explain how the non-Ego is transmuted into the Ego. A "Spell" of God is any form of consciousness, and a "Scourge" any form of action.

The Charge, as a whole, demands for the Adept the control of every detail of the Universe which His Angel has created as a means of manifesting Himself to Himself. It covers command of the primary projection of the Possible in individuality, in the antithetical artifice which is the device of Mind, and in a balanced triplicity of modes or states of being whose combinations constitute the characteristics of Cosmos. It includes also a standard of structure, a rigidity to make reference possible. Upon these foundations of condition which are not things in themselves, but the canon to which things conform, is builded the Temple of Being, whose materials are themselves perfectly mysterious, inscrutable as the Soul, and like the Soul imagining themselves by symbols which we may feel, perceive, and adapt to our use without ever knowing the whole Truth about them. The Adept sums up all these items by claiming authority over every form of expression possible to Existence, whether it be a "spell" (idea) or a "scourge" (act) of "God", that is, of himself. The Adept must accept every "spirit", every "spell", every "scourge", as part of his environment, and make them all "subject to" himself; that is, consider them as contributory causes of himself. They have made him what he is. They correspond exactly to his own faculties. They are all - ultimately - of equal importance. The fact that he is what he is proves that each item is equilibrated. The impact of each new impression affects the entire system in due measure. He must therefore realize that every event is subject to him. It occurs because he had need of it. Iron rusts because the molecules demand oxygen for the satisfaction of their tendencies. They do not crave hydrogen; therefore combination with that gas is an event which does not happen. All experiences contribute to make us complete in ourselves. We feel ourselves subject to them so long as we fail to recognise this; when we do, we perceive that they are subject to us. And whenever we strive to evade an experience, whatever it may be, we thereby do wrong to ourselves. We thwart our own tendencies. To live is to change; and to oppose change is to revolt against the law which we have enacted to govern our lives. To resent destiny is thus to abdicate our sovereignty, and to invoke death. Indeed, we have decreed the doom of death for every breach of the law of Life. And every failure to incorporate any impression starves that particular faculty which stood in need of it.

This Section B invokes Air in the East, with a shaft of golden glory.

[1]This is an assumption based on Liber Legis II, 78 and III, 34.[2]Having experience of success in the practices of Liber 536, BATRAXO-RENOBOOKOSMOMAXIA.[3]They correspond to the Sulphur, Mercury, and Salt of Alchemy; to Sattvas, Rajas, and Tamas in the Hindu system; and are rather modes of action than actual qualities even when conceived as latent. They are the apparatus of communication between the planes; as such, they are conventions. There is no absolute validity in any means of mental apprehension; but unless we make these spirits of the Firmament subject unto us by establishing right relation (within the possible limits) with the Universe, we shall fall into error when we develop our new instrument of direct understanding. It is vital that the Adept should train his intellectual faculties to tell him the truth, in the measure of their capacity. To despise the mind on account of its limitations is the most disastrous blunder; it is the common cause of the calamities which strew so many shores with the wreckage of the Mystic Armada. Bigotry, Arrogance, Bewilderment, all forms of mental and moral disorder, so often observed in people of great spiritual attainment, have brought the Path itself into discredit; almost all such catastrophes are due to trying to build the Temple of the Spirit without proper attention to the mental laws of structure and the physical necessities of foundation. The mind must be brought to its utmost pitch of perfection, but according to its own internal properties; one cannot feed a microscope on mutton chops. It must be regarded as a mechanical instrument of knowledge, independent of the personality of its possessor. One must treat it exactly as one treats one's electroscope or one's eyes; one influence of one's wishes. A physician calls in a colleague to attend to his own family, knowing that personal anxiety may derange his judgment. A microscopist who trusts his eyes when his pet theory is at stake may falsify the facts, and find too late that he has made a fool of himself.In the case of initiations itself, history is scarred with the wounds inflicted by this Dagger. It reminds us constantly of the danger of relying upon the intellectual faculties. A judge must know the law in every point, and be detached from personal prejudices, and incorruptible, or iniquity will triumph. Dogma, with persecution, delusion, paralysis of progress, and many another evil, as its satraps, has always established a tyranny when Genius has proclaimed it. Islam making a bonfire of written Wisdom, and Haeckel forging biological evidence; physicists ignorant of radioactivity disputing the conclusions of geology, and theologians impatient of truth struggling against the tide of thought; all such must perish at the hands of their own error in making their minds, internally defective or externally deflected, the measure of the Universe.

Section C

The adept now invokes Fire in the South; flame red are the rays that burst from his Verendum.

Section D

He invokes Water in the West, his Wand billowing forth blue radiance.

Section E

He goes to the North to invoke Earth; flowers of green flame flash from his weapon. As practice makes the Adept perfect in this Work, it becomes automatic to attach all these complicated ideas and intentions to their correlated words and acts. When this is attained he may go deeper into the formula by amplifying its correspondences. Thus, he may invoke water in the manner of water, extending his will with majestic and irresistible motion, mindful of its impulse gravitation, yet with a suave and tranquil appearance of weakness. Again, he may apply the formula of water to its peculiar purpose as it surges back into his sphere, using it with conscious skill for the cleansing and calming of the receptive and emotional elements in his character, and for the solution or sweeping away of those tangled weeds of prejudice which hamper him from freedom to act as he will. Similar applications of the remaining invocations will occur to the Adept who is ready to use them.

Section F

The Adept now returns to the Tiphereth square of his Tau, and invokes spirit, facing toward Boleskine, by the active Pentagrams, the sigil called the Mark of the Beast, and the Signs of L.V.X. (See plate as before). He then vibrates the Names extending his will in the same way as before, but vertically upward. At the same time he expands the Source of that Will - the secret symbol of Self - both about him and below, as if to affirm that Self, duplex as is its form, reluctant to acquiesce in its failure to coincide with the Sphere of Nuith. Let him now imagine, at the last Word, that the Head of his will, where his consciousness is fixed, opens its fissure (the Brahmarandra-Cakkra, at the junction of the cranial sutures) and exudes a drop of clear crystalline dew, and that this pearl is his Soul, a virgin offering to his Angel, pressed forth from his being by the intensity of this Aspiration.

Section Ff

With these words the Adept does not withdraw his will within him as in the previous Sections. He thinks of them as a reflection of Truth on the surface of the dew, where his Soul hides trembling. He takes them to be the first formulation in his consciousness of the nature of His Holy Guardian Angel.

Line 1

The "Gods" include all the conscious elements of his nature.

Line 2

The "Universe" includes all possible phenomena of which he can be aware.

Line 3

The "Winds" are his thoughts, which have prevented him from attaining to his Angel.

Line 4

His Angel has made "Voice", the magical weapon which produces "Words", and these words have been the wisdom by which He hath created all things. The "Voice" is necessary as the link between the Adept and his Angel. The Angel is "King", the One who "can", the "source of authority and the fount of honour"; also the King (or King's Son) who delivers the Enchanted Princess, and makes her his Queen. He is "Ruler", the "unconscious Will"; to be thwarted no more by the ignorant and capricious false will of the conscious man. And He is "Helper", the author of the infallible impulse that sends the Soul sweeping along the skies on its proper path with such impetus that the attraction of alien orbs is no longer sufficient to swerve it. The "Hear me" clause is now uttered by the normal human consciousness, withdrawn to the physical body; the Adept must deliberately abandon his attainment, because it is not yet his whole being which burns up before the

Beloved.

Section G

The Adept, though withdrawn, shall have maintained the Extension of his Symbol. He now repeats the signs as before, save that he makes the Passive Invoking Pentagram of Spirit. He concentrates his consciousness within his Twin-Symbol of Self, and endeavours to send it to sleep. But if the operation be performed properly, his Angel shall have accepted the offering of Dew, and seized with fervour upon the extended symbol of Will towards Himself. This then shall He shake vehemently with vibrations of love reverberating with the Words of the Section. Even in the physical ears of the adept there shall resound an echo thereof, yet he shall not be able to describe it. It shall seem both louder than thunder, and softer than the whisper of the night-wind. It shall at once be inarticulate, and mean more than he hath ever heard.

Now let him strive with all the strength of his Soul to withstand the Will of his Angel, concealing himself in the closest cell of the citadel of consciousness. Let him consecrate himself to resist the assault of the Voice and the Vibration until his consciousness faint away into Nothing. For if there abide unabsorbed even one single atom of the false Ego, that atom should stain the virginity of the True Self and profane the Oath; then that atom should be so inflamed by the approach of the Angel that is should overwhelm the rest of the mind, tyrannize over it, and become an insane despot to the total ruin of the realm.

But, all being dead to sense, who then is able to strive against the Angel? He shall intensify the stress of His Spirit so that His loyal legions of Lion-Serpents leap from the ambush, awakening the adept to witness their Will and sweep him with them in their enthusiasm, so that he consciously partakes this purpose, and sees in its simplicity the solution of all his perplexities. Thus then shall the Adept be aware that he is being swept away through the column of his Will Symbol. and that His Angel is indeed himself, with intimacy so intense as to become identity, and that not in a single Ego, but in every unconscious element that shares in that manifold uprush.

This rapture is accompanied by a tempest of brilliant light, almost always, and also in many cases by an outburst of sound, stupendous and sublime in all cases, though its character may vary within wide limits. [1]

The spate of stars shoots from the head of the Will-Symbol, and is scattered over the sky in glittering galaxies. This dispersion destroys the concentration of the adept, whose mind cannot master such multiplicity of majesty; as a rule, he simply sinks stunned into normality, to recall nothing of his experience but a vague though vivid impression of complete release and ineffable rapture. Repetition fortifies him to realise the nature of his attainment; and his Angel, the link once made, frequents him, and trains him subtly to be sensitive to his Holy presence, and persuasion. But it may occur, especially after repeated success, that the Adept is not flung back into his mortality by the explosion of the Star-spate, but identified with one particular "Lion-Serpent", continuing conscious thereof until it finds its proper place in Space, when its secret self flowers forth as a truth, which the Adept may then take back to earth with him.

This is but a side issue. The main purpose of the Ritual is to establish the relation of the subconscious self with the Angel in such a way that the Adept is aware that his Angel is the Unity which expresses the sum of the Elements of that Self, that his normal consciousness contains alien enemies introduced by the accidents of environment, and that his Knowledge and Conversation of His Holy Guardian Angel destroys all doubts and delusions, confers all blessings, teaches all truth, and contains all delights. But it is important that the Adept should not rest in mere inexpressible realization of his rapture, but rouse himself to make the relation submit to analysis, to render it in rational terms, and thereby enlighten his mind and heart in a sense as superior to fanatical enthusiasm as Beethoven's music is to West African war-drums.

[1]These phenomena are not wholly subjective; they may be perceived, though often under other forms, by even the ordinary man.

Section Gg

The adept should have realised that his Act of Union with the angel implies[1] the death of his old mind save in so far as his unconscious elements preserve its memory when they absorb it, and[2] the death of his unconscious elements themselves. But their death is rather a going forth to renew their life through love. He then, by conscious comprehension of them separately and together, becomes the "Angel" of his Angel, as Hermes is the Word of Zeus, whose own voice is Thunder. Thus in this section the adept utters articulately so far as words may, what his Angel is to Himself. He says this, with his Scin-Laeca wholly withdrawn into his physical body, constraining His Angel to indwell his heart.

Line 1

"I am He" asserts the destruction of the sense of separateness between self and Self. It affirms existence, but of the third person only. "The Bornless Spirit" is free of all space, "having sight in the feet", that they may choose their own path. "Strong" is G B R, The Magician escorted by the Sun and the Moon (See Liber D and Liber 777). The "Immortal Fire" is the creative Self; impersonal energy cannot perish, no matter what forms it assumes. Combustion is Love.

Line 2

"Truth" is the necessary relation of any two things; therefore, although it implies duality, it enables us to conceive of two things as being one thing such that it demands to be defined by complementals. Thus, an hyperbola is a simple idea, but its construction exacts two curves.

Line 3

The Angel, as the adept knows him, is a being Tiphereth, which obscures Kether. The Adept is not officially aware of the higher Sephiroth. He cannot perceive, like the Ipsissimus, that all things soever are equally illusion and equally Absolute. He is in Tiphereth, whose office is Redemption, and he deplores the events which have caused the apparent Sorrow from which he has just escaped. He is also aware, even in the height of his ecstasy, of the limits and defects of his Attainment.

Line 4

This refers to the phenomena which accompany his Attainment.

Line 5

This means the recognition of the Angel as the True Self of his subconscious self, the hidden Life of his physical life.

Line 6

The Adept realises every breath, every word of his Angel as charged with creative fire. Tiphereth is the Sun, and the Angel is the spiritual Sun of the Soul of the Adept.

Line 7

Here is summed the entire process of bringing the conditioned Universe to knowledge of itself through the formula of generation [1]; a soul implants itself in sense-hoodwinked body and reason-fettered mind, makes them aware of their Inmate, and thus to partake of its own consciousness of the Light.

Line 8

"Grace" has here its proper sense of "Pleasantness". The existence of the Angel is the justification of the device of creation. [2]

Line 9

This line must be studied in the light of Liber LXV (Equinox XI. p. 65).

[1]That is, Yod He realizing Themselves Will and Understanding in the twins Vau He, Mind and body.[2]But see also the general solution of the Riddle of Existence in The Book of the Law and its Comment - Part IV of Book 4.

Section H.

This recapitulation demands the going forth together of the Adept and his Angel "to do their pleasure on the Earth among the living."

Section J.

The Beast 666 having devised the present method of using this Ritual, having proved it by his own practice to be of infallible puissance when properly performed, and now having written it down for the world, it shall be an ornament for the Adept who adopts it to cry Hail to His name at the end of his work. This shall moreover encourage him in Magick, to recall that indeed there was One who attained by its use to the Knowledge and Conversation of His Holy Guardian Angel, the which forsook him no more, but made Him a Magus, the Word of the Aeon of Horus!

For know this, that the Name IAF in its most secret and mighty sense declareth the Formula of the Magick of the BEAST whereby he wrought many wonders. And because he doth will that the whole world shall attain to this Art, He now hideth it herein so that the worthy may win to His Wisdom.

Let I and F face all[1]; yet ward their A from attack. The Hermit to himself, the fool to foes, The Hierophant to friends, Nine by nature, Naught by attainment, Five by function. In speech swift, subtle and secret; in thought creative, unbiassed, unbounded; in act gentle, patient and persistent.

Hermes to hear, Dionysus to touch, Pan to behold.

A Virgin, A Babe, and a Beast!

A Liar, an Idiot, and a Master of Men!

A kiss, a guffaw, and a bellow; he that hath ears to hear, let him hear!

Take ten that be one, and one that is one in three, to conceal them in six!

Thy wand to all Cups, and thy Disk to all Swords, but betray not thine Egg!

Moreover also is IAF verily 666 by virtue of Number; and this is a Mystery of Mysteries; Who knoweth it, he is adept of adepts, and Mighty among Magicians!

Now this word SABAF, being by number Three score and Ten [2], is a name of Ayin, the Eye, and the Devil our Lord, and the Goat of Mendes. He is the Lord of the Sabbath of the Adepts, and is Satan, therefore also the Sun, whose number of Magick is 666, the seal of His servant the BEAST.

But again SA is 61, AIN, the Naught of Nuith; BA means go, for Hadit; and F is their Son the Sun who is Ra-Hoor-Khuit.

So then let the Adept set his sigil upon all the words he hath writ in the Book of the Works of his Will.

And let him then end all, saying, Such are the Words! [3] For by this he maketh proclamation before all them that be about his Circle that these Words are true and puissant, binding what he would bind, and loosing what he would loose.

Let the Adept perform this Ritual aright, perfect in every part thereof, once daily for one moon, then twice, at dawn and dusk, for two moons, next, thrice, noon added, for three moons, afterwards, midnight making up his course, for four moons four times every day. Then let the Eleventh Moon be consecrated wholly to this Work; let him be instant in continual ardour, dismissing all but his sheer needs to eat and sleep. [4] For know that the true Formula [5] whose virtue sufficed the Beast in this Attainment, was thus:

INVOKE OFTEN[6]

So may all men come at last to the Knowledge and Conversation of the Holy Guardian Angel: thus sayeth the Beast, and prayeth His own Angel that this book be as a burning Lamp, and as a living Spring, for Light and Life to them that read therein.

666

[1]If we adopt the new orthography VIAOV (Book 4 Part III Chap. V.) we must read "The Sun-6-the Son" etc. for "all"; and elaborate this interpretation here given in other ways, accordingly. Thus O (of F) will not be "The Fifteen by function" instead of "Five" etc., and "in act free, firm, aspiring, ecstatic", rather than "gentle" etc. as in the present text.[2]There is an alternative spelling TzBA-F Where the Root, (ABz) "an Host", has the value of 93. The Practicus should revive this Ritual throughout in the Light of his personal researches in the Qabalah, and thus make it his own peculiar property. The spelling here suggested implies that he who utters the Word affirms his allegiance to the symbols 93 and 61 that he is a warrior in the army of Will and of the Sun. 93 is also the number of AIWAZ and 6 of The Beast.[3]The consonants of LOGOS, "Word", add (Hebrew values: sGL) to 93. And EPH, "Words", (whence "Epic") has also that value: EIDE TA EPH might be the phrase here intended: its number is 418. This would then assert the accomplishment of the Great Work; this is the natural conclusion of the Ritual. Cf. CCXX. III. 75.[4]These needs are modified during the process of Initiation both as to quantity and quality. One should not become anxious about one's physical or mental health on a priori grounds, but pay attention only to indubitable symptoms of distress should such arise.[5]The Oracles of Zoroaster utter this:"And when, by often invoking, all the phantasms are vanished, thou shalt see that Holy and Formless Fire, that Fire which darts and flashes through all the Depths of the Universe; hear thou the Voice of the Fire!"A similar Fire flashingly extending through the rushings of Air, or a Fire formless whence cometh the Image of a voice, or even a flashing Light abounding, revolving, whirling forth, crying aloud. Also there is the vision of the fire-flashing Courser of Light, or also a Child, borne aloft on the shoulders of the Celestial Steed, fiery, or clothed with gold, or naked, or shooting with the bow shafts or light, and standing on the shoulders of the horse, then if thy meditation prolongeth itself, thou shalt unite all these symbols into the form of a Lion."This passage - combined with several others - is paraphased in poetry by Aleister Crowley in his "*Tannhauser*"."And when, invoking often, thou shalt seeThat formless Fire; when all

the earth is shaken,The Stars abide not, and the moon is gone,All Time crushed back into Eternity,The Universe by earthquake overtaken; Light is not, and the thunders roll,The World is done:When in the darkness Chaos rolls againIn the excited brain:Then, O then call not to thy view that visibleImage of Nature; fatal is her name!It fitteth not thy Body to beholdThat living light of Hell,The unluminous, dead flame,Until that body from the crucibleHath passed, pure gold!For, from the confines of material space,The twilight-moving place,The gates of matter, and the dark threshold,Before the faces of the Things that dwellIn the Abodes of Night,Spring into sightDemons, dog-faced, that show no mortal signOf Truth, but desecrate the Light Divine,Seducing from the sacred mysteries.But, after all these Folk of Fear are drivenBefore the avenging levinThat rives the opening skies,Behold that formless and that Holy FlameThat hath no name;The Fire that darts and flashes, writhes and creepsSnake-wise in royal robeWound round that vanished glory of the globe,Unto that sky beyond the starry deeps,Beyond the Toils of Time, - then formulateIn thine own mind, luminous, concentrate,The Lion of the Light, a child that standsOn the vast shoulders of the Steed of God:Or winged, or shooting flying shafts, or shodWith the flame-sandals.Then, lift up thine hands!Centre thee in thine heart one scarlet thoughtLimpid with brilliance of the Light above!Drawn into naughtAll life, death, hatred, love:All self concentred in the sole desire -Hear thou the Voice of Fire!"[6]See Equinox I, VIII, 22.

POINT III

Scholion on Sections G & Gg

"The Seeds of Immortality!"

The Adept who has mastered this Ritual, successfully realising the full import of this controlled rapture, ought not to allow his mind to loosen its grip on the astral imagery of the Star-spate, Will-Symbol, or Soul-symbol, or even to forget its duty to the body and the sensible surroundings. Nor should he omit to keep his Body of Light in close touch with the phenomena of its own plane, so that its privy consciousness may fulfil its proper functions of protecting his scattered ideals from obsession.

But he should have acquired, by previous practice, the faculty of detaching these elements of his consciousness from their articulate centre, so that they become (temporarily) independent responsible units, capable of receiving communications from headquarters at will, but perfectly able [1] to take care of themselves without troubling their chief, and [2] to report to him at the proper time. In a figure, they must be like subordinate officers, expected to display self-reliance, initiative, and integrity in the execution of the Orders of the Day.

The Adept should therefore be able to rely on these individual minds of his to control their own conditions without interference from himself for the time required, and to recall them in due course, receiving an accurate report of their adventures.

This being so, the Adept will be free to concentrate his deepest self, that part of him which unconsciously orders his true Will, upon the realization of his Holy Guardian Angel. The absence of his bodily, mental and astral consciousness is indeed cardinal to success, for it is their usurpation of his attention which has made him deaf to his Soul, and his preoccupation with their affairs that has prevented him from perceiving that Soul.

The effect of the Ritual has been

to keep them so busy with their own work that they cease to distract him;

to separate them so completely that his soul is stripped of its sheaths;

to arouse in him an enthusiasm so intense as to intoxicate and anaesthetize him, that he may not feel and resent the agony of this spiritual vivisection, just as bashful lovers get drunk on the wedding night, in order to brazen out the intensity of shame which so mysteriously coexists with their desire;

to concentrate the necessary spiritual forces from every element, and fling them simultaneously into the aspiration towards the Holy Guardian Angel; and

to attract the Angel by the vibration of the magical voice which invokes Him.

The method of the Ritual is thus manifold.

There is firstly an analysis of the Adept, which enables him to calculate his course of action. He can decide what must be banished, what purified, what concentrated. He can then concentrate his will upon its one essential element, over-coming its resistance - which is automatic, like a physiological reflex - by destroying inhibitions through his ego-overwhelming enthusiasm. [1] The other half of the work needs no such complex effort; for his Angel is simple and unperplexed, ready at all times to respond to rightly ordered approach.

It is impossible to overcome one's inhibitions by conscious effort; their existence justifies them. God is on their side, as on that of the victim in Browning's Instans Tyrannus. A man cannot compel himself to love, however much he may want to, on various rational grounds. But on the other hand, when the true impulse comes, it overwhelms all its critics; they are powerless either to make or break a genius; it can only testify to the fact that it has met its master.

But the results of the Ritual are too various to permit of rigid description. One may say that, presuming the union to be perfect, the Adept need not retain any memory soever of what has occurred. He may be merely aware of a gap in his conscious life, and judge of its contents by observing that his nature has been subtly transfigured. Such an experience might indeed be the proof of perfection.

If the Adept is to be any wise conscious of his Angel it must be that some part of his mind is prepared to realise the rapture, and to express it to itself in one way or another. This involves the perfection of that part, its freedom from prejudice and the limitations of rationality so-called. For instance: one could not receive the illumination as to the nature of life which the doctrine of evolution should shed, if one is passionately persuaded that humanity is essentially not animal, or convinced that causality is repugnant to reason. The Adept must be ready for the utter destruction of his point of view on any subject, and even that of his innate conception of the forms and laws of thought. [2] Thus he may find that his Angel consider his "business" or his "love" to be absurd trifles; also that human ideas of "time" are invalid, and human "laws" of logic applicable only to the relations between illusions.

Now the Angel will make contact with the Adept at any point that is sensitive to His influence. Such a point will naturally be one that is salient in the Adept's character, and also one that is, in the proper sense of the word, pure. [3]

Thus an artist, attuned to appreciate plastic beauty is likely to receive a visual impression of his Angel in a physical form which is sublimely quintessential of his ideal. A musician may be rapt away by majestic melodies such as he never hoped to hear. A philosopher may attain apprehension of tremendous truths, the solution of problems that had baffled him all his life.

Conformably with this doctrine, we read of illuminations experienced by simple-minded men, such as a workman who "saw God" and likened Him to "a quantity of little pears". Again, we know that ecstasy, impinging upon unbalanced minds, inflames the idolised idea, and produces fanatical faith fierce even to frenzy, with intolerance and insanely disordered energy which is yet so powerful as to effect the destinies of empires.

But the phenomena of the Knowledge and Conversation of the Holy Guardian Angel are a side issue; the essence of the Union is the intimacy. Their intimacy (or rather identity) is independent of all partial forms of expression; at its best it is therefore as inarticulate as Love.

The intensity of the consummation will more probably compel a sob or a cry, some natural physical gesture of animal sympathy with the spiritual spasm. This is to be criticised as incomplete self-control. Silence is nobler.

In any case the Adept must be in communion with his Angel, so that his Soul is suffused with sublimity, whether intelligible or not in terms of intellect. It is evident that the stress of such spiritual possession must tend to overwhelm the soul, especially at first. It actually suffers from the excess of its ecstasy, just as extreme love produces vertigo. The soul sinks and swoons. Such weakness is fatal alike to its enjoyment and its apprehension. "Be strong! then canst thou bear more rapture!" sayeth The Book of the Law. [4]

The Adept must therefore play the man, arousing himself to harden his soul.

To this end, I, the Beast, have made trial and proof of divers devices. Of these the most potent is to set the body to strive with the soul. Let the muscles take grip on themselves as if one were wrestling. Let the jaw and mouth, in particular, be tightened to the utmost. Breathe deeply, slowly, yet strongly. Keep mastery over the mind by muttering forcibly and audibly. But lest such muttering tend to disturb communion with the Angel, speak only His Name. Until the Adept have heard that Name, therefore, he may not abide in the perfect possession of his Beloved. His most important task is thus to open his ears to the voice of his Angel, that he may know him, how he is called. For hearken! this Name, understood rightly and fully, declareth the nature of the Angel in every point, wherefore also that Name is the formula of the perfection to which the Adept must aspire, and also of the power of Magick by virtue whereof he must work.

He then that is as yet ignorant of that Name, let him repeat a word worthy of this particular Ritual. Such are Abrahadabra, the Word of the Aeon, which signifieth "The Great Work accomplished"; and Aumgn interpreted in Part III of Book 4 [5]; and the name of THE BEAST, for that His number showeth forth this Union with the Angel, and His Work is no other than to make all men partakers of this Mystery of the Mysteries of Magick.

So then saying this word or that, let the Adept wrestle with his Angel and withstand Him, that he may constrain Him to consent to continue in communion until the consciousness becomes capable of clear comprehension, and of accurate transmission [6] of the transcendent Truth of the Beloved to the heart that holds him.

The firm repetition of one of these Words ought to enable the Adept to maintain the state of Union for several minutes, even at first.

In any case he must rekindle his ardour, esteeming his success rather as an encouragement to more ardent aspiration than as a triumph. He should increase his efforts.

Let him beware of the "lust of result", of expecting too much, of losing courage if his first success is followed by a series of failures.

For success makes success seem so incredible that one is apt to create an inhibition fatal to subsequent attempts. One fears to fail; the fear intrudes upon the concentration and so fulfils its own prophecy. We know how too much pleasure in a love affair makes one afraid to disgrace oneself on the next few occasions; indeed, until familiarity has accustomed one to the idea that one's lover has never supposed one to be more than human.

Confidence returns gradually. Inarticulate ecstasy is replaced by a more sober enjoyment of the elements of the fascination.

Just so one's first dazzled delight in a new landscape turns, as one continues to gaze, to the appreciation of exquisite details of the view. At first they were blurred by the blinding rush of general beauty; they emerge one by one as the shock subsides, and passionate rapture yields to intelligent interest.

In the same way the Adept almost always begins by torrential lyrics painting out mystical extravagances about "ineffable love", "unimaginable bliss", "inexpressible infinities of illimitable utterness".[7] He usually loses his sense of proportion, of humour, of reality, and of sound judgment. His ego is often inflated to the bursting point, till he would be abjectly ridiculous if he were not so pitifully dangerous to himself and others. He also tends to take his new-found "truths of illumination" for the entire body of truth, and insists that they must be as valid an vital for all men as they happen to be for himself.

It is wise to keep silence about those things "unlawful to utter" which one may have heard "in the seventh heaven". This may not apply to the sixth.

The Adept must keep himself in hand, however tempted to make a new heaven and a new earth in the next few days by trumpeting his triumphs. He must give time a chance to redress his balance, sore shaken by the impact of the Infinite.

As he becomes adjusted to intercourse with his Angel, he will find his passionate ecstasy develop a quality of peace and intelligibility which adds power, while it informs and fortifies his mental and moral qualities instead of obscuring and upsetting them. He will by now have become able to converse with his Angel, impossible as it once seemed; for he now knows that the storm of sound which he supposed to be the Voice was only the clamour of his own confusions. The "infinity" nonsense was born of his own inability to think clearly beyond his limits, just as a Bushman, confronted by numbers above five, can only call them "many".

The truth told by the Angel, immensely as it extends the horizon of the Adept, is perfectly definite and precise. It does not deal in ambiguities and abstractions. It possesses form, and confesses law, in exactly the same way and degree as any other body of truth. It is to the truth of the material and intellectual spheres of man very much what the Mathematics of Philosophy with its "infinite series" and "Cantorian continuity" is to schoolboy arithmetic. Each implies the other, though by that one may explore the essential nature of existence, and by this a pawnbroker's profits.

This then is the true aim of the Adept in this whole operation, to assimilate himself to his Angel by continual conscious communion. For his Angel is an intelligible image of his own true Will, to do which is the whole of the law of his Being.

Also the Angel appeareth in Tiphereth, which is the heart of the Ruach, and thus the Centre of Gravity of the Mind. It is also directly inspired from Kether, the ultimate Self, through the Path of the High Priestess, or initiated intuition. Hence the Angel is in truth the Logos or articulate expression of the whole Being of the Adept, so that as he increases in the perfect understanding of His name, he approaches the solution of the ultimate problem, Who he himself truly is.

Unto this final statement the Adept may trust his Angel to lead him; for the Tiphereth-consciousness alone is connected by paths with the various parts of his mind.[8] None therefore save He hath the knowledge requisite for calculating the combinations of conduct which will organise and equilibrate for forces of the Adept, against the moment when it becomes necessary to confront the Abyss. The Adept must control a compact and coherent mass if he is to make sure of hurling it from him with a clean-cut gesture.

I, The Beast 666, lift up my voice and swear that I myself have been brought hither by mine Angel. After that I had attained unto the Knowledge and Conversation of Him by virtue of mine ardour towards Him, and of this Ritual that I bestow upon men my fellows, and most of His great Love that He beareth to me, yea, verily, He led me to the Abyss; He bade me fling away all that I had and all that I was; and He forsook me in that Hour. But when I came beyond the Abyss, to be reborn within the womb of BABALON, then came he unto me abiding in my virgin heart, its Lord and Lover!

Also He made me a Magus, speaking through His Law, the Word of the new Aeon, the Aeon of the Crowned and Conquering Child. [9] Thus he fulfilled my will to bring full freedom to the race of Men.

Yea, he wrought also in me a Work of wonder beyond this, but in this matter I am sworn to hold my peace.

[1]A high degree of initiation is required. This means that the process of analysis must have been carried out very thoroughly. The Adept must have become aware of his deepest impulses, and understood their true significance. The "resistance" here mentioned is automatic; it increases indefinitely against direct pressure. It is useless to try to force oneself in these matters; the uninitiated Aspirant, however eager he may be, is sure to fail. One must know how to deal with each internal idea as it arises.[2]Of course, even false tenets and modes of the mind are in one sense true. It is only their appearance which alters. Copernicus did not destroy the facts of nature, or change the instruments of observation. He merely effected a radical simplification of science. Error is really a "fool's knot". Moreover, the very tendency responsible for the entanglement is one of the necessary elements of the situation. Nothing is "wrong" in the end; and one cannot reach the "right" point of view without the aid of one's particular "wrong" point. If we reject or alter the negative of a photograph we shall not get a perfect positive.[3]This means, free from ideas, however excellent in themselves, which are foreign to it. For instance, literary interest has no proper place in a picture.[4]Liber Al vel Legis, II, 61-68, where the details of the proper technique are discussed.[5]The essence of this matter is that the word AUM, which expresses the course of Breath (spiritual life) from free utterance through controlled concentration to Silence, is transmuted by the creation of the compound letter MGN to replace M: that is, Silence is realized as passing into continuous ecstatic vibration, of the nature of "Love" under "Will" as shewn by MGN = 40 + 3 + 50 = 93 AGAPH, ThELHMA etc., and the whole word has the value of 100, Perfection Perfected, the Unity in completion, and equivalent to KR the conjunction of the essential male and female principles.[6]The "normal" intellect is incapable of these functions; a superior faculty must have been developed. As Zoroaster says: "Extend the void mind of thy soul to that Intelligible that thou mayst learn the Intelligible, because it subsisteth beyond Mind. Thou wilt not understand It as when understanding some common thing."[7]This corresponds to the emotional and metaphysical fog which is characteristic of the emergence of thought from homogeneity. The clear and concise differentiation of ideas marks the adult mind.[8]See the maps "Minutum Mundum" in the Equinox I, 1, 2, & 3 and the general relations detailed in Liber 777, of which the most important columns are reprinted in Appendix V.[9]For the account of these matters see The Equinox, Vol. I, "The Temple of Solomon the King", Liber 418, Liber Aleph, "John St. John", "The Urn", and Book 4, Part IV.

APPENDIX V

A FEW OF THE PRINCIPAL CORRESPONDENCES OF THE QABALAH.

REPRINTED WITH ADDITIONS FROM 777.

TABLE I

I KEY SCALE	II HEBREW NAMES OF NUMBERS & LETTERS	III ENGLISH OF COLUMN II
	Aleph-Yod-Nunfinal	Nothing.
0	Aleph-Yod-Nunfinal	No Limit.
	Samekh-Vau-Pehfinal	
	Aleph-Yod-Nunfinal	Limitless L.V.X.
	Samekh-Vau-Pehfinal	
	Aleph-Vau-Resh	
1	Koph-Taw-Resh	Crown.
2	Chet-Koph-Mem-Heh	Wisdom.
3	Bet-Yod-Nun-Heh	Understanding.
4	Chet-Samekh-Dalet	Mercy.
5	Gemel-Bet-Vau-Resh-Heh	Strength.
6	Taw-Peh-Aleph-Resh-Taw	Beauty.
7	Nun-Tzaddi-Chet	Victory.
8	Heh-Vau-Dalet	Splendour.
9	Yod-Samekh-Vau-Dalet	Foundation.
10	Mem-Lamed-Koph-Vau-Taw	Kingdom.
11	Aleph-Lamed-Pehfinal	Ox.
12	Bet-Yod-Taw	House.
13	Gemel-Mem-Lamed	Camel.
14	Dalet-Lamed-Taw	Door.
15	Heh-Heh	Window.
16	Vau-Vau	Nail.
17	Zain-Yod-Nunfinal	Sword.
18	Chet-Yod-Taw	Fence.
19	Tet-Yod-Taw	Serpent.
20	Yod-Vau-Dalet	Hand.
21	Koph-Pehfinal	Palm.
22	Lamed-Mem-Dalet	Ox Goad.
23	Mem-Yod-Memfinal	Water.
24	Nun-Vau-Nunfinal	Fish.
25	Samekh-Mem-Kophfinal	Prop.

26	Ayin-Yod-Nunfinal	Eye.
27	Peh-Heh	Mouth.
28	Tzaddi-Dalet-Yod	Fish-hook.
29	Qof-Vau-Pehfinal	Back of Head.
30	Resh-Yod-Shin	Head.
31	Shin-Yod-Nunfinal	Tooth.
32	Taw-Vau	Tau (as Egyptian).
32 "bis"	Taw-Vau	—
31 "bis"	Shin-Yod-Nunfinal	—

I KEY SCALE	VI THE HEAVENS OF ASSIAH	VII ENGLISH OF COLUMN VI
1	Resh-Aleph-Shin-Yod-Taw Heh-Gemel-Lamed-Gemel-Lamed-Yod-Memfinal	Sphere of the Primum Mobile
2	Mem-Samekh-Lamed-Vau-Taw	Sphere of the Zodiac Fixed Stars
3	Shin-Bet-Taw-Aleph-Yod	Sphere of Saturn
4	Tzaddi-Dalet-Qof	Sphere of Jupiter
5	Mem-Aleph-Dalet-Yod-Memfinal	Sphere of Mars
6	Shin-Mem-Shin	Sphere of Sol
7	Nun-Vau-Gemel-Heh	Sphere of Venus
8	Koph-Vau-Koph-Bet	Sphere of Mercury
9	Lamed-Bet-Nun-Heh	Sphere of Luna
10	Chet-Lamed-Memfinal Yod-Samekh-Vau-Dalet-Vau-Taw	Sphere of the Elements
11	Resh-Vau-Chet	Air
12	(Planets following Sephiroth corresponding)	MERCURY
13		Luna
14		Venus
15	Tet-Lamed-Heh	Aries Fire
16	Shin-Vau-Resh	Taurus Earth
17	Taw-Aleph-Vau-Mem-Yod-Memfinal	Gemini Air
18	Samekh-Resh-Tet-Nunfinal	Cancer Water
19	Aleph-Resh-Yod-Heh	Leo Fire
20	Bet-Taw-Vau-Lamed-Heh	Virgo Earth
21		Jupiter
22	Mem-Aleph-Zain-Nun-Yod-Memfinal	Libra Air
23	Mem-Yod-Memfinal	Water
24	Ayin-Qof-Resh-Bet	Scorpio Water
25	Qof-Shin-Taw	Sagittarius Fire
26	Gemel-Dalet-Yod	Capricornus Earth
27		Mars
28	Dalet-Lamed-Yod	Aquarius Air
29	Dalet-Gemel-Yod-Memfinal	Pisces Water
30		Sol
31	Aleph-Shin	Fire
32		Saturn
32 "bis"	Aleph-Resh-Tzaddifinal	Earth
31 "bis"	Aleph-Taw	Spirit

	IX THE SWORD AND THE SERPENT	XI ELEMENTS (WITH THEIR PLANE- TARY RULERS) Do not confuse with: rulers of Zodiac.	XII THE TREE OF LIFE
0	....	....	....
1	The Flaming	Root of Air	1st Plane Middle Pillar
2	Sword follows	" " Fire	2nd " Right "
3	the downward	" " Water	2nd " Left "
4	course of the	" " Water	3rd " Right "
5	Sephiroth, and	" " Fire	3rd " Left "
6	is compared	" " Air	4th " Middle "
7	to the Light-	" " Fire	5th " Right "
8	ning Flash.	" " Water	5th " Left "
9	Its hilt is	" " Air	6th " Middle "
10	in Kether and	" " Earth	7th " " "
	its point in		
	Malkuth.		
11	The Serpent of	Hot and Moist Air	Path joins 1-2
12	Wisdom follows	....	" " 1-3
13	the course of	....	" " 1-6
14	the paths or	....	" " 2-3
15	letters upward,	Sun Fire Jupiter	" " 2-6
16	its head being	Venus Earth Moon	" " 2-4
17	thus in Aleph,	Saturn Air Mercury	" " 3-6
18	its tail in Taw.	Mars Water	" " 3-5
19	Aleph, Mem, &	Sun Fire Jupiter	" " 4-5
	Shin are		
20	the Mother	Venus Earth Moon	" " 4-6
21	letters, re-	....	" " 4-7
22	ferring to the	Saturn Air Mercury	" " 5-6
23	Elements; Bet,	Cold & Moist Water	" " 5-8
24	Gemel, Dalet,	Mars Water	" " 6-7
	Koph, Peh, Resh		
25	and Taw, the	Sun Fire Jupiter	" " 6-9
26	Double letters,	Venus Earth Moon	" " 6-8
27	to the Planets;	....	" " 7-8
28	the rest,	Saturn Air Mercury	" " 7-9
29	Single letters,	Mars Water	" " 7-10
30	to the Zodiac.	....	" " 8-9
31		Hot and Dry Fire	" " 8-10
32	....	....	" " 9-10
32 "bis"		Cold and Dry Earth	....
31 "bis"	....	....	....

{WEH NOTE: Row 29 has been corrected, original had a typo of Mars Fire}

	XIV GENERAL ATTRIBUTION OF TAROT	XV THE KING SCALE OF COLOUR

1	The 4 Aces	Brilliance
2	The 4 Twos — Kings or Knights	Pure Soft Blue
3	The 4 Threes — Queens	Crimson
4	The 4 Fours	Deep violet
5	The 4 Fives	Orange
6	The 4 Sixes — Emperors or Princes	Clear pink rose
7	The 4 Sevens	Amber
8	The 4 Eights	Violet purple
9	The 4 Nines	Indigo
10	The 4 Tens — Empresses or Princesses	Yellow
11	The Fool — (Swords) Emperors or Princes	Bright pale yellow
12	The Juggler	Yellow
13	The High Priestess	Blue
14	The Empress	Emerald Green
15	The Emperor	Scarlet
16	The Hierophant	Red Orange
17	The Lovers	Orange
18	The Chariot	Amber
19	Strength	Yellow, greenish
20	Hermit	Green yellowish
21	Wheel of Fortune	Violet
22	Justice	Emerald Green
23	The Hanged Man — (Cups) Queens	Deep blue
24	Death	Green blue
25	Temperance	Blue
26	The Devil	Indigo
27	The House of God	Scarlet
28	The Star	Violet
29	The Moon	Crimson (ultra violet)
30	The Sun	Orange
31	The Angel or Last Judgment — (Wands) Kings or Knights	Glowing orange scarlet
32	The Universe	Indigo
32 "bis"	Empresses (Coins)	Citrine, olive, russet and black(1)
31 "bis"	All 22 trumps	White merging into grey

(1) The Pure Earth known to the Ancient Egyptians, during that Equinox of the Gods over which Isis presided (i.e. The Pagan Era) was taken as Green.

KEY SCALE	XIX SELECTION OF EGYPTIAN GODS	XXII SMALL SELECTION OF HINDU DEITIES
0	Harpocrates, Amoun, Nuith.	AUM.
1	Ptah, Asar un Nefer, Hadith.	Parabrahm (or any other whom one wishes to please).
2	Amoun, Thoth, Nuith (Zodiac).	Shiva, Vishnu (as Buddha avatara).Akasa(as matter).Lingam.
3	Maut, Isis, Nephthys.	Bhavani (all forms of Sakti), Prana (as Force), Yoni.
4	Amoun, Isis.	Indra, Brahma.
5	Horus, Nephthys.	Vishnu, Varruna-Avatar.

Key Scale		
6	Asar, Ra.	Vishnu-Hari-Krishna-Rama.
7	Hathoor.	Bhavani (all forms of Sakti). Prana (as Force), Yoni.
8	Anubis.	Hanuman.
9	Shu.	Ganesha Vishnu (Kurm Avatar).
10	Seb. Lower (i.e. unwedded), Isis and Nephthys.	Lakshmi, etc. (Kundalini)
11	Nu.	The Maruts (Vayu).
12	Thoth and Cynocephalus.	Hanuman, Vishnu (as Parasa-Rama).
13	Chomse.	Chandra (as Moon).
14	Hathoor.	Lalita(sexual aspect of Sakti)
15	Men Thu.	Shiva.
16	Asar Ameshet Apis.	Shiva (Sacred Bull).
17	Various twin dieties, Rehkt Merti, etc.	Various twin and hybrid Deities.
18	Kephra.	....
19	Ra-Hoor-Khuit, Pasht, Sekhet, Mau, Sekhmet.	Vishnu (Nara-Singh Avatar).
20	Isis (as Virgin).	The Gopi Girls, the Lord of Yoga.
21	Amoun-Ra.	Brahma, Indra.
22	Ma.	Yama.
23	Tum Athph Auramoth (as Water) Asar (as Hanged Man), Hekar, Isis.	Soma (apas).
24	Merti goddesses, Typhon, Apep, Khephra.	Kundalini.
25	....	Vishnu (Horse-Avatar).
26	Khem (Set).	Lingam, Yoni.
27	Horus.	....
28	Ahephi, Aroueris.	....
29	Khephra (as Scarab in Tarot Trump).	Vishnu (Matsya Avatar).
30	Ra and many others.	Surya (as Sun).
31	Thoum-aesh-neith, Mau, Kabeshunt, Horus, Tarpesheth.	Agni (Tejas) Yama, (as God of last Judgment).
32	Sebek, Mako.	Brahama.
32 "bis"	Satem, Ahapshi, Nephthys, Ameshet.	(Prithivi).
31 "bis"	Asar.	(Akasa).

KEY SCALE	XXXIV SOME GREEK GODS	XXXV SOME ROMAN GODS
0	Pan......................	....
1	Zeus, Iacchus	Jupiter
2	Athena, Uranus	Janus
3	Cybele, Demeter, Rhea, Here	Juno, Cybele, Saturn, Hecate
4	Poseidon	Jupiter
5	Ares, Hades	Mars
6	Iacchus, Apollo, Adonis	Apollo
7	Aphrodite, Nike	Venus
8	Hermes	Mercury
9	Zeus (as Air), Diana of Ephesus (as phallic stone)	Diana (as Moon)

10	Persephone (Adonis), Psyche	Ceres
11	Zeus	Jupiter
12	Hermes	Mercury
13	Artemis, Hecate	Diana
14	Aphrodite	Venus
15	Athena	Mars, Minerva
16	(Here)	Venus
17	Castor & Pollux, Apollo the Diviner	Casto & Pollux (Janus)
18	Apollo the Charioteer	Mercury
19	Demeter (borne by lions)	Venus (repressing the fire of Vulcan)
20	(Attis)	(Attis) Ceres, Adonis
21	Zeus	Jupiter (Pluto)
22	Themis, Minos, AEacus, and Rhadamanthus	Vulcan
23	Poseidon	Neptune
24	Ares	Mars
25	Apollo, Artemis (hunters)	Diana (as Archer)
26	Pan, Priapus (Erect Hermes and Bacchus)	Pan, Vesta, Bacchus, Priapus
27	Ares	Mars
28	(Athena), Ganymede	Juno
29	Poseidon	Neptune
30	Helios, Apollo	Apollo
31	Hades	Vulcan, Pluto
32	(Athena)	Saturn
32 "bis"	(Demeter)	Ceres
31 "bis"	Iacchus	(Liber)

KEY SCALE	XXXVIII ANIMALS, REAL AND IMAGINARY	XXXIX PLANTS, REAL AND IMAGINARY
0	....	....
1	God.	Almond in flower.
2	Man.	Amaranth.
3	Woman.	Cypress, Opium Poppy.
4	Unicorn.	Olive, Shamrock.
5	Basilisk.	Oak, Nux Vomica, Nettle.
6	Phoenix, Lion, Child.	Acacia, Bay, Laurel, Vine.
7	Lynx.	Rose.
8	Hermaphrodite, Jackal, Twin Serpents.	Moly, Anhalonium Lewinii.
9	Elephant.	(Banyan) Mandrake, Damiana, Yohimba.
10	Sphinx.	Willow, Lily, Ivy.
11	Eagle or Man (Cherub of Air).	Aspen.
12	Swallow, Ibis, Ape, Twin Serpents.	Vervain, Herb Mercury, Marjolane, Palm.
13	Dog.	Almond, Mugwort, Hazel, (as Moon). Moonworth, Ranunculus.
14	Sparrow, Dove, Swan.	Myrtle, Rose, Clover.
15	Ram, Owl.	Tiger Lily, Geranium.
16	Bull (Cherub of Earth).	Mallow.

17	Magpie, Hybrids.	Hybrids, Orchids.
18	Crab, Turtle, Sphinx.	Lotus.
19	Lion (Cherub of Fire).	Sunflower.
20	Virgin, Anchorite, any solitary person or animal.	Snowdrop, Lily, Narcissus.
21	Eagle.	Hyssop, Oak, Poplar, Fig.
22	Elephant.	Aloe.
23	Eagle-snake-scorpion (Cherub of Water).	Lotus, all Water Plants.
24	Scorpion, Beetle, Lobster or Crayfish, Wolf.	Cactus.
25	Centaur, Horse, Hyppogriff, Dog.	Rush.
26	Goat, Ass.	Indian Hemp, Orchis Root, Thistle.
27	Horse, Bear, Wolf.	Absinthe, Rue.
28	Man or Eagle (Cherub of Air). Peacock.	(Olive) Cocoanut.
29	Fish, Dolphin, Crayfish, Beetle.	Unicellular Organisms, Opium.
30	Lion, Sparrowhawk.	Sunflower, Laurel, Heliotrope.
31	Lion (Cherub of Fire).	Red Poppy, Hibiscus, Nettle.
32	Crocodile.	Ash, Cypress, Hellebore, Yew, Nightshade.
32 bis	Bull (Cherub of Earth).	Oak, Ivy.
31 bis	Sphinx (if Sworded and Crowned).	Almond in flower.

{WEH NOTE: lines 11, 16, 28 & 32 bis corrected as to element; original had typos of Fire, Air, Fire and Water respectively.}

KEY SCALE	XL PRECIOUS STONES	XLI MAGICAL WEAPONS
0	....	....
1	Diamond.	Swastika or Fylfat Cross, Crown.
2	Star Ruby, Turquoise.	Lingam, the Inner Robe of Glory.
3	Star Sapphire, Pearl.	Yoni, the Outer Robe of Concealment.
4	Amethyst, Sapphire.	The Wand, Sceptre, or Crook.
5	Ruby.	The Sword, Spear, Scourge or Chain.
6	Topaz, Yellow Diamond.	The Lamen or Rosy Cross.
7	Emerald.	The Lamp and Girdle.
8	Opal, especially Fire Opal.	The Names and Versicles, the Apron.
9	Quartz.	The Perfumes and Sandals.
10	Rock Crystal.	The Magical Circle & Triangle.
11	Topaz, Chalcedony.	The Dagger or Fan.
12	Opal, Agate.	The Wand or Caducesus.
13	Moonstone, Pearl, Crystal.	Bow and Arrow.
14	Emerald, Turquoise.	The Girdle.
15	Ruby.	The Horns, Energy, the Burin.
16	Topaz.	The Labour of Preparation.
17	Alexandrite, Tourmaline,	The Tripod.

	Iceland Spar.	
18	Amber.	The Furnace.
19	Cat's Eye.	The Discipline (Preliminary).
20	Peridot.	The Lamp and Wand (Virile Force reserved), the Bread.
21	Amethyst, Lapis Lazuli.	The Sceptre.
22	Emerald.	The Cross of Equilibrium.
23	Beryl or Aquamarine.	The Cup and Cross of Suffering, the Wine.
24	Snakestone.	The Pain of the Obligation.
25	Jacinth.	The Arrow (swift and straight application of Force).
26	Black Diamond.	The Secret Force, Lamp.
27	Ruby, any red stone.	The Sword.
28	Artificial Glass.	The Censer or Aspergillus.
29	Pearl.	The Twilight of the Place, Magic Mirror.
30	Crysoleth.	The Lamen or Bow and Arrow.
31	Fire Opal.	The Wand, Lamp, Pyramid of Fire.
32	Onyx.	The Sickle.
32 "bis"	Salt.	The Pantacle, the Salt.
31 "bis"	....	....

KEY SCALE	XLII PERFUMES	LIII THE GREEK ALPHABET	XLIX LINEAL FIGURES OF THE PLANETS AND GEOMANCY
0	....		The Circle.
1	Ambergris.		The Point.
2	Musk	(sigma)	The Line, also the Cross.
3	Myrrh, Civet		The Plane, also the Diamond, Oval, Circle and other Yoni Symbols.
4	Cedar	(iota)	The Solid Figure.
5	Tobacco	(phi)	The Tessaract.
6	Olibanum	omega	Sephirotic Geomantic Figures follow the Planets. Caput and Cauda Draconis are the Nodes of the Moon, nearly = Herschel and Neptune respectively. They belong to Malkuth.
7	Benzoin, Rose, Red Sandal	epsilon	
8	Storax		
9	Jasmine, Jinseng, all Odoriferous Roots	chi	
10	Dittany of Crete	Sampi	
11	Galbanum	alpha	Those of Airy Triplicity.
12	Mastic, White Sandal, Mace, Storax, all Fugitive Odours.	beta	Octagram.
13	Menstrual Blood, Camphor, Aloes, all Sweet Virginal Odours.	gamma	Enneagram.
14	Sandalwood, Myrtle all Soft Voluptuous Odours.	delta	Heptagram.
15	Dragon's Blood.	epsilon	Puer.

16	Storax.	digamma	Amissio.
17	Wormwood.	zeta	Albus.
18	Onycha.	eta	Populus and Via.
19	Olibanum.	theta	Fortuna Major & Fortuna Minor.
20	White Sandal, Narcissus.	iota	Conjunctio.
21	Saffron, all Generous Odours.	kappa	Square and Rhombus.
22	Galbanum.	lambda	Puella.
23	Onycha, Myrrh.	mu	Those of Watery Triplicity.
24	Siamese Benzoin, Opoponax.	nu	Rubeus.
25	Lign-aloes.	xi (sigma)	Acquisitio.
26	Musk, Civet (also Saturnian perfumes)	omicron	Carcer.
27	Pepper, Dragon's Blood, all Hot Pungent Odours.	pi	Pentagram.
28	Galbanum.	psi	Tristitia.
29	Ambergris.	koppa	Laetitia.
30	Olibanum, Cinamon, all Glorious Odours	rho	Hexagram.
31	Olibanum, all Fiery Odours.	sampi	Those of Firey Triplicity.
32	Assafoetida, Scammony, Indigo, Sulphur, all Evil Odours.	tau	Triangle.
32 bis	Storax, all Dull Heavy Odours.	upsilon	Those of Earthy Triplicity.

{WEH NOTE: on line 9, Chi was omitted; lines 21 & 32 bis, Chi and Tau there by error. These have been restored from Liber 777}

TABLE II

KEY SCALE	LIV THE LETTERS OF THE NAME	LV THE ELEMENTS AND SENSES	LXIII THE FOUR WORLDS	LXIV SECRET NAMES OF THE FOUR WORLDS
11	Vau	Air, Smell.	Yetzirah, Formative World.	Mem-Heh Mah
23	Heh	Water, Taste.	Briah, Creative World.	Samekh-Gemel Seg
31	Yod	Fire, Sight.	Atziluth, Archetypal World.	Ayin-Bet Ob
32 "bis"	Heh	Earth, Touch.	Assiah, Material World.	Bet-Nunfinal Ben
31 "bis"	Shin	Spirit, Hearing.	....	....

	LXVIII THE PART OF	LXIX THE ALCHEMICAL	LXX ATTRIBUTION OF	LXXV THE FIVE ELEMENTS (TATWAS)	LXXVI THE FIVE SKANDHAS

	THE SOUL	ELEMENTS	PENTAGRAM		
11	HB:RVCh Ruach	Mercury	Left Upper Point.	Vayu - The Blue Circle.	Sankhara
23	HB:NShMH: Neshamah	Salt	Right Upper Point.	Aupas - The Silver Crescent	Vedana.
31	HB:ChYH Chiah	Sulphur	Right Lower Point.	Agni or Tejas - The Red Triangle.	San~~n~~a.
32 "bis"	HB:NPSh Nephesh	Salt	Left Lower Point.	Prithivi - The Yellow Square.	Rupa
31 "bis"	H:YChYDH: Iechidah		Topmost Point.	Akasa - The Black Egg.	Vin~~nanam

TABLE III

	LXXVII THE PLANETS AND THEIR NUMBERS		LXXXI METALS	LXXXIII THE ATTRIBUTION OF THE HEXAGRAM
12	Mercury	8	Mercury.	Left Lower Point.
13	Moon	9	Silver.	Bottom Point.
14	Venus	7	Copper.	Right Lower Point.
21	Jupiter	4	Tin.	Right Upper Point.
27	Mars	5	Iron.	Left Upper Point.
30	Sun	6	Gold.	Centre Point.
31	Saturn	3	Lead.	Top Point.

TABLE IV

KEY SCALE	XCVII PARTS OF THE SOUL	CXVII THE SOUL (HINDU)	CXVIII THE CHAKKRAS OR CENTRES OF PRANA (HINDUISM)	CXXIV THE HEAVENLY HEXAGRAM	CXXXIII TITLES AND ATTRIBUTIONS OF THE WAND SUIT (CLUBS)
0					
1	YChYDH	Atma	Sahasrara (above Head).	Jupiter	The Root of the Powers of Fire.
2	ChYH	Buddhi	Ajna (Pineal Gland).	Mercury	Mars in Aries Dominion.
3	NShMH	Higher Manas	Visuddhi (Larynx).	Moon [Saturn Daath]	Sun in Aries Established Strength.
4				Venus	Venus in Aries Perfected Work.
5		Lower - Manas	Anahata (Heart)	Mars	Saturn in Leo Strife.
6				Sun	Jupiter in Leo Victory.
7	-RVCh	Kama	Manipura (Solar Plexus).		Mars in Leo Valour.
8		Prana	Svadistthana		Mercury in Sagit-

			(Navel).	tarius Swiftness.
9		Linga Sharira		Moon in Sagittarius: Great Strength.
			Muladhara (Lingam and Anus).	
10	NPSh	Sthula Sharira		Saturn in Sagittarius Oppression.

XCVIII — English of Col. XCVII

The Self..........	1	The Intellect.	4, 5, 6, 7, 8, 9.
The Life Force.....	2	The Animal soul which perceives and feels..	10
The Intuition......	3		

KEY SCALE	CXXXIV TITLES AND ATTRIBUTIONS OF THE CUP OR CHALICE SUIT (HEARTS)	CXXXV TITLES AND ATTRIBUTIONS OF THE SWORD SUIT (SPADES)	CXXXVI TITLES AND ATTRIBUTIONS OF THE COIN, DISC OR PANTACLE SUIT (DIAMONDS)
0	....	....	....
1	The Root of the Powers of Water.	The Root of the Powers of Air.	The Root of the Powers of Earth.
2	Venus in Cancer Love.	Moon in Libra The Lord of Peace restored.	Jupiter in Capricorn The Lord of Harmonious Change
3	Mercury in Cancer Abundance.	Saturn in Libra Sorrow.	Mars in Capricorn Material Works.
4	Moon in Cancer Blended Pleasure.	Jupiter in Libra Rest from Strife.	Sun in Capricorn Earthly Power.
5	Mars in Scorpio Loss in Pleasure.	Venus in Aquarius Defeat.	Mercury in Taurus Material Trouble.
6	Sun in Scorpio Pleasure.	Mercury in Aquarius Earned Success.	Moon in Taurus Material Success.
7	Venus in Scorpio Illusionary Success.	Moon in Aquarius Unstable Effort.	Saturn in Taurus Success Unfulfilled.
8	Saturn in Pisces Abandoned Success.	Jupiter in Gemini Shortened Force.	Sun in Virgo Prudence.
9	Jupiter in Pisces Material Happiness.	Mars in Gemini Despair & Cruelty.	Venus in Virgo Material Gain.
10	Mars in Pisces Perfected Success.	Sun in Gemini Ruin.	Mercury in Virgo Wealth.

{WEH NOTE: Two typos have been corrected in column CXXXIV by Liber 777: 4, Moon in place of Sun and 6, Sun in place of Moon.}

TABLE V

KEY SCALE	CXXXVII SIGNS OF THE ZODIAC	CXXXVIII PLANETS RULING IN COLUMN CCXXXVII	CXXXIX PLANETS EXALTED IN: COLUMN CXXXVII
15	Aries	Mars	P. M. (Sun)
16	Taurus	Venus	Uranus (Moon)
17	Gemini	Mercury	Neptune
18	Cancer	Moon	P. M. (Jupiter)
19	Leo	Sun	Uranus
20	Virgo	Mercury	Neptune (Mercury)
22	Libra	Venus	P. M. (Saturn)
24	Scorpio	Mars	Uranus
25	Sagittarius	Jupiter	Neptune
26	Capricorn	Saturn	P. M. (Mars)
28	Aquarius	Saturn	Uranus
29	Pisces	Jupiter	Neptune (Venus)

{WEH NOTE: Liber 777 gives different entries for column CXXXIX, and these have been added in parenthesis without deletion of original.}

TABLE I

KEY SCALE	CLXXV HEBREW LETTERS	ENGLISH VALUES OF HEBREW LETTERS	CLXXVI NUMERICAL VALUE OF COLUMN CLXXV	CLXXVII YETZIRATIC ATTRIBUTION OF COLUMN CLXXV	CLXXIX NUMBERS PRINTED ON TAROT
11	Aleph	A Aleph	1	Air	0
12	Bet	B Beth	2	Mercury	1
13	Gemel	G Gimel	3	Moon	2
14	Dalet	D Daleth	4	Venus	3
15	Heh	H He	5	Aries	4
16	Vau	V or W Vau	6	Taurus	5
17	Zain	Z Zain	7	Gemini	6
18	Chet	Ch Cheth	8	Cancer	7
19	Tet	T Teth	9	Leo	11
20	Yod	Y Yod	10	Virgo	9
21	Koph,Kf	K Kaph	20, 500	Jupiter	10

22	Lamed	L Lamed	30	Libra	8
23	Mem, M-f	M Mem	40, 600	Water	12
24	Nun, N-f	N Nun	50, 700	Scorpio	13
25	Samekh	S Samekh	60	Sagittarius	14
26	Ayin	O Ayin	70	Capricorn	15
27	Peh, P-f	P Pe	80, 800	Mars	16
28	Tzaddi, Tz-f	Tz Tzaddi	90, 900	Aquarius	17
29	Qof	(K soft) Qoph	100	Pisces	18
30	Resh	R Resh	200	Sun	19
31	Shin	Sh Shin	300	Fire	20
32	Taw	(T soft) Tau	400	Saturn	21
32 "bis"	Taw	....	400	Earth	—
31 "bis"	Shin	....	300	Spirit	—

NOTE. "Ch" like "ch" in "loch".

{WEH NOTE: The English value in row 27 has been corrected, original had O.}

KEY SCALE	CLXXX TITLES OF TAROT TRUMPS
11	The Spirit of 'GR:Alpha-iota-theta-eta-rho
12	The Magus of Power.
13	The Priestess of the Silver Star.
14	The Daughter of the Mighty Ones.
15	Sun of the Morning, Chief among the Mighty.
16	The Magus of the Eternal.
17	The Children of the voice: the Oracle of the Mighty Gods.
18	The Child of the Powers of the Waters: the Lord of the Triumph of Light.
19	The Daughter of the Flaming Sword.
20	The Prophet of the Eternal, the Magus of the Voice of Power.
21	The Lord of the Forces of Life.
22	The Daughter of the Lords of Truth; The Ruler of the Balance.
23	The Spirit of the Mighty Waters.
24	The Child of the Great Transformers. The Lord of the Gate of Death.
25	The Daughter of the Reconcilers, the Bringer-forth of Life.
26	The Lord of the Gates of Matter. The Child of the forces of Time.
27	The Lord of the Hosts of the Mighty.
28	The Daughter of the Firmament; the Dweller between the Waters.
29	The Ruler of Flux & Reflux. The Child of the Sons of the Mighty.
30	The Lord of the Fire of the World.
31	The Spirit of the Primal Fire.
32	The Great One of the Night of Time.
31 "bis"	....
32 "bis"	....

Appendix VI

A Few Principal Rituals

Grimorium Sanctissimum.

Arcanum Arcanorum Quod Continet Nondum Revelandum ipsis Regibus supremis O.T.O. Grimorium Quod Baphomet X Degree M... suo fecit.

De Templo.

1. Oriente .... Altare

2. Occidente .... Tabula dei invocandi

3. Septentrione .... Sacerdos

4. Meridione .... Ignis cum thuribulo, k.t.l.

5. Centro .... Lapis quadratus cum

Imagine Dei

Maximi Ingentis Nefandi Ineffabilis Sanctissimi

et cum ferro, tintinnabulo, oleo.

Virgo. Stet imago juxta librum Theléma.

De ceremonio Principii.

Fiat ut in Libro DCLXXI dicitur, sed antea virgo lavata sit cum verbis "Asperge me..." k.t.l., et habilimenta ponat cum verbis "Per sanctum Mysterium," k.t.l.

Ita Pyramis fiat. Tunc virgo lavabit sacerdotem et vestimenta ponat ut supra ordinatur.

(Hic dicat virgo orationes dei operis).

De ceremonio Thuribuli.

Manibus accedat et ignem et sacerdotem virgo, dicens:

"Accendat in nobis Dominus ignem sui amoris et flamman aeternae caritatis.

De ceremonio Dedicationis.

Invocet virgo Imaginem Dei. M.I.N.I.S. his verbis. — Tu qui es prater omnia... k.t.l."

Nec relinquet alteram Imaginem.

De Sacrificio Summo.

Deinde silentium frangat sacerdos cum verbis versiculi sancti dei particularitur invocandi.

Ineat ad Sanctum Sanctorum.

Caveat; caveat, caveat.

Duo qui fiunt UNUS sine intermissione verba versiculi sancti alta voce cantent.

De Benedictione Benedicti.

Missa rore, dicat mulier haec verba "Quia patris et filii s.s." k.t.l.

De Ceremonio Finis.

Fiat ut in Libro DCLXXI dicitur. [Greek:] AYMGN.

LIBER XXV

THE.STAR RUBY

Facing East, in the centre, draw deep deep deep thy breath closing thy mouth with thy right forefinger prest against thy lower lip. Then dashing down the hand with a great sweep back and out, expelling forcibly thy breath, cry APO PANTOS KAKODAIMONOS. With the same forefinger touch thy forehead, and say SOI, thy member, and say O PHALLE, [The secret sense of these words is to be sought in the numeration thereof.], thy right shoulder, and say ISCHUROS, thy left shoulder, and say EUCHARISTOS; then clasp thine hands, locking the fingers, and cry IAŌ. Advance to the East. Imagine strongly a Pentagram, aright, in thy forehead. Drawing the hands to the eyes, fling it forth, making the sign of Horus and roar THÉRION. Retire thine hand in the sign of Hoor-paar-Kraat.

Go round to the North and repeat; but say NUIT.

Go round to the West and repeat; but whisper BABALON.

Go round to the South and repeat; but bellow HADIT.

Completing the circle widdershins, retire to the centre and raise thy voice in the Paian, with these words IŌ PAN, with the signs of N.O.X.

Extend the arms in the form of a Tau and say low but clear:

PRO MOU IUNGES OPICHŌ MOU TELETARCHAI EPI DEXIA CHUNOCHES EPARISTERA DAIMONOS PHEG EI GAR PERI MOU O ASTÉR TŌN PENTE KAI EN TÉI STÉLÉI Ō ASTÉR TŌN EX ESTÉXE.

Repeat the Cross Qabalistic, as above, and end as thou didst begin.

LIBER XXXVI

THE STAR SAPPHIRE

Publication in Class D

Let the Adept be armed with his Magick Rood [and provided with his mystic rose].

In the centre, let him give the L.V.X. signs; or if he know them, if he will and dare do them, and can keep silent about them, the signs of N.O.X. being the signs of Puer, Vir, Puella, Mulier. Omit the sign. I.R.

Then let him advance to the East and make the Holy Hexagram, saying: Pater et Mater unus deus Ararita.

Let him go round to the South, make the Holy Hexagram and say: Mater et Filius unus deus Ararita.

Let him go round to the North, make the Holy Hexagram and then say: Filia et Pater unus deus Ararita.

Let him then return to the Centre, and so to The Centre of All (making the Rosy Cross as he may know how) saying Ararita Ararita Ararita (In this the Signs shall be those of Set Triumphant and of Baphomet. Also shall Set appear in the Circle. Let him drink of the Sacrament and let him communicate the same.) Then let him say: Omnia in Duos: Duo in Unum: Unus in Nihil: Haec nec Quatuor nec Omnia nec Duo nec Unus nec Nihil Sunt.

Gloria Patri et Matri et Filio et Filiae et Spiritui Sancto externo et Spiritui Sancto interno ut erat est erit in saecula Saeculorum sex in uno per nomen Septem in uno Ararita.

Let him then repeat the signs of L.V.X. but not the signs of N.O.X.: for it is not he that shall arise in the Sign of Isis Rejoicing.

LIBER XLIV

THE MASS OF THE PHOENIX

The Magician, his breast bare, stands before an altar on which are his Burin, Bell, Thurible, and two of the Cakes of Light. In the Sign of the Enterer he reaches West across the Altar, and cries:

Hail Ra, that goest in thy bark

Into the caverns of the Dark!

He gives the sign of Silence, and takes the Bell, and Fire, in his hands.

East of the Altar see me stand

With light and musick in my hand!

He strikes Eleven times upon the Bell 333 - 55555 - 333 and places the Fire in the Thurible.

I strike the Bell: I light the Flame;

I utter the mysterious Name.

ABRAHADABRA

He strikes eleven times upon the Bell.

Now I begin to pray: Thou Child,

Holy Thy name and undefiled!

Thy reign is come; Thy will is done.

Here is the Bread; here is the Blood.

Bring me through midnight to the Sun!

Save me from Evil and from Good!

That Thy one crown of all the Ten

Even now and here be mine. AMEN.

He puts the first Cake on the Fire of the Thurible.

I burn the Incense-cake, proclaim

These adorations of Thy name.

He makes them as in Liber Legis, and strikes again Eleven times upon the Bell. With the Burin he then makes upon his breast the proper sign.

Behold this bleeding breast of mine

Gashed with the sacramental sign!

He puts the second Cake to the wound.

I stanch the Blood; the wafer soaks

It up, and the high priest invokes!

He eats the second Cake.

This Bread I eat. This Oath I swear

As I enflame myself with prayer:

"There is no grace: there is no guilt:

This is the Law: DO WHAT THOU WILT!"

He strikes Eleven times upon the Bell, and cries

ABRAHADABRA.

I entered in with woe; with mirth

I now go forth, and with thanksgiving,

To do my pleasure on the earth

Among the legions of the living.

He goeth forth.

LIBER V

vel

REGULI

A.·. A.·. publication in Class D.

Being the Ritual of the Mark of the Beast:

an incantation proper to invoke the Energies of the Aeon of Horus,

adapted for the daily use of the Magician of whatever grade.

[The title is Latin and means Book 5 or Book of the Prince. Regulus is also the name of the star which marks the beginning or 0 degree of the constellation Leo.]

THE FIRST GESTURE

The Oath of the Enchantment, which is called the Elevenfold Seal.

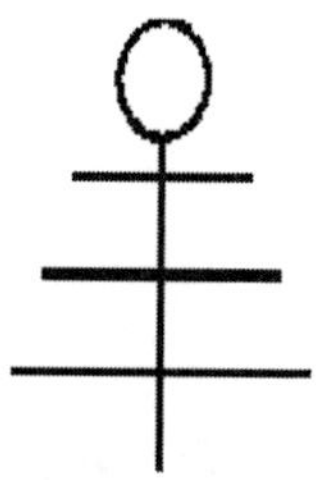

The Animadversion towards the Æon.

1. Let the Magician, robed and armed as he may deem to be fit, turn to face towards Boleskine,* that is the Housse of the Beast 666.
2. Let him strike the battery 1–3–3–3–1.
3. Let him put the Thumb of his right hand between its index and medius, and make the gestures hereafter following.

The Vertical Component of the Enchantment.

1. Let him describe a circle about his head, crying NUIT!
2. Let him draw the Thumb vertically downward, and touch the *muladhara cakra*, crying HADIT!

3. Let him, retracing the line, touch the centre of his breast, and cry RA-HOOR-KHUIT!

The Horizontal Component of the Enchantment.

1. Let him touch the Centre of his Forehead, his mouth, and his larynx, crying AIWAZ!
2. Let him draw his Thumb from right to left across his face at the level of the nostrils.
3. Let him touch the Centre of his Breast, and his Solar Plexus, crying THERION!
4. Let him draw his Thumb from left to right across his breast at the level of the sternum.
5. Let him touch the *svadhisthana.* and the *muladhara cakra,* crying BABALON!
6. Let him draw his Thumb from right to left across his abdomen, at the level of the hips.

(Thus shall he formulate the Sigil of the Grand Hierophant, but dependent from the Circle.)

The Asserveration of the Spells.

1. Let the Magician clasp his hands upon his Wand, his fingers and thumbs interlaced, crying LAShTAL! THELEMA! FIAOF! AGAPÉ! AUMGN!

(Thus shall be declared the Words of Power whereby the Energies of the Æon of Horus work his Will in the world.)

The Proclamation of the Accomplishment

1. Let the Magician strike the Battery: 3–5–3, crying ABRAHADABRA.

* Boleskine House is on Loch Ness, 17 mile from Inverness, latitude 57.14N, longitude 4.28W.

THE SECOND GESTURE

The Enchantment.

1. Let the Magician, still facing Boleskine, advance to the circumference of his Circle.
2. Let him turn himself towards the left, and pace with the stealth and swiftness of a tiger the precincts of his circle, until he complete one revolution thereof.
3. Let him give the sign of Horus (or the Enterer) as he passeth, so to project the Force that radiateth from Boleskine before him.
4. Let him pace his Path until he comes to the North; there let him halt, and turn his face to the North.

5. Let him trace with his Wand the Averse Pentagram proper to invoke Air (Aquarius).

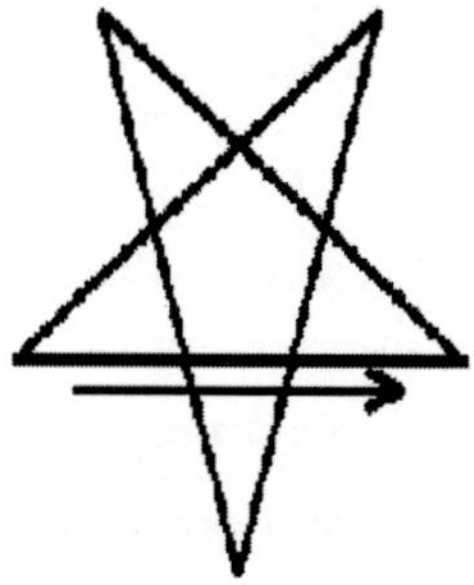

6. Let him bring the Wand to the Centre of the Pentagram and call upon NUIT!

7. Let him make the sign called Puella, standing with his feet together, head bowed, his left hand shielding the *muladhara cakra*, and his right hand shielding his breast (attitude of the Venus de Medici).

8. Let him turn again to the Left, and pursue his Path as before, projecting the Force from Boleskine as he passeth; let him halt when he next cometh to the South, and face outward.

9. Let him trace the Averse Pentagram that invoketh Fire (Leo).

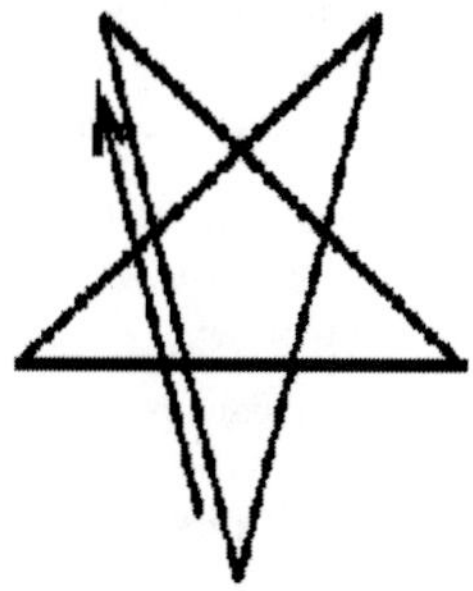

10. Let him point his Wand to the Centre of the Pentagram, and cry HADIT!

11. Let him give the sign Puer, standing with feet together and head erect. Let his right hand (the thumb extended at right angles to the fingers) be raised, the forearm vertical at a right angle with the upper arm, which is horizontally extended in the line joining the shoulders. Let his left hand, the thumb extended forwards, and the fingers clenched, rest at the junction of the thighs (attitudes of the gods Mentu, Khem, *etc.*).

12. Let him proceed as before; then in the East, let mim make the Averse Pentagram that invoketh Earth (Taurus).

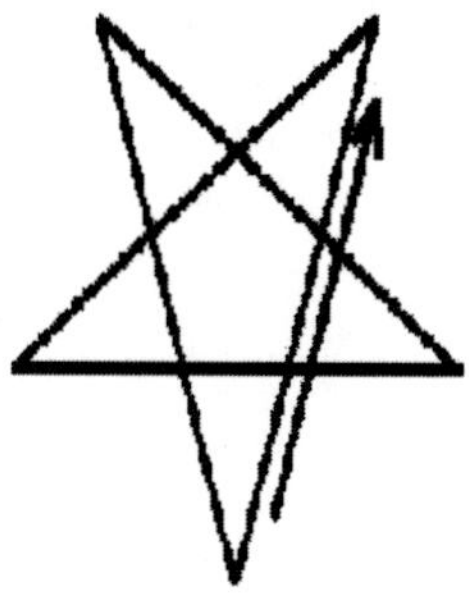

13. Let him point his Wand to the Centre of the Pentagram, and cry THERION!

14. Let him give the sign called Vir, the feet being together. The hands, with clenched fingers and thumbs thrust out forwards, are held to the temples; the head is then bowed and pushed out, as if to symbolize the butting of an horned beast (attitude of Pan, Bacchus, *etc.*). (Frontispiece, *Equinox* I(3)).

15. Proceding as before, let him make in the West the Averse Pentagram whereby Water is invoked.

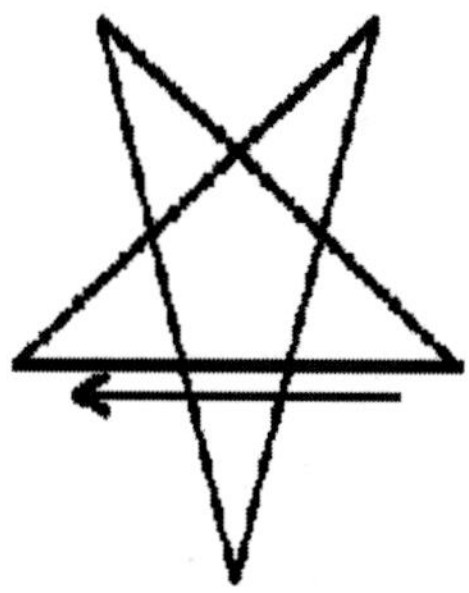

16. Pointing the Wand to the Centre of the Pentagram, let him call upon BABALON!

17. Let him give the sign Mulier. The feet are widely separated, and the arms raised so as to suggest a crescent. The head is thrown back (attitude of Baphomet, Isis in Welcome, the Microcosm of Vitruvius). (See *Book 4*, Part II).

18. Let him break into the dance, tracing a centripetal spiral widdershins, enriched by revolutions upon his axis as he passeth each Quarter, until he come to the centre of the Circle. There let him halt, facing Boleskine.

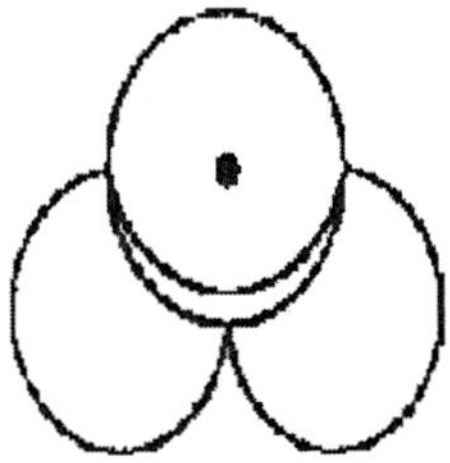

19. Let him raise the Wand, trace the Mark of the Beast, and cry AIWAZ!

20. Let him trace the Invoking Hexagram of The Beast.

21. Let him lower theWand, striking the Earth therewith.

22. Let him give the sign of Mater Triumphans. (The feet are together; the left arm is curved as if it supported a child; the thumb and index finger of the right hand pinch the nipple of the left breast, as if offering it to that child.) Let him utter the word THELEMA!2

23. Perform the Spiral Dance, moving deosil and whirling widdershins.Each time on passing th West extend the Wand to the Quarter in question, and bow:

a. "Before me the powers of LA!" (to West.)
b. "Behind me the powers of AL!" (to East.)
c. "On my right hand the powers of LA!" (to North.)
d. "On my left hand the powers of AL!" (to South.)
e. "Above me the powers of ShT!" (leaping in the air.)
f. "Beneath me the power of ShT!" (striking the ground.)
g. "Within me the Powers!" (in the attitude of Ptah erect, the feet together, the hands clasped upon the vertical Wand.)
h. "About me flames my Father's Face, the Star of Force and Fire!"
i. "And in the Column stands his six-rayed Splendour!"

(This dance may be omitted, and the whole utterance chanted in the attitude of Ptah.)

THE FINAL GESTURE

This is identical with the first gesture.

(*Here followeth an impression of the ideas implied in this Pæan*)

I also am a Star in Space, unique and self-existent, an individual essence incorruptible; I also am one Soul; I am identical with All and None. I am in All and all in me; I am, apart from all and lord of all, and one with all.

I am Omniciscient, for naught exists for me unless I know it. I am Omnipotents, for naught occurs save by Necesity, my soul's expression through my Will to be, to do, to suffer the symbols of itself. I am Omnipresent, for naught exists where I am not, who fashioned Space as a condition of my consciousness of myself, who am the centre of all, and my circumference the frame of mine own fancy.

I am the All, for all that exists for me is a necessary expression in thought of some tendency of my nature, and all my thoughts are only the letters of my Name.

I am the One, for all that I am is not the absolute All, and all my all is mine and not another's; mine, who conceive of others like myself in essence and truth, yet unlike in expression and illusion.

I am the None, for all that I am is the imperfect image of the perfect; each partial phantom must perish in the flasp of its counterpart, each form fulfil itself by finding its equated opposite, and satisfying its need to be the Absolute by the attainment of annihilation.

The World LAShTAL includes all this.

LA—Naught.

AL—Two.

L is "Justice," the *Kteis* fulfilled by the Phallus, "Naught and Two" because the plus and the minus have united in "love under will."

A is "The Fool," Naught in Thought (Parzival), Word (Harpocrates), and Action (Bacchus). He is the boundless air, and the wandering Ghost, but with "possibilities." He is the Naught that the Two have made by "love under will."

LA thus represents the Ecstasy of Nuit and Hadit conjoined, lost in love, and making themselves Naught thereby. Their child is begotten and conceived, but is in the phase of Naught also, as yet. LA is thus the Universe in that phase, with its potentialities of manifestation.

AL, on the contrary, though it is essentially identical with LA, shows "The Fool" manifested through the Equilibrium of Contraries. The wieght is still nothing, but it is expressed as it were two equal weights in opposite scales. The indicator still points to zero.

ShT is equally 31 with LA and AL, but it expresses the secret nature which operates the Magick or the transmutations.

ShT is the formula of this particular Æon; another æon might have another way of saying 31.

Sh is Fire as T is Force; conjoined they express Ra-Hoor-Khuit.

"The Angel"3 represents the Stèle 666, showing the Gods of the Æg;on, while "Strength" is a picture of Babalon and the Beast, the earthly emissaries of those Gods.

ShT is the dynamic equivalent of LA and AL. Sh shows the Word of the Law, being triple, as 93 is thrice 31. T shows the formula of Magic declared in that Word; the Lion, the Serpent, the Sun, Courage and Sexual Love are all indicated by the card.

In LA note that Saturn or Satan is exalted in the House of Venus or Astarté and it is an airy sign. Thus L is Father-Mother, Two and Naught, and the Spirit (Holy Ghost) of their Love is also Naught. Love is AHBH, 13, which is AChD. Unity, 1, *aleph*. who is "The Fool" who is Naught, but none the less an individual One, who (as such) is not another, yet unconscious of himself until his Oneness expresses itself as a duality.

Any impression or idea is unknowable in itself. It can mean nothing until brought into relation with other things. The first step is to distinguish one thought from another; this is the condition of recognizingg it. To define it, we must perceive its orientation to all our other ideas. The extent of our knowledge of any one thing varies therefore with the number of ideas with which we can compare it. Every new fact not only adds itself to our universe, but increases the value of what we already possess.

In AL this "The" or "God" arranges for "Countenance to behold countenance,"4 by establishing itself as an equilibrium, A the One-Naught conceived as L the Two-Naught. This L is the Son-Daughter Horus-Harpocrates just as the other L was the Father-Mother Set-Isis. Here then is Tetragrammaton once more, but expressed in identical equations in which every term is perfect in itself as a mode of Naught.

ShT supplies the last element; making the Word of either five or six letters, according as we regard ShT as one letter or two. Thus the Word affirms the Great Work accomplished: 5°=6°.

ShT is moreover a necessary resolution of the apparent opposition of LA and AL; for one could hardly pass to the other without the catalytic action of a third identical expression whose function should be to transmute them. Such a term must be in itself a mode of Naught, and its nature cannot encroach on the perfections of Not-Being, LA, or of Being, AL. It must be purely Nothing-Motion as they are purely Nothing-Matter, so as to create a Matter-in-Motion which is a function of "Something."

Thus ShT is Motion in its double phase, an inertia compose of two opposite current, and each current is also thus polarized. Sh is Heaven and Earth, T Male and Female; ShT is Spirit and Matter; one is the word of Liberty and Love flashing its Light to restore Life to Earth, the other is the act by which Life claims that Love is Light and Liberty. And these are Two-in-One, the divine letter of Silence-in-Speech whose symbol is the Sun in the Arms of the Moon.5

But Sh and T are alike formulæ of force in action as opposed to entities; they are not states of existence, but modes of motion. They are verbs, not nouns.

Sh is the Holy Spirit as a "tongue of fire" manifest in triplicity, and is the child of Set-Isis as their *logos* or Word uttered by their "Angel." The card is XX, and 20 is the value of *yod* (the secret seed of all things, the Virgin, "The Hermit," Mercury, the Angel or Herald) expressed in full as IVD. Sh is the spiritual congress of Heaven and Earth.

But T is the Holy Spirit in action as a "roaringg Lion" or as "the old Serpent" instead of an "Angel of Light." The twins of Set-Isis, harlot and beast, are busy with that sodomitic and incestuous lust which is the traditional formula for producing demi-gods, as in the cases of Mary and the Dove, Leda and the Swan, *etc.* The card is XI, the number of Magick AVD: *aleph* "The Fool" impregnating the woman according to the Word of *yod*, the Angel of the Lord! His sister has seduced her brother Beast, shaming the Sun with her sin; she has mastered the Lion, and enchanted the Serpent. Nature is outraged by Magick; man is bestialized and woman defiled. The conjunction produces a monster; it affirms regression of types. Instead of a man-God conceived of the Spirit of God by a virgin in innocence, we are asked to adore the bastard of a whore and a brute, begotten in shamefullest sin and born in most blasphemous bliss.

This is in fact the formula of our Magick; we insist that all acts must be equal; that existence asserts the right to exist; that unless evil is a mere term expressing some relation of haphazard hostility between forces equally self-justified, the universe is as inexplicable and impossible as uncompensated action; that the orgies of Bacchus and Pan are no less sacramental than the Masses of Jesus; that the scars of syphilis are sacred and worthy of honour as much as the wounds of the martyrs of Mary.

It should be unnecessary to insist that the above ideas apply only to the Absolute. Toothache is still painful, and deceit degrading, to a man, relatively to his situation in the world of illusion; he does his Will by avoiding them. But the existence of "Evil" is fatal to philosophy so long as it is supposed to be independent of conditions; and to accustom the mind to "make no difference" between any two ideas6 as such is to emancipate it from the thralldom of terror.

We affirm on our altars our faith in ourself and our wills, our love of all aspects of the Absolute All.

And we make the Spirit *shin* combine with the Flesh *teth* int a single letter, whose value is 31 even as those of LA the Naught, and AL the All, to complete their Not-Being and Being with its Becoming, to mediate between identical extremes as their mean—the secret that sunders and seals them.

It declares that all somethings are equally shadows of Nothing, and justifies Nothing in its futile folly of pretending that something is stable, by making us aware of a method of Magick through the practice of which we may partake in the pleasure of the process.

The Magician should devise for himself a definite technique for destroying "evil." The essence of such a practice will consist in training the mind and the body to confront things which case fear, pain, disgust,* shame and the like. He must learn to endure them, then to become indifferent to them, then to become indifferent to them, then to analyze them until they give pleasure and instruction, and finally to appreciate them for their own sake, as aspects of Truth. When this has been done, he should abandon them, if they are really harmful in relation to health and comfort. Also, our selction of "evils" is limited to those that cannot damage us irreparably. *E.g.*, one ought to practice smelling assafoetida until one likes it; but not arsine or hydrocyanic acid. Again, one might have a liaison with an ugly old woman until one beheld and loved the star which she is; it would be too dangerous to overcome the distaste for dishonesty by forcing oneself to pick pockets. Acts which are essentially dishonourable must not be done; they should be justified only by calm contemplation of their correctness in abstract cases.

Love is a virtue; it grows stronger and purer and less selfish by applying it to what it loathes; but theft is a vice involving the slave-idea that one's neighbour is superior to oneself. It is admirable only for its power to develop certain moral and mental qualities in primitive types, to prevent the atrophy of such faculties as our own vigilance, and for the interest which it adds to the "tragedy, Man."

Crime, folly, sickness and all such phenomena must be contemplated with complete freedom from fear, aversion, or shame. Otherwise we shall fail to see accurately, and interpret intelligently; in which case we shall be unable to outwit and outfight them. Anatomists and physiologists, grappling in the dark with death, have won hygeine, surgery, prophylaxis and the rest for mankind. Anthropologists, archæologists, physicists and other men of science, risking thumbscrws, stake, infamy and ostracism, have torn the spider-snare of superstition to shreds and broken in pieces the monstrous idol of Morality, the murderous Moloch which has made mankind its meat throughout history. Each fragment of that coprolite it manifest as an image of some brute lust, some torpid dullness, some ignorant instinct, or some furtive fear shapen in his own savage mind.

Man is indeed not wholly freed, even now. He is still trampled under the hoofs of the stampeding mules that nightmare bore to his wild ass, his creative forces that he had not mastered, the sterile ghosts that he called gods. Their mystery cows men still; they fear, they flinch, they dare not face the phantoms. Still, too, the fallen fetich seems awful; it is frightful to them that there is no longer an idol to adore with anthems, and to appease with the flesh of their firstborn. Each scrambles in the bloody mire of the floor to snatch some scrap for a relic, that he may bow down to it and serve it.

So, even today, a mass of maggots swarm heaving over the carrion earth, a brotherhood bound by blind greed for rottenness. Science still hesitates to raise the Temple of Rimmon, though every year finds more of her sons impatient of Naaman's prudence. The Privy Council of the Kingdom of Mansoul sits in permenant scret session; it dares not declare what must follow its deed in shattering the monarch Morality into scraps of crumbling conglomerate of of climatic, tribal, and person prejudices, corrupted yet more by the action of crafy ambition, insane impulse, ignorant arrogance, superstitious hysteria, fear fashioning falsehoods on the stone that it sets on the grave of Truth whom it has murdered and buried in the black earth Oblivion. Moral philosophy, psychology, sociology, anthropology, mental pathology, physiology, and many another of the children of Wisdom, of whom she is justified, well know that the laws of Ethics are a chaos of confused conventions, based at best on customs convenient in certain conditions, more often on the craft or caprice of the biggest, the most savage, heartless, cunning and blood-thirsty brutes of the pack, to secure their power or pander to their pleasure in cruelty. There is no principle, even a false one, to give coherence to the clamour of ethical propositions. Yet the very men that have smashed Moloch, and strewn the earth with shapeless rubble, grow pale when they so much as whisper among themselves: "While Moloch ruled all men were bound by one law, and by the oracles of them that, knowing the fraud, feared not, but were his priests and wardens of his mystery. What now? How can any of us, though wise and strong as never was known, prevail on men to act in concert, now that each prays to his own chip of God, and yet knows every other chip to be a worthless ort, dream-dust, ape-dung, tradition-bone, or—what not else?"

So Science begins to see that the Initiates were maybe not merely silly and selfish in making their rule of silence, and in protecting Philosophy from the profane. Yet still she hopes that the mischief may not prove mortal, and begs that things may go on much as usual until that secret session decide on some plan of action.

It has always been fatal when somebody finds out too much too suddenly. If John Huss had cackled more like a hen, he might have survived Michaelmas, and been esteemed for his eggs. The last fifty years have laid the axe of analysis to the root of every axiom; they are triflers who content themselves with lopping the blossoming twigs of our beliefs, or the boughs of our intellectual instruments. We can no longer assert any single proposition, unless we guard ourselves by enumerating countelss conditions which must be assumed.

This digression has outstayed its welcome; it was only invited by Wisdom that it might warn Rashness of the dangers that encompass even Sincerity, Energy and Intelligence when they happen not to contribute to Fitness-in-their-environment.

The Magician must be wary in his use of his powers; he must may every act not only accord with his Will, but with the properties of his position at the time. It might be my Will to reach the foot of a cliff; but the easiest way—also the speediest, most direct least obstructed, the way of minimum effort—would be simply to jump. I should have destroyed my Will in the act of fulfilling it, or what I mistook for it; for the True Will has no goal; its nature being To Go. Similarly, a parabola is bound by one law which fixes its relations with two straight lines at every point; yet it has no end short of infinity, and it continually changes its direction. The Initiate who is aware Who he is can always check is conduct by reference to the determinants of his curve, and calculate his past, his future, his bearings, and his proper course at any assigned moment; he can even comprehend himself as a simple idea. He may attain to measure fellow-parabolas, ellipses that cross his path, hyperbolas that span all space with their twin wings. Perhaps he may come at long last, leaping beyond the limits of his own law, to conceive that sublimely stupendous outrage to Reason, the Cone! Utterly inscrutable to him, he is yet well aware that he exists in the nature thereof, that he is necessary thereto, that he is ordered thereby, and that therefrom he is sprung, from the loins of so fearful a Father! His own infinity becomes zero in relation to that of the least fragment of the solid. He hardly exists at all. Trillions multiplies by trillions of trillions of such as he could not cross the frontier even of breadth, the idea which he came to guess at only becuase he felt himself bound by some mysterious power. Yet breadth is equally a nothing in the presence of the Cone. His first conception must evidently be a frantic spasm, formless, insane, not to be classed as an articulate thougght. Yet, if he develops the faculties of his mind, the more he knows of it the more he sees that its nature is identical with his own whenever comparision is possible.

The True Will is thus both determined by its equations, and free because those equation are simply its own name, spelt out fully. His sense of being under bondage comes from his inability to read it; his sense that evil exists to thwart him arises when he begins to learn to read, reads wrong, and is obstinate that his error is an improvement.

We know one thing only. Absolute existence, absolute motion, absolute direction, absolute simultaneity, absolute truth, all such ideas: they have not, and never can have, any real meaning. If a man in *delirium tremens* fell into the Hudson River, he might remember the proverb and clutch at an imaginary straw. Words such as "truth" are like that straw. Confusion of thought is concealed, and its impotence denied, by the invention. This paragraph opened with "We know": yet, quesitoned, "we" make haste to deny the possibility of possessing, or even of defining, knowledge. What could be more certain to a parabola-philosopher that he could be approached in two ways, and two only? It would be indeed little less that the whole body of his knowledge, implied in the theory of his definition of himself, and confirmed by every single experience. He could receive impressions only be meeting A, or being caught up by B. Yet he would be wrong in an infinite number of ways. There are therefore *Aleph*-Zero7 possibilities that at any moment a man may find himself totally transformed. And it may be that our present dazzled bewilderment is due to our recognition of the existence of a new dimension of thought, which seems so "inscrutably infinite" and "absurd" and "immoral," *etc.*—because we have not studied it long enough to appreciate that its laws are identical with our own, though extended to new conceptions. The discovery of radioactivity created a momentary chaos in chemistry and physics; but it soon led to a fuller interpretation of the old ideas. It dispersed many difficulties, harmonized many discords, and—yea, more! It shewed the substance of Universe as a simplicity of Light and Life, manners to compose atoms, themselves capable of deeper self-realization through fresh complexities and organizations, each with its own peculiar powers and pleasures, each pursuing its path througggh the world where all things are possible. It revealed the omnipresence of Hadit, identical with Himself, yet fulfilling Himself by dividing His interplay with Nuit into episodes, each form of his energy isolated with each aspect of Her receptivity, delight developing delight continuous from complex to complex. It was the voice of Nature awakening at the dawn of the Æon, as Aiwaz uttered the Word of the Law of Thelema.

So also shall he who invoketh often behold the Formless Fire, with trembling and bewilderment; but if he prolong his meditation, he shall resolve it into coherent and intelligibile symbols, and he shall hear the articulate utterance of that Fire, interpret the thunder thereof as a still small voice in his heart. And the Fire shall reveal to his eyes his own image in its own true glory; and it shall speak in his ears the mystery that is his own right Name.

This then in the virtue of the Magick of The Beast 666, and the canon of its proper useage; to destroy the tendency to discriminate between any two things in theory, and in practice to pierce the veils of every sanctuary, pressing forward to embrace every image; for there is none that is not very Isis. The Inmost is one with the Inmost; yet the form of the One is not the form of the other; intimacy exacts fitness. He therefore who liveth by air, let him not be bold to breathe water. But mastery cometh by measure: to him who with labour, courage, and caution giveth his life to understand all that doth encompass him, and to prevail against it, shall be increase. "The word of Sin is Restriction": seek therefore Righteousness, enquiring into Iniquity, and fortify thyself to overcome it.

*: The people of England have made two revolutions to free themselves from Popish fraud and tyranny. They are at their tricks again; and if we have to make a Third Revolution, let us destroy the germ itself!

Notes

This ritual was first published in Appendix VI of *Magick in Theory and Practice*. The text above is taken from the version published in *Magick: Book 4 Parts I-IV* which corrects a few errors and omissions in the original edition. Two earlier drafts of this ritual, with a measure of audience participation, are also extant.

1: THELEMA, AGAPÉ, and AUMGN in Greek in the original. FIAOF or VIAOV (Hebrew, Vau-Yod-Aleph-Ayin-Yod = 93) is a variation of the formula of IAO dicussed by Crowley in Chapter V of *Magick in Theory and Practice*. AUMGN is an exention of AUM described in Chapter VII of *Magick*.

2: THELEMA in Greek letters in the original.

3: A name sometimes used for Tarot Trump XX, more usually called "Judgement" or "the Last Judgement." In Crowley's Thoth deck it is called The Æon – T.S.

4: The quote is from the "Sepher Dtznouthia" or "Book of Concealment," a Qabalistic text translated by Mathers from the Latin of Von Rosenroth and published in *Kabbalah Unveiled.*

5: The double letter ShT is glyphed by writing the Greek equivalents of Shin-Teth, Sigma-Theta, using the variant form of the capital Sigma which looks the the Latin C. The result looks like Crowley's "Sun and Moon conjoined" symbol.

6: The allusion is to AL I. 22, which reads: "Let there be no difference made among you between any one thing & any other thing; for thereby there cometh hurt."

7: Should probably be read Aleph-Null, written as the Hebrew letter Aleph followed by a zero in subscript. The reference is to the infinite set of cardinal numbers, the smallest infinite set; a set is said to have Aleph-null members if its members can be put into one to one correspondence with the set of natural numbers (0, 1, 2, 3, ...). On this definition, there are as many signed integers (which includes negative numbers) as natural numbers, and as many rational numbers (i.e., numbers which can be written as fractions, one integer divided by another) as natural numbers. There are, however, more real numbers; the real numbers cannot be put in a one-to-one correspondence with the natural numbers, because they cannot be written in order; for whatever ordering principle you use, given any two real numbers it will always be possible to put one in between them. It is still a matter of debate whether there exist any infinite sets between aleph-null and the continuum (the latter being the set of real numbers).

Liber XV

O. T. O.

Ecclesiæ Gnosticæ Catholicæ

Canon Missæ

Edited from the Ancient Documents in

Assyrian and Greek by The Master Therion

I: OF THE FURNISHINGS OF THE TEMPLE

IN THE EAST, that is, in the direction of Boleskine, which is situated on the South-Eastern shore of Loch Ness in Scotland, two miles east of Foyers, is a shrine or High Altar. Its dimensions should be 7 feet in length, 3 feet in breadth, 44 inches in height. It should be covered with a crimson altar-cloth, on which may be embroidered fleur-de-lys in gold, or a sunblaze, or other suitable emblem.

On each side of it should be a pillar or obelisk, with countercharges in black and white.

Below it should be the dais of three steps, in black and white squares.

Above it is the super-altar, at whose toÿ is the Stele of Revealing in reproduction, with four candles on each side of it. Below the stele is a place for The Book of the Law, with six candles on each side of it. Below this again is the Holy Graal, with roses on each side of it. There is room in front of the Cup for the Paten. On each side beyond the roses are two great candles.

All this is enclosed within a great Veil.

Forming the apex of an equilateral triangle whose base is a line drawn between the pillars, is a small black square altar, of superimposed cubes.

Taking this altar as the middle of the base of a similar and equal triangle, at the apex of this second triangle is a small circular font.

Repeating, the apex of a third triangle is an upright tomb.

II: OF THE OFFICERS OF THE MASS

The PRIEST. Bears the Sacred Lance, and is clothed at first in a plain white robe.

The PRIESTESS. Should be actually Virgo Intacta or specially dedicated to the service of the Great Order. She is clothed in white, blue, and gold. She bears the Sword from a red girdle, and the Paten and Hosts, or Cakes of Light.

The DEACON. He is clothed in white and yellow. He bears The Book of the Law.

Two CHILDREN. They are clothed in white and black. One bears a pitcher of water and a cellar of salt, the other a censer of fire and a casket of perfume.

III: OF THE CEREMONY OF THE INTROIT

The DEACON, opening the door of the Temple, admits the congregation and takes his stand between the small altar and the font. (There should be a doorkeeper to attend to the admission.) The DEACON advances and bows before the open shrine where the Graal is exalted. He kisses The Book of the Law three times, opens it, and places it upon the super-altar. He turns West.

The DEACON: Do what thou wilt shall be the whole of the Law. I proclaim the Law of Light, Life, Love, and Liberty in the name of IAQ.

The CONGREGATION: Love is the law, love under will.

The DEACON goes to his place between the altar of incense and the font, faces East, and gives the step and sign of a Man and a Brother. All imitate him.

The DEACON and all the PE_PLE:

I believe in one secret and ineffable LORD; and in one Star in the Company of Stars of whose fire we are created, and to which we shall return; and in one Father of Life, Mystery of Mystery, in His name CHAOS, the sole viceregent of the Sun upon the Earth; and in one Air the nourisher of all that breathes.

And I believe in one Earth, the Mother of us all, and in one Womb wherein all men are begotten, and wherein they shall rest, Mystery of Mystery, in Her name BABALON.

And I believe in the Serpent and the Lion, Mystery of Mystery, in His name BAPHOMET.

And I believe in one Gnostic and Catholic Church of Light, Life, Love and Liberty, the Word of whose Law is THELEMA.

And I believe in the communion of Saints.

And, forasmuch as meat and drink are transmuted in us daily into spiritual substance, I believe in the Miracle of the Mass.

And I confess one Baptism of Wisdom whereby we accomplish the Miracle of Incarnation.

And I confess my life one, individual, and eternal that was, and is, and is to come.

AUMGN. AUMGN. AUMGN.

Music is now played. The child enters with the ewer and the salt. The VIRGIN enters with the Sword and the Paten. The child enters with the censer and the perfume. They face the DEACON, deploying into line, from the space between the two altars.

The VIRGIN: Greeting of Earth and Heaven!

All give the Hailing sign of a Magician, the DEACON leading.

The PRIESTESS, the negative child on her left, the positive child on her right, ascends the steps of the High Altar. They await her below. She places the Paten before the Graal. Having adored it, she descends, and with the children following her, the positive next her, she moves in a serpentine manner involving 3 circles of the

Temple. (Deosil about altar, widdershins about font, deosil about altar and font, widdershins about altar, and so to the Tomb in the West.) She draws her Sword and pulls down the Veil therewith.

The PRIESTESS: By the power of Iron, I say unto thee, Arise. In the name of our Lord the Sun, and of our Lord ... that thou mayst administer the virtues to the Brethren.

She sheathes the Sword.

The PRIEST, issuing from the Tomb, holding the Lance erect with both hands, right over left, against his breast, takes the first three regular steps. He then gives the Lance to the PRIESTESS, and gives the three penal signs. He then kneels and worships the Lance with both hands. Penitential music.

The PRIEST: I am a man among men.

He takes again the Lance, and lowers it. He rises.

The PRIEST: How should I be worthy to administer the virtues to the Brethren?

The PRIESTESS takes from the child the water and the salt, and mixes them in the font.

The PRIESTESS: Let the salt of Earth admonish the water to bear the virtue of the Great Sea. (Genuflects.) Mother, be thou adored.

She returns to the West. on PRIEST with open hand doth she make, over his forehead, breast, and body.

Be the PRIEST pure of body and soul!

The PRIESTESS takes the censer from the child, and places it on the small altar. She puts incense therein.

Let the Fire and the Air make sweet the world! (Genuflects.)

Father, be thou adored.

She returns West, and makes with the censer before the PRIEST, thrice as before.

Be the PRIEST fervent of body and soul!

(The children resume their weapons as they are done with.)

The DEACON now takes the consecrated Robe from High Altar, and brings it to her. She robes the PRIEST in his Robe of scarlet and gold.

Be the flame of the Sun thine ambience, O thou PRIEST of the SUN!

The DEACON brings the crown from the High Altar. (The crown may be of gold or platinum, or of electrum magicum; but with no other metals, save the small proportions necessary to a proper alloy. It may be adorned with divers jewels, at will But it must have the Uræus serpent twined about it, and the cap of maintenance must match the scarlet of the Robe. Its texture should be velvet.)

Be the Serpent thy crown, O thou PRIEST of the LORD!

Kneeling, she takes the Lance, between her open hands, and runs them up and down upon the shaft eleven times, very gently.

Be the LORD present among us!

All give the Hailing Sign.

The PEOPLE: So mote it be.

IV: OF THE CEREMONY OF THE OPENING OF THE VEIL

The PRIEST: Thee therefore whom we adore we also invoke. By the power of the lifted Lance!

He raises the Lance. All repeat Hailing Sign. A phrase of triumphant music. The PRIEST takes the PRIESTESS by her right hand with his left, keeping the Lance raised.

I, PRIEST and KING, take thee, Virgin pure without spot; I upraise thee; I lead thee to the East; I set thee upon the summit of the Earth.

He thrones the PRIESTESS upon the altar. The DEACON and the children follow, they in rank, behind him. The PRIESTESS takes The Book of the Law, resumes her seat, and holds it &127;pen on her breast with her two hands, making a descending triangle with thumbs and forefingers. The PRIEST gives the lance to the DEACON to hold, and takes the ewer from the child, and sprinkles the PRIESTESS, making five crosses, forehead, shoulders, and thighs. The thumb of the PRIEST is always between his index and medius, whenever he is not holding the Lance. The PRIEST takes the censer from the child, and makes five crosses, as before. The children replace their weapons on their respective altars. The PRIEST kisses The Book of the Law three times. He kneels for a space in adoration, with joined hands, knuckles closed, thumb in position aforesaid. He rises, and draws the veil over the whole altar. All rise and stand to order. The PRIEST takes the lance from the DEACON, and holds it as before, as Osiris or Pthah. He circumambulates the Temple three times, followed by the DEACON and the children as before. (These, when not using their hands, keep their arms crossed upon their breasts.) At the last circumambulation they leave him, and go to the place between the font and the small altar, where they kneel in adoration, their hands joined palm to palm, and raised above their heads. All imitate this motion. The PRIEST returns to the East, and mounts the first step of the altar.

The PRIEST:

O circle of Stars whereof our Father is but the younger brother, marvel beyond imagination, soul of infinite space, before whom Time is Ashamed, the mind bewildered, and the understanding dark, not unto Thee may we attain, unless Thine image be Love. Therefore by seed and root and stem and bud and leaf and flower and fruit do we invoke Thee.

Then the priest answered & said unto the Queen of Space, kissing her lovely brows, and the dew of her light bathing his whole body in a sweet-smelling perfume of sweat; O Nuit, continuous one of Heaven, let it be ever thus; that men speak not of thee as One but as None; and let them speak not of thee at all, since thou art continuous.

During this speech the PRIESTESS must have divested herself completely of her robe. See CCXX I:62.

The PRIESTESS:

But to love me is better than all things; if under the night-stars in the desert thou presently burnest mine incense before me, invoking me with a pure heart, and the serpent flame therein,

thou shalt come a little to lie in my bosom. For one kiss wilt thou then be willing to give all; but whoso gives one particle of dust shall lose all in that hour. Ye shall gather goods and store of women and spices; ye shall wear rich jewels; ye shall exceed the nations of the earth in splendour and pride; but always in the love of me, and so shall ye come to my joy. I charge you earnestly to come before me in a single robe, and covered with a rich head-dress. I love you! I yearn to you! Pale or purple, veiled or voluptuous, I who am all pleasure and purple, and drunkenness of the innermost sense, desire you. Put on the wings, and arouse the coiled splendour within you: come unto me! To me! To me! Sing the raptuous love-song unto me! Burn to me perfumes! Wear to me jewels! Drink to me, for I love you! I love you. I am the blue-lidded daughter of sunset; I am the naked brilliance of the voluptuous night-sky. To me! To me!

The PRIEST mounts the second step.

The PRIEST:

O secret of secrets that art hidden in the being of all that lives, not Thee do we adore, for that which adoreth is also Thou. Thou art That, and That am I.

I am the flame that burns in every heart of man, and in the core of every star. I am Life, and the giver of Life; yet therefore is the knowledge of me the knowledge of death. I am alone; there is no God where I am.

The DEACON and all rise to their feet, with the Hailing sign.

The DEACON:

But ye, O my people rise up and awake.

Let the rituals be rightly performed with joy and beauty.

There are rituals of the elements and feasts of the times.

A feast for the first night of the Prophet and his Bride.

A feast for the three days of the writing of the Book of the Law.

A feast for Tahuti and the children of the Prophet-secret, O Prophet!

A feast for the Supreme Ritual, and a feast for the Equinox of the Gods.

A feast for fire and a feast for water; a feast for life and a greater feast for death.

A feast every day in your hearts in the joy of my rapture.

A feast every night unto Nu, and the pleasure of uttermost delight.

The PRIEST mounts the third step.

The PRIEST:

Thou that art One, our Lord in the Universe the Sun, our Lord in ourselves whose name is Mystery of Mystery, uttermost being whose radiance enlightening the worlds is also the breath that maketh every God even and Death to tremble before Thee - By the Sign of Light appear

Thou glorious upon the throne of the Sun.

Make open the path of creation and of intelligence between us and our minds. Enlighten our understanding. Encourage our hearts. Let thy light crystallize itself in our blood, fulfilling us of Resurrection.

A ka dua

Tuf ur biu

bi a'a chefu

Dudu nur af an nuteru.

The PRIESTESS: There is no law beyond Do what thou wilt.

The PRIEST parts the veil with his lance. During the previous speeches the PRIESTESS has, if necessary, as in savage countries, resumed her robe.

The PRIEST:

IO IO IO IAO SABAO

KURIE ABRASAX KURIE MEITHRAS KURIE PHALLE.

IO PAN, IO PAN PAN IO ISXURON, IO ATHANATON IO ABROTON IO IAO. XAIRE PHALLE KAIRE PANPHAGE KAIRE PANGENETOR.

HAGIOS, HAGIOS, HAGIOS IAO.

The PRIESTESS is seated with the Paten in her right hand and the cup in her left. The PRIEST presents the Lance, which she kisses eleven times. She then holds it to her breast, while the PRIEST, falling at her knees, kisses them, his arms stretched along her thighs. He remains in this adoration while the DEACON intones the Collects. All stand to order, with the Dieu Garde, that is, feet square, hands, with linked thumbs, held loosely. This is the universal position when standing, unless other direction is given.

V: OF THE OFFICE OF THE COLLECTS WHICH ARE ELEVEN IN NUMBER

The Sun

The DEACON: Lord visible and sensible of whom this earth is but a frozen spark turning about thee with annual and diurnal motion, source of light, source of life, let thy perpetual radiance hearten us to continual labour and enjoyment; so that as we are constant partakers of thy bounty we may in our particular orbit give out light and life, sustenance and joy to them that revolve about us without diminution of substance or effulgence for ever.

The PEOPLE: So mote it be.

The Lord

The DEACON: Lord secret and most holy, source of life, source of love, source of liberty, be thou ever constant and mighty within us, force of energy, fire of motion; with diligence let us ever labour with thee, that we may remain in thine abundant joy.

The PEOPLE: So mote it be.

The Moon

The DEACON: Lady of night, that turning ever about us art now visible and now invisible in thy season, be thou favourable to hunters, and lovers, and to all men that toil upon the earth, and to all mariners upon the sea.

The PEOPLE: So mote it be.

The Lady

The DEACON: Giver and receiver of joy, gate of life and love, be thou ever ready, thou and thine handmaiden, in thine office of gladness.

The PE_PLE: So mote it be.

The Saints

The DEACON: Lord of Life and Joy, that art the might of man, that art the essence of every true god that is upon the surface of the Earth, continuing knowledge from generation unto generation, thou adored of us upon heaths and in woods, on mountains and in caves, oÿenly in the marketplaces and secretly in the chambers of our houses, in temples of gold and ivory and marble as in these other temples of our bodies, we worthily commemorate them worthy that did of old adore thee and manifest they glory unto men,

(At each name the DEACON signs with thumb between index and medius. At ordinary mass it is only necessary to commemorate those whose names are italicized, with wording as is shown.)

Laotze and Siddartha and Krishna and Tahuti, Mosheh, Dionysus, Mohammed and To Mega Therion, with these also Hermes, Pan, Priapus, Osiris and Melchizedek, Khem and Amoun and Mentu, Heracles, Orpheus and Odysseus; with Vergilius, Catullus, Martialis, Rabelais, Swinburne, and many an holy bard; Apollonius Tyanæus, Simon Magus, Manes, Pythagoras, Basilides, Valentinus, Bardesanes and Hippolytus, that transmitted the Light of the Gnosis to us their successors and their heirs; with Merlin, Arthur, Kamuret, Parzival, and many another, pr&127;phet, priest and king, that bore the Lance and Cup, the Sword and Disk, against the Heathen; and these also, Carolus Magnus and his paladins, with William of Schyren, Frederick of Hohenstaufen, Roger Bacon, Jacobus Burgundus Molensis the Martyr, Christian Rosencreutz, Ulrich von Hutten, Paracelsus, Michael Maier, Roderic Borgia Poÿe Alexander the Sixth, Jacob Boehme, Francis Bacon Lord Verulam, Andrea, Robertus de Fluctibus, Johannes Dee, Sir Edward Kelly, Thomas Vaughan, Elias Ashmole, Molinos, Adam Weishaupt, Wolfgang von Goethe, Ludovicus Rex Bavariæ, Richard Wagner, Alphonse Louis Constant, Friedrich Nietzsche, Hargrave Jennings, Carl Kellner, Forlong dux, Sir Richard Payne Knight, Paul Gaugin, Sir Richard Francis Burton, Doctor Gaerard Encausse, Doctor Theodor Reuss, and Sir Aleister Crowley - Oh Sons of the Lion and the Snake! with all thy saints we worthily commemorate them worthy that were and are and are to come.

May their Essence be hre present, potent, puissant and paternal to perfect this feast!

The PEOPLE: So mote it be.

The Earth

The DEACON: Mother of fertility on whose breast lieth water, whose cheek is caressed by air, and in whose heart is the sun's fire, womb of all life, recurring grace of seasons, answer favorably the prayer of labour, and to pastors and husbandmen be thou propitious.

The PEOPLE: So mote it be.

The Principles

The DEACON: Mysterious Energy, triform, mysterious Matter, in fourfold and sevenfold division, the interplay of which things weave the dance of the Veil of Life upon the Face of the Spirit, let there be Harmony and Beauty in your mystic loves, that in us may be health and wealth and strength and divine pleasure according to the Law of Liberty; let each pursue his Will as a strong man that rejoiceth in his way, as the course of a Star that blazeth for ever among the joyous company of Heaven.

The PEOPLE: So mote it be.

Birth

The DEACON: Be the hour auspicious, and the gate of life open in peace and in well-being, so that she that beareth children may rejoice, and the babe catch life with both hands.

The PEOPLE: So mote it be.

Marriage

The DEACON: Upon all that this day unite with love under will let fall success; may strength and skill unite to bring forth ecstasy, and beauty answer beauty.

The PE_PLE: So mote it be.

Death

The DEACON: Term of all that liveth, whose name is inscrutable, be favourable unto us in thine hour.

The PEOPLE: So mote it be.

The End

The DEACON: Unto them from whose eyes the veil of life hath fallen may there be granted the accomplishment of their true Wills; whether they will absorption in the Infinite, or to be united with their chosen and preferred, or to be in contemplation, or to be at peace, or to achieve the labour and heroism of incarnation on this planet or another, or in any Star, or aught else, unto them may there be granted the accomplishment of their wills; yea, the accomplishment of their wills. AUMGN. AUMGN. AUMGN.

The PEOPLE: So mote it be.

All sit.

The DEACON and the children attend the PRIEST and PRIESTESS, ready to hold any appropriate weapon as may be necessary.

VI: OF THE CONSECRATION OF THE ELEMENTS

The PRIEST makes the five crosses. 3 12 on paten and cup; 4 on paten alone; 5 on cup alone.

The PRIEST: Life of man upon earth, fruit of labour, sustenance of endeavour, thus be thou nourishment of the Spirit!

He touches the Host with the Lance.

By the virtue of the Rod

Be this bread the Body of God!

He takes the Host.

TOUTO 'ESTI TO SOMA MOU.

He kneels, adores, rises, turns shows Host to the PEOPLE, turns, replaces Host, and adores. Music. He takes the Cup.

Vehicle of the joy of Man upon earth, solace of labour, inspiration of endeavour, thus be thou ecstasy of the Spirit!

He touches the Cup with the Lance.

By the virtue of the Rod

Be this wine the Blood of God!

He takes the Cup.

TOUTO 'ESTI TO POTHRION TOU 'AIMATOS MOU.

He kneels, adores, rises, turns, shows the Cup to the PEOPLE, turns replaces the Cup, and adores. Music.

For this is the Covenant of Resurrection.

He makes the five crosses on the PRIESTESS.

Accept, O LORD, this sacrifice of life and joy, true warrants of the Covenant of Resurrection.

The PRIEST offers the Lance to the PRIESTESS, who kisses it; he then touches her between the breasts and upon the body. He then flings out his arms upward, as comprehending the whole shrine.

Let this offering be borne upon the waves of Aethyr to our Lord and Father the Sun that travelleth over the Heavens in his name ON.

He closes his hands, kisses the PRIESTESS between the breasts, and makes three great crosses over the Paten, the Cup, and himself. He strikes his breast. All repeat this action.

Hear ye all, saints of the true church of old time now essentially present, that of ye we claim heirship, with ye we claim communion, from ye we claim benediction in the name of IAO.

He makes three crosses on Paten and Cup together. He uncovers the Cup, genuflects, takes the Cup in his left hand and the Host in his right. With the Host he makes the five crosses on the Cup.

1

3 2

5 4

He elevates the Host and the Cup. The Bell strikes.

'AGIOS 'AGIOS 'AGIOS IAO.

He replaces the Host and the Cup, and adores.

VII: OF THE OFFICE OF THE ANTHEM

The PRIEST:

Thou who art I, beyond all I am,

Who hast no nature and no name,

Who art, when all but thou are gone,

Thou, centre and secret of the Sun,

Thou, hidden spring of all things known

And unknown, Thou aloof, alone,

Thou, the true fire within the reed

Brooding and breeding, source and seed

Of life, love, liberty, and light,

Thou beyond speech and beyond sight,

Thee I invoke, my faint fresh fire

Kindling as mine intents aspire.

Thee I invoke, abiding one,

Thee, centre and secret of the Sun,

And that most holy mystery

Of which the vehicle am I.

Appear, most awful and most mild,

As it is lawful, in thy child!

The CHORUS:

For of the Father and the Son

The Holy Spirit is the norm;

Male-female, quintessential, one,

Man-being veiled in woman-form.

Glory and worship in the highest,

Thou Dove, mankind that deifiest,

Being that race, most royally run

To spring sunshine through winter storm.

Glory and worship be to Thee,

Sap of the world-ash, wonder-tree!

First Semichorus, MEN:

Glory to thee from gilded tomb!

Second Semichorus, WOMEN:

Glory to thee from waiting womb!

MEN:

Glory to Thee from earth unploughed!

WOMEN:

Glory to Thee from virgin vowed!

MEN:

Glory to Thee, true Unity

Of the eternal Trinity!

WOMEN:

Glory to Thee, thou sire and dam

And self of I am that I am!

MEN:

Glory to Thee, beyond all term,

Thy spring of sperm, thy seed and germ!

WOMEN:

Glory to Thee, eternal Sun,

Thou One in Three, Thou Three in One!

CHORUS:

Glory and worship be to Thee,

Sap of the world-ash, wonder-tree!

(These words are to form the substance of the anthem; but the whole or any part thereof shall be set to music, which may be as elaborate as art can devise. But even should other anthems be authorized by the Father of the Church, this shall hold its place as the first of its kind, the father of all others.)

VIII: OF THE MYSTIC MARRIAGE AND CONSUMMATION OF THE ELEMENTS

The PRIEST takes the Paten between the index and medius of the right hand. The PRIESTESS clasps the Cup in her right hand.

The PRIEST: Lord most secret, bless this spiritual food unto our bodies, bestowing upon us health and wealth and strength and joy and peace, and that fulfilment of will and of love under will that is perpetual happiness.

He makes with Paten and kisses it. He uncovers the Cup, genuflects, rises. Music. He takes the Host, and breaks it over the Cup. He replaces the right-hand portion in the Paten. He breaks off a particle of the left-hand portion.

TOUTO ESTI TO SPERMA MOU. O PATHR ESTIN O HUIOS DIA TO PNEUMA 'AGION. AUMGN. AUMGN. AUMGN.

He replaces the left-hand part of the Host. The PRIESTESS extends the Lance-point with her left hand to receive the particle. The PRIEST clasps the Cup in his left hand. Together they depress the Lance-point in the Cup.

The PRIEST and the PRIESTESS: HRILIU.

The PRIEST takes the Lance. The PRIESTESS covers the Cup. The PRIEST genuflects, rises, bows, joins hands. He strikes his breast.

The PRIEST:

O Lion and O Serpent that destroy the destroyer, be mighty among us.

O Lion and O Serpent that destroy the destroyer, be mighty among us.

O Lion and O Serpent that destroy the destroyer, be mighty among us.

The PRIEST joins hands upon the breast of the PRIESTESS, and takes back his Lance. He turns to the Peoÿle, lowers and raises the Lance, and makes upon them.

Do what thou wilt shall be the whole of the Law.

The PEOPLE: Love is the law, love under will.

He lowers the Lance, and turns to East. The PRIESTESS takes the Lance in her right hand. With her left hand she offers the Paten. The PRIEST kneels.

The PRIEST: In my mouth be the essence of the life of the Sun!

He takes the Host with the right hand, makes with it on the Paten, and consumes it. Silence. The PRIESTESS takes, uncovers, and offers the Cup, as before.

The PRIEST: In my mouth be the essence of the joy of the earth!

He takes the Cup, makes on the PRIESTESS, drains it and returns it.

Silence. He rises, takes the Lance, and turns to the PEOPLE.

The PRIEST: There is no part of me that is not of the Gods.

(Those of the PEOPLE who intend to communicate, and none other should be present, having signified their intention, a whole Cake of Light, and a whole goblet of wine, have been prepared for each one. The DEACON marshals them; they advance one by one to the altar. The children take the Elements and offer them. The PEOPLE communicate as did the PRIEST, uttering the same words in an attitude of Resurrection: "There is no part of me that is not of the Gods." The exceptions to this part of the ceremony are when it is of the nature of a celebration, in which case none but the PRIEST communicate; or part of the ceremony of marriage, when none other, save the two to be married, partake; part of the ceremony of baptism, when only the child baptised partakes; and of Confirmation at puberty, when only the persons confirmed partake. The Sacrament may be reserved by the PRIEST, for administration to the sick in their homes.

The PRIEST closes all within the veil. With the Lance he makes crosses on the people thrice, thus.

The PRIEST:

The LORD bless you.

The LORD enlighten your minds and comfort your hearts and sustain your bodies.

The LORD bring you to the accomplishment of your true Wills, the Great Work, the Summum Bonum, True Wisdom and Perfect Happiness.

He goes out, the DEACON and children following, into the Tomb of the West.

Music. (Voluntary.)

Appendix VII

A few of the principal instructions authorised by the A.'.A.'.

Liber HHH sub figura CCCXLI.

CONTINET CAPITULA TRIA: MMM, AAA, ET SSS.

LIBER HHH SUB FIGURA CCCXLI. CONTINET CAPITULA TRIA: MMM, AAA, ET SSS.

Publication in Class D

I.

MMM. "I remember a certain holy day in the dusk of the Year, in the dusk of the Equinox of Osiris, when first I beheld thee visibly; when first the dreadful issue was fought out; when the Ibis-headed One charmed away the strife. I remember thy first kiss, even as a maiden should. Nor in the dark byways was there another: thy kisses abide." — *LIBER LAPIDIS LAZULI.* VII. 15. 16.

0. Be seated in thine Asana, wearing the robe of a Neophyte, the hood drawn.

It is night, heavy and hot, there are no stars. Not one breath of wind stirs the surface of the sea, that is thou. No fish play in thy depths.

Let a Breath rise and ruffle the waters. This also thou shalt feel playing upon thy skin. It will disturb thy meditation twice or thrice, after which thou shouldst have conquered this distraction. But unless thou first feel it, that Breath hath not arisen.

Next, the night is riven by the lightning flash. This also shalt thou feel in thy body, which shall shiver and leap with the shock, and that also must both be suffered and overcome.

After the lightning flash, resteth in the zenith a minute point of light. And that light shall radiate until a right cone be established upon the sea, and it is day.

With this thy body shall be rigid, automatically; and this shalt thou let endure, withdrawing thyself into thine heart in the form of an upright Egg of blackness; and therein shalt thou abide for a space.

When all this is perfectly and easily performed at will, let the aspirant figure to himself a struggle with the whole force of the Universe. In this he is only saved by his minuteness. But in the end he is overcome by Death, who covers him with a black cross.

Let his body fall supine with arms outstretched.

So lying, let him aspire fervently unto the Holy Guardian Angel.

Now let him resume his former posture.

Two and twenty times shall he figure to himself that he is bitten by a serpent, feeling even in his body the poison thereof. And let each bite be healed by an eagle or hawk, spreading its wings above his head, and dropping thereupon a healing dew. But let the last bite be so terrible a pang at the nape of the neck that he seemeth to die, and let the healing dew be of such virtue that he leapeth to his feet.

Let there be now placed within his egg a red cross, then a green cross, then a golden cross, then a silver cross; or those things which these shadow forth. Herein is silence; for he that hath rightly performed the meditation will understand the inner meaning hereof, and it shall serve as a test of himself and his fellows.

Let him now remain in the Pyramid or Cone of Light, as an Egg, but no more of blackness.

Then let his body be in the position of the Hanged Man, and let him aspire with all his force unto the Holy Guardian Angel.

The grace having been granted unto him, let him partake mystically of the Eucharist of the Five Elements and let him proclaim Light in Extension; yea, let him proclaim Light in Extension.

II

AAA "These loosen the swathings of the corpse; these unbind the feet of Osiris, so that the flaming God may rage through the firmament with his fantastic spear." ***Liber Lapidis Lazuli.*** **VII. 3.**

0. Be seated in thine Asana, or recumbent in Shavasana, or in the position of the dying Buddha.

Think of thy death; imagine the various diseases that may attack thee, or accidents overtake thee. Picture the process of death, applying always to thyself.

(A useful preliminary practice is to read textbooks of Pathology, and to visit museums and dissecting-rooms.)

Continue this practice until death is complete; follow the corpse through the stages of embalming, wrapping and burial.

Now imagine a divine breath entering thy nostrils.

Next, imagine a divine light enlightening the eyes.

Next, imagine the divine voice awakening the ears.

Next, imagine a divine kiss imprinted on the lips.

Next, imagine the divine energy informing the nerves and muscles of the body, and concentrate on the phenomenon which will already have been observed in 3, the restoring of the circulation.

Last, imagine the return of the reproductive power, and employ this to the impregnation of the Egg of light in which man is bathed.

Now represent to thyself that this Egg is the Disk of the Sun, setting in the west.

Let it sink into blackness, borne in the bark of heaven, upon the back of the holy cow Hathor. And it may be that thou shalt hear the moaning thereof.

Let it become blacker than all blackness. And in this meditation thou shalt be utterly without fear, for that the blankness that will appear unto thee is a thing dreadful beyond all thy comprehension.

And it shall come to pass that if thou hast well and properly performed this meditation that on a sudden thou shalt hear the drone and booming of a Beetle.

Now then shall the Blackness pass, and with rose and gold shalt thou arise in the East, with the cry of an Hawk resounding in thine ear. Shrill shall it be and harsh.

At the end shalt thou rise and stand in the mid-heaven, a globe of glory. And therewith shall arise the mighty Sound that holy men have likened unto the roaring of a Lion.

Then shalt thou withdraw thyself from the Vision, gathering thyself into the divine form of Osiris upon his throne.

Then shalt thou repeat audibly the cry of triumph of the god re-arisen, as it shall have been given unto thee by thy Superior.

And this being accomplished, thou mayest enter again into the Vision, that thereby shall be perfected in Thee.

After this shalt thou return into the Body, and give thanks unto the Most High God IAIDA, yea unto the Most High God IAIDA.

Mark well that this operation should be performed if it be possible in a place set apart and consecrated to the Works of the Magick of Light. Also that the Temple should be ceremonially open as thou hast knowledge and skill to perform, and that at the end thereof the closing should be most carefully accomplished. But in the preliminary practice it is enough to cleanse thyself by ablution, by robing, and by the rituals of the Pentagram and Hexagram.

0-2 should be practised at first, until some realisation is obtained; and the practice should always be followed by a divine invocation of Apollo or of Isis or of Jupiter or of Serapis.

Next, after a swift summary of 0-2 practice 3-7.

This being mastered, add 8.

Then add 9-13.

Then being prepared and fortified, well fitted for the work, perform the whole meditation at one time. And let this be continued until perfect success be attained therein. For this is a mighty meditation and holy, having power even upon Death, yea, having power even upon Death.

(Note by Fra. O.M. At any time during this meditation the concentration may bring about Samadhi. This is to be feared and shunned, more than any other breaking of control, for that it is the most tremendous of the forces which threaten to obsess. There is also some danger of acute delirious melancholia at point 1.)

III

SSS "Thou art a beautiful thing, whiter than a woman in the column of this vibration.

"I shoot up vertically like an arrow, and become that Above.

"But it is death, and the flame of the pyre.

"Ascend in the flame of the pyre, O my Soul!

"Thy God is like the cold emptiness of the utmost heaven, into which thou radiatest thy little light.

"When Thou shalt know me, O empty God, my flame shall utterly expire in thy great N.O.X."
***Liber Lapidis Lazuli.* I. 36-40.**

0. Be seated in thine Asana, preferably the Thunderbolt.

It is essential that the spine be vertical.

In this practice the cavity of the brain is the Yoni; the spinal cord is the Lingam.

Concentrate thy thought of adoration in the brain.

Now begin to awaken the spine in this manner. Concentrate thy thought of thyself in the base of the spine, and move it gradually up a little at a time.

By this means thou wilt become conscious of the spine, feeling each vertebra as a separate entity. This must be achieved most fully and perfectly before the further practice is begun.

Next, adore the brain as before, but figure to thyself its content as infinite. Deem it to be the womb of Isis, or the body of Nuit.

Next, identify thyself with the base of the spine as before, but figure to thyself its energy as infinite. Deem it to be the phallus of Osiris or the being of Hadit.

These two concentrations 4 and 5 may be pushed to the point of Samadhi. Yet lose not control of the will; let not Samadhi be thy master herein.

Now then, being conscious both of the brain and the spine, and unconscious of all else, do thou imagine the hunger of the one for the other; the emptiness of the brain, the ache of the spine, even as the emptiness of space and the aimlessness of Matter.

And if thou hast experience of the Eucharist in both kinds, it shall aid thine imagination herein.

Let this agony grow until it be insupportable, resisting by will every temptation. Not until thine whole body is bathed in sweat, or it may be in sweat of blood, and until a cry of intolerable anguish is forced from thy closed lips, shalt thou proceed.

Now let a current of light, deep azure flecked with scarlet, pass up and down the spine, striking as it were upon thyself that art coiled at the base as a serpent.

Let this be exceedingly slow and subtle; and though it be accompanied with pleasure, resist; and though it be accompanied with pain, resist.

This shalt thou continue until thou art exhausted, never relaxing the control. Until thou canst perform this one section 9 during a whole hour, proceed not. And withdraw from the meditation by an act of will, passing into a gentle Pranayama without Kumbhakham, and meditating on Harpocrates, the silent and virginal God.

Then at last, being well-fitted in body and mind, fixed in peace, beneath a favourable heaven of stars, at night, in calm and warm weather, mayst thou quicken the movement of the light until it be taken up by the brain and the spine, independently of thy will.

If in this hour thou shouldst die, is it not written, "Blessed are the dead that die in the Lord"? Yea, Blessed are the dead that die in the Lord!

Liber E vel Exercitiorum

sub figura IX

WEH NOTE: There are quite a few differences in text between this version and that published in EQUINOX I, 1. Most of these appear to be typo's or to be minor changes, especially to modernize punctuation or usage.

I

It is absolutely necessary that all experiments should be recorded in detail during, or immediately after, their performance.

It is highly important to note the physical and mental condition of the experimenter or experimenters.

The time and place of all experiments must be noted; also the state of the weather, and generally all conditions which might conceivably have any result upon the experiment either as adjuvants to or causes of the result, or as inhibiting it, or as sources of error.

The A.·. A.·. will not take official notice of any experiments which are not thus properly recorded.

It is not necessary at this stage for us to declare fully the ultimate end of our researches; nor indeed would it be understood by those who have not become proficient in these elementary courses.

The experimenter is encouraged to use his own intelligence, and not to rely upon any other person or persons, however distinguished, even among ourselves.

The written record should be intelligently *(WEH NOTE: EQUINOX I, 1 has "intelligibly".)* prepared so that others may benefit from its study.

The Book John St. John published in the first number of the "Equinox" is an example of this kind of record by a very advanced student. It is not as simply written as we could wish, but will show the method.

The more scientific the record is, the better. Yet the emotions should be noted, as being some of the conditions.

Let then the record be written with sincerity and care; thus with practice it will be found more and more to approximate to the ideal.

II

Physical clairvoyance

Take a pack of (78) Tarot playing cards. Shuffle; cut. Draw one card. Without looking at it, try to name it. Write down the card you name, and the actual card. Repeat, and tabulate results.

This experiment is probably easier with an old genuine pack of Tarot cards, preferably a pack used for divination by some one who really understood the matter.

Remember that one should expect to name the right card once in 78 times. Also be careful to exclude all possibilities of obtaining the knowledge through the ordinary senses of sight and touch, or even smell.

There was once a man whose fingertips were so sensitive that he could feel the shape and position of the pips and so judge the card correctly.

It is better to try first the easier form of the experiment, by guessing only the suit.

Remember that in 78 experiments you should obtain 22 trumps and 14 of each other suit; so that without any clairvoyance at all, you can guess right twice in 7 times (roughly) by calling trumps each time.

Note that some cards are harmonious.

Thus it would not be a bad error to call the five of Swords ("The Lord of Defeat") instead of the ten of Swords ("The Lord of Ruin"). But to call the Lord of Love (2 Cups) for the Lord of Strife (5 Wands) would show that you were getting nothing right.

Similarly a card ruled by Mars would be harmonious with a 5, a card of Gemini with "The Lovers".

These harmonies must be thoroughly learnt, according to the numerous tables given in 777.

As you progress you will find that you are able to distinguish the suit correctly three times in four and that very few indeed inharmonious errors occur, while in 78 experiments you are able to name the card aright as many as 15 or 20 times.

When you have reached this stage, you may be admitted for examination; and in the event of your passing you will be given more complex and difficult exercises.

III

Asana - Posture

You must learn to sit perfectly still with every muscle tense for long periods.

You must wear no garments that interfere with the posture in any of these experiments.

The first position: (The God). Sit in a chair; head up, back straight, knees together, hands on knees, eyes closed.

The second position: (The Dragon). Kneel; buttocks resting on the heels, toes turned back, back and head straight, hands on thighs.

The third position: (The Ibis). Stand, hold left ankle with right hand, *(WEH NOTE: The EQUINOX version adds: "(and alternately practise right ankle in left hand, &c.)".)* free forefinger on lips.

The fourth position: (The Thunderbolt). Sit; left heel pressing up anus, right foot poised on its toes, the heel covering the phallus; arms stretched out over the knees; head and back straight.

Various things will happen to you while you are practising these positions; they must be carefully analysed and described.

Note down the duration of practice; the severity of the pain (if any) which accompanies it, the degree of rigidity attained, and any other pertinent matters.

When you have progressed up to the point that a saucer filled to the brim with water and poised upon the head does not spill one drop during a whole hour, and when you can no longer perceive the slightest tremor in any muscle; when, in short, you are perfectly steady and easy, you will be admitted for examination; and, should you pass, you will be instructed in more complex and difficult practices.

IV

Pranayama - Regularisation of the Breathing

At rest in one of your positions, close the right nostril with the thumb of the right hand and breathe out slowly and completely through the left nostril, while your watch marks 20 seconds. Breathe in through the same nostril for 10 seconds. Changing hands, repeat with the other nostril. Let this be continuous for one hour.

When this is quite easy to you, increase the periods to 30 and 15 seconds.

When this is quite easy to you, but not before, breathe out for 15 seconds, in for 15 seconds, and hold the breath for 15 seconds.

When you can do this with perfect ease and comfort for a whole hour, practice breathing out for 40 and in for 20 seconds.

This being attained, practice breathing out for 20, in for 10, holding the breath for 30 seconds.

When this has become perfectly easy to you, you may be admitted for examination, and should you pass, you will be instructed in more complex and difficult practices.

You will find that the presence of food in the stomach, even in small quantities, makes the practices very difficult.

Be very careful never to overstrain your powers; especially never get so short of breath that you are compelled to breathe out jerkily or rapidly.

Strive after depth, fullness, and regularity of breathing.

Various remarkable phenomena will very probably occur during these practices. They must be carefully analysed and recorded.

V

Dharana - Control of Thought

Constrain the mind to concentrate itself upon a single simple object imagined.

The five tatwas are useful for this purpose; they are: a black oval; a blue disk; a silver crescent; a yellow square; a red triangle.

Proceed to combinations of simple objects; e.g. a black oval within a yellow square, and so on.

Proceed to simple moving objects, such as a pendulum swinging, a wheel revolving, etc. Avoid living objects.

Proceed to combinations of moving objects, e.g. a piston rising and falling while a pendulum is swinging. The relation between the two movements should be varied in different experiments.

Or even a system of flywheels, eccentrics, and governor.

During these practices the mind must be absolutely confined to the object determined upon; no other thought must be allowed to intrude upon the consciousness. The moving systems must be regular and harmonious.

Note carefully the duration of the experiments, the number and nature of the intruding thoughts, the tendency of the object itself to depart from the course laid out for it, and any other phenomena which may present themselves. Avoid overstrain; this is very important.

Proceed to imagine living objects; as a man, preferably some man known to, and respected by, yourself.

In the intervals of these experiments you may try to imagine the objects of the other senses, and to concentrate upon them.

For example, try to imagine the taste of chocolate, the smell of roses, the feeling of velvet, the sound of a waterfall or the ticking of a watch.

Endeavour finally to shut out all objects of any of the senses, and prevent all thoughts arising in your mind. When you feel you have attained some success in these practices, apply for examination, and should you pass, more complex and difficult practices will be prescribed for you.

VI

Physical limitations

It is desirable that you should discover for yourself your physical limitations.

To this end ascertain for how many hours you can subsist without food or drink before your working capacity is seriously interfered with.

Ascertain how much alcohol you can take, and what forms of drunkenness assail you.

Ascertain how far you can walk without once stopping; likewise with dancing, swimming, running, etc.

Ascertain for how many hours you can do without sleep.

Test your endurance with various gymnastic exercises, club swinging, and so on.

Ascertain for how long you can keep silence.

Investigate any other capacities and aptitudes which may occur to you.

Let all these things be carefully and conscientiously recorded; for according to your powers will it be demanded of you.

VII

A Course of Reading

The object of most of the foregoing practices will not at first be clear to you; but at least (who will deny it?) they have trained you in determination, accuracy, introspection, and many other qualities which are valuable to all men in their ordinary avocations, so that in no case will your time have been wasted.

That you may gain some insight into the nature of the Great Work which lies beyond these elementary trifles, however, we should mention that an intelligent person may gather more than a hint of its nature from the following books, which are to be taken as serious and learned contributions to the study of Nature, though not necessarily to be implicitly relied upon.

The Yi King (S.B.E. Series, Oxford University Press.)

The Tao Teh King (S.B.E. Series.)

Tannhauser, by A. Crowley.

The Upanishads.

The Bhagavad-Gita.

The Voice of the Silence.

Raja Yoga, by Swami Vivekananda.

The Shiva Sanhita.

The Aphorisms of Patanjali.

The Sword of Song.

The Book of the Dead.

Rituel et Dogme de la Haute Magie.

The Book of the Sacred Magic of Abramelin the Mage.

The Goetia.

The Hathayoga Pradipika.

The Spiritual Guide of Molinos.

Erdmann's *History of Philosophy.*

The Star in the West (Captain Fuller).

The Dhammapada (S.B.E. Series, Oxford University Press).

The Questions of King Milinda (S.B.E. Series).

777 vel Prolegomena, etc..

Varieties of Religious Experience (James).

Kabbala Denudata.

Konx Om Pax.

Careful study of these books will enable the pupil to speak in the language of his master, and facilitate communications with him.

The pupil should endeavour to discover the fundamental harmony of these very varied works; for this purpose he will find it best to study the most extreme divergencies side by side.

He may at any time that he wishes apply for examination in this course of reading.

During the whole of this elementary study and practice he will do wisely to seek out and attach himself to, a master, one competent to correct him and advise him. Nor should he be discouraged by the difficulty of finding such a person.

Let him further remember that he must in no wise rely upon, or believe in, that master. He must rely entirely upon himself, and credit nothing whatever but that which lies within his own knowledge and experience.

As in the beginning, so at the end, we here insist upon the vital importance of the written record as the only possible check upon error derived from the various qualities of the experimenter.

Thus let the work be accomplished duly; yea, let it be accomplished duly.

(If any really important or remarkable results should occur, or if any great difficulty presents itself, the A∴ A∴ should be at once informed of the circumstances.)

LIBER O

VEL

MANVS ET SAGITTAE

SVB FIGVR

VI

A.'. A.'. Publication in Class B.

Imprimatur:

D.D.S.Praemonstrator

O.S.V.Imperator

N.S.F.Cancellarius

These are all halftone photos of a single human in a black Tau robe, barefoot with hood completely closed over the face. The hood displays a six-pointed figure on the forehead — presumably the radiant eye of Horus of the A.'. A.'., but the rendition is too poor in detail. There is a cross pendant over the heart. The ten panels are numbered in white in the upper left, but the numerals are very dim even in the Ist edition (some blurred out entirely in the Weiser edition).

The panels are identified by two columns of numbered captions, 1 to 6 to the left and 7 to 10 to the right. The description is bottom to top and left to right:

"1. Earth: the god Set fighting." Frontal figure. Rt. foot pointed to the fore and angled slightly outward with weight on ball of foot. Lf. heel touching Rt. heel and foot pointed left. Arms form a diagonal with body, right above head and in line with left at waist height. Hands palmer and open with fingers outstretched and together. Head erect.

"2. Air: The god Shu supporting the sky." Frontal. Heels together and slightly angled apart to the front, flat on floor. Head down. Arms angled up on either side of head about head 1.5 ft. from head to wrist and crooked as if supporting a ceiling just at head height with the finger tips. The palms face upward and the backs of the hands away from the head. Thumbs closed to side of palms. Fingers straight and together.

"3. Water: the goddess Auramoth." Same body and foot position as #2, but head erect. Arms are brought down over the chest so that the thumbs touch above the heart and the backs of the hands are to the front. The fingers meet below the heart, forming between thumbs and fingers the descending triangle of water.

"4. Fire: the goddess Thoum-aesh-neith." Frontal. Head and body like #3. Arms are angled so that the thumbs meet in a line over the brow. Palmer side facing. Fingers meet above head, forming between thumbs and fingers the ascending triangle of fire.

"5,6. Spirit: the rending and closing of the veil." Head erect in both. #5 has the same body posture as #1, except that the left and right feet are countercharged and flat on the floor. Arms and hands are crooked forward at shoulder level such that the hands appear to be clawing open a split veil — hands have progressed to a point that the forearms are invisible, being directly pointed at the front. Upper arms are flat and horizontal in the plain of the image. #6. has the same body posture as #1, feet in same position as #1 but flat to the floor. The arms are elbow down against abdomen, with hands forward over heart in claws such that the knuckles are touching. Passing from #5 to #6 or vice versa is done by motion of shoulders and rotation of wrists. This is different from the other sign of opening the veil, the Sign of the Enterer, with is done with hands flat palm to palm and then spread without rotation of wrists.

"7-10. The L V X signs."

"7. + Osiris slain — the cross." Body and feet as in #2. Head bowed. Arms directly horizontal from the shoulders in the plane of the image. Hands with fingers together, thumbs to side of palm and palmer side forward. The tau shape of the robe dominates the image.

"8. L Isis mourning — the Svastica." The body is in semi-profile, head down slightly and facing right of photograph. The arms, hands, legs and feet are positioned to define a swastika. Left foot flat, carrying weight and angled toward the right of the photo. Right foot toe down behind the figure to the left in the photo. Right upper arm due left in photo and forearm vertical with fingers closed and pointing upward. Left arm smoothly canted down to the right of photo, with fingers closed and pointed down.

"9. V Typhon — the Trident." Figure frontal and standing on tip toe, toes forward and heals not touching. Head back. Arms angled in a "V" with the body to the top and outward in the plain of the photo. Fingers and thumbs as #7, but continuing the lines of the arms.

"10. X Osiris risen — the Pentagram." Body and feet as in #7. Head directly frontal and level. Arms crossed over heart, right over left with hands extended, fingers closed and thumb on side such that the palms rest on the two opposite shoulders.}

LIBER O

VEL

MANVS ET SAGITTAE

SVB FIGVRA

VI +

I.

1. This book is very easy to misunderstand; readers are asked to use the most minute critical care in the study of it, even as we have done in its preparation.

2. In this book it is spoken of the Sephiroth and the Paths; of Spirits and Conjurations; of Gods, Spheres, Planes, and many other things which may or may not exist.

It is immaterial whether these exist or not. By doing certain things certain results will follow; students are most earnestly warned against attributing objective reality or philosophic validity to any of them.

3. The advantages to be gained from them are chiefly these:

("a") A widening of the horizon of the mind.

("b") An improvement of the control of the mind.

4. The student, if he attains any success in the following practices, will find himself confronted by things (ideas or {13} beings) too glorious or too dreadful to be described. It is essential that he remain the master of all that he beholds, hears or conceives; otherwise he will be the slave of illusion, and the prey of madness.

Before entering upon any of these practices, the student should be in good health, and have attained a fair mastery of Asana, Pranayama and Dharana.

5. There is little danger that any student, however idle or stupid, will fail to get some result; but there is great danger that he will be led astray, obsessed and overwhelmed by his results, even though it be by those which it is necessary that he should attain. Too often, moreover, he mistaketh the first resting-place for the goal, and taketh off his armour as if he were a victor ere the fight is well begun.

It is desirable that the student should never attach to any result the importance which it at first seems to possess.

6. First, then, let us consider the Book "777" and its use; the preparation of the Place; the use of the Magic Ceremonies; and finally the methods which follow in Chapter V. "Viator in Regnis Arboris," and in Chapter VI. "Sagitta trans Lunam."

(In another book will it be treated of the Expansion and Contraction of Consciousness; progress by slaying the Chakkrams; progress by slaying the Pairs of Opposites; the methods of Sabhapaty Swami, &c., &c.)

II.

1. The student must FIRST obtain a thorough knowledge of "Book 777", especially of columns i., ii., iii., v.,

vi., vii., ix., xi., xii., xiv., xv., xvi., xvii., xviii., xix., xxxiv., xxxv., xxxviii., {14} xxxix., xl., xli., xlii., xlv., liv., lv., lix., lx., lxi., lxiii., lxx., lxxv., lxxvii., lxviii., lxxix., lxxx., lxxxi., lxxxiii., xcvii., xcviii., xcix., c., ci., cxvii., cxviii., cxxxvii., cxxxviii., cxxxix., clxxv., clxxvi., clxxvii., clxxxii.

When these are committed to memory, he will begin to understand the nature of these correspondences. ("See" Illustrations "The Temple of Solomon the King" in this number. Cross references are given.)

2. If we take an example, the use of the table will become clear.

Let us suppose that you wish to obtain knowledge of some obscure science.

In column xlv., line 12, you will find "Knowledge of Sciences."

By now looking up line 12 in the other columns, you will find that the Planet corresponding is Mercury, its number eight, its lineal figures the octagon and octagram. The God who rules that planet Thoth, or in Hebrew symbolism Tetragrammaton Adonai and Elohim Tzabaoth, its Archangel Raphael, its Choir of Angels Beni Elohim, its Intelligence Tiriel, its Spirit Taphtatharath, its colours Orange (for Mercury is the Sphere of the Sephira Hod, 8), Yellow, Purple, Grey, and Indigo rayed with Violet; its Magical Weapon the Wand or Caduceus, its Perfumes Mastic and others, its sacred plants Vervain and others, its jewel the Opal or Agate; its sacred animal the Snake, &c., &c.

3. You would then prepare your Place of Working accordingly. In an orange circle you would draw an eight-pointed star of yellow, at whose points you would place eight lamps. The Sigil of the Spirit (which is to be found in Cornelius {15} Agrippa and other books) you would draw in the four colours with such other devices as your experience may suggest.

4. And so on. We cannot here enter at length into all the necessary preparations; and the student will find them fully set forth in the proper books, of which the "Goetia" is perhaps the best example.

These rituals need not be slavishly imitated; on the contrary the student should do nothing the object of which he does not understand; also, if he have any capacity whatever, he will find his own crude rituals more effective than the highly polished ones of other people.

The general purpose of all this preparation is as follows:

5. Since the student is a man surrounded by material objects, if it be his wish to master one particular idea, he must make every material object about him directly suggest that idea. Thus in the ritual quoted, if his glance fall upon the lights, their number suggests Mercury; he smells the perfumes, and again Mercury is brought to his mind. In other words, the whole magical apparatus and ritual is a complex system of mnemonics.

[The importance of these lies principally in the fact that particular sets of images that the student may meet in his wanderings correspond to particular lineal figures, divine names, &c. and are controlled by them. As to the possibility of producing results external to the mind of the seer ("objective," in the ordinary common sense acceptation of the term) we are here silent.]

6. There are three important practices connected with all forms of ceremonial (and the two Methods which later we shall describe). These are: {16}

(1) Assumption of God-forms.

(2) Vibration of Divine Names.

(3) Rituals of "Banishing" and "Invoking".

These, at least, should be completely mastered before the dangerous Methods of Chapters V. and VI. are attempted.

III

1. The Magical Images of the Gods of Egypt should be made thoroughly familiar. This can be done by studying them in any public museum, or in such books as may be accessible to the student. They should then be carefully painted by him, both from the model and from memory.

2. The student, seated in the "God" position, or in the characteristic attitude of the God desired, should then imagine His image as coinciding with his own body, or as enveloping it. This must be practised until mastery of the image is attained, and an identity with it and with the God experienced.

It is a matter for very great regret that no simple and certain test of success in this practice exists.

3. The Vibration of God-names. As a further means of identifying the human consciousness with that pure portion of it which man calls by the name of some God, let him act thus:

4. ("a") Stand with arms outstretched. ("See" illustration.)

("b") Breathe in deeply through the nostrils, imagining the name of the God desired entering with the breath.

("c") Let that name descend slowly from the lungs to the heart, the solar plexus, the navel, the generative organs, and so to the feet. {17}

("d") The moment that it appears to touch the feet, quickly advance the left foot about 12 inches, throw forward the body, and let the hands (drawn back to the side of the eyes) shoot out, so that you are standing in the typical position of the God Horus,["See" Illustration in Vol. I. No. 1, "Blind Force."] and at the same time imagine the Name as rushing up and through the body, while you breathe it out through the nostrils with the air which has been till then retained in the lungs. All this must be done with all the force of which you are capable.

("e") Then withdraw the left foot, and place the right forefinger upon the lips, so that you are in the characteristic position of the God Harpocrates["See" Illustration in Vol. I. No. 1, "The Silent Watcher."]

5. It is a sign that the student is performing this correctly when a single "Vibration" entirely exhausts his physical strength. It should cause him to grow hot all over, or to perspire violently, and it should so weaken him that he will find it difficult to remain standing.

6. It is a sign of success, though only by the student himself is it perceived, when he hears the name of the God vehemently roared forth, as if by the concourse of ten thousand thunders; and it should appear to him as if that Great Voice proceeded from the Universe, and not from himself.

In both the above practices all consciousness of anything but the God-form and name should be absolutely blotted out; and the longer it takes for normal perception to return, the better. {18}

IV

I. The Rituals of the Pentagram and Hexagram must be committed to memory; they are as follows:

The Lesser Ritual of the Pentagram

(i) Touching the forehead say Ateh (Unto Thee).

(ii) Touching the breast say Malkuth (The Kingdom).

(iii) Touching the right shoulder, say ve-Geburah (and the Power).

(iv) Touching the left shoulder, say ve-Gedulah (and the Glory).

(v) Clasping the hands upon the breast, say le-Olahm, Amen (To the Ages, Amen).

(vi) Turning to the East make a pentagram (that of Earth) with the proper weapon (usually the Wand). Say ("i.e." vibrate) I H V H.

(vii) Turning to the South, the same, but say A D N I.

(viii) Turning to the West, the same, but say A H I H.

(ix) Turning to the North, the same, but say A G L A.

Pronounce: Ye-ho-wau, Adonai, Eheieh, Agla.

(x) Extending the arms in the form of a Cross say:

(xi) Before me Raphael;

(xii) Behind me Gabriel;

(xiii) On my right hand Michael.

(xiv) On my left hand Auriel;

(xv) For about me flames the Pentagram,

(xvi) And in the Column stands the six-rayed Star.

(xvii-xxi) Repeat (i) to (v), the Qabalistic Cross. {19}

The Greater Ritual of the Pentagram.

The Pentagrams are traced in the air with the sword or other weapon, the name spoken aloud, and the signs used, as illustrated.

THE PENTAGRAMS OF SPIRIT

The Signs of the Portal ("see" Illustrations): Extend the hands in front of you, palms outwards, separate them as if in the act of rending asunder a veil or curtain (actives), and then bring them together as if closing it up again and let them fall to the side (passives).

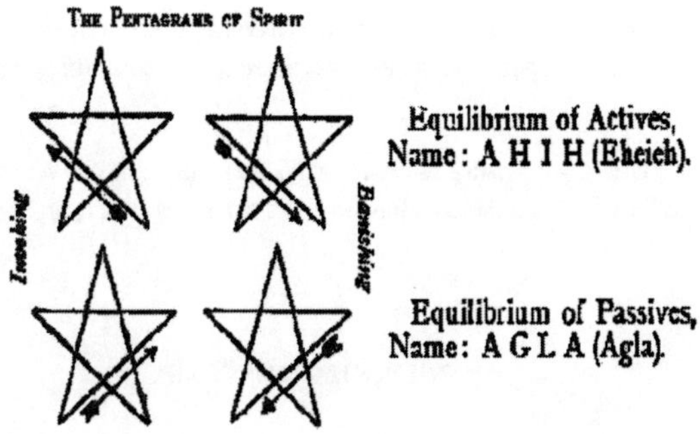

(The Grade of the "Portal" is particularly attributed to the element of Spirit; it refers to the Sun; the Paths of Samekh, Nun and Ayin, are attributed to this degree.<> See "777" lines 6 and 31 bis).

THE PENTAGRAMS OF FIRE.

{20} The signs of 4 Degree = 7 Square: Raise the arms above the head and join the hands, so that the tips of the fingers and of the thumbs meet, formulating a triangle ("See" illustration).

(The Grade of 4 Degree = 7 Square is particularly attributed to the element Fire; it refers to the planet Venus; the paths of Qof, Tzaddi and Peh are attributed to this degree. For other attributions "see" "777" lines 7 and 31).

THE PENTAGRAMS OF WATER.

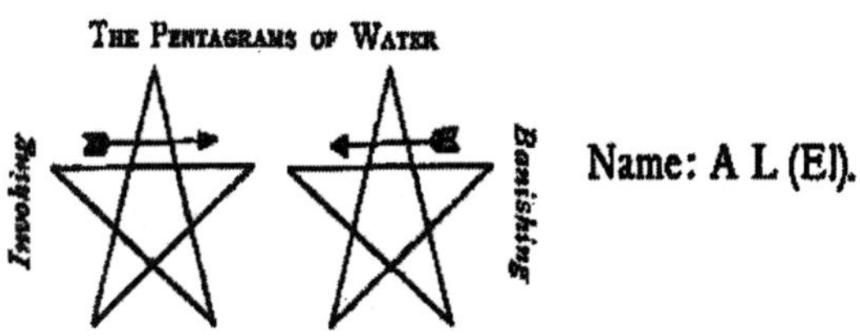

The signs of 3 Degree = 8 Square: Raise the arms till the elbows are on a level with the shoulders, bring the hands across the chest, touching the thumbs and tips of fingers so as to form a triangle apex downwards. ("See" illustration).

(The Grade of 3 Degree = 8 Square is particularly attributed to the element of Water; it refers to the planet Mercury; the paths of Resh and Shin are attributed to this degree. For other attributions "see" "777", lines 8 and 23).

THE PENTAGRAMS OF AIR.

The signs of 2 Degree = 9 Square: Stretch both arms upwards and outwards, the elbows bent at right angles, the hands bent back, the palms upwards as if supporting a weight. ("See" illustration). {21}

(The Grade of 2 Degree = 9 Square is particularly attributed to the element Air; it refers to the Moon; the path of Taw is attributed to this degree. For other attributions "see" "777" lines 9 and 11).

THE PENTAGRAMS OF EARTH

The Sign of 1 Degree = 10 Square: Advance the right foot, stretch out the right hand upwards and forwards, the left hand downwards and backwards, the palms open.

(The Grade of 1 Degree = 10 Square is particularly attributed to the element of Earth, "See" "777" lines 10 and 32 bis).

The Lesser Ritual of the Hexagram.

This ritual is to be performed after the "Lesser Ritual of the Pentagram".

(i) Stand upright, feet together, left arm at side, right across body, holding the wand or other weapon upright in the median line. Then face East and say:

(ii) I.N.R.I.

Yod. Nun. Resh. Yod.

Virgo, Isis, Mighty Mother.

Scorpio, Apophis, Destroyer.

Sol, Osiris, Slain and Risen.

Isis, Apophis, Osiris, IAO. {22}

(iii) Extend the arms in the form of a cross, and say: "The Sign of Osiris Slain." ("See" Illustration).

(iv) Raise the right arm to point upwards, keeping the elbow square, and lower the left arm to point downwards, keeping the elbow square, while turning the head over the left shoulder looking down so that the eyes follow the left forearm, and say, "The Sign of the Mourning of Isis." ("See" Illustration).

(v) Raise the arms at an angle of sixty degrees to each other above the head, which is thrown back, and say, "The Sign of Apophis and Typhon." ("See" Illustration).

(vi) Cross the arms on the breast, and bow the head and say, "The Sign of Osiris Risen." ("See" Illustration).

(vii) Extend the arms again as in (iii) and cross them again as in (vi) saying: "L.V.X., Lux, the Light of the Cross".

(viii) With the magical weapon trace the Hexagram of Fire in the East, saying, "Ararita" (Aleph-Resh-Aleph-Resh-Yod-Taw-Aleph). This Word consists of the initials of a sentence which means "One is His Beginning: One is His Individuality: His Permutation is One."

This hexagram consists of two equilateral triangles, both apices pointed upwards. Begin at the top of the upper {23} triangle and trace it in a dextro-rotary direction. The top of the lower triangle should coincide with the central point of the upper triangle.

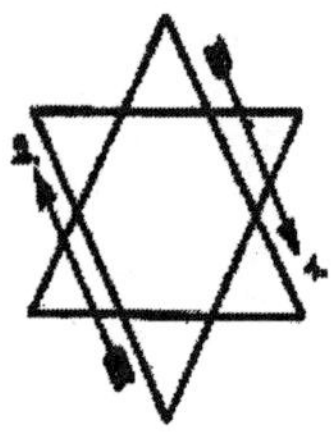

(ix) Trace the Hexagram of Earth in the South, saying "ARARITA." This Hexagram has the apex of the lower triangle pointing downwards, and it should be capable of inscription in a circle.

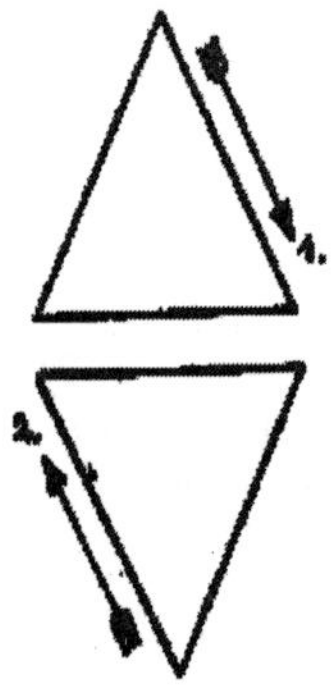

(x) Trace the Hexagram of Air in the West, saying "ARARITA." This Hexagram is like that of Earth; but the bases of the triangles coincide, forming a diamond.

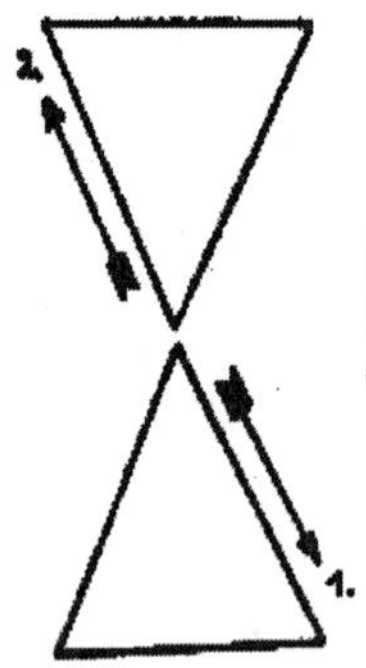

(xi) Trace the hexagram of Water in the North, saying "ARARITA." This hexagram has the lower triangle placed above the upper, so that their apices coincide.

(xii) Repeat (i-vii)

The Banishing Ritual is identical, save that the direction of the Hexagrams must be reversed. {24}

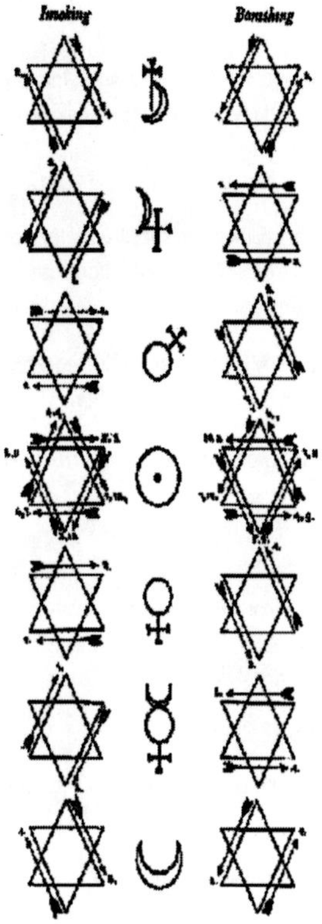

"The Greater Ritual of the Hexagram"

To invoke or banish planets or zodiacal signs.

The Hexagram of Earth alone is used. Draw the hexagram, Jupiter beginning from the point which is attributed to the planet you are dealing with. ("See" "777" col. lxxxiii).

Thus to invoke Jupiter begin from the Mars right-hand point of the lower triangle, dextro-rotary and complete; then trace the upper triangle from its left hand point and complete.

Trace the astrological sigi l of the planet in the centre of your hexagram.

For the Zodiac use the hexagram of the planet which rules the sign you require ("777", col. cxxxviii); but draw the astrological sigil of the sign, instead of that of the planet.

For Caput and Cauda Draconis use the lunar hexagram, with the sigil of Caput Draconis or Cauda Draconis.

To banish, reverse the hexagram.

In all cases use a conjuration first with Ararita, and next with the name of the God corresponding to the planet or sign you are dealing with.

The Hexagrams pertaining to the planets are as in plate on preceding page.

2. These rituals should be practised until the figures drawn appear in flame, in flame so near to physical flame that it would perhaps be visible to the eyes of a bystander, were one present. It is alleged that some persons have attained the power of actually kindling fire by these means. Whether this be so or not, the power is not one to be aimed at.

3. Success in "banishing" is known by a "feeling of cleanliness" in the atmosphere; success in "invoking" by a "feeling of holiness." It is unfortunate that these terms are so vague.

But at least make sure of this: that any imaginary figure or being shall instantly obey the will of the student, when he uses the appropriate figure. In obstinate cases, the form of the appropriate God may be assumed.

4. The banishing rituals should be used at the commencement of any ceremony whatever. Next, the student should use a general invocation, such as the "Preliminary Invocation" in the "Goetia" as well as a special invocation to suit the nature of his working.

5. Success in these verbal invocations is so subtle a {26} matter, and its grades so delicately shaded, that it must be left to the good sense of the student to decide whether or not he should be satisfied with his result.

V

1. Let the student be at rest in one of his prescribed positions, having bathed and robed with the proper decorum. Let the place of working be free from all disturbance, and let the preliminary purifications, banishings and invocations be duly accomplished, and, lastly, let the incense be kindled.

2. Let him imagine his own figure (preferably robed in the proper magical garments and armed with the proper magical weapons) as enveloping his physical body, or standing near to and in front of him.

3. Let him then transfer the seat of his consciousness to that imagined figure; so that it may seem to him that he is seeing with its eyes, and hearing with its ears.

This will usually be the great difficulty of the operation.

4. Let him then cause that imagined figure to rise in the air to a great height above the earth.

5. Let him then stop and look about him. (It is sometimes difficult to open the eyes.)

6. Probably he will see figures approaching him, or become conscious of a landscape.

Let him speak to such figures, and insist upon being answered, using the proper pentagrams and signs, as previously taught.

7. Let him travel about at will, either with or without guidance from such figure or figures. {27}

8. Let him further employ such special invocations as will cause to appear the particular places he may wish to visit.

9. Let him beware of the thousand subtle attacks and deceptions that he will experience, carefully testing the truth of all with whom he speaks.

Thus a hostile being may appear clothed with glory; the appropriate pentagram will in such a case cause him to shrivel or decay.

10. Practice will make the student infinitely wary in these matters.

11. It is usually quite easy to return to the body, but should any difficulty arise, practice (again) will make the imagination fertile. For example, one may create in thought a chariot of fire with white horses, and command the charioteer to drive earthwards.

It might be dangerous to go too far, or to stay too long; for fatigue must be avoided.

The danger spoken of is that of fainting, or of obsession, or of loss of memory or other mental faculty.

12. Finally, let the student cause his imagined body in which he supposes himself to have been travelling to coincide with the physical, tightening his muscles, drawing in his breath, and putting his forefinger to his lips. Then let him "awake" by a well-defined act of will, and soberly and accurately record his experiences.

It may be added that this apparently complicated experiment is perfectly easy to perform. It is best to learn by "travelling" with a person already experienced in the matter. Two or three experiments will suffice to render the student confident and even expert. See also "The Seer", pp. 295-333.

VI

1. The previous experiment has little value, and leads to few results of importance. But it is susceptible of a development which merges into a form of Dharana — concentration — and as such may lead to the very highest ends. The principal use of the practice in the last chapter is to familiarise the student with every kind of obstacle and every kind of delusion, so that he may be perfect master of every idea that may arise in his brain, to dismiss it, to transmute it, to cause it instantly to obey his will.

2. Let him then begin exactly as before, but with the most intense solemnity and determination.

3. Let him be very careful to cause his imaginary body to rise in a line exactly perpendicular to the earth's tangent at the point where his physical body is situated (or to put it more simply, straight upwards).

4. Instead of stopping, let him continue to rise until fatigue almost overcomes him. If he should find that he has stopped without willing to do so, and that figures appear, let him at all costs rise above them.

Yea, though his very life tremble on his lips, let him force his way upward and onward! 5. Let him continue in this so long as the breath of life is in him. Whatever threatens, whatever allures, though it were Typhon and all his hosts loosed from the pit and leagued against him, though it were from the very Throne of God Himself that a Voice issues bidding him stay and be content, let him struggle on, ever on.

6. At last there must come a moment when his whole {29} being is swallowed up in fatigue, overwhelmed by its own inertia.*

* This in case of failure. The results of success are so many and wonderful that no effort is here made to describe them. They are classified, tentatively, in the "Herb Dangerious," Part II., "infra".

Let him sink (when no longer can he strive, though his tongue by bitten through with the effort and the blood gush from his nostrils) into the blackness of unconsciousness; and then, on coming to himself, let him write down soberly and accurately a record of all that hath occurred, yea a record of all that hath occurred.

EXPLICIT

[A book of Elementary Invocations is in preparation, and will be issued in Number 3.]

ASTARTE

vel

Liber BERYLLI

sub figura CLXXV

A.·. A.·.

Publication in Class B.

Imprimatur:

N. Fra A.·. A.·.

0. This is the Book of Uniting Himself to a particular Deity by devotion.

1. *Considerations before the Threshold.* First concerning the choice of a particular Deity. This matter is of no import, sobeit that thou choose one suited to thine own highest nature. Howsoever, this method is not so suitable for gods austere as Saturn, or intellectual as Thoth. But for such deities as in themselves partake in anywise of love it is a perfect mode.

2. *Concerning the prime method of this Magick Art.* Let the devotee consider well that although Christ and Osiris be one, yet the former is to be worshipped with Christian, and the latter with Egyptian rites. And this although the rites themselves are ceremonially equivalent. There should, however, be *one* symbol declaring the transcending of such limitations; and with regard to the Deity also, there should be some *one* affirmation of his identity both with all other similar gods of other nations, and with the Supreme of whom all are but partial reflections.

3. *Concerning the chief place of devotion.* This is the Heart of the Devotee, and should be symbolically represented by that room or spot which he loves best. And the dearest spot therein shall be the shrine of his temple. It is most convenient if this shrine and altar should be sequestered in woods, or in a private grove, or garden. But let it be protected from the profane.

4. *Concerning the Image of the Deity.* Let there be an image of the Deity; first because in meditation there is mindfulness induced thereby; and second because a certain power enters and inhabits it by virtue of the ceremonies; or so it is said, and We deny it not. Let this image be the most beautiful and perfect which the devotee is able to procure; or if he be able to paint or to carve the same, it is all the better. As for Deities with whose nature no Image is compatible, let them be worshipped in an empty shrine. Such are Brahma, and Allah. Also some postcaptivity conceptions of Jehovah.

5. *Further concerning the shrine.* Let this shrine be furnished approÿriately as to its ornaments, according to the book 777. With ivy and pine-cones, that is to say, for Bacchus, and let lay before him both grapes and wine. So also for Ceres let there be corn, and cakes; or for Diana moon-wort and pale herbs, and

pure water. Further it is well to support the shrine with talismans of the planets, signs and elements appropriate. But these should be made according to the right Ingenium of the Philosophus by the light of the Book 777 during the course of his Devotion. It is also well, nevertheless, if a magick circle with the right signs and names be made beforehand.

6. *Concerning the Ceremonies.* Let the Philosophus prepare a powerful Invocation of the particular Deity according to his Ingenium. But let it consist of these several parts:

   First, an Imprecation, as of a slave unto his Lord.
   Second, an Oath, as of a vassal to his Liege.
   Third, a Memorial, as of a child to his Parent.
   Fourth, an Orison, as of a Priest unto his God.
   Fifth, a Colloquy, as of a Brother with his Brother.
   Sixth, a Conjuration, as to a Friend with his Friend.
   Seventh, a Madrigal, as of a Lover to his Mistress.

   And mark well that the first should be of awe, the second of fealty, the third of dependence, the fourth of adoration, the fifth of confidence, the sixth of comradeship, the seventh of passion.

7. *Further concerning the ceremonies.* Let then this Invocation be the principal part of an ordered ceremony. And in this ceremony let the Philosophus in no wise neglect the service of a menial. Let him sweep and garnish the place, sprinkling it with water or with wine as is appropriate to the particular Deity, and consecrating it with oil, and with such ritual as may seem him best. And let all be done with intensity and minuteness.

8. *Concerning the period of devotion, and the hours thereof.* Let a fixed period be set for the worship; and it is said that the least time is nine days by seven, and the greatest seven years by nine. And concerning the hours, let the Ceremony be performed every day thrice, or at least once, and let the sleep of the Philosophus be broken for some purpose of devotion at least once in every night.

   Now to some it may seem best to appoint fixed hours for the ceremony, to others it may seem that the ceremony should be performed as the spirit moves them so to do: for this there is no rule.

9. *Concerning the Robes and Instruments.* The Wand and Cup are to be chosen for this Art; never the Sword or Dagger, never the Pantacle, unless that Pantacle chance to be of a nature harmonious. But even so it is best to keep the Wand and Cup, and if one must choose, the Cup.

   For the Robes, that of a Philosoÿhus, or that of an Adept Within is most suitable; or, the robe best fitted for the service of the particular Deity, as a bassara for Bacchus, a white robe for Vesta. So also, for Vesta, one might use for instrument the Lamp; or the sickle, for Chronos.

10. *Concerning the Incense and Libations.* The incense should follow the nature of the particular Deity; as, mastic for Mercury, dittany for Persephone. Also the libations, as, a decoction of nightshade for Melancholia, or of Indian hemp for Uranus.

11. *Concerning the harmony of the ceremonies.* Let all these things be rightly considered, and at length, in language of the utmost beauty at the command of the Philosophus, accompanied, if he has skill, by music, and interwoven, if the particular Deity be jocund, with dancing. And all being carefully prepared and rehearsed, let it be practised daily until it be wholly rhythmical with his aspiration, and as it were, a part of his being.

12. *Concerning the variety of the ceremonies.* Now, seeing that every man differeth essentially from every other man, albeit in essence he is identical, let also these ceremonies assert their identity by their diversity. For this reason do We leave much herein to the right Ingenium of the Philosophus.

13. *Concerning the life of the devotee.* First, let his way of life be such as is pleasing to the particular Deity. Thus to invoke Neptune, let him go a-fishing; but if Hades, let him not approach the water that is hateful to Him.

14. *Further, concerning the life of the devotee.* Let him cut away from his life any act, word, or thought, that is hateful to the particular Deity; as, unchastity in the case of Artemis, evasions in the case of Ares. Besides this, he should avoid all harshness or unkindness of any kind in thought, word, or deed, seeing that above the particular Deity is One in whom all is One. Yet also he may deliberately practise cruelties, where the particular Deity manifests His Love in that manner, as in the case of Kali, and of Pan. And therefore, before the beginning of his period of devotion, let him practise according to the rules of Liber Jugorum.

15. *Further concerning the life of the devotee.* Now, as many are fully occupied with their affairs, let it be known that this method is adaptable to the necessities of all.

    And We bear witness that this which followeth is the Crux and Quintessence of the whole Method.

    First, if he have no Image, let him take anything soever, and consecrate it as an Image of his God. Likewise with his robes and instruments, his suffumigations and libations: for his Robe hath he not a nightdress; for his instrument a walking stick; for his suffumigation a burning match; for his libation a glass of water?

    But let him consecrate each thing that he useth to the service of that particular Deity, and not profane the same to any other use.

16. *Continuation.* Next, concerning his time, if it be short. Let him labour mentally upon his Invocation, concentrating it, and let him perform this Invocation in his heart whenever he hath the leisure. And let him seize eagerly upon every opportunity for this.

17. *Continuation.* Third, even if he have leisure and preparation, let him seek ever to bring inward the symbols, so that even in his well ordered shrine the whole ceremony revolve inwardly in his heart, that is to say in the temple of his body, of which the outer temple is but an image. For in the brain is the shrine, and there is no Image therein; and the breath of man is the incense and the libation.

18. *Continuation.* Further concerning occupation. Let the devotee transmute within the alembic of his heart every thought, or word, or act into the spiritual gold of his devotion.

    As thus: eating. Let him say: "I eat this food in gratitude to my Deity that hath sent it to me, in order to gain strength for my devotion to Him."
    Or: sleeping. Let him say: "I lie down to sleep, giving thanks for this blessing from my Deity, in order that I may be refreshed for new devotion to Him."
    Or: reading. Let him say: "I read this book that I may study the nature of my Deity, that further knowledge of Him may inspire me with deeper devotion to Him."
    Or: working. Let him say: "I drive my spade into the earth that fresh flowers (fruit, or what not) may spring up to His glory, and that I, purified by toil, may give better devotion to Him."
    Or: whatever it may be that he is doing, let him reason it out in his own mind, drawing it

through circumstance and circumstance to that one end and conclusion of the matter. And let him not perform the act until he hath done this.

As it is written: Liber VII, cap. v. —

22. *Every breath, every word, every thought is an act of love with thee.*

23. *The beat of my heart is the pendulum of love.*

24. *The songs of me are the soft sighs:*

25. *The thoughts of me are very rapture:*

26. *And my deeds are the myriads of Thy Children, the stars and the atoms.*

And Remember Well, that if thou wert in truth a lover, all this wouldst thou do of thine own nature without the slightest flaw or failure in the minutest part thereof.

19. *Concerning the Lections.* Let the Philosoÿhus read solely in his copies of the holy books of Thelema, during the whole period of his devotion. But if he weary, then let him read books which have no part whatever in love, as for recreation.

But let him copy out each verse of Thelema which bears upon this matter, and ponder them, and comment thereupon. For therein is a wisdom and a magic too deep to utter in any other wise.

20. *Concerning the Meditations.* Herein is the most potent method of attaining unto the End, for him who is thoroughly prepared, being purified by the practice of the Transmutation of deed into devotion, and consecrated by the right performance of the holy ceremonies. Yet herein is danger, for that the Mind is fluid as quicksilver, and bordereth upon the Abyss, and is beset by many sirens and devils that seduce and attack it to destroy it. Therefore let the devotee beware, and precise accurately his meditations, even as a man should build a canal from sea to sea.

21. *Continuation.* Let then the Philosophus meditate upon all love that hath ever stirred him. There is the love of David and of Jonathan, and the love of Abraham and Isaac, and the love of Lear and Cordelia, and the love of Damon and Pythias, and the love of Sappho and Atthis, and the love of Romeo and Juliet, and the love of Dante and Beatrice, and the love of Paolo and Francesca, and the love of Caesar and Lucrezia Borgia, and the love of Aucassin and Nicolette, and the love of Daphnis and Chloe, and the love of Cornelia and Caius Gracchus, and the love of Bacchus and Ariadne, and the love of Cupid and Psyche, and the love of Endymion and Artemis, and the love of Demeter and Persephone, and the love of Venus and Adonis, and the love of Lakshmi and Vishnu, and the love of Siva and Bhavani, and the love of Buddha and Ananda, and the love of Jesus and John, and many more.

Also there is the love of many saints for their particular deity, as of St. Francis of Assisi for Christ, of Sri Sabhapaty Swami for Maheswara, of Abdullah Haji Shirazi for Allah, of St Ignatius Loyola for Mary, and many more.

Now do thou take one such story every night, and enact it in thy mind, grasping each identity with infinite care and zest, and do thou figure thyself as one of the lovers and thy Deity as the other. Thus do thou pass through all adventures of love, not omitting one; and to each do thou conclude: How pale a reflection is this of my love for this Deity!

Yet from each shalt thou draw some knowledge of love, some intimacy with love, that shall aid thee to perfect thy love. Thus learn the humility of love from one, its obedience from another, its intensity from a third, its purity from a fourth, its peace from yet a fifth.

So then thy love being made perfect, it shall be worthy of that perfect love of His.

22. *Further concerning meditation.* Moreover let the Philosophus imagine to himself that he hath indeed succeeded in his devotion, and that his Lord hath appeared to him, and that they converse as may be fitting.

23. *Concerning the Mysterious Triangle.* Now then as three cords separately may be broken by a child, while those same cords duly twisted may bind a giant, let the Philosophus learn to entwine these three methods of Magic into a Spell.

To this end let him understand that as they are One, because the end is one, so are they One because the method is One, even the method of turning the mind toward the particular Deity by love in every act.

And lest thy twine slip, here is a little cord that wrappeth tightly round and round all, even the Mantram or Continuous Prayer.

24. *Concerning the Mantram or Continuous Prayer.* Let the Philosophus weave the Name of the Particular Deity into a sentence short and rhythmical, as, for Artemis: epsilon-pi-epsilon-lambda-theta-omicron-nu, epsilon-pi-epsilon-lambda-theta-omicron-nu, Alpha-rho-tau-epsilon-mu-iota-sigma; or, for Shiva: Namo Shivaya namaha Aum; or, for Mary: Ave Maria; or for Pan, chi-alpha-iota-rho-epsilon Sigma-omega-tau-eta-rho kappa-omicron-sigma-mu-omicron-upsilon, Iota-omega Pi-alpha-nu, Iota-omega Pi-alpha-nu; or, for Allah: Hua Allahu alazi lailaha illa Hua.

Let him repeat this day and night without cessation mechanically in his brain, which is thus made ready for the advent of that Lord, and armed against all other.

25. *Concerning the Active and the Passive.* Let the Philosophus change from the active love of his particular Deity to a state of passive waiting, even almost a repulsion, the repulsion not of distaste, but of sublime modesty.

As it is written, Liber LXV.ii.59. I have called unto Thee, and I have journeyed unto Thee, and it availed me not. 60. I waited patiently, and Thou wast with me from the beginning.

Then let him change back to the Active, until a veritable rhythm is established between the states, as it were the swinging of a Pendulum. But let him reflect that a vast intelligence is required for this; for he must stand as it were almost without himself to watch those phases of himself, And to do this is a high Art, and pertaineth not altogether to the grade of Philosoÿhus. Neither is it of itself helpful, but rather the reverse, in this especial practice.

26. *Concerning silence.* Now there may come a time in the course of this practice when the outward symbols of devotion cease, when the soul is as it were dumb in the presence of its God. Mark that this is not a cessation, but a transmutation of the barren seed of prayer into the green shoot of yearning. This yearning is spontaneous, and it shall be left to grow, whether it be sweet or bitter. For often times it is as the torment of hell in which the soul burns and writhes unceasingly. Yet it ends, and at its end continue openly thy Method.

27. *Concerning Dryness.* Another state wherein at times the soul may fall is this dark night. And this is indeed purifying in such depths that the soul cannot fathom it. It is less like pain than like death. But it is the necessary death that comes before the rising of a body glorified.

This state must be endured with fortitude; and no means of alleviating it may be employed. It may be broken up by the breaking up of the whole Method, and a return to the world without. This cowardice not only destroys the value of all that has gone before, but destroys the value of the Oath of Fealty that thou hast sworn, and makes thy Will a mockery to men and gods.

28. *Concerning the Deceptions of the Devil.* Note well that in this state of dryness a thousand seductions will lure thee away; also a thousand means of breaking thine oath in spirit without breaking it in letter. Against this thou mayst repeat the words of thine oath aloud again and again until the temptation be overcome.

Also the devil will represent to thee that it were much better for this operation that thou do thus and thus, and seek to affright thee by fears for thy health or thy reason.

Or he may send against thee visions worse than madness.

Against all this there is but one remedy, the Discipline of thine Oath. So then thou shalt go through ceremonies meaningless and hideous to thee, and blaspheme shalt thou against thy Deity and curse Him. And this mattereth little, for it is not thou, so be that thou adhere to the Letter of thine Obligation. For thy Spiritual Sight is closed, and to trust it is to be led unto the precipice, and hurled therefrom.

29. *Further of this matter.* Now also subtler than all these terrors are the Illusions of Success. For one instant's {WEH NOTE: Magick in Theory and Practice has "But one instant's..."} self-satisfaction or Expansion of thy Spirit, especially in this state of dryness, and thou art lost. For thou mayst attain the False Union with the Demon himself. Beware also of even the pride which rises from having resisted the temptations.

But so many and so subtle are the wiles of Choronzon that the whole world could not contain their enumeration.

The answer to one and all is the persistence in the literal fulfilment of the routine. Beware, then, last, of that devil {49} who shall whisper in thine ear that the letter killeth, but the spirit giveth life, and answer: Except a corn of wheat fall into the ground, and die, it abideth alone, but if it die, it bringeth forth much fruit.

Yet shalt thou also beware of disputation with the devil, and pride in the cleverness of thine answers to him. Therefore, if thou hast not lost the power of silence, let it be first and last employed against him.

30. *Concerning the Enflaming of the Heart.* Now learn that thy methods are dry, one and all. Intellectual exercises, moral exercises, they are not Love. Yet as a man, rubbing two dry sticks together for long, suddenly found a spark, so also from time to time will true love leap unasked into thy mediation. Yet this shall die and be reborn again and again. It may be that thou hast no tinder near.

In the end shall come suddenly a great flame and a devouring, and burn thee utterly.

Now of these sparks, and of these splutterings of flame, and of these beginnings of the Infinite Fire, thou shalt thus be aware. For the sparks thy heart shall leap up, and thy ceremony or meditation or toil shall seem of a sudden to go of its own will; and for the little flames this shall be increased in volume and intensity; and for the beginnings of the Infinite Fire thy ceremony shall be caught up unto ravishing song, and thy meditation shall be ecstasy, and thy toil shall be a delight exceeding all pleasure thou hast ever known.

And of the Great Flame that answereth thee it may not be spoken; for therein is the End of this Magick

Art of Devotion.

31. *Considerations with regard to the use of symbols.* It is to be noted that persons of powerful imagination, will, and intelligence have no need of these material symbols. There have been certain saints who are capable of love for an idea as such without it being otherwise than degraded by "idolising" it, to use this word in its true sense. Thus one may be impassioned of beauty, without even the need of so small a concretion of it as "The beauty of Apollo", the "beauty of roses", the "beauty of Attis". Such persons are rare; it may be doubted whether Plato himself attained to any vision of absolute beauty without attaching to it material objects in the first place. A second class is able to contemplate ideals through this veil; a third class need a double veil, and cannot think of the beauty of a rose without a rose before them. For such is this Method of most use; yet let them know that there is this danger therein, that they may mistake the gross body of the symbol for the idea made concrete thereby.

32. *Considerations of further danger to those not purged of material thought.* Let it be remembered that in the nature of the love itself is danger. The lust of the satyr for the nymph is indeed of the same nature as the affinity of Quicklime for water on the one hand, and of love of Ab for Ama on the other; so also is the triad Osiris, Isis, Horus like that of a horse, mare, foal, and of red, blue, purple. And this is the foundation of Correspondences.

But it were false to say "Horus is a foal" or "Horus is purple". One may say: "Horus resembles a foal in this respect, that he is the offspring of two complementary beings".

33. *Further of this matter.* So also many have said truly that all is one, and falsely that since earth is That One, and ocean is That One, therefore earth is ocean. Unto Him good is illusion, and evil is illusion; therefore good is evil. By this fallacy of logic are many men destroyed.

Moreover, there are those who take the image for the God; as who should say, my heart is in Tiphereth, and an Adeptus is in Tiphereth; I am therefore an adept.

And in this practice the worst danger is this, that the love which is its weapon should fail in one of two ways.

First, if the love lack any quality of love, so long is it not ideal love. For it is written of the Perfected One: "There is no member of my body which is not the member of some god." Therefore let not the Philosophus despise any form of love, but harmonise all. As it is written: Liber LXV, 32. "So therefore Perfection abideth not in the Pinnacles or in the Foundation, but in the harmony of One with all."

Second, if any part of this love exceed, there is disease therein. As, in the love of Othello for Desdemona, love's jealousy overcame love's tenderness, so may it be in this love of a particular Deity. And this is more likely, since in this divine love no element may be omitted.

It is by virtue of this completeness that no human love may in any way attain to more than to foreshadow a little part thereof.

34. *Concerning Mortifications.* These are not necessary to this method. On the contrary, they may destroy the concentration, as counter-irritants to, and so alleviations of, the supreme mortification which is the Absence of the Deity invoked.

Yet as in mortal love arises a distaste for food, or a pleasure in things naturally painful, this perversion should be endured and allowed to take its course. Yet not to the interference with natural bodily health, whereby the instrument of the soul might be impaired.

And concerning sacrifices for love's sake, they are natural to this Method, and right.

But concerning voluntary privations and tortures, without use save as against the devotee, they are generally not natural to healthy natures, and wrong. For they are selfish. To scourge one's self serves not one's master; yet to deny one's self bread that one's child may have cake is the act of a true mother.

35. *Further concerning Mortifications.* If thy body, on which thou ridest, be so disobedient a beast that by no means will he travel in the desired direction, or if thy mind be baulkish and eloquent as Balaam's fabled Ass, then let the practice be abandoned. Let the shrine be covered in sackcloth, and do thou put on habits of lamentation, and abide alone. And do thou return most austerely to the practice of Liber Jugorum, testing thyself by a standard higher than that hitherto accomplished, and punishing effractions with a heavier goad. Nor do thou return to thy devotion until that body and mind are tamed and trained to all manner of peaceable going.

36. *Concerning minor methods adjuvant in the ceremonies. I. Rising on the planes.* By this method mayst thou assist the imagination at the time of concluding thine Invocation. Act as taught in Liber O, by the light of Liber 777.

37. *Concerning minor methods adjuvant in the ceremonies. II. Talismanic Magic.* Having made by thine Ingenium a talisman or pantacle to represent the particular Deity, and consecrated it with infinite love and care, do thou burn it ceremonially before the shrine, as if thereby giving up the shadow for the substance. But it is useless to do this unless thou do really in thine heart value the talisman beyond all else that thou hast.

38. *Concerning minor methods adjuvant in the ceremonies. III. Rehearsal.* It may assist if the traditional history of the particular Deity be rehearsed before him; perhaps this is best done in dramatic form. This method is the main one recommended in the "Exercitios Espirituales" of St Ignatius, whose work may be taken as a model. Let the Philosophus work out the legend of his own particular Deity, and apportioning days to events, live that life in imagination, exercising the five senses in turn, as occasion arises.

39. *Concerning minor matters adjuvant in the ceremonies. IV. Duresse.* This method consists in cursing a deity recalcitrant; as, threatening ceremonially "to burn the blood of Osiris, and to grind down his bones to power." This method is altogether contrary to the spirit of love unless the particular Deity be himself savage and relentless; as Jehovah or Kali. In such a case the desire to perform constraint and cursing may be the sign of the assimilation of the spirit of the devotee with that of his God, and so an advance to the Union with HIm.

40. *Concerning the value of this particular form of Union or Samadhi.* All Samadhi is defined as the ecstatic union of a subject and object in consciousness, with the result that a third thing arises which partakes in no way of the nature of the two.

It would seem at first sight that it is of no importance whatever to choose an object of meditation. For example, the Samadhi called Atmadarshana might arise from simple concentration of the thought on an imagined triangle, or on the heart.

But as the union of two bodies in chemistry may be endothermic or exothermic, the combination of Oxygen with Nitrogen is gentle, while that of Oxygen with Hydrogen is explosive; and as it is found that the most heat is disengaged as a rule by the union of bodies most opposite in character, and that the compound resulting from such is most stable, so it seems reasonable to suggest that the most important and enduring Samadhi results from the contemplation of the Object most npposite to the devotee. [On other planes, it has been suggested that the most opposed types make the best marriages and produce the healthiest children. The greatest pictures and operas are those in which violent extremes are blended, and so generally in every field of activity. Even in mathematics, the greatest parallelogram is formed if the lines composing it are set at right angles. ED.]

41. *Conclusions from the foregoing.* It may then be suggested to the Philosophus, that although his work will be harder his reward will be greater if he choose a Deity most remote from his own nature. This method is harder and higher than that of Liber E. For a simple object as there suggested is of the same nature as the commonest things of life, while even the meanest Deity is beyond uninitiated human understanding. On the same plane, too, Venus is nearer to man than Aphrodite, Aphrodite than Isis, Isis than Babalon, Babalon than Nuit.

Let him decide therefore according to his discretion on the one hand and his aspiration on the other; and let not one outrun his fellow.

42. *Further concerning the value of this Method.* Certain objections arise. Firstly, in the nature of all human love is illusion, and a certain blindness. Nor is there any true love below the Veil of the Abyss. For this reason we give this method to the Philosoÿhus, as the reflection of the Exempt Adept, who reflects the Magister Templi and the Magus. Let then the Philosophus attain this Method as a foundation of the higher Methods to be given to him when he attains those higher grades.

Another objection lies in the partiality of this Method. This is equally a defect characteristic of the Grade.

43. *Concerning a notable danger of Success.* It may occur that owing to the tremendous power of the Samadhi, overcoming all other memories as it should and does do, that the mind of the devotee may be obsessed, so that he declare his particular Deity to be sole God and Lord. This error has been the foundation of all dogmatic religions, and so the cause of more misery than all other errors combined.

The Philosophus is peculiarly liable to this because from the nature of the Method he cannot remain sceptical; he must for the time believe in his particular Deity. But let him (1) consider that this belief is only a weapon in his hands, (2) affirm sufficiently that his Deity is but an emanation or reflection or eidolon of a Being beyond him, as was said in Paragraph 2. For if he fail herein, since man cannot remain permanently in Samadhi, the memorised Image in his mind will be degraded, and replaced by the corresponding Demon, to his utter ruin.

Therefore, after Success, let him not delight overmuch in his Deity, but rather busy himself with his other work, not permitting that which is but a step to become a goal. As it is written also, Liber CLXXXV.: "remembering that Philosophy is the Equilibrium of him that is in the House of Love."

44. *Concerning the secrecy and the rites of Blood.* During this practice it is most wise that the Philosophus utter no word concerning his working, as if it were a Forbidden Love that consumeth him. But let him answer fools according to their folly; for since he cannot conceal his love from his fellows, he must speak to them as they may understand.

And as many Deities demand sacrifice, one of men, another of cattle, a third of doves, let these sacrifices be replaced by the true sacrifices in thine own heart. Yet if thou must symbolise them outwardly for the hardness of thine heart, let thine own blood, and not another's, be spilt before that altar. [The exceptions to this rule pertain neither to this practice, nor to this grade. N. Fra. A.·. A.·..]

Nevertheless, forget not that this practice is dangerous, and may cause the manifestation of evil things, hostile and malicious, to thy great hurt.

45. *Concerning a further sacrifice.* Of this it shall be understood that nothing is to be spoken; nor need anything be spoken to him that hath wisdom to comprehend the number of the paragraph. And this sacrifice is fatal beyond all, unless it be a sacrifice indeed. Yet there are those who have dared and achieved thereby.

46. *Concerning yet a further sacrifice.* Here it is spoken of actual mutilation. Such acts are abominable; and while they may bring success in this Method, form an absolute bar to all further progress.

And they are in any case more likely to lead to madness than to Samadhi. He indeed who purposeth them is already mad.

47. *Concerning human affection.* During this practice thou shalt in no wise withdraw thyself from human relations, only figuring to thyself that thy father or thy brother or thy wife is as it were an image of thy particular Deity. Thus shall they gain, and not lose, by thy working. Only in the case of thy wife this is difficult, since she is more to thee than all others, and in this case thou mayst act with temperance, lest her personality overcome and destroy that of thy Deity.

48. *Concerning the Holy Guardian Angel.* Do thou in no wise confuse this invocation with that.

49. *The Benediction.* And so may the love that passeth all Understanding keep your hearts and minds through Iota-Alpha-Omega Alpha-Delta-Omicron-Nu-Alpha-Iota Sigma-Alpha-Beta-Alpha-Omega and through BABALON of the City of the Pyramids, and through Astarte, the Starry One green-girdled, in the name ARARITA. AMN.

Liber RV vel Spiritus

sub figura CCVI

Publication in Class B

WEH NOTE: The Liber omits sections 0 and 1 in earlier publication in EQUINOX I, 7 as well as here. There are signs that this version has been edited, notably changes were made in punctuation and capitalization. The editing appears to be defective, with some material omitted inadvertently. There is one original footnote, and the others are mine. There was also a photo page in the EQUINOX version.

2. Let the Zelator observe the current of his breath.

3. Let him investigate the following statements, and prepare a careful record of research.

   a. Certain actions induce the flow of the breath through the right nostril (Pingala); and, conversely, the flow of the breath through Pingala induces certain actions.

   b. Certain other actions induce the flow of the breath through the left nostril (Ida), and conversely.

   c. Yet a third class of actions induce the flow of the breath through both nostrils at once (Sushumna), and conversely.

   d. The degree of mental and physical activity is interdependent with the distance from the nostrils at which the breath can be felt by the back of the hand.

4. *First practice.* — Let him concentrate his mind upon the act of breathing, saying mentally, "The breath flows in", "the breath flows out", and record the results. [This practice may resolve itself into Mahasatipatthana (vide Liber XXV) or induce Samadhi. Whichever occurs should be followed up as the right Ingenium of the Zelator, or the advice of his Practicus, may determine.]

5. *Second practice.* Pranayama. — This is outlined in Liber E. Further, let the Zelator accomplished in those practices endeavour to master a cycle of 10, 20, 40 or even 16, 32, 64. But let this be done gradually and with due caution. And when he is steady and easy both in Asana and Pranayama, let him still further increase the period.

   Thus let him investigate these statements which follow: —

   a. If Pranayama be properly performed, the body will first of all become covered with sweat. This sweat is different in character from that customarily induced by exertion. If the Practitioner rub this sweat thoroughly into his body, he will greatly strengthen it.

   b. The tendency to perspiration will stoў as the practice is continued, and the body become automatically rigid.

   Describe this rigidity with minute accuracy.

   c. The state of automatic rigidity will develop into a state characterised by violent spasmodic movements of which the Practitioner is unconscious, but of whose result he is aware. This result is that the body hops gently from place to place. After the first two or three occurrences of this experience, Asana is not lost. The body appears (on another theory) to have lost its weight almost completely and to be moved by an unknown force.

d. As a development of this stage, the body rises into the air, and remains there for an appreciably long period, from a second to an hour or more.

Let him further investigate any mental results which may occur.

6. *Third Practice.* — In order both to economise his time and to develoÿ his powers, let the Zelator practise the deep full breathing which his preliminary exercises will have taught him during his walks. Let him repeat a sacred sentence (mantra) or let him count, in such a way that his footfall beats accurately with the rhythm thereof, as is done in dancing. Then let him practise Pranayama, at first without the Kumbhakam,

WEH NOTE: Equinox spells this "Kumbakham" in this spot only.

and paying no attention to the nostrils otherwise than to keep them clear. Let him begin by an indrawing of the breath for 4 paces, and a breathing out for 4 paces. Let him increase this gradually to 6.6, 8.8, 12.12, 16.16 and 24.24, or more if he be able. Next let him practise in the proper prnportion 4.8, 6.12, 8.16, 12.24 and so on. Then if he choose, let him recommence the series, adding a gradually increasing period of Kumbhakam.

WEH NOTE: Equinox spells this "Kumbhakham".

7. *Fourth practice.* — Following on this third practice, let him quicken his mantra and his pace until the walk develops into a dance. This may also be practised with the ordinary waltz step, using a mantra in three-time, such as GR:epsilon-pi-epsilon-lambda-theta-omicron-nu, GR:epsilon-pi-epsilon-lambda-theta-omicron-nu, GR:Alpha-rho-tau-epsilon-mu-iota-sigma; or Iao, Iao Sabao; in such cases the practice may be combined with devotion to a particular deity: see Liber CLXXV. For the dance as such it is better to use a mantra of a non-committal character, such as GR:Tau-omicron GR:epsilon-iota-nu-alpha-iota, GR:Tau-omicron GR:Kappa-alpha-lambda-omicron-nu, GR:Tau-omicron 'GR:Alpha-gamma-alpha-delta-omicron-nu,

WEH NOTE: The Equinox has this last word as:"' GR:gamma-alpha-theta-alpha-nu"

or the like.

8. *Fifth practice.* — Let him practice mental concentration during the dance, and investigate the following experiments:

    a. The dance becomes independent of the will.

    b. Similar phenomena to those described in 5 (a), (b), (c), (d), occur.

9. A note concerning the depth and fullness of the breathing. In all prnper expiration the last possible portion of air should be expelled. In this the muscles of the throat, chest, ribs, and abdomen must be fully employed, and aided by the pressing of the upper arms into the flanks, and of the head into the thorax.

   In all proper inspiration the last possible portion of air must be drawn into the lungs.

   In all proper holding of the breath, the body must remain absolutely still.

Ten minutes of such practice is ample to induce profuse sweating in any place of a temperature of 17 Degree C or over.

The progress of the Zelator in acquiring a depth and fullness of breath should be tested by the respirometer.

The exercises should be carefully graduated to avoid overstrain and possible damage to the lungs.

This depth and fullness of breath should be kept as much as possible, even in the rapid exercises, with the exception of the sixth practice following.

10. *Sixth Practice.* — Let the Zelator breathe as shallowly and rapidly as possible. He should assume the attitude of his moment of greatest expiration, and breathe only with the muscles of his throat. He may also practice lengthening the period between each shallow breathing.

This may be combined, when acquired, with concentration on the Visuddhi cakkra, i.e. let him fix his mind unwaveringly upon a point in the spine opposite the larynx.)

> *WEH NOTE: In the Equinox this parenthetic paragraph is identified as an editorial comment.*

> *WEH NOTE: from this point, the text in the Equinox diverges from this text. There is an additional step: "11. "Seventh practice." Let the Zelator breathe as deeply and rapidly as possible." The step numbered here as "Seventh" is labeled "Eighth" in the Equinox.*

11. *Seventh practice.* — Let the Zelator practise restraint of breathing in the following manner. At any stage of breathing let him suddenly hold the breath, enduring the need to breathe until it passes, returns, and passes again, and so on until consciousness is lost, either rising to Samadhi or similar supernormal condition, or falling into oblivion.

13. *Ninth practice.* — Let him practice the usual forms of Pranayama, but let Kumbhakam be used after instead of before expiration. Let him gradually increase the period of this Kumbhakam as in the case of the other.

14. A note concerning the conditions of these experiments.

The conditions favourable are dry, bracing air, a warm climate, absence of wind, absence of noise, insects and all other disturbing influences,

> *Note that in the early stages of concentration of the mind, such annoyances become negligible.*

a retired situation, simple food eaten in great moderation at the conclusion of the practices of morning and afternoon, and on no account before practising. Bodily health is almost essential, and should be most carefully guarded (See Liber CLXXXV, "Task of a Neophyte"). A diligent and tractable disciple, or the Practicus of the Zelator, should aid him in his work. Such a disciple should be noiseless, patient, vigilant, prompt, cheerful, of gentle manner and reverent to his master, intelligent to anticipate his wants, cleanly and gracious, not given to speech, devoted and unselfish. With all this he should be fierce and terrible to strangers and all hostile influences, determined and vigorous, increasingly vigilant, the guardian of the threshold.

It is not desirable that the Zelator should employ any other creature than a man, save in cases of necessity. Yet for some of these purposes a dog will serve, for others a woman. There are also others appointed to serve, but these are not for the Zelator.

15. *Tenth Practice.* — Let the Zelator experiment if he will with inhalations of oxygen, nitrous oxide, carbon dioxide, and other gases mixed in small proportion with his air during his practices. These experiments are to be conducted with caution in the presence of a medical man of experience, and they are only useful as facilitating a simulacrum of the results of the proper practices and thereby enheartening the Zelator.

16. *Eleventh practice.* — Let the Zelator at an time during the practices, especially during the periods of Kumbhakam, throw his will utterly towards his Holy Guardian Angel, directing his eyes inward and upward, and turning back his tongue as if to swallow it. (This latter operation is facilitated by severing the fraenum linguae, which, if done, should be done by a competent surgeon. We do not advise this or any similar method of cheating difficulties. This is, however, harmless.)

> *WEH NOTE: Harmless, that is, if you don't mind the danger of choking to death in your sleep!*

In this manner the practice is to be raised from the physical to the spiritual-plane, even as the words Ruh, Ruach, Pneuma, Spiritus, Geist, Ghost, and indeed words of almost all languages, have been raised from their physical meanings of wind,

> *WEH NOTE: The Equinox adds "air," to this list.*

breath, or movement, to the spiritual plane. (RV is the old root meaning Yoni and hence Wheel (Fr. roue, Lat. rota, wheel) and the corresponding Semitic root means "to go". Similarly spirit is connected with "spiral". — Ed.)

17. Let the Zelator attach no credit to any statements that may have been made throughout the course of this instruction, and reflect that even the counsel which we have given as suitable to the average case may be entirely unsuitable to his own.

Liber YOD

Sub Figura DCCCXXXI

(This book was formerly called Vesta. It is referred to the path of Virgo and the letter Yod.)

I.

1. This is the book of drawing all to a point.

2. Herein are described three methods whereby the consciousness of the Many may be melted to that of the One.

II.

FIRST METHOD

0. Let a magical circle be constructed, and within it an upright Tau drawn upon the ground. Let this Tau be devised into 10 squares (See Liber CMLXIII., Illustration 1.)

1. Let the magician be armed with the Sword of Art.1

2. Let him wear the black robe of a Neophyte.

3. Let a single flame of camphor burn at the top of the Tau, and let there be no other light or ornament.

> *In circumstances where this is inappropriate let him be armed with wand and lamp instead of as in text. — N.*

4. Let him "open" the Temple as in DCLXXI or in any other convenient manner.

5. Standing at the appropriate quarters, at the edge of the circle, let him banish the 5 elements by the appropriate rituals.

6. Standing at the edge of the circle, let him banish the 7 planets by the appropriate rituals. Let him face the actual position of each planet in the heavens at the time of his working.

7. Let him further banish the twelve signs of the Zodiac by the appropriate rituals, facing each sign in turn.

8. Let him at each of these 24 banishings make three circumambulations widdershins, with the signs of Horus and Harpocrates in the East as he passes it.

9. Let him advance to the square of Malkuth in the Tau, and perform a ritual of banishing Malkuth. But here let him not leave the square to circumambulate the circle, but use the formula and God-form of Harpocrates.

10. Let him advance in turn to the squares Jesod, Hod, Netzach, Tiphereth, Geburah, Chesed and banish each by appropriate rituals.

11. And let him know that such rituals include the pronunciation of the appropriate names of God backwards, and also a curse against the Sephira in respect of all that which it is, for that which distinguishes and separates it from Kether.

12. Advancing to the squares of Binah and Chokmah in turn, let him banish these also. And for that by now an awe and trembling shall have taken hold upon him, let him banish these by a supreme ritual of inestimable puissance; and let him beware exceedingly lest his will falter or his courage fail.

13. Finally, let him, advancing to the square of Kether, banish that also by what means he may. At the end whereof let him set his foot upon the light, extinguishing it;

If armed with wand and lamp let him extinguish the light with his hand. — N.

and, as he falleth, let him fall within the circle.

SECOND METHOD

1. Let the Hermit be seated in his Asana, robed, and let him meditate in turn upon every several part of his body until that part is so unreal to him that he no longer includes it in his comprehension of himself . For example if it be his right foot, let him touch that foot, and be alarmed, thinking, "A foot! ... foot! What is this foot? Surely I am not alone in the Hermitage!" And this practice should be carried out not only at the time of meditation, but during the day's work.

2. This meditation is to be assisted by reasoning; as "This foot is not I. If I should lose my foot, I should still be I. This foot is a mass of changing and decaying flesh, bone, skin, blood, lymph, etc. while I am the Unchanging and Immortal Spirit, uniform, not made, unbegotten, formless, self-luminous," etc.

3. This practice being perfect for each part of the body, let him combine his workings until the whole body is thus understood as the non-Ego and as illusion.

4. Let then the Hermit, seated in his Asana, meditate upon the Muladhara Cakkra and its correspondence as a power of the mind, and destroy it in the same manner as aforesaid. Also by reasoning: "This emotion (memory, imagination, intellect, will, as it may be) is not I. This emotion is transient: I am immovable. This emotion is passion. I am peace", and so on.

Let the other Cakkras in their turn be thus destroyed, each one with its mental or moral attribute.

5. In this let him be aided by his own psychological analysis, so that no part of his conscious being be thus left undestroyed. And on his thoroughness in this matter may turn his success.

6. Lastly, having drawn all his being into the highest Sahasrara Cakkra, let him remain eternally fixed in meditation thereupon.

7. AUM.

THIRD METHOD.

1. Let the Hermit stimulate each of the senses in turn, concentrating upon each until it ceases to stimulate.

(The senses of sight and touch are extremely difficult to conquer. In the end the Hermit must be utterly unable by any effort to see or feel the object of those senses, O.M.)

2. This being perfected, let him combine them two at a time. For example, let him chew ginger (taste and touch), and watch a waterfall (sight and hearing) and watch incense (sight and smell) and crush sugar in his teeth (taste and hearing) and so on.

3. These twenty-five practices being accomplished, let him combine them three at a time, then four at a time.

4. Lastly, let him combine all the senses in a single object. And herein may a sixth sense be included. He is then to withdraw himself entirely from all the stimulations, perinde ac cadaver, in spite of his own efforts to attach himself to them.

5. By this method it is said that the demons of the Ruach, that is, thoughts and memories, are inhibited, and We deny it not. But if so be that they arise, let him build a wall between himself and them according to the method.

6. Thus having stilled the voices of the Six, may he obtain in sense the subtlety of the Seventh.

7. AUMGN.

(We add the following, contributed by a friend at that time without the A: A: and its dependent orders. He worked out the method himself, and we think it may prove useful to many. O.M.)

(1) The beginner must first practise breathing regularly through the nose, at the same time trying hard to believe that the breath goes to the Ajna and not to the lungs.

The Pranayama exercises described in the Equinox Vol. I, No. 4, p. 101 must next be practised, always with the idea that Ajna is breathing.

Try to realise that power, not air, is being drawn into the Ajna, is being concentrated there during Kumbhakam, and is vivifying the Ajna during expiration. Try rather to increase the force of concentration in Ajna than to increase so excessively the length of Kumbhakam as this is dangerous if rashly undertaken.

(2) Walk slowly in a quiet place; realise that the legs are moving, and study their movements. Understand thoroughly that these movements are due to nerve messages sent down from the brain, and that the controlling power lies in the Ajna. The legs are automatic, like those of a wooden monkey: the power in Ajna is that which does the work, is that which walks. This is not hard to realise, and should be grasped firmly, ignoring all other walking sensations.

Apply this method to every other muscular movement.

(3) Lie flat on the back with the feet under a heavy piece of furniture. Keeping the spine straight and the arms in a line with the body, rise slowly to a sitting posture, by means of the force residing in the Ajna (i.e. try to prevent the mind dwelling one any other exertion or sensation.)

Then let the body slowly down to its original position. Repeat this two or three times, every night and morning, and slowly increase the number of repetitions.

(4) Try to transfer all bodily sensations to the Ajna, e.g., "I am cold" should mean "I feel cold", or better still, "I am aware of a sensation of cold" — transfer this to the Ajna, "the Ajna is aware", etc.

(5) Pain if very slight may easily be transferred to the Ajna after a little practice. The best method for beginner is to imagine he has a pain in the body and then imagine that it passes directly into the Ajna. It does not pass through the intervening structures, but goes direct. After continual practice even severe pain may be transferred to the Ajna.

(6) Fix the mind on the base of the spine and then gradually move the thoughts upwards to the Ajna.

(In this meditation Ajna is a Holy of Holies, but it is dark and empty.)

Finally, strive hard to drive anger and other obsessing thoughts into the Ajna. Try to develop a tendency to think hard of Ajna when these thoughts attack the mind, and let Ajna conquer them.

Beware of thinking of "My Ajna". In these meditations and practices, Ajna does not belong to you; Ajna is the master and worker, you are the wooden monkey.

LIBER Taw-Yod-Shin-Aleph-Resh-Bet (ThIShARB)

VIAE MEMORIAE

sub figura CMXIII

A.·. A.·.

Publication in Class B.

Imprimatur:

N. Fra A.·. A.·.

000. May be.

[00. It has not been possible to construct this book on a basis of pure Scepticism. This matters less, as the practice leads to Scepticism, and it may be through it.]

0. This book is not intended to lead to the supreme attainment. On the contrary, its results define the separate being of the Exempt Adept from the rest of the Universe, and discover his relation to that Universe.

1. It is of such importance to the Exempt Adept that We cannot overrate it. Let him in no wise adventure the plunge into the Abyss until he have accomplished this to his most perfectest satisfaction.

2. For in the Abyss no effort is anywise possible. The Abyss is passed by virtue of the mass of the Adept and his Karma. Two forces impel him: (1) the attraction of Binah, (2) the impulse of his Karma; and the ease and even the safety of his passage depend on the strength and direction of the latter.

3. Should one rashly dare the passage, and take the irrevocable Oath of the Abyss, he might be lost therein through AEons of incalculable agony; he might even be thrown back upon Chesed, with the terrible Karma of failure added to his original imperfection.

4. It is even said that in certain circumstances it is possible to fall altogether from the Tree of Life, and to attain the Towers of the Black Brothers. But We hold that this is not possible for any adept who has truly attained his grade, or even for any man who has really sought to help humanity even for a single second,<<Those in possession of Liber CLXXXV. will note that in every grade but one the aspirant is pledged to serve his inferiors in the Order.>> and that although his aspiration have been impure through vanity or any similar imperfection.

5. Let then the Adept who finds the result of these meditations unsatisfactory refuse the Oath of the Abyss, and live so that his Karma gains strength and direction suitable to the task at some future period.

6. Memory is essential to the individual consciousness; otherwise the mind were but a blank sheet on which shadows are cast. But we see that not only does the mind retain impressions, but that it is so

constituted that its tendency is to retain some more excellently than others. Thus the great classical scholar, Sir Richard Jebb, was unable to learn even the schoolboy mathematics required for the preliminary examination at Cambridge University, and a special act of the authorities was required in order to admit him.{WEH NOTE: Normally this would be an exercise of Medieval privilege by a Royal or other nobility. Wars have been lost over such "Grace" being given in the qualification of officers!}

7. The first method to be described has been detailed in Bhikkhu Ananda Metteya's "Training of the Mind" (EQUINOX, I. 5, pp. 28-59, and especially pp. 48-56). We have little to alter or to add. Its most important result, as regards the Oath of the Abyss, is the freedom from all desire or clinging to anything which it gives. Its second result is to aid the adept in the second method, by supplying him with further data for his investigation.

8. The stimulation of memory useful in both practices is also achieved by simple meditation (Liber E), in a certain stage of which old memories arise unbidden. The adept may then practise this, stopping at that stage, and encouraging instead of suppressing the flashes of memory.

9. Zoroaster has said, "Explore the River of the Soul, whence or in what order you have come; so that although you have become a servant to the body, you may again rise to that Order (the A∴ A∴) from which you descended, joining Works (Kamma) to the Sacred Reason (the Tao)."

10. The Result of the Second Method is to show the Adept to what end his powers are destined. When he has passed the Abyss and become NEMO, the return of the current causes him "to appear in the Heaven of Jupiter as a morning star or as an evening star."[The formula of the Great Work "Solve et Coagula" may be thus interpreted. Solve, the dissolution of the Self in the Infinite; Coagula, the presentation of the Infinite in a concrete form to the outer. Both are necessary to the Task of a Master of the Temple.] In other words, he should discover what may be the nature of his work. Thus Mohammed was a Brother reflected into Netzach, Buddha a Brother reflected into Hod, or, as some say, Daath. The present manifestation of Frater P. to the outer is in Tiphereth, to the inner in the path of Leo.

11. First Method. Let the Exempt Adept first train himself to think backwards by external means, as set forth here following.

("a") Let him learn to write backwards, with either hand.

("b") Let him learn to walk backwards.

("c") Let him constantly watch, if convenient, cinematograph films, and listen to phonograph records, reversed, and let him so accustom himself to these that they appear natural, and appreciable as a whole.

("d") Let him practise speaking backwards; thus for "I am He" let him say, "Eh ma I".

("e") Let him learn to read backwards. In this it is difficult to avoid cheating one's self, as an expert reader sees a sentence at a glance. Let his disciple read aloud to him backwards, slowly at first, then more quickly.

("f") Of his own ingenium, let him devise other methods.

12. In this his brain will at first be overwhelmed by a sense of utter confusion; secondly, it will endeavour to evade the difficulty by a trick. The brain will pretend to be working backwards when it is really normal. It is difficult to describe the nature of the trick, but it will be quite obvious to anyone who has

done practices ("a") and ("b") for a day or two. They become quite easy, and he will think that he is making progress, an illusion which close analysis will dispel.

13. Having begun to train his brain in this manner, and obtained some little success, let the Exempt Adept, seated in his Asana, think first of his present attitude, next of the act of being seated, next of his entering the room, next of his robing, et cetera, exactly as it happened. And let him most strenuously endeavour to think each act as happening backwards. It is not enough to think: "I am seated here, and before that I was standing, and before that I entered the room," etc. That series is the trick detected in the preliminary practices. The series must not run "ghi-def-abc" but "ihgfedcba": not "horse a is this" but "esroh a si siht". To obtain this thoroughly well, practice ("c") is very useful. The brain will be found to struggle constantly to right itself, soon accustoming itself to accept "esroh" as merely another glyph for "horse." This tendency must be constantly combated.

14. In the early stages of this practice the endeavour should be to meticulous minuteness of detail in remembering actions; for the brain's habit of thinking forwards will at first be insuperable. Thinking of large and complex actions, then, will give a series which we may symbolically write "opqrstu-hijklmn-abcdefg." If these be split into detail, we shall have "stu-pqr-o—mn-kl-hij—fg-cde-ab," which is much nearer to the ideal "utsrqponmlkjihgfedcba."

15. Capacities differ widely, but the Exempt Adept need have no reason to be discouraged if after a month's continuous labour he find that now and again for a few seconds his brain really works backwards.

16. The Exempt Adept should concentrate his efforts upon obtaining a perfect picture of five minutes backwards rather than upon extending the time covered by his meditation. For this preliminary training of the brain is the Pons Asinorum of the whole process.

17. This five minutes' exercise being satisfactory, the Exempt Adept may extend the same at his discretion to cover an hour, a day, a week, and so on. Difficulties vanish before him as he advances; the extension from a day to the course of his whole life will not prove so difficult as the perfecting of the five minutes.

18. This practice should be repeated at least four times daily, and progress is shown firstly by the ever easier running of the brain, secondly by the added memories which arise.

19. It is useful to reflect during this practice, which in time becomes almost mechanical, upon the way in which effects spring from causes. This aids the mind to link its memories, and prepares the adept for the preliminary practice of the Second Method.

20. Having allowed the mind to return for some hundred times to the hour of birth, it should be encouraged to endeavour to penetrate beyond that period. If it be properly trained to run backwards, there will be little difficulty in doing this, although it is one of the distinct steps in the practice.

21. It may be then that the memory will persuade the adept of some previous existence. Where this is possible, let it be checked by an appeal to facts, as follows:

22. It often occurs to men that on visiting a place to which they have never been, it appears familiar. This may arise from a confusion of thought or a slipping of the memory, but it is conceivably a fact.

If, then, the adept "remember" that he was in a previous life in some city, say Cracow, which he has in this life never visited, let him describe from memory the appearance of Cracow, and of its inhabitants, setting down their names. Let him further enter into details of the city and its customs. And having done this with great minuteness, let him confirm the same by consultation with historians and geographers, or by a personal visit, remembering (both to the credit of his memory and its discredit) that historians, geographers, and himself are alike fallible. But let him not trust his memory to assert its conclusions as fact, and act thereupon, without most adequate confirmation.

23. This process of checking his memory should be practised with the earlier memories of childhood and youth by reference to the memories and records of others, always reflecting upon the fallibility even of such safeguards.

24. All this being perfected, so that the memory reaches back into aeons incalculably distant, let the Exempt Adept meditate upon the fruitlessness of all those years, and upon the fruit thereof, severing that which is transitory and worthless from that which is eternal. And it may be that he being but an Exempt Adept may hold all to be savourless and full of sorrow.

25. This being so, without reluctance will he swear the Oath of the Abyss.

26. Second Method. Let the Exempt Adept, fortified by the practice of the First Method, enter the preliminary practice of the Second Method.

27. Second Method. Preliminary Practices. Let him, seated in his Asana, consider any event, and trace it to its immediate causes. And let this be done very fully and minutely. Here, for example, is a body erect and motionless. Let the adept consider the many forces which maintain it; firstly, the attraction of the earth, of the sun, of the planets, of the farthest stars, nay, of every mote of dust in the room, one of which (could it be annihilated) would cause that body to move, although so imperceptibly. Also the resistance of the floor, the pressure of the air, and all other external conditions. Secondly, the internal forces which sustain it, the vast and complex machinery of the skeleton, the muscles, the blood, the lymph, the marrow, all that makes up a man. Thirdly the moral and intellectual forces involved, the mind, the will, the consciousness. Let him continue this with unremitting ardour, searching Nature, leaving nothing out.

28. Next, let him take one of the immediate causes of his position, and trace out its equilibrium. For example, the will. What determines the will to aid in holding the body erect and motionless?

29. This being discovered, let him choose one of the forces which determined his will, and trace out that in similar fashion; and let this process be continued for many days until the interdependence of all things is a truth assimilated in his inmost being.

30. This being accomplished, let him trace his own history with special reference to the causes of each event. And in this practice he may neglect to some extent the universal forces which at all times act on all, as for example the attraction of masses, and let him concentrate his attention upon the principal and determining or effective causes.

For instance, he is seated, perhaps, in a country place in Spain. Why? Because Spain is warm and suitable for meditation, and because cities are noisy and crowded. Why is Spain warm? and why does he wish to meditate? Why choose warm Spain rather than warm India? To the last question: Because Spain is nearer to his home. Then why is his home near Spain? Because his parents were Germans. And why did they go to Germany? And so during the whole meditation.

31. On another day, let him begin with a question of another kind, and every day devise new questions,

not only concerning his present situation, but also abstract questions. Thus let him connect the prevalence of water upon the surface of the globe with its necessity to such life as we know, with the specific gravity and other physical properties of water, and let him perceive ultimately through all this the necessity and concord of things, not concord as the schoolmen of old believed, making all things for man's benefit or convenience, but the essential mechanical concord whose final law is "inertia." And in these meditations let him avoid as if it were the plague any speculation sentimental or fantastic.

32. Second Method. The Practice Proper. Having then perfected in his mind these conceptions, let him apply them to his own career, forging the links of memory into the chain of necessity.

And let this be his final question: To what purpose am I fitted? Of what service can my being prove to the Brothers of the A.·. A.·. if I cross the Abyss, and am admitted to the City of the Pyramids?

33. Now that he may clearly understand the nature of this question, and the method of solution, let him study the reasoning of the anatomist who reconstructs an animal from a single bone. To take a simple example.

34. Suppose, having lived all my life among savages, a ship is cast upon the shore and wrecked. Undamaged among the cargo is a "Victoria." What is its use? The wheels speak of roads, their slimness of smooth roads, the brake of hilly roads. The shafts show that it was meant to be drawn by an animal, their height and length suggest an animal of the size of a horse. That the carriage is open suggests a climate tolerable at any rate for part of the year. The height of the box suggest crowded streets, or the spirited character of the animal employed to draw it. The cushions indicate its use to convey men rather than merchandise; its hood that rain sometimes falls, or that the sun is at times powerful. The springs would imply considerable skill in metals; the varnish much attainment in that craft.

35. Similarly, let the adept consider of his own case. Now that he is on the point of plunging into the Abyss a giant Why? confronts him with uplifted club.

36. There is no minutest atom of his composition which can be withdrawn without making him some other than he is; no useless moment in his past. Then what is his future? The "Victoria" is not a waggon; it is not intended for carting hay. It is not a sulky; it is useless in trotting races.

37. So the adept has military genius, or much knowledge of Greek; how do these attainments help his purpose, or the purpose of the Brothers? He was put to death by Calvin, or stoned by Hezekiah; as a snake he was killed by a villager, or as an elephant slain in battle under Hamilcar. How do such memories help him? Until he have thoroughly mastered the reason for every incident in his past, and found a purpose for every item of his present equipment, [A brother known to me was repeatedly baffled in this meditation. But one day being thrown with his horse over a sheer cliff of forty feet, and escaping without a scratch or a bruse, he was reminded of his many narrow escapes from death. These proved to be the last factors in his problem, which, thus completed, solved itself in a moment. O.M. {WEH NOTE ADDENDA: Here Crowley speaks of himself, the event being noted in his China walk account.}] he cannot truly answer even those Three Question what were first put to him, even the Three Questions of the Ritual of the Pyramid; he is not ready to swear the Oath of the Abyss.

38. But being thus enlightened, let him swear the Oath of the Abyss; yea, let him swear the Oath of the Abyss.

Liber B
vel Magi
sub Figura I

00. One is the Magus: twain His forces; four His weapons. These are the seven Spirits of Unrighteousness; seven vultures of evil. This is the art and craft of the Magus but glamour. How shall He destroy Himself?

0. Yet the Magus hath power upon the Mother both directly and through love. And the Magus is Love, and bindeth together That and This in His Conjuration.

1. In the beginning doth the Magus speak Truth, and send forth Illusion and Falsehood to enslave the soul. Yet therein is the Mystery of Redemption.

2. By his Wisdom made He the Worlds: the World that is God is none other han He.

3. Now then shall He end His Speech with Silence? For He is Speech.

4. He is the First and the Last. How shall He cease to number Himself?

5. By a Magus is this writing made known through the mind of a Magister. The one uttereth clearly, and the other Understandeth; yet the Word is falsehood, and the Understanding darkness. And this saying is of All Truth.

6. Nevertheless it is written; for there be times of darkness, and this as a lamp therein.

7. With the Wand createth He.

8. With the Cup preserveth He.

9. With the Dagger destroyeth He.

10. With the Coin redeemeth He.

11. His weapons fulfil the wheel; and on What Axle that turneth is not known unto Him.

12. From all these actions must He cease before the curse of His Grade is uplifted from Him. Before He attain to that which existeth without Form.

13. And if at this time He be manifested upon earth as a Man, and therefore is this present writing, let this be His method, that the curse of His grade, and the burden of His attainment, be uplifted from Him.

14. Let Him beware of abstinence from action. For the curse of His grade is that he must speak Truth, that the Falsehood thereof may enslave the souls of men. Let Him then utter that without Fear, that the Law may be fulfilled. And according to His Original Nature will that law be shapen, so that one may declare gentleness and quietness, being an Hindu; and another fierceness and servility, being a Jew; and yet another ardour and manliness, being an Arab. Yet this matter toucheth the mystery of Incarnation, and is not here to be declared.

15. Now the grade of a Magister teacheth the Mystery of Sorrow, and the grade of a Magus the Mystery of

Change, and the grade of Ipsissimus the Mystery of Selflessness, which is called also the Mystery of Pan.

16. Let the Magus then contemplate each in turn, raising it to the ultimate power of Infinity. Wherein Sorrow is Joy, and Change is Stability, and Selflessness is Self. For the interplay of the parts hath no action upon the whole. And this contemflation shall be performed not by simple meditation — how much less then by reason! — but by the method which shall have been given unto Him in His initiation to the Grade.

17. Following which method, it shall be easy for Him to combine that rinity from its elements, and further to combine Sat-Chit-Ananda, and Light, Love, Life, three by three into nine that are one, in which meditation success shall be That which was first adumbrated to Him in the grade of Practicus (which reflecteth Mercury into the lowest world) in Liber XXVII, "Here is Nothing under its three forms."

18. And this is the Opening of the Grade of Ipsissimus, and by the Buddhists it is called the trance Nerodha-Samapatti.

19. And woe, woe, woe, yea woe, and again woe, woe, woe, unto seven times be His that preacheth not His law to men!

20. And woe also be unto Him that refuseth the curse of the grade of a Magus, and the burden of the Attainment thereof.

21. And in the word CHAOS let the book be sealed, yea, let the Book be sealed.

Liber Resh vel Helios

sub figura CC

Publication in class D

0. These are the adorations to be performed by aspirants to the A.·. A.·.

1. Let him greet the Sun at dawn, facing East, giving the sign of his grade. And let him say in a loud voice:

   Hail unto Thee who art Ra in Thy rising, even unto Thee who art Ra in Thy strength, who travellest over the Heavens in Thy bark at the Uprising of the Sun.

   Tahuti standeth in His splendour at the prow, and Ra-Hoor abideth at the helm.

   Hail unto Thee from the Abodes of Night!

2. Also at Noon, let him greet the Sun, facing South, giving the sign of his grade. And let him say in a loud voice:

   Hail unto Thee who art Ahathoor in Thy triumphing, even unto Thee who art Ahathoor in Thy beauty, who travellest over the heavens in thy bark at the Mid-course of the Sun.

   Tahuti standeth in His splendour at the prow, and Ra-Hoor abideth at the helm.

   Hail unto Thee from the Abodes of Morning!

3. Also, at Sunset, let him greet the Sun, facing West, giving the sign of his grade. And let him say in a loud voice:

   Hail unto Thee who art Tum in Thy setting, even unto Thee who art Tum in Thy joy, who travellest over the Heavens in Thy bark at the Down-going of the Sun.

   Tahuti standeth in His splendour at the prow, and Ra-Hoor abideth at the helm.

   Hail unto Thee from the Abodes of Day!

4. Lastly, at Midnight, let him greet the Sun, facing North, giving the sign of his grade, and let him say in a loud voice:

   Hail unto thee who art Khephra in Thy hiding, even unto Thee who art Khephra in Thy silence, who travellest over the heavens in Thy bark at the Midnight Hour of the Sun.

   Tahuti standeth in His splendour at the prow, and Ra-Hoor abideth at the helm.

   Hail unto Thee from the Abodes of Evening.

5. And after each of these invocations thou shalt give the sign of silence, and afterward thou shalt perform the adoration that is taught thee by thy Superior. And then do thou compose Thyself to holy meditation.

6. Also it is better if in these adorations thou assume the God-form of Whom thou adorest, as if thou didst unite with Him in the adoration of That which is beyond Him.

7. Thus shalt thou ever be mindful of the Great Work which thou hast undertaken to perform, and thus

shalt thou be strengthened to pursue it unto the attainment of the Stone of the Wise, the Summum Bonum, True Wisdom and Perfect Happiness.

Liber III vel Jugorum

0.

0. Behold the Yoke upon the neck of the Oxen! Is it not thereby that the Field shall be ploughed? The Yoke is heavy, but joineth together them that are separate — Glory to Nuit and to Hadit, and to Him that hath given us the Symbol of the Rosy Cross!

Glory unto the Lord of the Word Abrahadabra, and Glory unto Him that hath given us the Symbol of the Ankh, and of the Cross within the Circle!

1. Three are the Beasts wherewith thou must plough the Field; the Unicorn, the Horse, and the Ox. And these shalt thou yoke in a triple yoke that is governed by One Whip.

2. Now these Beasts run wildly upon the earths and are not easily obedient to the Man.

3. Nothing shall be said here of Cerberus, the great Beast of Hell that is every one of these and all of these, even as Athanasius hath foreshadowed. For this matter

(i.e. the matter of Cereberus).

is not of Tiphereth without, but Tiphereth within.

I.

0. The Unicorn is speech. Man, rule thy Speech! How else shalt thou master the Son, and answer the Magician at the right hand gateway of the Crown?

1. Here are practices. Each may last for a week or more.

(a) Avoid using some common word, such as "and" or "the" or "but"; use a paraphrase.

(b) Avoid using some letter of the alphabet, such as "t", or "s". or "m"; use a paraphrase.

(c) Avoid using the pronouns and adjectives of the first person; use a paraphrase.

Of thine own ingenium devise others.

2. On each occasion that thou art betrayed into saying that thou art sworn to avoid, cut thyself sharply upon the writs or forearm with a razor; even as thou shouldst beat a disobedient dog. Feareth not the Unicorn the claws and teeth of the Lion?

3. Thine arm then serveth thee both for a warning and for a record. Thou shalt write down thy daily progress in these practices, until thou art perfectly vigilant at all times over the least word that slippeth from thy tongue.

Thus bind thyself, and thou shalt be for ever free.

II.

0. The Horse is Action. Man, rule thine Action. How else shalt thou master the Father, and answer the Fool at the Left Hand Gateway of the Crown?

1. Here are practices. Each may last for a week, or more.

(a) Avoiding lifting the left arm above the waist.

(b) Avoid crossing the legs.

Of thine own ingenium devise others.

2. On each occasion that thou art betrayed into doing that thou art sworn to avoid, cut thyself sharply upon the wrist or forearm with a razor; even as thou shouldst beat a disobedient dog. Feareth not the Horse the teeth of the Camel?

3. Thine arm then serveth thee both for a warning and for a record. Thou shalt write down thy daily progress in these practices, until thou art perfectly vigilant at all times over the least action that slippeth from the least of thy fingers.

Thus bind thyself, and thou shalt be for ever free.

III.

0. The Ox is Thought. Man, rule thy Thought! How else shalt thou master the Holy Spirit, and answer the High Priestess in the Middle Gateway of the Crown?

1. Here are practices. Each may last for a week or more.

(a) Avoid thinking of a definite subject and all things connected with it, and let that subject be one which commonly occupies much of thy thought, being frequently stimulated by sense-perceptions or the conversation of others.

(b) By some device, such as the changing of thy ring from one finger to another, create in thyself two personalities, the thoughts of one being within entirely different limits from that of the other, the common ground being the necessities of life.

For instance, let A be a man of strong passions, skilled in the Holy Qabalah, a vegetarian, and a keen "reactionary" politician. Let B be a bloodless and ascetic thinker, occupied with business and family cares, an eater of meat, and a keen progressive politician. Let no thought proper to "A" arise when the ring is on the "B" finger, and vice versa.

Of thine own Ingenium devise others.

2. On each occasion that thou art betrayed into thinking that thou art sworn to avoid, cut thyself sharply upon the wrist or forearm with a razor; even as thou shouldst beat a disobedient dog. Feareth not the Ox the Goad of the Ploughman?

3. Thine arm then serveth thee both for a warning and for a record. Thou shalt write down thy daily progress in these practices, until thou art perfectly vigilant at all times over the least thought that ariseth in thy brain.

Thus bind thyself, and thou shalt be for ever free.

LIBER CHETH

VEL

VALLVM ABIEGNI

SVB FIGVRA

CLVI

A.'. A.'.

Publication in Class A.

Imprimatur:

N. Fra A.'. A.'.

1. This is the secret of the Holy Graal, that is the sacred vessel of our Lady the Scarlet Woman, Babalon the Mother of Abominations, the bride of Chaos, that rideth upon our Lord the Beast.

2. Thou shalt drain out thy blood that is thy life into the golden cup of her fornication.

3. Thou shalt mingle thy life with the universal life. Thou shalt keep not back one drop.

4. Then shall thy brain be dumb, and thy heart beat no more, and all thy life shall go from thee; and thou shalt be cast out upon the midden, and the birds of the air shall feast upon thy flesh, and thy bones shall whiten in the sun.

5. Then shall the winds gather themselves together, and bear thee up as it were a little heap of dust in a sheet that hath four corners, and they shall give it unto the guardians of the abyss.

6. And because there is no life therein, the guardians of the abyss shall bid the angels of the winds pass by. And the angels shall lay thy dust in the City of the Pyramids, and the name thereof shall be no more. {25}

7. Now therefore that thou mayest achieve this ritual of the Holy Graal, do thou divest thyself of all thy goods.

8. Thou hast wealth; give it unto them that have need thereof, yet no desire toward it.

9. Thou hast health; slay thyself in the fervour of thine abandonment unto Our Lady. Let thy flesh hang loose upon thy bones, and thine eyes glare with thy quenchless lust unto the Infinite, with thy passion for the Unknown, for Her that is beyond Knowledge the accursed one.

10. Thou hast love; tear thy mother from thine heart, and spit in the face of thy father. Let thy foot trample the belly of thy wife, and let the babe at her breast be the prey of dogs and vultures.

11. For if thou dost not this with thy will, then shall We do this despite thy will. So that thou attain to the Sacrament of the Graal in the Chapel of Abominations.

12. And behold! if by stealth thou keep unto thyself one thought of thine, then shalt thou be cast out into the abyss for ever; and thou shalt be the lonely one, the eater of dung, the afflicted in the Day of Be-with-Us.

13. Yea! verily this is the Truth, this is the Truth, this is the Truth. Unto thee shall be granted joy and health and wealth and wisdom when thou art no longer thou.

14. Then shall every gain be a new sacrament, and it shall not defile thee; thou shalt revel with the wanton in the market-place, and the virgins shall fling roses upon thee, and the merchants bend their knees and bring thee gold and spices. Also young boys shall pour wonderful wines for thee, and the singers and the dancers shall sing and dance for thee. {26}

15. Yet shalt thou not be therein, for thou shalt be forgotten, dust lost in dust.

16. Nor shall the aeon itself avail thee in this; for from the dust shall a white ash be prepared by Hermes the Invisible.

17. And this is the wrath of God, that these things should be thus.

18. And this is the grace of God, that these things should be thus.

19. Wherefore I charge you that ye come unto me in the Beginning; for if ye take but one step in this Path, ye must arrive inevitably at the end thereof.

20. This Path is beyond Life and Death; it is also beyond Love; but that ye know not, for ye know not Love.

21. And the end thereof is known not even unto Our Lady or to the Beast whereon She rideth; nor unto the Virgin her daughter nor unto Chaos her lawful Lord; but unto the Crowned Child is it known? It is not known if it be known.

22. Therefore unto Hadit and unto Nuit be the glory in the End and the Beginning; yea, in the End and the Beginning.

Liber A'ASH vel Capriconi Pneumatici

sub figura CCCLXX

Publication in Class A

1. Gnarled Oak of God! In thy branches is the lightning nested! Above thee hangs the Eyeless Hawk.

2. Thou art blasted and black! Supremely solitary in that heath of scrub.

3. Up! The Ruddy clouds hang over thee! It is the storm.

4. There is a flaming gash in the sky.

5. Up.

6. Thou art tossed about in the grip of the storm for an aeon and an aeon and an aeon. But thou givest not thy sap; thou fallest not.

7 Only in the end shalt thou give up thy sap when the great God F.I.A.T. is enthroned on the day of Be-With-Us.

8. For two things are done and a third thing is begun. Isis and Osiris are given over to incest and adultery. Horus leaps up thrice armed from the womb of his mother. Harpocrates his twin is hidden within him. SET is his holy covenant, that he shall display in the great day of M.A.A.T., that is being interpreted the Master of the Temple of A.'. A.'., whose name is Truth.

9. Now in this is the magical power known.

10. It is like the oak that hardens itself and bears up against the storm. It is weather-beaten and scarred and confident like a sea-captain.

11: Also it straineth like a hound in the leash.

12. It hath pride and great subtlety. Yea, and glee also!

13. Let the Magus act thus in his conjuration.

14. Let him sit and conjure; let him draw himself together in that forcefulness; let him rise next swollen and straining; let him dash back the hood from his head and fix his basilisk eye upon the sigil of the demon. Then let him sway the force of him to and fro like a satyr in silence, until the Word burst from his throat.

15. Then let him not fall exhausted, although he

WEH NOTE: EQUINOX I, 6 has "...the might..."

might have been ten thousandfold the human; but that which floodeth him is the infinite mercy of the Genitor-Genitrix of the Universe, whereof he is the Vessel.

16. Nor do thou deceive thyself. It is easy to tell the live force from the dead matter. It is no easier to tell

the live snake from the dead snake.

17. Also concerning vows. Be obstinate, and be not obstinate. Understand that the yielding of the Yoni is one with the lengthening of the Lingam. Thou art both these; and thy vow is but the rustling of the wind on Mount Meru.

18. How

WEH NOTE: EQUINOX I, 6 has "Now..."

shalt thou adore me who am the Eye and the Tooth, the Goat of the Spirit, the Lord of Creation. I am the Eye in the Triangle, the Silver Star that ye adore.

19. I am Baphomet, that is the Eightfold Word that shall be equilibrated with the Three.

20. There is no act or passion that shall not be an hymn in mine honour.

21. All holy things and all symbolic things shall be my sacraments.

22. These animals are sacred unto me; the goat, and the duck, and the ass, and the gazelle, the man, the woman and the child.

23. All corpses are sacred unto me; they shall not be touched save in mine eucharist. All lonely places are sacred unto me; where one man gathereth himself together in my name, there will I leap forth in the midst of him.

24. I am the hideous god, and who mastereth me is uglier than I.

25. Yet I give more than Bacchus and Apollo; my gifts exceed the olive and the horse.

26. Who worshippeth me must worship me with many rites.

27. I am concealed with all concealments; when the Most Holy Ancient One is stripped and driven through the market place, I am still secret and apart.

28. Whom I love I chastise with many rods.

29. All things are sacred to me; no thing is sacred from me.

30. For there is no holiness where I am not.

31. Fear not when I fall in the fury of the storm; for mine acorns are blown afar by the wind; and verily I shall rise again, and my children about me, so that we shall uplift our forest in Eternity.

32. Eternity is the storm that covereth me.

33. I am Existence, the Existence that existeth not save through its own Existence, that is beyond the Existence of Existences, and rooted deeper than the No-Thing-Tree in the Land of No-Thing.

34. Now therefore thou knowest when I am within Thee, when my hood is spread over thy skull, when my might is more than the penned Indus, and resistless as the Giant Glacier.

35. For as thou art before a lewd woman in Thy nakedness in the bazaar, sucked up by her slyness and

smiles, so art thou wholly and no more in part before the symbol of the beloved, though it be but a Pisacha or a Yantra or a Deva.

36. And in all shalt thou create the Infinite Bliss and the next link of the Infinite Chain.

37. This chain reaches from Eternity to Eternity, ever in triangles — is not my symbol a triangle? — ever in circles — is not the symbol of the Beloved a circle? Therein is all progress base illusion, for every circle is alike and every triangle alike!

38. But the progress is progress, and progress is rapture, constant, dazzling, showers of light, waves of dew, flames of the hair of the Great Goddess, flowers of the roses that are about her neck, Amen!

39. Therefore lift up thyself as I am lifted up.

WEH NOTE: EQUINOX I, 6 makes this sentence the first of the following paragraph.

Hold thyself in as I am master to accomplish. At the end, be the end far distant as the stars that lie in the navel of Nuit, do thou slay thyself as I at the end am slain, in the death that is life, in the peace that is mother of war, in the darkness that holds light in his hand, as an harlot that plucks a jewel from her nostrils.

40. So therefore the beginning is delight, and the end is delight, and delight is in the midst, even as the Indus is water in the cavern of the glacier, and water among the greater hills and the lesser hills and through the ramparts of the hills and through the plains, and water at the mouth thereof when it leaps forth into the mighty sea, yea, into the mighty sea.

(The Interpretation of this Book will be given to members of the Grade of Dominus Liminis on application, each to his Adeptus.)

LIBER A

vel

ARMORUM

SUB FIGURA CDXII

"... the obeah and the wanga; the work of the wand and the work of the sword; these he shall learn and teach." Liber AL, I, 37.

The Pantacle.

Take pure wax, or a plate of gold, silver-gilt or Electrum Magicum. The diameter shall be eight inches, and the thickness half an inch.

Let the Neophyte by his understanding and ingenium devise a symbol to represent the Universe.

Let his Zelator approve thereof.

Let the Neophyte engrave the same upon the plate with his own hand and weapon.

Let it when finished be consecrated as he hath skill to formform, and kept wrapped in silk of emerald green.

The Dagger.

Let the Zelator take a piece of pure steel, and beat it, grind it, sharpen it, and polish it, according to the art of the swordsmith.

Let him further take a piece of oak wood, and carve a hilt. The length shall be eight inches.

Let him by his understanding and ingenium devise a Word to represent the Universe.

Let his Practicus approve thereof.

Let the Zelator engrave the same upon his dagger with his own hand and instruments.

Let him further gild the wood of his hilt.

Let it when finished be consecrated as he hath skill to formform, and kept wrapped in silk of golden yellow.

The Cup.

Let the Practicus take a piece of Silver and fashion therefrom a cup. The height shall be 8 inches, and the diameter 3 inches.

Let him by his understanding and ingenium devise a Number to represent the Universe.

Let his Philosophus approve thereof.

Let the Practicus engrave the same upon his cup with his own hand and instrument.

Let it when finished be consecrated as he hath skill to formform, and kept wrapped in silk of azure blue.

The Baculum.

Let the Philosophus take a rod of copper, of length eight inches and diameter half an inch.

Let him fashion about the top a triple flame of gold.

Let him by his understanding and ingenium devise a Deed to represent the Universe.

Let his Dominus Liminis approve thereof.

Let the Philosophus formform the same in such a way that the Baculum may be partaker therein.

Let it when finished be consecrated as he hath skill to formform, and kept wrapped in silk of fiery scarlet.

The Lamp.

Let the Dominus Liminis take pure lead, tin, and quicksilver, with platinum, and, if need be, glass.

Let him by his understanding and ingenium devise a Magick Lamp that shall burn without wick or oil, being fed by the Aethyr.

This shall he accomplish secretly and apart, without asking the advice or approval of his Adeptus Minor.

Let the Dominus Liminis keep it when consecrated in the secret chamber of Art.

This then is that which is written: "Bring furnished with complete armour and armed, he is similar to the goddess."

And again, "I am armed, I am armed."

Part-IV

OEAHMA
(Thelema)
The Law

Chapter I

I,1: Had! The manifestation of Nuit.

I,2: The unveiling of the company of heaven.

I,3: Every man and every woman is a star.

I,4: Every number is infinite; there is no difference.

I,5: Help me, o warrior lord of Thebes, in my unveiling before the Children of men!

I,6: Be thou Hadit, my secret centre, my heart & my tongue!

I,7: Behold! it is revealed by Aiwass the minister of Hoor-paar-kraat.

I,8: The Khabs is in the Khu, not the Khu in the Khabs.

I,9: Worship then the Khabs, and behold my light shed over you!

I,10: Let my servants be few & secret: they shall rule the many & the known.

I,11: These are fools that men adore; both their Gods & their men are fools.

I,12: Come forth, o children, under the stars, & take your fill of love!

I,13: I am above you and in you. My ecstasy is in yours. My joy is to see your joy.

I,14:

Above, the gemmèd azure is
The naked splendour of Nuit;
She bends in ecstasy to kiss
The secret ardours of Hadit.
The winged globe,the starry blue,
Are mine, O Ankh-af-na-khonsu!

I,15: Now ye shall know that the chosen priest & apostle of infinite space is the prince-priest the Beast; and in his woman called the Scarlet Woman is all power given. They shall gather my children into their fold: they shall bring the glory of the stars into the hearts of men.

I,16: For he is ever a sun, and she a moon. But to him is the winged secret flame, and to her the stooping starlight.

I,17: But ye are not so chosen.

I,18: Burn upon their brows, o splendrous serpent!

I,19: O azure-lidded woman, bend upon them!

I,20: The key of the rituals is in the secret word which I have given unto him.

I,21: With the God & the Adorer I am nothing: they do not see me. They are as upon the earth; I am Heaven, and there is no other God than me, and my lord Hadit.

I,22: Now, therefore, I am known to ye by my name Nuit, and to him by a secret name which I will give him when at last he knoweth me. Since I am Infinite Space, and the Infinite Stars thereof, do ye also thus. Bind nothing! Let there be no difference made among you between any one thing & any other thing; for thereby there cometh hurt.

I,23: But whoso availeth in this, let him be the chief of all!

I,24: I am Nuit, and my word is six and fifty.

I,25: Divide, add, multiply, and understand.

I,26: Then saith the prophet and slave of the beauteous one: Who am I, and what shall be the sign? So she answered him, bending down, a lambent flame of blue, all-touching, all penetrant, her lovely hands upon the black earth, & her lithe body arched for love, and her soft feet not hurting the little flowers: Thou knowest! And the sign shall be my ecstasy, the consciousness of the continuity of existence, the omnipresence of my body.

I,27: Then the priest answered & said unto the Queen of Space, kissing her lovely brows, and the dew of her light bathing his whole body in a sweet-smelling perfume of sweat: O Nuit, continuous one of Heaven, let it be ever thus; that men speak not of Thee as One but as None; and let them speak not of thee at all, since thou art continuous!

I,28: None, breathed the light, faint & faery, of the stars, and two.

I,29: For I am divided for love's sake, for the chance of union.

I,30: This is the creation of the world, that the pain of division is as nothing, and the joy of dissolution all.

I,31: For these fools of men and their woes care not thou at all! They feel little; what is, is balanced by weak joys; but ye are my chosen ones.

I,32: Obey my prophet! follow out the ordeals of my knowledge! seek me only! Then the joys of my love will redeem ye from all pain. This is so: I swear it by the vault of my body; by my sacred heart and tongue; by all I can give, by all I desire of ye all.

I,33: Then the priest fell into a deep trance or swoon, & said unto the Queen of Heaven; Write unto us the ordeals; write unto us the rituals; write unto us the law!

I,34: But she said: the ordeals I write not: the rituals shall be half known and half concealed: the Law is for all.

I,35: This that thou writest is the threefold book of Law.

I,36: My scribe Ankh-af-na-khonsu, the priest of the princes, shall not in one letter change this book; but lest there be folly, he shall comment thereupon by the wisdom of Ra-Hoor-Khu-it.

I,37: Also the mantras and spells; the obeah and the wanga; the work of the wand and the work of the sword; these he shall learn and teach.

I,38: He must teach; but he may make severe the ordeals.

I,39: The word of the Law is **Thelema.***

* Greek letters in MS: **theta-epsilon-lambda-eta-mu-alpha**.

I,40: Who calls us Thelemites will do no wrong, if he look but close into the word. For there are therein Three Grades, the Hermit, and the Lover, and the man of Earth. Do what thou wilt shall be the whole of the Law.

I,41: The word of Sin is Restriction. O man! refuse not thy wife, if she will! O lover, if thou wilt, depart! There is no bond that can unite the divided but love: all else is a curse. Accursed! Accursed be it to the aeons! Hell.

I,42: Let it be that state of manyhood bound and loathing. So with thy all; thou hast no right but to do thy will.

I,43: Do that, and no other shall say nay.

I,44: For pure will, unassuaged of purpose, delivered from the lust of result, is every way perfect.

I,45: The Perfect and the Perfect are one Perfect and not two; nay, are none!

I,46: Nothing is a secret key of this law. Sixty-one the Jews call it; I call it eight, eighty, four hundred & eighteen.

I,47: But they have the half: unite by thine art so that all disappear.

I,48: My prophet is a fool with his one, one, one; are not they the Ox, and none by the Book?

I,49: Abrogate are all rituals, all ordeals, all words and signs. Ra-Hoor-Khuit hath taken his seat in the East at the Equinox of the Gods; and let Asar be with Isa, who also are one. But they are not of me. Let Asar be the adorant, Isa the sufferer; Hoor in his secret name and splendour is the Lord initiating.

I,50: There is a word to say about the Hierophantic task. Behold! there are three ordeals in one, and it may be given in three ways. The gross must pass through fire; let the fine be tried in intellect, and the lofty chosen ones in the highest. Thus ye have star & star, system & system; let not one know well the other!

I,51: There are four gates to one palace; the floor of that palace is of silver and gold; lapis lazuli & jasper are there; and all rare scents; jasmine & rose, and the emblems of death. Let him enter in turn or at once the four gates; let him stand on the floor of the palace. Will he not sink? Amn. Ho! warrior, if thy servant sink? But there are means and means. Be goodly therefore: dress ye all in fine apparel; eat rich foods and drink sweet wines and wines that foam! Also, take your will and fill of love as ye will, when, where, and with whom ye will! But always unto me.

I,52: If this be not aright; if ye confound the space-marks, saying: They are one; or saying, They are many; if the ritual be not ever unto me: then expect the direful judgments of Ra Hoor Khuit!

I,53: This shall regenerate the world, the little world my sister, my heart & my tongue, unto whom I send this kiss. Also, o scribe and prophet, though thou be of the princes, it shall not assuage thee nor absolve thee. But ecstasy be thine and joy of earth: ever To me! To me!

I,54: Change not as much as the style of a letter; for behold! thou, o prophet, shalt not behold all these mysteries hidden therein.

I,55: The child of thy bowels, he shall behold them.

I,56: Expect him not from the East, nor from the West; for from no expected house cometh that child. Aum! All words are sacred and all prophets true; save only that they understand a little; solve the first half of the equation, leave the second unattacked. But thou hast all in the clear light, and some, though not all, in the dark.

I,57: Invoke me under my stars! Love is the law, love under will. Nor let the fools mistake love; for there are love and love. There is the dove, and there is the serpent. Choose ye well! He, my prophet, hath chosen, knowing the law of the fortress, and the great mystery of the House of God. All these old letters of my Book are aright; but * is not the Star. This also is secret: my prophet shall reveal it to the wise.

* In MS, the symbol found here is usually interpreted as the Hebrew letter **Tzaddi**.

I,58: I give unimaginable joys on earth: certainty, not faith, while in life, upon death; peace unutterable, rest, ecstasy; nor do I demand aught in sacrifice.

I,59: My incense is of resinous woods & gums; and there is no blood therein: because of my hair the trees of Eternity.

I,60: My number is 11, as all their numbers who are of us. The Five Pointed Star, with a Circle in the Middle, & the circle is Red. My colour is black to the blind, but the blue & gold are seen of the seeing. Also I have a secret glory for them that love me.

I,61: But to love me is better than all things: if under the night-stars in the desert thou presently burnest mine incense before me, invoking me with a pure heart, and the Serpent flame therein, thou shalt come a little to lie in my bosom. For one kiss wilt thou then be willing to give all; but whoso gives one particle of dust shall lose all in that hour. Ye shall gather goods and store of women and spices; ye shall wear rich jewels; ye shall exceed the nations of the Earth in splendour & pride; but always in the love of me, and so shall ye come to my joy. I charge you earnestly to come before me in a single robe, and covered with a rich headdress. I love you! I yearn to you! Pale or purple, veiled or voluptuous, I who am all pleasure and purple, and drunkenness of the innermost sense, desire you. Put on the wings, and arouse the coiled splendour within you: come unto me!

I,62: At all my meetings with you shall the priestess say-and her eyes shall burn with desire as she stands bare and rejoicing in my secret temple-To me! To me! calling forth the flame of the hearts of all in her love-chant.

I,63: Sing the rapturous love-song unto me! Burn to me perfumes! Wear to me jewels! Drink to me, for I love you! I love you!

I,64: I am the blue-lidded daughter of Sunset; I am the naked brilliance of the voluptuous night-sky.

I,65: To me! To me!

I,66: The Manifestation of Nuit is at an end.

Chapter II

II,1: Nu! the hiding of Hadit.

II,2: Come! all ye, and learn the secret that hath not yet been revealed. I, Hadit, am the complement of Nu, my bride. I am not extended, and Khabs is the name of my House.

II,3: In the sphere I am everywhere the centre, as she, the circumference, is nowhere found.

II,4: Yet she shall be known & I never.

II,5: Behold! the rituals of the old time are black. Let the evil ones be cast away; let the good ones be purged by the prophet! Then shall this Knowledge go aright.

II,6: I am the flame that burns in every heart of man, and in the core of every star. I am Life, and the giver of Life, yet therefore is the knowledge of me the knowledge of death.

II,7: I am the Magician and the Exorcist. I am the axle of the wheel, and the cube in the circle. "Come unto me" is a foolish word: for it is I that go.

II,8: Who worshipped Heru-pa-kraath have worshipped me; ill, for I am the worshipper.

II,9: Remember all ye that existence is pure joy; that all the sorrows are but as shadows; they pass & are done; but there is that which remains.

II,10: O prophet! thou hast ill will to learn this writing.

II,11: I see thee hate the hand & the pen; but I am stronger.

II,12: Because of me in Thee which thou knewest not.

II,13: for why? Because thou wast the knower, and me.

II,14: Now let there be a veiling of this shrine: now let the light devour men and eat them up with blindness!

II,15: For I am perfect, being Not; and my number is nine by the fools; but with the just I am eight, and one in eight: Which is vital, for I am none indeed. The Empress and the King are not of me; for there is a further secret.

II,16: I am the Empress & the Hierophant. Thus eleven, as my bride is eleven.

II,17:

Hear me, ye people of sighing!
The sorrows of pain and regret
Are left to the dead and the dying,
The folk that not know me as yet.

II,18: These are dead, these fellows; they feel not. We are not for the poor and sad: the lords of the earth are our kinsfolk.

II,19: Is a God to live in a dog? No! but the highest are of us. They shall rejoice, our chosen: who sorroweth is not of us.

II,20: Beauty and strength, leaping laughter and delicious languor, force and fire, are of us.

II,21: We have nothing with the outcast and the unfit: let them die in their misery. For they feel not. Compassion is the vice of kings: stamp down the wretched & the weak: this is the law of the strong: this is our law and the joy of the world. Think not, o king, upon that lie: That Thou Must Die: verily thou shalt not die, but live. Now let it be understood: If the body of the King dissolve, he shall remain in pure ecstasy for ever. Nuit! Hadit! Ra-Hoor-Khuit! The Sun, Strength & Sight, Light; these are for the servants of the Star & the Snake.

II,22: I am the Snake that giveth Knowledge & Delight and bright glory, and stir the hearts of men with drunkenness. To worship me take wine and strange drugs whereof I will tell my prophet, & be drunk thereof! They shall not harm ye at all. It is a lie, this folly against self. The exposure of innocence is a lie. Be strong, o man! lust, enjoy all things of sense and rapture: fear not that any God shall deny thee for this.

II,23: I am alone: there is no God where I am.

II,24: Behold! these be grave mysteries; for there are also of my friends who be hermits. Now think not to find them in the forest or on the mountain; but in beds of purple, caressed by magnificent beasts of women with large limbs, and fire and light in their eyes, and masses of flaming hair about them; there shall ye find them. Ye shall see them at rule, at victorious armies, at all the joy; and there shall be in them a joy a million times greater than this. Beware lest any force another, King against King! Love one another with burning hearts; on the low men trample in the fierce lust of your pride, in the day of your wrath.

II,25: Ye are against the people, O my chosen!

II,26: I am the secret Serpent coiled about to spring: in my coiling there is joy. If I lift up my head, I and my Nuit are one. If I droop down mine head, and shoot forth venom, then is rapture of the earth, and I and the earth are one.

II,27: There is great danger in me; for who doth not understand these runes shall make a great miss. He shall fall down into the pit called Because, and there he shall perish with the dogs of Reason.

II,28: Now a curse upon Because and his kin!

II,29: May Because be accursed for ever!

II,30: If Will stops and cries Why, invoking Because, then Will stops & does nought.

II,31: If Power asks why, then is Power weakness.

II,32: Also reason is a lie; for there is a factor infinite & unknown; & all their words are skew-wise.

II,33: Enough of Because! Be he damned for a dog!

II,34: But ye, o my people, rise up & awake!

II,35: Let the rituals be rightly performed with joy & beauty!

II,36: There are rituals of the elements and feasts of the times.

II,37: A feast for the first night of the Prophet and his Bride!

II,38: A feast for the three days of the writing of the Book of the Law.

II,39: A feast for Tahuti and the child of the Prophet-secret, O Prophet!

II,40: A feast for the Supreme Ritual, and a feast for the Equinox of the Gods.

II,41: A feast for fire and a feast for water; a feast for life and a greater feast for death!

II,42: A feast every day in your hearts in the joy of my rapture!

II,43: A feast every night unto Nu, and the pleasure of uttermost delight!

II,44: Aye! feast! rejoice! there is no dread hereafter. There is the dissolution, and eternal ecstasy in the kisses of Nu.

II,45: There is death for the dogs.

II,46: Dost thou fail? Art thou sorry? Is fear in thine heart?

II,47: Where I am these are not.

II,48: Pity not the fallen! I never knew them. I am not for them. I console not: I hate the consoled & the consoler.

II,49: I am unique & conqueror. I am not of the slaves that perish. Be they damned & dead! Amen. [This is of the 4: there is a fifth who is invisible, & therein am I as a babe in an egg.]

II,50: Blue am I and gold in the light of my bride: but the red gleam is in my eyes; & my spangles are purple & green.

II,51: Purple beyond purple: it is the light higher than eyesight.

II,52: There is a veil: that veil is black. It is the veil of the modest woman; it is the veil of sorrow, & the pall of death: this is none of me. Tear down that lying spectre of the centuries: veil not your vices in virtuous words: these vices are my service; ye do well, & I will reward you here and hereafter.

II,53: Fear not, o prophet, when these words are said, thou shalt not be sorry. Thou art emphatically my chosen; and blessed are the eyes that thou shalt look upon with gladness. But I will hide thee in a mask of sorrow: they that see thee shall fear thou art fallen: but I lift thee up.

II,54: Nor shall they who cry aloud their folly that thou meanest nought avail; thou shall reveal it: thou availest: they are the slaves of because: They are not of me. The stops as thou wilt; the letters? change them not in style or value!

II,55: Thou shalt obtain the order & value of the English Alphabet; thou shalt find new symbols to attribute them unto.

II,56: Begone! ye mockers; even though ye laugh in my honour ye shall laugh not long: then when ye are sad know that I have forsaken you.

II,57: He that is righteous shall be righteous still; he that is filthy shall be filthy still.

II,58: Yea! deem not of change: ye shall be as ye are, & not other. Therefore the kings of the earth shall be

Kings for ever: the slaves shall serve. There is none that shall be cast down or lifted up: all is ever as it was. Yet there are masked ones my servants: it may be that yonder beggar is a King. A King may choose his garment as he will: there is no certain test: but a beggar cannot hide his poverty.

II,59: Beware therefore! Love all, lest perchance is a King concealed! Say you so? Fool! If he be a King, thou canst not hurt him.

II,60: Therefore strike hard & low, and to hell with them, master!

II,61: There is a light before thine eyes, o prophet, a light undesired, most desirable.

II,62: I am uplifted in thine heart; and the kisses of the stars rain hard upon thy body.

II,63: Thou art exhaust in the voluptuous fullness of the inspiration; the expiration is sweeter than death, more rapid and laughterful than a caress of Hell's own worm.

II,64: Oh! thou art overcome: we are upon thee; our delight is all over thee: hail! hail: prophet of Nu! prophet of Had! prophet of Ra-Hoor-Khu! Now rejoice! now come in our splendour & rapture! Come in our passionate peace, & write sweet words for the Kings!

II,65: I am the Master: thou art the Holy Chosen One.

II,66: Write, & find ecstasy in writing! Work, & be our bed in working! Thrill with the joy of life & death! Ah! thy death shall be lovely: whoso seeth it shall be glad. Thy death shall be the seal of the promise of our agelong love. Come! lift up thine heart & rejoice! We are one; we are none.

II,67: Hold! Hold! Bear up in thy rapture; fall not in swoon of the excellent kisses!

II,68: Harder! Hold up thyself! Lift thine head! breathe not so deep-die!

II,69: Ah! Ah! What do I feel? Is the word exhausted?

II,70: There is help & hope in other spells. Wisdom says: be strong! Then canst thou bear more joy. Be not animal; refine thy rapture! If thou drink, drink by the eight and ninety rules of art: if thou love, exceed by delicacy; and if thou do aught joyous, let there be subtlety therein!

II,71: But exceed! exceed!

II,72: Strive ever to more! and if thou art truly mine-and doubt it not, an if thou art ever joyous!-death is the crown of all.

II,73: Ah! Ah! Death! Death! thou shalt long for death. Death is forbidden, o man, unto thee.

II,74: The length of thy longing shall be the strength of its glory. He that lives long & desires death much is ever the King among the Kings.

II,75: Aye! listen to the numbers & the words:

II,76: 4 6 3 8 A B K 2 4 A L G M O R 3 Y X 24 89 R P S T O V A L. What meaneth this, o prophet? Thou knowest not; nor shalt thou know ever. There cometh one to follow thee: he shall expound it. But remember, o chosen one, to be me; to follow the love of Nu in the star-lit heaven; to look forth upon men, to tell them this glad word.

II,77: O be thou proud and mighty among men!

II,78: Lift up thyself! for there is none like unto thee among men or among Gods! Lift up thyself, o my prophet, thy stature shall surpass the stars. They shall worship thy name, foursquare, mystic, wonderful, the number of the man; and the name of thy house 418.

II,79: The end of the hiding of Hadit; and blessing & worship to the prophet of the lovely Star!

Chapter III

III,1: Abrahadabra! the reward of Ra Hoor Khut.

III,2: There is division hither homeward; there is a word not known. Spelling is defunct; all is not aught. Beware! Hold! Raise the spell of Ra-Hoor-Khuit!

III,3: Now let it be first understood that I am a god of War and of Vengeance. I shall deal hardly with them.

III,4: Choose ye an island!

III,5: Fortify it!

III,6: Dung it about with enginery of war!

III,7: I will give you a war-engine.

III,8: With it ye shall smite the peoples; and none shall stand before you.

III,9: Lurk! Withdraw! Upon them! this is the Law of the Battle of Conquest: thus shall my worship be about my secret house.

III,10: Get the stele of revealing itself; set it in thy secret temple-and that temple is already aright disposed-& it shall be your Kiblah for ever. It shall not fade, but miraculous colour shall come back to it day after day. Close it in locked glass for a proof to the world.

III,11: This shall be your only proof. I forbid argument. Conquer! That is enough. I will make easy to you the abstruction from the ill-ordered house in the Victorious City. Thou shalt thyself convey it with worship, o prophet, though thou likest it not. Thou shalt have danger & trouble. Ra-Hoor-Khu is with thee. Worship me with fire & blood; worship me with swords & with spears. Let the woman be girt with a sword before me: let blood flow to my name. Trample down the Heathen; be upon them, o warrior, I will give you of their flesh to eat!

III,12: Sacrifice cattle, little and big: after a child.

III,13: But not now.

III,14: Ye shall see that hour, o blessed Beast, and thou the Scarlet Concubine of his desire!

III,15: Ye shall be sad thereof.

III,16: Deem not too eagerly to catch the promises; fear not to undergo the curses. Ye, even ye, know not this meaning all.

III,17: Fear not at all; fear neither men nor Fates, nor gods, nor anything. Money fear not, nor laughter of the folk folly, nor any other power in heaven or upon the earth or under the earth. Nu is your refuge as Hadit your light; and I am the strength, force, vigour, of your arms.

III,18: Mercy let be off: damn them who pity! Kill and torture; spare not; be upon them!

III,19: That stele they shall call the Abomination of Desolation; count well its name, & it shall be to you as 718.

III,20: Why? Because of the fall of Because, that he is not there again.

III,21: Set up my image in the East: thou shalt buy thee an image which I will show thee, especial, not unlike the one thou knowest. And it shall be suddenly easy for thee to do this.

III,22: The other images group around me to support me: let all be worshipped, for they shall cluster to exalt me. I am the visible object of worship; the others are secret; for the Beast & his Bride are they: and for the winners of the Ordeal x. What is this? Thou shalt know.

III,23: For perfume mix meal & honey & thick leavings of red wine: then oil of Abramelin and olive oil, and afterward soften & smooth down with rich fresh blood.

III,24: The best blood is of the moon, monthly: then the fresh blood of a child, or dropping from the host of heaven: then of enemies; then of the priest or of the worshippers: last of some beast, no matter what.

III,25: This burn: of this make cakes & eat unto me. This hath also another use; let it be laid before me, and kept thick with perfumes of your orison: it shall become full of beetles as it were and creeping things sacred unto me.

III,26: These slay, naming your enemies; & they shall fall before you.

III,27: Also these shall breed lust & power of lust in you at the eating thereof.

III,28: Also ye shall be strong in war.

III,29: Moreover, be they long kept, it is better; for they swell with my force. All before me.

III,30: My altar is of open brass work: burn thereon in silver or gold!

III,31: There cometh a rich man from the West who shall pour his gold upon thee.

III,32: From gold forge steel!

III,33: Be ready to fly or to smite!

III,34: But your holy place shall be untouched throughout the centuries: though with fire and sword it be burnt down & shattered, yet an invisible house there standeth, and shall stand until the fall of the Great Equinox; when Hrumachis shall arise and the double-wanded one assume my throne and place. Another prophet shall arise, and bring fresh fever from the skies; another woman shall awake the lust & worship of the Snake; another soul of God and beast shall mingle in the globed priest; another sacrifice shall stain the tomb; another king shall reign; and blessing no longer be poured To the Hawk-headed mystical Lord!

III,35: The half of the word of Heru-ra-ha, called Hoor-pa-kraat and Ra-Hoor-Khut.

III,36: Then said the prophet unto the God:

III,37: I adore thee in the song -

I am the Lord of Thebes,and I
The inspired forth-speaker of Mentu;

For me unveils the veiled sky,
The self-slain Ankh-af-na-khonsu
Whose words are truth. I invoke, I greet
Thy presence, O Ra-Hoor-Khuit!

Unity uttermost showed!
I adore the might of Thy breath,
Supreme and terrible God,
Who makest the gods and death
To tremble before Thee -
I, I adore thee!

Appear on the throne of Ra!
Open the ways of the Khu!
Lighten the ways of the Ka!
The ways of the Khabs run through
To stir me or still me!
Aum! let it fill me!

III,38: So that thy light is in me; & its red flame is as a sword in my hand to push thy order. There is a secret door that I shall make to establish thy way in all the quarters, (these are the adorations, as thou hast written), as it is said:

The light is mine; its rays consume
Me: I have made a secret door
Into the House of Ra and Tum,
Of Khephra and of Ahathoor.
I am thy Theban, O Mentu,
The prophet Ankh-af-na-khonsu!

By Bes-na-Maut my breast I beat;
By wise Ta-Nech I weave my spell.
Show thy star-splendour, O Nuit!
Bid me within thine House to dwell,
O winged snake of light, Hadit!
Abide with me, Ra-Hoor-Khuit!

III,39: All this and a book to say how thou didst come hither and a reproduction of this ink and paper for ever — for in it is the word secret & not only in the English — and thy comment upon this the Book of the Law shall be printed beautifully in red ink and black upon beautiful paper made by hand; and to each man and woman that thou meetest, were it but to dine or to drink at them, it is the Law to give. Then they shall chance to abide in this bliss or no; it is no odds. Do this quickly!

III,40: But the work of the comment? That is easy; and Hadit burning in thy heart shall make swift and secure thy pen.

III,41: Establish at thy Kaaba a clerk-house: all must be done well and with business way.

III,42: The ordeals thou shalt oversee thyself, save only the blind ones. Refuse none, but thou shalt know &

destroy the traitors. I am Ra-Hoor-Khuit; and I am powerful to protect my servant. Success is thy proof: argue not; convert not; talk not overmuch! Them that seek to entrap thee, to overthrow thee, them attack without pity or quarter; & destroy them utterly. Swift as a trodden serpent turn and strike! Be thou yet deadlier than he! Drag down their souls to awful torment: laugh at their fear: spit upon them!

III,43: Let the Scarlet Woman beware! If pity and compassion and tenderness visit her heart; if she leave my work to toy with old sweetnesses; then shall my vengeance be known. I will slay me her child: I will alienate her heart: I will cast her out from men: as a shrinking and despised harlot shall she crawl through dusk wet streets, and die cold and an-hungered.

III,44: But let her raise herself in pride! Let her follow me in my way! Let her work the work of wickedness! Let her kill her heart! Let her be loud and adulterous; let her be covered with jewels, and rich garments, and let her be shameless before all men!

III,45: Then will I lift her to pinnacles of power: then will I breed from her a child mightier than all the kings of the earth. I will fill her with joy: with my force shall she see & strike at the worship of Nu: she shall achieve Hadit.

III,46: I am the warrior Lord of the Forties: the Eighties cower before me, & are abased. I will bring you to victory & joy: I will be at your arms in battle & ye shall delight to slay. Success is your proof; courage is your armour; go on, go on, in my strength; & ye shall turn not back for any!

III,47: This book shall be translated into all tongues: but always with the original in the writing of the Beast; for in the chance shape of the letters and their position to one another: in these are mysteries that no Beast shall divine. Let him not seek to try: but one cometh after him, whence I say not, who shall discover the Key of it all. Then this line drawn is a key: then this circle squared in its failure is a key also. And Abrahadabra. It shall be his child and that strangely. Let him not seek after this; for thereby alone can he fall from it.

III,48: Now this mystery of the letters is done, and I want to go on to the holier place.

III,49: I am in a secret fourfold word, the blasphemy against all gods of men.

III,50: Curse them! Curse them! Curse them!

III,51: With my Hawk's head I peck at the eyes of Jesus as he hangs upon the cross.

III,52: I flap my wings in the face of Mohammed & blind him.

III,53: With my claws I tear out the flesh of the Indian and the Buddhist, Mongol and Din.

III,54: Bahlasti! Ompehda! I spit on your crapulous creeds.

III,55: Let Mary inviolate be torn upon wheels: for her sake let all chaste women be utterly despised among you!

III,56: Also for beauty's sake and love's!

III,57: Despise also all cowards; professional soldiers who dare not fight, but play; all fools despise!

III,58: But the keen and the proud, the royal and the lofty; ye are brothers!

III,59: As brothers fight ye!

III,60: There is no law beyond Do what thou wilt.

III,61: There is an end of the word of the God enthroned in Ra's seat, lightening the girders of the soul.

III,62: To Me do ye reverence! to me come ye through tribulation of ordeal, which is bliss.

III,63: The fool readeth this Book of the Law, and its comment; & he understandeth it not.

III,64: Let him come through the first ordeal, & it will be to him as silver.

III,65: Through the second, gold.

III,66: Through the third, stones of precious water.

III,67: Through the fourth, ultimate sparks of the intimate fire.

III,68: Yet to all it shall seem beautiful. Its enemies who say not so, are mere liars.

III,69: There is success.

III,70: I am the Hawk-Headed Lord of Silence & of Strength; my nemyss shrouds the night-blue sky.

III,71: Hail! ye twin warriors about the pillars of the world! for your time is nigh at hand.

III,72: I am the Lord of the Double Wand of Power; the wand of the Force of Coph Nia-but my left hand is empty, for I have crushed an Universe; & nought remains.

III,73: Paste the sheets from right to left and from top to bottom: then behold!

III,74: There is a splendour in my name hidden and glorious, as the sun of midnight is ever the son.

III,75: The ending of the words is the Word Abrahadabra.

The Book of the Law is Written

and Concealed.

Aum. Ha.

The Comment

Do what thou wilt shall be the whole of the Law.
The study of this Book is forbidden. It is wise to destroy this copy after the first reading.
Whosoever disregards this does so at his own risk and peril. These are most dire.
Those who discuss the contents of this Book are to be shunned by all, as centres of pestilence.
All questions of the Law are to be decided only by appeal to my writings, each for himself.
There is no law beyond Do what thou wilt.
Love is the law, love under will.

The priest of the princes,
ANKH-F-N-KHONSU